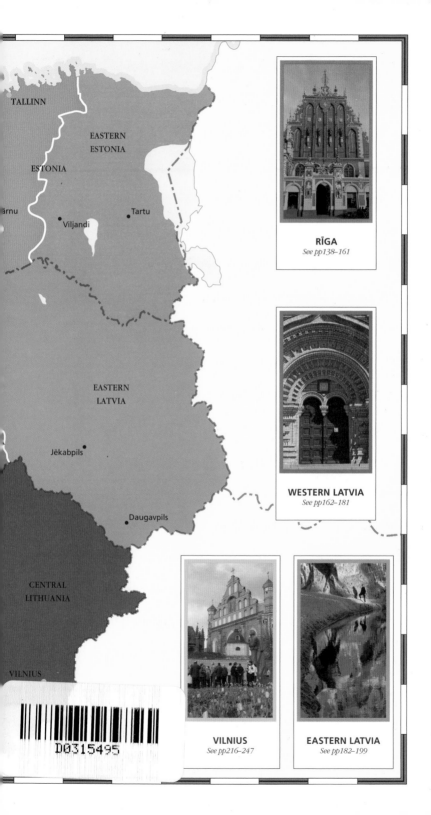

TALLINN

EASTERN
ESTONIA

ESTONIA

ärnu

Viljandi

Tartu

RĪGA
See pp138–161

EASTERN
LATVIA

Jēkabpils

Daugavpils

WESTERN LATVIA
See pp162–181

CENTRAL
LITHUANIA

VILNIUS

VILNIUS
See pp216–247

EASTERN LATVIA
See pp182–199

EYEWITNESS TRAVEL
ESTONIA, LATVIA AND LITHUANIA

DK

LONDON, NEW YORK,
MELBOURNE, MUNICH AND DELHI
www.dk.com

MANAGING EDITOR Aruna Ghose
DESIGN MANAGERS Sunita Gahir, Priyanka Thakur
PROJECT EDITOR Alka Thakur
PROJECT DESIGNER Rajnish Kashyap
EDITORS Jyoti Kumari, Ipshita Nandi
DESIGNERS Namrata Adhwaryu, Anchal Kaushal
SENIOR CARTOGRAPHIC MANAGER Uma Bhattacharya
CARTOGRAPHERS Mohammad Hassan, Jasneet Kaur
SENIOR PICTURE RESEARCHER Taiyaba Khatoon
PICTURE RESEARCHER Sumita Khatwani
ASSISTANT PICTURE RESEARCHER Shweta Andrews
SENIOR DTP DESIGNER Vinod Harish
DTP DESIGNER Azeem Siddiqui

CONTRIBUTORS
Howard Jarvis, John Oates, Tim Ochser, Neil Taylor

PHOTOGRAPHERS
Demetrio Carrasco, Nigel Hicks, Linda Whitwam

ILLUSTRATORS
Chinglemba Chingtham, Sanjeev Kumar, Surat Kumar Mantoo,
Arun Pottirayil, Suman Saha, Mark Warner,
Chapel Design & Marketing Ltd

Printed and bound by South China Printing Co. Ltd., China

First published in the UK in 2009
by Dorling Kindersley Limited
80 Strand, London WC2R 0RL

13 14 15 16 10 9 8 7 6 5 4 3 2 1

Reprinted with revisions 2011, 2013

Copyright © 2009, 2013 Dorling Kindersley Limited, London
A Penguin Company

ISBN 978-1-40938-625-4

Front cover main image: Alexander Nevsky Cathedral, Estonia

◁ **A splendid overview of the colourful buildings of Riga, Latvia**

CONTENTS

Door knocker, Tallinn

**St Nicholas's Orthodox Cathedral in
Karosta, near Liepāja, Latvia**

Picturesque Island Castle at Trakai, Lithuania

Statue of King Gustav Adolphus of
Sweden, Tartu, Estonia

Amber jewellery, sold in souvenir
shops all over the Baltic region

The spectacular Vilnius Cathedral, Lithuania

HOW TO USE THIS GUIDE

This guide helps you get the most from your visit to the Baltic States. It provides detailed practical information and expert recommendations. *Introducing Estonia, Latvia and Lithuania* maps the three countries and sets them in their historical and cultural context, and describes events throughout the year. Each country has its own chapter, with its portrait, history and descriptions of important sights using visuals and maps. Information about hotels, restaurants, shops and markets, entertainment and sports is found in *Travellers' Needs*. The *Survival Guide* has tips on everything from making a telephone call to using local transportation.

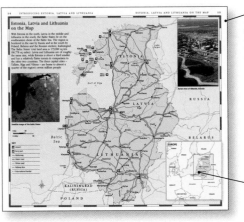

ESTONIA, LATVIA AND LITHUANIA ON THE MAP

The orientation map shows the location of the Baltic States in relation to their neighbouring countries. In this book, each country is divided into three main sightseeing areas that are covered in a full chapter, such as *Estonia Region by Region* and so on. These areas are highlighted on other maps throughout the book.

A locator map shows where you are in relation to the other European countries.

ESTONIA, LATVIA AND LITHUANIA REGION BY REGION

Each country has been divided into three regions with a map at the start of the section. The key to the symbols is on the back flap.

Sights at a Glance lists the chapter's sights by category, such as Churches and Cathedrals, Towns, Resorts and Villages and Islands and National Parks.

1 Introduction
The landscape, history and character of each region is described here, explaining how they have changed over the centuries and what they have to offer to the visitor today.

2 Regional Map
This map shows the road network and gives an overview of the topography of the entire region. All the sights are numbered and there are also useful tips on getting around by car, bus and train.

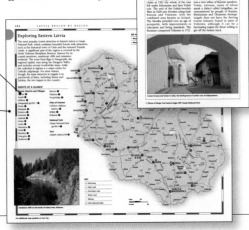

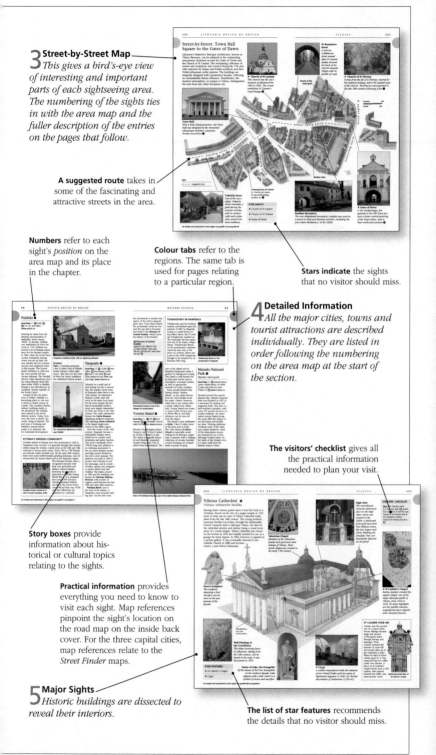

3 Street-by-Street Map
This gives a bird's-eye view of interesting and important parts of each sightseeing area. The numbering of the sights ties in with the area map and the fuller description of the entries on the pages that follow.

A suggested route takes in some of the fascinating and attractive streets in the area.

Numbers refer to each sight's *position* on the area map and its place in the chapter.

Colour tabs refer to the regions. The same tab is used for pages relating to a particular region.

Stars indicate the sights that no visitor should miss.

4 Detailed Information
All the major cities, towns and tourist attractions are described individually. They are listed in order following the numbering on the area map at the start of the section.

The visitors' checklist gives all the practical information needed to plan your visit.

Story boxes provide information about historical or cultural topics relating to the sights.

Practical information provides everything you need to know to visit each sight. Map references pinpoint the sight's location on the road map on the inside back cover. For the three capital cities, map references relate to the *Street Finder* maps.

5 Major Sights
Historic buildings are dissected to reveal their interiors.

The list of star features recommends the details that no visitor should miss.

INTRODUCING ESTONIA, LATVIA AND LITHUANIA

DISCOVERING ESTONIA, LATVIA AND LITHUANIA

The Baltic States all share a fairly similar landscape. Their western coastline is a sinuous and seemingly endless pristine beach stretching from Lithuania to Latvia and into Estonia, with beautiful resort towns such as Palanga, Jūrmala and Pärnu. Estonia's islands embody the diversity of all aspects of nature in the Baltics, while the southeastern part of the country has some of the hilliest and most picturesque terrain in the entire region. Western Latvia and Lithuania are rich in virgin forests and gently undulating landscapes that become wilder further east. The capital cities, while bound by many historical affinities, each have a distinctly different character, from the medieval splendour of Tallinn, to the decadent Art Nouveau of Rīga and the elegant Baroque of Vilnius.

Splendid outburst of autumn yellow at Kadriorg Park, Tallinn, Estonia

TALLINN

- Medieval Old Town
- Excellent museums
- Lively art scene
- Exhilarating nightlife

Tallinn's medieval Old Town is the heart of the city and an ideal starting point for visitors. **Town Hall Square** (see pp58–9) gloriously personifies Tallinn's medieval past and is an easy walk from the Old Town's other attractions. With spectacular views over the city, **Toompea** (see pp68–9) is the seat of the Estonian government. The city boasts some small but fascinating museums, especially the **Tallinn City Museum** (see p63), with its concise overview of the city's history. The **Estonian Open-Air Museum** (see p81) offers a glimpse into traditional Estonian life. The magnificent surroundings of **Kadriorg Park** (see pp74–7) include many small specialist museums as well as the impressive **Kumu Art Museum** (see p76). Beyond the park stands the popular **TV Tower** (see p80).

Tallinn strikes a perfect balance between cultural refinement and youthful hedonism. An abundance of good restaurants, cafés and bars are concentrated in and around the Old Town.

WESTERN ESTONIA

- Unspoiled islands
- Marvellous beach resorts
- Stunning nature parks
- Paldiski's Soviet relics

Western Estonia is rich in natural beauty. The amazingly untouched islands here offer numerous scenic drives and splendid hiking routes. **Saaremaa Island** (see pp92–5) is the largest and its capital **Kuressaare** (see p94) is home to the Bishop's Castle. **Kihnu Island** (see p101) is one of the few remaining places where a traditional Estonian way of life still persists.

Pärnu (see pp98–9) is a gorgeous resort town with delightful architecture and an extremely attractive long stretch of beach. The resort town of **Haapsalu** (see p88) has not altered much since its 19th-century heyday as a fashionable spa resort.

Soomaa National Park (see pp100–101) and **Matsalu National Park** (see p89) are notable wildlife sanctuaries with exceptionally intricate ecosystems, and are surrounded by some historic sights.

The former Soviet naval base at **Paldiski** (see p88) has some spectacular coastal scenery full of relics of the country's Soviet past.

Windmill Tavern in Kuressaare, Saaremaa Island, Western Estonia

Eastern Estonia's sweeping coastline, with Narva-Jõesuu beachside resort hidden among pine trees

EASTERN ESTONIA

- Lahemaa National Park
- Picturesque towns
- Religious heritage
- Setu culture

Eastern Estonia has a wealth of diverse attractions. The stunning scenery of **Lahemaa National Park** *(see pp106–10)* includes little fishing villages and stately manor houses.

The coast passes through some intriguing industrial areas, such as the former Soviet town of **Sillamäe** *(see p111)*, before culminating in the historic Russian border city of **Narva** *(see p112)*. The resort of **Narva-Jõesuu** *(see p112)* boasts of one of the country's prettiest beaches.

The village of **Kuremäe** *(see p112)* is visited for its spectacular Russian Orthodox Pühtitsa Convent. **Lake Peipsi** *(see p123)* dominates Estonia's eastern border and its atmospheric shores are home to a community of Old Believers *(see p122)*.

Both historic and modern, the vibrant city of **Tartu** *(see pp114–17)* in the southeast lies at the very heart of Estonian culture. The beautiful landscape of this region abounds with little villages and towns, such as **Rõuge** *(see p120)* and **Viljandi** *(see p118)*, and is also generously strewn with countless historic sights.

In the far southeast corner of Estonia the unique Setu people *(see p120)* still hold on to their old way of life.

RĪGA

- Atmospheric Old Town
- Excellent dining
- Art Nouveau architecture
- Vibrant cultural scene

Rīga's colourful Old Town is full of historic sights, shops and museums as well as cafés, bars and restaurants. The superb **Dome Cathedral** *(see p142)* dominates Dome Square, while the imposing **St Peter's Church** *(see p149)* is one of Rīga's most recognized landmarks. Of the many museums in the area, the **Museum of the Occupation of Latvia** *(see p148)* is one of

the best and should not be missed. The imposing **Freedom Monument** *(see p150)*, the revered symbol of Latvian nationhood, serves as a border between the Old Town and the city centre.

Art Nouveau architecture *(see pp152–3)* can be seen throughout the city centre, but is most impressive on Alberta Street. The elegant neighbourhood of **Mežaparks** *(see p156)* is close to Rīga Zoo and the venerable **Rīga's Cemeteries** *(see p157)*.

Across the Daugava river lies **The Left Bank** *(see p155)*, which is home to several intriguing sights, including **Victory Park** *(see p155)* and the **Railway Museum** *(see p155)*. Further afield is the **Latvian Ethnographic Open-Air Museum** *(see p159)*, among Rīga's best.

Cobblestoned street with historic buildings in Rīga, Latvia

Rundāle Palace set in verdant surroundings, Western Latvia

WESTERN LATVIA

- **Beach resorts of Jūrmala**
- **Delightful towns**
- **The Livonian Coast**
- **Exquisite palaces**

Some of the Baltic region's best sights can be found in Western Latvia. A string of pretty resort towns, **Jūrmala** (see pp170–71) has a pine forest-lined beach. Its tightly clustered summer houses, which include rare examples of wooden Art Nouveau, are architectural marvels.

Ventspils (see pp176–7), a coastal city, has an immaculately renovated historic centre. **Liepāja** (see pp180–81) is arguably Latvia's most attractive city besides its capital and is famed for its vibrant music scene. The region's lush landscape is also filled with delightful small towns, such as **Tukums** (see p171), wine-producing **Sabile** (see p178) and **Kuldīga** (see p179).

The Livonian Coast, along the Gulf of Rīga and Baltic Sea, is a scenic drive and is lined with countless pretty old fishing villages before ending in **Cape Kolka** (see p173). Kolka is part of the densely forested Slītere National Park, which is also home to the Livs (see p172), the oldest of Latvia's indigenous peoples.

The Baroque-Rococo **Rundāle Palace** (see pp168–9) and the Neo-Classical palace,

Mežotne Palace (see p166), are just some of the sights attesting to the distinguished history of Western Latvia.

EASTERN LATVIA

- **Gauja National Park**
- **Unspoiled coastline**
- **Abundant lakes**
- **Historic Daugavpils**

The country's most stunning landscape can be experienced in **Gauja National Park** (see pp186–9). The park encompasses the Gauja Valley, a vast forested basin with steep sandstone banks and jaw-dropping cliffs. The sharply winding and deceptively placid-looking Gauja river is ideal for kayaking and canoeing, while the entire park is well served by a range of nature trails.

Girls in traditional outfits, near the castle at Cēsis, Eastern Latvia

Sigulda (see p188) is the perfect starting point for exploring the area, although the historic town of **Cēsis** (see pp188–9) on the eastern border of the park is another good entry point.

The coastline east of Rīga is not quite as popular as Jūrmala, but it is no less beautiful. The pleasant resort town of **Saulkrasti** (see p192) serves as the main focal point of a whole string of small coastal villages that line the amazingly unspoiled stretch of beach here.

In southeastern Latvia, the area known as **Latgale** (see p198) is famed for its abundance of lakes, all of which are used by locals for fishing or taking a refreshing dip.

The predominantly Russian-speaking city of **Daugavpils** (see pp196–7) is rich in architecture and places of historic interest.

VILNIUS

- **Well-preserved Old Town**
- **Baroque architecture**
- **Impressive environs**
- **Cheery nightlife**

The Lithuanian capital's UNESCO-protected Old Town holds the majority of the city's sights, such as the labyrinthine courtyards of **Vilnius University** (see pp220–22) and the Chapel of St Casimir inside **Vilnius Cathedral** (see pp224–5). The spires and interiors of Catholic churches such as **St John's** (see p222), **St Anne's** (see p228) and **St Theresa's** (see p234) and the mystical **Gates of Dawn** (see p235) have survived the ravages of the centuries.

The Baroque architecture that characterizes Vilnius sets it apart from any other city in Europe. The **Church of Sts Peter and Paul** (see pp242–3), one of Vilnius's finest Baroque jewels, lies within easy walking distance of the Old Town.

The bohemian quarter of **Užupis** (see p240) and the views from **Verkiai Palace** (see

Vilnius Cathedral and Gedimino Bell Tower lit up at night, Vilnius

p245) make a good day-trip. On the city's fringes, the **Pushkin Museum** *(see p244)* and the **Paneriai Holocaust Memorial** *(see pp244–5)* draw the more serious visitors.

In addition to its lively nightlife, Vilnius is famed for its rich cultural life. It has two symphony orchestras and hosts several important music festivals.

CENTRAL LITHUANIA

- **Trakai Island Castle**
- **Sprawling national parks**
- **Idyllic spa towns**
- **Museums of Kaunas**

The ideal day-trip from Vilnius is **Trakai** *(see pp252–3)*, with its fairytale Island Castle set amid a lake that is dotted with countless islands. Exploring the castle, renting a rowing boat, going for a swim and sampling the village's distinctive Karaim dishes all make for memorable experiences.

The region is blessed with a verdant landscape and crystal-clear lakes. The amazingly untouched **Aukštaitija National Park** *(see pp266–7)*, with its network of lakes and rivers, attracts canoeists. The ancient forests of **Dzūkija National Park** *(see p256)* are interspersed with secluded villages with bubbling streams and thatched cottages.

One of Lithuania's major spa resorts, **Druskininkai** *(see p255)* is located in a bend in the Nemunas river, lined with towering pines. It is famed for its mineral muds and healing waters. The quiet spa town of **Birštonas** *(see p257)* is popular for Birštonas Jazz, Lithuania's oldest jazz festival.

The heart of Central Lithuania is **Kaunas** *(see pp258–61)*, arguably the most intriguing of the Baltic region's second cities. The city's varied collection of museums offers insights into the Lithuanian character.

WESTERN LITHUANIA

- **Unique spit and lagoon**
- **Serene Palanga resort**
- **Lively port city of Klaipėda**
- **Žemaitija National Park**

Western Lithuania may be comparatively isolated, being well away from Vilnius, but it has, nonetheless, plenty of captivating places to see. The main highlight is the unique coastal landscape, particularly the **Curonian Spit National Park** *(see pp284–5)*, a thin wedge of land covered in towering dunes and pine forest that stretches almost 100 km (60 miles) into the Baltic Sea. Its fishing villages and yachting harbours facing the sheltered Curonian Lagoon make the area extremely beautiful. The sublime little town of Nida, and a sandy beach that extends along the edge of the sea, provide the spit with an appealing coastal scenery. In contrast to this peaceful, UNESCO-protected landscape, the resort of **Palanga** *(see p282)* further north is packed in summer with holidaying families and fun-loving teenagers and youngsters. In or out of season, Palanga is worth visiting for attractions such as the Amber Museum.

The port city of **Klaipėda** *(see pp280–81)*, with timber-framed houses and a quaint Old Town, has retained its old Prussian atmosphere. The city's love of festivities is epitomized in the Sea Festival, which draws tourists in droves every year.

The region's secluded nature is most apparent in and around **Žemaitija National Park** *(see pp278–9)*. Isolated villages and wooden farmsteads carry a mystical blend of Catholic and pagan imagery, seen in the wayside crosses and shrines, or at the **Orvidas Garden** *(see p277)*.

One of the popular beaches around Palanga, Western Lithuania

Estonia, Latvia and Lithuania on the Map

With Estonia in the north, Latvia in the centre and Lithuania in the south, the Baltic States lie on the southeastern shore of the Baltic Sea. The region is bordered in the east by Russia and in the south by Poland, Belarus and the Russian enclave, Kaliningrad. The Baltic States' total land area is 173,000 sq km (66,778 sq miles). Latvia and Lithuania are of roughly equal size, while Estonia is about a third smaller and has a relatively flatter terrain in comparison to the other two countries. The three capital cities – Tallinn, Rīga and Vilnius – are home to almost a quarter of the region's 7 million people.

TALLINN

Vormsi Island   Riisipere
Kärdla
Hiiumaa Island   Haapsalu

Muhu Island   Lihula

Saaremaa Island   Pärnu

Kuressaare   Kihnu Island

Gulf of Rīga

Cape Kolka

Ventspils   Talsi   Gau

A10   Tukums   Jūrmala   RĪGA
Kuldīga   Sabile
Pāvilosta   Jelgava
A9   Saldus   Dobele
Liepāja   A9

Joniškis

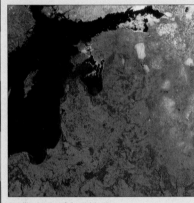

Satellite image of the Baltic States

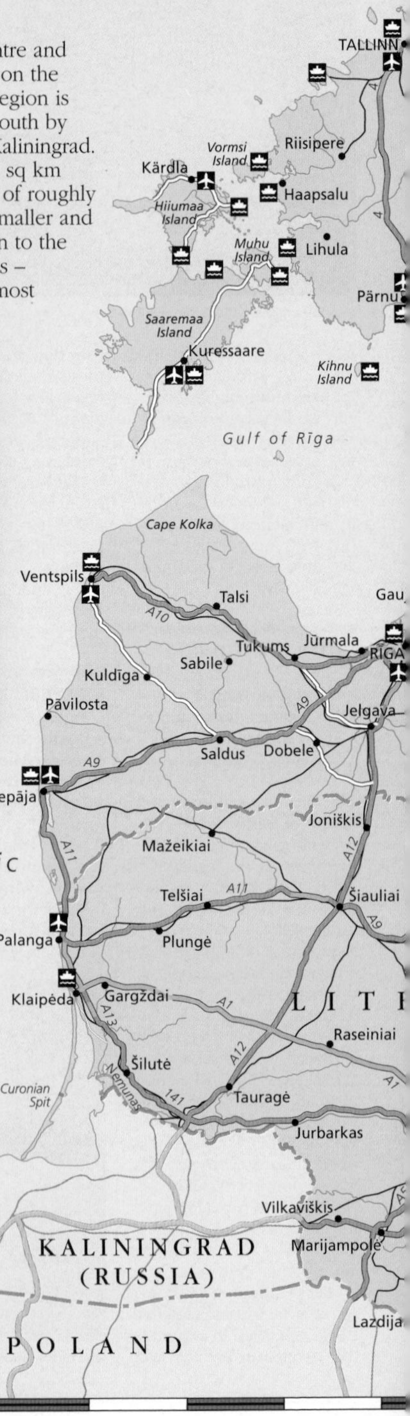

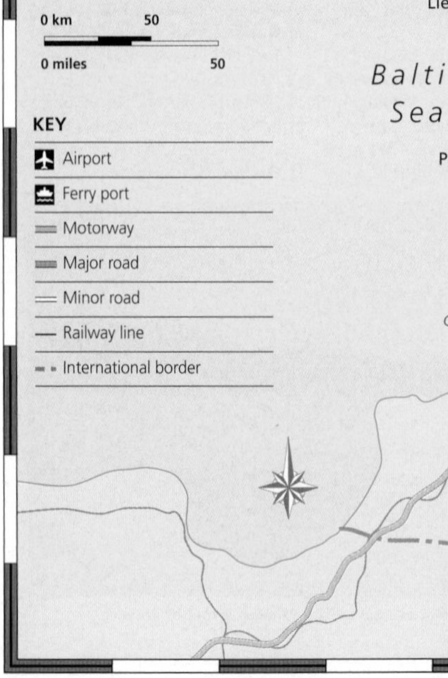

0 km   50

0 miles   50

KEY

✈ Airport

⛴ Ferry port

▬ Motorway

▬ Major road

═ Minor road

— Railway line

–·– International border

Baltic Sea

Mažeikiai

Telšiai   A11   Šiauliai
Palanga   A9
Plungė

Klaipėda   Gargždai   A1   L I T H
A13   Raseiniai
Šilutė   A12
Curonian Spit   141   Tauragė
Jurbarkas

Vilkaviškis
KALININGRAD   Marijampolė
(RUSSIA)
Lazdija
P O L A N D

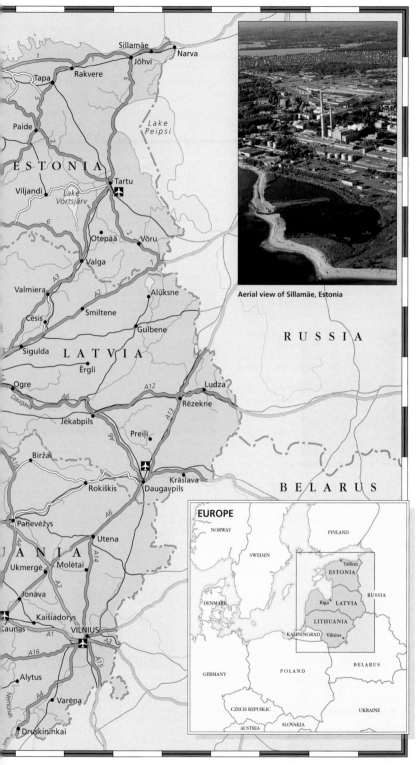

Aerial view of Sillamäe, Estonia

Architectural Styles

Ever since the wooden fortifications of the Baltic tribes were replaced by stone castles in the 13th and 14th centuries, foreign influences have dominated the architecture of Estonia, Latvia and Lithuania. Today, the Baltic capitals are architectural treasure troves, with Tallinn particularly noted for its medieval buildings, Vilnius for its Italian Baroque and Rīga for its Art Nouveau. The Soviet era saw the building of inexpensive mass housing. Since independence private investment has funded ambitious new projects.

Detail of the extravagant Gothic brickwork of Perkūnas House, Kaunas

ROMANESQUE AND GOTHIC

Brought to Tallinn and Rīga by medieval German invaders, the Romanesque style, with its heavy vaulting, round arches and restrained ornamentation, lasted briefly in the region. The ornate Gothic ribbed vaults, pointed arches and decorative façades were more popular. Tallinn boasts the finest examples, while most of Rīga's were destroyed as part of the 19th-century rebuilding of the city.

Estonian History Museum *was built in Tallinn for the Great Guild, a powerful organization of German-speaking merchants. This early 15th-century building has a stern Gothic façade and vaulted halls.*

Church of St Anne, *Vilnius's most celebrated Gothic building, was constructed using 33 types of red brick. So impressed was Napoleon Bonaparte that he is said to have wanted to take it back to Paris.*

Kuressaare Castle, *on Saaremaa Island, is the only intact Gothic-style medieval castle in the Baltic States. It is built in local dolomite.*

RENAISSANCE AND BAROQUE

The 15th- and 16th-century revival of Classical learning, which favoured architectural features such as regularity, symmetry and a central axis, found little expression in Lithuania. In Latvia and Estonia, however, it led to the addition of new façades to existing buildings. The bold 17th- and 18th-century Baroque style, endorsed by the Catholic church, found favour in the religious climate of Vilnius.

Pažaislis Monastery, *in Kaunas, is one of Eastern Europe's most prominent Baroque monuments. Built in the 17th century by Italian architects, the monastery church has a twin-towered façade, behind which soars the 52-m (171-ft) dome. A wealth of marble enriches the interior.*

House of Blackheads, *in Tallinn, was used by the Brotherhood of Blackheads. It was formerly a 14th-century building, which was redesigned in a Renaissance style in 1597. The interiors were renovated in Neo-Classical style in 1908.*

NEO-CLASSICAL AND HISTORICIST

The Neo-Classical style arrived in the Baltic States as late as the 1780s. The style had a strong influence on Tartu, as well as some of the finest manor houses throughout Estonia. However, most examples today are found in Tallinn, often as façades on earlier buildings; some Latvian and Lithuanian palaces also exhibit the style. Around 1820, the Historicist movement became popular, drawing inspiration from various styles including Gothic, Renaissance and Neo-Baroque.

Tartu's Town Hall *is an elegant Neo-Classical edifice, eye-catchingly painted in lilac and orange. It was designed in the 18th century by J H B Walter for the Pistohlkors family.*

Kaunas's Town Hall, *locally known as the "White Swan", was renovated in 1870 in Neo-Classical style. It also bears Baroque traces, most obviously in its 53-m (174-ft) tall stepped tower.*

Latvian National Theatre, *in Rīga, was designed in a superb Neo-Baroque style. It was completed in 1902 by architect Augusts Reinbergs under the influence of Historicist aesthetics.*

ART NOUVEAU, MODERNIST AND CONTEMPORARY

The second half of the 19th century saw Art Nouveau gaining a hold in Riga. After World War I there was a reaction against earlier flamboyant styles, with Modernists emphasizing function and Soviets favouring severe Functionalism. Since independence, further construction has taken place in the capitals, but it is not always in harmony with old architectural styles.

Alberta iela 13, *in Rīga, is a fine example of eclectic Art Nouveau, blending Classical and Symbolist imagery and Neo-Baroque stylistic features.*

Europa Tower, *in Vilnius, is one of a growing number of skyscrapers in the Baltic capitals, marking the return of the private sector.*

National Library, *in Tallinn, is one of the architectural triumphs of the late Soviet period. Raine Karp, the Estonian architect who designed it, used local dolomitic limestone.*

Landscape and Wildlife

The three Baltic countries are heavily forested with pine, spruce and birch and enjoy a predominantly flat terrain, although there are hilly areas such as the Vidzeme Upland in Latvia. The highest point in the region is Estonia's Suur Munamägi peak, which rises to about 318 m (1,043 ft) above sea level. The Baltic States are known for a dramatic coastline, innumerable lakes and rivers as well as extensive wetlands which, along with forests, provide habitats for a wide range of wildlife. The countries are also on major bird migration paths, making them popular with ornithologists all over the world. All three countries are still extensively covered with peat bogs, marshes and lakes.

Erratic boulders, *some of them very large, are common on the coastline of Estonia's Käsmu Peninsula (see p110). They were dragged there by glaciers during the last Ice Age.*

FOREST
Around 40 per cent of the total landscape in Estonia, Latvia and Lithuania is forested. Pine, spruce and birch are the main species, alongside other trees such as oak, ash, elm and maple. Trees were highly valued in the region's pre-Christian religions.

WETLANDS
The extensive wetlands of the region are ideal habitats for migrating birds, and for supporting plants such as cranberries and orchids. In Estonia, raised bogs in which thick layers of peat have built up are common. Many are protected by national parks.

FAUNA
The Baltic States are home to large mammals such as lynx, elk, deer, wolves and brown bears. With the region lying on major migration routes there are numerous nesting bird species including white stork, crane, barn swallow and grouse. The rivers and lakes teem with fish such as perch, trout and carp.

Bees *are highly valued in the region, as apiculture is an important industry and a part of the Baltic States' cultural heritage.*

White storks *are emblematic of the region and are often found nesting atop chimney pots or telegraph poles. Black storks are a relatively rare sight.*

Wolves *are found in the region's forests, especially in Lithuania. However, they are a rare sight, as hunting has resulted in the dwindling numbers of this predatory animal.*

FLORA

The Baltic States' forests and wetlands provide an environment in which a diverse range of plants can thrive. Many edible varieties of fungi and berries grow here. There is an orchid trail near Lake Engure, in Latvia, and yellow rattle and sea holly grow on Saaremaa and the Curonian Spit.

Arctic lichen *is a type of fungus found in Hiiumaa Island's Landscape Reserve. Like other lichen, it usually grows in two layers with a growth of algae in between.*

Mushrooms *are mostly wood decomposers or parasites. As the virgin forests are depleting, species of the former are becoming rarer.*

Orchids *grow mostly in the wetlands and woods. Those found here include rare North European species that are facing extinction.*

Berries, *such as cranberries, are eaten and also turned into wine.*

LAKES AND RIVERS

The region is dotted with lakes, of which Lake Peipsi in Estonia is the largest. There are a number of short rivers in the area. The low salinity of the Baltic Sea limits the number of plants and animal species it can support. Thus many of those present are freshwater species.

COASTLINE

Estonia has a sprawling coastline. It includes a stretch of the Baltic Klint, which is a long erosional escarpment stretching from Sweden to Russia. Another striking coastal feature is the Curonian Spit, a long sandy strip in Lithuania stretching to Kaliningrad.

The barn swallow, *the national bird of Estonia, often builds its nests in man-made structures.*

Ringed seals *are protected and can be found off the coast of Saaremaa and other Estonian islands.*

Brown bears *are omnivores and can be spotted in the forests of Estonia and Latvia, although they are usually sighted only with the help of a guide.*

Elk *is a game species that usually lives in forests and wetlands. It often appears on restaurant menus in the Baltic States.*

Religion

Although the Baltic lands were officially Christian by the end of the 14th century, pagan beliefs persisted and mingled with the new religion. Protestantism left its mark in the 16th century, but Lithuania soon returned to the Catholic fold. Today, it is the only country where the church plays a major public role. In Estonia and Latvia, the surge in religious participation after independence in 1991 proved short-lived. A significant number of ethnic Russians belong to the Russian Orthodox church, while other minority religious groups include Jews and Muslims.

Aerial view of the Orthodox Cathedral in Rīga, Latvia

Priest performing a Romuvan ritual, a popular modern religion

PAGANISM

Christianity came late to the Baltic region, with the Grand Duchy of Lithuania holding out until 1387, a year after Grand Duke Jogaila was baptized. The details of pagan beliefs are sparse, and scholars rely on surviving traditions and folk songs. Animism, the belief that plants and animals possess spirits, prevailed. Trees had great significance, with prayers offered at sacred groves.

Shamans communicated with the gods, but there was no organized priesthood. For Latvians and Lithuanians major deities included Dievs (the Sky God), Saule (the Sun), Pērkons or Perkūnas (Thunder), Velns (Trickster), Mēness (the Moon) and Laima (Fate). The Estonians and Livs (see p172) worshipped Taara (War), Uku (Thunder and Lightning), Vanetooni (the Dead), Maaema (Land), Ahti (Water) and Vanejumi (Fertility). Some scholars argue that these various

deities show aspects of one divine being. Pagan overtones are still present in a number of Christian celebrations.

The first period of independence of the 20th century saw attempts to revive old traditions. Some local organizations, such as Dievturība in Latvia, were nationalist in tone. After years of Soviet marginalization, Dievturība has now been revived, and in Lithuania, the pagan group Romuva has a fairly strong following.

ORTHODOX CHRISTIANITY

Orthodox missionaries arrived in the region as early as the 10th century but had little success, and Orthodox Christianity was largely eclipsed by Catholicism except among the Setu (see p120). This changed only under Russian rule in the 19th century, with many magnificent Orthodox churches built at that time.

Today, almost all Orthodox worshippers in the region are ethnic Russians. Their churches are known for the abundance of icons – images of Christ, Mary and various saints – often displayed in rows on a screen called an iconostasis. The region also contains small communities of Old Believers (see p122), descendants of worshippers who broke away from the Orthodox Church in protest against reforms introduced by Patriarch Nikon in 1652. Bringing Russian Orthodox rites in line with the Greek, his motives were both

Devotees lined up in Alexander Nevsky Church, Tallinn, Estonia

religious and political. The Old Believers sought to retain the purity of their faith, and the result was a schism (*raksol* in Russian) and their subsequent persecution. Many Old Believers fled from Russia, and today the main communities in the Baltic States are around Lake Peipsi (*see p123*) in Estonia and in the Latgale region of Latvia. Differences in rites include making the sign of the cross with two fingers (the Orthodox church now uses three) and changes to the wording of the Creed. Old Believers regard shaving a man's beard as sinful, and there are restrictions on smoking tobacco. Members often wear long traditional Russian shirts.

Catholic Church of the Holy Spirit, Vilnius, Lithuania

Old Believers' Church made of wood near Lake Peipsi

CATHOLICISM

Catholicism was brought to the region by force, with Pope Innocent III authorizing a crusade against the northern pagans in 1198. The areas which are now known as Estonia and Latvia fell first, with Lithuania hanging on until 1387.

The new religion was regarded as alien by the indigenous population, a feeling exacerbated by the use of Latin in services. Catholicism found its strongest roots in Eastern Latvia and Lithuania, both under the influence of Poland. These foundations were strengthened by the Counter-Reformation, the Catholic Church's response to the threat posed by Lutheranism. The newly established Jesuit order built schools and made efforts to use the native language, also emphasizing the importance of the Virgin Mary in an attempt to win back worshippers. Today Lithuania is the only country out of the three Baltic States where religion is central to national identity.

PROTESTANTISM

The Reformation was quickly felt in Estonia and Western Latvia, with the introduction of the revolutionary ideas of Lutheranism, a major branch of Protestant Christianity. The offshoot emphasized receiving God's grace through faith alone, rather than through good works. It first appeared in Estonian urban centres during the 1520s. Initially, the landowners resisted the change, but soon they recognized it as a useful way to resist the influence of the Pope. Peasants were expected to follow the faith of their landlords. The new beliefs were further bolstered by Swedish rule in the 17th century, when more pastors were trained and there was an increased use of indigenous languages for religious activities. The first Bible in Latvian was published in 1689 by the Lutheran theologian Ernst Glück (1654–1705).

There was a brief revival in religious activity after independence from the oppressive regime of the Soviet era, when many churches were converted to be used for other purposes. Although many Estonians and Latvians still follow Lutheranism, participation has declined in recent years and there are now marginally more Catholics than Lutherans in Latvia.

Virgin Mary's Lutheran Church, Otepää

Famous People

A history of cultural domination by other nations explains why only a handful of figures from the Baltic States are internationally known. It was only with the 19th-century national awakening movements that the notion of distinctive Baltic cultures gained popularity. After the brief confidence of the first independence, the restrictions of the Soviet era meant that most famous people from the region were either of Russian heritage or were living outside their native countries. In the years since independence in 1991, the arts have been hampered by reduced state funding and a population with little disposable income.

A portrait by Michael Sittow, a 15th-century Tallinn-born artist

VISUAL ARTS

Estonia's best-known painter was Eduard Wiiralt (1898–1954), while in the 20th century animators Elbert Tuganov (1920–2007) and Priit Pärn (b.1946) gained international praise. Within Latvia, painter Janis Rozentāls (1866–1916) remains most beloved, although Mark Rothko *(see p196)* is more famed abroad. Lithuania has produced several notable photographers, including Antanas Sutkus (b.1939).

Sergei Eisenstein *(1898–1948), one of the most influential film directors and theorists of all time, was born in Rīga. His groundbreaking use of editing is best seen in his early Marxist cinematic works, including* Strike! *(1924) and* Battleship Potemkin *(1925).*

Mikalojus Konstantinas Čiurlionis *(1875–1911), Lithuania's pre-eminent composer, was also an accomplished artist. His work draws extensively upon Symbolism and the influence of music can be found in his emphasis on mood, interest in harmony and development of themes across a series of paintings. The tempera on canvas shown above is entitled* The Offering *(1909).*

LITERATURE

Key to the 19th-century national awareness was the preservation of traditional stories and the creation of new myths by authors such as Latvian Andrejs Pumpurs (1841–1902), Estonian Friedrich Kreutzwald (1803–82) and Lithuanian Jonas Mačiulis (1862–1932). Modern literature is equally celebrated and famous authors include Estonian poets Jaan Kaplinski (b.1941) and Jaan Kross (1920–2007), and Lithuanian novelist Ričardas Gavelis (b.1950).

Anton Hansen Tammsaare *(1878–1940) is regarded as the greatest Estonian writer. His work,* Truth and Justice, *is a five-volume series of novels covering subjects that include rural Estonia and the Russian Revolution of 1905.*

Czesław Miłosz *(1911–2004) was born into a Polish aristocratic family and educated in Vilnius. Poet and intellectual, Miłosz won the Nobel Prize for Literature in 1980. He is perhaps best known for* The Captive Mind, *a prose critique of Communist ideology.*

MUSIC

Estonia has a strong tradition of classical composition. Veljo Tormis (b.1930) is influenced by Estonian folk music, while Erkki-Sven Tüür (b.1959) mixes avant-garde techniques with early music and progressive rock. The father of Latvian classical music is Jāzeps Vītols (1863–1948), and the country is also known for pop and rock performers such as the band Brainstorm. Lithuania is renowned for jazz musicians including the Ganelin Trio, while its finest classical composer was M K Čiurlionis.

Arvo Pärt *(b.1935), an Estonian composer, experimented with Schoenberg's 12-tone technique and the use of chance early on in his career. He is internationally known for "sacred minimalism", drawing on medieval traditions and Orthodox Christianity. Pärt describes his music as tintinnabuli* (like bells).

THEATRE AND DANCE

Professional theatre was once the domain of the ruling classes, but from the mid-19th century plays were written by authors such as Estonia's Eduard Vilde (1865–1933) and Latvia's Rūdolfs Blaumanis (1863–1908). Lithuania's lively theatre scene is dominated by director E Nekrošius (b.1952). Ballet thrived during the Soviet era, with the Rīga Ballet promoting Alexander Godunov (1949–95).

Mikhail Baryshnikov *(b.1948), born in Rīga, is of Russian descent. Baryshnikov began his ballet studies in the Latvian city before progressing to Leningrad (now St Petersburg). He defected while on tour in Canada in 1974. He later became a citizen of the USA and founded a dance centre in New York.*

Voldemar Panso *(1920–77), the famous theatre director, rejected Soviet ideology in favour of complex characters and the ambiguity of Symbolism. He also founded the Estonian Youth Theatre (later the Tallinn City Theatre).*

SPORT

The talent of Baltic athletes was, for many decades, obscured by their status as Soviet citizens. Estonia's most famous Olympian was heavyweight wrestler Kristjan Palusalu (1908–87), while Latvian long-distance walker Jānis Daliņš (1904–78) won the Olympic silver in 1932. Lithuania's top Olympic athlete is discus-thrower Virgljus Alekna (b.1972). The region has also produced exceptional basketball players, including Lithuanian Arvydas Sabonis (b.1964), Latvian Uljana Semjonova (b.1952) and Estonian Tiit Sokk (b.1964).

Erki Nool *(b.1970) won a gold medal in the decathlon at the 2000 Sydney Olympics, a controversial result since a judge had disallowed all three of his discus attempts before the competition referee overruled him. In 2007, he was elected to the Estonian Parliament.*

Uljana Semjonova *(b.1952), a basketball player of Russian-Latvian origin, won two Olympic gold medals in 1976 and 1980. She dominated the world basketball scene throughout the 1970s and 80s and never lost any official international match.*

Folk Songs and Music

The traditional songs of Estonia, Latvia and Lithuania typically deal with everyday events, calendar rituals and rites of passage, though stories of epic heroism and grandeur also exist. These songs are sung by women. Efforts to compile the songs began in earnest in the late 19th century and this was an important facet of the region's growing national awareness. Later, between 1987 and 1990, the struggle for freedom from the Soviet Union came to be known as the Singing Revolution, partly due to the role played by huge open-air concerts.

Cover of the 1998 album *Beyond the River: Seasonal Songs of Latvia*

Traditional Lithuanian songs, *or* dainos, *deal with daily life. They are sung solo, in unison or polyphonically. One of the best-known forms is the duophonic* sutartinė *from the northeast.*

Monophonic Estonian songs, *or* runo, *are related to those from Finland, and their roots are much older than those of Latvia and Lithuania. The Setu people of Eastern Estonia have their own distinctive polyphonic singing traditions.*

BALTICA FESTIVAL

This annual international folklore festival was first held in Estonia in 1987 and is hosted cyclically by the Baltic States. The three Baltic flags were hoisted together for the first time during the second festival in 1987. Today, the festival brings together around 3,000 participants and includes concerts, parades and workshops.

Latvian folk songs, *or* dainas, *consist of one or two stanzas each with two non-rhyming couplets. This singing tradition is lyrical and usually draws inspiration from pagan mythology or daily life. Traditionally, these songs were accompanied by instruments such as bagpipes and psalteries, with accordions and fiddles added in the 17th century.*

Veljo Tormis
(b.1930) is a celebrated composer of choral music based on the folk songs of his native Estonia. Many of his more political pieces of the 1970s and 80s were censored by the Soviet government.

Iļģi, *the famous Latvian folk music band, was formed in 1981. Like most folk musicians of the country, they revived forgotten traditions and developed into a band that used folklore as an impulse for creating music of their own.*

BALTIC FOLK SINGERS

The Soviet era saw government-approved performers refine folk songs with classical harmonies and accompaniment, but enthusiasts worked to preserve genuine traditions. Today, a number of festivals are held all over the region.

Veronika Povilionienė
(b.1946) has enjoyed success since the late 1960s, promoting folk singing as a mode of anti-Soviet protest. In recent years, she has also recorded pop and jazz albums.

THE BALTIC PSALTERY

The most characteristic instrument used by the region's folk singers is the Baltic psaltery. It exists in numerous variations, and is known as *kokle* in Latvia, *kanklės* in Lithuania and *kannel* in Estonia. In the late 19th century, hybrids influenced by German and Austrian zithers were developed.

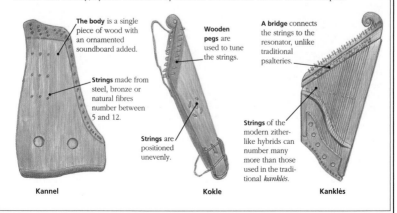

The body is a single piece of wood with an ornamented soundboard added.

Strings made from steel, bronze or natural fibres number between 5 and 12.

Wooden pegs are used to tune the strings.

Strings are positioned unevenly.

A bridge connects the strings to the resonator, unlike traditional psalteries.

Strings of the modern zither-like hybrids can number many more than those used in the traditional *kanklės*.

Kannel

Kokle

Kanklės

Baltic Amber

Amber has been valued for millennia, with amber jewellery found dating back to the early Neolithic period (around 7000 BC). Many medical authorities of the ancient world, including Hippocrates, believed that amber had healing properties. A trade network, now known as the Amber Route, arose at the height of the Roman Empire. In the medieval period, amber was used to make rosaries. Today, it still washes up on Latvian and Lithuanian shores, although 90 per cent of the world's amber is mined in the Curonian Spit of neighbouring Kaliningrad.

One of the many amber stalls found in tourist areas

IDENTIFYING AMBER

Sellers may pass off copal or plastic as genuine amber. Genuine amber floats in salt water and exudes a pine scent when touched with a red-hot needle, but only laboratory tests are conclusive.

Unpolished amber of different colours and shapes

Amber-catchers *in the Baltic Sea are shown in this lithograph from the 1850s. In the 13th century, local amber-gathering was forbidden by the Teutonic Knights. Their monopoly was lifted only in the 19th century, reviving amber-working traditions.*

Amber pieces *are regularly washed ashore in Pāvilosta (see p179), a small port town in Latvia. There are a handful of professional amber-catchers, and tourists can arrange to go out with them.*

FORMATION OF AMBER

Before it is washed up on the coasts of the Baltic States, especially after raging storms, amber takes millions of years to transform from pine resin into a sought-after substance. Often clear, it can also have pine needles or insects trapped in the resin before it solidified.

Tree Exuding Resin
Certain trees exude a sticky resin, which has a range of defensive functions. Its antiseptic qualities kill bacteria and fungi, while its stickiness inhibits physical attack from insects.

Insects Trapped in Amber
Any insects stuck in the resin are prevented from decaying, as the substance is antiseptic and lacking in water. Slowly, the volatile components evaporate, leaving behind copal.

Copal Formation
Copal, or hardened resin, becomes incorporated into the ground after the tree dies. The solidification process continues for millions of years, until the inert substance becomes amber.

USES OF AMBER

In addition to its decorative value, amber was once considered to have healing powers and even today some Lithuanians consider it to be a cure for goitre. The Aztecs and Maya are known to have burnt amber as incense.

Knife decorated with amber

Delicately crafted amber jewellery

Typical amber box

Exquisite brooch fashioned in amber

THE AMBER ROUTE

An EU-funded project has devised a modern-day Amber Route that links a series of cities along the Baltic Coast. Starting from Ventspils *(see pp176–7)*, the route takes in Palanga *(see p282)*, Liepāja *(see pp180–81)* and Klaipėda *(see pp280–81)*. While some of these towns have amber museums, Palanga also has an amber-processing workshop. Nida in Lithuania has a museum that exhibits amber. The route also takes in Karklė and Pāvilosta, with professional amber-catchers. Juodkrantė, once the site of major amber-mining activity, boasts a collection of prehistoric amber artifacts. Further south is Kaliningrad, a Russian outpost, which is the source of the vast majority of the world's amber.

Amber Museum in Palanga
(see p282) *features a stunning collection of amber pieces with prehistoric insects trapped inside, as well as amber jewellery. There is also a display presenting the natural history of amber.*

An amber-polishing workshop,
held by experts, offers participants the opportunity to create their own jewellery. Some amber museums across the Baltic States conduct these workshops.

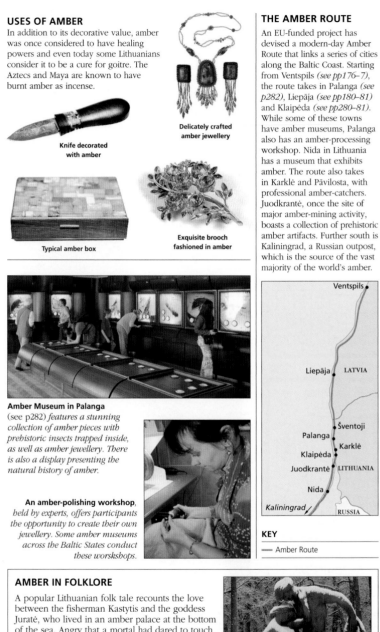

Ventspils

Liepāja   LATVIA

Šventoji

Palanga
            Karklė

Klaipėda

Juodkrantė   LITHUANIA

Nida

Kaliningrad   RUSSIA

KEY

— Amber Route

AMBER IN FOLKLORE

A popular Lithuanian folk tale recounts the love between the fisherman Kastytis and the goddess Juratė, who lived in an amber palace at the bottom of the sea. Angry that a mortal had dared to touch a goddess, the god Perkūnas sent lightning to destroy the palace and drown Kastytis. It is believed that pieces of the palace have been washing up on the shore ever since. The well-known story was first recorded in writing by Liudvikas Adomas Jucevičius in 1842, and the tale has even been adapted into a rock opera.

Jūratė kaj Kastytis by Nijolė Ona Gaigalaitė

The Climate of Estonia, Latvia and Lithuania

With the Baltic Sea as a moderating influence, the Baltic region has a temperate climate without the extremes that afflict neighbouring Russia. Winters are gloomy, however, with short days and bitter winds. The first snow usually falls in November, and inland there can be constant snow cover from December to April. The snowy season is shorter on the coast, where temperatures are noticeably lower in summer and higher in winter. At other times the weather is unpredictable, with rain even in the middle of summer when days are long and warm.

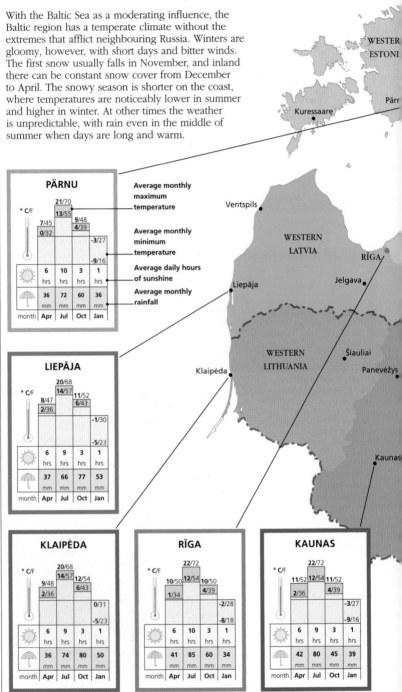

PÄRNU

°C/F

	21/70 13/55	9/48 4/39		
7/45 0/32			-3/27	
			-9/16	

☀	6 hrs	10 hrs	3 hrs	1 hrs
☂	36 mm	72 mm	60 mm	36 mm
month	Apr	Jul	Oct	Jan

Average monthly maximum temperature

Average monthly minimum temperature

Average daily hours of sunshine

Average monthly rainfall

LIEPĀJA

°C/F

	20/68 14/57	11/52 6/43		
8/47 2/36			-1/30	
			-5/23	

☀	6 hrs	9 hrs	3 hrs	1 hrs
☂	37 mm	66 mm	77 mm	53 mm
month	Apr	Jul	Oct	Jan

KLAIPĖDA

°C/F

	20/68 14/57	12/54 6/43		
9/48 2/36			0/31	
			-5/23	

☀	6 hrs	9 hrs	3 hrs	1 hrs
☂	36 mm	74 mm	80 mm	50 mm
month	Apr	Jul	Oct	Jan

RĪGA

°C/F

	22/72 10/50 12/54 10/50			
1/34		4/39	-2/28	
			-8/18	

☀	6 hrs	10 hrs	3 hrs	1 hrs
☂	41 mm	85 mm	60 mm	34 mm
month	Apr	Jul	Oct	Jan

KAUNAS

°C/F

	22/72 11/52 12/54 11/52			
2/36		4/39	-3/27	
			-9/16	

☀	6 hrs	9 hrs	3 hrs	1 hrs
☂	42 mm	80 mm	45 mm	39 mm
month	Apr	Jul	Oct	Jan

WESTERN ESTONIA

Kuressaare

Pärnu

Ventspils

WESTERN LATVIA

RĪGA

Jelgava

Liepāja

Klaipėda

WESTERN LITHUANIA

Šiauliai

Panevėžys

Kaunas

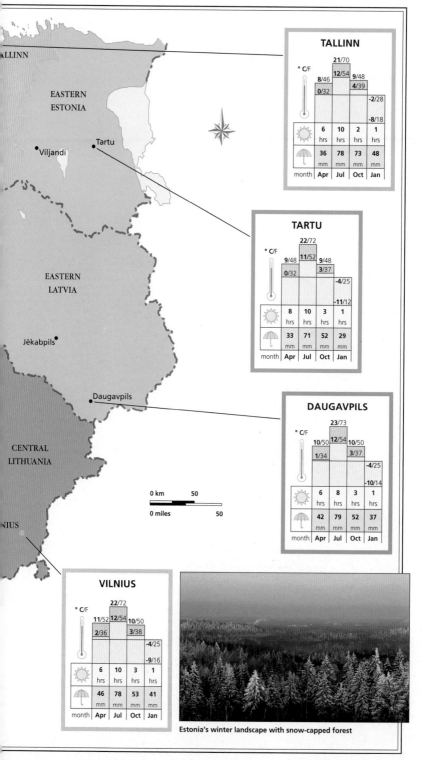

TALLINN

°C/F

21/70
12/54
8/46   9/48
0/32   4/39
        -2/28
        -8/18

☀	6 hrs	10 hrs	2 hrs	1 hrs
☂	36 mm	78 mm	73 mm	48 mm
month	Apr	Jul	Oct	Jan

TARTU

°C/F

22/72
11/52
9/48   9/48
0/32   3/37
        -4/25
        -11/12

☀	8 hrs	10 hrs	3 hrs	1 hrs
☂	33 mm	71 mm	52 mm	29 mm
month	Apr	Jul	Oct	Jan

DAUGAVPILS

°C/F

23/73
10/50 12/54 10/50
1/34   3/37
              -4/25
              -10/14

☀	6 hrs	8 hrs	3 hrs	1 hrs
☂	42 mm	79 mm	52 mm	37 mm
month	Apr	Jul	Oct	Jan

VILNIUS

°C/F

22/72
11/52 12/54 10/50
2/36   3/38
              -4/25
              -9/16

☀	6 hrs	10 hrs	3 hrs	1 hrs
☂	46 mm	78 mm	53 mm	41 mm
month	Apr	Jul	Oct	Jan

Map labels: TALLINN, EASTERN ESTONIA, Viljandi, Tartu, EASTERN LATVIA, Jēkabpils, Daugavpils, CENTRAL LITHUANIA, VILNIUS

0 km   50
0 miles   50

Estonia's winter landscape with snow-capped forest

THE HISTORY OF ESTONIA, LATVIA AND LITHUANIA

he history of the Baltic region begins only in 2000 BC with the arrival of the early Baltic tribes, the ancestors of today's Estonians, Latvians and Lithuanians. Despite a shared experience of conquests, foreign occupations and struggles for independence, the three countries have preserved their distinct cultural identities, emerging in 1991 as sovereign states.

Archaeological evidence suggests that the Baltic region was inhabited as early as 10,000 BC, at the end of the Ice Age. The earliest occupied site, at Kernavė in Lithuania, dates back to 9000 BC. These Stone Age people used bows, arrows and spears for hunting and fishing. It was not until 3000 BC, however, that the ancestors of the current inhabitants began to arrive. Surviving by hunting and fishing, the Finno-Ugrians – the future Finns and Estonians – were among the first to drift across Europe from Asia. They were pushed back by the Indo-European groups that arrived in 2000 BC. The Indo-Europeans, who introduced crop cultivation and animal rearing to the traditional modes of subsistence, mingled with the existing groups, eventually forming the races now known collectively as the Balts.

During the first centuries AD, distinctive regional tribes began to form. These were the Samogitians (Lowlanders) and Aukštaitijans (Highlanders) in western and eastern Lithuania, the Curonians along the

Coin dedicated to Kernavė, Lithuania

coast, the Prussians beyond the Nemunas river, the Zemgalians in central Latvia and the Selonians and Latgalians further east. For several centuries, the Balts remained firmly rural, living off the land. Until the early 1200s, there were similar but unrelated settlements all along the coast from what is now Klaipėda as far as St Petersburg. There are very few records of life at that time as the local communities used wood rather than stone for all their fortifications and housing. Archaeological research has shown that there were extensive trading networks across the sea from this area to Sweden and Germany and inland towards Russia. The little written material from that time talks about the Balts as good boat-builders and dreaded pirates.

At a time when the rest of Europe had embraced Christianity, the Balts staunchly practised paganism. After haphazard attempts by small groups of Western European missionaries to convert the area to Christianity failed, the first Baltic crusade was sanctioned by Pope Innocent III in 1198.

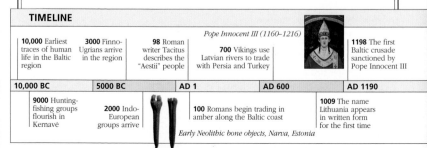

TIMELINE

10,000 Earliest traces of human life in the Baltic region

3000 Finno-Ugrians arrive in the region

98 Roman writer Tacitus describes the "Aestii" people

Pope Innocent III (1160–1216)

700 Vikings use Latvian rivers to trade with Persia and Turkey

1198 The first Baltic crusade sanctioned by Pope Innocent III

10,000 BC	5000 BC	AD 1	AD 600	AD 1190

9000 Hunting-fishing groups flourish in Kernavė

2000 Indo-European groups arrive

100 Romans begin trading in amber along the Baltic coast

Early Neolithic bone objects, Narva, Estonia

1009 The name Lithuania appears in written form for the first time

◁ **Detail from Jan Matejko's *Battle of Grünwald* (1878) showing Grand Duke Vytautas defeating the Teutonic Knights**

GERMANS IN ESTONIA AND LATVIA

After the papal declaration of the crusade, the Teutonic Knights, or the German warrior-monks who called themselves the Brotherhood of the Sword, began to venture along the Baltic coast. The phrase *"Drang nach Osten"* ("Thrust Eastwards"), which would become notorious in World War II, dates from this time. Religious and commercial zeal drove the crusaders to establish colonies along the Baltic coast. In 1201, a bishopric was set up in Rīga, which became the basis for the Baltic conquest. Expanding into Estonia from the south, the Knights created Livonia in 1207. Comprising Latvia and Estonia, Livonia was recognized as part of the Holy Roman Empire, with Rīga as the capital. Estonia's largest island,

Saaremaa, was subjugated in 1227. A fortress built in 1260 at its capital, Kuressaare, is the only one in the Baltic region to be preserved largely as the Teutonic Knights built it. Livonia flourished under the Knights, as they built cities throughout the region. After joining the Hanseatic League, a trading confederation of German port-cities and merchants' associations, Tallinn and Rīga began to thrive. The new social order, dominated by the Germans, excluded the local inhabitants not only from mercantile activities, but also agriculture, where they could only be hired as serfs.

POLISH DOMINATION IN LITHUANIA

Lithuania had a very different history from that of the area to its north. While Christianity was dominant in much of the Baltic region, Lithuania continued to be resolutely pagan until 1385, when Duke Jogaila married a Polish princess, embraced Christianity and assumed the crowns of Poland and Lithuania. Long before him, in 1251, Mindaugas had briefly adopted Christianity so that he could be crowned by the Pope. In 1410, Jogaila and his cousin Vytautas (r.1410–30), Grand Prince of Lithuania, decisively defeated the Teutonic Knights in the Battle of Žalgiris, or Grünwald. Under Vytautas, the Grand Duchy of Lithuania *(see pp212–13)* emerged as one of the largest states in Europe. Eventually, however, it came increasingly under the control of the Poles, with the relationship culminating in the creation of Polish-Lithuanian Commonwealth in 1569. With

A 19th-century lithograph showing the Battle of Grünwald (1410)

TIMELINE

1201 German crusaders set up a bishopric in Rīga	**1237** The Brotherhood of the Sword becomes Livonian Order			**1372** German replaces Latin as the official language in Rīga and Tallinn	**1410** Lithuanians and Poles defeat the Teutonic Knights at the Battle of Žalgiris (Grünwald)
		1260 Building of Kuressaare Castle starts	*Kuressaare Castle*		

1200	1250	1300	1350	1400	1450

	1230 Mindaugas unites the Grand Duchy of Lithuania	**1282** Rīga joins the Hanseatic League; Tallinn follows three years later	**1385** Lithuania united with Poland under Jogaila		**1430** The Grand Duchy reaches the Black Sea
1207 Livonia becomes part of the Holy Roman Empire					

Siege of Narva by the Russians in 1558 during the Livonian Wars

the Polish takeover, the right to own land was lost, privileges of the peasantry were curbed and serfdom was firmly established in Lithuania.

THE SWEDES AND THE RUSSIANS

Sweden and Russia fought two major wars to ensure control over the Baltic Sea and the surrounding land. In the Livonian Wars (1558–83), Poland and Lithuania were involved in resisting the armies of Russia's Ivan the Terrible (r.1533–84), in view of the destruction he had wrought in Livonia. The immediate aftermath of the war resulted in most of Estonia coming under Swedish rule, while Latvia endured a Polish occupation and Lithuania's full union with Poland was formalized. Southern and Eastern Latvia, commonly known as Courland and Latgale respectively, became duchies owing allegiance to Poland.

War soon broke out again, this time between the Poles and the Swedes, and in 1621, the Swedes seized Rīga and northern Latvia. The Duchy of Courland stayed in Polish hands, although the dukes almost became rulers in their own right. The most prominent of them, Duke Jakob Kettler (r.1642–82), brought the duchy to the pinnacle of its wealth and

power. The Swedish occupation, regarded as the gentlest Livonia ever endured, was marked by a benign governance. The Germans, meanwhile, continued to hold sway in Livonia, socially and culturally. When an alternative to Latin was needed in the churches, German was the obvious choice. The universities at Rīga and Tartu taught exclusively in German. German merchants were granted special rights by the Swedish rulers, Charles XI (r.1660–97) and Charles XII (r.1697–1718), to ensure the continuity of commerce.

After the German barons' estates were expropriated by the Swedish crown, they turned to Russia for help. In 1700, Charles XII defeated Peter the Great of Russia at Narva, marking the beginning of the Great Northern War (1700–21). The loss at Narva inspired the Tsar to create a modern army and, in 1709, using a bitter winter to his advantage, he defeated the Swedes at the Battle of Poltava. In 1710, Tallinn and Rīga were occupied and soon Estonia and Latvia were brought under Russian control.

Battle of Poltava, a work by M Lomonosov (1711–65)

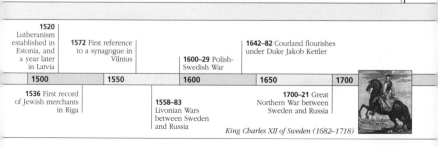

1520 Lutheranism established in Estonia, and a year later in Latvia	1572 First reference to a synagogue in Vilnius	1600–29 Polish-Swedish War	1642–82 Courland flourishes under Duke Jakob Kettler	
1500	**1550**	**1600**	**1650**	**1700**
1536 First record of Jewish merchants in Rīga		1558–83 Livonian Wars between Sweden and Russia	1700–21 Great Northern War between Sweden and Russia	

King Charles XII of Sweden (1682–1718)

Tsar Alexander I with a soldier holding the Imperial Standard

1812, Napoleon's Grand Army marched through Vilnius en route to Moscow, and was greeted by the people as liberators. In the same year Napoleon returned there, retreating ignominiously, not because the Russians had fought him successfully, but because they denied him supplies. In a pre-emptive move, the Russians burnt down the wooden suburbs of Rīga to give them a clear firing line for defending the town. Eventually, the French army was forced to retreat.

UNDER TSARIST RULE

Peter the Great treated his new conquests with respect, as the Swedes had done before him. He continued to give the local German community considerable autonomy, both with their trading rights in the towns and with their manor houses in the countryside. After his death in 1725, a unique century of peace followed. There were neither invasions nor local uprisings. The Jews *(see pp36–7)*, who had flourished under the Duchy of Lithuania, gradually spreading into Latvia and parts of Estonia, continued to thrive. By the 18th century, Vilnius had become the Jewish capital of Eastern Europe, referred to as Vilna. Under Catherine the Great (r.1762–96), the Russian Empire expanded to include Lithuania's Grand Duchy, which resulted from the third, and final, partition of Poland in 1795.

Tsar Alexander I (r.1801–25) was forced to forsake his dreams of reconstituting the Grand Duchy, when, in

A CENTURY OF UNEASY PEACE

Under Alexander I, a series of agrarian laws were passed. Serfdom was abolished between 1816 and 1819, and peasants were allowed to buy and sell land. Civil unrest, however, came from the intelligentsia in the towns, dissatisfied by the religious domination of the Orthodox Church and the increasing use of the Russian language. Between 1830 and 1831, the movement was at its strongest in Lithuania and one of the countermeasures taken by the Russian authorities was to close Vilnius University in 1832, hoping that this would quell the unrest. In 1864, they resorted to banning the publication of books in Lithuanian using the Latin alphabet; books were now to be transcribed into Cyrillic. This encouraged publishers in Prussia to produce books in the Latin

An 1864 print in Lithuanian using the Latin alphabet

TIMELINE

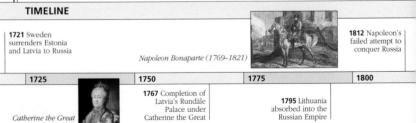

1721 Sweden surrenders Estonia and Latvia to Russia

Napoleon Bonaparte (1769–1821)

1812 Napoleon's failed attempt to conquer Russia

1725	1750	1775	1800

1767 Completion of Latvia's Rundāle Palace under Catherine the Great

Catherine the Great (1729–96)

1795 Lithuania absorbed into the Russian Empire

alphabet and to smuggle them across the border. By the 1860s, nationalist movements were equally active in Latvia and Estonia. In 1869, the first Estonian Song Festival was held, and in the following year, the writer Lydia Koidula produced her first play in Estonian, having previously only written in German. It is significant that both events took place in Tartu and not in Tallinn, where German and Russian influence was still too strong. The Latvian writer Krišjānis Valdemārs also caused a stir in Tartu by printing his name-card in Latvian. It was not until 1900, however, that Estonians, Latvians and Lithuanians could freely proclaim their nationalities in their capital cities.

Latvian writer Krišjānis Valdemārs (1825–91)

In the 19th century, as in the 18th, the Russians delegated local administration to the Germans. It was, therefore, the Germans, and not the Russians, who gained from the commercial potential of mass production, railways and steamships. Rīga and Tallinn expanded hugely as ports and manufacturing centres. The prospect of work drew many people from rural areas into the larger towns.

WAR RETURNS

Strikes and demonstrations took place in 1905 in many cities throughout Russia, to pressurize the Tsarist regime to grant civil rights and improve social conditions. Given the size of its industrial workforce at this time, Rīga was an active participant in this unrest. In the countryside, protests were directed against the German landed gentry and manor houses all over the region were attacked. These were social rather than nationalistic movements, partly as the Balts were now able to use their own languages openly and could also take part in local administration. National aspirations were, however, forcibly dampened at the outbreak of World War I (1914–18). The Russian Revolution of 1917, which resulted in the collapse of Tsarist Russia and which brought the Bolsheviks to power, played a significant role in changing the course of the region's history. The Civil War that followed soon after was seen as an opportunity for the Baltic States to take control of their destiny.

A turn-of-the-19th-century postcard impression of Rīga, one of Eastern Europe's most vibrant cities

1854 Crimean War breaks out; British Navy blockades Russian Baltic ports

1870 Tallinn–St Petersburg railway opens

1917 Russian Revolution and Civil War stimulate Baltic independence movements

| 1825 | 1850 | 1875 | 1900 |

1832 Russians close Vilnius University to curtail spread of nationalist ideas

Liepāja tram 1 at Liela iela, Latvia

1899 First Baltic electric tram line opens in Liepāja

1905 Urban and rural attacks on German and Russian business

1916 Election of first Latvian mayor of Rīga

Jewish History

Star worn by Jews during the Holocaust

The history of Jewish settlement in the Baltic region began in the 14th century, when King Gediminas invited merchants and craftsmen into the Grand Duchy of Lithuania. Estonia only ever had a small Jewish population, while Jews arrived in Latvia in the 15th century, but were only allowed to settle in Rīga much later. During World War II, almost all Jews who did not flee were killed. Although some returned, the Jewish communities today are dwindling, partly due to emigration to Israel.

Jewish Vilna's itinerant clothes-sellers photographed in 1915

The Gaon of Vilna (1720–97) *was Lithuania's most famous Jewish scholar, whose writing and research still guide many in the Jewish community today. In 1997, the celebration of the bicentenary of his birth brought Litvaks, former Lithuanian Jews, back to Vilnius from all over the world.*

JEWS IN THE BALTIC REGION

Banned from buying property and taking up professions until the late 19th century, the Jewish population lived largely as itinerant tradesmen and market stall-holders. After World War I, Jews were granted full rights as citizens. Until their persecution by the Nazis in 1941, when they were killed in large numbers, the Jews were active in the professions, business and politics.

Rīga's Great Choral Synagogue *was built in 1869 for the city's Jews, who thrived after the laws restricting Jewish residence were lifted in 1840. The site of a Jewish massacre executed by the Nazis in 1941, the synagogue no longer exists.*

Children celebrating Purim *were photographed in 1933 in Vilnius. Purim, a joyful festival in the Jewish calendar, is still celebrated by the Jewish community in the Baltic region today.*

Kenesa, a 20th-century synagogue in Trakai, *is where the Karaim* (see p253) *congregate. An ethnically Turkish community from the northern shores of the Black Sea, they first settled in Trakai in the 14th century.*

Makkabi Sports Association *was one of the Jewish organizations that thrived in independent Latvia between 1920 and 1940, when the government worked hard to eliminate anti-Semitism.*

The Paneriai Holocaust Memorial (see p244), *just outside Vilnius, commemorates the 70,000 Jews who were murdered here during the Nazi occupation (1941–44). In Latvia, 66,000 Jews were massacred, while Estonia, where 4,300 Jews lived prior to World War II, was declared "Jew free".*

Rīga's Museum of the Jews in Latvia *documents 500 years of Jewish history in the region, and includes this poster used by anti-Semitic groups.*

Tallinn's Beit Bella Synagogue *was opened on 16 May 2007. The city had been without a synagogue since the destruction of an earlier one during World War II. Today, a 3,000-strong Jewish community lives in Estonia, while in Latvia and Lithuania, Jews now number over 9,000 and 4,000 respectively.*

Estonia's Constituent Assembly in session, 1919

INDEPENDENCE DECLARED

As Western Europe welcomed peace in November 1918, the Baltic area was one enormous battlefield. Anti-Bolsheviks still hoped to overthrow the new Soviet regime, and the Germans wanted to make up for losses in the West with victories in the East. The Poles were keen to form another commonwealth with Lithuania. As a result, there was little interest in supporting the declarations of independence made by the three Baltic States early that year. Only a large British fleet, stationed off the Estonian coast, was happy to supply arms to Estonia and Latvia and, therefore, help them achieve independence.

By early 1920, Estonia and Latvia were able to fight off all their enemies and get them to agree to borders, which would hold until 1940. Lithuania was forced to give up Vilnius, after the Poles seized it later that year. Subsequently, Kaunas was made the

temporary capital. Lithuanians compensated themselves to some extent by seizing Memel (Klaipėda) in 1923 from French troops.

For the next 20 years, the three countries operated in a very similar manner. Weak, ever-changing governments in the 1920s gave way in the 1930s to strong statesmen who ran the state on Mussolini's corporatist model. Even though nobody in any Baltic government had had a senior position before independence, it was remarkable what they were able to achieve in such a short period of time. In Estonia and Latvia, the German estates were seized but the many successful urban businesses that had been established in the previous century were allowed to continue as before.

THE SOVIET OCCUPATION

On 17 June 1940, the Baltic countries fell to the Russians, as agreed in the Molotov-Ribbentrop Pact, a non-aggression treaty signed between Germany and the USSR. All traces of the previous 20 years of independence were removed. Senior members of the three governments were executed. Flags, national anthems and Bibles were banned. The Soviet Union did not want to be reminded of its failure to conquer the Baltic States at the end of World War I. In June 1941, a massive deportation to Siberia was organized of around 10,000 Estonians, 15,000 Latvians and 30,000 Lithuanians, most of whom died. A week later, Germany invaded the Baltic States, violating the Molotov-Ribbentrop Pact.

The USSR and Germany signing the Molotov-Ribbentrop Pact of 1939

TIMELINE

1918 The three Baltic States declare independence

1922 Russia becomes Soviet Union (USSR)

1920 Russia recognizes independence of the three Baltic States

1939 Molotov-Ribbentrop Pact signed between the USSR and Germany

1940 The three Baltic countries incorporated into the USSR

1925

1935

1941 German occupation of the Baltics begins

1945 Soviet reoccupation

1945

1956 Baltic deportees allowed back from Siberia

1960 Foreign tourists begin to be allowed to visit the Baltic capitals

1955

196

Soviet tanks in Riga, 1940

A chain of people joining hands to form the "Baltic Way" across the three Baltic States

Soviet forces, who called themselves "liberators", slowly reconquered most of the Baltic region during the autumn of 1944, as they drove the Germans westwards. In anticipation of their return, many locals fled to Sweden or Germany. Others who stayed joined the partisans based in the countryside. Known as Forest Brothers, they were a very effective guerrilla force until the mid-1950s, disrupting the Soviet administration throughout the region. All the links with the outside world were broken, including trading routes.

Aware that it had only minimal popular support, the Soviet government knew that the incorporation of the Baltic States could only be achieved and maintained with brute force. In each country, the Russian military occupied large parts to which access was strictly controlled and all the paperwork needed was only in Russian. The Russification policies followed by the Tsars were enforced once again in order to stamp out the national identities of Estonia, Latvia and Lithuania. They imposed such uniformity that it became challenging for an outsider to distinguish one Baltic State from the other. In 1989, a human chain, referred to as the "Baltic Way",

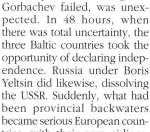

Soviet President Mikhail Gorbachev

was formed across the three Baltic States to draw the world's attention to their shared history of suffering.

INDEPENDENCE RETURNS

Perestroika (reform) and *glasnost* (openness), the two buzz words of Mikhail Gorbachev's regime (1985–91), had a dramatic effect in the Baltic region. Independence could be discussed openly and national flags reappeared. By 1990, independence for Estonia, Latvia and Lithuania could be predicted, but only in the long term. However, its sudden arrival on 21 August 1991, when an attempted coup in Moscow against Gorbachev failed, was unexpected. In 48 hours, when there was total uncertainty, the three Baltic countries took the opportunity of declaring independence. Russia under Boris Yeltsin did likewise, dissolving the USSR. Suddenly, what had been provincial backwaters became serious European countries, with their own airlines, currencies and, above all, recognition on a worldwide basis. In 2004, the three Baltic States joined the EU and NATO (North Atlantic Treaty Organization), and in 2007, acceded to the Schengen Agreement.

1994 Last Russian troops leave the Baltic region

1991 Independence restored to the three Baltic countries

2002 Eurovision Song Contest held in Tallinn; a year later in Riga

Eurovision Song Contest 2002

2011 Estonia joins the Eurozone

| 1975 | 1985 | 1995 | 2005 | 2015 |

1980 Moscow Olympics' sailing events held in Tallinn

1989 Two million people hold hands from Tallinn to Vilnius, known as the "Baltic Way"

2004 Baltic States join EU and NATO; accede to the Schengen Agreement three years later

Coin issued in 1999 to mark the tenth anniversary of the "Baltic Way"

ESTONIA

Estonia at a Glance

The smallest of the Baltic States, Estonia is divided
into two geographical regions, Western Estonia
and Eastern Estonia. Apart from the hilly region in
the southeast, most of the country is low-lying and
is punctuated with innumerable lakes and rivers.
Estonia's deeply indented coastline and archipelago of many islands offer some dramatic
scenery. The country's predominantly flat landscape
is sparsely populated and made up of forests, wetlands and peatbogs that teem with wildlife.

Tallinn (see pp54–83), *the
capital of Estonia, is among
the best-preserved cities in
Northern Europe. The city is
a compact and harmonious
blend of medieval
and modern
architecture.*

TALLINN
(see pp54–83)

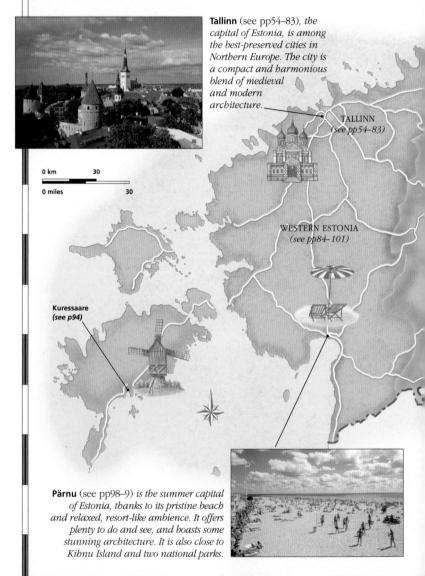

0 km   30

0 miles   30

WESTERN ESTONIA
(see pp84–101)

Kuressaare
(see p94)

Pärnu (see pp98–9) *is the summer capital
of Estonia, thanks to its pristine beach
and relaxed, resort-like ambience. It offers
plenty to do and see, and boasts some
stunning architecture. It is also close to
Kihnu Island and two national parks.*

◁ Street in Old Town Tallinn, with St Nicholas's Orthodox Church in the background

Lahemaa National Park (see pp106–109), *the largest national park in Estonia, has diverse terrain criss-crossed by hiking trails. It is dotted with villages such as Palmse, whose manor house contains the park's information centre.*

Narva (see p112) *has a fortified medieval castle that illustrates how this largely Russian-speaking city was at the frontline of regional power struggles for centuries.*

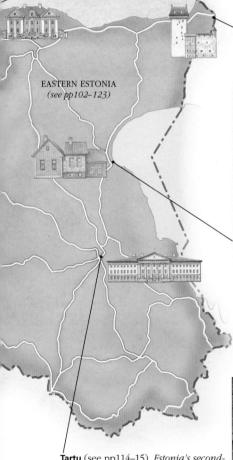

EASTERN ESTONIA
(see pp102–123)

Lake Peipsi (see p123) *is a huge body of water bordering Russia. A number of settlements with wooden houses mark the lakeshore. The Old Believers live in numerous little lakeshore villages towards the north, while the Setu live in the southern environs.*

Tartu (see pp114–15), *Estonia's second-largest city, is famed for its university and has an exciting cultural and nightlife scene. The city rivals Tallinn in charm and splendour, as well as historic significance.*

A PORTRAIT OF ESTONIA

*P*resenting a heady mix of medieval heritage and technological advancement, Estonia has rebuilt itself in the post-Soviet era, adapting to the demands of the modern world while preserving a distinct cultural identity. With its rich historic architecture, natural landscapes and dynamic culture, the country makes a significant impression on the ever-growing number of visitors that it attracts.

Estonia's tumultuous history has resulted from its geographical position as a crossroads between Eastern and Western Europe. With Russia dominating its eastern border, Scandinavia surrounding it to the north and west and the other two Baltic States to its south, Estonia was considered a prize strategic asset among the regional powers through the centuries.

Sign outside Olde Hansa restaurant

After regaining independence from the Soviet Union in 1991, Estonia was left severely dilapidated. During the long slog towards NATO and EU membership throughout the 1990s, Estonia was often held up by Eastern Europe as an example of how to rapidly modernize while preserving national heritage and improving overall living conditions. Estonia is sometimes referred to as e-Estonia due to its reputation for technological innovation. It has almost total Wi-Fi coverage and one of the highest rates of mobile phone usage in the world. Although the rural areas still lag behind the cities in raising living standards, Estonia has grown into a major travel destination. Its forests and marshlands, pristine islands and traditional villages are as alluring as its capital Tallinn, a pulsating city with a medieval Old Town.

Estonia's typical river scenery with yellow leaves and green mossy stones

◁ A group of Estonian folk dancers performing in national costume

Participants awaiting their turn at the All-Estonian Song Festival

significant icon for the nation, rousing affirmation of Estonian identity.

Religion does not play a particularly large part in Estonian life, although hundreds of years of foreign occupation led to many people converting to Christianity, including Lutheranism and Russian Orthodoxy. The most important aspects of Estonian culture are distinctly pagan in origin. The hugely popular midsummer festival Jaanipäev (John's Day), characterized by drinking, dancing and revelry, has a pagan origin.

SOCIETY AND CULTURE

In general, Estonians are more strongly influenced by Scandinavian culture than by that of their Baltic neighbours. Finns and Estonians also share close linguistic links through the Finno-Ugric language family. A sizeable Russian-speaking minority remained in Estonia after the Soviet withdrawal, leading to some diplomatic skirmishes with Russia over the years. Today, there are fewer instances of conflict between Russians and Estonians.

Estonians take great pride in their heritage. The country's medieval past is visible not only in some of its architecture, but also in festivals that have their roots in that era. Folk culture is central to national identity, as Estonians were predominantly reduced to serfdom, with no right to own land or property, until the country's first spell of independence in 1918. The All-Estonian Song Festival, which was first held in 1869 and has since taken place every five years, remains a

POLITICAL LIFE

Estonia underwent a major political transition in the 1990s, adopting a parliamentary democracy which introduced neo-liberal economic and political policies.

In the early years of independence, there was a lingering cynicism towards politics, as many former Communist Party leaders continued to hold high offices, and corruption was a regular part of the political process. This changed in 2000, as the nation prepared to join the European Union and decisions from Brussels now have just as much effect as local ones.

Parliamentary session in progress

Tallinn's new modern city centre, with the Radisson Blu Hotel *(left)* and SEB bank buildings *(right)*

Estonia is governed by a coalition of parties. The major parties are the centre-right Reform Party and the populist Center Party, while several smaller parties often hold the balance of power.

ECONOMY

Until about 2005, Estonia had a large GDP growth and low unemployment. Its capital, Tallinn, underwent a transition with the economic boom, with office towers shooting up and expensive new shops and restaurants enjoying good trade. The property market boomed, as did the market for new cars, paid for mostly on credit borrowed from Swedish banks.

This changed with the global financial crisis, which wiped out the growth rate and pushed unemployment to 10 per cent. The government cut its spending as it attempted to meet the economic criteria necessary to enter the eurozone, and in July 2010 the EU gave approval for the adoption of the euro in Estonia with effect from January 2011.

Income levels are still below the EU average, although consumer prices are relatively similar to those in the richer western EU countries. The main industries are real estate, manu-facturing, retail, transport and communication. There is also a large focus on information technology.

TOURISM

Tourism has been instrumental in transforming Estonia from a drab post-Soviet state into a thriving nation, and the private sector has been quick to adapt and respond to the business opportunities this has opened up. Tallinn was inevitably the first part of the country to benefit. Tourism has stimulated a social renaissance in parts of the country that had languished in poverty for many years, and towns throughout the country have seen a steady increase in tourism-related investment.

Tourists enjoying Tallinn's roof-top panorama

ESTONIA THROUGH THE YEAR

Estonians celebrate a host of seasonal festivals through the year. These encompass everything from religion, folk culture and handicrafts to art, music, dance and theatre, making the festival calendar both colourful and remarkable. Much of the festive frenzy occurs in the summer, peaking with the Midsummer's Eve

Estonian folk dancers

celebrations. Summer is also the time when a series of concerts are held throughout the country, and when the Folklore Baltica Festival *(see p132),* which showcases the region's distinct traditional culture, takes place. In addition to the annual festivals, a number of commemorative days are observed throughout Estonia.

SPRING

As expected from a country so attuned to the seasons, spring is a joyful time marked by a lively range of long-established festivals.

MARCH

Estonian Film Days *(late Mar),* Tallinn. The best in all Estonian film genres are given awards. Selected movies are shown with English subtitles.
Estonian Music Days *(Mar).* Contemporary Estonian classical music is showcased in Tallinn and other cities.

APRIL

Jazzkaar *(late Apr).* The biggest jazz festival held throughout Estonia includes local and international names.
Tartu Student Days *(late Apr–early May).* During this festival, Tartu's students hold bizarre concerts,

Saxophonist playing at a concert during Jazzkaar

Horse-riders in medieval costumes, celebrating Tallinn Old Town Days

shows and parties open to everybody.

MAY

Tallinn Literature Festival *(early May),* Tallinn. Local and international authors gather in the Old Town.
Tallinn Old Town Days *(late May–early Jun).* Tallinn's medieval past is celebrated with re-enactments of old traditions like jousting. The streets are filled with market stalls and people in costume.
Spring Farm Days *(mid-May),* Tallinn. The Estonian Open Air Museum replicates the traditional spring farming tasks, such as growing crops and rearing livestock.

SUMMER

After months of wintry gloom and darkness, Estonians make the best of their short but resplendent summers, with an abundance of festivals.

JUNE

Midsummer's Eve *(23 Jun).* This summer celebration is marked by a night of joyous drinking, eating and age-old rituals around a bonfire.
Pärnu Hanseatic Days *(late Jun).* This two-day festival includes a procession, craft fair and knights' tournament.
Juu Jääb Muhu Music Festival *(late Jun),* Muhu Island. A small and enjoyable weekend of local and international music, tending towards jazz and world music. Camping is available.

JULY

Haapsalu Early Music Festival *(early Jul).* Set in the pretty surroundings of Haapsalu Castle, this is a celebration of early classical music.
Õllesummer Festival *(early Jul),* Tallinn. This huge beer festival also features major concerts, from jazz to rock, as well as sideshows.

Audience watching performers on stage, Viljandi Folk Festival

Old Town Medieval Market *(early Jul)*, Tallinn. An exciting series of concerts, workshops, costumed performers and traditional market stalls.
Viljandi Folk Festival *(late Jul)*. Folk music ensembles from all over Estonia perform in the castle grounds.

AUGUST

Birgitta Festival *(mid-Aug)*, Tallinn. Operas, concerts and recitals are held in the ruins of Pirita Convent. Food is served on the summer terrace.
August Dance Festival *(late Aug)*, Tallinn. The best in contemporary dance, including guest performances by famous international troupes.

AUTUMN

The festival season winds down a bit in the autumn, though most cities have a few annual events on offer.

SEPTEMBER

Credo International Festival of Orthodox Sacred Music *(early–late Sep)*, Tallinn. Orthodox sacred music concerts held in churches and concert halls.
Matsalu Nature Film Festival *(late Sep)*. An unusual festival screening the works of various nature-filmmakers.

OCTOBER

NYYD *(mid-Oct)*, Tallinn. The best in experimental compositions from Estonia and abroad are featured.

NOVEMBER

Black Nights Film Festival *(Nov–Dec)*, Tallinn. A comprehensive selection of independent and world cinema celebrating the best in film. Most films are screened with English subtitles. Tickets can be purchased from Piletilevi outlets. The festival also runs smaller events in other towns.

WINTER

Despite the long and bitterly cold spells, winter also holds the promise of a wonderful snow-blanketed landscape and a season of festivity.

DECEMBER

Christmas Jazz Festival *(early Dec)*. A series of jazz concerts held in Tallinn and several other towns in the run-up to Christmas.

Old Town Christmas Market *(Dec–early Jan)*, Tallinn. Equally popular with tourists and locals, the market has a variety of goods on sale from the traditional to the novel.

JANUARY

Pärnu Contemporary Music Days *(mid–late Jan)*. An outstanding festival of classical music, which also features lectures, workshops and theatre performances.

Skiiers participating in the popular Tartu Ski Marathon

FEBRUARY

Baroque Music Festival *(early–mid-Feb)*, Tallinn. A festival favourite offering a series of Baroque music concerts in various venues around the Old Town.
Tartu Ski Marathon *(early Feb)*. This hugely popular ski-fest features events and competitions but the highlight is the 63-km (39-mile) ski marathon.

PUBLIC HOLIDAYS
New Year's Day (1 Jan)
Independence Day (24 Feb)
Good Friday (Mar/Apr)
May Day (1 May)
Võidupüha Victory Day (23 Jun)
St John's Day (24 Jun)
Restoration of Independence (20 Aug)
Christmas (24–26 Dec)

A brightly illuminated Christmas tree, Tallinn

THE HISTORY OF ESTONIA

*H*istorical references to Estonia date from the early 13th century, when the Teutonic Knights arrived, introducing a new social order in which the Germans dominated for several centuries. A brief benevolent Swedish rule in the 17th century was followed by Russian and German oppression, which continued with a short-lived inter-war independence. Estonia became a republic only in 1991.

The German Knights, or the Brotherhood of the Sword, started a bitter struggle for the control of Estonia that lasted from 1208, when they established their hold over Otepää, until 1211. The Danes, too, were contending for the control of Estonia. In 1206, they tried in vain to subjugate Saaremaa, the country's largest and most prosperous island. Denmark's King Valdemar II (r.1202–41) occupied Tallinn in 1219, but his attempts to expand the Danish territory further were unsuccessful.

Fragment of a seal of Danish King Valdemar II

which the Germans owned manor estates and the local inhabitants were obliged to work as serfs, survived until the 19th century.

Tallinn was acquired again by the Germans in 1346, when large-scale protests against feudal exactions forced the Danes to relinquish their possessions in Estonia. During this time, many guilds and merchants' associations emerged, and towns such as Tallinn, Tartu, Viljandi and Pärnu thrived as members of the Hanseatic League. Tallinn, particularly, prospered as one of Northern Europe's largest towns.

GERMAN CONQUEST

In 1227, the Teutonic Knights conquered the whole of Estonia, also controlling Tallinn until 1238, when it was returned to the Danes. The Knights took over a stone castle built by the Danes and rebuilt it as the Toompea Castle the same year. The foundations for a new social order were laid, with the Germans serving as the nobility, as well as merchants and craftsmen. The Estonians were forcibly converted to Christianity and their land given away to the Knights and bishops. The feudal system, in

An impression of Tallinn's Toompea Castle in 1227

TIMELINE

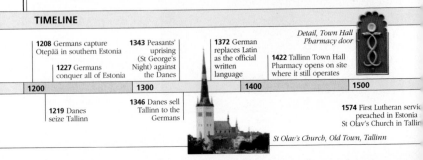

1208 Germans capture Otepää in southern Estonia

1227 Germans conquer all of Estonia

1219 Danes seize Tallinn

1343 Peasants' uprising (St George's Night) against the Danes

1346 Danes sell Tallinn to the Germans

1372 German replaces Latin as the official written language

1422 Tallinn Town Hall Pharmacy opens on site where it still operates

Detail, Town Hall Pharmacy door

1574 First Lutheran servic[e] preached in Estoni[a] St Olav's Church in Tallin[n]

St Olav's Church, Old Town, Tallinn

1200   1300   1400   1500

Tartu University, Estonia's prestigious seat of learning

THE SWEDISH RULE

The 16th century saw Estonia as the major battleground between Russia and Sweden in the Livonian Wars *(see p33)*. By 1629, the whole country was in Swedish hands. The Swedes achieved much over the next 50 years, including the establishment of Tartu University, the introduction of schools all around the country, printing of books in Estonian and the construction of several buildings, especially in Narva and Tartu. Narva was built as the second Swedish capital. The social system created by the Germans was left undisturbed, however. Later Swedish kings interfered by seizing German-owned estates, incurring the wrath of the Germans who turned to Russia's Peter the Great for help.

STRUGGLE AGAINST THE RUSSIANS

Although the Swedish troops were initially able to resist the Russians, in 1709, the final battle between the Swedish King Charles XII and Peter the Great sealed Estonia's fate for the next 200 years, during which time there would be little threat to Tsarist rule. The Russians as well as the Baltic Germans actively kept Estonians out of any positions of responsibility, besides curbing the Estonian language. The discontent of the intelligentsia found expression in the rebellion led by the students of Tartu University in the 19th century.

In 1905, in common with many other places in Russia, Estonia witnessed unrest that spread to the towns. The factory-workers lent support to the nascent Bolshevik movement, while several German manors were burnt down in the countryside. During World War I (1914–18), the prospect of Estonian independence seemed bleak. However, the 1917 Revolution that ended the Tsarist regime in Russia and the chaos that followed in Moscow, encouraged Estonia to declare independence in February 1918, in Pärnu. The Treaty of Tartu, signed with Russia in February 1920, formally confirmed Estonian independence.

Estonian Army recruiting poster, 1918

Declaration of independence in February 1918, Pärnu

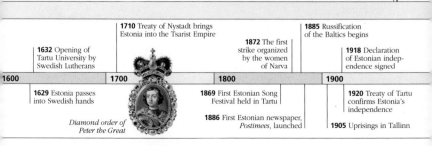

1632 Opening of Tartu University by Swedish Lutherans

1710 Treaty of Nystadt brings Estonia into the Tsarist Empire

1872 The first strike organized by the women of Narva

1885 Russification of the Baltics begins

1918 Declaration of Estonian independence signed

1600	1700	1800	1900

1629 Estonia passes into Swedish hands

Diamond order of Peter the Great

1869 First Estonian Song Festival held in Tartu

1886 First Estonian newspaper, *Postimees*, launched

1920 Treaty of Tartu confirms Estonia's independence

1905 Uprisings in Tallinn

President Konstantin Päts *(centre)* in 1939

FREEDOM AND WORLD WAR II

Although there were 20 coalition governments between 1919 and 1933, they all agreed to immediately distribute the Baltic-German landholdings among the local community. Education and state pension systems were introduced nationwide. People who had been active in the national movement before World War I took senior positions in government. The most prominent of these politicians was Konstantin Päts, who staged a coup in February 1934 and dissolved Parliament, although he began to restore democratic institutions in 1938. Day-to-day life for most Estonians was hardly affected by these developments. Industry, agriculture and international trade continued as before. Päts ruled until the Soviet invasion on 16 June 1940, which brought a sudden and brutal end to independent Estonia. The Russians executed several prominent Estonians, including Päts himself, and many others were deported to Siberia. The German invasion,

Soviet tanks thwarting the Germans' landing attempt in Estonia in September 1941

which came a year later, was seen by many in Estonia as a sort of liberation. Tallinn-born Alfred Rosenberg, who was appointed by Nazi Germany to run the Baltic States, treated the general population less harshly compared to most other countries subjected to Nazi occupation. In September 1944, the advancing Red Army returned to Estonia, forcing the Nazis to surrender and Estonia once again became part of the Soviet Union.

SOVIET ESTONIA

The ten years which followed the Soviet reoccupation were traumatic for Estonia. The deportation programme, restarted in 1944, saw its climax in March 1949 with the arrest of 20,000 Estonians. The Soviets wanted to curb any opposition to the establishment of collective farms. The deportations were also meant to sabotage the successful guerrilla campaign run by the Forest Brothers, a resistance group active until the early 1950s throughout Estonia. Stalin's death in 1953 led to a slightly less oppressive regime in Estonia, as it did throughout the USSR. From the 1960s, Estonia's link with the non-Soviet world began to grow. A ferry link between Tallinn and Helsinki was started twice a week. The 1980 Moscow Olympics turned out to be invaluable for Estonia, when it staged the yachting events, which brought thousands of foreign visitors to Tallinn. As a

TIMELINE

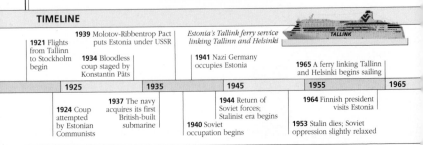

1921 Flights from Tallinn to Stockholm begin

1939 Molotov-Ribbentrop Pact puts Estonia under USSR

1934 Bloodless coup staged by Konstantin Päts

Estonia's Tallink ferry service linking Tallinn and Helsinki

TALLINK

1941 Nazi Germany occupies Estonia

1965 A ferry linking Tallinn and Helsinki begins sailing

| 1925 | 1935 | 1945 | 1955 | 1965 |

1924 Coup attempted by Estonian Communists

1937 The navy acquires its first British-built submarine

1940 Soviet occupation begins

1944 Return of Soviet forces; Stalinist era begins

1964 Finnish president visits Estonia

1953 Stalin dies; Soviet oppression slightly relaxed

Olympic torch inaugurating the yachting events held in 1980, Tallinn

INDEPENDENCE

The years 1992 and 1993 turned out to be a challenging time for Estonia. The immediate reintroduction of the kroon as the national currency wiped out savings accumulated in Soviet roubles and inflation was not immediately curtailed. Prime Minister Mart Laar, who served the first term from 1992 to 1994, coined the phrase "the little country that can" and it did, very quickly. Many suffered temporarily, as factories closed and collective farms were abandoned, but few suffered long-term as tourism, Finnish assembly plants and international call centres quickly absorbed any spare labour. Returning to power in 1999, Laar was able to steer the country out of the financial crisis that stemmed from the collapse of Russia's economy in 1998.

result, foreign newspapers, direct-dial international phone calls and a range of consumer goods not seen in Tallinn since 1940 were introduced. After the Games, all these quickly disappeared, but the memory of them did not; frustration with the USSR turned in the 1980s to total disillusionment as Finnish TV showed what a different style of life was being enjoyed just 50 km (31 miles) from Tallinn.

When Mikhail Gorbachev came to power in 1985 as General Secretary of the Communist Party of the Soviet Union, Estonians took advantage of his liberal policies to revitalize the cultural scene and to restructure factories and small businesses. Plans to reform the economy were made, the key element of which was the introduction of a stable currency. At the time of the collapse of the USSR in 1991, Estonians were better prepared, at least in theory, for a capitalist economy than were any of the other Soviet republics.

Former Estonian Prime Minister Mart Laar

From 2000 onwards, Estonia enjoyed record growth and increased prosperity. Many public works projects were built with European Union funds and foreign banks gave generous private loans. This ended with the global financial crisis, and although Estonia was not as badly affected as other Baltic nations, the economy slowed considerably. In July 2010, Estonia was given approval to enter the eurozone. From January 2011 the euro replaced the kroon as legal tender. Relations with Russia have improved markedly, although diplomatic, cultural and even trade hiccups still occur occasionally.

1980 Olympics sailing and yachting events open in Tallinn

1992 Lennart Meri elected as president

President Lennart Meri (1929–2006)

2004 Estonia joins NATO and EU

2011 The euro replaces the kroon as Estonia's currency

1975	1985	1995	2005	2015

1991 Estonia declares independence

1994 Russian troops withdrawn; Estonia sinks, claiming 850 lives

2007 World's first national Internet election held

Pirita Yachting Centre, venue for Olympics yachting events in 1980

TALLINN

In little over a decade, the Estonian capital has grown into a dynamic, chic and exciting city. An architectural wonder, Tallinn has some stunning examples of modern architecture that reflect the newfound confidence of its people. In addition to restoring the medieval architecture of its Old Town, the city has experienced a major construction boom.

An overview of Tallinn from Toompea Hill shows how the city has made the best of its extraordinary historic foundations. Tallinn first appeared on the Western European map in 1154. The city came to be known as Tallinn after the Danes conquered it in 1219 and built a stronghold on Toompea Hill. "Tallinn" is an abbreviation of the Estonian name Taani Linnus, meaning "Danish stronghold". However, Tallinn officially bore the Teutonic name of Reval until Estonia's first period of independence in 1918. With the arrival of German merchants in 1230, the city was divided into the Upper Town (Toompea) and the Lower Town.

In 1346, the Danish king sold Tallinn to Germany. The city flourished in the 14th and 15th centuries, when it was one of the leading members of the powerful Hanseatic League. The brilliantly restored Old Town, a UNESCO World Heritage Site since 1991, is a living monument to this golden period of Tallinn's history.

Tallinn was relatively stagnant during the Tsarist Russian period, which began in 1710 under the rule of Peter the Great. For most of the 19th century, it was little more than a summer resort for wealthy Russians. However, the introduction of the Tallinn–St Petersburg railway in 1870 restored the city's former glory as a major trading centre. During the Soviet occupation a vast influx of predominantly Russian-speaking workers swelled Tallinn's population.

Since independence in 1991, improving air and sea transport links with Western Europe has made Tallinn easily accessible. The city has forged close ties with neighbouring Finland and the Tallinn–Helsinki ferry line is among the busiest in the world.

Young ballerinas performing in a street in Tallinn during the summer festivities held in June

◁ **Striking domes of Alexander Nevsky Cathedral soaring above the trees**

Exploring Tallinn

The vast majority of sights in Tallinn are concentrated in and around Town Hall Square and Toompea, in medieval Old Town. Relatively easy to explore on foot, the winding cobbled streets are dotted with elegant back alleys, courtyards and spired churches, as well as fascinating museums that present the city's historic and cultural traditions. There are also many notable buildings around the fringes of the Old Town, all within easy walking distance. On the eastern section of the city wall, Viru Gate serves as one of the main access points into the Old Town.

Viru Gate, one of the best-known landmarks in Tallinn

SIGHTS AT A GLANCE

Churches and Monasteries

Alexander Nevsky Cathedral ⑲
Cathedral of St Mary
  the Virgin ⑳
Church of the Transfiguration
  of Our Lord ⑭
Dominican Monastery ⑩
Holy Spirit Church ③
Niguliste Church pp64–5 ⑥
St Olav's Church ⑮

Museums

Adamson-Eric Museum ㉔
Estonian Museum of Applied
  Art and Design ⑬
Great Guild Hall ④
Museum of Estonian
  Photography ⑤
Museum of Occupations ㉑
Museum of Theatre
  and Music ⑦
Tallinn City Museum ⑪

**Historic Buildings and
Sites of Interest**

Fat Margaret Tower ⑰
House of Blackheads ⑫
Kiek-in-de-Kök ㉓
Knights' House ㉒
St Catherine's Passageway ⑨
Three Sisters ⑯
Toompea Castle ⑱
Town Hall ①
Town Hall Pharmacy ②
Viru Gate ⑧

0 metres		200
0 yards		200

SEE ALSO

• *Where to Stay* pp292–4

• *Where to Eat* pp322–5

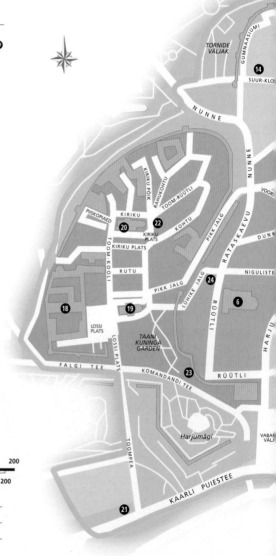

KEY

■ Street-by-Street map *pp58–9*

■ Street-by-Street map *pp68–9*

ℹ️ Tourist information

✝ Church

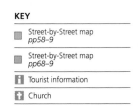

Pikk Hermann Tower, in the scenic Toompea area

GETTING AROUND

Walking is the best way to explore Tallinn's Old Town. However, motorized transport is required to see some major sights, such as Kadriorg Park east of the Old Town, as well as Pirita, the TV Tower and the Botanical Gardens, which are all situated to the northeast of Kadriorg Park. The city's public transport system is a network of buses, trolleybuses and trams. Nearly all buses and trolleybuses leave from Vabaduse Square or the Viru Keskus terminal, while most tram lines pass by the Old Town. Tallinn has transport links with all major towns and cities in Estonia.

View of the city's skyline from Toompea Hill

Street-by-Street: Around Town Hall Square

Medieval carving, Town Hall Square

In the heart of the Old Town, the magnificent Town Hall Square has, for centuries, served as a marketplace. Gently sloping, the cobblestoned square is surrounded by a ring of elegantly designed medieval buildings. The early 14th-century Town Hall is Northern Europe's only surviving late Gothic town hall. A meeting point for locals and visitors, the square captures the essence of the Old Town. In summer, it is filled with open-air cafés and restaurant tables.

Busy market in Town Hall Square, seen from the Town Hall tower

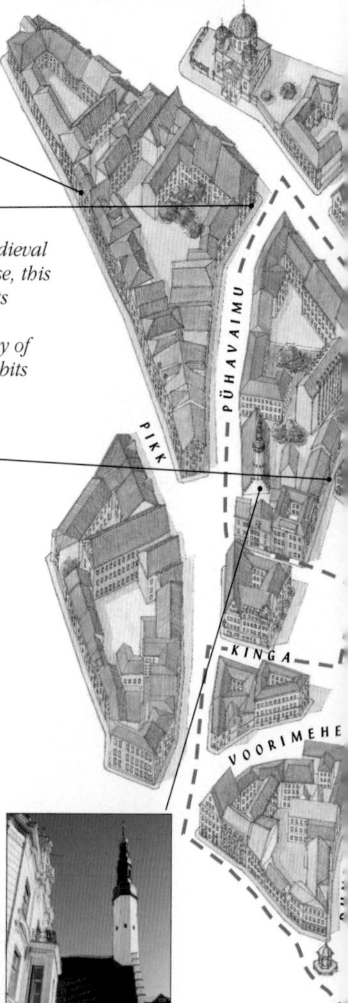

House of Blackheads

Tallinn City Museum

Housed in a medieval merchants' house, this museum presents Tallinn's history through a variety of fascinating exhibits and artifacts ⑪

★ **Town Hall Pharmacy**
Worth a visit just for the impressive interior, this long-running pharmacy also has a charming little museum displaying old curiosities ②

KEY

– – – Suggested route

STAR SIGHTS

★ Town Hall Pharmacy

★ Town Hall

Holy Spirit Church
Regarded as one of Tallinn's most attractive churches, this splendidly preserved structure houses a treasure trove of medieval and Renaissance features ③

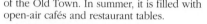

Dominican Monastery
Among Tallinn's oldest buildings, the monastery complex also includes an atmospheric museum which has some beautiful stone carvings ❿

Viru Street
One of the most famous in the Old Town, this busy street is packed with a variety of restaurants, bars, cafés and shops.

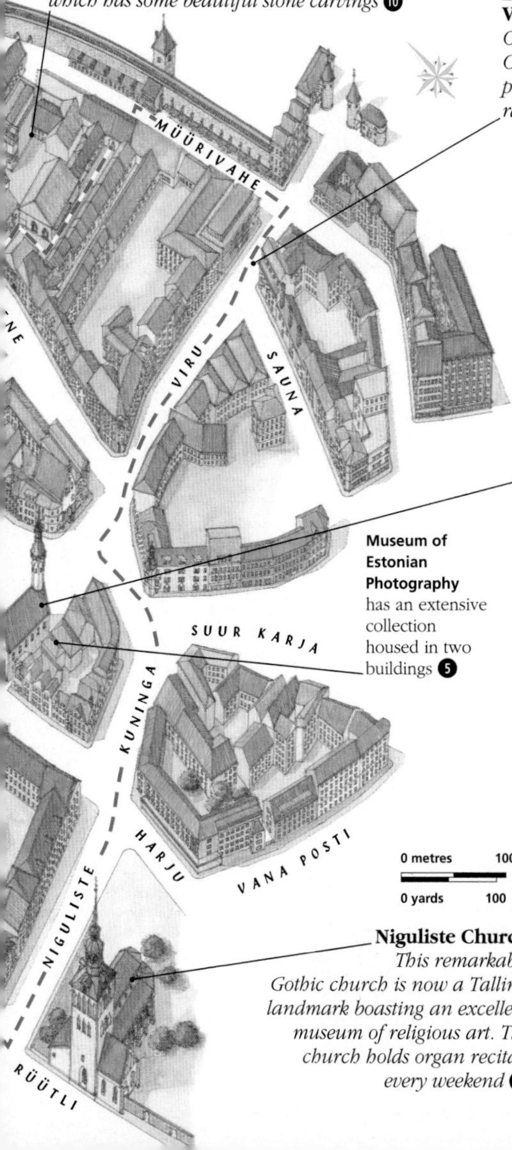

★ Town Hall
Taking pride of place in Town Hall Square, this imposing Gothic building with an octagonal tower has been the focus of civic life since the Middle Ages ❶

Museum of Estonian Photography has an extensive collection housed in two buildings ❺

0 metres 100
0 yards 100

Niguliste Church
This remarkable Gothic church is now a Tallinn landmark boasting an excellent museum of religious art. The church holds organ recitals every weekend ❻

MÜÜRIVAHE

VIRU

SAUNA

SUUR KARJA

KUNINGA

HARJU

VANA POSTI

NIGULISTE

RÜÜTLI

Town Hall ❶
Tallinna raekoda

Raekoja plats 1. **Map** 1 C2. **Tel** 645 7900. 🚌 5, 40. 🚋 1, 2, 3, 4. ⏰ Jul–Aug: 10am–4pm Mon–Sat; Sep–May: by appointment. Tower: May–Aug: 11am–6pm daily. 🅿️ 🔲 🔲
www.tallinn.ee/raekoda

One of the most revered symbols of Tallinn, the Town Hall dates back to 1404. Its high-pitched roof is supported by two tall gables and a late-Renaissance spire crowns the slender octagonal tower. The narrow windows and crenellated parapet complete the building's impressive appearance. Facing Town Hall Square, a vaulted arcade runs along the north façade, where a small café puts out tables in the summer. Inside, it is possible to see the Citizens' Hall and the Council Hall, although most visitors head straight for the tower and the 115-step ascent to the top.

Town Hall Pharmacy ❷
Raeapteek

Raekoja plats 11. **Map** 1 C2. **Tel** 631 4860. 🚌 5, 40. 🚋 1, 2, 3, 4. ⏰ 10am–6pm Tue–Sat. 🔲
www.raeapteek.ee

The Town Hall Pharmacy is famed for being one of the oldest-established pharmacies in Europe. The building's exterior dates back to the 17th century but there is evidence that a pharmacy existed on the site as long ago as 1422. In one corner of the shop's interior there is a

modest museum with a small selection of historical exhibits including medical instruments and curative treatments. Ask to try the spiced wine, which was a popular purchase in medieval times. According to a local legend, marzipan was accidentally created here and named Martin's Bread.

Graceful Baroque tower of Holy Spirit Church

Holy Spirit Church ❸
Pühavaimu kirik

Pühavaimu 2. **Map** 1 C2. **Tel** 644 1487. 🚌 5, 40. 🚋 1, 2, 3, 4. ⏰ Oct–Apr: 10am–2pm Mon–Fri; May–Sep: 9am–5pm Mon–Sat. 🅿️ ➕ 3pm Sun (in English).
www.eelk.ee/tallinna.puhavaimu

The 13th-century Holy Spirit Church is one of the most beautiful churches in Tallinn. The Gothic building served as the Town Hall chapel before being converted into a

church. Its whitewashed exterior includes the oldest public clock in Tallinn, with carvings dating from 1684. The stepped gable is topped by a striking Baroque tower. The spire was nearly destroyed by fire in 2002, but was restored within a year. Inside, the church is a treasure trove of religious artifacts and architecture, from the magnificently intricate Baroque pews to the Renaissance-era pulpit. The sublime altar triptych, *The Descent of the Holy Ghost* (1483), by Lübeck artist Berndt Notke, is the main highlight. The church holds a special place in Estonian history, as the first Estonian-language sermons were delivered here in 1535 following the Reformation.

Great Guild Hall ❹
Suurgildi hoone

Pikk jalg 17. **Map** 1 C2. **Tel** 641 1630. 🚌 5, 40. 🚋 1, 2, 3, 4. ⏰ 11am–6pm Thu–Tue. 🅿️ 🔲
www.ajaloomuuseum.ee

One the most important buildings in medieval Tallinn, the Great Guild Hall was constructed in 1417. It was owned by a powerful union of wealthy merchants. The building holds a significant place in the town's history. It was mainly used as the gathering place for its members but at times it was also rented out for wedding parties and court sessions. It was the starting as well as the end point of most festive processions of Tallinn. The late-Gothic building has retained its original appearance through the centuries, although the windows were remodelled in the 1890s.

The Great Guild Hall's majestic interior provides a perfect setting for a branch of the **Estonian History Museum** *(see p78).* The museum's collection of historical artifacts covers Estonian history from the Stone Age to the mid-19th century in fine detail. The exhibits, which include everything from jewellery to weaponry, are accompanied by explanatory texts in Estonian, Russian and English.

Interior of the Town Hall Pharmacy, with well-stocked shelves

Medieval Architecture

Tallinn's Old Town is one of the best-preserved examples of medieval architecture in Northern Europe. With its winding cobblestoned streets and rows of elegantly gabled façades, the Old Town retains the true character of a medieval town centre. The labyrinthine street structure developed in relation to the power seat of Toompea above and the harbour below, with the all-important Town Hall Square and marketplace at the heart of it. Although Tallinn flourished as a centre of trade in medieval times, it was relatively quiet in the 19th century, which is probably why the Old Town was spared from being demolished. Tallinn's medieval fortifications are also very well preserved, with some 2 km (1 mile) of the town wall and half of the original 46 towers still intact.

Door knocker, Estonian History Museum

The gabled upper storey was used for storage, with a winch used to hoist up merchandise.

A model of a medieval merchant's house *can be seen at the Tallinn City Museum (see p63), a 14th-century building. The upper storey was used to store merchandise, and guests were entertained on the first floor.*

Medieval towers *are famous symbols of the city's history. Kiek-in-de-Kök (see p71) and Fat Margaret Tower (see p67) are now museums. Visitors can get a view of the area by climbing the adjoining Nunna, Sauna and Kuldjala towers.*

Saiakang alley, *which is just off Town Hall Square, is one of the narrow medieval streets and passageways that make the Old Town so fascinating.*

Lühike jalg, *also known as the "Short Leg", is a steep, atmospheric passageway that was built in the 13th century as a link between the stronghold of Toompea, or the Upper Town, and the rest of Tallinn. In the Middle Ages, a number of coppersmiths and locksmiths had their workshops on Lühike jalg.*

A dragonhead waterspout *can be seen just below the Town Hall's roof. The delightful waterspouts of the Town Hall are fine examples of the mischievous details that adorn many of Tallinn's medieval buildings.*

An 1898 photograph, Museum of Estonian Photography

Museum of Estonian Photography ❺
Fotomuuseum

Raekoja tänav 4/6. **Map** 1 C3. **Tel** 644 8767. 🚌 5, 40. 🚊 1, 2, 3, 4. ◯ Mar–Oct: 10:30am–6pm Thu–Tue; Nov–Feb: 10am–5:30pm Thu–Tue. 🗓 🖼 🏛 www.linnamuuseum.ee

Tucked away behind the Town Hall, the Museum of Estonian Photography consists of two separate buildings, one dating back to the 14th century and the other to the 18th century. They once served as the town prisons and were also used to hold court sessions. The buildings now house an extensive collection of Estonian photography covering the period from 1840 to 1940. The display, which includes rare daguerreotypes, ambrotypes and ferrotypes, showcases some of the finest works by well-known early Estonian photographers including H Tiidermann, B Lais and N Nyländer. Pride of place is given to the tiny Minox camera which was reputedly invented in Estonia in 1936. The gallery also hosts temporary exhibitions of contemporary works.

Niguliste Church ❻
Niguliste kirik

See pp64–5.

Museum of Theatre and Music ❼
Teatri-ja muusikamuuseum

Müürivahe 12. **Map** 1 C3. **Tel** 644 6407. 🚌 5, 40. 🚊 3, 4. ◯ 10am–6pm Wed–Sat. 🖼 🗓 call in advance. www.tmm.ee

This museum focuses on a much-loved part of the country's cultural heritage, and also serves as an academic centre. Founded in 1924, the music museum was combined with a theatre museum in 1941. There is much for music and theatre aficionados to enjoy, from a fine selection of folk instruments to a collection of original theatre production programmes. The papers and instruments of the eminent Estonian composer, Peeter Süda (1883–1920), form a small part of the museum's collection. The staff are happy to play the instruments for a small fee. The museum owns the copyright to the work of composer Heino Eller (1887–1970) and since 1998, has been awarding the prestigious Heino Eller Music Prize to distinguished figures.

Viru Gate ❽

Viru tänav. **Map** 2 D3. 🚌 5, 40. 🚊 1, 2, 3, 4.

On the eastern section of the city wall, the Viru Gate serves as one of the main access points into the Old Town. A picturesque sight, its slightly skewed stone towers are one of Tallinn's best-known images. The pair of towers that make up the gate were built in the 14th century and were part of a larger gate-system. The surrounding stretch of city wall dates back to the 16th century. A moat and water mill, which once existed between the foregates and the main gate, were demolished in 1843. In the early 20th century, Viru Street was regarded as one of the city's most fashionable and is now a major tourist spot.

Stone towers of Viru Gate, one of the most renowned images of Tallinn

St Catherine's Passageway ❾
Katariina käik

Katariina käik. **Map** 2 D2. 🚌 *5, 40.* 🚊 *1, 2, 3, 4.*

A fascinating medieval alleyway with uneven stone walls and overhead vaulting, St Catherine's Passageway joins Vene and Müürivahe Streets. A string of arts and crafts workshops line the passage, where it is possible to watch resident artisans working with jewellery, ceramics and glass or binding books. The passage runs along the surviving wall of St Catherine's Church, which was built in 1246. The church was Tallinn's largest in its day and several gravestones, some dating from the 14th century, still line this narrow passageway.

The cobblestoned St Catherine's Passageway

Dominican Monastery ❿
Dominiiklaste klooster

Vene 16/18. **Map** 2 D2. **Tel** 515 5489 or 511 2536. 🚌 *5, 40.* 🚊 *1, 2, 3, 4.* 🕐 *No regular opening hours. Call to arrange a visit.* 📷 🎫 *tour offered to the monastery's inner chambers through the cloister.* 🌐 **www**.kloostri.ee *or* **www.** claustrum.eu

Founded by Dominican monks in 1246, this monastery was a renowned centre of learning. It thrived until the Reformation riots broke

A passageway in the medieval Dominican Monastery, Old Town

out in 1524. The Lutherans destroyed the monastery and forced the monks into exile. In 1531, a fire damaged most of the desecrated St Catherine's Church, which had formed its south wing.

After suffering neglect for four centuries, the ruined monastery was renovated in 1954. Today a serene cloister, its atmospheric passageways and its pretty inner garden draw visitors. The star attraction, however, is the fine **Dominican Monastery Museum**, with Estonia's largest collection of medieval and Renaissance stone carvings by local stone-masons. One of the prominent works, a decorative relief of an angel on a triangular slab, is attributed to Hans von Aken, the 16th-century German Mannerist painter.

🏛 **Dominican Monastery Museum**
🕐 *mid-May–mid-Sep: 10am–6pm daily.* 📷

Tallinn City Museum ⓫
Tallinna linnamuuseum

Vene 17. **Map** 1 C2. **Tel** 615 5195. 🚌 *5, 40.* 🚊 *1, 2, 3, 4.* 🕐 *Mar–Oct: 10:30am–6pm Wed–Mon; Nov–Feb: 10:30am–5pm Wed–Mon.* 📷 💻 **www**.linnamuuseum.ee

Located in a 14th-century merchant's house, the Tallinn City Museum was opened in 1937 to introduce locals to the city's rich cultural heritage. Today, the vast collection, set over three floors, offers a fascinating overview of Tallinn's history. Highlights include a cutaway model of a 16th-century merchant's house and a fine model recreating a 19th-century domestic interior. There is also a replica model of Old Thomas, the famous weather-vane that sits atop the Town Hall steeple. The floors are interspersed with lifelike wax figures, dressed in period costumes. Also on view are a collection of silverware, porcelain and pewter and numerous tapestries.

The museum's display of 20th-century exhibits includes photographs of the vast crowds that congregated in the Old Town after Estonia regained its independence from the Soviet Union in 1991. One of the main draws is the intriguing exhibit entitled *The Town That Will Never Be Ready.* It was inspired by a local legend that claims Tallinn will disappear the moment someone proclaims it is finally completed as a city.

Model of Tallinn from the 1820s displayed in the Tallinn City Museum

Niguliste Church ❻
Niguliste kirik

Dedicated to St Nicholas, Niguliste Church was originally built in the 13th century, although nearly all that remains today is from the 15th century. Most of Tallinn's medieval artworks were destroyed in the Reformation riots of 1524. However, according to legend, Niguliste Church escaped being ransacked due to the laudable efforts of the church warden, who sealed the door with melted lead. Today, Tallinn's most impressive collection of medieval religious artworks are housed here. The building has served as a museum ever since it was extensively rebuilt during Soviet times after being damaged by Soviet air raids in World War II. The church regularly holds organ and choral concerts.

Exterior of the Niguliste Church, one of Tallinn's medieval treasures

★ Altarpiece Depicting St Nicholas
Painted in 1482 by Hermen Rode of Lübeck, this superbly detailed altarpiece shows a variety of scenes from the life of St Nicholas, as well as the beheading of St George.

A collection of bells from churches all over Estonia is displayed inside the church.

Altar Triptych of St Mary and the Brotherhood of Blackheads
The main panel shows St George and St Maurice standing beside the Madonna, while St Francis and St Gertrude stand in the wings.

The Silver Chamber is located on the extreme corner of the church.

Stone Figure
This sculpture is one of the wonderfully evocative stone figures that are part of the original design of Niguliste Church.

Entrance

STAR FEATURES

★ Altarpiece Depicting St Nicholas

★ Bernt Notke's Danse Macabre

The spire, originally built in 1696, was finally restored in 1984.

Stone Carving

Carved in stone, the skull and crossbones can be seen at the entrance to the chapel near the church's main door. Stone carving, a vital element in Estonian architecture, was largely done in dolomite and sandstone.

VISITORS' CHECKLIST

Niguliste 3. **Map** 1 C3. **Tel** 631 4330. ☐ 10am–5pm Wed–Sun. 🎫 tickets available until 4:30pm (call 644 9903 for bookings). 🎧 book in advance; extra charges for guided tour (up to 35 people) in a foreign language. www.ekm.ee **Silver Chamber** ☐ 10am–5pm Wed–Sun. 🎧 extra charges (up to 10 people). **Organ Music** Sat & Sun at 4pm for 30 mins.

★ Bernt Notke's Danse Macabre

The 15th-century frieze by Bernt Notke (1440–1509) is widely considered the pièce de résistance of the church. Only a fragment of the 30-m (98-ft) original remains.

Display, Silver Chamber

The small side chamber contains a fascinating display of ornate silverware that belonged to various guilds and organizations, such as the influential and wealthy Brotherhood of Blackheads.

DANCING WITH DEATH

Part of a 15th-century frieze by Bernt Notke, *Danse Macabre* is considered one of Estonia's most prized works of art, as it is the only known surviving example of its genre on canvas. Skeletal figures of death are shown as enticing a king and nobles to dance along with them. No one knows exactly how the painting came to Tallinn, but it is possible that Notke had reproduced a similar frieze he completed in 1461 in his native Lübeck in Germany.

Detail showing a king

Bernt Notke's frieze, *Danse Macabre*, which is kept inside the church, depicts the universality of death.

Renaissance-style House of Blackheads, with ornate front door

House of Blackheads 🔞
Mustpeade maja

Pikk 26. **Map** 1 C2. **Tel** 631 3199.
🚌 5, 40. 🚊 1, 2, 3, 4. ◯ only
for chamber music concerts (call for
timings). **www**.mustpeademaja.ee

This 15th-century Renaissance
building was the meeting
place of the Brotherhood of
Blackheads, an association
of unmarried merchants and
shipowners, who were then
able to join the more powerful Great Guild upon marriage.
The unusual name was der-
ived from the North African
St Maurice, the organization's
patron saint, whose image
can be seen on the ornate
front door of the building.
   Unlike their counterparts in
Rīga (see p148), the Tallinn
Blackheads were obliged to
defend the city in times of
strife and proved themselves
especially formidable adver-
saries during the Livonian
Wars (1558–82). However,
in general, it seems that the
wealthy young Blackheads
lived somewhat leisurely and
hedonistic lives. The association survived until the Soviet
invasion in 1940, and today,

the House of Blackheads
regularly hosts chamber music
concerts in its elegant main
hall, which is noted for its
wood-panelled interior.

Estonian Museum of Applied Art and Design 🔞
Eesti tarbekunsti ja
disainimuuseum

Lai 17. **Map** 1 C2. **Tel** 627 4600.
🚌 3. 🚊 1, 2. ◯ 11am–6pm Wed–
Sun. 📷 🛈 **www**.etdm.ee

Housed in a converted
17th-century granary, the
Estonian Museum of Applied
Art and Design features the
best in Estonian design from
the early 20th century to the
present day. The vast selection
of exhibits, which include
jewellery, ceramics, glass, furniture and textiles, is a splendid
example of the pride that
Estonia takes in applied arts.
   Many of the exhibits meld
Scandinavian-style refinement
with subtle Baltic irony to
excellent effect. Some of the
fantastic examples of furniture
are especially eye-catching
and a delight for art collectors.
There are also some fine

pieces of porcelain, dating
from the 1930s to the 1960s,
by the legendary Estonian
artist Adamson-Eric (see p71).
   Since the museum opened
in 1980 it has done a formidable job of promoting Estonian
design at home and abroad.
Be sure to pick up a copy
of the map, which highlights
some notable examples of
public design around Tallinn.

Church of the Transfiguration of Our Lord 🔞
Issandamuutmise kirik

Suur-Kloostri 14–1. **Map** 1 C2.
Tel 646 4003. 🚌 3. 🚊 1, 2.
◯ 9am–1pm Sun. 📷 🛈 10am
Sun. **www**.teelistekirikud.ekn.ee

Located close to a stretch
of the medieval city wall,
the secluded Church of the
Transfiguration of Our Lord
has an impressive Baroque-
style spire and a richly
decorated interior. The
church originally belonged
to St Michael's Convent of
the Cistercian Order but
was closed down during
the Reformation. Briefly
serving as a church for the
Swedish garrison, it was
handed over to the Orthodox
Church in 1716 during the
rule of Peter the Great, who
donated the extraordinary
iconostasis by Russian architect
Ivan Zarudny. The church
also has a bell dating from
1575, the oldest in Tallinn.

Baroque spire of the Church of
the Transfiguration of Our Lord

View of Tallinn and the Baltic Sea from St Olav's Church

St Olav's Church ⓯
Oleviste kirik

Lai 50. **Map** 1 C1. **Tel** 641 2241.
🚌 3. 🚃 1, 2. ◯ Apr–Oct: 10am–6pm daily. 🎧 ⬛ www.oleviste.ee

St Olav's 124-m (407-ft) spire is a major Tallinn landmark and the church holds a proud place in local history. The legend goes that Tallinners wanted to build the tallest spire in the world to attract merchant ships and a complete stranger promised to help them. As payment he wanted the city people to guess his name. When the church was nearing completion, the city fathers sent a spy to his home and found out his name. They called out "Olev" when he was fixing the cross and he lost his balance and fell. In fact, the name of the church was in homage to King Olav II of Norway. The 159-m (522-ft) spire made the church the tallest building in the world until a lightning-strike burned it down in 1625. Amazingly, the church was struck by lightning six times and burned down twice between then and 1820.

Detail of stone carving on rear of St Olav's Church

The original 16th-century structure of the church was renovated extensively in the 19th century. St Olav's interior is not especially striking, although the vaulted ceiling is impressive and the church tower has a viewing platform with breathtaking vistas of the city. The exterior rear wall features an elaborately carved 15th-century tombstone of Johann Ballivi, a victim of the plague.

Three Sisters ⓰
Kolm õde

Pikk 71. **Map** 2 D1. 🚌 3. 🚃 1, 2.

Situated at the northern end of Pikk Street, the Three Sisters are three adjoining medieval merchants' houses that have been tastefully converted into a single luxury hotel (*see p294*). The houses were built in 1362 and were functional commercial premises, complete with loading hatches and winches to hoist sacks of goods up and down. The houses' original owners, who were mostly guild elders, town councillors and burgomasters, also used their premises to entertain foreign guests whom they met on their business trips abroad. The elegant gabled houses are among the best-preserved buildings from the 14th century and form a valuable addition to the magnificent surroundings of Pikk Street. The Three Sisters Hotel proudly counts Queen Elizabeth II and the singer Sting among the many luminaries who have stayed there.

Fat Margaret Tower ⓱
Paks Margareeta

Pikk 70. **Map** 2 D1. **Tel** 641 1408.
🚌 3. 🚃 1, 2. ◯ 10am–6pm Wed–Sun. 🎧 ⬛ call in advance. ⬛ www.meremuuseum.ee

The 16th-century tower's evocative name derives from the fact that it was the largest part of the city's fortifications, with walls measuring 4 m (13 ft) thick. It was originally built to defend the harbour as well as to impress visitors arriving by sea. Later, the tower was transformed into a prison and was the scene of an outbreak of violence during the 1917 Revolution, when the prison guards were murdered by a mob of workers, soldiers and sailors.

Fat Margaret Tower now serves the more peaceful function of housing the **Estonian Maritime Museum** (Eesti meremuuseum), with a curious collection of nautical paraphernalia spread out over four storeys. The exhibits include an insight into shipbuilding and historical accounts of Estonia's harbours. There is also a scale model of the *Estonia*, the car and passenger ferry that sank between Tallinn and Stockholm in 1994. There are gorgeous views of the Old Town and Tallinn's harbour and bay from the top of the tower.

🏛 **Estonian Maritime Museum**
Pikk 70. **Tel** 641 1408. ◯ 10am–6pm Wed–Sun. 🎧

Metal ship replica on the entrance wall, Estonian Maritime Museum

Street-by-Street: Toompea

Set on Toompea Hill, some 50 m (164 ft) above sea level, Toompea lies southwest of the Old Town. It dates back to the 13th century, when the Danes erected a stone castle on the site. The hill has changed hands many times over the centuries, but still remains enclosed in the impressive limestone fortifications built during the Livonian War (1558–82). The eclectic complex of Toompea Castle now houses the Riigikogu, Estonia's Parliament, in Castle Square. The centre of the square is dominated by the imposing Alexander Nevsky Cathedral. Toompea Hill offers a spectacular vantage point of the Old Town and makes an ideal starting point for a tour of Tallinn.

Pikk Hermann Tower, one of Tallinn's main landmarks

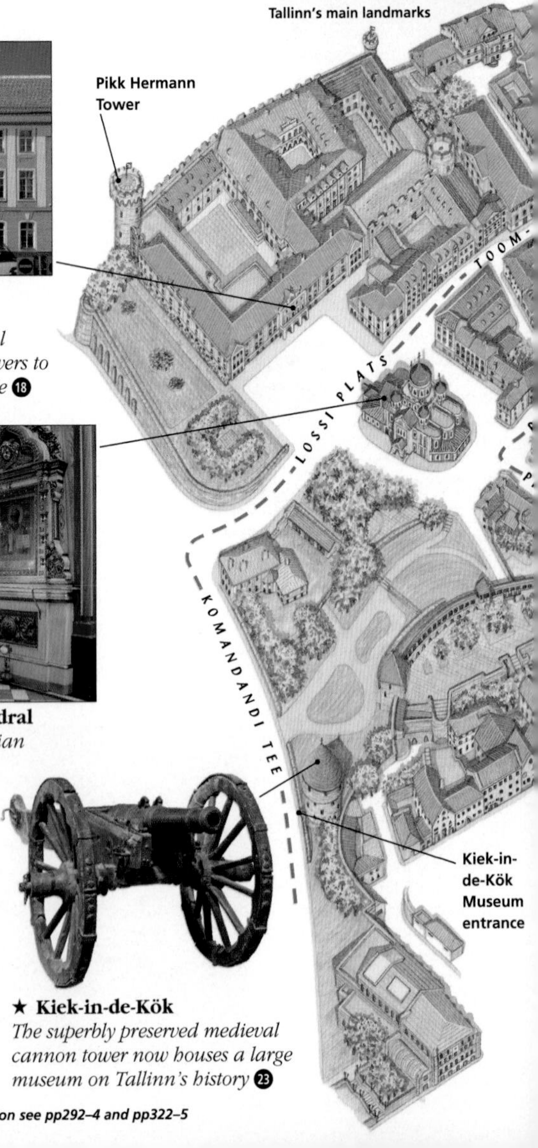

Pikk Hermann Tower

★ Toompea Castle
This hilltop castle compound comprises several architectural styles, from medieval stone towers to a vibrant pink Baroque façade ⓲

★ Alexander Nevsky Cathedral
Tallinn's most grandiose Russian Orthodox cathedral was named after the war hero who victoriously led Russian soldiers into battle at Lake Peipsi in 1242 ⓳

Kiek-in-de-Kök Museum entrance

STAR SIGHTS

★ Toompea Castle

★ Alexander Nevsky Cathedral

★ Kiek-in-de-Kök

★ Kiek-in-de-Kök
The superbly preserved medieval cannon tower now houses a large museum on Tallinn's history ㉓

Cathedral of St Mary the Virgin
Originally built as a wooden church by the Danes in 1240, St Mary's is the oldest church in mainland Estonia. Most of its austere Gothic exterior, however, dates from the 14th century 🏛

Patkuli Viewing Platform
One of Toompea's secluded hideaways, this picturesque spot has great panoramic views of the Old Town's red roofs as well as of the harbour.

KEY

– – – Suggested route

Pikk Jalg Gate Tower
With a striking red roof, the tower at the end of cobbled Pikk jalg dates from the 14th century.

Kohtuotsa viewing platform, swarming with postcard sellers and tour groups, looks out over the Old Town.

metre   100
yards   100

Knights' House
The Neo-Renaissance building was built in 1848 to serve as the headquarters of the Knighthood, the then local aristocracy. The well-preserved interior is a blend of various styles 🔟

The Neo-Byzantine Alexander Nevsky Cathedral

Toompea Castle ⑱
Toompea loss

Lossi plats 1a. **Map** 1 B3. **Tel** 631
6345. 🚋 3, 4. ⬜ 10am–4pm
Mon–Fri. 🎫 call in advance. ♿ 🚫
www.riigikogu.ee

The elegant and unassuming
pink Classical façade of
Toompea Castle belies the
history behind this vital seat
of power. The castle is now
home to Riigikogu (Estonia's
Parliament), but for some 700
years it belonged to various
occupying foreign powers.
In the 9th century, a wooden
fortress stood on the site,
which was conquered by the
Danes in 1219, who then
constructed the stone fortifications around the hill,
much of which still survives.

The architecturally diverse
castle complex features the
50-m (164-ft) Pikk Hermann
Tower, above which flies the
Estonian flag. The unique-
looking Riigikogu, which was
built in 1922, is situated in the
castle courtyard. Toompea as

a whole enjoyed its own
rights and privileges until
1878, when it was officially
merged with the rest of
the town below.

Alexander Nevsky Cathedral ⑲
Aleksander Nevski katedraal

Lossi plats 10. **Map** 1 B3. **Tel** 644
3484. 🚋 3, 4. ⬜ 8am–8pm Sat,
8am–7pm Sun–Fri. ✝ 8:30am
Mon–Sat, 10am Sun. 🚫 📷
www.teelistekirikud.ekn.ee

The imposing Alexander
Nevsky Cathedral was built
between 1894 and 1900, under
orders from Tsar Alexander III.
As intended, the Neo-Byzantine
edifice dominates Castle Square
with its towering onion domes
and golden crosses.

Legend has it that the cathedral was built on the grave of
the Estonian folk hero Kalev. It
is named after the sainted Russian duke Alexander Nevsky
(1219–63), who defeated the
Livonian Knights on the banks

of Lake Peipsi in 1242. Disliked
by many Estonians as a symbol
of the Russification policies
carried out by Alexander III, it
was due to be demolished in
1924, but the controversial plan
was never carried out.

The extravagant altar is
made up of a dazzling display
of icons, while the sheer scale
of the cathedral's interior is
equally impressive.

Cathedral of St Mary the Virgin ⑳
Toomkirik

Toomkooli 6. **Map** 1 B2. **Tel** 644
4140. 🚋 3, 4. ⬜ Jun–Aug: 9am–
5pm daily; Sep–May: 9am–5pm Tue–
Sun. **www**.eelk.ee/tallinna.toom

Popularly known as Dome
Church, St Mary's is believed
to be the oldest church in
Estonia. It was built in 1240
by the Danes and underwent
extensive rebuilding over the
years. The somewhat plain
Gothic exterior dates from
the 14th century, while the
beautiful interior boasts an
elaborate Baroque pulpit and
a widely admired organ built
in 1878. Other significant
features include 107 aristocratic coats of arms and the
fine Renaissance tomb of
the French-born mercenary,
Pontus de la Gardie, who captured Narva for the Swedes
from the Russians in 1581,
during the Great Northern
War (1558–82). In 1684, the

**Intricately designed Baroque pulpit,
Cathedral of St Mary the Virgin**

church was badly damaged in a fire that swept Toompea and had to be substantially reconstructed. Today, the church remains at the very heart of Estonian Lutheranism.

Museum of Occupations ㉑
Okupatsioonide muuseum

Toompea 8. **Map** 1 B3. **Tel** 668 0250. ⬚ 3, 4. ⬚ 11am–6pm Tue–Sun. ⬚ ⬚ call in advance. ⬚ ⬚ ⬚
www.okupatsioon.ee

This comprehensive museum provides a look at life in Estonia under both the Nazi and Soviet occupations. The fascinating exhibits include examples of bureaucratic paperwork, gut-wrenching accounts of mass deportation and execution, as well as poster-art propaganda, which was an essential weapon for the occupying forces.

The open-space museum remembers the countless victims of the occupations, and its symbolic location at the foot of Toompea adds a certain poignancy. It was partly founded by Kistler-Ritso, an Estonian World War II refugee to the United States. He donated 2 million dollars to the museum, the largest private donation in Estonian history.

Knights' House ㉒
Rüütelkonna hoone

Kiriku plats 1. **Map** 1 B2. ⬚ 3, 4.

Built in 1848, the Knights' House originally served as a meeting place for the knight-hood, an influential segment of the Toompea gentry. It was home to the Foreign Ministry during the first independent republic, which lasted from 1920 to 1940. During Soviet times, the building housed the Estonian National Library.

It temporarily accommodated the main collection of the Art Museum of Estonia before it moved to its new permanent home in the Kumu Art Museum *(see p76).* The

Exterior of the 19th-century Knights' House, now a venue for concerts

building, which did occasion-ally host concerts, is currently closed to the public.

Kiek-in-de-Kök ㉓

Komandandi 2. **Map** 1 B3. **Tel** 644 6686. ⬚ 3, 4. ⬚ Mar–Oct: 10:30am–6pm Tue–Sun; Nov–Feb: 10am–5:30pm Tue–Sun. ⬚ ⬚ call 644 6686 for a guided group tour of secret tunnels under the bastion. ⬚
www.linnamuuseum.ee

One of the most powerful cannon towers in 16th century Northern Europe, Kiek-in-de-Kök was built in 1475 as Toompea's main bastion. The tower stands 38 m (125 ft) tall and its walls are 4 m (13 ft) thick. The curious Low German name means "to peek into the kitchen", suggesting that soldiers had a good vantage point over the enemy. Some, however, believe that they literally peeked into people's kitchens. The tower fell into

Painted porcelain plate, **Adamson-Eric Museum**

Bitter Death, a cannon replica displayed in Kiek-in-de-Kök

disuse in the mid-18th century and now houses a five-floor museum devoted to Tallinn's history. The highlights include medieval artillery and a plague doctor's protective uniform.

Adamson-Eric Museum ㉔

Lühike jalg 3. **Map** 1 C3. **Tel** 644 5838. ⬚ 3, 4. ⬚ 11am–6pm Wed–Sun. ⬚ ⬚ group tours of 10–35; call in advance. ⬚ allowed only with-out the flash. ⬚ www.ekm.ee

Located in a medieval house on a narrow stairway con-necting the Old Town with Toompea, the Adamson-Eric Museum is a branch of the Art Museum of Estonia. Adamson-Eric (1902–68) is one of the key figures of 20th-century Estonian art. His idiosyn-cratic and diverse body of work spanned several decades and influenced countless artists after him.

The Tartu-born artist was primarily a painter, but also worked with ceramics, metal forms, jewellery and leather, among other media. Although he held several prominent positions in various Soviet art committees during the latter part of his life, he was thrown out of the Communist Party in 1949 and forced into fac-tory work for four years. After suffering a stroke in 1955 and losing the use of his right hand, he taught himself to paint using his left hand. The collection on display was donated to the Art Museum of Estonia by the artist's widow.

Exploring Beyond the Old Town

There is much more to Tallinn than its tourist-packed Old Town. A little way east is Kadriorg Park, with its splendid palace, the Kumu Art Museum and the nearby Song Festival Grounds. Further east is Maarjamäe Palace, which houses the Estonian History Museum. Just off lies the fascinating Pirita Convent. A short distance west of the Old Town is the Estonian Open-Air Museum with some of Estonia's oldest rural architecture. The well-connected suburb of Nõmme to the south is also worth exploring. Most places are within easy reach of public transport.

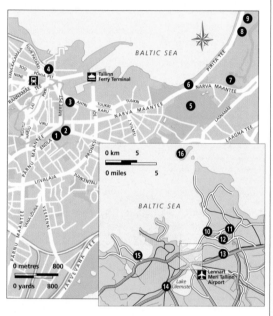

KEY

🛬 Airport

🚉 Railway station

⚓ Ferry port

▬ Motorway

▬ Main road

▬ Minor road

SIGHTS AT A GLANCE

Theatres, Concert Halls and Museums
Energy Centre ❹
Estonian Drama Theatre ❶
Estonian National Opera ❷
Estonian Open-Air Museum ⓯

Maarjamäe Palace ❽
Song Festival Grounds ❼

Historic Buildings
Pirita Convent ❿
Rotermanni Quarter and
    Salt Storage Warehouse ❸
Russalka Memorial ❻
Soviet War Memorial ❾
TV Tower ⓫

Parks and Gardens
Kadriorg Park pp74–7 ❺
Tallinn Botanical Gardens ⓬

Islands and Suburbs
Aegna Island ⓰
Lasnamäe ⓭
Nõmme ⓮

Estonian Drama Theatre ❶
Eesti draamateater

Pärnu mnt 5. **Tel** 680 5555.
🚌 5, 36, 40. 🚊 3, 4. ⏲
10am–5pm Mon–Fri. 📷 ♿ 🚫 📶
www.draamateater.ee

This popular theatre occupies one of the most striking buildings on the fringes of the Old Town. Built in 1910 as a German-language theatre, it was purchased by the Estonian Drama Theatre in 1939.

The elegant Art Nouveau exterior combines rustic-style features in a manner unique to the Baltic States. Under Soviet occupation, the theatre's name was changed to the Tallinn Drama Theatre, in an effort to remove nationalist affinities associated with it. However, in 1989 it reverted to its original name.

The theatre is the largest in Estonia with a 40-member company and an average of 500 performances per season. The productions are usually in Estonian, with rare exceptions during theatre festivals.

Grand entrance of the Estonian Drama Theatre

Estonian National Opera ❷
Rahvusooper Estonia

Estonia pst 4. **Tel** 683 1215. 🚌 5, 36, 40. 🚊 3, 4. ⏲ 11am–7pm daily (box office). 📷 ♿ 🚫 📶
www.opera.ee

The imperious bulk of the Estonian National Opera dominates the view along the stretch of Estonia Avenue, skirting the eastern edge of the Old Town.

Imposing façade of the Estonian National Opera

The sprawling building houses the Estonian National Opera and its ballet company in one wing and the Estonian National Symphony Orchestra in another, while the Winter Garden is regularly used to host state functions.

The Estonian National Opera was completed in 1913, through public donations, and was intended to serve as an impressive showcase for Estonian culture that would overshadow similar German and Russian institutions in Tallinn. In recent years, the opera company has gained an outstanding international reputation and its cutting-edge productions can be seen for a fraction of the price visitors would pay in most European capitals.

Charles Abraham Rotermann

Rotermanni Quarter and Salt Storage Warehouse ❸
Eesti arhitektuurimuuseum

Ahtri 2. **Tel** 625 7007. 🚌 all buses to Viru Bus Terminal. 🚊 1, 2, 3, 4. **Museum of Estonian Architecture Tel** 625 7007. ⬭ 11am–6pm Wed–Sun. 🏷 🎫 ♿ 📷 📷
www.arhitektuurimuuseum.ee

The Rotermanni Quarter is situated east of Mere Avenue on the fringes of Tallinn's port area and within comfortable walking distance of the Old Town. The district is named after Charles Abraham Rotermann, a 19th-century industrialist, and was a major industrial hub before most of its factories and warehouses fell into disuse and disrepair during the Soviet era. In 2007 the district underwent a major redevelopment. Several buildings with brave architectural designs were constructed to house boutique shops, offices and restaurants.

The impressive limestone building of the Salt Storage Warehouse, located nearby, is home to the **Museum of Estonian Architecture**. It was once used as the city's salt warehouse. Today, it houses a range of architecture-related exhibits, spread out over its vast three-floor interior.

Energy Centre ❹
Tehnika-ja teaduskeskus

Põhja pst 29. **Tel** 715 2650. 🚌 3. 🚊 1, 2. ⬭ 10am–6pm Mon–Fri, noon–5pm Sat. 🏷 🎫 📷
www.energiakeskus.ee

Situated in a former power station, the Energy Centre is an enormous museum that forms part of the Tallinn Science and Technology Centre. It has numerous interactive exhibits which are used to demonstrate the rudiments of science.

The centre is charmingly old-fashioned and relies on the joy of learning through entertainment, rather than the slick presentation and hi-tech gadgetry used by most modern-day institutes. There is an especially enjoyable array of hands-on exhibits downstairs. The centre also hosts various other more serious science-related exhibitions and seminars.

Salt Storage Warehouse, home to the Museum of Estonian Architecture

Kadriorg Park ❺

Kadriorg Park is one of Tallinn's most interesting features outside the Old Town. It centres on the magnificent 18th-century Baroque palace built as a summer residence for Peter the Great and boasts a wealth of small museums, historic monuments and art galleries. The park stretches for 1.5 km (1 mile) from its southwest corner to the northeast. It is a popular and picturesque place for a leisurely stroll. The elegant and affluent residential streets near the south entrance are also well worth a look and include museums dedicated to Eduard Vilde and Anton Hansen Tammsaare, two of Estonia's most prominent 20th-century literary figures.

Statue of Friedrich Reinhold Kreutzwald
This grand statue honours the writer of Kalevipoeg, considered the founding work of Estonian literature.

Swan Lake
The Swan Lake is one of the park's focal points, although its elegant island pavilion is mostly enjoyed by swans.

Anton Hansen Tammsaare Museum
The museum offers an insight into how the writer Tammsaare (1878–1940) lived and also exhibits his literary works.

0 metres   200
0 yards   200

Eduard Vilde Memorial Museum
This attractive summer house serves as a living memorial to one of Estonia's most revered writers. Vilde lived and worked here until his death in 1933.

STAR SIGHTS

★ Kadriorg Palace

★ Kumu Art Museum

★ Kadriorg Palace
Peter the Great's Baroque palace now houses the Estonian Art Museum's foreign collection. However, the museum's main exhibits are displayed at the Kumu Art Museum.

VISITORS' CHECKLIST

2 km (1 mile) E of the Old Town.
1a, 5, 8, 19, 34a, 35, 38.
1, 3. Note: Visitors can stroll through the park's residential streets to admire some architectural gems.

Russalka Memorial
This imposing monument (see p78) commemorates the sinking of the Russalka near Finland in 1893.

President's Palace

Peter the Great House Museum
The great Russian Tsar once used this cottage as a temporary residence.

★ Kumu Art Museum
Arguably the most architecturally impressive museum in the Baltic States, the magnificently designed Kumu houses the main exhibits of the Estonian Art Museum.

Mikkel Museum
The small museum is renowned for its porcelain vases and beautiful figurines.

Exploring Kadriorg Park

With forested paths, statues and ponds, Kadriorg Park is a charming place to explore. The area has a number of beautiful houses and manicured gardens and is also associated with art because of the number of museums, such as the Kumu Art Museum and Mikkel Museum, located here. Nearly all the park's main sights are on, or close to, Weizenbergi. Kadriorg Park is not very large and it is quite easy to cover its entire length on foot. A short distance from the Old Town, the park's quiet neighbourhood is, nevertheless, a pleasant 30-minute stroll away. Regular buses and trams connect Kadriorg Park with the Old Town.

The attractive garden of Kadriorg Palace

🏛 Kadriorg Palace

Weizenbergi 37. **Tel** 606 6400.
◯ May–Sep: 10am–5pm Tue–Sun;
Oct–Apr: 10am–5pm Wed–Sun. 🖼
🎫 ♿ 🖥 📷 www.ekm.ee
This palace was built in 1718 under orders from the Russian Tsar Peter the Great, who intended it to serve as a summer residence for the royal family. It was later named in honour of his wife Catherine. Kadriorg Palace was designed in the Northern Baroque style by the famous Italian master architect Nicola Michetti. The Russian emperor intended the three-winged palace to look like an Italian villa. No expense was spared in creating a magnificently lavish palace in the Italian Baroque style of which he was so fond.

After undergoing extensive renovation, the palace now houses the Estonian Art Museum's foreign collection.

Portrait of Thomas Chaloner by Van Dyck

Johannes Mikkel (1907–2006), whose collections are exhibited in the Mikkel Museum, donated some 600 works of foreign art to the Estonian Art Museum in 1994. The museum boasts a fine selection of European painting. However, the museum's main attraction is the astonishingly ornate Great Hall, which ranks among the finest examples of Baroque exuberance in Northern Europe. The well-manicured ornamental garden with fountains behind the palace is also open to the public.

🏛 Mikkel Museum

Weizenbergi 28. **Tel** 601 5844.
◯ 10am–5pm Wed–Sun. 🖼 🎫
www.ekm.ee
Located in the former kitchen of Kadriorg Palace, the Mikkel Museum comprises the private collection of Johannes Mikkel. He began collecting art during the inter-war period and over the years amassed a valuable collection. It is today considered one of the best private collections in Estonia.

The exhibits range from the 16th to 20th centuries and include an impressive selection of porcelain vases and figurines. There are some fine examples of classical European art, such as *Portrait of Thomas Chaloner*, attributed to the Flemish painter Anthony Van Dyck.

🏛 Kumu Art Museum

Weizenbergi 34. **Tel** 602 6000.
◯ May–Sep: 11am–6pm Tue–Sun;
Oct–Apr: 11am–6pm Wed–Sun. 🖼
🎫 ♿ 🍴 🖥 📷 www.ekm.ee
The Kumu Art Museum is the Estonian Art Museum's first purpose-built building; it was designed to provide a fitting home for the museum's main collection. The structure is built into a limestone bank on the edge of Kadriorg Park and is a work of art in itself.

The museum's enormous and beautifully designed interior is a labyrinth of artistic discovery with one exhibition hall leading to another. The exhibits in the rooms are arranged in chronological order. Among the many delights on show, Konrad Mägi's brilliantly coloured canvases stand out as a wonderful example of early 20th-century Estonian art. Eduard von Gebhardt's *Sermon on the Mount* is another painting to relish for both its epic excellence and

Row of busts on display in a room at the Kumu Art Museum

subtle irony. The fourth floor is devoted to a permanent exhibition entitled "Difficult Choices", exploring the complex relationship between art and the Soviet state, while the fifth floor is given over to the best in contemporary art. However, the most striking exhibition of all is the room filled with hundreds of busts eerily staring into space.

Catherine I's bedroom, Peter the Great House Museum

🏛 Peter the Great House Museum

Mäekalda 2. **Tel** 601 3136.
⬭ May–Aug: 10am–6pm Tue–Sun;
Sep–Apr: 10am–4pm Tue–Sun. 🖼
www.linnamuuseum.ee

This museum is housed in the 17th-century cottage which the Russian emperor used as a summer residence while Kadriorg Palace was being built. The cottage was purchased along with the surrounding land in 1713 and was enlarged with an additional wing so that it contained a hall, a kitchen and four rooms.

After Peter the Great died in 1725, his successors opted to stay in the more lavish Kadriorg Palace and the cottage fell into disrepair until Alexander I ordered it to be restored after a visit to Tallinn in 1804. The house contains few remains of Peter the Great's time, but it still affords an intriguing glimpse into the life of the enigmatic ruler. The bedroom has a four-poster bed and a pair of slippers which supposedly belonged to the Tsar himself. There is an exhibition in the basement about his life and achievements.

EDUARD VILDE (1865–1933)

Author of Estonian classics such as *The War in Mahtra* and *The Milkman from Mäeküla*, Eduard Vilde is one of the most revered figures in Estonian literature and is generally credited as being the country's first professional writer.

Eduard Vilde, writer and diplomat

Vilde spent a great deal of time travelling abroad and he lived for some time in Berlin in the 1890s, where he was influenced by materialism and socialism. His writings were also guided by the naturalism of the French writer Emile Zola (1840–1902). In addition to being a writer, Vilde was also an outspoken critic of Tsarist rule and of the German landowners. With the founding of the first Estonian republic in 1919, Vilde served as a diplomat in Berlin for several years. He spent the last years of his life editing and revising an enormous volume of his collected works.

🏛 A H Tammsaare Memorial Museum

Koidula 12a. **Tel** 601 3232.
⬭ 10am–5pm Wed–Mon. 🖼 🖼
www.linnamuuseum.ee

Anton Hansen Tammsaare (1878–1940) is Estonia's most important literary figure. His five-volume epic, *Truth and Justice*, takes a sweeping look at Estonian society from the 1870s to the 1930s.

The museum is situated in the attractive wooden house in Kadriorg where the novelist and his wife lived from 1932 until his death in 1940. The building was converted into a museum in 1978. On the first floor is the couple's five-room flat, while a separate wing serves as a museum dedicated

Exterior of the modest A H Tammsaare Memorial Museum

to Tammsaare's life and work. The collection of almost 6,000 artifacts includes several photographs, letters and manuscripts and even the writer's death mask.

🏛 Eduard Vilde Memorial Museum

Roheline aas 3. **Tel** 601 3181.
⬭ 11am–6pm Wed–Mon. 🖼 🖼
www.linnamuuseum.ee

The Eduard Vilde Memorial Museum is housed in a Neo-Baroque summer house beside Kadriorg Park which was presented to the writer as a 60th birthday gift by the Estonian government.

Vilde was one of Estonia's most prolific writers, and his works amount to a staggering 33 volumes. The museum showcases the six-room flat where Vilde lived with his wife from 1927 to 1933. The authentic furnishings are accompanied by period art pieces and provide a fascinating look at literary life in Tallinn in the 1920s. It is said that Vilde could often be seen enjoying long talks with his neighbour, the famous writer A H Tammsaare, in the nearby park.

The museum has been in existence since 1946 and is an interesting monument. The balusters of the wooden staircase, dating from the turn of the 19th century to the 20th century, have survived.

Russalka Memorial ❻

Near the junction of Pirita tee & Narva mnt. 🚌 1a, 34, 38. ⛟

This imposing memorial was erected in honour of the 177 soldiers who drowned when the Russian ship *Russalka*, or "Mermaid", sank en route to Finland in 1893. Designed by the renowned Estonian sculptor Amandus Adamson (1855–1929), the monument was erected in 1902. It features a bronze angel standing on tiptoe, holding aloft an Orthodox cross. The pedestal on which the angel stands is made of roughly hewn blocks of granite evoking stormy sea conditions. The monument is one of several locations around Tallinn which young couples visit to be photographed on their wedding day.

Angel with an Orthodox cross, standing atop Russalka Memorial

Song Festival Grounds ❼
Lauluväljak

Narva mnt 95. **Tel** 611 2102. 🚌 1a, 5, 8, 34a, 38 (to Lauluväljak); 19, 29, 35, 44, 51, 60, 63 (to Lasnamägi). ◯ daily. ⛟ www.lauluvaljak.ee

The centrepiece of the Song Festival Grounds is the **Song Festival Bowl**, the large shell-like amphitheatre, built in the 1960s. During the four-yearly all-Estonia Song Festival, the stage holds up to 15,000 choral singers, with room for many

Aerial view of the impressive shell-like Song Festival Bowl

more on an extra platform. It has been a strong symbol for Estonians ever since thousands of people gathered here during the 1988 Song Festival in a show of unity against Soviet occupation.

In summer, the venue hosts concerts, as well as the Beer Festival. The 42-m (138-ft) high Light Tower beside the Song Festival Bowl offers good views of the Old Town. On weekday evenings, the tower is used as a climbing post.

Maarjamäe Palace ❽

Pirita tee 56. **Tel** 622 8600. 🚌 5, 34, 38. ◯ 10am–5pm Wed–Sun. 📷 ⛟ call in advance. **www**.ajaloo muuseum.ee

An elegant Neo-Gothic summer house, Maarjamäe Palace was built in 1874 by the Russian Count Orlov-Davydov. The building has since served as a consulate, a hotel and restaurant, and a base for trainee pilots as well as the Soviet army. However, today, it houses another branch of the **Estonian History Museum** *(see p60)*.

The museum, inaugurated in 1987, picks up where its counterpart in the Old Town leaves off in the mid-19th century to cover the political and social upheavals of the 20th century. The exhibits include historically dressed

mannequins and recreations of domestic interiors. The 1940s and 50s are represented by army uniforms, photographs and weapons. There is an original hut used by the Forest Brothers *(see p118)*, the legendary partisans who fought against the Soviet occupation, and a replica of a desk used by a Communist Party secretary.

Visitors can go to the back of the palace to see some of the gigantic Soviet-era bronze monuments lying in an unceremonious heap.

🏛 **Estonian History Museum**
◯ 10am–5pm Wed–Sun.
Research: 9am–5pm Mon–Fri.

Maarjamäe Palace, housing a branch of the Estonian History Museum

Peter the Great (1672–1725)

Russia had long coveted Estonia as a much-needed outlet to Western Europe, but it was Peter the Great who finally achieved this. When the Treaty of Nystad ended the Great Northern War between Russia and Sweden in 1721, Estonia finally fell under Russian control. The Russian Tsar visited Tallinn 11 times during his reign and left an impressive legacy behind. From the magnificent Kadriorg Palace *(see p76),*

The Tsar's bust in Kadriorg Park

which was built as a royal summer residence, to the reconstruction of the ports in Tallinn and Paldiski, Peter the Great's formidable influence is still visible. The Tsar so loved Estonia that he once remarked, "If Tallinn and Rogewiek [Paldiski] had been mine in 1702, I would not have established my residence and the capital of European Russia on the low-lying river Neva but here."

Peter the Great *is represented as a great statesman in this portrait by Hippolyte Delaroche, painted in 1838. The Tsar's political intelligence and military prowess turned Russia into a major European power.*

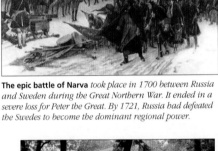

The epic battle of Narva *took place in 1700 between Russia and Sweden during the Great Northern War. It ended in a severe loss for Peter the Great. By 1721, Russia had defeated the Swedes to become the dominant regional power.*

The cottage in Kadriorg Park (see p77) *was used by Peter the Great and his wife Catherine I as a summer residence while Kadriorg Palace was being built. The cottage is now a museum.*

Portrait of Catherine I, painted by Jean-Marc Nattier in 1717

CATHERINE I (1684–1727)

Originally named Marta Skavronskaya, Catherine I was a Lithuanian peasant's daughter and is thought to have been born in present-day Estonia. A beautiful girl, Marta joined the household of Prince Aleksandr Menschikov, who introduced her to Peter the Great in 1703. They became lovers soon after that. In 1705, she converted to Orthodoxy, whereupon she changed her name to Catherine. The couple lived a modest life in a two-room log cabin during the construction of St Petersburg and were secretly married in 1707. In 1709, Catherine gave birth to Elizabeth, who later ruled Russia from 1741 to 1762. In 1724, Catherine was officially declared co-ruler of the Russian empire with her husband. Kadriorg *(see pp74–7)*, or Catherine's Valley, was named in her honour.

Soviet War Memorial ❾
Maarjamäe

Pirita tee. 🚌 1a, 8, 5, 34a, 38. ♿

The Soviet War Memorial is a typical example of Soviet war monuments in both its grand scale and rather kitsch-aesthetic appearance. The 35-m (115-ft) obelisk at the centre of the complex was erected in 1960 to commemorate the Russian sailors who died in 1918, during World War I. The surrounding features were built in the 1970s, in memory of the Soviet soldiers killed in 1941 under the Nazi onslaught. In a dilapidated state today, the site includes an eerie concrete amphitheatre and large concrete and iron figures.

A German cemetery filled with stone crosses lies just behind the memorial site, serving as yet another reminder of the fierce struggle for control over the region.

Pirita Convent ❿
Pirita klooster

Merivälja Tee 18. **Tel** 605 5044. 🚌 1a, 5, 8, 34a. ⭘ Nov–Mar: noon–4pm daily; Apr–May: 10am–6pm daily; Jun–Aug: 9am–7pm daily; Sep–Oct: 10am–6pm daily. 🎫 www.piritaklooster.ee

Founded in 1407 by the St Bridget Order, Pirita Convent was consecrated in 1436. It served as the largest convent in then Livonia (present-day Estonia and northern Latvia), until it was badly damaged in a siege by Ivan the Terrible in 1577. Over the following decades, the convent was reduced to a skeletal structure, as locals plundered it for building materials. In the 17th century, a cemetery was established in the compound.

Despite centuries of neglect and oblivion, the impressive ruins retain some splendour. The most striking feature is the perfectly intact 35-m (115-ft) high gable and the walls of the main hall. The site is run by Bridgettine nuns, who live in a state-of-the-art award-winning building close by. The nuns

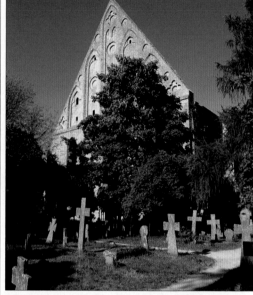

Pirita Convent screened by trees, with the cemetery in the foreground

offer lodgings in their home, continuing a tradition that has existed for hundreds of years.

TV Tower ⓫
Teletorn

Kloostrimetsa 58a. 🚌 34a, 38. ⭘ May–Sep: 10am–7pm daily; Oct–Apr: 11am–6pm Wed–Mon.

Inaugurated in 1980, the 314-m (1,030-ft) tall TV Tower, or Tallinn Tower, was designed as an impressive demonstration of superior Soviet engineering. It was the scene

TV Tower, a brilliant example of Russian engineering

of a tense stand-off between Estonians and Soviet troops in 1991, which was resolved peacefully when the Soviet troops withdrew. It is an amazing spectacle, despite its increasingly crumbling condition. There are great views from the observation deck.

Tallinn Botanical Gardens ⓬
Tallinna botaanikaaed

Kloostrimetsa tee 52, 10 km (6 miles) NE of city centre. **Tel** 606 2666. 🚌 34a, 38. ⭘ Apr–Sep: 11am–6pm; Oct–Mar: 11am–4pm. 🎫 📷 ♿ www.botaanikaaed.ee

Located in a beautiful stretch of woodland, the Tallinn Botanical Gardens have an exotic palm house as the main attraction. Adjoining the palm house are several greenhouses containing a superb selection of rare orchids and fascinating cacti. The outdoor collections include a rose garden, arboretum, limestone rock garden and a permanent display of "useful plants".

The grounds are set over 123 ha (304 acres) in a protected area of the Pirita River Valley and have a designated

4-km (2-mile) nature trail that goes through a lush range of habitats, from dry meadows to pine forests.

Lasnamäe ⓭

5 km (3 miles) NE of Tallinn.

A vast Soviet-era suburb founded on a limestone plateau in 1977, Lasnamäe houses almost a third of the city's population. The industrial part of the district is centred around Peterburi Street. Seemingly endless rows of housing blocks are lined up beside Laagna Street, which is a smaller road that passes through the so-called "Canyon", a road blasted through limestone.

The ambitious plans for the making of Lasnamäe were never finished and several aborted building projects that abruptly came to a halt when Estonia broke away from the Soviet Union, can still be seen. Although there is little of interest, the area as a whole is a strangely impressive sight and offers an intriguing glimpse of a side of the city that most visitors rarely see.

Nõmme ⓮

8 km (5 miles) S of Tallinn.
🚆 from Tallinn. 🚌 14, 18, 33.

The beautiful residential district of Nõmme was developed as a suburb after a railway station opened there in 1872. Soon after, wealthy Tallinners began building elegant summer villas with spacious gardens, and by 1926, the area had grown sufficiently to officially become a town. However, in 1940 the Soviets incorporated it into Tallinn.

Today, Nõmme is one of the most attractive areas of the city, with its own outdoor market, historic centre, cafés and restaurants, and some fine museums. The Kristjan Raud Museum is dedicated to the artist who illustrated the epic poem, *Kalevipoeg*, while the **Baron von Glehn Castle**, built by a Baltic-German landlord who largely founded the area,

Baron von Glehn Castle in lush surroundings, Nõmme

is an impressive sight. The castle is only open for special events but the surrounding park, with some particularly eye-catching statues, can be visited any time.

⚜ **Baron von Glenn Castle**
Vana-Mustimäe tee 48. *Tel 652 5076.* ◯ *by appointment only.*

Estonian Open-Air Museum ⓯
Eesti vabaõhumuuseum

Vabaõhumuuseumi tee 12.
Tel 654 9100. 🚌 *21, 21b.* ◯ *May–Sep: 10am–8pm daily; Oct–Apr: 10am–5pm daily.* 📷 📷 *call in advance.* ♿ 🏪 🏛 www.evm.ee

One of the few major sights outside the city centre, the Estonian Open-Air Museum is situated in the sprawling grounds of the former Rocco al Mare summer estate with a stunning backdrop of Kopli Bay. The museum is an enormous village made up of

historical rural buildings from all around the country. The exhibits range from the 18th to the 20th centuries and give a fascinating picture of how rural architecture developed in Estonia over the years. There are wooden windmills, thatched barns, a village inn and an 18th-century wooden church alongside numerous farmsteads and outbuildings.

A variety of activities are offered, including nature trails as well as horse and carriage rides, while regular music and theatre productions are held here. Annual highlights include the Midsummer's Eve celebrations *(see p48)* and the Autumn Fair.

Aegna Island ⓰
Aegna saar

14 km (9 miles) NE of Tallinn.
🚢 *from Pirita Harbour.*

The tiny 3-sq km (1-sq mile) island of Aegna is situated in the northeastern part of Tallinn Bay. However, its pristine sandy beaches and unspoiled nature may be the target for future development.

What few traces can be found of human activity are nearly all military. There was a cannon battery here during Tsarist rule, and after being briefly used by the Estonian army during the country's first period of independence, Aegna became a closed Soviet military zone.

The island is now governed by Tallinn City Council and improved ferry links have led to a steady increase in visitors. It is a popular place to pitch a tent in summer.

Old wooden house by the sea, Estonian Open-Air Museum

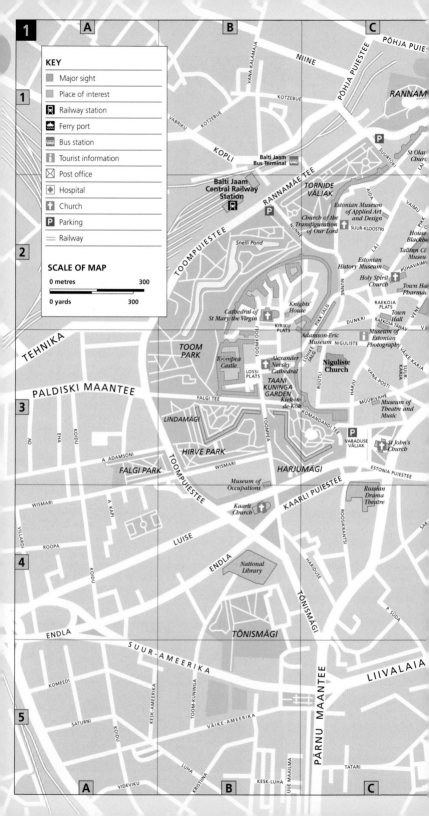

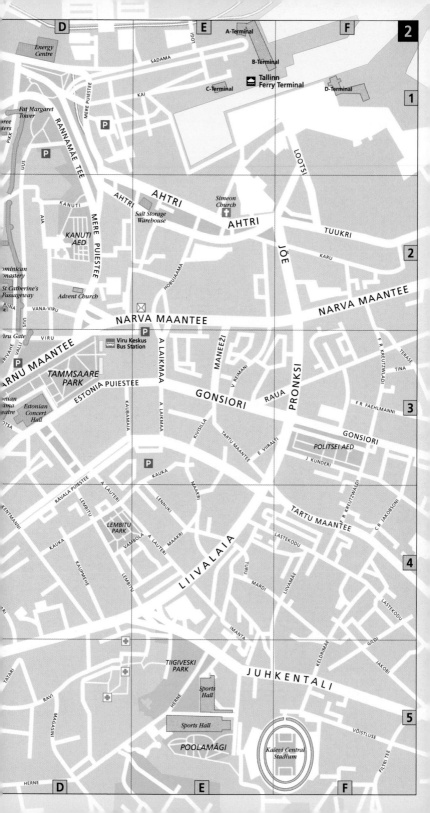

WESTERN ESTONIA

*T*he region enjoys some of the country's most stunning natural landscapes and is also historically entwined with the Estonian national identity in countless ways. The erratic, time-worn coastline is punctuated with numerous places of cultural interest as well as some lively summer resorts, while the archipelago is remarkable for its unspoiled, timeless beauty.

Estonia's history has, to a large extent, been shaped by its west coast. Swedes settled in large numbers on the islands and around Haapsalu, as they were in the path of Nordic trading routes. Peter the Great seized Estonia and, in 1718, built a port and navy base at Paldiski because he wanted a "window into the West". In Soviet times, the coastline served as a heavily guarded border zone.

Western Estonia's main coastal town is Pärnu in the south, the country's "Summer Capital". Further north, Haapsalu was a stylish 19th-century resort and has remained every bit as attractive today. Soomaa National Park, which lies just inland, is an enchanting waterworld of bogs and rivers, while Matsalu National Park is one of the biggest nesting grounds for birds in Europe. On the northwest coast, Paldiski offers testimony to the Soviet occupation in the form of countless crumbling buildings that once served the enormous submarine base there, while the beautiful cliffs around the peninsula make it a wonderful place for hiking. The whole coastline is dotted with tiny, picturesque villages, while countless manor houses, medieval churches, iconic lighthouses and other places of interest are strewn throughout this region.

Of the Estonian islands, Saaremaa is both the largest and the most popular. The island of Vilsandi is the remotest of all of Estonia's national parks but, covered with interesting sights, it is one of the most rewarding to visit. The islands of Hiiumaa, Vormsi and Muhu are less developed, but their rugged beauty is a strong attraction for visitors seeking the serenity of a pristine and somewhat remote environment.

Traditionally attired dancers forming a circle at a celebration on Hiiumaa Island

◁ Awe-inspiring icefall and rock formation near Paldiski

Exploring Western Estonia

Western Estonia offers an irresistible blend of cultural heritage and wild natural beauty. Pärnu is a good base from which to explore the bogs and wetlands of Soomaa National Park to the east and the flourishing bird sanctuary of Matsalu National Park to the north. The popular spa resort of Haapsalu is within easy driving distance of Tallinn and visitors can explore the ruggedly beautiful coastal area around Paldiski on the way. The islands of Kihnu, Muhu, Saaremaa, Vormsi and Hiiumaa are well connected to the mainland by ferry and can be reached from Pärnu and Haapsalu.

Wooden trail through a bog in Soomaa National Park

Row of old buildings in cobblestoned Rüütli Street, Pärnu

SIGHTS AT A GLANCE

Towns and Cities

Haapsalu ❷
Lihula ❻
Paldiski ❶
Pärnu pp98–9 ❾

National Parks and Reserves

Matsalu National Park ❹
Soomaa National Park pp100–101 ❿

Islands

Hiiumaa Island ❺
Kihnu Island ⓫
Muhu Island ❼
Saaremaa Island pp92–5 ❽
Vormsi Island ❸

Sights of Interest

Tori Stud Farm ⓬

KEY

▬▬	Motorway
▬▬	Main road
—	Secondary road
∷∷	Minor road
⊶	Railway
▬▬	International border

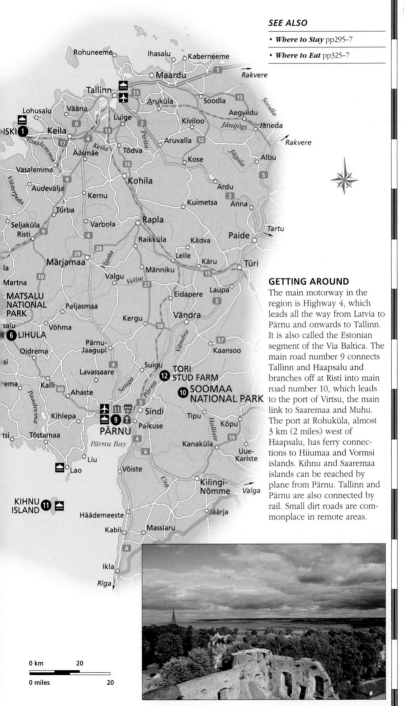

SEE ALSO
• *Where to Stay* pp295–7
• *Where to Eat* pp325–7

GETTING AROUND

The main motorway in the region is Highway 4, which leads all the way from Latvia to Pärnu and onwards to Tallinn. It is also called the Estonian segment of the Via Baltica. The main road number 9 connects Tallinn and Haapsalu and branches off at Risti into main road number 10, which leads to the port of Virtsu, the main link to Saaremaa and Muhu. The port at Rohuküla, almost 3 km (2 miles) west of Haapsalu, has ferry connections to Hiiumaa and Vormsi islands. Kihnu and Saaremaa islands can be reached by plane from Pärnu. Tallinn and Pärnu are also connected by rail. Small dirt roads are commonplace in remote areas.

View from the watchtower, Haapsalu Castle

Paldiski ❶

Road Map C1. 🏃 *4,000.* 🚉
🚌 *145 from Tallinn.* **www**.paldiski.ee

Deriving its name from the Estonian pronunciation of *baltiyskiy*, which means "Baltic" in Russian, Paldiski was established by Peter the Great in 1718. Paldiski was known to be of strategic importance for the Russian empire. In 1962, when the Soviet Navy nuclear submarine training centre was set up here, the area already had two nuclear reactors and employed some 16,000 people. The Soviets finally withdrew in 1994 and the town quickly fell into chronic disrepair. The Swedish director Lukas Moodysson shot his extraordinarily bleak film *Lilya-4-Ever* (2002) in Paldiski, though it was described as an unnamed "former republic of the Soviet Union".

Located 52 km (32 miles) west of Tallinn, Paldiski is a fascinating place to visit and it attracts a steady stream of tourists. The countless derelict military buildings testify to the prominent role Paldiski once played in the Soviet defence system. Today, however, the town is slowly, but surely, being revitalized. The port area is booming and Paldiski's natural beauty makes it an attractive site for residential development.

Haapsalu's medieval castle, with an adjoining cathedral

Environs
Pakri, a stunning peninsula 3 km (2 miles) west of Paldiski, boasts Estonia's tallest lighthouse. Also here are the ruins of Peter the Great's ambitious but unfinished fortress project.

The red-painted lighthouse at Pakri, near Paldiski

Haapsalu ❷

Road Map C2. 🏃 *12,000.* 🚉 *from Tallinn.* ⛴ *from Hiiumaa, Vormsi.* ℹ️ *Karja 15, 473 3248.* 🎵 *Early Music Festival (4–8 Jul), White Lady Days (Aug).* **www**.haapsalu.ee

Situated on a small spit of land jutting out into a narrow bay, the popular resort town of Haapsalu dates back to the 13th century. Its impressive Bishop's Castle ruins still serve as the main focal point for the town despite the fact that its formidable fortifications were largely dismantled by Peter the Great in the 18th century. The castle watchtower houses the **Castle Museum**, displaying medieval weaponry. The adjoining **Dome Cathedral** is the largest single-nave church in the Baltic region.

Over the course of the 19th century, Haapsalu became a fashionable holiday resort, famed for its curative mud treatments and pretty beaches. The town's landmark 216-m (709-ft) long train platform is an enduring monument to the era when Russian royalty and high society flocked to the town every summer. The platform was built in 1904 to receive Tsar Nicholas II and his entourage, and its ornate wooden canopy was designed to protect them from bad weather. The station closed in 1995 and the building now houses the **Estonian Railway Museum** with models of engines used between the late 19th and early 20th centuries.

Paralepa Beach, just to the west of the station, is Haapsalu's most popular bathing spot. On the east coast,

ESTONIA'S SWEDISH COMMUNITY

Swedish settlers in Estonia were first mentioned in 1294 in Haapsalu's town records. It is generally thought that Swedes settled along the western coastal areas in the 13th and 14th centuries to secure trade routes. From 1561 to 1700 Estonia was directly under Swedish rule. By the early 20th century, there were some 8,000 Swedish-speaking Estonians, most of whom lived on Vormsi Island and in the Haapsalu region.

Swedish circular crosses in St Olav's Church cemetery, Hullo

The Estonian-Swedes were a recognized minority with their own periodical and distinct cultural identity. However, the majority of them fled to Sweden during World War II. It is estimated that some 2,000 Estonian-Swedes remained behind, but life in the Soviet Union soon effaced their way of life and they effectively disappeared as a minority.

the promenade is another fine legacy of the town's imperial glory days. From Africa Beach the promenade winds its way past the spa hall at Kuursaal and leads to the **Museum of Coastal Swedes**, which traces the history of the Swedes.

🏛 **Museum of Coastal Swedes**
Sadama 31/32. **Tel** 473 7165.
⭘ 11am–4pm Tue–Sat. 🖼
www.aiboland.ee

Picturesque houses in one of the villages on Vormsi Island

Vormsi Island ❸

Road Map C1. 🏘 350. 🚌 from Haapsalu. ⛴ from Rohuküla, 10 km (6 miles) W of Haapsalu.
www.vormsi.ee

Estonia's fourth-largest island, Vormsi is only 10 km (6 miles) by 20 km (12 miles) in size. The island is ruggedly beautiful and blissfully unspoiled despite being only 3 km (2 miles)

TCHAIKOVSKY IN HAAPSALU

Tchaikovsky and his brothers Anatoly and Modest spent the summer of 1867 in Haapsalu. Living in a small house on Suur-Mere Street, the 27-year-old Tchaikovsky worked on *The Voyevoda*, his first opera and one of his major compositions. Tchaikovsky Bench on the promenade commemorates his stay and, at the press of a button, blares out a part of the Sixth Symphony, thought to be inspired by an Estonian folk song.

Tchaikovsky Bench on the promenade in Haapsalu

---

from the mainland. The size of the island and its beautiful landscapes make it perfect for hiking and cycling. The island is well known for its lush pine forests and an abundance of juniper bushes, as well as spectacular stretches of rocky coastline.

Some people believe that Vormsi means "Snakes Island", as the name derives from the old Swedish word for snake. Others, however, claim that it was named after a pirate called Orm. Either way, Vormsi Island was home to some 2,000 Swedes prior to World War II, and their influence can be seen all over the island.

The island's main settlement is **Hullo**, 3 km (2 miles) west of the ferry port at Sviby. The 14th-century **St Olav's Church** is especially worth visiting for its Baroque pulpit and a cemetery with a striking collection of circular Swedish crosses looming out of hand-made mounds of grass.

Matsalu National Park ❹
Matsalu rahvuspark

Road Map C2. 🛈 Matsalu Nature Centre, Penijõe Manor; 472 4236.
⭘ 9am–5pm Mon–Fri, 10am–6pm Sat & Sun. 🖼 www.matsalu.ee

Situated around the narrow Matsalu Bay, Matsalu National Park was founded in 1957 as a sanctuary for nesting and migratory birds. The area is a bird-watcher's paradise, with some 275 species found in its coastal wetlands. Six observation towers dotted along the coast offer the chance to see the fauna and birdlife up close. Viewing platforms overlook some of the islets and coastal meadows. Most of the observation towers are reached by car or bus, although Penijõe tower, on the bank of the Penijõe river, is a short walk from the Matsalu Nature Centre.

View of the Matsalu Bay islet, part of the idyllic Matsalu National Park

View of the pristine coastline of Hiiumaa Island

Hiiumaa Island ❺

Road Map C2. ✈ *Hiiesaare, 5 km (3 miles) E of Kärdla.* 🚌 *from Tallinn.* ⛴ *from Rohuküla, Triigi.* ℹ️ *Keskväljak 1, Kärdla, 462 2232.* 📅 *St John's Day (Jun).* **www**.hiiumaa.ee

Estonia's second-largest island, Hiiumaa is a paradise for nature-lovers due to its rugged and diverse landscape. Although it is only 22 km (14 miles) from the mainland, it is far less developed as a tourist destination than neighbouring Saaremaa *(see pp92–5)*. Over half the island is covered in forest that is home to an abundance of wildlife, such as elk, wild boar and lynx. The rest of the territory consists of meadows, peat bogs, heathland and endless miles of unspoiled coastline. Although there are plenty of interesting sights on the island, the majority of visitors come to Hiiumaa to enjoy its amazing

natural beauty and revitalizing atmosphere. The shallow waters off the northeast coast are very popular for canoeing and kayaking in the summer, and numerous hiking and cycling routes traverse the island. Public transport is limited and is best not relied on as the main means of getting around.

Kärdla

🏠 *4,000.* ℹ️ *Keskväljak 1, 462 2232.* **www**.hiiumaa.ee **Hiiumaa Museum** *Vabriku Väljak 8.* 🕙 *10am–5pm Mon–Fri.* 📷
This small town is of interest primarily as a base for exploring Hiiumaa. However, it is also a picturesque place, full of pretty wooden houses,

nearly all of which have well-tended gardens. A branch of the **Hiiumaa Museum** is housed in a one-storey wooden building, which was the home of a Swedish manager of a textiles factory in the 19th century. A seaside park lies just north of the museum and is filled with families and sunbathers throughout the summer.

The **Hill of Crosses** (Ristimägi), located 4 km (2 miles) west of Kärdla, is an impressive sight. The hill is packed with crosses made out of local wood. It is believed that the tradition of placing crosses at the site began with the deportation of Swedes in 1781 by the Russians. Today, most of the new crosses at the site are brought by tourists.

⛪ Suuremõisa Manor

Suuremõisa.
Although Estonians customarily refer to Suuremõisa (Big Manor) as a castle, it is actually a manor house. It was built in 1755 for Ebba Margaretha Stenbock, a relative of the powerful de la Gardie family, who owned much of Hiiumaa until the Russians acquired it in 1710. The widowed Stenbock lived in the manor with her children, after winning back the rights to her ancestral land.

In 1796, the manor was bought by a shipping magnate who was deported to Siberia in

KEY

━━ Major road

═══ Minor road

0 km   10

0 miles   10

Key to Symbols *see back flap*

Sprawling Suuremõisa Manor, fronted by a verdant lawn

1803 for murdering one of his ships' captains in the house. There are 64 rooms in this grand manor that currently houses two schools. Although the interior is not open to the public, it is possible to take a stroll around the manor's vast grounds.

Kassari

90. from Kärdla.
Hiiumaa Museum *May–Aug: 10am–5:30pm Mon–Sun.*
A small island connected to Hiiumaa by a causeway, Kassari is known for its natural beauty. The 18th-century Kassari chapel-turned-church is the only functioning church with a reed roof in Estonia. Near the church is the village of Kassari itself, home to the **Hiiumaa Museum**, which gives an overview of Hiiumaa from the Stone Age through to the present. The island culminates in the stunning Sääre Tirp peninsula in the south, a 2-km (1-mile) spit that can be covered on foot or by car.

The Orjaku Nature Trail explores Käina Bay, a major bird sanctuary. The coastal water around Kassari is said to be the warmest in Estonia and the island has plenty of good beaches, especially in the south. With only four villages, Kassari retains its peace even in the height of summer.

Kõpu Lighthouse

Kõpu village, 35 km (22 miles) W of Kärdla. *May–end Sep: 10am–8pm daily.* **Tel** 469 3474.
Midway along the rocky Kõpu peninsula, this is the world's third-oldest working lighthouse. Built on the highest hill of Hiiumaa, it was commissioned by the Hanseatic League in 1500

and completed in 1531. At the end of the 1980s, the crumbling edifice was reinforced with four thick sloping buttresses, giving it its highly distinctive appearance.

The equally distinct Ristna Lighthouse (1874) stands only 10 km (6 miles) further west, at the tip of the peninsula.

Kõpu Lighthouse, one of the world's oldest functioning lighthouses

Lihula ❻

Road Map C2. *1,600. Tiigi 5, 477 8214.* **www**.lihula.ee

The quiet town of Lihula leads to Matsalu National Park *(see p89)* and also serves as the last stopping-off point en

route to the islands of Muhu and Saaremaa. Lihula was the site of a major castle in the 13th century, which was almost destroyed during the Livonian Wars (1558–82). The impressive ruins stand atop a hill offering spectacular views of the region. Housed in an old manor house, the nearby **Lihula Museum** offers a comprehensive account of the town's history.

Lihula Museum

Linnuse tee 1. **Tel** 477 8880.
irregular hours; call for timings.

Muhu Island ❼

Road Map C2. *from Tallinn, Pärnu. from Virtsu.*
www.muhu.info

Most people generally pass through Muhu Island on their way to Saaremaa without spending much time here. However, Muhu is an extremely attractive island, whose small size makes it easy to explore. The village of Liiva, just 6 km (4 miles) from the ferry terminal, is home to the 13th-century St Catherine's Church, while the nearby coastal village of **Koguva** is a picturesque ensemble of stone farmhouses with thatched roofs.

Muhu Island has preserved its charming tradition of brightly painted farmhouse doors, some of which depict symbols that are said to keep evil spirits away.

The rugged natural beauty of the island also makes it a wonderful place for long walks, especially along the pristine coastline.

Stone farmhouses in the fishing village of Koguva, Muhu Island

Saaremaa Island ❽

Saaremaa is Estonia's largest island and the jewel of its archipelago. The capital, Kuressaare, is a strikingly picturesque town, whose relatively tranquil atmosphere makes it an ideal base from which to explore the island. The place has a lot to offer in terms of things to see and do, but its extraordinary natural beauty is the real attraction and the reason why so many people feel compelled to return here. The breathtaking landscape of Vilsandi National Park, the abundance of old churches and fascinating historical relics dotted throughout the island are just some of the main highlights *(see pp94–5)*.

Art Nouveau lion statues outside the information centre, Kuressaare

★ Vilsandi National Park
Known for its awe-inspiring landscapes, unspoilt islets and bird sanctuaries, this park was established in 1993 to preserve the ecology of Estonia's coast.

Kihelkonna Church, a splendid 13th-century place of worship, has an impressive steeple that was added in 1897.

Mihkli Farm Museum, an authentic 19th-century farmstead, offers a fascinating glimpse into rural life on the island in the past.

Mustj

Kihelkonna

Karla

Lümanda

Salme

77

Sõrve Peninsula

Mõntu

Sääre

Sõrve Peninsula
The scenery along Sõrve Peninsula is some of the most spectacular on the island, culminating in the magnificently wild and windswept tip. The best way to explore the ravishing coastline is to take a bike or car trip.

STAR SIGHTS
★ Vilsandi National Park

★ Angla Windmills

★ Bishop's Castle

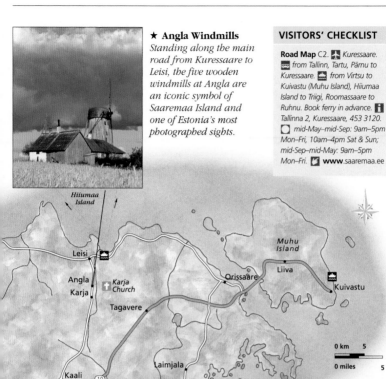

★ **Angla Windmills**
Standing along the main road from Kuressaare to Leisi, the five wooden windmills at Angla are an iconic symbol of Saaremaa Island and one of Estonia's most photographed sights.

VISITORS' CHECKLIST

Road Map C2. ✈ Kuressaare.
🚌 from Tallinn, Tartu, Pärnu to Kuressaare. ⛴ from Virtsu to Kuivastu (Muhu Island), Hiiumaa Island to Triigi, Roomassaare to Ruhnu. Book ferry in advance. ℹ Tallinna 2, Kuressaare, 453 3120.
🕐 mid-May–mid-Sep: 9am–5pm Mon–Fri, 10am–4pm Sat & Sun; mid-Sep–mid-May: 9am–5pm Mon–Fri. 💻 www.saaremaa.ee

Map showing Western Estonia region with locations including Hiiumaa Island, Leisi, Angla, Karja, Karja Church, Tagavere, Kaali, Kaarma, Upa, Koljala, Kuressaare, Laimjala, Orissaare, Liiva, Muhu Island, Kuivastu, Ruhnu Island, Bruka.

0 km 5
0 miles 5

Kaarma Church, which dates from the 13th century, has a striking 15th-century pulpit.

Poppy Fields
Due to its temperate climate and fertile soil, Saaremaa is rich in flora. Over 200 local species enjoy protection. Orchids and poppies grow wild in some parts.

KEY

✈	Airport
⛴	Ferry port
ℹ	Visitor information
✝	Church
▬	Major road
▭	Minor road
---	Ferry route
– –	Park boundary

★ **Bishop's Castle**
The formidable castle is the most important landmark in Kuressaare. It has Teutonic-order architecture with a powerful defence tower and a slender watchtower. The castle today houses an informative museum.

Exploring Saaremaa Island

The best way to explore Saaremaa Island is by car. The island's size makes it difficult to visit the major sights by bicycle, while public transport is extremely limited and erratic. Saaremaa has excellent, well-signposted roads on the whole, although bumpy dirt tracks are common in the more remote parts. The majority of visitors stay in Kuressaare but there is an abundance of excellent farmstead-style guest houses scattered throughout the island for a more authentic experience of rustic island life. All the major sights are within comfortable driving distance of the capital.

Buildings interspersed with greenery in the attractive town of Kuressaare

Kuressaare

🏙 16,000. ✈ 4 km (2 miles) SW of town centre. 🛈 Tallinna 2. 📅 St John's Eve (23 Jun).
www.kuressaare.ee

This small, but attractive and serene, town epitomizes the spirit of Saaremaa. Kuressaare's main thoroughfare, Lossi, which turns into Tallinna, is lined with a stunning stretch of beautiful buildings, including the green-domed St Nicholas's Church (Nikolai kirik) and the step-gabled Weigh House, which now serves as a pub known as Vaekoja. Most of all, though, the town makes a delightful place to stroll around, especially on a pleasant evening.

🏰 Bishop's Castle

Lossihoov 1, Kuressaare. **Tel** 455 7542. ⬛ May–Aug: 10am–6pm daily; Sep–Apr: 11am–6pm Wed–Sun. 💶 📷 call in advance. 📷
www.saaremaamuuseum.ee

Dating back to the 14th century, the Bishop's Castle (Piiskopilinnus) in Kuressare is one of the best-preserved medieval castles in the Baltic States. Built out of local dolomite, it is a spectacular sight, as visitors approach it through the surrounding landscaped park. The castle houses the intriguing Saaremaa Regional Museum, whose labyrinthine interior is a joy to explore. The exhibits about Saaremaa are well arranged and offer a vivid account of the island's epic history.

Highlights of the castle include the Bishop's Living Quarters with a dingy, spartan little room where the resident bishop could retire for reflection, and a particularly eye-catching medieval lavatory.

Kaali Meteor Crater

Kaali. 🚌 from Kuressaare to Kõnnu, 15 km (9 miles) NE, then walk for 3 km (2 miles). 🛈 Kaali Visitors' Centre, 459 1184. 🍴 📷
www.kaali.kylastuskeskus.ee

The meteor crater at Kaali is arguably one of the most extraordinary geological sights in Estonia. At a glance, it appears like a small lake, until visitors notice the perfectly rounded banks above the water and the shards of dolomite sticking out that were thrown up by the impact.

Scientists estimate that the meteor struck sometime between 4,000 and 7,500 years ago. With a diameter of 110 m (360 ft), it is the eighth-largest in the world. The crater exudes atmosphere, which inspires visitors to look upwards.

🌀 Angla Windmills

15 km (9 miles) N of Kaali. 🚌 from Kuressaare.

Lined up along the Upa–Leisi road, the five Angla Windmills (Angla tuulikud) are the last remaining group of windmills in Saaremaa. In the mid-19th century, there were 800 working windmills on the island.

Four of the Angla Windmills are constructed on the traditional Saaremaa model, while the largest is a wooden version of a Dutch windmill. Together, they form a mesmerizing sight amid the wide open landscape. Although the

Bishop's Living Quarters set in the lush grounds of the Bishop's Castle

Two of the five Angla Windmills, standing tall in an open landscape

windmills are not open to the public, there is a wonderful assortment of traditional play apparatus for children just behind them.

Karja Church

2 km (1 mile) NE of Angla Windmills, Karja village. ◯ *mid-May–mid-Sep: 10am–6pm daily.*

The medieval Karja Church (Karja kirik) is the smallest church in Saaremaa, but also one of the most beautiful. It is well known for its elaborate stone carvings, which include a relief of the Crucifixion above the side door and some remarkable figures inside depicting saints. There is also a famous bas relief showing Mary and John at Cavalry, along with the two thieves whose souls depart their bodies in the form of children.

Stone carving outside Karja Church

Kaarma Church

*15 km (9 miles) NW of Kuressaare, Kaarma village. **Tel** 459 5322.* ◯ *no regular opening hours.*

Dating from the 13th century, Kaarma Church (Kaarma kirik) is one of the oldest churches in Western Estonia. A stone tablet over the front portal attests to repairs made to the church in 1407 and is considered to be the first written example of the Estonian language. The 15th-century pulpit with a polychrome figure of Joseph beneath it is especially impressive. The church may appear incongruously large, standing in the middle of nowhere, but people once flocked here for Sunday services from the surrounding villages.

Mihkli Farm Museum

*28 km (17 miles) NW of Kuressaare. Viki. **Tel** 454 6613.* ◯ *mid-May–Aug: 10am–6pm daily; Sep–mid-Oct: 10am–6pm Wed–Sun.*

www.saaremaamuuseum.ee

In the sleepy village of Viki, the Mihkli Farm Museum (Mihkli talumuuseum) is a picturesque farmstead consisting of beautiful thatched cottages, a windmill, a brewery and even an old sauna. Most of the buildings date from 1827–56. The museum has one of the most authentic displays of rural architecture and traditional living styles. The farm was active until Soviet times, when collectivization broke it up. Today, visitors can learn traditional methods of making bread and butter.

Kihelkonna Church

3 km (2 miles) NW of Kihelkonna. **Tel** *454 6558.* ◯ *Jun–Aug: 10am–5pm daily.*

On the west coast of the island along the border of Vilsandi National Park, this 13th-century church is a treasure trove of religious architecture and artifacts. The organ, built in 1805, is the oldest in the country, while the beautiful pulpit dates from 1604. The altar triptych, *The Last Supper*, is a superb example of Renaissance church art.

Vilsandi National Park

10 km (6 miles) W of Kihelkonna. 🚤 *from Papisaare.* **Tel** *454 6510.* ℹ️ *Vilsandi National Park Visitors' Centre, Loona Manor.* ◯ *9am–5pm Mon–Fri.* www.vilsandi.ee

This huge national park comprises Vilsandi Island along with some 150 islets and a narrow strip of coast culminating in the rugged Harilaid Peninsula. The park was established thanks to a lighthouse keeper named Artur Toom, who set up a bird sanctuary here in 1910. The 23,880-ha (59,010-acre) park in its present form was founded in 1993.

The most significant bird sanctuaries are located on the Vaika Islands, off the western tip of Vilsandi, from where the imposing 40-m (131-ft) Vilsandi Lighthouse can be seen. For some of the most striking scenery, head to the Harilaid Peninsula. From here, it is possible to take an invigorating hike up to the leaning lighthouse. The trail offers evocative scenery.

Display showing the interior of a rural household, Mihkli Farm Museum

Tallinn's medieval city wall covered with snow in winter ▷

Pärnu 🌐

Wooden door carving

Often referred to as Estonia's summer capital, Pärnu has historic buildings, pastel-coloured wooden houses and elegant late 19th-century villas set along leafy streets. The town centre is situated on an estuary between the Pärnu river and the Baltic Sea, with all the main sights located within walking distance. The Old Town is centred around the pedestrianized Rüütli Street, with the most popular beach a ten-minute walk away. With an ultra-modern concert hall and high-quality theatre, Pärnu also has an exciting cultural scene.

🏛 Town Hall
Uus 4/Nikolai 3.
The elegant Neo-Classical building that is now the Town Hall was erected in 1797 as a wealthy merchant's residence. In 1819, the structure was slightly altered to serve as the house for the town's governor and, in 1839, it took on its current function as Pärnu's Town Hall. What makes it worth visiting is the magnificent Art Nouveau extension built in 1911. Its brooding dark exterior is in total contrast to the bright yellow façade of the original structure and provides a fascinating juxtaposition of two radically different architectural styles.

🏛 Elizabeth's Church
Nikolai 22. **Tel** 443 1381.
⬜ Jun–Aug: 10am–6pm daily, Sep–May: 10am–2pm Mon–Fri.
🟥 www.eliisabet.ee
Another excellent example of local Baroque architecture, Elizabeth's Church (Eliisabeti kirik) has an elegant ochre exterior and maroon spire towering above the surrounding narrow side streets. It was founded specifically as a Lutheran church, in 1747, by the Russian Empress Elizabeth (1709–61). Today, it serves as the largest Protestant place of worship in Pärnu.

The wood-panelled interior is refined and understated, but all the more impressive for it. The church's spire was built by Johann Heinrich Wülbern, who also constructed Rīga's St Peter's Church. Elizabeth's Church is also renowned for its organ, one of the best in Estonia, built in 1929 by H Kolbe.

Green domes and yellow walls of St Catherine's Church

🏛 St Catherine's Church
Vee 16. **Tel** 444 3198.
⬜ 9am–5pm daily. 🟥
Built in 1768 for the Pärnu garrison during the reign of Catherine the Great, St Catherine's Church (Ekateriina kirik) is arguably the finest example of a Baroque-style church in Estonia. With bottle-green domes and lemon-yellow walls, the church boasts an elegant exterior and an equally opulent interior. Intended as an architectural showpiece, St Catherine's had a significant influence on Orthodox churches throughout the Baltic States.

🏛 Pärnu Concert Hall
Aida 4. **Tel** 445 5800.
⬜ 10am–6pm Mon–Fri, 10am–4pm Sat (box office). 🎫 ♿ 🏪
www.concert.ee
The Pärnu Concert Hall is a source of great pride for local people. The curvaceous glass and steel building is a strong example of modern architecture in the country and compares favourably with similar structures in other European cities. Its seashell-like shape was intended to symbolize Pärnu's status as a coastal town. The multifunctional building mostly hosts theatre performances and concerts, although it also houses an art gallery, music school and music shop.

🏛 Tallinn Gate
Mere pst.
The only trace of the 17th-century ramparts that protected Pärnu at one time, Tallinn Gate still offers a significant glimpse of the once impressive fortifications. Until 1710, when Swedish rule came to an end, it was known as Gustav's Gate, named after King Gustav Adolphus of Sweden (1594–1632).

Today, the Tallinn Gate's only function is to provide an elegant portal between the Old Town and the area leading to the sea. The cobble-stoned passageway offers a relaxed walk.

Verdant setting of the Tallinn Gate, formerly known as Gustav's Gate

Detail featuring an Art Nouveau mask, Ammende Villa

Ammende Villa

Mere pst 7. *Tel 447 3888.*
4–8pm Sun–Mon, 4–10pm Tue–Sat (restaurant). www.ammende.ee
Built in 1905 by a wealthy local merchant for the wedding party of his beloved daughter, Ammende Villa is one of the most impressive examples of Art Nouveau architecture in the country. Over the years, it has served as a casino, a health establishment and a library, before two Estonian businessmen renovated it and converted it into a luxury hotel *(see p296).* The villa is located a short walk from the sea and the Old Town.

Lydia Koidula Museum

J V Jannseni 37. *Tel 443 3313.*
10am–6pm Tue–Sat. *call in advance.* www.parnumuuseum.ee
Situated a short walk across the Pärnu river, the Lydia Koidula Museum provides a moving testimony to Estonia's most revered female poet. The museum, which was established in 1945, is situated in the building where her father, Johann Valdemar Jannsen, ran a primary school from 1857 to 1863.

One of the main highlights of the museum is a reconstruction of the bedroom where Koidula died of cancer in 1886 in the Russian town of Kronstadt. Although very little of Lydia Koidula's work is available in English, the museum is worth visiting for an interesting insight into the history of Estonian literature at that time.

VISITORS' CHECKLIST

Road Map D2. 44,000.
Riia mnt 116. Pikk tänav. Rüütli 16, 447 3000.
Pärnu Film Festival (Jul), Oistrakh Festival (Jul).
www.parnu.ee

LYDIA KOIDULA (1843–86)

Lydia Emilia Florentine Jannsen is a highly influential figure in Estonian history. Although she was forced to write anonymously in her day under the pseudonym Koidula, meaning "of the dawn", her poetry was ecstatically received. Her *My Country is My Love* became the unofficial national anthem during Soviet times. Some critics believe that Koidula's finest writing was her passionate correspondence with the writer Friedrich Reinhold Kreutzwald, although his jealous wife eventually put an end to it. Koidula later married a Latvian doctor. She died of cancer in Kronstadt, in the Gulf of Finland, pining for her country to the last.

Lydia Koidula, Estonia's beloved writer and poet

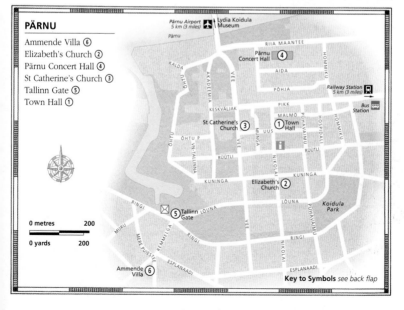

PÄRNU

Ammende Villa ⑥
Elizabeth's Church ②
Pärnu Concert Hall ④
St Catherine's Church ③
Tallinn Gate ⑤
Town Hall ①

0 metres 200
0 yards 200

Key to Symbols see back flap

Soomaa National Park ❿

Soomaa National Park, an enchanting self-enclosed world of bogs, rivers, swampland, meadows and virgin forest, was established in 1993. The 390-sq-km (151-sq-mile) park gets flooded in spring, which locals call the "fifth season". However, Soomaa's five bogs are its best natural feature. Approximately 6 m (20 ft) high in places, they can be accessed along a series of hiking trails set on wooden platforms. The park's stunning wildlife includes wolves, roe deer, brown bears, lynx, elk, wild boar and lesser spotted eagles.

ESTONIA

Area of the map illustrated

Pärnu • • Viljandi

KEY

☐ Soomaa National Park

Kuresoo Bog, at 11,000 ha (27,182 acres), is the largest bog. Birds come to nest here in spring.

Lemmjõgi River Spit Forest Trail is 5 km (3 mile) long.

★ Riisa Bog Trail
The 5-km (3-mile) long bog trail, close to the border of the park, culminates in a group of bog pools.

Ingatsi Bog Trail
Half of the 4-km (2-mile) trail is a boardwalk that leads through swamp forest and bog pools.

Meiekose Hiking Trail, a 5-km (3-mile) trail, is also suitable for cycling.

Karuskose Farm
Close to hiking trails and bog-land, this farm offers guided walks, fishing, canoeing and traditional canoe-building courses.

Kuuraniidu Study Trail has information boards describing the local flora.

★ Tõramaa Wooded Meadow Trail
A 2-km (1-mile) walk leads to this pretty trail, which allows visitors to explore the park and its well-preserved meadow.

STAR SIGHTS

★ Riisa Bog Trail

★ Tõramaa Wooded Meadow Trail

VISITORS' CHECKLIST

Road Map D2. 🚉 *from Tallinn.*
🚌 *from Pärnu.* ℹ️ *National Park
Visitors' Centre, Tõramaa, 435
7164.* 🕐 *Easter–Oct: 10am–6pm
daily; Oct–Easter: 10am–4pm
Tue–Sat.* 🚗 *Aivar Ruukel, 506
1896.* **www**.soomaa.com 📧
🔺 🍴 *Karuskose Farm.*

**Hüpassaare Hiking
Trail** is 5 km
(3 miles) long, and
passes through forest
and bog pools before
culminating at the
Mart Saar House
Museum.

Flora
*The peat moss of the bogs
is ideal for heather, cranberries and Labrador
tea. The sundew plant
gets additional nutrition
by catching insects.*

Öördi Hiking Trail, a 7-km
(4-mile) forest trail, starts from
Iia village on the Kõpu-Jõesuu
road and leads to Lake Öördi.

KEY

ℹ️	Visitor information
🔺	Campsite
🌿	Viewpoint
═	Minor road
- -	Trail
▬ ▬	Park boundary

Kihnu Jõnn's grave on Linaküla,
the main village on Kihnu Island

Kihnu Island ⓫

Road Map C2. 👥 *600.* 🚢 *from
Pärnu.* ⛴ *from Munalaid, 40 km (25
miles) SW of Pärnu.* **www**.kihnu.ee

The tiny island of Kihnu has
a significant place in Estonian
culture. It is the only part of
the country where women
still wear traditional dress
and the islanders continue
to live largely traditional life-
styles. Fishing remains a
major source of livelihood,
as do the much-admired
handmade clothing and
mittens. There are four villages on the island, but as it
is only 7 km (4 miles) long
and 3.5 km (2 miles) wide,
it is easy to get around.

In the main village of
Linaküla lies the grave of
the legendary Kihnu Jõnn
(1848–1913), the island's most
famous inhabitant. Born on
Kinhu, Jõnn was a larger-
than-life, hard-drinking sailor
who sailed around the globe.

Tori Stud Farm ⓬
Tori hobusekasvandus

Pärnu mnt 13, Tori. **Road Map** D2.
🚌 *from Pärnu.* **Tel** *503 1892.*
🕐 *8am–5pm Mon–Fri.* 🚫 📷 *call one
day in advance.* **www**.torihobune.ee

Situated in the beautiful
village of Tori, Tori Stud Farm
is a good stopping-off point
on the way to nearby Soomaa
National Park. Estonia's oldest
horse farm, it was established
in 1856 by the Livonian gentry with the aim of breeding
a strong local stock. After
several failed attempts at
improving the local breed,
a crossbred Norfolk-Roadster
horse was brought in, which
became the basis for the
new breed. The stud farm is
still used for breeding purposes today, although its
horses are far more likely
to be used for giving horse-
riding lessons than for
ploughing the fields.

Tori Stud Farm is also a
worthwhile excursion in
itself. Visitors to the farm
can partake in a range of
activities, including a guided
tour of the farm which
introduces them to some of
the 90-odd horses. Those
interested in old-fashioned
transport can take a tour of
the farm and village in a
horse-driven carriage for a
small fee charged on an
hourly basis. It is possible to
go sleigh-riding in winter.

The farm also boasts a
wonderful little museum situated in a thatched wooden
barn. Its collection features a
fascinating assortment of exhibits relating to the history of
horse-breeding as well as the
history of the local village.

Tori Stud Farm, breeder of some of Estonia's finest horses

EASTERN ESTONIA

The landscape of Eastern Estonia, punctuated with rolling hills, lush forests, limestone escarpments and pristine lakes, is more diverse than the country's western part. This truly fascinating region combines idyllic scenery with picturesque old manor houses and the unique cultural heritage of the Setu people and Old Believers, which have survived through the centuries.

Despite being geographically stunning, some parts of Eastern Estonia are less frequented by tourists, especially the far northeast, southeast and around Lake Peipsi. The vast mass of Lake Peipsi dominates the central part of this region. The western shores of the lake are dotted with the sizeable settlements of Russian Old Believers who have been living here for countless generations.

Captured and conquered repeatedly by Russians since 1558, the historic fortress town of Narva still bears testimony to the enormous role Russia has played in shaping Estonia's history. During World War II, the value of oil-shale mining rose significantly, bringing Kohtla-Järve into sharp focus. Today, this heavily industrial town serves as a vast, sprawling, living monument to Soviet-era industry.

East of Tallinn, Lahemaa National Park is arguably the most beautiful of the country's nature reserves for the variety of its landscape and natural features. Further along, the Ontika coastline, with its huge limestone escarpments and cascading waterfalls, is breathtaking.

Social, cultural and political history abounds in the southeast as a whole. Viljandi hosted the country's very first Song Festival, while Estonia's national flag was sanctified in Otepää. Tartu, Estonia's second-largest city and its spiritual capital, is at the heart of the country's history and culture.

With attractions such as the grand Sangaste Manor and the captivating Suur Munamägi viewing tower at the country's highest point, the south and southeast are among Estonia's most scenic areas. In the far southeast, the ethnographically distinct Setu people continue to live traditionally.

Migrating flock of gulls flying across Lake Peipsi

◁ Stretch of the Jägala river on its course through the lush landscape of Lahemaa National Park

Exploring Eastern Estonia

Eastern Estonia has strikingly diverse
attractions. Lahemaa National Park boasts
some of the country's most beautiful
landscapes, with countless villages dotted
throughout the area. A stunning coastline
stretches to the medieval city of Narva and
the pristine beach at Narva-Jõesuu. To the
south is Lake Peipsi. The picturesque landscape
of the southeast provides a beautiful backdrop
to attractive towns such as Viljandi and Otepää,
as well as to countless places of historic
significance. Tartu makes an ideal base from
which to explore the region.

SIGHTS AT A GLANCE

Towns, Cities and Resorts
Kuremäe ❼
Narva ❺
Narva-Jõesuu ❻
Otepää ⓰
Paide ⓫
Põltsamaa ⓬
Põlva ㉓
Rakvere ❽
Rõuge ⓳
Sillamäe ❹
Tartu pp114–17 ⓭
Väike-Maarja ❾
Vastseliina ㉑
Viljandi ⓯
Võru ㉒

**Buildings and
Sites of Interest**
Kohtla Underground
   Mining Museum ❷
Kiidjärve Watermill ㉔
Mõniste Open-Air Museum ⓲
Sangaste Manor ⓱

**National Parks
and Reserves**
Endla Nature Reserve ❿
*Lahemaa National
   Park pp106–109* ❶

Areas of Natural Beauty
Lake Võrtsjärv ⓮
Ontika Coast ❸
Suur Munamägi ⓴
Taevaskoja Sandstone Cliffs ㉕

Tour
Lake Peipsi p123 ㉖

Medieval Ivangorod Castle, seen from Narva

SEE ALSO

• **Where to Stay** pp297–9

• **Where to Eat** pp327–9

GETTING AROUND

Highway 1 (the E20 under the European system) leads east out of Tallinn and skirts Lahemaa National Park before following the coast to Narva. Highway 2 (E263) connects Tartu and Võru and Highway 3 (E264) links Tartu and Valga, skirting the northern part of Lake Peipsi along the way. The town of Rakvere also has a road leading to Tartu. A railway connects Tallinn with Rakvere, Narva, Tartu and Viljandi. Tartu also has a small airport. In the southeast an intricate network of signposted dirt roads connects most of the villages in the area.

Fishing village in Lahemaa National Park

0 km	20
0 miles	20

KEY

▬▬▬	Motorway
▬▬▬	Main road
▬▬▬	Secondary road
▭▭▭	Minor road
▬▬▬	Scenic route
⌐⌐⌐	Railway
▬▬▬	International border
△	Peak

Lahemaa National Park ❶

Extending across the north coast of Estonia, Lahemaa National Park, or Lahemaa Rahvuspark, is a nature-lover's paradise. It is the largest park in Estonia and also the first area to be designated a national park in the erstwhile Soviet Union. The diverse terrain covers four peninsulas jutting out into the Gulf of Finland and stretches inland over an area of 725 sq km (280 sq miles). The park teems with wildlife and has several marked trails through its forests and bogs and along its meandering coastline. Many impressive manor houses and picturesque villages can be found throughout the area *(see pp108–9)*.

KEY

☐ Lahemaa National Park

Viinistu
Once a fishing village, Viinistu has developed into a local cultural centre. It is home to an impressive art gallery.

★ Käsmu Peninsula
The rugged coastline of Käsmu Peninsula, strewn with giant boulders left behind by retreating glaciers after the last Ice Age, has an ethereal beauty.

Flora and Fauna
With forest covering more than 70 per cent of Lahemaa, the area is rich in flora and fauna. The landscape has many raised bogs, including the 7,000-year-old Laukasoo Reserve. The thriving wildlife includes a population of wolves, bear and lynx.

0 km   2

0 miles   2

STAR SIGHTS

★ Käsmu Peninsula

★ Altja Village

★ Palmse Manor House

For hotels and restaurants in this region see pp297–9 and pp327–9

Võsu
A beautiful stretch of beach, tranquil atmosphere and stunning natural surroundings make this historic village a very popular holiday resort.

VISITORS' CHECKLIST

Road Map D1. 🚌 from Tallinn to Võsu, Altja, Käsmu, Viinistu. ℹ️ National Park Visitors' Centre, Palmse, 329 5555. ⬤ May–Sep: 10am–6pm Mon–Fri; Oct–Apr: 9am–5pm Mon–Fri. 🚻 🖥 📷 ⛺ available at Võsu (May–Sep). **www**.keskkonnaamet.ee

The Oandu Forest Trail is a well-signposted, 5-km (3-mile) long route. Foraging wildlife can be seen along the mostly moss-covered path.

Käsmu Bay

smu

Lame

Pihlaspea

Vergi Peninsula

Altja

⛺🚌 Võsu

Oandu

Koljaku

Sagadi Manor

Sagadi

Vihula

Metsanurga

ℹ️ mse

★ Altja Village
With its ornately thatched roofs and timber houses, the fishing village of Altja provides an authentic glimpse of a bygone era, when its survival depended on the sea.

Sagadi Manor
The grounds of Sagadi Manor, one of the most attractive in the region, are covered with sculptures, while its numerous outhouses include the Forestry Museum.

★ Palmse Manor House
The stately Baroque house has now been restored as a museum, while its converted outhouses and extensive grounds offer several other attractions.

KEY

🚌	Bus station
ℹ️	Visitor information
⛺	Campsite
═══	Minor road
– –	Trail
▪ ▪	Park boundary

Exploring Lahemaa National Park

The sheer size of Lahemaa National Park makes getting around it by bike or car the best option. When driving to Lahemaa along the Tallinn-Narva Highway, turn off at the crossroads at Viitna and head north towards Palmse village, where there is a National Park Visitors' Centre. From Palmse, it is a relatively short drive to all the main villages, sites and areas of natural beauty. Käsmu and Võsu make convenient hiking and cycling bases with plenty of good accommodation, although most places are often booked up well in advance during summer.

Regal interior of the ornately decorated Palmse Manor House

🏛 Palmse Manor House

8 km (5 miles) N of Viitna. *Tel 324 0070.* ☐ *May–Sep: 10am–7pm daily, Oct–Apr: 10am–6pm daily.* 📷 🎫 *call in advance.* ♿ 🍴 🛍
www.palmse.ee

The attractive village of Palmse is the ideal starting point for a tour of the enchanting Lahemaa National Park. It also has a well-run visitors' centre. The focus of the village is the splendid Palmse Manor House, an elegant Baroque building that originally served as a Cistercian convent. In 1677, it became the family home of the von Pahlens, a leading family of Baltic barons.

Today, the manor house serves as a museum, offering an interesting overview of the estate's history. The old distillery has been converted into a hotel with an excellent restaurant, while a lovely café now occupies the bathhouse.

The manor house organizes a wine tour, where visitors can enjoy a glass of sparkling wine or locally produced wine made from berries grown in the nearby Brest Pavilion. The manor grounds are beautifully landscaped. In summer, visitors can take a boat tour of the serene Swan Lake and soak up the surrounding tranquility.

🏖 Võsu

8 km (5 miles) N of Palmse. 🚌 *from Tallinn.* ☐ *hours vary, check website.* 🍴 🛍 **www**.lahemaa.ee

A charming and quiet little coastal village, Võsu is a popular holiday resort. Its peaceful ambience and stunning natural beauty have made it a favourite summer getaway for families since the late 19th century. The resort

Tourists enjoying themselves at the pine-fringed beach in Võsu

is 2 km (1 mile) long and packed with elegant wooden houses from end to end.

The most distinctive building in the village is the old Fire Tower, which now houses an art gallery. Its beach, with Blue Flag status, is also one of the most attractive along the north coast. With its soft white sand and pine-fringed dunes, it offers gentle shade during the hot summer days. It is also a convenient base for further explorations of Oandu and Altja.

🏖 Käsmu

16 km (10 miles) N of Palmse.) 🍴
🏛 **Käsmu Maritime Museum**
☐ *May–Sep: 10am–7pm daily; Oct–Apr: 10am–5pm Mon–Fri.*
www.kasmu.ee

Approximately 6 km (4 mile) long and 3 km (2 mile) wide, Käsmu village is situated on the smallest of the four peninsulas in Lahemaa National Park. It is often referred to as the prettiest village in the region due to its distinguished history and proudly kept homesteads.

Käsmu was a shipbuilding centre of repute in the 19th century, while the largely ice-free bay made it a regular place of anchor in winter. A maritime school was set up in the village in 1884 which now houses the **Käsmu Maritime Museum**. The museum's emphasis is on the 1920s and 30s through World War II and the Soviet era. It has an eclectic collection of artifacts honouring the village's seafaring past.

The village is also called the Captain's Village, because of the 62 captains that resided in Käsmu between World War I and World War II. Käsmu was decimated by the Soviets in the 1940s, with many families sent to Siberia and others fleeing across the sea.

Today, the village enjoys the reputation for being one of the best holiday resorts in the park. Käsmu also boasts a fascinating coastline strewn with giant boulders, a large and erratic scattering of which lie in a stone field near the village. This is the highlight of the famous Käsmu Boulder Walk *(see p110).*

🎣 Altja

15 km (9 miles) E of Võsu. **Altja Tavern Tel** 520 9156. ⬜ *May–Sep: 11am–9pm daily; Oct–Apr: 11am–8pm Sun–Thu, 11am–9pm Fri–Sat.* 🔟 **Oandu** 10 km (6 miles) S of Võsu. 🅰 *free National Park campsite.* **www**.altja.ee

Situated to the east of Lahemaa National Park, Altja is a lovely fishing village that skirts the rugged coastline of the park. Its main landmark is a large wooden swing that stands in an open space, at the eastern end of the village. Just beyond, along the beach, are the abandoned huts of fishermen. The timber houses with thatched roofs make the village seem like an open-air museum. There is a picturesque wooden suspension bridge in the same corner.

Water barrel, Viinistu Art Museum

Beyond Altja, in nearby **Oandu**, there are two fantastic nature trails where visitors can get a taste of Lahemaa National Park's varied forest landscape. The 2-km (1-mile) long Oandu Beaver Trail passes by several beaver dams and countless skilfully gnawed tree stumps. The 5-km (3-mile) long circular Oandu Forest Nature Trail, passes through sweet-smelling and lush pine forest. Visitors are likely to spot tracks left by foraging wild boar, elk and brown bears.

Viinistu

9 km (6 miles) W of Käsmu. ⬜ *no regular opening hours.* 🔟 ⬜ **Viinistu Art Museum Tel** 608 6422. ⬜ *11am–6pm Wed–Sun.* 🌐 **www**.lahemaa.ee

Lying on the eastern tip of the Pärispea Peninsula, the village of Viinistu is an intriguing little place. It profited from the smuggling of vodka to Finland during prohibition in the 1920s, but during the Soviet era it was incorporated into the nearby Loksa industrial complex.

Today, it has been reinvented due to the efforts of Jaan Manitsky (b.1943), a wealthy local businessman who opened a hotel and the **Viinistu Art Museum** by the harbour. The museum has an impressive collection of 20th-century Estonian art and uses two converted water-towers for temporary exhibitions.

The harbour has been restored and it is possible to travel northeast from Viinistu to the barren Mohni Island.

View of the beautiful 18th-century manor house at Sagadi Manor

🏛 Sagadi Manor

8 km (5 miles) NE of Palmse. **Tel** 676 7878. ⬜ *May–Sep: 10am–6pm daily; Oct–Apr: by prior arrangement.* 🌐 📷 *call in advance.* ♿ ⬜ **www**.sagadi.ee

Built in 1749, the Sagadi Manor (Sagadi mõis) consists of several buildings symmetrically laid out around a sprawling courtyard in front, with a manicured park and pond to the rear. The attractive 18th-century Baroque manor house is now home to a museum which offers an authentic glimpse of the lives of the Baltic-German aristocratic family who lived in the region in the mid-18th century. The manor house later served as a primary school and part of a collective farm until it finally opened as a museum in 1987.

The Baroque gatehouse, which used to be the main entrance to the manor house, is particularly grand. There are also some truly fascinating sculptures scattered around the grounds.

Today, the outhouses on one side of the courtyard are occupied by the Forestry Museum (Metsamuuseum), which provides a detailed overview of the diverse flora and fauna of Estonia's forests. Housed in the building nearby is a hotel called Sagadi Manor *(see p298)*. A former bailiff's residence now serves as the Sagadi hostel. The historic estate is also home to a Nature School where ecological research is carried out.

Landmark wooden swing at the quaint fishing village of Altja

Käsmu Boulder Walk

The smallest of the four peninsulas in Lahemaa, Käsmu boasts the most impressive chain of boulders. These form a formidable outcrop in the shallow waters, creating a dramatic coastline. Old Jüri, the tallest boulder at 5.5 m (18 ft), lies just off the northwest tip. Starting from Käsmu village, a path leads along the coast to the northwest tip of the peninsula before turning back towards the village through dense forest. There are clearly marked hiking trails and a cycling route.

Cosy wooden cottage snuggled in the heart of Käsmu village

Scenic Views ③
One of the most stunning routes in the park, this path follows the whole length of the coast.

Cycle Route ④
The scenic bicycle route is about 14 km (9 miles) long and is marked with blue ribbons.

Saartneem Island

GULF OF FINLAND

Eru Bay

Käsmu Bay

KÄSMU PENINSULA

LAKE KÄSMU

Võsu

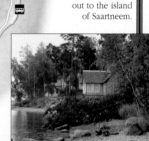

Saartneem ②
A path leads from Käsmu village to the northwest tip of the peninsula, where a chain of erratic boulders stretches out to the island of Saartneem.

Käsmu Village ①
Käsmu village is one of the most popular resorts in Lahemaa. With plenty of B&B accommodation, it is an ideal base for exploring the Käsmu Peninsula as a whole, as well as the other regions of Lahemaa.

KEY

🚌	Bus station
ℹ	Visitor information
⛺	Campsite
- -	Walk route
—	Bicycle route
==	Other road

TIPS FOR WALKERS

Starting point: Käsmu village.
Length: 11 km (7 miles).
Walking trails: An 11-km (7-mile) long path marked with red ribbons leads north of Käsmu village from Old Jüri. A shorter walk is the path west of Käsmu village which leads through the Stone Plantation.

Erratic Boulders ⑤
The Stone Plantation on the trail west of Käsmu village has a bizarre expanse of boulders. These attract a large number of visitors to the area.

0 km	1
0 miles	1

Kohtla Underground Mining Museum ❷

Kohtla kaevanduspark-muuseum

Road Map E1. *Tel 332 4017.*
🚌 from Kohtla-Järve. ⏰ 9am–5pm
Mon–Fri, 11am–3pm Sat & Sun. 📷
✂ book in advance. 🍴 summer
only. **www**.kaevanduspark.ee

Undoubtedly one of the
most fascinating museums in
Estonia, Kohtla Underground
Mining Museum is located
in the sprawling industrial
area of Kohtla-Nõmme. Set
in a massive oil-shale mining
complex, the museum
operates guided tours where
the history, technology
and purpose of mining are
explained before visitors are
taken to explore the dark,
damp labyrinth of the mines.
    Visitors can see the infernal
mining machines at work and
can even attempt to drill or
ride an underground bike.
There is also the added
option of sampling a miner's
lunch under ground.
    The outdoor tour continues
on to the very impressive
mountains of mined stone
and it is possible to see one
of the biggest diggers in the
world. Wall and mountain
climbing are some of the
adventure sports offered
here. Located nearby is the
vast industrial town of
Kohtla-Järve. A small town

**Exhibit at the intriguing Kohtla
Underground Mining Museum**

before World War II, it saw
speedy development during
the Soviet era with the
expansion of the oil-shale
mines in the area.

Ontika Coast ❸

Road Map E1. 🚌 from Tallinn
to Jõhvi, then bus or taxi to Toila,
Ontika. **www**.ida-virumaa.ee

The coastal limestone cliffs
of Ontika make it one of the
most striking areas of natural
beauty in Estonia. Sprawling
over almost 20 km (12 miles)
between Saka and Toila, the
plateau is the highest point of
the North-Estonian limestone
escarpment. At Ontika, the
cliff reaches a height of 57 m
(184 ft) and offers a view
across the Gulf of Finland.
Valaste, which lies 5 km
(3 miles) east, has Estonia's
highest waterfall. The 26-m

(85-ft) stream of cascading
water has carved its way
through a bed of 470 to 570
million-year-old rocks to
create an amazing sight.

Environs
The beautiful **Oru Park, Toila**
is located 14 km (9 miles) east
of Ontika Coast and is worth
visiting. The park is spread
out over an area of 105 ha
(260 acres) along the coast.

Sillamäe ❹

Road Map E1. 🏠 17,000. 🚌 from
Tallinn, Narva. **www**.sillamae.ee

Situated midway between
Kohtla-Järve and Narva,
Sillamäe makes for a
fascinating excursion. This
Soviet-era town was the site
of a uranium mine for the
Soviet nuclear programme.
However, it was so secret
that it was not even marked
on official maps.
    The town is a living
example of the more elegant
side of late-Stalinist residential
architecture. Many of the
ornately decorated apartment
blocks set along tree-lined
boulevards and manicured
parks are very attractive. The
mine was closed in 1991 and
a number of other industries
have since moved in. Sillamäe
is slowly but surely reinvent-
ing itself as an upcoming
coastal and historic tourist
destination of interest.

View of the limestone cliffs set against the azure Baltic Sea, Ontika Coast

For hotels and restaurants in this region see pp297–9 and pp327–9

Narva ❺

Road Map E1. 🏠 65,000. 🚆 *from Tallinn.* 🚌 *from Tallinn, Tartu.* ℹ️ *Puškini 13, 356 0184.* 🎭 *Narva Days (early Jun), Narva Historic Festival (Aug).* **www**.narva.ee

After centuries of being bitterly fought over, Narva now marks the EU border with Russia. Although most of the city's much-admired medieval centre was levelled by the Soviet air force towards the end of World War II, there is still plenty to see and do.

On the west coast of the Narva river stands the impressive Narva Castle, whose main tower, Tall Hermann, houses the predominantly war-themed **Narva Museum**. A splendid riverside park surrounds the castle.

With a population that is 96 per cent Russian-speaking, Narva has a different feel from Tallinn. The city is also close to a number of attractions in the area.

🏛 **Narva Museum**
Tel 359 9230. ⏰ *10am–6pm Wed–Sun.* 🌐 www.narvamuuseum.ee

Narva Castle, home to the war-themed Narva Museum

Narva-Jõesuu ❻

Road Map E1. 🚌 *from Narva.* ℹ️ 🌐 www.narva-joesuu.ee

The attractive summer resort of Narva-Jõesuu is famed for its pristine beach. Lined with pine trees and old wooden houses, the beach stretches for 7 km (4 miles) from Narva-Jõesuu to Meriküla. The area was a fashionable spa resort in the 19th century and was popular with St Petersburg's

Exterior of Pühtitsa Convent in Kuremäe, partially hidden by trees

high society. Present-day Narva-Jõesuu enjoys a beach, a lively nightlife and a booming water-sports industry.

Kuremäe ❼

Road Map E1. 🚌 *from Tallinn, Narva.*

The small village of Kuremäe is celebrated for its Russian Orthodox **Pühtitsa Convent**, one of the most notable sights in Estonia. The convent was founded in 1891 and today some 150 nuns live there. There are six churches in the complex which is dominated by the striking Dormition Cathedral, built in 1910. The convent is surrounded by a thick granite wall and has a majestic entrance gate with seven large bells. The bright façade and pristine appearance of the place gives it a

Statue of a bull on Vallimägi Hill, Rakvere

cheerful air. The convent also has a hostel for guests and pilgrims.

🛐 **Pühtitsa Convent**
Tel 337 0715. ⏰ *8am–8pm daily.* 📷 ✝️ 🅿️ **www**.orthodox.ee

Rakvere ❽

Road Map D1. 🏠 17,000. 🚆 *from Tallinn, Narva.* ℹ️ *Laada 14, 324 2734.* **www**.rakvere.ee

The town of Rakvere, with restored historic buildings and a striking main square, has been transformed into an attractive tourist destination. Its most famous landmark, the 13th-century **Rakvere Castle** on Linnamägi Hill, is a medieval theme park now. The exhibits cover the castle's history from its early existence until it fell to ruins. A grand and slightly Picasso-esque statue of a bull, created by local artist Tauno Kangro (b.1966), stands on top of Vallimägi Hill and is a new symbol for the town. Rakvere's inhabitants are proud of the fact that the renowned composer Arvo Pärt (see p23) went to school and had begun his music studies here.

⚔ **Rakvere Castle**
Vallimägi. *Tel* 322 5500.
⬜ *May–Sep: 11am–7pm daily.* 🖼
www.svm.ee

Väike-Maarja ➒

Road Map D1. 🏘 5,000. 🚌 *from Rakvere.* 🛈 *Pikk 3, 326 1625.*
www.v-maarja.ee

A typical parochial Estonian town, Väike-Maarja is steeped in history and has a number of quirky sights of interest. Housing the local tourism information centre, the **Väike-Maarja Museum** offers an eclectic and detailed overview of the town's history, including a fascinating tour of how the Forest Brothers (see p118) used to live. It is also possible to have a "Forest Brothers' picnic" in a reconstructed bunker. Other interesting sights include a Soviet missile base, the Vao Stronghold Tower Museum and the 14th-century town church.

🛈 **Väike-Maarja Museum**
Pikk 3. *Tel* 326 1625. ⬜ *May–Sep: 10am–5pm Tue–Sat; Oct–Apr: 10am–5pm Mon–Fri.*

Endla Nature Reserve ➓
Endla looduskaitseala

Road Map D1. 🚌 *from Tartu.*
🛈 *Reserve Headquarters, Tooma, 70 km (43 miles) NW of Tartu, 676 7999.* 📷 *call in advance.*
www.endlakaitseala.ee

A scenic maze of peat bogs, rivers, swamp forests and lakes, the Endla Nature Reserve is considered to be one of the most important freshwater systems in the country. Although the reserve straddles three counties, its relatively small size makes

it much easier to explore than the larger national parks. One of the six hiking trails, the stunning **Männikjärve Trail** stretches for 1 km (0.5 mile) over a long plank platform. To the east of the reserve, **Emumägi Hill** is the area's highest point. Its observation tower offers a superb view of the countryside.

The medieval octagonal tower amid castle ruins, Paide

Paide ⓫

Road Map D1. 🏘 9,000. 🚌 *from Tallinn.* 🛈 *Pärnu 6, 385 0400.*
www.paide.ee

Located in the centre of Estonia, Paide makes the ideal base from which to explore the heartland of the country. To emphasize its central location, the town has adopted a heart shape as its official logo. Paide's biggest tourist draw is the beautifully restored 13th-century octagonal castle tower and surrounding ruins. The tower houses a museum

focusing on the town's early history, while the **Järvamaa Museum** offers a much broader look at the nature and history of the area. The Town Hall Square is the focal point of the well-kept town centre and offers a small variety of decent restaurants and cafés.

🏛 **Järvamaa Museum**
Lembitu 5. *Tel* 385 1867.
⬜ *Apr–Oct: 11am–6pm Tue–Sat; Nov–Mar: 10am–5pm Tue–Sat.*
🖼 www.jarva.ee/muuseum

Põltsamaa ⓬

Road Map D2. 🏘 5,000. 🚌 *from Tallinn, Tartu.* 🛈 *Lossi 1, 775 1390.*
www.poltsamaa.ee

The idyllic town of Põltsamaa is set amid the ruins of Põltsamaa Castle. Once the centre of power for Duke Magnus, the King of Livonia in the 16th century, the castle stronghold is an amazingly eclectic jigsaw of historical pieces. The exquisite Rococo palace was built in the 18th century on the site of an old convent, while the elegant Lutheran **St Nicholas's Church** dates from 1633 and was reconstructed in 1952. Located in an old storehouse in the castle yard, the **Põltsamaa Museum** boasts some fine exhibits.

🛈 **St Nicholas's Church**
Lossi 3. *Tel* 776 9915. ⬜ *Jun–Aug: 10am–3pm daily.* 🛐 *11am Sun.* 🖼

🏛 **Põltsamaa Museum**
Loss tänav 1. *Tel* 775 1390.
⬜ *May–Sep: 10am–6pm daily; Oct–Apr: 10am–4pm Mon–Sat.* 🖼

Well-maintained building inside the castle grounds at Põltsamaa

Tartu  ⑬

Best known for being home to the venerable Tartu University, the town is frequently referred to as the intellectual capital of Estonia. The university was founded in 1632 by King Gustav Adolphus of Sweden (1594–1632) and has played a major role in Estonian history ever since. With the second-largest population in the country, Tartu has a thriving cultural scene and exciting nightlife, and makes a convenient base from which to explore the southeast of the country.

Statue of King Gustav Adolphus

🏛 Town Hall Square

Tartu's historic centre is set around Town Hall Square (Raekoja plats), with the Emajõgi river in the front and Toomemägi (*see pp116–17*) just behind it. The gently sloping cobblestoned square is distinctly Neo-Classical, with the pink Town Hall overlooking it from the top. The Great Fire of 1775 burned down most of the city and today the square's Neo-Classical look is in sync with the rest of the city centre. The famous **Kissing Students Fountain**, in front of the Town Hall, was erected in 1998.

🏛 Tartu University Main Building

Ülikooli 18. **Tel** 737 5384. ⬜ 11am–5pm Mon–Fri. 🖼 🎫 ♿ www.ut.ee
Finished in 1809, Tartu University Main Building (Tartu ülikooli peahoone) is one of Estonia's finest Neo-Classical buildings. It contains the impressive Art Museum, from which the imposing Assembly Hall and the far more amusing Lock-Up can be seen. Unruly students were confined to the Lock-Up as punishment. Their scribbling and doodling on the walls makes for amusing reading.

⛪ St John's Church

Jaani 5. **Tel** 744 2229. ⬜ May–Sep: 10am–6pm Mon–Sat, 10am–1pm Sun. 🖼 ✝ 11am Sun. www. jaanikirik.ee
Dating from 1330, St John's Church (Jaani kirik) was severely damaged by bombing during World War II. However, even after extensive renovations and having a new spire added in 1999, the church remains one of the best examples of brick Gothic architecture in Northern Europe. Hundreds of elaborate terracotta figures, dating from the Middle Ages, adorn the church interior. It is believed that there were originally more than 1,000 of them.

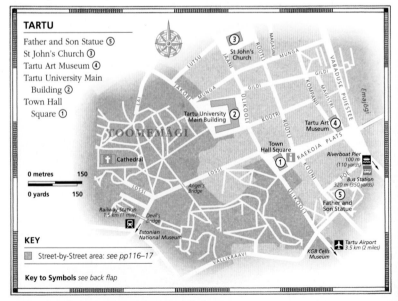

TARTU

Father and Son Statue ⑤
St John's Church ③
Tartu Art Museum ④
Tartu University Main Building ②
Town Hall Square ①

St John's Church ③
Tartu University Main Building ②
TOOMEMÄGI
Cathedral
Tartu Art Museum ④
Town Hall Square ①
Emajõgi
Riverboat Pier 100 m (110 yards)
Bus Station 320 m (350 yards)
Angel's Bridge
RAEKOJA PLATS
Father and Son Statue ⑤
Railway Station 1.5 km (1 mile)
Devil's Bridge
Estonian National Museum
KGB Cells Museum
Tartu Airport 3.5 km (2 miles)
VALLIKRAAVI

0 metres   150
0 yards   150

KEY

⬛ Street-by-Street area: see pp116–17

Key to Symbols *see back flap*

Leaning building in which the Tartu Art Museum is housed

🏛 Tartu Art Museum

Raekoja plats 18. **Tel** 744 1080.
◯ 11am–6pm Wed–Sun. 📷
📹 call in advance. 💻
www.tartmus.ee

Housing one of the finest collections in the country, Tartu Art Museum (Tartu kunstimuuseum) features the works of prominent Estonian artists such as Elmar Kits (1913–72), Ülo Sooster (1924–70) and Marko Mäetamm (b.1965). A thorough and captivating overview of Estonian art, which spans the 19th century through to the present, is also provided. The museum's other impressive aspect is the building that houses it. Leaning conspicuously to one side, it belonged to the famous Russian Field Marshal Barclay de Tolly (*see p118*), who successfully led the Russian army against Napoleon in 1812.

Father and Son Statue

Küüni (close to Poe St).
Originally planned for Tallinn, this delightful little statue by Ülo Õun (1940–88) was conceived in 1977. It was cast in bronze in 1987, purchased by the Tartu Town Government in 2001 and, finally, unveiled on Children's Day (1 June) in 2004. The father figure is modelled after the sculptor, and the child is modelled after his son Kristjan, when he was around one-and-a-half years old. Interestingly, both father and son are proportionately equal in this highly unusual and extremely touching monument.

🏛 KGB Cells Museum

Riia 15b. **Tel** 746 1717.
◯ 11am–4pm Tue–Sat. 📷 📹
www.linnamuuseum.tartu.ee

Situated in the basement of the regional headquarters of the KGB/NKVD, the KGB Cells Museum (KGB kongid) offers grim testimony to the nightmare of the Soviet occupation. Some of the former cells have been turned into exhibition spaces, while others have been restored to their original condition to provide a picture of what so many Estonians suffered under the Soviet regime. Much attention is paid to the mass deportations that took place between 1940 and 1949, including the official plans for carrying them out. There are gut-wrenching artifacts from the Gulags, the notorious correction camps where thousands of Estonians died.

A desk in the KGB Museum, with Stalin's portrait on the wall

VISITORS CHECKLIST

Road Map E2. 🏙 100,000. ✈
🚉 A3, Vaksali 6, 1.5 km (1 mile) W of centre. 🚌 C2, Soola 2, E of the centre. 🚍 Narva mnt 2.
ℹ Raekoja plats 9, 744 2111.
🎉 Tartu City Day (29 Jun), Student Days (around 1 May).
www.tartu.ee

🏛 Estonian National Museum

Kuperjanovi 9. **Tel** 735 0445.
◯ 11am–6pm Tue–Sun. 📷
📹 call in advance. 🚻 💻 📷
www.erm.ee

Estonia's most important ethnological centre, the Estonian National Museum (Eesti rahva muuseum) boasts over one million artifacts collected since 1909. The museum focuses on Estonia and other Finno-Ugric cultures, and its collection covers every imaginable aspect of life. From chairs made of gnarled birch wood to warped wooden beer tankards, the displayed objects eloquently attest to a way of life that seems quaintly anachronistic in today's times.

In addition, there are vast photographic and documental archives, including a punk jacket (circa 1982–85), among the fascinating collection of costumes. The museum is dedicated to the great Estonian folklorist and linguist Jakob Hurt (1839–1907). The museum occasionally holds temporary exhibitions that encompass themes from furniture to photography.

KARL ERNST VON BAER (1792–1876)

A Baltic-German biologist, Karl Ernst von Baer was one of the founders of embryology. His pioneering work in this area was recognized by Darwin, although Baer himself was extremely critical of the evolutionary theory. Baer studied at Tartu University and later taught at Königsberg and the St Petersburg Academy of Sciences, before living out his last years in Tartu. A statue of him sitting pensively atop a large plinth has pride of place on Toomemägi. A rather endearing tradition takes place every year, on the eve of St Philip's Day (1 May), when Tartu University students wash Baer's bronze hair.

Statue of Karl Ernst von Baer on Toomemägi

Street-by-Street: Toomemägi

With its labyrinthine layout of narrow, winding streets and elegant historic buildings, Toomemägi (Cathedral Hill) is full of delightful surprises. In medieval times a fortress and cathedral stood on the hill but both were abandoned during the Livonian Wars (1558–82). Today, Toomemägi is home to a variety of prominent public buildings. Many of them belong to Tartu University, which was re-established here in 1802. There are several impressive monuments to some of the university's most esteemed graduates in the landscaped parks dotted around the hillside. The hill also commands some wonderful rooftop views of the city of Tartu spread out below.

Statue of two Wildes outside Irish pub, Eduard Vilde Lokaal

Devil's Bridge
The bridge was built in 1913 to honour three centuries of rule by the Russian Romanov dynasty. The bridge was dedicated to Tsar Alexander I.

KEY

– – – Suggested route

0 metres   100
0 yards   100

★ University Observatory
When it was built in 1820, the observatory had the most powerful achromatic telescope in the world. It was separated from the university in 1946 and now serves as a science centre.

STAR SIGHTS

★ University Observatory

★ Angel Bridge

★ Statue of Karl Ernst von Baer

★ Angel Bridge
According to tradition, making a wish and holding one's breath while crossing this 19th-century yellow-and-black bridge will fulfil it.

Cathedral Ruins
The massive ruins bear testimony to the original grandeur of the cathedral. Damaged during the Livonian Wars, it was rebuilt as a library after the reopening of the university in 1802. Visitors can climb the renovated towers.

The sacrifical stone was the site of worship for pagan Estonians.

★ Statue of Karl Ernst von Baer
This impressive monument befits Tartu University's most eminent graduate and founder of modern embryology.

Tartu University
When the first students registered here in 1632, it was only the second university in the province of Swedish Livonia. Since its establishment, the university has played a crucial role in Estonia's history.

Town Hall
Dating back to 1786, the current Town Hall is the third of its kind to occupy this position at the heart of Tartu. The elegant early Classicist architecture was considered very fashionable in the 18th century.

JAKOBI

LOSSI

Lake Võrtsjärv ⑭

Road Map D2. 🚌 *from Viljandi, Otepää.* ℹ️ *Visitor Centre, Rannu, 527 5630.* ☐ *May–Sep: 10am–6pm Tue–Sat, 10am–4pm Sun; Oct–Apr: 10am–5pm Tue–Fri.* 🖥️ *www.vortsjarv.ee*

Straddling the counties of Viljandi, Tartu and Valga, Lake Võrtsjärv is the second-largest lake in Estonia after Lake Peipsi *(see p123)*. The northern part of the lake has some beautiful sandy beaches, while the southern part is swampier.

The Visitor Centre is a great place to gather information before your visit, and you can also rent a canoe or boat from here. There are several attractions scattered around the lake. The mausoleum of Barclay de Tolly (1757–1818), the Russian general credited with helping to defeat Napoleon, is in **Jõgeveste**, south of the lake. The bagpipe farm in Riidaja, at the southwest corner of the lake, is one of the area's more unusual sights. A popular summer activity is to take a tour of the lake aboard a *kalepurjekas*, a boat that was used in the olden days.

Magnificent view of Otepää, set amid lush landscape

surrounding landscape. A crucial staging post on the Hanseatic trade route *(see p32)*, Viljandi emerged as one of Estonia's leading strongholds in the 16th century. By the end of the 19th century, the local area had become one of the wealthiest in Estonia.

Viljandi is notable for its well-preserved historic buildings, with an abundance of pretty timber cottages and early 20th-century brick houses.

In the small plaza, at the junction of Lossi and Tartu, is a statue that pays homage to Carl Robert Jakobson (1841–82). This zealous 19th-century Estonian nationalist helped get the National Awakening underway by founding the Estonian-language newspaper *Sakala* in Viljandi in 1878. The statue is also the main focal point for the town.

Viljandi is also a major centre for folk art and music, with a large music academy and a popular yearly festival.

A section of the medieval castle on Castle Hill, Viljandi

Viljandi ⑮

Road Map D2. 👥 *20,000.* 🚌 *from Tallinn.* 🚆 *from Tartu.* ℹ️ *Vabaduse 6, 433 0442.* 🎭 *Viljandi Folk Festival (late Jul).* **www**.viljandi.ee

The pleasant town of Viljandi is centred on the medieval castle ruins sitting atop Castle Hill, which affords spectacular views of the nearby lake and

Otepää ⑯

Road Map E2. 👥 *2,300.* 🚌 *from Tartu, Võru, Tallinn.* ℹ️ *Tartu mnt 1, 766 1200.* 🎭 *Tartu Marathon (Feb).* **www**.otepaa.ee

Situated amid the beautiful rolling hills of southeast Estonia, Otepää is equally popular as a summer and winter holiday retreat. The town also holds a special place in Estonian history. In 1884 the national flag was consecrated in the parish church, which now houses the **Flag Museum**. The totemic Energy Column at Mäe Street is an intriguing reminder of how strongly pagan beliefs prevail in Estonia.

Lake Pühajärv, 3 km (2 miles) south of Otepää, has some splendid beaches and dining spots to enjoy the magnificent scenery.

🏛️ **Flag Museum**
Tel 504 0424. ☐ *by appointment.*

THE FOREST BROTHERS

After the Soviet Union reoccupied Estonia in 1944, thousands of men fled to the woods to take up arms. They became known as the Forest Brothers and fought a guerrilla-style campaign against the Soviet system, most prominently in Viljandi and Tartu, with strong support from locals. However, the NKVD units ruthlessly targeted the partisans' families and by 1949 their support network had largely been broken. By 1953, only a few of the Forest Brothers were left. The last active member died in 1980.

Illustration of an underground bunker used by Forest Brothers

Skiing and Snowboarding

Skiing is a popular winter pastime in Estonia. When Estonia won three gold medals for skiing events at the 2006 Winter Olympics, the medallists were hailed as national heroes and "ski fever" gripped the country. Although Estonia has a flat terrain, there are numerous ski hills, such as the 318-m (1,043-ft) high Suur Munamägi, that offer snowboarding and downhill skiing. There are many

Snow-boarding

ski resorts around Otepää. However, since Estonia is blanketed in snow throughout winter, the ski resorts are crowded until spring. The annual Tartu Ski Marathon *(see p49)* is held at Kuutsemäe Ski Resort and has seen as many as 10,000 participants Snowboarding is also fast gaining popularity in the region and Baltic snowboarders compete with the best in Europe in "trick park" acrobatics.

The Tartu Ski Marathon *is one of the highlights of the winter sports calendar in Estonia. This 63-km (39-mile) WorldLoppet series event attracts competitors from all over the world. The festive proceedings also provide plenty of other skiing activities for non-professionals as well as children.*

Winter time in Otepää *draws hordes of ski-lovers, as this idyllic "Winter Capital" has several resorts, such as the one on Väike Munamägi (Small Egg Hill), 2 km (1 mile) from Otepää. Snowboarding, ice skating and snowtubing are popular in this attractive southern town.*

KRISTINA ŠMIGUN-VÄHI (B.1977)

A cross-country skier, Tartu-born Kristina Šmigun has achieved remarkable success in her field, which has made her a national hero among sports enthusiasts in Estonia. Her parents, Anatoli Šmigun and Rutt Rehemaa, were also successful skiers. Kristina has won six medals at the FIS Nordic World Championships, including a gold medal in 2003.

Her greatest success to date, however, was to become the first Estonian woman to win two gold medals at the 2006 Turin Winter Olympic Games. She won the 2 X 7.5 km (4.5 miles) double pursuit and the 10 km (6 miles) classical.

Kristina Šmigun at the Turin Winter Olympic Games

Kuutsemäe Ski Resort *is a seven-slope skiing facility about 14 km (9 miles) outside Otepää. Its cross-country skiing tracks are well marked out.*

Andrus Veerpalu, *winner of two Olympic gold medals and one silver medal, is Estonia's most successful Olympic athlete. The cross-country skier has also won gold and silver in the World Championships.*

The English Gothic Revival-style exterior of Sangaste Manor

Sangaste Manor ⑰
Sangaste loss

Road Map D2. **Tel** 767 9300.
🚌 from Tartu, Otepää. ⬤ 10am–4pm
daily. 🅿️ 🎫 call in advance. ♿ ⑪
💻 www.sangasteloss.ee

One of the most attractive
buildings of its kind in
Estonia, Sangaste Manor was
built in the English Gothic
Revival style between 1879
and 1883. It was commis-
sioned by Count Friedrich
von Berg to prove to an
English aristocrat, whose
daughter he was wooing,
that he was not the "savage
from Russia" that the preju-
diced nobleman deemed him
to be. Sangaste's striking
red-brick façade, crenellated
gables and elegant towers
lend it the appearance of a
whimsical castle rather than
a parochial manor house. The
arched vestibule Dome Hall

on the ground floor used
to hold grand balls and still
retains an air of grandeur,
while the spacious dining
room, which is criss-crossed
with Tudor-style rafters, is
particularly impressive.
Sangaste is surrounded by a
75-ha (185-acre) forest park,
making it a favourite place
for wedding receptions.

Mõniste Open-Air Museum ⑱
Mõniste muuseum

Road Map E2. Kuutsi, Mõniste
village. **Tel** 789 0622. 🚌 from Tartu.
⬤ May–Sep: 10am–5pm daily,
Oct–Apr: 10am–4pm Mon–Fri. 🅿️
🎫 www.hot.ee/monistem

Established in 1948, Mõniste
Open-Air Museum is the
oldest museum of its kind
in the country. The museum
is located in 19th- and

early 20th-century farm
buildings, which are sur-
rounded by the tranquil
and beautiful forests of the
Võru countryside. The
museum offers plenty of
activities for visitors. Special
days are regularly held
throughout the summer,
which focus on the essential
aspects of traditional rural
life such as milking cows,
working with wood and
flax and baking bread. Apart
from authentic farm work,
visitors can also spin yarn,
roll linen and make rope.
One of the most interesting
activities provided here is
learning how Estonian
farmers used local plants
and trees to treat ailments.

St Mary's Church, set in lush
rolling fields, Rõuge

Rõuge ⑲

Road Map E2. 🚌 from Võru.
ℹ️ Haanja mnt, 785 9245.
⬤ May–Sep: 10am–6pm Mon–Fri.
http://rouge.kovtp.ee

The small village of Rõuge
perfectly embodies the
languid charm of southeast
Estonia and is considered by
many Estonians to be the
most beautiful village in the
country. Situated on the
shores of Lake Rõuge
Suurjärv, the deepest in the
country at 38 m (125 ft), and
with the magnificent Valley of
the Nightingales looming in
the background, it is an
exceptionally tranquil place.
There are a series of nature
trails through the valley which
start from behind **St Mary's
Church**. The church dates
back to 1730 and was the site

THE SETU PEOPLE

A Setu woman wearing
traditional clothes

Living in the southeast of Estonia,
the Setu people form a distinct
ethnographic group. Unlike the
majority of Estonians, the Setu are
Orthodox, having lived in a region
that was Christianized by the
Russian Orthodox Church. They
also have their own unique language known as Võru-Setu, which
differs considerably from standard
Estonian. Traditional Setu folk
music is among the most beautiful
in Estonia, although its plaintive
polyphonic form is strikingly
Slavic-sounding. The Setu people
are also famous for their traditional costumes and handicrafts.
The best starting point to explore Setu culture is Obinitsa.
Located at the centre of Setumaa, or "the Land of the Setu",
the little village celebrates several Setu festivals.

of an Estonian stronghold until the 12th century. Adjacent to the church is an old wooden school dating from 1888, which has some beautiful wooden carvings and sculptures on its exterior. Opposite the church is a monument honouring those Estonians who lost their lives in the war of independence (1918–20).

Suur Munamägi 20

Road Map E2. **Tel** 786 7514. from Võru. Apr–Aug: 10am–8pm daily; Sep–Oct: 10am–5pm daily; Nov–Mar: noon–3pm Sat & Sun. www.suurmunamagi.ee

Situated just south of the village of Haanja, Suur Munamägi (Great Egg Hill) is the highest point in the Baltic States. At a mere 318 m (1,043 ft) above sea level, it gives an idea of how flat the Baltic region is. However, the surrounding landscape of farmsteads, forests and hills is breathtaking enough to merit a trip to the top of the hill. On clear days, it is possible to see all the way to Russia and Latvia.

At the peak, there is an elegant observation tower which was built in 1939 and renovated to include the glass-fronted Suur Munamägi Tower Café (see p329) and a lift. Delightfully quirky wooden carvings, which peer down from the trees, can be seen while walking up the steep path to the top of the forested hill.

Kreutzwald Memorial Monument in Võru

F R KREUTZWALD (1803–82)

One of Estonia's best-loved writers, Friedrich Reinhold Kreutzwald is revered by Estonians as one of the most pivotal figures in the National Awakening of the 19th century. The enormous body of literature created by him in the Estonian language still instils a strong sense of identity and confidence among patriotic Estonians. Despite being impoverished, he studied medicine at Tartu University, where he developed a passionate interest in national folklore. He wrote many epics based on Estonian folklore, the most celebrated of which is *Kalevipoeg* (Son of Kalev). Published between 1857 and 1859, it was part fiction, part influenced by existing folk stories.

Vastseliina 21

Road Map E2. from Võru. www.vastseliina.ee

The small town of Vastseliina is visited mainly for the 14th-century castle located 4 km (2 miles) east of it. The castle was originally a border stronghold built by the Germans as a defence against the Russians. It became the site of a miracle in 1353, when a cross was seen suspended in the middle of the castle's chapel altar. The incident was reported by the Bishop of Rīga to Pope Innocent and the castle subsequently became a place of pilgrimage. In 1702, the castle was completely destroyed during the Northern War (1700–21), but the ruins are a vivid reminder of this once fiercely-contested area.

In Vana-Vastseliina, at the foot of the castle hill, **Piiri Tavern** – first mentioned in 1695 – still serves food.

Wooden houses lining Jüri Street in Võru

Võru 22

Road Map E2. 14,000. Tartu 31, 782 1881. Võru Folklore Festival (mid-Jul). www.voru.ee

Situated in the centre of the southeast corner of Estonia, Võru is a good base for exploring the surrounding region. The town is best known for its impressive 18th-century wooden architecture.

Võru's main sight is the **Kreutzwald Memorial Museum**, the former house of writer F R Kreutzwald, who had a medical practice in the town. The sandy shores of Lake Tamula almost reach the town centre and are perfect for walks.

Environs
Obinitsa, 30 km (19 miles) east of Võru, is the largest village of the Setu community.

Kreutzwald Memorial Museum
Apr–Sep: 10am–6pm Wed–Sun; Oct–Mar: 11am–5pm Wed–Sun.

View from the observation tower, Suur Munamägi

Sweeping view of Lake Põlva with the spire of St Mary's Church in the background

Põlva ㉓

Road Map E2. 🏘 6,500. 🚌 from Tartu. 🛈 Kesk 42, 799 5001. 📅 Town Days (first weekend in June). **www**.polva.ee

The town is set around the artificial Lake Põlva, whose sandy shores are crowded with sunbathers in summer. Legend has it that a girl was immured in a kneeling position in **St Mary's Church** to keep the devils away. This is reputedly how Põlva, meaning "knee" in Estonian, got its name.

The town was developed around St Mary's Church, which lay in ruins for a long period until it was rebuilt after the Northern War (see p33). Nearby, the Cultural Centre, an award-winning building, houses an art gallery, concert hall and café, and offers panoramic views of the town from its terraced roof. Põlva is also famous for the Intsikurmu Song Festival Grounds. Set in a small forested area on the west side of the town, it regularly hosts concerts.

Kiidjärve Watermill ㉔

Road Map E2. 🚌 from Põlva. 🛈 Kiidjärve village, 799 2122. 🖥 **www**.polvamaa.ee

Built in 1914, the Kiidjärve Watermill is situated in the Kiidjärve-Taevaskoja Recreational Area, a 32-sq-km (12-sq-mile) pocket of

stunning natural beauty that also includes sandcliffs. The watermill is the largest red-brick structure of its kind in the Baltic region. There are many hiking trails that start at Kiidjärve village. Horse-riding, cycling and canoeing are also popular ways to see the area. The famous Akste Anthills, some of which stand 2 m (7 ft) high, are among the area's most fascinating sights.

Taevaskoja Sandstone Cliffs ㉕

Road Map E2. 🚌 from Põlva. 🚌 from Tartu. 🛈 Taevaskoja Tourism & Holiday Centre, 5373 6406. **www**.taevaskoja.ee

Taevaskoja, meaning "Heaven's Hall", is famous for its sandstone cliffs and natural beauty. The Big and Small Taevaskoja cliffs are among the main attractions in the Põlva area. They run along the striking Ahja river, which is regarded

as one of Estonia's most beautiful. Close to the Small Taevaskoja is the Maiden's Cave, which was carved by the spring water flowing out of the Devonian sandstone and is also a source of numerous legends and myths. Nearby is the Big Taevaskoja, a striking sandstone wall, widely regarded as a national symbol.

Sandstone cliffs at Taevaskoja, along the Ahja river

THE RUSSIAN OLD BELIEVERS

Opposing the sweeping reforms brought about by Patriarch Nikon (1605–81), the Old Believers split from the Russian Orthodox Church in the 17th century. Due to persecution, many moved to southeast Estonia, especially near Lake Peipsi where they have adhered to their traditional way of life ever since. Today, there are 11 congregations of Old Believers in Estonia, comprising about 15,000 members. They are known for their love of onions which they grow in abundance. It is a local belief that onions ward off various ills if eaten in large amounts.

Congregation of Old Believers

Lake Peipsi ㉖

Setu craftwork

The fifth-largest lake in Europe, Lake Peipsi stretches across a large part of the eastern border with Russia. It is a tranquil place steeped in history and tradition, with the immense lake dominating every aspect of life. The region is famous for being home to the Old Believers as well as the Setu people *(see p120)*. The lakeshore has beautiful stretches of sandy beaches dotted with small fishing villages.

Fishing, a common activity on the coast of Lake Peipsi

Mustvee ①
A small museum dedicated to the Old Believers and three churches are the main sights here.

Raja ②
Famed for its Old Believers' Church, the 4.5-km (3-mile) long Raja is considered to be the longest village in Estonia.

Kolkja ③
The Museum of Old Believers is the highlight of Kolkja. The village also has a good restaurant that offers a taste of local cuisine.

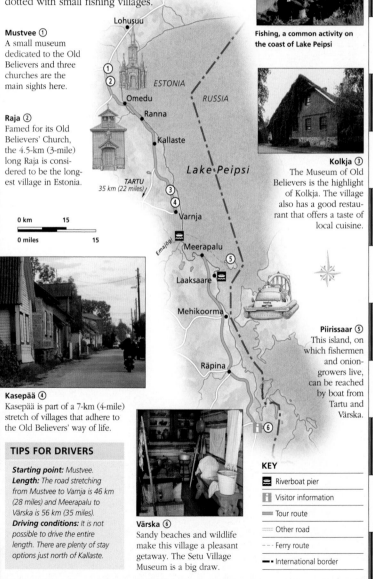

Lohusuu

ESTONIA

RUSSIA

Omedu
Ranna
Kallaste

Lake Peipsi

TARTU
35 km (22 miles)

Varnja

Emajõgi

Meerapalu

Laaksaare

Mehikoorma

Räpina

Piirissaar ⑤
This island, on which fishermen and onion-growers live, can be reached by boat from Tartu and Värska.

0 km   15

0 miles   15

Kasepää ④
Kasepää is part of a 7-km (4-mile) stretch of villages that adhere to the Old Believers' way of life.

TIPS FOR DRIVERS

Starting point: Mustvee.
Length: The road stretching from Mustvee to Varnja is 46 km (28 miles) and Meerapalu to Värska is 56 km (35 miles).
Driving conditions: It is not possible to drive the entire length. There are plenty of stay options just north of Kallaste.

Värska ⑥
Sandy beaches and wildlife make this village a pleasant getaway. The Setu Village Museum is a big draw.

KEY

🚢	Riverboat pier
ℹ	Visitor information
▬	Tour route
═══	Other road
---	Ferry route
▬·▬	International border

LATVIA

Latvia at a Glance

Latvia is traditionally divided into four regions, roughly corresponding to the territories of the old Baltic tribes. Its long sandy coastline includes two of the country's largest ports, while the western region of Kurzeme is heavily forested in the north. To the south, the flat and fertile plains of Zemgale border Lithuania. In the north, Vidzeme has the most varied landscape, with a long coastline as well as forests, wetlands and hills. Bordering Russia and Belarus, the culturally distinct easternmost Latgale region remains largely rural and undeveloped.

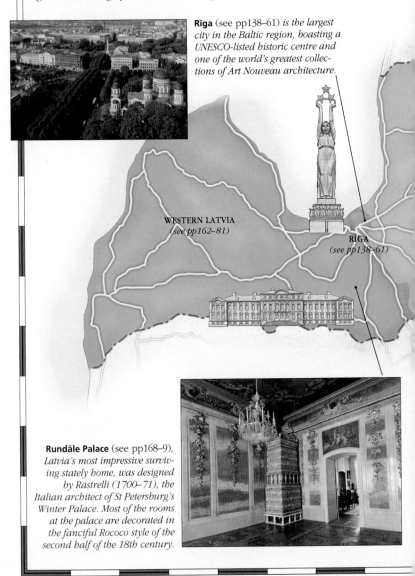

Rīga (see pp138–61) *is the largest city in the Baltic region, boasting a UNESCO-listed historic centre and one of the world's greatest collections of Art Nouveau architecture.*

WESTERN LATVIA
(see pp162–81)

RĪGA
(see pp138–61)

Rundāle Palace (see pp168–9), *Latvia's most impressive surviving stately home, was designed by Rastrelli (1700–71), the Italian architect of St Petersburg's Winter Palace. Most of the rooms at the palace are decorated in the fanciful Rococo style of the second half of the 18th century.*

◁ **View of the sandstone cliffs on the Salaca river, in Eastern Latvia**

Gauja Valley (see pp186–9) *is one of the most attractive parts of the country and a popular destination for both local and foreign tourists. In addition to providing a compelling mix of natural attractions and historic sites, it also offers some of Latvia's best opportunities for outdoor activities, from canoeing to bobsleighing.*

0 km 25

0 miles 25

EASTERN LATVIA
(see pp182–99)

Latgale lake area
(see p198) *is studded with almost 5,000 lakes. Although the Latgale upland rises no higher than 300 m (984 ft), the crystal-clear lakes enhance the beauty of this region, which is blessed with unspoiled countryside.*

Aglona (see p195), *the most important site of Catholic pilgrimage in the region, is famed for a 17th-century icon of the Virgin Mary which is only displayed on special occasions. The busiest day of the year is the feast of the Assumption, on 15 August, when thousands of visitors flock to the Baroque church.*

A PORTRAIT OF LATVIA

ying between the other two Baltic States, Latvia is characterized by delightful forests and lakes, fascinating historical towns and dynamic cities, which are, by and large, unexplored. Nonetheless, the country's exciting capital, Rīga, draws hordes of Western Europeans round the year. The largest city in the Baltic region, Rīga revels in its cultural treasures and hedonistic nightlife.

Much before the arrival of the German crusaders in 1201, local Latvian tribes had established trading links with merchants as far afield as Byzantium, while Orthodox Christianity had made inroads from the East. Yet, it was the crusaders who were responsible for ushering in eight centuries of foreign domination. A short period of self-determination in the early 20th century ended with occupation first by Nazi Germany and then by Soviet Russia. The Soviet era brought rapid industrialization, while the restoration of independence in 1991 further hastened the pace of the country's modernization. Nonetheless, a distinctively Latvian culture developed and survived, assimilating foreign influences and substantial regional differences. A connection with nature, reflecting centuries of rural toil, has remained intact at the same time. While still trying to come to terms with the social, economic and political legacies of the 20th century, the country entered the 21st century with confidence. The historic cores of Rīga and other major cities have been restored, while the rural areas are being developed for ecotourism.

Statue on the House of Blackheads, Rīga

A splendid view of the countryside in Sigulda, Gauja National Park

◁ Latvian women in traditional dress in Cathedral Square, Rīga

Traditional Latvian folk dancers performing at the Latvian Ethnographic Open-Air Museum, near Rīga

PEOPLE

The most obvious ethnic divide is between the country's Latvian and Russian communities that make up 60 and 30 per cent respectively, of the country's population of 2.3 million. Although Russians form the majority in Latvia's major cities, a significant proportion of them are not citizens, as they have not passed the mandatory language and citizenship tests. They cannot vote in national elections, nor are they allowed to travel and work freely in the EU.

Other minorities include Lithuanians, Poles, Belarusians and Ukranians. Most of Latvia's Jews were executed or fled during World War II, although some of the survivors returned and small communities exist today.

SOCIETY AND CULTURE

Latvians are, by and large, socially conservative, and although employment levels are equal for women and men, the latter are usually better paid. Women have played prominent public roles, also making a mark in Latvian politics. Yet, the female domain is still often considered to be the home.

The strict social hierarchy, imposed by the Baltic Germans, ensured the survival and adaptation of many folk traditions. Echoes of Latvia's

pagan past remain to this day, most obviously in the passionate celebration of Midsummer, and even city-dwellers profess a connection with nature. This is also reflected in the popularity of flowers as gifts, although it is important to give bunches with an odd number of stems, as even numbers are associated with funerals.

Latvians never took strongly to organized religion and today only around a third of the population identify themselves as Christians, mostly Evangelical Lutheran.

POLITICS AND ECONOMY

Since the restoration of independence, Latvia has seen the birth of dozens of political parties that have formed a succession of short-lived centre-right coalition governments. The end of

People attending the anniversary of the proclamation of the Republic of Latvia in Rīga

of Communist rule has not meant the end of widespread corruption, with a small number of powerful oligarchs using political influence to promote vested financial interests. All this has bred a general sense of scepticism towards the political system.

Ships docked at Liepāja harbour, a former Soviet naval base

The Soviet authorities took a primarily agricultural economy and transformed it to one based largely around heavy industry, with an associated influx of Russian workers into the cities. The collapse of the Soviet planned economy meant a sudden loss of markets for Latvia's goods, and the country was plunged into further crisis when four newly privatized banks crashed in 1995. From then until the economic crisis of 2008, privatization, economic reform and low wages fostered rapid growth. Most raw materials are imported, with the exception of timber, but industry has thrived on foreign investment. Exports include pharmaceuticals, timber, textiles, electrical and electronic goods, ships, dairy products, beef and grains. Latvia has capitalized on its status as an East–West trade hub, with oil transit from the former USSR to Western Europe particularly lucrative.

Although money has been flooding into Latvia, the living conditions of the ordinary people has not improved much. A lack of opportunities has precipitated migration from rural areas, either to Latvian cities or to other EU countries.

TOURISM

One very evident change in recent years has been the rapid growth in tourism. While much of the country remains under-explored by foreign visitors, Rīga has established itself firmly on the tourist map. The area around the Old Town is transforming to accommodate the growing number of visitors. The city is striving to recover its prized epithet of "Paris of the North", which it once shared with several other European cities.

However, the most fertile area for growth lies probably outside of the urban areas, where the forests, rivers and lakes seem serenely untouched. Even though the infrastructure is still developing, tourism offers genuine opportunities for reviving rural economies, with some farm-steads already embracing the possibilities of ecotourism.

A group of rafters in the forested Kurzeme region

LATVIA THROUGH THE YEAR

With the pagan past never entirely erased by the German crusaders, the Latvian calendar is punctuated by celebrations which mark the rhythm of passing seasons. Many folk traditions are incorporated into Christian festivals, and they provide a chance to experience traditional activities. International cultural events are concentrated in Rīga, although other cities, particularly Liepāja, have their share, and many smaller towns celebrate folk festivals. The best time to visit is from May to mid-September. Rīga, however, gets plenty of tourists throughout the year due to its vibrant cultural life and it can look very attractive on a clear winter's day.

Violinist performing at a concert

SPRING

The rain and mud of early spring can dampen the spirits. However, by April the countryside comes alive with dance and music.

MARCH

Piano Stars *(early Mar)*, Liepāja. This festival was established in 1993 and attracts pianists from around the world.

APRIL

International Baltic Ballet Festival *(Apr–May)*. The festival, which features styles of dance ranging from classical to avant-garde, is held in Rīga as well as other towns.

MAY

Rīga Opera Festival *(May–Jun)*, Rīga. An international festival marking the end of the season for the Latvian National Opera, with an overview of the previous year.

Livonian Festival *(late May)*, Cēsis. Highlights include medieval music, food, craft workshops and battle re-enactments held in the town's Livonian Order castle.
Art Days and Museum Nights. At this lively festival, artists display their work in streets and squares across the country. Concerts and theatre performances are held, and many museums stay open into the night.

SUMMER

The summer months are the best time to visit, not only because the weather is at its most enjoyable, but because it is festival season.

JUNE

Artisans' Festival and Fair *(first weekend)*, Rīga. This event has been in existence since 1971, with music, theatre, dance and traditional craft demonstrations at the Ethnographic Open-Air Museum *(see p159)*.

Knights fighting in the Baltic Medieval Festival

Midsummer *(23–24 Jun)*. On Herb Day (Līgo), houses and barns are decorated with branches, flowers and leaves. In the evening, songs are sung around fires which remain lit until the dawn of St John's Day (Jāņi).

JULY

Sea Festival *(second week-end)*. Fishermen are honoured along with the God of the Sea in this festival.
Latvian Song and Dance Festival, Rīga. A major event in the calendar, this festival is held every five years and will next take place in 2013.
Folklore Baltica Festival, Rīga. The three Baltic capitals host the event in turns.
Rīgas Ritmi, Rīga. Jazz and world-music artists descend on Rīga for this music festival.
Summer Sound, Liepāja. This festival confirms the city's claim to be the home of Latvian rock music.

Performers at the Rīga Opera Festival

Dancers in a street performance during Rīga City Festival

Positivus, Mazsalaca. Latvia's biggest rock festival is held next to the Baltic Sea and attracts international artists.

AUGUST

Assumption of the Blessed Virgin Mary *(15 Aug)*, Aglona. Thousands of pilgrims visit Latvia's most important Catholic place of worship.
Rīga City Festival *(mid-Aug)*. First held in 2001 to celebrate the 800th anniversary of the city's founding, the festival consists of concerts.

AUTUMN

Autumnal colours can make this season a pleasant time to see the countryside, but temperatures fall rapidly from mid-September.

SEPTEMBER

Railway Festival *(first Sat)*, Gulbene–Alūksne Narrow-Gauge Line. Events are held at various stops along this railway line, with a restored steam engine as the star attraction.

OCTOBER

New Music Festival Arēna *(Oct–Nov)*, Rīga. A month-long showcase for contemporary compositions.

NOVEMBER

Mārtiņdiena *(10 Nov)*. This marks the beginning of winter. Events take place at Rīga's Ethnographic Open-Air Museum *(see p159)*.
Lāčplēsis Day *(11 Nov)*. A number of events are held on this day in honour of Latvian freedom fighters.

WINTER

Short days and poor weather can make travelling in winter a challenging proposition, but on a clear day Latvia's snow-bound landscape can be beautiful.

DECEMBER

Christmas *(25–26 Dec)*. Yule logs are dragged from house to house, collecting the misfortune of the previous year before being ceremonially burnt.
Old Town Christmas Market *(Dec–early Jan)*, Rīga. Popular with tourists and local people, this festive market has a variety of goods on sale.

JANUARY

Silver Bells International Sacred Music Festival *(mid-Jan)*, Daugavpils. A competition with performances from a range of choirs, ensembles and soloists.

Exhibit at the International Ice Sculpture Festival, Jelgava

FEBRUARY

International Ice Sculpture Festival *(early Feb)*, Jelgava. One of the largest festivals of its kind in the world. After the event, the sculptures remain on display until they melt in the sun.

PUBLIC HOLIDAYS

New Year's Day (1 Jan)
Good Friday (March/April)
Easter Sunday and Monday (March/April)
Labour Day (1 May)
Restoration of the Independence of the Republic of Latvia (4 May)
Mother's Day (second Sunday in May)
Midsummer (23–24 June)
Proclamation of the Republic of Latvia (18 Nov)
Christmas (24–26 Dec)

Visitors enjoying the beautiful city of Rīga in autumn

THE HISTORY OF LATVIA

*L*atvia's history is traditionally considered to begin with the advent of the Teutonic Knights in 1201, which started German dominance of the area for three centuries. From the mid-16th to the early 18th century, Latvia was divided between Poland and Sweden. By 1795, all of Latvia had been absorbed into Russia. Final independence from foreign domination was only achieved in 1991.

Latvia's strategic geographical position, which prompted its more powerful neighbours to gain control over the region, largely decided the course of its history. By the late 12th century, Latvia's trade route up the Daugava river was increasingly visited by merchants from Western Europe. The Teutonic Knights, German warrior-monks, who first arrived in 1200, were looking for conquests as well as new converts in a pagan land. In 1201, they founded Rīga, which grew into an important centre for trade between the Baltic region and Western Europe.

Teutonic Knight in battle gear

THE GERMANS AND THE SWEDES
The power of the Germans quickly extended across all of Latvia. Castles were built in Cēsis (1209), Kuldīga (1242) and Valmiera (1283) to prevent any local resistance. Meanwhile, Rīga, Cēsis and Ventspils began to thrive as members of the Hanseatic League *(see p32)*. The beneficiaries of this growth were the Germans, who also owned large manors in the countryside. The Latvians, on the other hand, were dispossessed and forced to become serfs.

The early 16th century saw the townspeople lending zealous support to the Reformation movement, and soon after Protestantism was declared as the state religion. In 1561, during the Livonian Wars *(see p33)*, Poland conquered Latvia and Catholicism was firmly established. The separate Duchy of Courland, owing allegiance to Poland, was created in the south and west.

The clash between the Protestant Swedes and Catholic Poles in the late 16th century resulted in Swedish rule in

King Gustav Adolphus landing near the Baltic Coast in 1630

TIMELINE

Stone coat of arms of the Hanseatic League

1201 Riga founded by Bishop Albert of Bremen

1282 Rīga joins the Hanseatic League

1561 Latvia occupied by Poland

1558 Livonian Wars begin

1200	1300	1400	1500

1211 Building of Riga Cathedral begins

1372 German replaces Latin as official language

1520 First Lutheran service held

1536 F record Jewish mercha in Riga

Rīga Cathedral

northern Latvia for much of the 17th century. The Swedes were responsible for spreading education in the Latvian language throughout the country. Under Gustav Adolphus (r.1611–32), Sweden consolidated its hold over Livonia, which was then under Polish rule. Around the same period, the Duchy of Courland flourished under Jakob Kettler (r.1642–82), who built a powerful navy at Ventspils and also founded Latvia's only colony, the Caribbean island of Tobago.

Jakob Kettler, Duke of Courland

THE RUSSIAN EMPIRE
In 1710, during the Great Northern War *(see p33)*, the Swedes surrendered Rīga to Peter the Great of Russia. The Russians introduced 200 years of stability. Serfdom was abolished in 1819, which enabled farmhands to migrate to the towns as industrialization and the railways created a wide range of new employment. Power and money would, however, stay firmly in German and Russian hands. German merchants still enjoyed the privileges that they had secured from the Swedish rulers.

Towards the end of the 19th century, the Russians attempted to replace German with Russian as the national language. This infuriated the Latvian intelligentsia, who saw it as a sign of oppression. They began organizing political movements hostile to the Tsarist regime and continuing

German control of many businesses and farms. The 1905 uprisings in Russia found a sympathetic echo in Rīga and across the Latvian countryside, where over 100 manor houses were burnt down.

THE FIGHT FOR FREEDOM
When World War I broke out in 1914, Latvia became the main battleground between Germany and Russia, neither ever seizing its entire territory. Latvia's national aspirations took a blow as many Latvians were forced to join the Russian army. The Latvians, who were permitted to form their own army in 1915, put up a spirited fight against the Germans at the Battle of Christmas, which began on 23 December 1916. However, the Latvians were ultimately defeated and the Germans captured Rīga. The Allied victory in 1918 forced the German troops to withdraw. Within a few days, on 18 November, Latvian independence was declared.

A 19th-century oil painting of ships at a Latvian port

1621 Riga seized by King Gustav Adolphus of Sweden

King Gustav Adolphus of Sweden (1594–1632)

1680 Rīga's first newspaper, in German, started

1689 Bible translated into Latvian

1822 First Latvian newspaper printed

1873 First Latvian Song Festival held

1905 Socialist revolution demands independence

1917 Russian Revolution

1629 Sweden colonizes Latvia

1710 Riga conquered by Peter the Great

1817 Serfdom outlawed in Kurzeme

1850s National Awakening Movement formed

1914 German occupation of Latvia begins

1918 Formal declaration of Latvian independence

1600   1700   1800   1900

THE FIRST INDEPENDENCE

Latvia's newly formed government was forced to flee to Liepāja in January 1919, returning to Rīga in July, when the city had been freed of Bolshevik troops. Throughout that year, many forces were ranged against Latvian independence and against each other, including the Germans, Poles and Russians. Latvia was only assured of its independence when it signed a peace treaty with Russia on 11 August 1920.

President Kārlis
Ulmanis (1877–1942)

Despite the constantly changing governments that ruled until 1934, much was achieved during this period of independence. Trade was re-directed westwards and away from Russia, the Latvian language was used throughout the country and Rīga came to be regarded as the Baltic region's capital. The leading political figure throughout this period was Kārlis Ulmanis (1877–1942), who staged a coup in 1934 and abolished parliament. He proclaimed himself president, taking Mussolini as his role-model.

Progress came to a grinding halt with the Soviet invasion on 17 June 1940, making Latvia a part of the USSR. Anyone who had played a significant role in "bourgeois" Latvia was either executed or deported to Siberia. The German invasion followed a year later in June 1941, and most of Latvia was occupied within ten days. The Nazi regime was as brutal, but with different targets. Most of its victims were from the Jewish community, which had grown considerably after the laws which restricted Jewish residence were lifted in 1840.

THE RETURN OF THE RUSSIANS

The Soviets returned to Eastern Latvia and Rīga as "liberators" in autumn 1944, though the Germans held out until May 1945 in the country's west. This enabled nearly 100,000 Latvians to escape to Germany and Sweden, from where many continued on to Britain, Canada and Australia. In March 1949, the Russians carried out more deportations; this time their victims were mostly farmers unwilling to join the new collectives. As Latvians were forcibly removed from their own country, Russians were happy to take their place, and their numbers grew throughout the Soviet era. By 1990, half the population of the country was Russian-speaking and there was a serious threat that Latvian would disappear as the national language. The first public protest took place in 1987, when a crowd gathered around the Freedom Monument in Rīga, to commemorate the 1941 deportations to Siberia. New political groups began to emerge a year later. The most forceful

Soldiers marching through Rīga in 1940

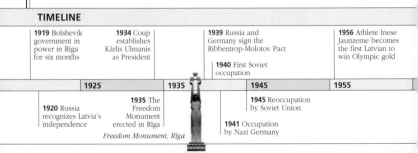

PLF supporters campaigning during the 1990 elections

of them, the Popular Front of Latvia (PLF), demanded full independence and won the elections in 1990.

INDEPENDENCE AT LAST

The violence that broke out in January 1991 showed the determination of the Latvians for independence. Eight people were killed in clashes with Soviet forces in Rīga. In August, Moscow's conservative Communists staged a coup against President Mikhail Gorbachev, but it collapsed within two days and Latvia suddenly found itself free.

Latvia was led during the first eight years of independence by Guntis Ulmanis (b.1939). Governments came and went as they had done in the 1920s, but they largely agreed on a slower policy of privatization than the Estonians were practising. The poor salaries being paid in the public sector continued the low-level corruption prevalent in the Soviet era and introduced it at higher levels too.

The beginning of the 21st century saw the effective integration of Latvia into Western Europe, particularly with its joining the EU (European Union) in 2004. Nonetheless, Latvia has still managed to maintain its trading links with Russia. The citizenship of half of Latvia's population, who speak Russian as their first language, is a problem likely to trouble its post-independence governments. However, sensitive handling of this issue can ensure the country's long-term security.

JEWS IN LATVIA

In the early 19th century, Jews in the Russian Empire were barred from the academic world, government and the army officer corps. Anti-Semitism worsened under Tsar Alexander III (1881–94). Between the two World Wars, President Ulmanis firmly suppressed the activities of fringe groups that wanted to promote anti-Semitism. As part of its Latvian invasion in June 1941, Nazi Germany put its extermination policies into practice at once. The genocide was carried out in two phases that year. By 1945, only about 1,000 Jews, from a pre-war population of 95,000, had survived. Jewish institutions were

Pro-German Latvian militia standing guard over captured Jews in Liepāja in 1941

re-established in 1988, at the end of the Soviet era. A proper evaluation of Jewish history in all eras could only be carried out after independence in 1991.

President Vaira Vīķe-Freiberga (b.1937)

1991 Latvian independence re-established

1999 Vaira Vīķe-Freiberga becomes Latvia's first woman president

2007 Valdis Zatlers sworn in as president

2009 A riot in Riga leads to the dismissal of the government, as economic crisis hits Latvia

1975	1985	1995	2005	2015

'70 Latvia's Jewish population ⌐ows to 50,000, ⌐st of whom ⌐e in Rīga

1990 PLF wins elections

1993 A democratic constitution adopted

2001 Rīga celebrates its 800th anniversary

2004 Latvia joins NATO and EU

2006 Latvia hosts the 70th IIHF Ice Hockey Championships

2014 Rīga is the European Capital of Culture

RĪGA

With its long history as a mercantile centre, Rīga is the largest and most cosmopolitan city in the Baltic States. This is reflected in the buildings that line its streets and squares. The Old Town boasts an engaging array of medieval warehouses and Dutch Renaissance apartments. Remarkable Art Nouveau buildings, which secured the city UNESCO World Heritage Site status, can also be found.

When German crusader Bishop Albert von Buxhoevden chose Rīga as a strategic location for his fortress in 1201, the area was already inhabited by tribes who traded with Russian and Scandinavian merchants. The German settlement became the headquarters for the subjugation of the region and prospered as a member of the Hanseatic League of trading cities. Ruled by Sweden from 1621 to 1710, Rīga experienced a 19th-century heyday under the Russians. New suburbs were built for incoming workers, the harbour was expanded, a ring of boulevards was created in place of the old fortifications, and in the 20th century, industries such as automobile construction were developed.

The capital of an independent Latvia between the World Wars, Rīga suffered heavily during both conflicts and many of its oldest buildings were devastated. Several, including the striking House of Blackheads, have been rebuilt or restored. The "liberation" of Rīga by the Red Army in 1944 ushered in almost five decades of Communist rule, and there are still more ethnic Russians than Latvians in Rīga; relations between the two communities are cordial but rarely warm.

Since Latvia regained independence in 1991, Rīga has flourished, becoming a vibrant tourist destination with an impressive range of museums and a spirited nightlife. Change has been rapid and not always smooth, with the arrival of low-cost airlines in particular bringing its own challenges. Fashionable new bars and restaurants cater to growing crowds of visitors, and new glass and steel buildings have sprung up alongside the cobbled streets and church spires of the medieval Old Town. This is not a picture-perfect city stuck in time, but a lively metropolis intent on shedding the trappings of Soviet rule.

Outdoor café lining Cathedral Square (Doma laukums)

◁ Dutch Renaissance façade of the House of Blackheads, Rīga's Old Town

Exploring Rīga

For many centuries Rīga was largely contained within the city walls on the right bank of the Daugava river. Now known as the Old Town, this area contains most of the city's sites of interest. The main route through the tangle of picturesque streets and squares is Kaļķu Street, leading from the Stone Bridge (Akmens tilts) to Brīvības Street and the Freedom Monument. When the city walls were removed in the mid-19th century, the space was developed into a ring of boulevards and parks. The main train and bus stations lie on the southeastern edge of this ring. To the north is the late 19th- and early 20th-century extension of the city known as the Quiet Centre, which includes some of the city's most impressive Art Nouveau architecture.

Town Hall Square, Rīga

KEY

▨	Street-by-Street map *pp146–7*
🛈	Tourist information
⊠	Post office
🚓	Police station
✝	Church
🅿	Parking

SEE ALSO

• *Where to Stay* pp300–2

• *Where to Eat* pp330–32

GETTING AROUND

The Old Town is compact and best seen on foot: cars are only allowed on a few streets, and there is no public transport. The main Art Nouveau district is within walking distance of the Old Town, while a network of trams, trolleybuses and buses provides access to further-flung attractions. Taxis are also abundant outside the Old Town. The two tourist information offices can offer advice on guided tours.

0 metres   200

0 yards   200

SIGHTS AT A GLANCE

Churches and Cathedrals
Dome Cathedral **1**
Orthodox Cathedral **29**
St Jacob's Cathedral **8**
St John's Church **24**
St Peter's Church **21**
St Saviour's Church **4**

Museums and Galleries
Arsenal Museum of Art **10**
Art Museum Rīga Bourse **7**
Art Nouveau Museum **33**
Krišjānis Barons Memorial
  Museum **28**

Latvian National Museum of Art **30**
Museum of the Barricades of 1991 **2**
Museum of Decorative Arts and
  Design **22**
Museum of Jews in Latvia **31**
Museum of the Occupation
  of Latvia **18**
Museum of Rīga's History and
  Navigation **3**
Pauls Stradiņš Museum of
  the History of Medicine **32**
Photography Museum **25**
Porcelain Museum **23**
Powder Tower/Latvian War
  Museum **13**

Buildings and Monuments
Bastejkalns **26**
Cats' House **14**
Freedom Monument **27**
Great Guild **15**
House of Blackheads **17**
Latvian Riflemen Monument **19**
Mentzendorff House **20**
Parliament **9**
Rīga Castle **5**
Small Guild **16**
St Jacob's Barracks **12**
Swedish Gate **11**
Three Brothers **6**

Panoramic view of Rīga's Old Town and the Daugava river

Impressive Cross-Vaulted Gallery of the Dome, Dome Cathedral

Dome Cathedral ❶
Doma baznīca

Doma laukums 1. **Map** 1 C3.
Tel 6722 7573. ◯ May–Sep:
9am–6pm daily (to 5pm Wed & Fri);
Oct–Apr: 9am–5pm daily.
◉ for special events. ⬛ 🎵 8am
Mon–Sat; noon Sun. **www**.doms.lv

Founded as St Mary's in 1211 by Bishop Albert von Buxhoevden, the cathedral became one of the city's three seats of power alongside the town hall and the castle. It gained its current name from the German word *Dom*, meaning "cathedral", during the Reformation. The cathedral looks as if it has sunk, but in fact the land around it has been raised to keep out flood-water from the Daugava river.

The largest place of worship in the Baltic region, the cathedral has been altered over the years and its bulky structure exhibits a variety of styles. The altar alcove and the east wing crossing are Romanesque, with a cross-vaulted ceiling and rows of semi-circular windows. Simpler Neo-Gothic additions are characterized by pointed arches, large windows and lierne vaulting, while the eastern pediment and the steeple are in an 18th-century Baroque style. The portal was added in the 19th century, followed by an Art Nouveau vestibule in the 20th century.

Most of the interior decor was destroyed during the Reformation, and it is now very plain except for the tombs of merchants and the

19th-century stained glass. The woodwork of the 17th-century pulpit is ornate, however, as is the organ case, which is Mannerist with Baroque and Rococo additions. It is possible to visit the **Cross-Vaulted Gallery of the Dome**, a Romanesque cloister and courtyard all year round.

Museum of the Barricades of 1991 ❷
1991 Gada barikāžu muzejs

Krāmu iela 3. **Map** 1 C4. **Tel** 6721
3525. ◯ 10am–5pm Mon–Fri. ⬛
donations. 🎵 **www**.barikades.lv

This museum recalls the pivotal days of January 1991 when the people of Rīga took to the streets, following the threat of direct presidential rule from Moscow and the stationing of Soviet tanks outside the Supreme Council in Vilnius. Most fascinating of

the exhibits is video footage shot around the barricades, showing people installing huge blocks of concrete to defend strategic points, including the Interior Ministry and TV Tower. Scenes shot at night are punctuated by gunfire and shouting. A final room is dedicated to the people who were killed in Bastejkalns *(see p150)*.

Museum of Rīga's History and Navigation ❸
Rīgas vēstures un kuģniecības muzejs

Palasta iela 4. **Map** 1 C4. **Tel** 6721
1358. ◯ Oct–Apr: 11am–5pm
Wed–Sun; May–Sep: 10am–5pm
daily. ⬛ 🎵 **www**.rigamuz.lv

Founded in 1773, this museum is the oldest in Rīga. Housed in an impressive building with tiled stoves and stained-glass windows, it is also one of the city's most interesting and varied museums. The exhibition on navigation stresses the strong maritime history of the city up until World War I, and includes several large model ships and material on Krišjānis Valdemārs *(see p191)*. Other rooms cover everything from prehistory to independence. Highlights from the Middle Ages include the *Madonna on a Crescent Moon*, a sculpture of the patroness of the Great Guild which was taken to Germany during World War II, and *Big Kristaps*, a large 16th-century statue of St Christopher.

Interior of the Museum of the Barricades of 1991

St Saviour's Church ❹
Anglikāņu baznīca

Anglikāņu iela 2a. **Map** 1 C3.
Tel 6722 2259. 🛉 *11am first Sun
of the month. Free lunchtime concerts are held at 1pm every Wed.*
www.anglicanriga.lv

Funded by British merchants,
this small Neo-Gothic church,
built in 1857, is the only
Anglican place of worship
in the city. The English
bricks were brought as ballast
on trading ships, and the
church was even built on a
layer of British soil. During
the Soviet era it was used
by students as a disco and
recording studio, but since
the second independence in
1991 it has been reopened for
worship with a congregation
including English-speaking
expatriates.

Rīga Castle ❺
Rīgas pils

Pils laukums 3. **Map** 1 C3. **History
Museum of Latvia** *Tel* 6722 1357.
⬜ *10am–5pm Wed–Sun.* 🖼️ 📷
www.history-museum.lv

The city's original Livonian
Order castle was destroyed by
Rīga's citizens during a war
against the Order lasting from
1297 to 1330. After losing, the
townspeople were forced to
build a new castle on the
present site just outside the
city. Continuing quarrels led
the Master of the Order to
leave the capital, but Rīga
Castle was destroyed by the
citizens once more in 1484.
Again they were defeated and
the next castle the townspeople were compelled to
build forms the core of the
current structure and was the
headquarters of the Livonian
Order until 1561.

   As well as being the
official residence of Latvia's
president, the building houses
the **History Museum of Latvia**
(Latvijas vēstures muzejs).
The exhibits take in religious
sculpture, traditional regional
costumes and consumer
goods from the first period
of independence.

Three Brothers ❻
Trīs brāļi

17–21 Mazā pils iela. **Map** 1 C3.
Museum of Architecture *Tel* 6722
0779. ⬜ *9am–6pm Mon, 9am–5pm
Tue–Thu, 9am–4pm Fri.* 🖼️ *donations.*
www.archmuseum.lv

This row of buildings on
Mazā pils Street covers three
distinct architectural styles.
Number 17, with a stepped
gable and Gothic niches,
dates from the 15th century
and is Rīga's oldest stone
residential building. The ears
of wheat on the stones beside
the door indicate that it was
owned by a baker. The
wooden interior of the 17th-
century building at number
19 now houses the small
Museum of Architecture.
The green building at
number 21 was built in the
18th century.

Art Museum Rīga Bourse ❼
Mākslas muzejs Rīgas Birža

Doma laukums 6. **Map** 1 C3.
Tel 6722 3434. ⬜ *10am–6pm Tue–
Sun (to 8pm Fri).* **www**.rigasbirza.lv

This impressive building,
built in the ornate Venetian
Renaissance style in 1856, was
one of the city's most elegant
edifices. However, years of
neglect and a fire in 1979
destroyed much of its beauty.
After three years of renovation
work, it opened its doors in
2011 as Latvia's most modern
museum. The museum's main
focus is foreign art, including
European paintings dating

from the 16th to the 20th
centuries, and 19th century
paintings from China and
Japan. There is also a collection
of porcelain and glass, which
features pieces from the
Danish Royal Porcelain Factory.

Entrance of St Jacob's Cathedral, the
seat of Rīga's Catholic archbishop

St Jacob's Cathedral ❽
Sv Jēkaba katedrāle

Klostera iela 1. **Map** 1 C3. *Tel* 6732
6419. ⬜ *May–Sep: 9am–7pm; Oct–
Apr: 9am–6pm.* 🛉 *8am.*

Sited outside the old city walls,
St Jacob's was built in 1225 to
serve the surrounding villages.
The church was renowned
for having its bell not in the
Gothic steeple but hanging
from a cupola, which is still
visible on the southern side
although the bell has gone. It
was rung to signal that an execution was taking place in the
city, although another story
insists that it was heard when
unfaithful women passed by
the church. Today, it is the seat
of Rīga's Catholic archbishop.

Changing of the guard outside Rīga Castle

Parliament ⑨
Saeima

Jēkaba 11. **Map** 1 C3.
www.saeima.lv

This rather anonymous building, constructed from 1863 to 1867 with Florentine Renaissance features, and renovated several times since, was originally used for meet-ings of the local landed gentry. From 1919 to 1934, as today, it served as the seat of Latvia's parliament, while during World War II it was the headquarters of Friedrich Jeckeln – the SS officer who oversaw the killing of Latvia's Jews, Roma and other "undesirables". Later it was used by the Supreme Soviet of Latvia. Nearby stands a monument that was built to commemorate those who died in the Barricades of 1991 *(see p137)*.

Arsenal Museum of Art ⑩
Mākslas muzejs Arsenāls

Torņa 1. **Map** 1 C3. **Tel** 6735 7527. ◻ noon–6pm Tue, Wed & Fri; noon–8pm Thu; noon–5pm Sat & Sun. 🖼 **www**.lnmm.lv

This is Rīga's premier venue for shows of cutting-edge art. There is no permanent collection, but the temporary exhibitions are generally of high quality. The emphasis is on art from the middle of the 20th century onwards, either produced in Latvia or by Latvians living abroad. The imposing one-storey building

Imposing façade of Latvia's Parliament

on Jēkaba Square was built between 1828 and 1832 in the style of Russian Classicism as a customs house. The name "Arsenal" comes from a previous building on the same spot, built by the Swedes. The downstairs exhibition space particularly benefits from airy rooms and high ceilings.

Swedish Gate ⑪
Zviedru vārti

Between Torņa iela & Aldaru iela. **Map** 1 C3.

The sole remnant of eight city gates, the Swedish Gate was built in 1698 during a period of Swedish rule in Rīga. It runs through the ground floor of the house at Torņa 11, and legend has it that the gate was created illegally by a wealthy mer-chant to give him more direct access to his warehouse. More likely, it was built for the use of the soldiers stationed at St Jacob's Barracks. Today the gate provides access between the popular strip of shops

and bars on Torņa Street and the quieter, but pleasant, Aldaru Street. Newly married couples include the gate on their tour of the city, as passing through it is said to bring good luck.

Swedish Gate, built through the ground floor of an old house

St Jacob's Barracks ⑫
Jēkaba kazarmas

Torņa iela. **Map** 2 D3.

Built in the 17th century to house Swedish soldiers, this yellow block is now home to shops and restaurants. The barracks also played a brief role in the nation's cultural development, as the site of an artists' commune opened in 1917, although the building retained its military purpose. Many of the members went on to join the influential Rīga Artists' Group of the 1920s and 30s. Opposite is the oldest remaining stretch of the city wall, dating from the 13th to 16th centuries but restored during the Soviet era.

Paintings and sculpture exhibited at the Arsenal Museum of Art

Powder Tower/ Latvian War Museum ⓭

Pulvertornis/Latvijas kara muzejs

Smilšu 20. **Map** 2 D3. **Tel** 6722 3743. May–Sep: 10am–6pm daily; Oct–Apr: 10am–5pm daily. donations. www.karamuzejs.lv

The cylindrical Powder Tower is all that remains from a total of 18 towers that were once part of the city's defences. Its 14th-century foundations are among the oldest in the city, but the rest of the structure dates from 1650, being rebuilt after it was destroyed by the Swedish army in 1621. The 2.5-m (8-ft) thick walls were intended to protect the gun-powder stored inside, after which the tower was named. Nine Russian cannon-balls remain embedded in the walls as proof of the tower's strength.

The tower was bought by a German student fraternity at the end of the 19th century and in 1919 it housed a military museum reflecting on the then-recent fight for independence as well as on World War I. The annexe building was constructed from 1937 to 1940, but the Soviet occupation meant that it did not fulfil its function until several decades later. From 1957 the tower housed the Museum of the Revolution in the Soviet Republic of Latvia.

The current museum, the Latvian War Museum, occupies both the tower and the annexe. While the oldest exhibit – part of a cannon discovered during the 1930s – dates from the 15th century, the museum largely concen-trates on 20th-century war-fare. World War I is covered with interesting displays of weapons, uniforms and propaganda posters, as well as items made by the Latvian Riflemen *(see p148)*. Other rooms examine the role of Latvians in the Russian Revolution, the Latvian War of Independence, World War II and the Soviet occupation.

Old issue of Lāčplēsis magazine at the Latvian War Museum

Cats' House ⓮

Kaķu māja

Meistaru iela 10. **Map** 2 D3.

This yellow Art Nouveau building on the corner of Meistaru and Amatu streets is a popular image of Rīga for its two feline statues. The story goes that before World War I a merchant who owned the building was refused entry to the Great Guild because he was Latvian and membership was reserved for Germans only. In retaliation, he put two statues of black cats – with arched backs and tails up – onto the roof, positioning them so that their backsides faced the guildhall. After a lengthy court battle the merchant eventually gained entry into the guild and turned the cats around.

Statue on the roof of Cats' House

Great Guild ⓯

Lielā Ģilde

Amatu 6. **Map** 2 D3. **Tel** 6721 3798.

Established in the 13th century, the Great Guild had a monopoly on trade in Rīga for centuries. The building that served as the guild's headquarters was built from 1853 to 1860. An old guild chamber displays symbols of Hanseatic cities and the bridal chamber was once used by guild members' children on their wedding nights. Today, the building holds concerts by the Philharmonic Orchestra.

Small Guild ⓰

Mazā Ģilde

Amatu iela 5. **Map** 2 D3. **Tel** 6722 3772. for concerts and conferences only. www.gilde.lv/maza

While the Great Guild counted the city's merchants as its members, the less powerful Small Guild existed to promote the interests of Rīga's German artisans. This guild may have been less prestigious than its neighbour, but with its turret and spire it is a more attractive building. The Italian mosaic floor in the entrance hall is particularly noteworthy. The current structure was started between 1864 and 1866, and then completed after an interval of 20 years.

Splendid exterior of the Small Guild

Street-by-Street: Around Town Hall Square

The Blackheads' patron

Until a local government reform in 1877, the Town Hall Square was Rīga's administrative centre. Built in 1334, the Town Hall was one of three focuses of power alongside Dome Cathedral and Rīga Castle, representing the interests of the city's residents. The square has functioned as a marketplace and a site where festivals were held and executions carried out. The impressive step-gabled House of Blackheads has been completely rebuilt, while the Town Hall is a modern building behind a Neo-Classical façade. Out of place at the square's edge is a Soviet-era building housing the Museum of the Occupation of Latvia.

Statue of Roland
A legendary medieval figure and one of Charlemagne's knights, Roland became a symbol of the independence of cities from the local nobility.

KEY

 — — — Suggested route

Town Hall

Town Hall Square
Many of the square's elaborate buildings, destroyed by German bombs during World War II, have benefited from a restoration project tied to the city's 800th anniversary in 2001.

GRĒCINIEKU IEL

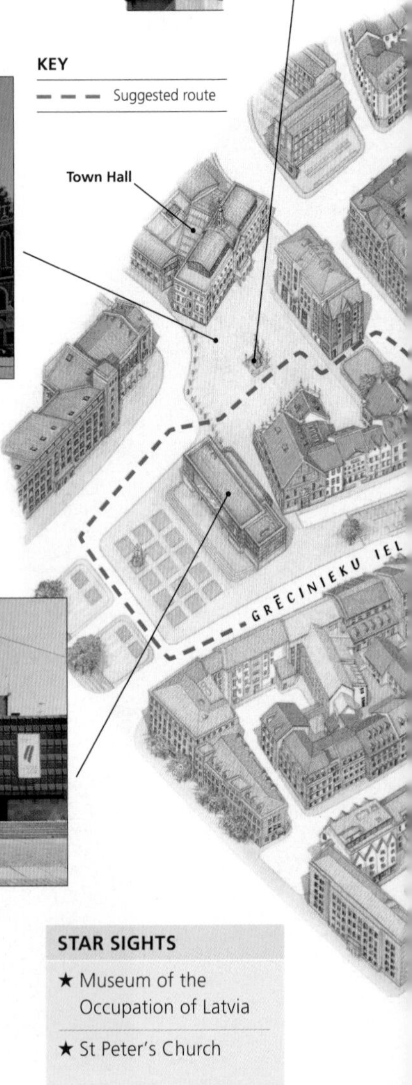

★ Museum of the Occupation of Latvia
This incongruous slab of concrete houses a chilling and detailed testament to the suffering of Latvians during the Soviet and Nazi occupations in the 20th century ⑱

STAR SIGHTS

★ Museum of the Occupation of Latvia

★ St Peter's Church

★ St Peter's Church
This striking building has been destroyed and rebuilt several times over since its original 13th-century incarnation ㉑

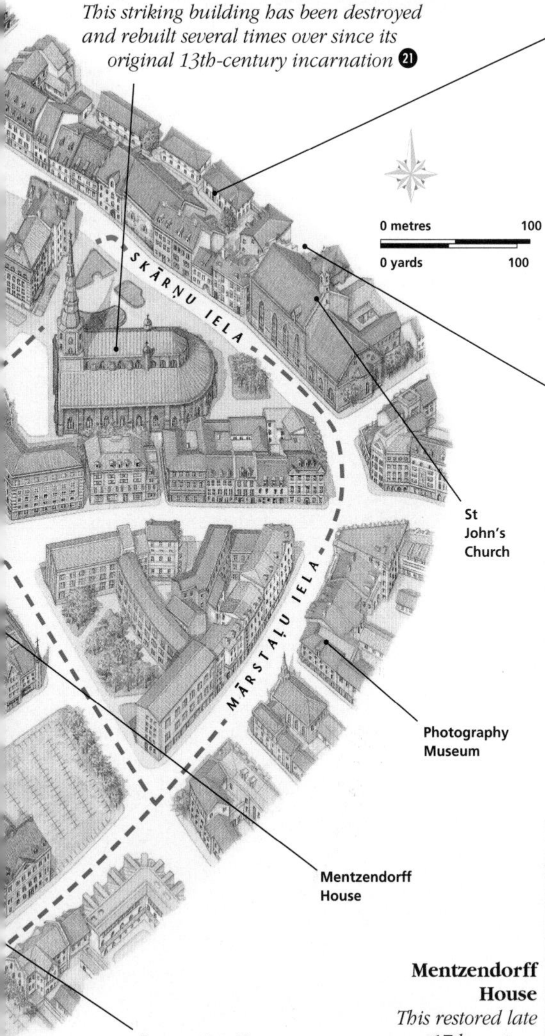

Konventa Sēta
The winding Convent Courtyard has been renovated and is now home to shops, galleries and the Porcelain Museum (see p149).

SKĀRŅU IELA

MĀRSTAĻU IELA

| 0 metres | 100 |
| 0 yards | 100 |

St John's Church

Jāņa Sēta
The courtyard of St John's Church is lined with tables and chairs in summer.

Photography Museum

Mentzendorff House

Dannenstern House
was the largest dwelling in 17th-century Rīga.

Mentzendorff House
This restored late 17th-century building is home to a museum of the merchant class ⑳

House of Blackheads, set behind Schwab House

House of Blackheads ⑰

Melngalvju nams

Rātslaukums 7. **Map** 1 C4.
Tel 6704 4300. 🛈 Schwab House.
◑ until 2016.

Together with the adjoining
Schwab House, the House of
Blackheads is one of Rīga's
most impressive reconstruction
projects. It was originally built
in 1334 for the city's guilds,
after the Livonian Order seized
the existing guild buildings.
Over time, the Blackheads, a
guild of unmarried foreign
merchants, became the sole
occupants. Their name derives
from their patron, St Maurice
(who was often depicted as a
Moor), and they were known
for their riotous parties.

The building's ground floor
housed shops, while the guildhall was on the first floor. The
step-gabled Dutch Renaissance
façade was added in the late
1500s, the astronomical clock
in 1622, and the Hanseatic
emblems and the four figures
(Neptune, Mercury, Unity and
Peace) in 1896. Schwab House
was built to complement its
neighbour in 1891.

The Blackheads disbanded
when the Baltic Germans
were asked by Hitler to return
home at the beginning of
World War II. Both buildings
were devastated by bombing
in 1941 and the Soviet authorities demolished the remnants seven years later; the
current structures date from
1999. The building will serve
as a temporary presidential
residence until 2016, while

renovation work is carried
out at Rīga Castle *(see p143)*.
The city's main tourist
information office can be
found in Schwab House.

Museum of the Occupation of Latvia ⑱

Latvijas okupācijas muzejs

Strēlnieku laukums 1. **Map** 1 C4.
Tel 6721 2715. ◑ for renovations
until 2014; temporarily housed in US
Embassy building, Raina bulvaris 7.
🎫 donations. 🎞 📷
www.occupationmuseum.lv

This Soviet-era concrete
structure was built to house a
museum honouring the Latvian
Riflemen, but since 1993 it has
provided a sobering account
of Latvians' suffering at the
hands of Nazi Germany in
World War II and the later
Soviet occupation. The collection includes photographs
and eyewitness accounts of
deportations and political

represssion. The replica of a
Gulag barracks room offers
an insight into the hardship
experienced by deportees. The
renovated building will include
a memorial to the victims of
Communist occupation.

Latvian Riflemen Monument ⑲

Strēlnieku piemineklis

Strēlnieku laukums. **Map** 1 C4. ♿

Depicting three brooding
Latvian Riflemen, this controversial granite sculpture has
stood in the square bearing its
name since 1970. The Riflemen
were a unit of the Russian
army, formed to defend their
homeland against Germany in
1915. Radicalized by the heavy
losses they suffered during
fierce fighting, they went on to
support Lenin during the 1917
Revolution. Some of the Riflemen later returned to Latvia,
while others became Lenin's
most trusted troops. Some
local people see the Riflemen
as Latvian military heroes,
while for others they recall the
repressive Soviet period.

Mentzendorff House ⑳

Mencendorfa nams

Grēcinieku 18. **Map** 2 D4. **Tel** 6721
2951. ◑ May–Sep: 10am–5pm daily;
Oct–Apr: 11am–5pm Wed–Sun. 🎫
📷 **www**.mencendorfanams.com

Constructed in 1695 as the
premises for a glass-cutter,
this tall building got its current
name from a delicatessen

Beautifully restored wall paintings in a room of Mentzendorff House

based on the ground floor in the early 20th century. Extensively restored in the 1980s and 90s, the building is now a museum devoted to the life of Rīga's merchant class in the 17th and 18th centuries. Each room is decorated in period style. One highlight is the wall paintings, influenced by the work of French artist Antoine Watteau, depicting the wealthy relaxing.

Vera Viduka's 1977 textile at the Museum of Decorative Arts and Design

St Peter's Church ㉑
Pēterbaznīca

Skārņu 19. **Map** 2 D4. *Tel* 6722 9426. ☐ 10am–6pm Tue–Sun. ♿ except tower. 📷 for tower www.peterbaznica.riga.lv

First mentioned in 1209, St Peter's Church was, unlike other churches, largely built by the Livs *(see p172)* and not by foreigners. None of the original wooden church remains, but parts of the walls date from the 1200s. The semi-circular apse and its three chapels were built in the 15th century, while the three Baroque dolomite entrance portals were added in the late 17th century. The church, which had become Lutheran in 1523, was damaged by fire in 1721, when Peter the Great is said to have headed the failed efforts to rescue it.

Lenin plate, Porcelain Museum

The church's steeple has been rebuilt several times over. The current one was built in 1973. Reaching a height of 123 m (403 ft), it provides excellent views across the city.

Museum of Decorative Arts and Design ㉒
Dekoratīvās mākslas un dizaina muzejs

Skārņu iela 10/20. **Map** 2 D4. *Tel* 6722 2235. ☐ 11am–5pm Tue & Thu–Sun; 11am–7pm Wed. 📷 📷 📷 www.lnmm.lv

This museum is housed in the former St George's Church, Rīga's oldest surviving stone

building. It was constructed as the chapel for Rīga's original Livonian Order castle in 1208, and became a separate church after the castle was destroyed in 1297. After the Reformation it was used as a warehouse, and traces of sacred and profane uses have been retained in the building.

The museum gives an overview of decorative arts from the 1890s to the present day. Temporary exhibitions are shown on the ground floor, while the first floor, covering the 1890s to the 1960s, is the most interesting part of the main collection. Highlights include painted ceramics from the Baltars studio and carpet designs by Jūlijs Madernieks.

Porcelain Museum ㉓
Rīgas porcelāna muzejs

Kalēju 9/11. **Map** 2 D4. *Tel* 6701 2944. ☐ 11am–6pm Tue–Sun. 📷 www.porcelanamuzejs.riga.lv

Situated in the Convent Courtyard, this museum reflects the history of porcelain manufacturing in Latvia, which dates back to the late 19th century. The 6,000 exhibits include a wide range of dinner services, as well as a huge red-and-gold vase made to celebrate the city's 700th anniversary in 1901. Of historic importance is a display of vases and statues portraying Soviet leaders.

St John's Church ㉔
Jāņa baznīca

Jāņa 7. **Map** 2 D4. *Tel* 6722 4028. ☐ 10am–5pm Tue–Sat. 🕐 6:30pm Wed, 10am Sun.

Built as the cloister chapel for a Dominican Order monastery in 1234, St John's was devastated by 15th-century fighting between the Livonian Order and the city. Only the main door and porch remain, with the rest rebuilt in Gothic style, including a web-vaulted red-brick nave with an apse, choir and tower. In 1582, the Polish king Stefan Bathory gave the church to the Lutherans, and it was further expanded in the Mannerist style. The interior includes a Baroque altar dating from 1769 and a painting, *Krustā sistais* (The Crucified, 1912), by Janis Rozentāls in the sacristy.

Impressive ceiling and nave of St John's Church

Boating on the city canal in Bastejkalns park

Photography Museum 25
Latvijas fotogrāfijas muzejs

Mārstaļu iela 8. **Map** 2 D4. **Tel** 6722 2713. ☐ May–Sep: 10am–5pm Wed & Fri–Sun, noon–7pm Thu; Oct–Apr: 11am–5pm Wed & Fri–Sun, noon–7pm Thu. 🌐 🚇 www.fotomuzejs.lv

This museum traces the development of photography from 1839 to 1941 through displays of photographs and camera equipment. The images also serve to illustrate life in Latvia, depicting events such as the 1905 Revolution *(see p135)* and scenes of daily life during the first period of independence. In one room, an early 20th-century photographic studio has been re-created and in another there is a display dedicated to the Minox, or "spy" camera, invented by Rīga-born Walter Zapp (1905–2003). More unusual items include stereoscopic images and viewers and there is also a gallery that holds temporary exhibitions.

Large plate camera, exhibited at the Photography Museum

Bastejkalns 26

Basteja bulvāris. **Map** 2 D3.

Situated next to the Freedom Monument, this leafy park was set out in the mid-19th century on the mound of a 17th-century bastion. It is a pleasant place to relax, but it also contains a reminder that the path to Latvia's independence was not without bloodshed. On the night of 20 January 1991, OMON troops – also known as the Black Berets – tried to storm barricaded government buildings. Two filmmakers (Gvido Zvaigzne and Andris Slapiņš), two militiamen (Sergejs Kononenko and Vladimirs Gomanovics) and a schoolboy (Edijs Riekstiņš) were killed in the ensuing gunfire in Bastejkalns. Local people regularly renew the flowers on the memorial stones which bear their names, located close to a small bridge.

Freedom Monument 27
Brīvības piemineklis

Brīvības bulvāris. **Map** 2 D3. ♿

Built in 1935 on a site previously occupied by a statue of Peter the Great, the 42-m (138-ft) tall Freedom Monument is a potent symbol of Latvian independence. It was designed by the sculptor Kārlis Zāle, also responsible for the ensemble at the Brothers' Cemetery *(see p157)*. The granite base is decorated with reliefs and statues representing four virtues – work, spiritual life, family and

protection of the fatherland – as well as Latvian heroes including Lāčplēsis. It also bears the motto "*Tēvzemei un brīvībai*" (For Fatherland and Freedom). The slender granite column is topped by a female figure, commonly known as Milda, holding aloft three golden stars, which represent the three cultural regions of Latvia – Kurzeme, Vidzeme and Latgale. During the Soviet era the authorities banned people from laying flowers at the base of the monument and placed a statue of Lenin a short distance away.

Imposing Freedom Monument, designed by Kārlis Zāle

Krišjānis Barons Memorial Museum 28
Krišjāņa Barona memoriālais muzejs

Kr Barona iela 3. **Map** 2 E3. **Tel** 6728 4265. ☐ 11am–6pm Wed–Sun. 🌐 🚇 🏠 www.baronamuzejs.lv

Located in an apartment where the famous folklorist spent the last years of his life, this museum displays photographs and documents relating to Barons's life and work. The most important exhibit is the *Dainu skapis* (Cabinet of Latvian Folk Songs), a specially designed chest of drawers in which

KRIŠJĀNIS BARONS

In a nation where singing is one of the most important forms of cultural expression, Krišjānis Barons (1835–1923) is perceived as a hero. Influenced by Krišjānis Valdemārs *(see p191)* and part of the group of nationalist intellectuals known as the Young Latvians, Barons is

Photograph of Krišjānis Barons

known for systematizing Latvia's four-line folk songs (*dainas*). He did not collect them in person, but by selecting certain songs as central and then enlisting to the differences between them, he was able to include 217,996 songs in the six-volume work he published between 1894 and 1915.

Barons organized the texts of over 350,000 four-line folk songs sent by thousands of singers and informants. Each was written according to Barons's instructions on a slip of paper the same size as cigarette-paper boxes, which he used for storage before the cabinet was built. Contrary to popular belief, not all the slips were rewritten by Barons.

Orthodox Cathedral ㉙

Pareizticīgo katedrāle

Brīvības iela 23. **Map** 2 D3.
Tel 6721 2901. 🕇 8am, 6pm Mon–Sat; 6:30am, 8:30am, 6pm Sun.

Situated on the edge of Esplanade Park (Esplanāde), this Neo-Byzantine Russian cathedral is officially called the Cathedral of Christ's Nativity (Kristus dzimšanas katedrāle). An attractive structure topped by five domes, it was built from 1876 to 1884 for the city's growing Russian community and was part of a deliberate process of Russification. It became a Lutheran church during the brief German occupation of Rīga in World War I, and once again an Orthodox church in 1921.

As with many places of worship, the Soviet authorities found alternative uses for the building during their occupation. In the 1960s they turned it into a lecture hall and planetarium. The interior decorations were nearly destroyed, and are still being replaced.

Latvian National Museum of Art ㉚

Latvijas Nacionālais mākslas muzejs

Kr Valdermāra 10a. **Map** 2 D2.
Tel 6732 4461. 🕐 11am–5pm Wed–Mon (to 8pm Fri). 📷 📹
www.lnmm.lv

The interior of this early 20th-century Neo-Baroque building still has its original gilt and marble embellishments. While the collection was originally eclectic, in the 1920s and 30s the director Vilhelms Purvītis (1872–1945), himself one of the country's most famous artists, decided to focus on Latvian works. The first floor, therefore, traces the development of Latvian art from the mid-19th century to 1945, while the ground floor displays 18th- and 19th-century Balto-Germanic and Russian art. The latter collection also includes

many icons from the 16th to 20th centuries.

There are, unsurprisingly, many paintings by Latvia's best-known artist Janis Rozentāls *(see p22)* and his works on display include *Leaving the Cemetery* (1895), and *Portrait of Malvīne Vīgnere-Grinberga* (1916). Other Latvian artists represented include Jēkabs Kazaks (1895–1920) and Romāns Suta (1896–1943), who were both members of the Rīga Artists' Group.

Museum of Jews in Latvia ㉛

Muzejs Ebreji Latvijā

Skolas iela 6. **Map** 2 D2.
Tel 6728 3484. 🕐 noon–5pm Mon–Thu, Sun. 📷 donations.
www.jewishmuseum.lv

Housed inside a Jewish community centre, this museum is based around the collections of Holocaust survivors Zalman Elelson and Marģers Vestermanis. It tells the story of the Jewish community in Latvia, which begins in the 16th century with the first records of Jews in the country and progresses to photographs of early 20th-century family life. Inevitably, though, the focus is on the horrific years of the Nazi occupation. The museum does not shy away from distressing images of the Holocaust, and it even includes footage of the massacre of Jews on Liepāja beach.

View of the elaborate domed roof of the Orthodox Cathedral

Pauls Stradiņš Museum of the History of Medicine ㉜

Paula Stradiņa medicīnas vēstures muzejs

Antonijas iela 1. **Map** 2 D2.
Tel 6722 2665. ▥ 2, 24. Trolleybus 1, 19. ◯ 11am–5pm Tue–Sat (to 7pm Thu). ● last Fri of the month.
▨ ▧ www.mvm.lv

Opened in 1961, this museum is based around the collection of cancer specialist Dr Pauls Stradiņš and is one of the world's three biggest medical museums. Its aim is to explore the history of medicine in relation to scientific development. Ancient uses of medicinal herbs, trepanning (the oldest known surgery, which involves making a hole in the patient's skull) and Soviet developments in space biology and medicine are covered. The oddest exhibit is a stuffed two-headed dog, which was the result of experimental grafting.

Art Nouveau Museum ㉝

Jūgendstila muzejs

Albert iela 12. **Map** 2 D2. **Tel** 6718 1464. ◯ 10am–6pm Tue–Sun. ▨ ▧ www.jugendstils.riga.lv

This museum celebrates the Art Nouveau movement for which Rīga is most famous. It is located in the former apartment of the building's architect, Konstantīns Pekšēns (1859–1928), who lived here around 1900.

Before you enter the apartment, note the elaborately decorated balconies and corner tower. Once indoors, it is worth climbing the staircase to the fifth floor in order to view the paintings that adorn the ceilings. The interior is furnished throughout as it would have been during the time when Pekšēns lived here, although few of the items are original.

Visitors are guided by staff in period costume, and there is a short film about Art Nouveau buildings in Rīga.

Art Nouveau Architecture

Owl motif,
Elizabetes iela 10b

Rīga's collection of Art Nouveau buildings has been recognized by UNESCO as unparalleled anywhere in the world, with most found in the Quiet Centre (Klusais Centrs). Many of the early examples – dating from the turn of the 20th century – are categorized as eclectic Art Nouveau, making use of asymmetry, symbolic ornamentation and details drawn from nature. Two other Art Nouveau styles found here are perpendicular, which placed emphasis on vertical composition, and National Romanticism, which incorporated folk motifs and the use of natural materials.

| 0 metres | 100 |
| 0 yards | 100 |

VIDUS IELA
AUSEKĻA IELA
VILANDES IELA
RŪPNIEZĪBAS IELA
⑬ ⑫
ELIZABETES IEL

Elizabetes iela 13 ⑫
Less ornately decorated than others in the area, and judicious in its use of space, the façade of this building illustrates the principle of *amor vacui* (love of space).

Strēlnieku iela 4a ⑨
Symbols of victory adorn this eclectic Art Nouveau edifice, including maidens clutching wreaths and bald eagles. The building, designed by Mikhail Eisenstein, now houses a private school.

Strēlnieku iela 2 ⑪
An example of perpendicular Art Nouveau, the architectural design of this building is relatively restrained, with ornamental details integrated into the structure, including carvings of grain at the top.

Elizabetes iela 23 ⑩
This building has anthropomorphic carvings and a pediment with the words *"Labor vinvit omnia"* (Work conquers all), which commemorates architect Mārtiņš Nukša.

Alberta iela 13 ⑧
Numerous female figures on this building display a range of emotions.

Alberta iela 4 ④
Lions are uncommon in Art Nouveau, but in this eclectic building their wings indicate their traditional connection with the sun.

KEY LIST OF SITES

Elizabetes iela 33 ②
This early experiment with Art Nouveau by Mikhail Eisenstein, one of the foremost proponents of the eclectic style, draws upon Historicist architecture.

Alberta iela 11 ⑥
A fine example of National Romanticism, this building, constructed in natural stone, has bay windows resembling turrets.

ELSEWHERE IN THE CITY

Although the Quiet Centre includes some of Rīga's finest examples of Art Nouveau, there are many other buildings worth visiting elsewhere in the city. Examples in the Old Town include Kalēju iela 23, with its tree-shaped portal, and the city's oldest Art Nouveau building at Audēju iela 7. There are excellent examples of National Romanticism at Tērbatas iela 15/17 and A Čaka iela 26, and several impressive buildings on Brīvības iela and Hamburgas iela. *Art Nouveau in Rīga* (Silvija Grosa, published by Jumava) has good walks of the city.

Brightly coloured façade, Kalēju iela 23

Further Afield

Although primarily residential, Rīga's suburbs include numerous places of interest for visitors. The Moscow Suburb, southeast of the Old Town, has long been home to immigrant communities, including many Jews before World War II. In contrast, the exclusive Mežaparks to the north was built for wealthy Baltic Germans. Across the Daugava river is the Left Bank, where old wooden buildings and a variety of museums can be found.

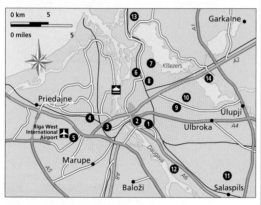

Moscow Suburb ❶
Maskavas forštate

🚌 *A18, T15.* 🚊 *3, 7, 9.*

The area to the east of the Central Market has long been known as the Moscow Suburb, for the road to Moscow ran through it and many of its inhabitants were impoverished Russians. They were joined by Jews – who had previously been banned from settling in the city – in the second half of the 19th century. When the German army arrived in 1941, they established a Jewish ghetto in the suburb, bounded by Kalna, Lauvas, Ebreju, Jersikas and Daugavpils streets.

Still home to many non-Latvians today, it is a quiet area with cobbled side-streets and numerous wooden and religious buildings. The nearby **Rīga Ghetto Museum** attempts to depict life inside the Jewish ghetto, with barbed-wire fences, original cobblestones and other artifacts. A memorial was unveiled at the **Choral Synagogue Ruins** on 4 July 2007, exactly 66 years after German soldiers had filled the building with Jewish families and burned it to the ground.

The memorial includes the names of the 270 Latvians known to have rescued Jews during the war and the image of Žanis Lipke who, with his wife Johanna, saved more than 50 lives.

Other religious buildings in the area include the small and atmospheric **Russian Orthodox Church of the Annunciation** (Tserkva blagoveshtenya) and the domed Grebenshchikov Church (Grebenščikova baznīca) where Old Believers *(see p122)* worship. The distinctive octagonal Lutheran **Jesus Church** (Jēzus baznīca), the largest wooden church in the city, is also worth visiting.

The **Academy of Sciences** (Latvijas zinātņu akadēmija) is a more controversial landmark. Rīga's first skyscraper, it was built between 1953 and 1957 in a pseudo-Baroque style which earned it the nickname "Stalin's Birthday Cake". The ornamentation includes both Latvian folk imagery and hammer-and-sickle motifs, and while parts of it are in need of repair it remains an impressive structure. The balcony on the 17th floor is open to the public.

🏛 **Rīga Ghetto Museum**
Maskavas 14a. *Tel* 6727 0827.
⬜ 10am–6pm Sun–Fri.

⛪ **Choral Synagogue Ruins**
Corner of Gogoļa & Dzirnavu iela.

⛪ **Russian Orthodox Church of the Annunciation**
Gogoļa iela 9. *Tel* 6722 0566.

⛪ **Jesus Church**
Elijas iela 18. *Tel* 6722 4123.
⏰ 6pm Thu, 10am Sun.

🏛 **Academy of Sciences**
Akadēmijas laukums 1.
Tel 6722 9350. **Balcony**
⬜ May–Sep: 9am–6pm daily. 🎫

Academy of Sciences, nicknamed "Stalin's Birthday Cake"

Well-maintained locomotives on show at the Railway Museum, Left Bank

teātra muzejs), which is set in the former home of engineer-turned-actor Smiļģis (1886–1966). The centrepiece is the small private theatre in which he rehearsed, and there are also exhibits relating to stage actors from the nation's first period of independence.

🏛 **Railway Museum**
2–4 Uzvaras bulvāris. *Tel* 6723 2849.
⬜ 10am–5pm Tue–Sun (to 6pm Thu). 🖼 www.railwaymuseum.lv

🏛 **Eduards Smiļģis Theatre Museum**
Smiļģa iela 37/39. *Tel* 6761 1893.
⬜ 11am–6pm Wed–Sun. 🖼

Central Market ❷
Centrāltirgus

Centrāltirgus 1. ⬜ 8am–5pm daily.
📵 www.centraltirgus.lv

Housed in five Zeppelin hangars, Rīga's Central Market is one of the most distinctive in Europe. The hangars, which the German Kaiser's army had abandoned in Kurzeme during World War I, were moved to their current site during the 1920s. The market building sells mostly fresh food, while the area around it is crammed with stalls selling other goods.

Left Bank ❸
Pārdaugava

🚌 A8, T9. 🚊 2, 4, 5, 10.

Although most sites of interest lie on the right bank of the Daugava river, the Left Bank includes specialist museums

and some of the country's best wooden architecture found in Āgenskalns district.

Just across the Stone Bridge (Akmens tilts) is the city's **Railway Museum** (Latvijas dzelzceļa muzejs), the highlight of which is the collection of rolling stock in the yard outside. Exhibits housed inside a renovated engine warehouse include photographs of Latvian stations, old tickets and posters, railway staff uniforms and signalling equipment.

Close by is **Victory Park** (Uzvaras parks), named after the Red Army's victory over the Nazis, which was depicted by the Soviet regime as a "liberation" of the city. The war memorial depicting soldiers being greeted by a welcoming figure of Victory is controversial and Latvian nationalists have twice tried to blow it up.

Also on this bank is the **Eduards Smiļģis Theatre Museum** (Eduarda Smiļģa

Botanical Gardens ❹
Botāniskais dārzs

Kandavas iela 2. *Tel* 6745 0852.
🚊 5 to Konsula iela. ⬜ May–Sep: 9am–7pm; Oct–Apr: 9am–4:30pm. 🖼 🗣 in English, Russian or German by arrangement. ♿ www.botanika.lu.lv

Founded in 1922 as part of the University of Latvia, the Botanical Gardens have been in their current location since 1926. The site includes 5,400 species of plants, with approximately 400 of them native to Latvia; many of them are rare or endangered. In the centre of the garden is a complex of five greenhouses, including a palm house, a large collection of ferns, and a greenhouse devoted to cacti and other succulents. The gardens are particularly attractive from spring through to summer.

Greenhouse set amid the lush grounds of Rīga's Botanical Gardens

Aviation Museum ❺
Aviācijas muzejs

Rīga Airport. **Tel** 2686 2707.
◯ Apr–Nov: 8am–7pm Tue–Sun;
Dec–Mar: 8am–5pm Tue–Sat. 🗐
🗐 🖵 🗐 www.aviamuseum.org

Located just beside Rīga's airport, this private open-air museum claims to have the largest collection of Soviet aircraft outside the Commonwealth of Independent States. The impressive array of aeroplanes and helicopters is the legacy of the Young Pilot's Club, an organization founded in 1956, which was granted used military aircraft for training purposes. After the break-up of the Soviet Union, funding dried up, but in 1998 the equipment was moved onto airport territory. In addition to the aircraft, both military and civilian, there is a small exhibition of uniforms and other equipment. Opening hours can be erratic so visitors should call ahead.

M16 airplane, on show at the Aviation Museum

Dauderi ❻

Sarkandaugavas iela 30. **Tel** 6739
1780, 6739 2229. 🚌 5 or 9 to
Aldaris. ◯ 11am–5pm Wed–Sun. 🗐
www.history-museum.lv

This late 19th-century Neo-Gothic mansion, 6 km (4 miles) from Rīga's city centre, was the summer residence of Latvian president Kārlis Ulmanis from 1937 to

Neo-Gothic façade of Dauderi mansion dating from the 19th century

1940, although he only ever stayed here for short periods of time. The Soviet army later occupied the building, and in turn the Germans placed anti-aircraft guns in the grounds. The mansion has also been used as a kindergarten and as tasting rooms for the Ministry of Food.

Now converted into a museum, the rooms are decorated and furnished in the style of the 1920s and 30s. There are displays dedicated to the life of Ulmanis, the nation's first period of independence and the cultural activities of Latvian exiles during World War II and the subsequent Soviet occupation. The collection is eclectic and includes photographs, medals, puppets and folk costumes. The mansion is surrounded by a park containing sculptures and artificial ruins.

Cherubs decorating the ceiling of Dauderi mansion

Mežaparks ❼

🚋 11.

Previously called Kaiserwald (German for "Emperor's Forest") in reference to its use as a base by the invading Swedish king Gustav Adolphus in the 17th century, this part of northeast Rīga became Europe's first garden city in the early 20th century. Renamed Mežaparks, meaning "Forest Park", it was designed as a suburb for wealthy Baltic

Germans, most of whom later returned to Germany at the beginning of World War II. During the war a concentration camp was set up in the area by the Nazis, housing Jews brought from liquidated ghettos across Eastern Europe. The camp was closed when the Red Army invaded in 1944 and nothing remains of it today. During the Soviet period many of the suburb's buildings fell into disrepair. Since independence, however property prices in Mežaparks have risen, and the area is now predominantly Latvian with a significant number of foreign owners including several embassies. Some of the new residents are building homes which are grand, if not always tasteful, while others are restoring older buildings. The area is fascinating to walk around for its mix of contemporary, Modernist and Art Nouveau buildings, with Hamburgas Street a particular highlight of the area.

Another reason to visit the area is **Rīga Zoo** (Rīgas zooloģiskais dārzs), a well-maintained site which is popular with families. It is known for its bears and has an excellent tropical house, although the zoo's star attraction is a pair of rare Amur tigers. Rides in a horse-drawn carriage are available during the summer, and special events take place throughout the year, including the weighing of the zoo's tortoises in June, and Wolves' Day in September.

Close to the zoo is the **Song Stadium** (Mežaparka estrāde), which was built to host the National Song Festival, held every five years. With the finale including more than 10,000 singers on stage at one time, the. stadium is built on a very large scale.

✗ Rīga Zoo
Meža prospekts 1. **Tel** *6751 8409.*
⬜ *May–Sep: 10am–6pm daily;*
Oct–Apr: 10am–4pm daily. 🎦 🅿
www.rigazoo.lv

Rīga's Cemeteries ❽

Aizsaules iela. 🚌 *A9.* 🚃 *11.* ⬜ *daily.*

Rīga's three most interesting cemeteries are located just south of Mežaparks along Aizsaules Street. The grandest is the **Brothers' Cemetery** (Brāļu kapi), built for Latvians who died defending their country during World War I and the War of Independence. The best-known sculptures are three patriotic works by Kārlis Zāle: *Two Brothers, The Wounded Horseman* and *Mother Latvia.* The memorial features the 19 coats of arms

of the Latvian administrative districts as well as soil from every *pagasts* (parish).

The **Rainis Cemetery** (Raiņa kapi) existed before the writer and atheist Janis Pliekšāns, known as Rainis, was buried there in 1929, but it was renamed in his honour. His memorial allegorically depicts a youthful Latvia awakening from its slumber. Rainis's wife Elza Rozenberga, who wrote under the name Aspazija, lies beside him, and many other Latvian artists and musicians have also been buried here.

The **Woodlands Cemetery** (Meža kapi) opened in 1913 and is the burial place for many political figures from Latvia's first period of independence. It was intended that the main alley would lead straight to the memorial to Latvia's first president Janis Čakste (1859–1927), but during the Soviet era smaller gravestones were put in the way. Janis Rozentāls *(see p22)* is also laid to rest at the site, while the most famous sculpture is the *Grieving Mother*, which marks the suspicious death of the nation's foreign minister in 1925.

Mother Latvia statue, Brothers' Cemetery

Biķernieki Forest ❾
Biķernieku mežs

🚌 *A16, T14.*

This site was chosen by the Nazis for the execution and burial of around 40,000 Jews and other "undesirables" brought from Germany and several occupied European countries between 1941 and 1944. The memorial is the most moving of those in the Rīga area.

A path leads from Biķernieki Street under a white concrete arch, revealing a field of jagged stones huddled together into sections, each representing a city from which Jews were deported. The centre-piece is a concrete canopy under which a black stone stands, with an inscription reading "*O earth, cover not thou my blood, and let my cry have no place*" (Job 16:18). Further smaller memorials nearby mark mass graves. The site can be reached on foot from the Motor Museum *(see p158)* although the route is not signposted; the trolleybus stop is about 1 km (0.6 miles) from the memorial.

Evocative jagged stones of the Holocaust Memorial, Biķernieki Forest

Auto Union V16 racing car on display at the Motor Museum

Motor Museum ⑩
Rīgas motormuzejs

S Eizenšteina 6. **Tel** 6702 5888. 🚌 5, 15; minibus 207, 263. ◯ 10am–6pm daily. 🎦 📷 in English or Russian. 🖥 🏠 www.motormuzejs.lv

Row after row of gleaming cars, motorcycles and bicycles are housed in this modern hangar-like building. There are over 240 vehicles in total – both Latvian-made and foreign. The highlight is a series taken from the Kremlin's collection. The former Soviet president Leonid Brezhnev, in particular, was a motor enthusiast and one of the exhibits is a 1966 Rolls Royce Silver Shadow which he crashed in Moscow – a startled-looking waxwork sits behind the wheel. There is also a heavy armoured ZIS 115S limousine used by Stalin. Small panels give background information on the vehicles and tell the story of the automotive industry in Latvia. The museum shop sells model cars.

Salaspils ⑪

15 km (9 miles) SE of central Rīga. 🚇 Dārziņi. www.salaspils.lv

Although its history stretches back to the 12th century, Salaspils is notorious as the location of a World War II German concentration camp. Its original inmates were prisoners of war, but they were joined by Jews brought from several occupied countries after Rīga's main ghetto was closed. The number of people who died in the camp is disputed as the Soviet regime subsequently exaggerated the figures as a propaganda tool, but it is thought that hundreds were either killed directly or died as a result of the camp's harsh conditions.

The entrance to the camp is marked by a long, sloping concrete block placed at an angle to the ground, intended to symbolize the boundary between life and death. The text on the block reads "*Behind this gate the earth groans*" – a line from a poem by Eižens Vēveris, who was a prisoner of the camp. Inside the block is a small exhibition which, like the rest of the site, has a rather neglected air. Beyond this, the shape of the camp has been indicated, and a metronome ticks inside a block of stone – its slow beat seemingly coming from deep inside the earth. Dominating the site is a series of huge sculptures erected in 1967, with titles such as *The Humiliated* and *The Unbroken*.

Sculpture at Salaspils

Rumbula Forest ⑫
Rumbulas mežs

11 km (7 miles) from central Rīga, along Maskavas iela. 🚇

At least 25,000 Jews were murdered in Rumbula Forest on 30 November and 8 December 1941. The victims, mostly women, children and the elderly from the Rīga ghetto, were shot and their bodies dumped in five mass graves. Just three people are known to have survived. The location of the killings came to light after the war, when two local people tried to sell jewellery found in the area.

Until the late 1980s, the memorials identified the dead as Soviet citizens, although members of the Jewish community illegally tended the site and were eventually allowed to add a modest stone bearing Hebrew text. The focal point of the memorial, constructed in 2002, is a large menorah (seven-branched candlestick), surrounded by broken stones, each of which is inscribed with the names of a murdered family.

Vecāķi ⑬

15 km (9 miles) NE of central Rīga. 🚇 🚌 A24.

This stretch of coast is a popular escape from the city during summer, although its beach is rarely crowded. At the eastern end there is an area reserved for naturists. It is worth walking west along the coast, towards the mouth of the Daugava river, for the remains of fortifications built to protect what was one of Europe's biggest ports. Many of the bunkers date from the time of the Napoleonic Wars, but were last used during World War I. The fortifications have not been well maintained, so exercise caution.

Vast sandy coastline of Vecāķi, northeast of central Rīga

Latvian Ethnographic Open-Air Museum ⑭
Latvijas Etnogrāfiskais brīvdabas muzejs

Occupying 86 ha (213 acres) of woodland on the shores of Lake Jugla, this site includes over 118 homesteads, churches, windmills and other structures from across Latvia. Founded in 1924, the site is organized according to Latvia's ethnographic regions – Vidzeme, Kurzeme, Zemgale and Latgale – drawing attention to variations in building design and living arrangements in different parts of the country. With craftspeople working on-site during the summer, and many buildings containing everyday artifacts, the museum offers an insight into 19th-century rural life and takes at least 2 hours to explore.

VISITORS' CHECKLIST

Brīvības gatve 440.
Tel 6799 4510. 🚌 1.
🕙 10am–5pm daily. 📷 📹
🛈 10am Sun. 📷
www.brivdabasmuzejs.lv

Dutch Windmill
The windmill (1890) is from Latgale and can operate two grindstones simultaneously.

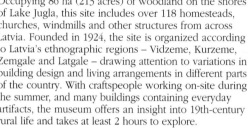

Vidzeme Spinning Wheel-Maker's Homestead

★ **Kurzeme Peasants' Homestead**
This wooden building with a reed-thatched roof is typical of 19th-century rural architecture in southwest Kurzeme.

Zemgale Peasants' Homestead includes a dwelling-house, a bath-house, granaries and a threshing barn.

★ **Usma Church**
Most wooden churches were replaced by stone buildings in the 19th century, making this a rare example.

Handicrafts
Handicraft displays include traditional wickerwork.

Kurzeme Fishermen's Village

Entrance

STAR SIGHTS

★ Kurzeme Peasants' Homestead

★ Usma Church

Old Believers' House
Located in a Latgale village, the house exhibits a loom for weaving thread and a samovar used to boil water for tea.

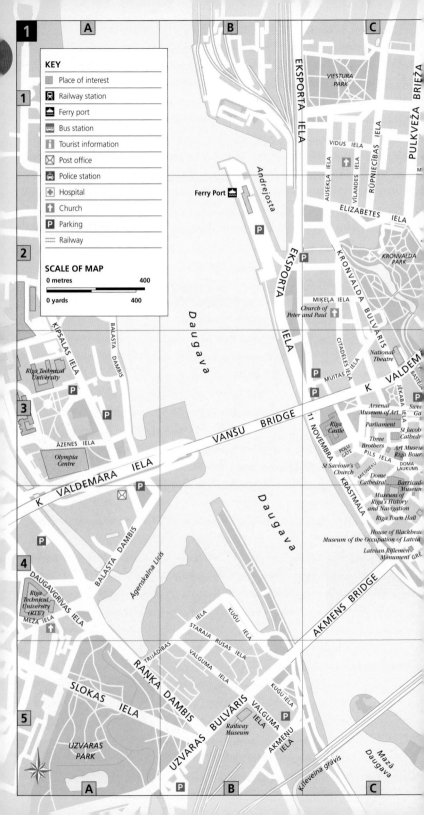

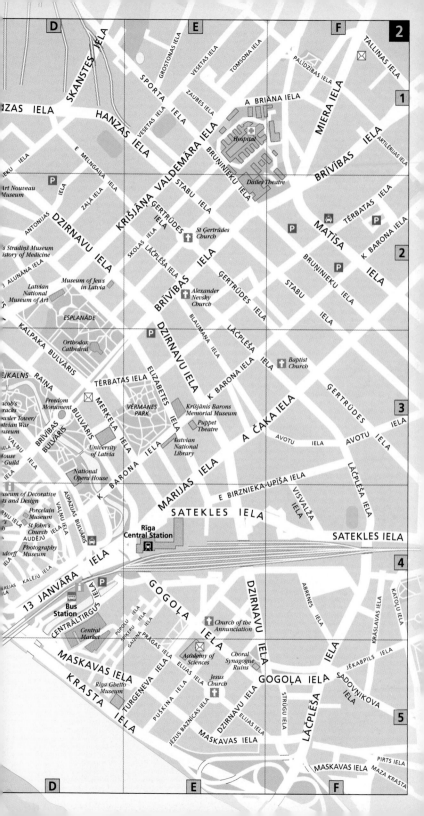

WESTERN LATVIA

*K*nown for its dense forests and fertile plains, lively cities and sleepy rural towns, Western Latvia enchants visitors with its contrasts. The Kurzeme region is quiet and sparsely populated, with the major exceptions of the busy ports of Ventspils and Liepāja. Running along the Lithuanian border, the largely agricultural Zemgale region is dotted with castles and manor houses recalling past glories.

Prior to the arrival of the German crusaders, the heavily forested western region now called Kurzeme was dominated by the Kurši tribe, while the Livs inhabited its northern coast. The fertile and well-drained terrain running along the Lielupe river in the south was home to the Zemgaļi; together with an eastern region formerly called Selonia, this area is now known as Zemgale. The Kurzeme tribes were defeated in 1267 and just over two decades later the same fate befell the Zemgaļi – the last of the Latvian tribes to surrender.

When the Livonian Order collapsed in the 16th century its last master, Gotthard Kettler, retained control of the entire region as a largely independent fiefdom of Poland. With Jelgava as its capital, the Duchy of Courland and Semigallia reached its zenith under Duke Jakob Kettler (r.1640–81). The Duchy was incorporated into the Russian Empire in 1795, and its fate was thereafter tied up with that of the rest of what is now Latvia.

Today, most of Kurzeme retains its rural character, although the cities of Liepāja and Ventspils are among the largest and most vibrant in the country. The few remaining speakers of the Liv language continue their fishing traditions on the northern coast. The area has several picturesque small towns, including Kuldiga and Talsi. The Zemgale countryside consists mainly of flat farmland, with exceptions such as forest parks in the hills around Tērvete. Jelgava's old town was devastated during World War II, although the duke's palace is still standing. The most popular tourist attraction, however, is Rundāle Palace with its Baroque exterior and restored Rococo interior.

Splendid yellow rape fields in full bloom, Kurzeme

◁ Entrance of the beautiful St Nicholas's Orthodox Cathedral in Karosta, Liepāja

Exploring Western Latvia

Kurzeme's long, unspoiled coastline has some tranquil villages as well as the cities of Ventspils and Liepāja. Ventspils is one of Latvia's busiest ports, while Liepāja has transformed from a derelict port to a vibrant cultural centre. Further inland, Kuldīga is among the country's most attractive small towns and makes a good base for exploration, while Pedvāle is popular for its outdoor sculptures. In Zemgale, Rundāle Palace, Bauska Castle and a Neo-Classical palace at Mežotne are highlights. Jelgava, a major transport hub, is a good base from which to explore the region.

SIGHTS AT A GLANCE

Towns and Cities

Bauska ❹
Dobele ❼
Dundaga ❸
Jelgava ❶
Ķemeri ❾
Kuldīga ㉑
Liepāja pp180–81 ㉓
Sabile ⑱
Saldus ⑳
Talsi ⑰
Tukums ❿
Ventspils pp176–7 ⑮

Sites and Buildings of Interest

Jaunpils Castle ❽
Mežotne Palace ❷
Pedvāle Open-Air Museum ⑲
Rundāle Palace pp168–9 ❸
Skaistkalne Roman
   Catholic Church ❺
VIRAC ⑯

Park and Reserve

Lake Pape Nature Reserve ㉔
Tērvete Nature Park ❻

Area of Natural Beauty

Lake Engure ⑫

Beaches and Resorts

Jūrmala pp170–71 ⓫
Pāvilosta ㉒

Tour

The Livonian Coast p173 ⑭

Ruins of the 15th-century Bauska Castle standing on a grass mound

Kolka

Ģipka

Roja
Kaltene

'aldemārpils Mērsrags
P127
le   Krievragciems   Bērzciems
12 LAKE
TALSI   ENGURE
Nurmuiža
žstende   P128   Engure
A10 Cēre Sēme   Apšuciems
BILE   Kandava   P131   P131
PEDVĀLE   TUKUMS **10**   **JŪRMALA**   Rīga *Jēkabpils*
OPEN-AIR   A10 **9** Sloka   *Lake*
MUSEUM   P121   ĶEMERI   *Babītes*   Baloži
P109   Sāti   Slampe   Tireļi   A5   A8
Zante   Vaski   Kalnciems   Ķekava
P104   Džūkste   A9   Olaine   Misa
Viesati   Jaunbērze   P99   A7   Stūri
8 JAUNPILS   P98   *Zemgale*   Klāvi
va Pilsblīdene Annenieki   CASTLE   **JELGAVA 1**   Garoza   Iecava   P88 Stelpe
0 SALDUS   A9 Upenieki   DOBELE **7**   Svēte   A8   Emburga   P94   Bārbele
Striķi   P104   P96   Zaļenieki   SKAISTKALNE
Puijas   Skares   TĒRVETE   MEŽOTNE   ROMAN **5**
rsīši   Auce   Bēne   NATURE   **6** Tērvete   PALACE **2**   **4** CATHOLIC
Grivaši P96   PARK   Eleja   BAUSKA   CHURCH
Ruba   Bukaiši   Augstkalne   A12 RUNDĀLE   Kamārde   A7
Ukri   *Šiauliai*   PALACE **3**   *Panevēžys*

GETTING AROUND

To explore Western Latvia's remote towns and villages, it is generally best to travel by car. By contrast, it is also possible to visit the region's many other attractions by using public transport. While buses are a good option for reaching Bauska and most of Kurzeme's sights, taking a train is preferable for trips to Jelgava and Tukums. However, as there are no direct rail links between Rīga and Rundāle, travellers must change at Bauska. The port towns of Ventspils and Liepāja have good ferry connections with Rīga as well as with other European cities. There are also airports at Liepāja and Ventspils.

KEY

▬▬▬	Motorway
▬▬▬	Main road
▬▬▬	Secondary road
▭▭▭	Minor road
⌁⌁⌁	Railway
▬▬▬	International border

Jelgava Palace, built on an island in the Lielupe river, Jelgava

Jelgava ❶

Road Map C4. 🏛 66,000.
🚌 from Rīga. 🚆 from Rīga.
ℹ️ Akadēmijas iela 1, 6300 5445.
🎭 International Ice Sculpture Festival
(Feb). **www**.visit.jelgava.lv

Between 1578 and 1795,
Jelgava was the capital of the
Duchy of Courland. Much of
the town was damaged during
the two World Wars. The most
prominent remnant of the
duchy period is the **Jelgava
Palace** (Jelgavas pils), the winter residence of Ernst Johann
Biron *(see p169)*. Built in the
18th century by Francesco
B Rastrelli, the building today
houses the Latvian University
of Agriculture. None of the
original interiors remain
intact, but a small museum
houses archive photographs
of the palace's pre-war state.
Museum staff also provide
access to the burial vault
of the Dukes of Courland.
  The old town offers a
handful of interesting sights.
The impressively restored
**Orthodox Cathedral of
St Simeon and St Anna** (Sv
Sīmaņa un Annas pareizticīgo
katedrāle) was designed by
Rastrelli for Biron's patron,
Anna Ivanovna. A Baroque
building houses the **History
and Art Museum** (Vēstures un
mākslas muzejs), which documents local history, while the
quirky little **Latvian Railway
Museum** (Latvijas dzelzceļu
muzejs) attracts rail enthusiasts.

Environs
The small **Nikolai Cemetery**,
4 km (2 miles) southeast of
Jelgava, contains the graves of
36 British soldiers and sailors

who died in 1917 in Latvia
as German prisoners of war
during World War I.

⚓ **Jelgava Palace**
Lielā iela 2. **Tel** 6396 2197.
🕐 May–Oct: 9am–5pm daily. 🎫

✝️ **Orthodox Cathedral of
St Simeon and St Anna**
Raiņa iela 5. **Tel** 6302 0207.
🕐 9am–5pm daily. 🕔 5pm.

🏛 **History and Art Museum**
Akadēmijas iela 10. **Tel** 6302 3383.
🕐 10am–5pm Wed–Sun. 🎫

🏛 **Latvian Railway Museum**
Stacijas iela 3. **Tel** 6309 6494.
🕐 11am–3pm Wed, Fri, Sat;
1–6pm Thu. 🎫

Mežotne Palace ❷

Road Map D4. **Tel** 6396 0711. 🕐
May–Aug: 8am–9pm; Sep–Apr: 9am–
6pm. 🎫 🍴 **www**.mezotnespils.lv

This restored Neo-Classical
structure was built in 1802 for
Charlotte von Lieven, govern-
ess to the grandchildren of the

Pastel-coloured exterior of the
Neo-Classical Mežotne Palace

Russian Tsarina Catherine II.
The original design by Italian
architect Giacomo Quarenghi
was developed by local architect J G Berlitz. The Lieven
family lost the manor in 1920
during the agrarian reforms,
and it was partly destroyed
during World War II. Today,
the palace is used for functions
and as a hotel *(see p304)*, but
it is also open to visitors. The
highlight is the Dome Hall,
with artificial marble pillars
and walls, and a dome painted
to give the illusion of three-
dimensional decoration. The
grounds are in the style of an
English park, and in summer
boats take visitors across the
Lielupe river. On the other side
of the river is a castle mound,
site of one of the largest
Semigallian castles and scene
of their final battle against the
German crusaders (1290).

Rundāle Palace ❸

See pp168–9.

Bauska ❹

Road Map D4. 🏛 11,000. 🚌 from
Rīga. ℹ️ Rātslaukums 1, 6392 3797.
🎭 Early Music Festival (Jul),
International Country Music Festival
(Jul). **www**.tourism.bauska.lv

A small country town, Bauska
is known mainly for its 15th-
century **Bauska Castle** (Bauskas
pils), which was built at the
confluence of the Mēmele and
Mūsa rivers to help control the
trade route between Rīga and
Lithuania. Later, it became the
property of the Duchy of
Courland and Semigallia and

a fortified residence was added for the duke. Restoration work has reversed inauthentic Soviet alterations, including the renewal of the original sgraffito decoration on the towers. It is possible to climb one of the towers for a small fee.

Besides a number of fine wooden buildings, the town also boasts a 16th-century Lutheran church and the riverside **Bauskas Alus** brewery.

⚓ Bauska Castle
Tel 6392 3793. ◯ May–Sep: 9am–7pm daily; Oct: 9am–6pm daily; Nov–Apr: 11am–5pm Tue–Sun. ⬛
www.bauskaspils.lv

Bauskas Alus
Tel 2945 1942. ◯ by appointment. ⬛ www.bauskasalus.lv

Embellished altarpiece, Skaistkalne Roman Catholic Church

Skaistkalne Roman Catholic Church ❺
Skaistkalnes Romas katoļu baznīca

Road Map D4. Slimnīcas iela 2, Skaistkalne. *Tel* 6393 3154. ⬛

Built for the Jesuits in 1692 and now maintained and administered by monks of the Paulian Order, Skaistkalne Church is Latvia's most popular place of pilgrimage after Aglona *(see p195)*. Raised on a mound, the white building has a red roof and a rounded apse. The Baroque interior features artificial marble palisades and an ornate altarpiece. Plump pastel-painted cherubs decorate the pulpit and organ, and

two sets of paintings represent the Stations of the Cross. Call ahead, as the church is often locked.

Tērvete Nature Park ❻
Tērvetes dabas parks

Road Map C4. ⬛ ⓘ *Tērvetes Sils, 6372 6212.* ◯ 9am–7pm daily (Nov–Feb: to 5pm). ⬛ ⬛ ⬛ ⬛ partial.
www.tervetesnov.lv

This popular nature park was developed in the forest around Tērvete, which was famous as the home of Sprīdītis, a Tom Thumb-like character in the beloved fairytale by Anna Brigadere (1861–1933). Her summer house has been preserved as the **Anna Brigadere Museum**.

The theme of the fairytale is evident throughout the park, with its Dwarf Forest and Fairytale Forest dotted with carved wooden creatures. Summertime attractions include the park's own witch, and there are quieter paths through the Old Pine Forest. Nearby are a Livonian Order castle mound with replica fort and the **Tērvete History Museum**, which displays a collection of farm utensils and textiles.

🏛 Anna Brigadere Museum
Sprīdīši. *Tel* 2653 2691. ◯ May–Oct: 10am–5pm Wed–Sun. ⬛

🏛 Tērvete History Museum
Lielķēniņi. *Tel* 2989 6804. ◯ May–Nov: 10am–5pm Wed–Sun. ⬛

Wooden figure, Tērvete Nature Park

Dobele ❼

Road Map C4. 🏘 *11,100.* 🚌 🚉 ⓘ *Baznīcas iela 6, 6372 3074.* www.zemgaletourism.lv

Situated on the banks of the Bērze river, Dobele is visited mainly for its ruined Livonian Order castle, built in 1335. Destroyed several times during the Polish-Swedish Wars (1600–29), the castle began to be restored only in 2002. The small **Dobele History Museum** recounts the town's history and mounts temporary exhibitions. On the edge of town, the **Dobele Horticultural Plant Breeding Experimental Station** houses a museum dedicated to noted horticulturalist Pēteris Upītis (1896–1976). One of the largest lilac collections in the world can also be found here. Classical music concerts are held in the gardens every spring while the flowers are in bloom.

Environs
A drive of 13 km (8 miles) down a gravel road west of town, the **Pokaiņi Forest** is an area of spiritual significance due to its numerous unusual rock formations.

🏛 Dobele History Museum
Brīvības 7. *Tel* 6372 1309. ◯ 11am–6pm Tue–Fri, 11am–4pm Sat. ⬛

🌸 Dobele Horticultural Plant Breeding Experimental Station
Graudu iela 1. *Tel* 6372 2294. ◯ 8am–5pm Mon–Fri.

Ruins of the 14th-century Livonian Order castle in Dobele

Rundāle Palace ❸

Designed by Francesco Bartolomeo Rastrelli (1700–71), Rundāle is one of the finest palaces in the Baltic region. Work began in 1736 on a Baroque summer residence for Ernst Johann Biron, but was left unfinished when he was exiled. Following Biron's return, the interiors were renovated in the Rococo style. Biron's son removed most of the furnishings when he left in 1795, after Courland was annexed by Russia. The structure suffered damages during the 20th century, and the rooms have served as an elementary school and a granary. Restoration began in 1972 and is still in progress.

Detail, Rose Room
Rococo touches, such as fake marble, silver detailing and floral motifs, adorn the room.

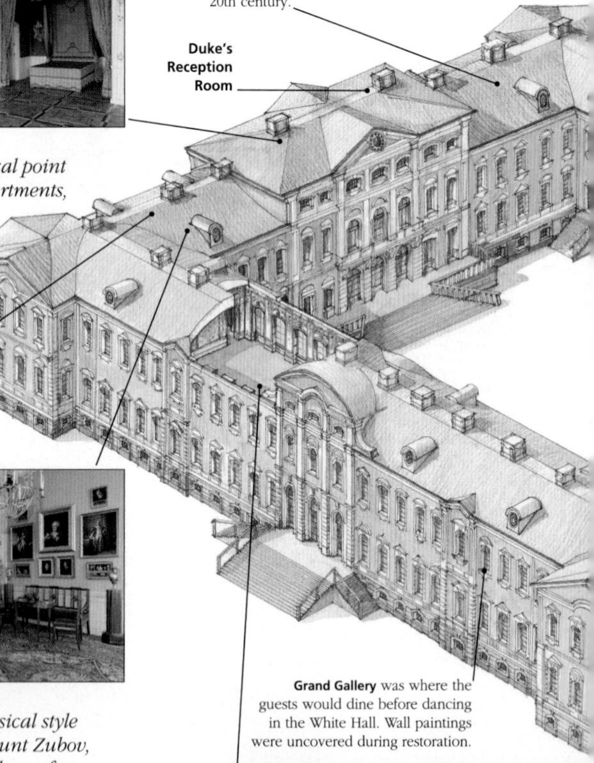

Marble Hall was used as a school gym in the 20th century.

Duke's Reception Room

★ Duke's Bedroom
This room was the focal point of Biron's private apartments, which occupied the central block of the palace.

Rose Room

The Corner Room
The Russian Neo-Classical style reflects the taste of Count Zubov, who inhabited the palace after Courland was absorbed into the Russian Empire.

Grand Gallery was where the guests would dine before dancing in the White Hall. Wall paintings were uncovered during restoration.

★ Gold Hall
The initials of the palace's owner, "EJ", can be seen amid the ornate gilt scrolls.

STAR FEATURES

★ Duke's Bedroom

★ Gold Hall

★ White Hall

Formal French-style gardens, re-created from the original plans

VISITORS' CHECKLIST

Road Map D4. 🚌 *from Bauska.*
Tel 6396 2197. 🕐 *May–Oct:*
10am–6pm daily; Nov–Apr:
10am–5pm daily. 📷 🅿 🍴
www.rundale.net
Park 🕐 *May–Oct: 10am–7pm*
daily (Jun–Aug: to 9pm Fri–Sun);
Nov–Apr: 10am–5pm daily.

The history of the palace's construction is exhibited in the building's basement.

Duchess's Boudoir
The duchess could rest and receive visitors during the day in the splendidly decorated boudoir, which has now been restored. The duchess and other family members lived in the western wing.

The exhibition of period clothes fills three rooms with fashion from the 17th and 18th centuries.

The courtyard has gateposts topped by the duke's emblem – a heraldic lion.

The Oval Porcelain Cabinet, made by Johann Michael Graff, was designed to exhibit exquisite artifacts.

★ White Hall
This ballroom boasts lavish stucco work by German sculptor Johann Michael Graff. The restrained colour scheme gives the room its name.

ERNST JOHANN BIRON

The son of a minor landlord, Ernst Johann Biron was asked to leave the academy in Königsberg (present-day Kaliningrad) for bad behaviour. Failing to establish himself in the Russian court, he returned to Jelgava and became close to the widowed Duchess of Courland, Anna Ivanovna. In 1730, Anna became empress of Russia, and three years later Biron was appointed Duke of Courland. After his patron died in 1740, the unpopular Biron was sent into exile, returning only in 1763. A year later, Catherine II made him duke once more but he abdicated in 1769 in favour of his son Peter.

Duke of Courland, Ernst Johann Biron (1690–1772)

Jaunpils Castle **8**
Jaunpils pils

Road Map C4. **Tel** 6310 7082.
◯ 10am–6pm daily. 🏛 🖼
www.jaunpilspils.lv

Built by the Livonian Order in 1301, with its distinctive round tower added in the 15th century, Jaunpils Castle was owned by the German von der Recke family from 1561 to 1922. On 24 December 1905, the castle was burnt down by revolutionaries (see p135), and the current structure is almost entirely the result of subsequent reconstruction. The small museum inside includes replicas of weapons and armour, as well as some interesting photographs of the castle before 1905. Across the courtyard from the museum is a pub, and the castle also has eight atmospheric hotel rooms (see p303). Guided tours also take in Jaunpils town's Evangelical Lutheran Church and the early-19th-century watermill.

One of a dozen bridges across the Vēršupīte river, Ķemeri Park

Ķemeri **9**

Road Map C3. 🚌 from Rīga.
🛈 Meža Māja, 6773 0078. 🛶 canoe trips & wildlife tours arranged at visitors' centre. **www**.daba.gov.lv

A popular resort in the early 20th century, Ķemeri is considered part of Jūrmala, although it has not seen the same scale of rejuvenation experienced further east. The town's main attraction, **Ķemeri Park** encompasses an Orthodox church, pavilions and bridges across the Vēršupīte river.

Ķemeri is also the entry point to **Ķemeri National Park**, which has rivers, lakes, meadows, inland dunes, sulphur springs and forests. A 3-km (2-mile) wooden pathway traverses the park's 6,000-ha (14,830-acre) bog, which attracts bird-watchers.

Jūrmala **⑪**

Literally meaning "seaside" in Latvian, Jūrmala is an attractive stretch of beaches, pine forests and small towns alongside the Gulf of Rīga. During the 19th century, the area became famous for its medicinal mud and sulphur-rich spring water. Jūrmala soon grew into a popular resort and it became fashionable to own a summerhouse here. The wooden houses as well as older sanitaria still dot the area, standing alongside modern guest houses and upmarket spas.

Jomas Street in Majori is a pedestrianized strip that forms the heart of Jūrmala. It is lined with a large number of outdoor cafés, restaurants and hotels, as well as a variety of shops.

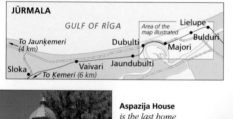

JŪRMALA

GULF OF RĪGA
Area of the map illustrated
Lielupe
To Jaunķemeri (4 km)
Dubulti
Bulduri
Majori
Sloka
To Ķemeri (6 km)
Vaivari
Jaundubulti

GULF RĪGA

Marienbāde Sanitarium was built in 1870.

Majori Beach

Z MEIEROVIČA PROSPEKTS

Lielupe

JŪRAS IELA

JOMAS

Aspazija House is the last home of one of Latvia's most famous poets, Elza Rozenberga (1865–1943), nicknamed as "Aspazija". The house is now a branch of the Jūrmala Town Museum.

DUBULTI
DUBULTU PROSPEKTS
SLOKAS IELA

Jūrmala City Museum charts the growth of the seaside resort from the early 19th century to today.

Tukums ⑩

Road Map C3. 🏠 *19,000.* 🚌 *from Rīga.* 🚗 🛈 *Talsu 5, 6312 4451.* 🗓 *Tue, Thu, Sat.* 🎭 *Festival of Female Choirs and Men's Choruses (Jun).* **www**.visittukums.lv

Meaning the "Land of the End" in Livonian, Tukums stands at the point where the Zemgale plains meet the Kurzeme uplands. Little remains of the town's history as an ancient Liv settlement, while the only remnant of the Livonian Order castle is the Palace Tower (Pils tornis). Restored in 1767 to serve as a granary and jail, it now houses the **Local History Museum**, which displays dioramas and temporary exhibitions.

Monument to freedom fighters, Tukums

The oldest buildings in the old town date from the late 19th and early 20th centuries. The main highlight, **Tukums Art Museum**, houses Latvian art from the 1920s and 30s. It is considered to be Latvia's foremost gallery outside Rīga.

Environs
Durbes Pils, a manor house on the eastern edge of Tukums, is an 1820s Neo-Classical building with a 17th-century core. The restored rooms include displays on local history, but the foremost exhibition is the ethnological collection in the former servants' quarters.

About 5 km (3 miles) east of Tukums is the 15th-century Šlokenbeka Manor. It is home to the **Latvian Road Museum**. Many exhibits are of specialist interest but the collections of horse-drawn carriages and road building machines have a more general appeal.

Jaunmoku Pils (*see p303*), 5 km (3 miles) west of Tukums, is a distinctive red-brick manor house with step gables and chimneys. Many of the rooms of this former hunting lodge are decorated in an ornate style. A highlight is a large tiled stove bearing images of Rīga and Jūrmala. The forest museum upstairs includes oddities such as a collection of silver cigarette holders. It is possible to climb the tower for stunning views of the surrounding countryside.

🏛 **Local History Museum**
Brīvības laukums 19a. **Tel** 6312 4348. ⏰ 10am–5pm Tue–Sat, 10am–4pm Sun. 📷

🏛 **Tukums Art Museum**
Harmonijas 7. **Tel** 6318 2392. ⏰ 11am–5pm Tue–Fri, 11am–4pm Sat & Sun. 📷

⚓ **Durbes pils**
Mazā parka 7. **Tel** 6312 2633. ⏰ 10am–5pm Tue–Sat, 11am–4pm Sun. 📷 📷 📷

🏛 **Latvian Road Museum**
Milzkalne. **Tel** 6318 2354. ⏰ Nov–Apr: 10am–3pm Mon–Fri; May–Oct: 9am–4pm Mon–Fri. 📷

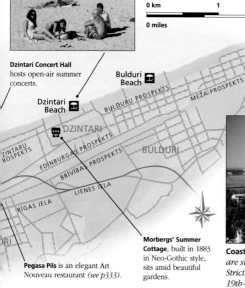

Dzintari Beach, *a popular stretch of sand in summer, draws hordes of tourists. It is dotted with beer tents and volleyball nets during this time.*

0 km 1
0 miles 1

Dzintari Concert Hall hosts open-air summer concerts.

Bulduri Beach

Dzintari Beach

DZINTARI

ZINTARU PROSPEKTS
EDINBURGAS PROSPEKTS
BRĪVĪBAS PROSPEKTS
BULDURU PROSPEKTS
MEŽA PROSPEKTS
BULDURI
LIENES IELA
RĪGAS IELA

Morbergs' Summer Cottage, built in 1883 in Neo-Gothic style, sits amid beautiful gardens.

Pegasa Pils is an elegant Art Nouveau restaurant (*see p333*).

Key to Symbols *see back flap*

VISITORS' CHECKLIST

Road Map C3. 🚌 *from Rīga.* 🛈 *Jomas iela 50, Majori, 6776 4276.* **Aspazija House** Meierovica prosp 20, Dubulti. **Tel** 6776 9445. **Jūrmala City Museum** Tirgoņu iela 29, Majori. **Tel** 6776 4746. **Dzintari Concert Hall** Turaidas iela 1. **Tel** 6776 2086. **Morbergs' Summer Cottage** Dzintaru Prospekts 52/54. **Tel** 6722 7175. **Pegasa Pils** Jūras iela 60, Majori. **Tel** 2923 6425.

Coastal towns, *which make up Jūrmala, are situated among picturesque pine forests. Strict building regulations preserve the 19th-century wooden summerhouses and restrict construction in the area.*

Reed-filled part of Lake Engure, with boats moored along the shore

Lake Engure 🔢
Engures ezers

Road Map C3. 🚤 *for boating: Abragciems Kempings, 4 km (2 miles) N of Engure, 6316 1668; for fishing permits: Ornithological Centre, Bērzciems, 6947 4420 (open by appointment only).* **www**.eedp.lv

Latvia's third-largest lake, Engure is a significant bird habitat. Around 160 species have been spotted in the wetlands, including cranes and grey herons. A road leads around the western edge of the lake between the towns Mērsrags and Engure, while the **Ornithological Centre** on the eastern side of the lake can be reached by turning inland just north of Bērzciems. One bird-watching tower is situated close to the centre, while another is directly opposite it across the lake. A 3.5-km (2-mile) orchid trail

starts close to the Ornithological Centre, running through dry pine forest and a chalky grass swamp in which 22 species of orchid can be found.

Many parts of the lake are choked with reeds as a result of pollution by chemical fertilizers, and a number of fish species have disappeared, although fishing permits can still be obtained at the centre.

Coat of arms at the castle, Dundaga

Environs
The small fishing port of **Roja**, 26 km (16 miles) northwest of Mērsrags, offers more accommodation options than most places on the coastal route from Rīga to Ventspils. Exhibits in the town's **Sea-Fishing Museum** (Rojas jūras zvejniecības muzejs) look at the naval schools of Krišjānis

Valdemārs *(see p191),* sailing ships in the late 19th and early 20th centuries, fish canning and the local Banga fishermen's collective.

🏛 **Sea-Fishing Museum**
Selgas iela 33. **Tel** 6326 9594.
🕐 *Jun–Sep: 10am–6pm Tue–Sun; Oct–May: 10am–5pm Tue–Sat.*

Dundaga 🔢

Road Map C3. 🏘 4,000. 🚌
ℹ️ *Pils iela 14, 6323 2293.*
www.ziemelkurzeme.lv

First recorded in 1245, Dundaga has a restored 13th-century Livonian Order castle that today houses the tourist office. The seven coats of arms inscribed on the castle belong to its owners. The Lutheran church nearby has an altarpiece by Janis Rozentāls (1866–1916). The church's 19th-century wooden organ case is unusual, as it is the work of Latvian craftsmen who generally produced functional items while foreign masters made decorative pieces.

Dundaga features a large, bizarre sculpture of a crocodile at the corner of Talsu and Dinsberga streets, honouring local crocodile hunter Arvīds Blūmentāls (1925–2006). He emigrated to Australia during World War II and is said to be the inspiration for the film *Crocodile Dundee* (1986).

Large concrete crocodile sculpture on a bed of stones in Dundaga

THE COAST-DWELLING LIVS
A Finnic people related to the Estonians, the Livs settled along the Gulf of Rīga around 5,000 years ago, long before the arrival of the Latvian tribes. They referred to themselves as *raandalist* (coast-dwellers) and *kalāmied* (fishermen), and the sea has always been central to their way of life.

German crusaders devastated Livonian culture in the 13th century and the Livs were gradually assimilated into the other Baltic tribes. During the 19th and 20th centuries, children were educated in German and later Russian rather than in Livonian. Many of the remaining Livs were forced to leave the region when the Soviets declared the coast a military zone. Since 1991 there have been concerted efforts to preserve and strengthen Liv culture. Today, not more than 200 people are officially registered as Livs.

Monument to Livonian Culture in Mazirbe

The Livonian Coast

A narrow strip of land running along the edge of the Gulf of Rīga and the Baltic Sea and dominated by sand dunes and pine forests, the Livonian Coast is separated from the rest of Kurzeme by the Zilie kalni (Blue Hills). It is home to one of Europe's smallest ethnic groups, the Livs. The coastal route also provides access to some of Latvia's most beautiful scenery. It is only a short walk between fishing villages and attractively secluded beaches.

TIPS FOR DRIVERS

Tour length: 60 km (37 miles).
Stopping-off points: There are small guest houses and campsites in several of the coastal villages. Booking ahead is advisable.
Road conditions: Conditions can be difficult once off the main roads, particularly in poor weather.

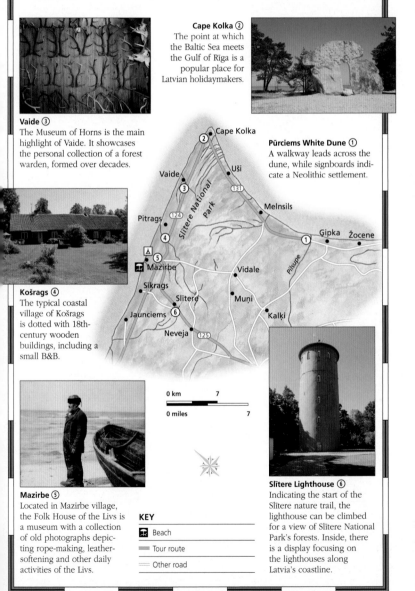

Cape Kolka ②
The point at which the Baltic Sea meets the Gulf of Rīga is a popular place for Latvian holidaymakers.

Vaide ③
The Museum of Horns is the main highlight of Vaide. It showcases the personal collection of a forest warden, formed over decades.

Pūrciems White Dune ①
A walkway leads across the dune, while signboards indicate a Neolithic settlement.

Košrags ④
The typical coastal village of Košrags is dotted with 18th-century wooden buildings, including a small B&B.

Mazirbe ⑤
Located in Mazirbe village, the Folk House of the Livs is a museum with a collection of old photographs depicting rope-making, leather-softening and other daily activities of the Livs.

Slītere Lighthouse ⑥
Indicating the start of the Slītere nature trail, the lighthouse can be climbed for a view of Slītere National Park's forests. Inside, there is a display focusing on the lighthouses along Latvia's coastline.

KEY

🏖 Beach

— Tour route

═ Other road

0 km   7
0 miles   7

Picturesque view of the village of Sabile, known as the Switzerland of Latvia ▷

Ventspils ⑮

Founded in 1290, Ventspils has long been a trading centre and was a member of the Hanseatic League. In the 18th century, war and plague ravaged the city, but it later thrived as part of the Russian Empire.

A hub for Russian oil tankers till recently, Ventspils has gained an air of affluence since independence. In order to limit its reliance on Russia, the city has been spruced up to boost tourism. Enlivened by parks, flower beds and fountains, Ventspils has a bustling modern centre and a well-restored old town. The historic core is best explored on foot and a walk along Ostas Street gives a chance to see bovine sculptures left after the 2012 Cow Parade.

Exterior of the 13th-century Livonian Order castle, Ventspils Castle

🏛 Ventspils Castle

Jāṇa iela 17. **Tel** 6362 2031.
⬚ 10am–6pm Tue–Sun.
📷 🎫 ♿ 🍴
www.muzejs.ventspils.lv

On the bank of the Venta river, this Livonian Order castle is one of the finest in Latvia. Although it began life as a late 13th-century stone tower, its current form largely dates from the 14th century. Devastated by the Swedish army in 1659, the castle has been restored many times since. Parts of the red-brick gallery in the inner courtyard were built as recently as the 1870s.

The museum inside the castle recounts its history through engaging displays and touch screens. As a Livonian Order stronghold, it was a self-contained world complete with a dormitory, refectory, chapel and meeting hall. Later, the chapel was used as a Lutheran church, while the building served as a prison at various times from 1824 to 1959. It became the barracks for the German army during World War I and for Soviet border guards from 1962 to 1983. The rooms in which the exhibits are laid out bear fragments of wall paintings from the 15th to 17th centuries, and there are also displays of traditional costumes and jewellery.

The pleasant restaurant on the premises, Melnais Sivēns *(see p335)*, is one of the best places to eat in the city. During summer, it is possible to try archery and, by arrangement, fire a small cannon in front of the castle.

⛪ Russian Orthodox Church of St Nicholas

Plosta iela 10. **Tel** 6362 1616.
The onion-domed Russian Orthodox Church of St Nicholas (Sv Nikolaja pareizticīgo baznīca) was consecrated in the early 20th century. Although the Neo-Byzantine exterior needs to be restored, the interior has an excellent collection of icons.

Venta

⑥ Ventspils Beach

Venta

① Ventspils Castle

OSTAS IELA
PILS IELA
JĀŅA IELA

K VALDEMĀRA
AVOTU
RĪGAS IELA
KATOŅU IELA
MEŽA IELA
LIEPU
SAULES IELA
PLA

OSTGALS

KARLINES
LIVU
JŪRAS IELA

⑤ Aqua Park

OĻU IELA
KRONA IELA
VILŅU IELA
MEDNU IELA

KATOŅU IELA
LIEPĀJAS
MEŽA IELA
LIELĀDZIRNAVU

LIELAIS PROSPEKTS

LIELAIS PROSPEK

PARKA IELA
VASARNĪCU IELA
Children's City
PĒTERA IELA

INŽENIERU IELA
LAIMAS
ATPŪTAS
STRAZDU

Seaside Open-Air Museum
④
RĪNKA IELA

0 metres	500
0 yards	500

Key to Symbols see back flap

⛪ Lutheran Church of St Nicholas

Tirgus 2. **Tel** 6362 2750.
🕐 9am–4pm daily.

With a portico at the front and a tower with an observation platform, this attractive yellow-and-white church (Sv Nikolaja Luterāļu baznīca) stands on the old market square. Dating from 1835, it was built according to the wishes of Tsar Nicholas I.

🏛 Seaside Open-Air Museum

Riņķa 2. **Tel** 6362 4467. 🕐 May–Oct: 10am–6pm Wed–Sun. 🖼 ♿ 📷 www.ventspilsmuzejs.lv **Narrow-Gauge Railway** May–Oct: Sat & Sun.

The Seaside Open-Air Museum (Piejūras brīvdabas muzejs) was opened in 1954 to preserve the heritage of Latvia's fishing villages, which began to disappear as the Soviet authorities regarded the shores as areas of military importance. Buildings were moved from their original location and reassembled here and the site now includes homesteads, smokehouses, curing cabins, net sheds and even a large windmill.

Traditional crafts are displayed around the site in summer. There are also large collections of fishing

boats and anchors, and a **Narrow-Gauge Railway**. Until the 1960s, the steam engine linked seaside villages, but now it takes a 1.4-km (0.8-mile) trip through Seaside Park.

Water slides and swimming pools at the Aqua Park

🏊 Aqua Park

Medņu iela 19. **Tel** 2642 9684.
🕐 May–Sep: 10am–9pm daily. 🖼 📷

With three pools, several slides, Jacuzzis and saunas as well as a variety of water playgrounds, the Aqua Park (Akvaparks) is popular with families. Swimming gear can be rented on site.

🏖 Ventspils Beach

2 km (1 mile) S of town. ♿
The residents of Ventspils are proud of their beach, particularly the 1.2-km (0.7-mile) stretch that received an EU Blue Flag in 1999 for meeting international standards. This was a remarkable achievement, since the coast had been contaminated by industrial pollution during the Soviet era. Parts of the beach have been set aside for windsurfers, nudists and smokers, and there are playgrounds for children. At the northern end of the beach is a breakwater, with a promenade leading to a lighthouse at the end.

VIRAC (Ventspils International Radio Astronomy Centre) ⑯

Ventspils Starptautiskais Radioastronomijas Centrs

Road Map B3. **Tel** 2923 0818.
🕐 Mar–Nov: 6am–6pm daily.
🖼 📷 call in advance.
www.virac.venta.lv

Situated in a former Russian army town, the 1970s military installation is believed to have spied on communications between Europe and the USA for at least a decade. When they left in 1994, the Russians took the smallest dish, leaving the two heavier ones which are 16 m (52 ft) and 32 m (105 ft) in diameter. The bigger one is the largest radio telescope in Northern Europe and the world's eighth largest.

A combination of size and precision engineering makes the larger dish especially valuable to scientists. Guided tours of it begin with the ground-floor laboratory. Visitors can climb up to a viewing platform and then step into one of the suspended laboratory pods. The structure was built by a naval factory in the Ukraine, and the interiors are reminiscent of a ship.

The unmarked road to VIRAC, leading past eerily empty residential buildings, is just east of an electrical substation on the P124. Book in advance for a guided tour.

Radio telescope at VIRAC, the largest in Northern Europe

Talsi ⑰

Road Map C3. 12,500.
Liela iela 19–21, 6322 4165.
Mara's Craft Market Fair (Aug).
www.talsitourism.lv

The administrative centre of
northern Kurzeme and a
transport hub for the region,
Talsi is an attractive town
spread out around two lakes
and across nine hills. It was
originally a Liv settlement,
captured by the Kurši during
the 10th century, and then by
the Livonian Order in 1263. A
mound remains where the
Order's castle stood on
Watermill Hill (Dzirnavkalns).

Talsi's oldest surviving
building is the 18th-century
Lutheran church, atop Church
Hill (Baznīckalns). The most
noted pastor of the church
was Karl Amenda (1771–1836),
a close friend of composers
Beethoven and Mozart.
Nearby, the cobblestoned
Kalēju and Ūdens streets are
notable for water troughs.

The **Talsi Regional Museum**
(Talsu novada muzejs), housed
in a late 19th-century Neo-
Classical residence, features
an interesting exhibition on
the Livs. The building's
original painted ceiling can
be seen in one of the rooms.

Environs
Laumas Nature Park, 20 km
(12 miles) north, has several
walking and cycle paths.
Guided tours are available,
including one focusing on
bees. It also has a campsite.

🏛 Talsi Regional Museum
K Mīlenbaha 19. **Tel** 2910 2628.
10am–5pm Tue–Sun.
www.talsumuzejs.lv

Picturesque view of Talsi with a canopy of trees rising behind

Vīna Kalns, Sabile's renowned
vineyard

Sabile ⑱

Road Map C3. 3,500.
Pilskalna iela 6, 6325 2344.
Wine Festival (Jul). www.sabile.lv

A small town on the banks of
the Abava river, Sabile was first
mentioned in 1253, by which
time it had long been inhabited
by the Kurši tribe. Only a
mound remains of the tribe's
castle, although the stones
were used to repair the town's
17th-century Lutheran church,
which houses Latvia's oldest
bell, made
in 1450.

Just 1 km
(0.6 mile) from
Sabile centre is the
**Drubazas Botany
Trail**, a 2-km
(1 mile) guided
walk through
forests and marshes.

Sabile's wine hill,
Vīna Kalns, is said to be the
northernmost vineyard in the
world. The strong and sour
wine was popular in the
court of the Kurzeme Duchy

Sculpture, Pedvāle
Open-Air Museum

(1561–1795), but viniculture
may have begun long before.
In the 1930s, the vineyard
was used to experiment with
grape varieties, but this ceased
during the Soviet period. Work
began again in 1989, and there
are now 650 vines of 15 varieties. Wine-tasting is possible
at the annual wine festival.

Environs
Mara's Caves (Māras kambari),
named after an ancient
Latvian goddess, are located
12 km (7 miles) southwest of
Sabile. In the Middle Ages,
these sandstone caves were
the hiding place of bandits.

🌿 Drubazas Botany Trail
"Drubazas" Abavas pagasts. **Tel**
2647 3783. 9am–6pm daily.

Pedvāle Open-Air Museum ⑲
Pedvāles brīvdabas
mākslas muzejs

Road Map C4. Strauta 4. **Tel** 6325
2249. May–Oct: 10am–6pm
daily. www.pedvale.lv

The near-derelict buildings
and grounds of
Pedvāle Manor,
a short walk
uphill from
Sabile, were
bought by sculptor
Ojars Feldbergs in
1991. A year later,
they were opened
as the Pedvāle
Open-Air Museum,
one of Latvia's most interesting
museums. Scattered around
the 100-ha (247-acre) site are
over 150 works by Latvian and
international artists. Many of
the artworks are designed
specifically for the museum
during conferences and workshops. The on-site ticket office
provides a map to help
visitors in their exploration.
Some of Feldbergs's own
work can be found exhibited
in the attractively decaying
estate buildings at the far end
of the site, while other
buildings have been renovated
to accommodate visiting
artists. The former manor
house is now a guest house
open to the public.

Rows of crosses marking the graves of German soldiers, near Saldus

Saldus ⑳

Road Map C4. 🚍 🛈 *Striķu iela 3, 6380 7443.*

Set amid scenic countryside, close to Lake Ciecere, Saldus is best known for the **Janis Rozentāls Museum of History and Art** (Jaņa Rozentāla Saldus Vēstures un Mākslas Muzejs). Rozentāls *(see p152)*, who was born near Saldus, reconstructed the building in 1900. The artist's home till 1901, it is now a museum that showcases his works. Temporary art exhibitions are housed in an adjacent building.

Environs
Vācu Karavīru Kapi, 7 km (4 miles) south of town, is a war cemetery where German soldiers who died in Latvia were re-buried in a single place.

🏛 **Janis Rozentāls Museum of History and Art**
Striķu iela 22. *Tel 6388 1547.*
⭘ *9am–5pm Tue–Fri, 10am–4pm Sat & Sun.* 📷

Kuldīga ㉑

Road Map B3. 🚶 *14,000.* 🚍 🛈 *Baznīcas iela 5, 6332 2259.* 🎑 *Town Festival (mid-Jul).* **www**.visit.kuldiga.lv

With a well-preserved old town and an attractive location alongside the Venta river, Kuldīga is one of Latvia's most alluring provincial towns. It was founded in 1242 by the Livonian Order, who chose the site to capitalize on

the river and a land route linking Prussia with the lower Daugava Valley.

In the 16th century, Kuldīga's castle was one of the residences of Duke Gothard Kettler and the town traded with Rīga and Jelgava. The streets near the attractive old town hall square, running alongside the Alekšupīte river, feature 17th- and 18th-century timber buildings. Also here are a couple of attractive churches, St Catherine's (Sv Katrīnas baznīca) and the Holy Trinity (Sv Trīsvienības Katoļu baznīca). A short walk away is the Venta Waterfall (Ventas rumba), the widest in Europe. Close by is a 164-m (538-ft) brick bridge, one of Europe's longest. Overlooking the river is **Kuldīga District Museum** (Kuldīgas novada muzejs), best known for its collection of playing cards.

Statue of Janis Rozentāls, Saldus

Environs
The **Riežupe Sand Caves** (Riežupes smilšu alas), 4 km (2 miles) north of Kuldīga, form the longest cave system in Latvia. A quarter of the 2-km (1-mile) site is open to visitors.

🏛 **Kuldīga District Museum**
Pils iela 5. *Tel 6332 2364.*
⭘ *11am–5pm Tue–Sun.* 📷

Pāvilosta ㉒

Road Map B4. 🛈 *Dzintaru iela 2, 6349 8229.* 🎑 *Sea Festival (Jul).*

Founded in 1879, the small port town of Pāvilosta was named after Paul Lilienfeld, Governor of Kurzeme from 1868 to 1885. Tourist activities in Pāvilosta revolve around the sea, including yacht and canoe hire and trips out in a fishing boat. The surrounding area is also a popular spot for windsurfing and is home to the country's first world-class yacht marina, **Pāvilosta Marina**.

The **Regional Studies Museum** (Pāvilostas novadpētniecības muzejs), located in the town's oldest building, exhibits everyday items from the region and Latvian-only displays about local history.

⚓ **Pāvilosta Marina**
Ostmalas iela 4. *Tel 6349 8581.*
www.pavilostamarina.lv

🏛 **Regional Studies Museum**
Dzintaru iela 1. *Tel 6349 8276.*
⭘ *mid-May–mid-Sep: 11am–5pm Wed–Fri, noon–4pm Sat & Sun; mid-Sep–mid-May: 9am–5pm Mon–Fri.* 📷

Ferries anchored at the harbour in the port town of Pāvilosta

Liepāja ㉓

Although Liepāja was officially declared a town in 1625, it expanded only in the early 19th century. The deepening of the ice-free port and the building of a railway link were followed, in 1890, by the foundation of a Tsarist naval port at Karosta. Today, Liepāja is Latvia's third-largest city with a vibrant cultural life. It is dotted with many interesting sights, most of which are located in its historic core. Many of the city's older buildings have been extensively restored.

Wooden sculpture, Liepāja Museum

Beautifully carved Baroque altar of St Anne's Basilica

🏛 Holy Trinity Church

Baznīcas 1. **Tel** 6342 2208. ◯ 10am–6pm daily. 🎟 donations. **Organ recital** Jul: Sat (call for timings).
The modest exterior of the mid-18th-century Holy Trinity Church (Svētās Trīsvienības baznīca) belies one of the finest interiors in the Baltic region, adorned with gilt

Details on the exterior of Holy Trinity Church

detailing and woodcarvings. The centrepiece is an organ built in 1773 by H A Contius, a favourite of composer J S Bach. Expanded in 1885, it was the world's largest organ until 1912. Wooden steps lead up the clock tower for views.

House of Craftsmen

Dārza iela 4–8. **Tel** 2654 1424. ◯ 9am–5pm Mon–Sat. 📷
With a wide variety of fine handicrafts on sale, the House of Craftsmen (Amatnieku namiņš) is a place where one can watch skilled artisans as they weave traditional textiles. The world's longest amber necklace, 123 m (404 ft) long and weighing 60 kg (132 lb), is also on display along with photographs documenting its creation.

🏛 St Anne's Basilica

Veidenbauma iela 1. **Tel** 2922 7566.
First documented in 1508, the current Neo-Gothic St Anne's Basilica (Sv Annas baznīca) dates only from the end of the 19th century. The plain interior is dominated by the huge Baroque altar, carved for Duke Jakob Kettler (*see p135*) in 1697 by Nicolas Sefrens. The altar painting depicts the Passion of Christ in three panels, with the Crucifixion at the bottom, the wrapping of his body in the centre and the Ascension at the top.

🏛 Occupation Museum

K Ukstiņa iela 7/9. **Tel** 6342 0274.
◯ 10am–6pm daily. 📷
The interesting Occupation Museum (Okupāciju režīms) offers an absorbing account

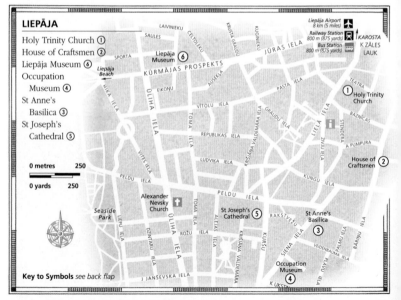

LIEPĀJA

Holy Trinity Church ①
House of Craftsmen ②
Liepāja Museum ⑥
Occupation Museum ④
St Anne's Basilica ③
St Joseph's Cathedral ⑤

0 metres   250
0 yards   250

Key to Symbols *see back flap*

of the city's treatment at the hands of Nazi Germany and the Soviet Union, with copious notes available in English. Exhibits include everyday objects left behind by repatriated Baltic Germans at the start of World War II, photographs of people deported en masse by the Soviets in June 1941 and an account of the killing of the city's Jews and other "undesirables".

The exhibits end with a display about the events leading up to independence. The offices of the Popular Front, which was based in the building, have been left intact. Rooms upstairs house an exhibition of antique photographic equipment.

St Joseph's Cathedral

Rakstvežu iela 16/18. *Tel* 6342 9775. Decorated inside with scenes from the Bible, the yellow St Joseph's Cathedral (Sv Jāzepa katedrāle) attained its current towering form in the 19th century. The congregation needed a larger church, but had no land on which to build, which is why they simply expanded the existing building upwards.

Liepāja Museum

Kūrmājas prospekts 16/18. *Tel* 6342 2327. ☐ 11am–7pm Wed–Sun. www.liepajasmuzejs.lv
Set amid a small sculpture garden, the Liepāja Museum (Liepājas muzejs) is housed in an ornate early 20th-century building with an impressive galleried hall. The displays trace local history, with exhibits including the heads of stone cherubs from St Anne's Basilica, a series of pewter drinking vessels topped by human figures and traditional southern Kurzeme costumes. Also here is a reconstruction of the workshop of the famous sculptor Mikelis Pankoks (1894–1983), who vanished in 1944 and was presumed dead. He had fled the country incognito, and ended his days in a Swiss mental hospital.

Liepāja Beach

Although the coast here was once an environmental disaster area, it has now been thoroughly cleaned up and proudly flies its EU Blue Flag.

VISITORS' CHECKLIST

Road Map B4. 85,750. Cimdenieki, Lidostas iela 8. Rīgas iela. Rīgas iela. Rožu Laukums 5/6, 6348 0808. daily. Piano Star Festival (Mar), Summer Sound (Jul), International Organ Music Festival (Sep). www.liepaja turisms.lv

The long, sandy Liepāja Beach (Liepājas pludmale) is separated from the Old Town by the wooded **Seaside Park** (Jūrmalas parks). The nearby streets are lined with elegant Art Nouveau buildings that used to be summer houses.

Façade of St Nicholas's Orthodox Cathedral, Karosta

Karosta

4 km (2 miles) N of town. 3, 4, 7. www.karosta.lv **St Nicholas's Orthodox Church** Katedrāles 7. **Military Prison** Invalīdu 4.
A military harbour built by the Russians during the late 19th century, Karosta was off-limits to civilians. In its heyday, it housed 40,000 personnel. Today, it has a ghost-town feel, with streets of huge unoccupied buildings.

One reason for visiting Karosta is to see the striking onion-domed **St Nicholas's Orthodox Cathedral** (Sv Nikolaja pareizticīgo catedrāle), used as a cinema and gym by the Soviets. The old **Military Prison** (Karostas cietums) is now the Kurzeme region's major tourist attraction, offering a chance to be locked up and yelled at by "guards" for a couple of hours or overnight.

Lake Pape Nature Reserve ㉔

Papes dabas parks

Road Map B4. *Tel* 2922 4331. Buši, Rucava village, 2913 4903; Bārtas iela 6, Nica, 2945 8532. www.pdf-pape.lv

Just 10 km (6 miles) from the Lithuanian border, the wetlands, pine forests, dunes, grasslands and coastline of the Lake Pape area make an excellent trip from Liepāja. Sponsored by the World Wide Fund for Nature, the reserve covers around 52,000 ha (128,495 acres), and is best known for its *savvaļas zirgi* (semi-wild horses) and *sumbru ganības* (European bison). Guided tours, taking around 90 minutes, are available from the ticket office at the entrance to the signposted grazing area.

The reserve is popular with bird-watchers, due to its location on a migration path. Some 271 species have been sighted here, 15 of which are on the European Red List of endangered species. The area is sparsely populated, although there are three villages within the reserve. One of them is the dune-enclosed settlement of Pape, home to **Vītolnieki**, a branch of the Latvian Ethnographic Open-Air Museum (see p159).

Vītolnieki

Pape village. *Tel* 2926 2283. ☐ May–Sep: 10am–6pm Fri–Wed. by appointment.

Bird-watching tower at the Lake Pape Nature Reserve

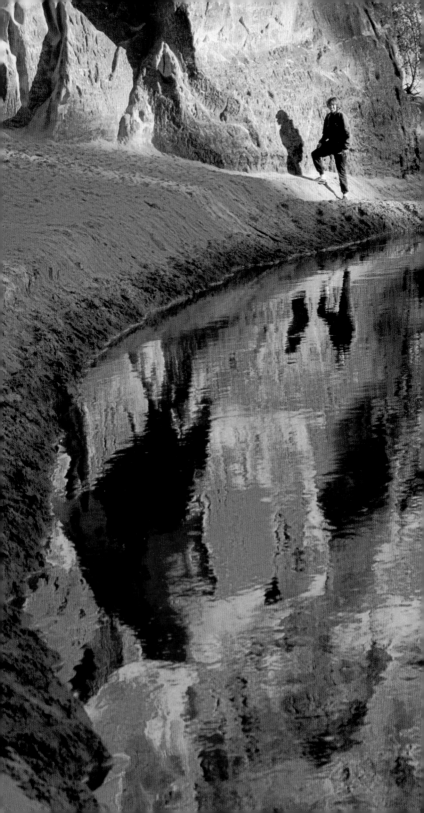

EASTERN LATVIA

*T*he eastern part of Latvia includes some of the country's most popular attractions, both natural and man-made, as well as rarely visited rural districts. Although far from mountainous, the terrain is not as flat as in the west and there are two extensive upland areas dotted with myriad lakes, some of which have well-developed tourist facilities, while others remain isolated and untouched.

When the German crusaders arrived, they found the Livs and Lettgallians inhabiting the region which now forms Vidzeme, while Latgallians and Selians lived further east in what is now Latgale. The Bishop of Rīga took control of the west and east of Vidzeme, while central Vidzeme and most of Latgale was claimed by the Livonian Order. After the collapse of the Livonian Order in 1561 the whole of the east fell under Lithuanian, and later Polish, rule.

The end of the Polish-Swedish Wars in 1629 saw Sweden ruling both Estonia and Vidzeme. The Russians conquered Vidzeme in 1721. Reliant economically on agriculture, forestry and wood processing, the region is sometimes claimed as the cradle of Latvian culture as it produced many of the country's best-known writers and musicians. Today Vidzeme is second only to Rīga as a travel destination, with the Gauja National Park combining natural beauty and historical attractions.

Latgale, on the other hand, was ruled by Poland until 1772. The Polish influence fostered a strong Catholic tradition, particularly evident in the pilgrimage centre of Aglona. Latgale was later absorbed directly into the Russian Empire, unlike other Latvian regions which were ruled as separate provinces. This isolation delayed the national awakening in Latgale, and today it is neglected as a predominantly Russian backwater. Despite this, its villages and lakes charm visitors and the regional capital Daugavpils is slowly shaking off its image as a grey Soviet throwback.

Old houses and tower in Cēsis, a town steeped in history

◁ Bank of the Gauja river below Eagle Cliff, Gauja National Park

Exploring Eastern Latvia

The most popular tourist attraction in Eastern Latvia is Gauja
National Park, which combines beautiful forests with attractions
such as the historic town of Cēsis and the restored Turaida
Castle. A significant part of the region is covered by the
North Vidzeme Biosphere Reserve, famous for its
coastal meadows, sandstone cliffs and extensive
wetlands. The route from Rīga to Daugavpils, the
regional capital, runs along the Daugava Valley
and includes several worthwhile stops, while
the cathedral at Aglona is a major centre for
Catholic pilgrimage. For most visitors,
though, the main attraction in Latgale is its
patchwork of lakes, including Rāzna and
Lubāns, the two largest in the country.

SIGHTS AT A GLANCE

Towns, Resorts and Villages
Aglona **17**
Ainaži **3**
Alūksne **23**
Daugavpils pp196–7 **15**
Dunte **7**
Jēkabpils **13**
Krāslava **16**
Lielvārde **10**
Limbaži **6**
Līvāni **14**
Ludza **21**
Mazsalaca **5**
Preiļi **18**
Rēzekne **19**
Salacgrīva **4**
Saulkrasti **8**

Skrīveri **11**
Valmiera **2**
Vecpiebalga **22**

Sites of Interest
Gulbene–Alūksne
Railway **24**
Ikšķile **9**
Koknese **12**

National Park
*Gauja National Park
pp186–9* **1**

Tour
Latgale Lakes p198 **20**

Sandstone cliffs on the banks of Salaca river, Vidzeme

KEY

- Motorway
- Main road
- Secondary road
- Minor road
- Railway
- International border

SEE ALSO

- *Where to Stay* pp305–7
- *Where to Eat* pp335–7

GETTING AROUND

The highlights of Gauja National Park are easily reached by bus or train from Rīga, while even small towns in Vidzeme usually have at least one bus a day. Rīga and Daugavpils are well connected by buses and trains that run several times a day. The public transport network elsewhere in Latgale is not well developed and it is easier to use a private vehicle, particularly when exploring the lakes. Bus services link all the towns but services are not very frequent.

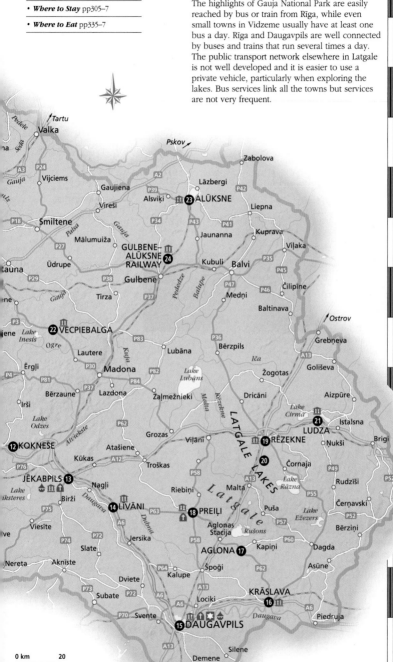

0 km 20

0 miles 20

Gauja National Park ❶

Latvia's first and most popular national park was established in 1973, stretching for about 100 km (62 miles) along the Gauja River Valley. But the area has been attracting tourists to its so-called "Alpine trails" since the 19th century. Almost half of the 92,000-ha (227,337-acre) park is forested, and it is home to about 900 plant, 149 bird and 48 mammal species. Around 4 per cent of the park forms a closed nature reserve, but the rest is accessible by road. Canoeing and boating are great ways to see the caves, cliffs and ravines carved out by the river since the glaciers receded 12,000 years ago. In addition to its natural attactions, the area also has some of Latvia's most fascinating historic sites (see pp188–9).

KEY

☐ Gauja National Park

★ Turaida Museum Reserve
The extensively restored Turaida Castle houses historical exhibitions, while the grounds include outbuildings and a sculpture park.

New Castle in Sigulda
This fanciful manor house was built in 1867 near the ruins of a Livonian Order Castle, where there is now an open-air stage.

STAR SIGHT

★ Turaida Museum Reserve

★ Līgatne Education and Recreation Centre

★ Cēsis

Bobsleigh Run
Sigulda offers a rare chance to experience the thrill of a world-class bobsleigh run at a reasonable price. In summer, a slower, wheeled vehicle is used.

★ **Līgatne Education and Recreation Centre**
Inside the park, footpaths and tracks for vehicles wind past spacious enclosures housing animals, including elk, brown bears and European bison.

VISITORS' CHECKLIST

Road Map D3. 🚉 *from Rīga.*
🚌 *from Rīga.* ℹ️ *Gauja National Park Visitors' Centre, Turaidas iela 2a, Sigulda, 2665 7661.*
🛶 *guided canoe trips organized by Campo in Rīga (2922 2339), Makars in Sigulda (2924 4948).*
△ **www**.gnp.lv

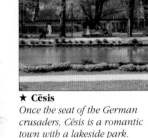

★ **Cēsis**
Once the seat of the German crusaders, Cēsis is a romantic town with a lakeside park.

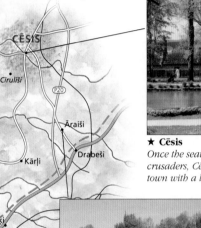

CĒSIS
Raiskums
Cirulīši
P14
P20
Āraiši
Gauja
Drabeši
Kārļi
Amata
Skaļupe   Zvārte Rock
Ieriķi
Līgatne
A2
Ligatne
Augšlīgatne

Lake Āraiši
Archaeologists found remains of a fortress on the lake bed. This reconstruction offers a glimpse into Latgallian life in the 9th and 10th centuries.

Zvārte Rock, a 35-m (115-ft) high sandstone outcrop, boasts excellent views. It is locally believed to be a haunt of witches and demons.

KEY

🚉 Railway station

ℹ️ Visitor information

🚠 Cable car

△ Campsite

🔭 Viewpoint

▬ Major road

▬ Minor road

▬ Other road

— Railway line

- - Park boundary

ROSE OF TURAIDA

According to a popular legend, in 1601 a young orphan girl, found in the aftermath of a battle between the Swedish and Polish armies, was named Maija and raised in Turaida Castle. She fell in love with Viktor, a gardener from Sigulda Castle. One day a deserter from the Polish army lured her into the nearby Gūtmaņa Cave under false pretences, but she tricked him into killing her rather than surrendering her chastity. The so-called grave of the Turaida Rose in the Turaida Museum Reserve is considered a romantic spot for newlyweds.

Gravestone of the Turaida Rose, the beautiful Maija

Exploring Gauja National Park

The park follows the Gauja River Valley as it flows southwest from Valmiera. Road access to the park is good, with the A2 and A3 running alongside. The most convenient access points from Rīga are Sigulda, where the park information office is located, and Cēsis. In addition to hotels and guest houses along the major routes and close to the tourist sites, the park includes a network of 22 campsites. They are arranged along the Gauja, Amata and Brasla rivers, making canoeing an appealing way to see the area. The stretch between Sigulda and Cēsis is particularly attractive.

Sigulda

from Rīga. from Rīga. Train station, Ausekla iela, 6797 1335. www.sigulda.lv
A spacious town set in scenic woodland, Sigulda is a centre for outdoor activities and is also a good base for visiting Krimulda and Turaida. After the Brotherhood of the Sword subdued the Liv population in 1207, they gave the valley's right bank to the Bishop of Rīga and built their own castle on the left bank. The Brotherhood, renamed the Livonian Order, lost the town to the Poles in 1562, and it passed between the Poles and Swedes for 150 years, until it was taken by Russia in the Great Northern War (1700–21).

The castle ruins are tucked away behind the 19th-century New Castle (Jaunā pils) and its fine gardens. Close by is a Lutheran church and the impressive viewpoint called Artists' Hill (Gleznotāju kalns). Paths run through the woodland to Satzele Castle Mound, once a Liv fortress, and Peter's Cave on the bank of the Vējupīte river.

Krimulda

from Sigulda. from Sigulda 9am–5pm Mon–Fri. 6797 2232. www.krimuldaspils.lv
The Bishop of Rīga had a castle built in Krimulda after taking control of the right bank of the Gauja Valley in 1207. Krimulda Castle (Krimuldas pils) was destroyed by the Swedish army in 1601, and little remains of the ruins. It is easier to spot the nearby 19th-century Neo-Classical manor house (Krimuldas muižas pils). It is now a

Cable car carrying visitors from Sigulda to Krimulda

rehabilitation centre for children, with a café and basic accommodation.

⛰ Turaida Museum Reserve

6 km (4 miles) N of Sigulda. from Sigulda. **Tel** 6797 2376. May–Oct: 9am–8pm daily; Nov–Apr: 10am–5pm daily. 11am Sun. www.turaida-muzejs.lv
The Turaida Museum Reserve mainly consists of a castle and a group of outbuildings. Turaida Castle was built by the Brotherhood of the Sword in 1214. It was left in ruins

after a fire in 1776 and has since been extensively restored. Plaques help visitors to understand the site, while exhibitions inside deal with the history of the castle and illustrate the restoration process. Near the museum entrance are the remains of the Turaida estate, including a working smithy and exhibitions on farming and woodcraft.

Close to the castle is the Turaida Church. Built in 1750, it is one of the oldest churches in Latvia. Outside the church is a memorial to the Turaida Rose *(see p187)*. Tucked away behind the church is the Folk Song Park (Dainu kalns), where 25 sculptures celebrate the work of Krišjānis Barons *(see p151)*. Nature trails lead down slopes from the park.

Cēsis

35 km (22 miles) NE of Sigulda. from Rīga. from Rīga. Pils laukums 9, 6412 1815. www. tourism.cesis.lv **Museum of Art and History** Pils laukums 9. May–Sep: 10am–6pm daily; Oct–Apr: 10am–5pm Tue–Sun. inc New Castle.
One of the oldest towns in Latvia, Cēsis has winding streets lined with attractive wooden and stone buildings. It was once an important trading centre, becoming a member of the Hanseatic League in 1383. The town served as the headquarters of the Brothers of the Sword, and later the Livonian Order, for much of the period between 1237 and 1561.

In 1577, Ivan the Terrible took Cēsis. Further damage was inflicted during the Great Northern War and the town

Row of wooden and stone houses in the old town, Cēsis

Picturesque view of the wooden dwellings of Āraiši Lake Fortress

also witnessed extremely fierce fighting during the War of Independence (1918–20).

The Cēsis castle complex is the town's major attraction. Visitors are given builders' helmets and lanterns for the tour of the 15th- to 16th-century towers of the 13th-century Old Castle. The pink New Castle, built in 1777, is home to the **Museum of Art and History** (Cēsu vēstures un mākslas muzejs). The highlight is the well-presented "Treasures of Cēsis" exhibition. Cēsis Exhibition House (Cēsu izstāžu nams), a renovated 18th-century coach house, stands on the square in front of the New Castle. To the north, the Castle Park is a popular place to relax in the summer, while the Old Town is to the southeast of the castle.

Other attractions include the 19th-century Cēsis Brewery, although the beer is now brewed outside the town.

⛪ Āraiši Lake Fortress
10 km (6 miles) S of Cēsis. **Tel** 6410 7080. ◻ Apr–Oct: 9am–7pm daily; Nov–Mar: 9am–4pm daily. 🖼️ ✔️
Tales of sunken castles are common in Latvian folklore, appearing to stem from the 9th- to 10th-century Latgallian practice of building settlements on islets. In 1965, archaeologists found one such settlement in Lake Āraiši, now

reconstructed as a tourist sight. A wooden platform holds 16 single-room dwellings with log walls and bark roofs. Each of them could accommodate three to eight people. A clay stove was used for heating and cooking, while a small structure to the right of each doorway was used for storage or to keep cattle.

Today, guides in costume re-create the atmosphere of the settlement, and a dug-out boat can be hired. Back on shore is a ruined Livonian Order castle and several reconstructed Stone, Bronze and Iron Age dwellings.

Sign, Līgatne Education and Recreation Centre

🍃 Līgatne Education and Recreation Centre
15 km (9 miles) NE of Sigulda. 🚌 from Cēsis. **Tel** 6415 3313. ◻ May–Sep: 9am–6pm Mon–Fri, 9am–7pm Sat & Sun; Oct–Apr: 10am–5pm daily. 🖼️ **www**.gnp.lv
A wooded nature park, Līgatne Education and Recreation Park (Līgatnes mācību un atpūtas parks), is home to the likes of brown bears, lynx, beavers, elk and European bison. Large enclosures are connected by 5.5 km (3.4 miles) of walking trails and a 5-km (3-mile) route for vehicles. The site includes a 22-m (72-ft) viewing tower, horse-riding facilities, spots for campfires and several car parks. Dogs are not allowed on the trails.

THE LATVIAN FLAG

According to tradition, the Latvian national flag was born in Cēsis around 1280. The story goes that warriors from one of the Latvian tribes wrapped their dying chieftain in a white flag, which they had captured from their Estonian enemies. After a stirring speech, the chieftain died and the warriors removed the flag from his body to find that his blood had left two red stripes on it; the white stripe in the middle was where he had lain. The warriors took the new flag into battle and defeated their enemies. The present-day version of the flag was designed by artist Ansis Cīrulis in May 1917. The Museum of Art and History in Cēsis has an exhibition dedicated to the Latvian flag.

Latvian flag hoisted on the New Castle, Sigulda

Forlorn remains of the Livonian Order castle in Valmiera

Valmiera ❷

Road Map D3. 🏘 *30,000.*
🚂 *from Rīga.* 🚌 *from Cēsis.*
ℹ️ *Rīgas iela 10, 6420 7177.*
🎭 *Winter Music Festival (Jan), City Festivities (Jul), Craftsmen's Festival (Aug), St Simeon's Fair of the Middle Ages (Oct).* **www**.visit.valmiera.lv

Once a Hanseatic League member, Valmiera was founded in 1283 and has a distinguished history of trade due to its position on the Gauja river. Today, it is the second-largest city in Vidzeme after Rīga, but its old town was devastated in World War II. Most sights of interest are clustered together beside the river, just east of the city's main roundabout.

The 13th-century **St Simon's Church** (Sv Sīmaņa baznīca) has been destroyed several times and its current appearance dates from 1739. The altarpiece shows a depiction of the Temptation of Christ by Christiana Vogels-Vogelstein. Visitors can climb the church tower for a view of the city.

Just beyond the church lie the ruins of the Livonian Order castle and the **Museum of Local Studies** (Valmieras novadpētnieciības muzejs). The museum covers local history and hosts exhibitions. Close by is the city's oldest wooden building, a former pharmacy built in 1735.

🏠 **St Simon's Church**
Bruņinieku iela 2. *Tel 6420 0333.*
⏰ *11am–5pm Tue–Sun.*

🏛 **Museum of Local Studies**
Bruņinieku iela 3. *Tel 6422 3620.*
⏰ *10am–5pm Tue–Sat.* 🎫

Ainaži ❸

Road Map D2. 🏘 *1,800.*
🚌 *from Cēsis.* ℹ️ *Valdemara iela 50a, 6404 3241.*

Close to the Estonian border, Ainaži occupies a crucial place in Latvia's maritime history. For centuries, the coastline was sparsely inhabited, justifying the town's name, which is derived from the Livonian word *ainagi* meaning "solitary". However, by the 19th century, it had become an important fishing centre, and in 1864, was chosen by Krišjānis Valdemārs as the location for his naval school, which closed only in 1919 during the civil war. The original school building is now the **Naval College Museum** (Ainažu jūrskolas muzejs), which displays photographs, documents, model ships and a collection of anchors. Ainaži also boasts the **Fire-fighters' Museum** (Ainažu ugunsdzēsības muzejs). Exhibits in the main building include hand-operated water pumps, uniforms and insignia, while the garage displays fire trucks. The museum staff are former fire-fighters.

🏛 **Naval College Museum**
Valdemāra iela 47. *Tel 6404 3349.*
⏰ *May–Sep: 10am–5pm Wed–Sun; Oct–Apr: 11am–5pm Tue–Sat.* 🎫

🏛 **Fire-fighters' Museum**
Valdemāra iela 69. *Tel 6404 3280.*
⏰ *May–Sep: 10am–4pm Tue–Sat, 10am–2pm Sun; Oct–Apr: 10am–4pm Tue–Fri, 10am–2pm Sat.*

Striking snowcapped Liv Sacrificial Caves near Salacgrīva

Salacgrīva ❹

Road Map D3. 🏘 *6,000.* 🚌 *from Rīga.* ℹ️ *Rīgas iela 10a, 6404 1254.* 🎭 *Positivus (Jul).* **www**.salacgriva.lv

Positioned at the mouth of the Salaca river, the fishing port of Salacgrīva officially became a town in 1928. There is evidence that German traders may have visited the Salaca before they reached the Daugava river. Salacgrīva is a good jumping-off point for exploring the area nearby.

Environs
On the banks of the Svētupe river, 10 km (6 miles) east of town, are the **Liv Sacrificial Caves** (Lībiešu upurala). Coins and artifacts dating from the 14th to 19th centuries have been found here, and there are runes carved into the walls. The **Randu Meadows** (Randu pļavas), about 8 km (5 miles) north of Salacgrīva, are rich in birdlife and rare plants.

Nautical objects displayed in the garden of Naval College Museum, Ainaži

For hotels and restaurants in this region see pp305–7 and pp335–7

Mazsalaca ❺

Road Map D2. 🚌 from Rīga.
ℹ️ Rīgas iela 1, 2837 4774.
www.mazsalaca.lv

This sleepy town has little to detain visitors, except for the **Mazsalaca Regional Museum**, with its unusual collection of woodcarvings on a Satanic theme by Valters Hirte. It is an ideal base, though, for nearby attractions, such as the spookily named Werewolf Pine and Devil's Caves, 2 km (1 mile) from Mazsalaca, where the spring water is said to have healing powers.

Skaņaiskalns (Sound Hill), a sandstone cliff southwest of Mazsalaca, is noted for its echoes. It can be reached via a park full of wooden sculptures, which can be viewed on the drive through, but are better seen on foot. The 2-km (1-mile) path begins at the Valtenburg manor house (now a school) on Parka Street.

🏛 **Mazsalaca Regional Museum**
Rīgas iela 1. **Tel** 6425 1781.
⏰ May–Oct: 11am–4pm Wed–Sun; Nov–Apr: 11am–4pm Tue–Thu.

Carved wooden soldiers in the park leading to Skaņaiskalns, Mazsalaca

Limbaži ❻

Road Map D3. 👥 9,200. 🚌 from Rīga. ℹ️ Torņa iela 3, 6407 0608.
www.visitlimbazi.lv

Although one of Latvia's oldest towns, Limbaži has retained little of its prosperous past. The area, which was known during the 13th century as Metsepole (Indriķis in Latvian), was one of three Liv territories mentioned in the early 13th-century chronicle written by Henry of Livonia.

Orthodox Church, dating back to the early 20th century, in Limbaži

Limbaži's stone castle, built by the Brotherhood of the Sword in 1223, served as the Archbishop of Rīga's residence. A town grew up around the castle and formed part of the Hanseatic League. The castle, now in ruins, was destroyed in the 1602 Polish-Swedish War.

Offering tours of the castle ruins is the **Museum of Regional Studies** (Limbažu muzejs), with its fascinating display of artifacts that recount the region's history. Close by is the 1903 **Orthodox Church**, which still retains some of its original splendour. A statue of Kārlis Baumanis, composer of the national anthem, stands in Jūras Street.

🏛 **Museum of Regional Studies**
Burtnieku iela 7. **Tel** 6407 0632.
⏰ May–Oct: 10am–6pm Tue–Sat; Nov–Apr: 10am–5pm Tue–Sat.
📷 for castle. 📷

KRIŠJĀNIS VALDEMĀRS

One of the key figures of the Latvian National Awakening, Krišjānis Valdemārs (1825–91) was a writer, educationist, political thinker and ideologist. During his time the majority of Latvian works were written by Baltic Germans, which he sought to change. From 1862 until its suppression in 1865, Valdemārs edited a Latvian-language publication, *Pēterburgas Avīzes*, alongside Krišjānis Barons and poet Juris Alunāns, which criticized the Baltic German sense of cultural superiority. He encouraged Barons and Fricis Brīvzemnieks to start a Latvian folk songs collection (*see pp24–5*), and was instrumental in establishing the Ainaži Naval College, where tuition was free and not dependent on social status.

Valdemārs's bust, Naval Museum

House set amid idyllic scenery reflected in one of the many clear-water lakes near Dunte

Dunte ❼

Road Map D3. 🚌 *from Valmiera.*

Otherwise unremarkable, Dunte is known for the **Münchausen Museum** dedicated to Karl Friedrich Hieronymus von Münchhausen (1720–97). An officer in the Russian cavalry, Baron Münchhausen married a local woman and visited Dunte on his honeymoon. He became unwittingly famous when a collection of fantastical stories featuring him was published anonymously in 1781, and his association with exaggeration continues to this day. Museum staff dress in period costumes, and one room is a fanciful reconstruction of his wife's boudoir. A screen shows a 1943 German film adaptation of his tales. Upstairs are waxworks of famous Latvians.

🏛 **Münchausen Museum**
Duntes Manor. *Tel* 6406 5633. ⭘
*May–Oct: 10am–5pm daily (to 6pm
Sat & Sun); Nov–Apr: 10am–5pm Sat
& Sun, by appt Wed–Fri.* 🖼 🎞 🏠

Saulkrasti ❽

Road Map D3. 🏠 5,550.
🚆 *from Rīga.* 🚌 *from Rīga.*
ℹ *Ainažu iela 13b, 6795 2641.*
🎭 *Town Festival (Jul), International
Jazz Festival (Jul), Organ Music
Festival (Sep).* **www**.saulkrasti.lv

A seaside resort since the 19th century, Saulkrasti is little more than a string of

homes and guest houses along the main road. Nonetheless, it remains a popular getaway for Rīga residents. The main activity is walking along the coastline, and a trail stretching for 4 km (2 miles) has several viewing points, including a platform on the White Dune (Baltā kāpa). The privately owned **Bicycle Museum** (Saulkrastu velosipēdu muzejs) is housed in a large shed in the owners' garden. The superb collection, a work of many years, features oddities such as a wooden bicycle made by an aeroplane engineer. There are also mock-ups of a workshop used for repairs and a shop of bicycle parts.

Cycle badges at Bicycle Museum, Saulkrasti

🏛 **Bicycle Museum**
Rīgas iela 44a. *Tel* 2888 3160.
⭘ *call in advance.* 🖼

Ikšķile ❾

Road Map D3. 🏠 6,250.
🚆 *from Rīga.* 🚌 *from Rīga.*

In the mid-12th century, the Augustinian monk Father Meinhard, the first Bishop of Ikšķile, accompanied German merchants along the Daugava river. He built **St Mary's Church** here, the first church in the territories of Latvia's tribes. The local Livs resisted being converted to Christianity and Meinhard made little headway. The church was the first stone building in the Baltics, and its ruins have been covered with a metal roof to protect them from the elements. Following the construction of a hydroelectric dam on the river, the ruins stand on an island, although there is nothing much to see.

Ruins of St Mary's Church in Ikšķile, one of Latvia's earliest churches

Lielvārde ⓾

Road Map D4. ⚑ 7,350. ⊞ from Rīga. ⓘ Edgara Kauliņa aleja 20, 6505 3759. 🎦 Regional Festival (Jul), Birthday of Andrejs Pumpurs (Sep). **www**.lielvarde.lv

The town of Lielvārde is best known as the site of the climactic battle between the heroic Lāčplēsis and the Black Knight. The conflict ended when the two warriors disappeared into the Daugava river close to an early 13th-century castle, the ruins of which stand on a hillock. Tall wooden sculptures nearby illustrate Lāčplēsis's story, while a pair of large stones are said to be the bed and blanket of the hero, who reputedly returns to the bank each night to sleep.

Also close to the river is the **Andrejs Pumpurs Museum** (Andreja Pumpura muzejs), dedicated to the eminent writer. A small display is devoted to *Lielvārdes josta*. These belts, used in traditional weddings, are for sale at the museum.

At the western end of town is **Uldevena Castle** (Uldevena pils), a reconstruction of a wooden Liv fortification. It was built in 1997 to the design of a local artist and takes elements from other structures, thus representing an "ideal" rather than a single castle.

Wooden sculpture of Lāčplēsis

🏛 **Andrejs Pumpurs Museum**
E Kauliņa aleja 20. **Tel** 6505 3759.
◷ 10am–5pm Tue–Sun (Nov–Apr: 11am–3pm Sun). 🎦 🅿

♣ **Uldevena Castle**
Parka iela 3. **Tel** 2946 5792. ◷ Apr–Nov: 10am–6pm Thu–Sun. 🎦 🅿

Skrīveri ⓫

Road Map D4. ⊞ from Rīga. ⓘ A Upīša 1, 2837 3530. **www**.skriveri.lv

Although the town has a long history, Skrīveri was devastated during World War I. Its main attraction is the **Andrejs Upīts Memorial Museum** (Andreja Upīša memoriālmajā), which draws visitors interested in Latvian literature. The exhibition about the noted author, critic and Communist polemicist is displayed in his former home. The **Tree Park** (Dendroloģiskais parks) close to Skrīveri is a pleasant place to wander, its paths running through almost 400 species of trees from around the world. Each tree has been tagged with both its Latvian and Latin names and, except for the occasional dog-walker, it is a surprisingly quiet

🏛 **Andrejs Upīts Memorial Museum**
Daugavas iela 58. **Tel** 6519 7221.
◷ mid-May–Oct: 10am–5pm Tue–Sun. 🎦 **www**.upisamuzejs.lv

ANDREJS PUMPURS AND LĀČPLĒSIS

Born in Birzgale, close to Lielvārde, Andrejs Pumpurs (1841–1902) was an unlikely literary figure. Working on the land before volunteering to fight in Serbia against the Ottoman Empire in 1876, he became a loyal officer in the Russian army but was also a staunch promoter of Latvian culture. Convinced of the need for a national epic, he chose the folk story of Lāčplēsis the Bear Slayer, whose mixed animal-human parentage is evident in his bear-like ears. Pumpurs also drew from Latvian folklore to create a strongly allegorical plot filled with demons and witches. Lāčplēsis defeats the Estonian giant Kalapuisis and convinces him of the need to work together against their foreign foes. Towards the end of the epic, Lāčplēsis unites the Latvian people and repels the invaders, but the wicked turncoat Kangars reveals the hero's secret – his strength is in his ears. The Black Knight, a Germanic giant, cuts off Lāčplēsis's ears, plunging Latvia into 700 long years of misery. The story goes that Lāčplēsis will rise again after he defeats his rival.

Mural of Lāčplēsis and Laimdota at the Andrejs Pumpurs Museum

Koknese ⓬

Road Map D4. ⊞ from Rīga. ⊞ ⓘ Melioratoru iela 1, 6516 1296. 🎦 International Folk Music Festival (Jul). **www**.koknese.lv

Once the main settlement of the Selonian tribe, which was subjugated by the Livonian Order in 1208, Koknese also appears in the tale of Lāčplēsis as the home of Laimdota – the beautiful and virtuous young woman with whom the hero falls in love. Today, the picturesque ruins of the Livonian Order castle, built in 1209 but destroyed during the Great Northern War (1700–21), makes Koknese popular with visitors. The site was even more attractive before a hydroelectric power station was built on the Daugava river in 1965.

Livonian Order castle with the Daugava river in the distance, Koknese

Neo-Byzantine St Nicholas's Orthodox Church in Jēkabpils

Jēkabpils 🔞

Road Map D4. 🏛 *28,000.*
🚌 *from Rīga.* 🚍 *from Rīga,*
Daugavpils. 🛈 *Brīvības iela 140/142,*
6523 3822. **www**.jekabpils.lv

Founded as a settlement for
Old Believers *(see p122),*
Jēkabpils received town rights
from Jakob Kettler, Duke of
Courland *(see p135),* in 1670.

In the town centre, the Neo-
Byzantine **St Nicholas's
Orthodox Church** (Sv Nikolaja
pareizticīgo baznīca) was built
in 1910. Close by, the large
private **Mans's Gallery** was one
of the first to open in post-
Soviet Latvia. East of the centre,
the **Selian Farmstead** (Sēļu
sēta) is an open-air museum
with 19th-century buildings,
including a farmhouse, a
smithy and a windmill.

On the opposite side of
the Daugava river lies the
13th-century **Krustpils Castle**
(Krustpils pils). Destroyed
during the Livonian Wars
(1558–82), it was reconstructed in 1585 and modified in
1849. Though the castle is
largely dilapidated, several of

its rooms have been restored,
and one of them displays
Russian military memorabilia.

**🏠 St Nicholas's
Orthodox Church**
Brīvības iela 202. **Tel** *6522 3886.*

🏛 Mans's Gallery
Brīvības iela 154. **Tel** *6523 1953.* 🕐
9am–6pm Mon–Sat. **www**.manss.lv

🏛 Selian Farmstead
Filozofu iela 6. **Tel** *6522 1042.*
🕐 *May–Oct: 9am–6pm Mon–Fri,*
10am–5pm Sat & Sun. 🖼

♣ Krustpils Castle
Rīgas iela 216b. **Tel** *6522 1042.*
🕐 *May–Oct: daily; Nov–Apr: Mon–*
Sat. **www**.jekabpilsmuzejs.lv

Līvāni 🔞

Road Map E4. 🏛 *11,000.* 🚌
🛈 *Domes iela 1b, 6538 1856.* 🖼
Town Festival (Jul), International Folk
Festival (Sep). **www**.livani.lv

With a long history as an
industrial centre, Līvāni takes
pride in its glass factory,
which opened in 1887. The
on-site **Glass Museum** (Stikla
muzejs) offers glass-blowing
demonstrations. During the

post-war era, the Soviet
regime built large biochemical
and construction facilities,
many of which became
obsolete after independence.
Recent efforts to improve the
town's fortunes include the
establishment of the **Latgale
Art and Craft Centre**, which
hosts exhibitions, besides con-
ducting ceramics and weaving
workshops for visitors.

🏛 Glass Museum
Domes 1b. **Tel** *6538 1855.* 🕐 *Jun–*
Aug: Tue–Sun; Sep–May: Tue–Sat.
🖼 🛈 **www**.latgalesamatnieki.lv

**🏛 Latgale Art and
Craft Centre**
Domes 1. **Tel** *6538 1855.*
🕐 *Tue–Sat.* 🖼 🛈

Daugavpils 🔞

See pp196–7.

Krāslava 🔞

Road Map E4. 🏛 *11,500.* 🚌 *from*
Daugavpils. 🛈 *Brīvības iela 13, 6562*
2201. **www**.visitkraslava.com

Attractively set alongside the
Daugava river, the town of
Krāslava is largely composed
of two-storey wooden buildings. Although there are few
specific sights to draw visitors,
it is a pleasant place to visit.

Standing on an artificial hill,
the 1750 Baroque Krāslava
Castle (Krāslavas pils) houses
the **Krāslava Museum**, dedicated to local arts and history.
The Catholic church (Katoļu
baznīca) stands on the town's
other hill. It is the finest of
the Baroque buildings in
Latgale. Its imposing fresco,
depicting St Ludovik leaving

Panoramic view of Krāslava town, with rows of pretty houses along the Daugava river

For hotels and restaurants in this region see pp305–7 and pp335–7

for the crusades, was painted by the Italian artist Philippo Kastaldi in the 18th century.

🏛 Krāslava Museum
Pils iela 8. **Tel** 6562 3586. ☐ May–Aug: Wed–Sun; Sep–Apr: Tue–Sat. ♿

Dazzling exterior of the majestic Aglona Basilica

Aglona ⑰

Road Map E4. 🚌 from Rīga. 🛈 Somersetas 34, 6532 2100. 🎉 Feast of the Assumption (15 Aug).

Catholic pilgrims from across the Baltic region and Russia flock to this otherwise unremarkable town to visit **Aglona Basilica** and attend the Feast of the Assumption. Lithuanian members of the Dominican Order were invited by a local landowner to build a monastery and school in 1697. The basilica, then a church, was built in the 18th century. Pope John Paul II declared it a basilica in 1980, marking the 200th anniversary of its completion, and visited it in 1993. The basilica is famous for its early 17th-century icon of the Virgin Mary, brought by the Dominicans and said to have healing powers. It is hidden behind a lesser icon, which slides down only during special services.

Preiļi ⑱

Road Map E4. 🚶 10,000. 🚌 from Rīga. 🛈 Kārsavas iela 4, 6532 2041. **www**.preili.lv

From about 1475 until 1866, the market town of Preiļi was under the control of the Borgh family, who were originally from Southern Italy. The most recent of the family's three manor houses still stands but is in poor condition. In the gatekeeper's house, the **History and Applied Arts Museum** (Preiļu vēstures un lientišķ mākslas muzejs) has exhibits including old photographs of the town and samples of the pottery for which Preiļi is renowned. More local ceramics can be found – and bought – at the **P Čerņavskis Pottery Workshop-Museum** (P Čerņavska keramikas darbnīca-muzejs). The late 19th-century **Roman Catholic Church** (Romas katoļu bazīca) contains an 18th-century crucifix, and two sculptures stand outside; one is dedicated to Mother Latvia and the other is a monument to the politically repressed during the Soviet regime.

Jug, Latgale Culture and History Museum

🏛 History and Applied Arts Museum
Raiņa 28. **Tel** 6532 2731. ☐ 11am–6pm Tue–Fri, 10am–4pm Sat. ♿

🏛 P Čerņavskis Workshop-Museum
Talsu iela 21. **Tel** 6532 2946. ☐ by appointment.

⛪ Roman Catholic Church
Tirgus laukums 11. **Tel** 6532 2041. ☐ by appointment.

Rēzekne ⑲

Road Map E4. 🚶 37,000. 🚌 from Rīga. 🚌 from Daugavpils. 🛈 Krasta iela 31, 6460 5005. **www**.rezekne.lv

Although most of its old buildings were destroyed during World War II, Rēzekne is one of the cultural centres of the Latgale region and also serves as good base for visiting the area's lakes.

The best-known sight, *Latgales Māra*, a statue created by Leons Tomašickis, stands in the centre of a large roundabout on Atbrīvošanas Avenue. The religious iconography of the statue depicting the pagan goddess Māra holding aloft a Christian cross may be ambiguous but the politics are not: the plinth simply reads "*Vienoti Latvija*" ("United for Latvia"). Unveiled in 1939, it commemorates the 1917 meeting in Rēzekne which decided that Latgale would no longer remain a part of Russia's Vitebsk province. Removed by the Russian authorities in 1940, the statue was reinstated by the occupying German army. Destroyed in 1950, the statue was rebuilt by Tomašickis's son after Latvia gained its independence in 1991. The inauguration of the replica took place in 1992.

Just north of the statue is the **Latgale Culture and History Museum** (Latgales kultūrvēstures muzejs), which focuses on the ceramics of the region, including traditional branched candelabra. South of the statue, on a small mound with excellent views of a Catholic church, are the ruins of the city's castle.

🏛 Latgale Culture and History Museum
Atbrīvošanas aleja 102. **Tel** 6462 2464. ☐ May–Sep: Wed–Sun; Oct–Apr: Tue–Sat. ♿

Exhibits displayed inside the History and Applied Arts Museum, Preiļi

Daugavpils ⑮

The second-most populous city in Latvia, Daugavpils is often regarded as a "Russian city" as the majority of its residents are Russian. Its history can be traced to 1275 and a Livonian Order castle called Dinaburga. In the 16th century, a settlement grew on the banks of the Daugava river, and was occupied by Poles, Russians and Swedes at various times. When the town was developed into a Tsarist fortress in the early 19th century, civilians were relocated southeast to the land that today forms the city centre. An industrial hub for the erstwhile Soviet Union, Daugavpils has suffered from economic neglect since independence, though the city's image is improving.

Stately exterior of the Museum of Regional Studies and Arts

🏛 Museum of Regional Studies and Arts

Rīgas iela 8. **Tel** 6542 4155.
⏱ 10am–6pm Tue–Sat. 📷
📷 📷 www.dnmm.lv

Housed in an attractive building dating from 1883, this museum is dedicated to local history from the 9th century BC to the present day, but focusing on the period between the second half of the 18th century and 1918. Paintings by the city's second-most famous artist, Leonīds Bauļins, occupy one room, while other rooms detail regional flora and fauna.

🔯 Synagogue

Cietokšņa 42. **Tel** 6542 0092.
⬜ by appointment.

Prior to World War I, over half of the town's population was Jewish. There were at one time 48 synagogues, of which only one remains in use. It was renovated in 2006 with the help of Mark Rothko's children, who had visited it in 2003, the centenary of their father's birth.

🔓 Cathedral of Sts Boris and Glebe

Tautas iela 2. **Tel** 6545 3544.

This blue-and-white building, resplendent with its ten golden cupolas, is the largest Russian Orthodox cathedral in the country. Built in 1905, it is named after the two saints on whose feast day the Russian army entered Daugavpils in 1656. The Russian name for the town, Borisoglebsk, was also taken from the saints' names. The icons and frescoes inside were copied from those in Sophia Cathedral in Kiev.

🔓 St Mary's Church

Puškina 16a. ⬜ services only. 📷

A solid pink structure with diminutive blue domes, this Old Believers' *(see p122)* church is rarely open to public. Visitors may, however, be able to look inside during services, when candles are lit in front of the dozens of icons that line the walls. The solemn chanting of the congregation adds to the atmosphere.

MARK ROTHKO (1903–70)

Mark Rothko was born Marcus Rothkowitz into a Jewish family in Daugavpils at a time when the Russian Empire was scarred by pogroms. His family emigrated to Portland, Oregon, in 1913. He received a scholarship to study at Yale University, but left after two years and trained in

art in New York. Rothko changed his name in 1940, and by 1950 he developed a unique style, in which soft-edged rectangular forms are aligned in front of coloured backgrounds. They are described as Abstract Expressionist, although Rothko insisted that he was interested in pure form. Following an aneurysm and the breakdown of his marriage, Rothko committed suicide in 1970.

Mark Rothko, Abstract Expressionist

Beautiful interior of the Cathedral of Sts Boris and Glebe

Rose-coloured façade of St Mary's Church

Martin Luther Church

18 Novembra iela 66. **Tel** 2957 4349. ☐ *Sun or by appointment.*
This red-brick, Neo-Gothic church dates from 1893 but has been completely renovated. During the Soviet regime, it was used as a boxing gym.

Virgin Mary Catholic Church

A Pumpura 11a. ☐ *evening mass.*
According to local legend the daughters of a rich merchant drowned in a lake on the spot where the church now stands.

VISITORS' CHECKLIST

Road Map E4. 🏘 *110,000.*
🚉 *Rīgas iela.* 🚌 *Viestura iela 10.*
ℹ *Rīgas 22a, 6542 2818.*
🎪 *City Festival (Jun).*

♠ Daugavpils Fortress

Cietokšņa iela. **Tel** 6542 4043.
☐ *8am–6pm.* 🎟
The construction of this self-contained Russian fortress began in 1810 but was interrupted when Napoleon's army attacked in July 1812. It is surrounded by earth walls. The moat encircling it once contained tunnels that connected it to the Daugava river, but they have since been blocked. The fortress served as a German concentration camp and was later occupied by the Soviet Army until 1993. While much of the fortress is now neglected and overgrown, the area is being rejuvenated. The Mark Rothko Art Centre, located in the former arsenal building, houses an artists' residence and provides space for exhibitions, as well as displaying original works by the world-famous artist, which were donated by his children. Guided tours and maps are available from the renovated water tower that now houses the fortress's culture and information centre.

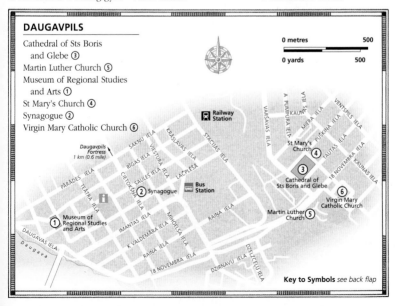

DAUGAVPILS

Cathedral of Sts Boris and Glebe ③
Martin Luther Church ⑤
Museum of Regional Studies and Arts ①
St Mary's Church ④
Synagogue ②
Virgin Mary Catholic Church ⑥

0 metres 500
0 yards 500

Daugavpils Fortress 1 km (0.6 mile)

Railway Station
Bus Station

St Mary's Church ④
Cathedral of Sts Boris and Glebe ③
Virgin Mary Catholic Church ⑥
Martin Luther Church ⑤
Museum of Regional Studies and Arts ①
Synagogue ②

Key to Symbols *see back flap*

Latgale Lakes ⑳

Latvia's relatively hilly southeastern corner, known as the Latgale Uplands (Latgales augstiene), is covered with a patchwork of more than 800 lakes. On a sunny day it is easy to see why this part is called the Land of Blue Lakes. Unfortunately, public transport is limited here, although if time permits the area can be explored by bus. The route also passes through Rēzekne, where the tourist office can provide advice on activities such as angling and bird-watching in the area, and a trip to Ludza en route is also possible.

Lake Lubāns, one of Latvia's favourite spots for bird-watchers

Lake Lubāns ⑧
One of the best places for bird-watching and fishing in the country, this is Latvia's largest lake by surface area.

Musical Instruments Workshop, Gaiglava ⑥
Visitors can watch artisans at work and learn to play traditional instruments.

Teirumnīki ⑦
A boardwalk circles the lake and runs through a swamp where cranberries grow.

Rēzekne ⑤
The cultural centre of Latgale, Rēzekne is known for its statue of pagan goddess Māra.

Mākoņkalns ③
Cloud Hill, at 248 m (814 ft), is a popular viewpoint, with ruins of a castle on the summit.

Lake Rāzna ④
The largest in Latvia by volume, Lake Rāzna offers a number of decent accommodation options.

KEY

ℹ️ Visitor information
▬ Tour route
⋯ Other road

Lielais Liepukalns ②
At 289 m (948 ft), this hill is the highest point in the region and the third-highest in the country.

Lake Ežezers ①
Translated as "Hedgehog Lake", Lake Ežezers is considered one of the most beautiful lakes in Latgale. Its 36 islands can be explored by boat.

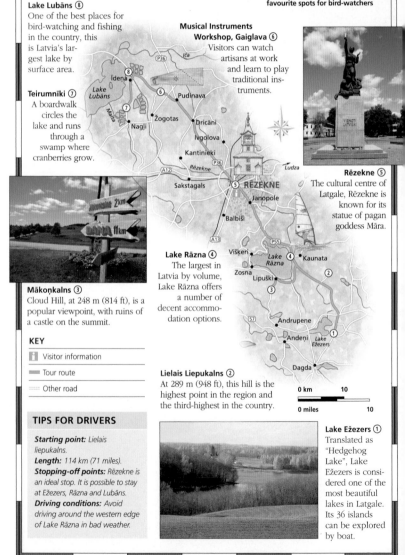

0 km   10

0 miles   10

TIPS FOR DRIVERS

Starting point: Lielais liepukalns.
Length: 114 km (71 miles).
Stopping-off points: Rēzekne is an ideal stop. It is possible to stay at Ežezers, Rāzna and Lubāns.
Driving conditions: Avoid driving around the western edge of Lake Rāzna in bad weather.

Ludza ㉑

Road Map E3. 🏘 10,500. 🚉
🚌 ℹ️ *Baznicas 42, 2946 7925.* ⛴

Perhaps the oldest town in Latvia, Ludza traces its foundation back to about 1177. The central square is home to the tourist information office and the Orthodox Cathedral.

The **Handicrafts Centre** (Ludzas amatnieku centrs), close to the central square, has a potter's kiln and space for artisans. Visitors can participate in workshops by prior arrangement. Handicraft objects are on sale here as well. There is also a monthly food and crafts market.

The town's **Museum of Local Studies** (Ludzas novadpētniecības muzejs) occupies the former villa of Jakov Kulnev (1764–1812), a Russian war hero who lived in Ludza. The grounds contain late 19th- and early 20th-century wooden buildings from various parts of Latgale.

🏛 **Handicrafts Centre**
Tālavijas iela 27a. *Tel 2946 7925.* ◯
Mon–Sat. **www**.ludzasamatnieki.lv

🏛 **Museum of Local Studies**
Kulneva iela 2. *Tel 6572 3931.*
◯ Mon–Sat. 📷

Vecpiebalga ㉒

Road Map D3. 🚌 ℹ️ *2611 0724.*
www.vecpiebalga.lv

With a history dating back to the early 14th century, this small town is famed as the home of prominent cultural figures. Notable among them were the brothers, Reinis (1839–1920) and Matīss Kaudzīte (1848–1926), who wrote *Mērnieku laiki* (The Times of the Land Surveyors). Among the best-loved Latvian novels, it is based on the sale of a landlord's estates to peasant farmers. The authors' home is now the **Kaudzīte Brothers Memorial Museum**.

Environs
There are other interesting sites close to Vecpiebalga. The Kārlis Skalbe Museum is about 4 km (2 miles) from the town. It occupies the

Statue of Liena, heroine of
***Mērnieku laiki*, in Vecpiebalga**

summerhouse of revolutionary writer Kārlis Skalbe (1878–1945). Further along the road is the Janskola Museum, housed in the former home of composer Emīls Dārziņš (1875–1910). The displays include works by Latvian poet Janis Sudrabkalns (1894–1975).

🏛 **Kaudzīte Brothers Memorial Museum**
Kalna kaibēni. *Tel 2618 5382.*
◯ mid-May–mid-Oct: daily. 📷

Alūksne ㉓

Road Map E3. 🏘 9,500. 🚉 *from Gulbene.* 🚌 *from Cēsis.* ℹ️ *Pils 25a, 6432 2804.* **www**.aluksne.lv

In 1342, the Knights of the Sword built a castle on an island in Lake Alūksne, after destroying the existing fortress. The Swedish army demolished the castle in 1702 rather than let it fall into Russian hands. Alūksne is best known for

its association with Ernst Glück (1654–1705), a German Lutheran clergyman who was the first to translate the Bible into Latvian. His home has been turned into the **Ernst Glück Museum of the Bible**.

The Museum of Local Studies and Art is housed in a manor house built in 1861 for Baron Vietinghoff. There are displays on local history, arts and crafts, and the museum can also arrange excursions.

🏛 **Ernst Glück Museum of the Bible**
Pils 25a. *Tel 6432 3164.* ◯ mid-May–mid-Oct: Tue–Sat; mid-Oct–mid-May: by appointment. 📷

Gulbene–Alūksne Narrow-Gauge Railway ㉔

Road Map E3. *Tel 6447 3037.*
🎏 *Railway Festival (first Sat in Sep).*
www.banitis.lv

This 33-km (21-mile) stretch of railway track constitutes the only functioning narrow-gauge railway within Latvia. The 90-minute journey has stops en route, including Stāmeriena, which has a manor house, and Umernieki.

The **Ates Mill Museum** is the primary incentive for visiting Umernieki. Around the mill is an ethnographic museum, consisting of 13 buildings which have been brought from around Vidzeme.

🏛 **Ates Mill Museum**
Ate, Kalncempji village. *Tel 2940 0393.* ◯ Tue–Sun (Nov–Apr: closed Sun). 📷 ♿ 🎏 Harvest Festival (Sep).

Old Soviet steam engine locomotive at Gulbene railway station

LITHUANIA

Lithuania at a Glance

An unblemished natural landscape of rolling hills, Lithuania is blessed with thousands of lakes that create a complex network of streams and rivers. In this low-lying post-glacial countryside, almost all the land lies at less than 200 m (656 ft) above sea level. The eastern half of the country is known as the "highlands" and the western half the "lowlands". The main features of the Lithuanian coast are its fascinating sandy dunes and beaches. Despite Lithuania's tumultuous history, many of the country's fine historic buildings have survived.

Hill of Crosses
(see p273)

Palanga (see p282)
is a popular beach resort that draws hundreds of visitors each summer. Once a quiet little fishing hamlet, today it is a vibrant place filled with innumerable bars and cafés.

WESTERN LITHUANIA
(see pp268–85)

Pažaislis Monastery
(see p261)

Parnidis Dune *towers over the fishing village of Nida, on the Curonian Spit (see pp284–5). Views from the summit take in both the Baltic Sea and the Curonian Lagoon and stretch southwards to Kaliningrad.*

◁ Statue of Jesus Christ amid thousands of crosses left by visitors on the Hill of Crosses, Western Lithuania

Kernavė (see p254) *is a UNESCO World Heritage Site, set in the Neris River Valley. Once the capital of the Grand Duchy of Lithuania, it is now one of the largest archaeological sites in the Baltic region. The state museum, established here in 1989, was converted into a cultural reserve in 2004.*

Vilnius Cathedral (see pp224–5), *a Neo-Classical structure, houses the lavish Baroque Chapel of St Casimir and a crypt that provides an insight into Lithuania's complex history.*

CENTRAL LITHUANIA
(see pp248–67)

VILNIUS
(see pp216–47)

Trakai Island Castle (see pp252–3), *in the picturesque village of Trakai, is a fairytale fortress that makes a beautiful day-trip from the capital during any season of the year. An optional trip by yacht or rowing boat rounds off the experience.*

0 km   25

0 miles   25

A PORTRAIT OF LITHUANIA

The largest of the three Baltic States and one of the hidden jewels of Europe, Lithuania takes pride in its relatively secluded landscape of clean lakes, ancient forests and coastal dunes. The capital Vilnius, which has a UNESCO-protected Old Town, combines the romance of its breathtaking Baroque architecture with the modern trappings of 21st-century Europe.

Lithuania successfully repelled the Germanic invaders as early as 1410 at the Battle of Grünwald. In the subsequent centuries, however, the country experienced a tumultuous series of invasions. Most recently, the two World Wars and the massacre of one of Europe's largest Jewish communities were followed by the neglect of the Soviet era.

The Vytis, emblem of Lithuania

Since its independence in 1991, Lithuania has strived to restore its national identity. Its capital Vilnius possesses one of Europe's finest old towns, with several Baroque masterpieces. Across the country, areas of serene natural beauty have become protected reserves teeming with wildlife. Excellent roads wind through attractive villages and towns that are remarkably tranquil. A resurgence in the popularity of folk culture is colouring every corner of the country, with wooden crosses, altars and shrines being crafted and folk song and dance traditions being explored. An explosion of printed and electronic materials in Lithuanian, a language related to Sanskrit, has taken place since the Singing Revolution (1987–90). At the same time, Lithuania is forging a positive political and cultural role for itself in the expanded European Union.

A sweeping view of Parnidis Dune, or the Great Dune, in the Curonian Spit National Park

◁ Dancers in traditional dress at a concert, Vilnius University

Catholics worshipping the Virgin Mary in Vilnius

ETHNIC AND RELIGIOUS IDENTITY

Lithuania is the most ethnically homogeneous of the Baltic countries. By staying largely agrarian it managed to stem the incoming tide of large numbers of Russians and other nationalities whom the Soviet authorities wanted to man the new factories being built across the Baltic region. Of its population of 3.3 million, 84 per cent are Lithuanian, while only 4.9 per cent are Russian and 6 per cent Polish. Other minorities include Belarusians and Ukrainians, besides a small group of Tatars and Karaim. In Vilnius, the most ethnically diverse city, Russian and Polish can commonly be heard.

Despite its pagan past, Lithuania has a strong Catholic identity that sets it apart from Estonia and Latvia, where the Germans introduced Lutheranism. The efforts of the Soviet authorities to stamp out religious worship by converting churches into warehouses, cinemas, art galleries and museums, destroying their interiors and deporting large numbers of priests to Siberia, failed. As a result, only 10 per cent of the people do not identify with any religious group today. Religious groups other than Catholics include Russian Orthodox (5 per cent) and small communities of Old Believers and Lutherans.

POLITICS

Since regaining independence in 1991, Lithuania has vacillated between left- and right-wing governments, while struggling to find its feet on the international stage. Achieving the goals of NATO and EU membership in 2004 was of huge significance for the Baltic region, wrenching it away from Russia's influence. The impeachment of President Rolandas Paksas for violating the constitution, also in 2004, was the climax of a wave of public scepticism in politics.

A Lithuanian folk dance group dressed in national costume

Former Lithuanian President Valdas Adamkus

High-profile corruption cases revealing how politicians have lobbied on behalf of business interests in exchange for money have created the feeling that moral leadership in Lithuania is waning. Some politicians, however, including two-time president Valdas Adamkus, remained untainted by scandal.

ECONOMY

The Lithuanian economy is one of the fastest-growing in Europe. A dynamic private sector feeds strongly on niche industries including laser optics and biotechnology, as well as core industries such as construction and energy. Lithuanian laser and biotech companies are among the strongest in Europe. Lithuania's largest company by turnover is the Mažeikių Nafta oil refinery near Mažeikiai. The Soviet-era Ignalina Nuclear Power Plant has been decommissioned, but a new nuclear power plant is likely to be constructed to reduce reliance on Russian energy.

Agriculture was rapidly privatized after independence, and heavily subsidized after EU membership. Although this has made much of the land more productive, negative results include large swathes of abandoned land and widespread rural poverty. However, ways are being found to invest in sustainable industries such as tourism. Many small farms have been turned into attractive countryside farmsteads providing tourist activities and accommodation.

MODERN LIFE

The countless art galleries in the cities and towns reveal the importance of art and culture to Lithuania. The walls of most households are adorned with real paintings and graphics rather than framed reproductions. Cultural figures, such as M K Čiurlionis and adored novelist and painter Jurga Ivanauskaitė, have apportioned their skills to more than one medium. Symphonies, chamber concerts, classical ballets and operas are performed regularly throughout the country. On the stage, the dark, post-industrial version of *Hamlet*, by acclaimed theatre director Eimuntas Nekrošius, is one of the most popular theatrical pieces.

In sport, although Lithuania has produced achievers such as the discus-thrower Virgilijus Alekna and ice-dancer Margarita Drobiazko, basketball remains its national obsession. While the Kaunas-based Žalgiris team and Vilnius-based Lietuvos Rytas team dominate the domestic scene, the Lithuanian Olympic basketball team has put Lithuania on the world map.

The 2006 Euroleague basketball match in progress

LITHUANIA THROUGH THE YEAR

Lithuanians celebrate a host of festivals where traditional events and folk culture blend with ancient pagan and Catholic rituals. Most of the year's events take place in summer, when after months of wintry gloom the country comes alive with music, dance, cinema, folk culture, handicraft and food festivals. Music is at the centre of most of the country's events, and it ranges from classical, jazz and blues to electronic and contemporary. Christmas is usually white but the thick snows fail to thwart the merrymaking, which culminates in New Year's Eve celebrations. A number of commemorative days are observed in addition to the traditional annual events.

Lithuanian accordonist

Kaziuko Crafts Fair, held every year to mark St Casimir's Day

SPRING

Lithuanians welcome spring with joyful celebrations. The warmer weather wakes the country up to a new season of fairs and festivals.

MARCH

Kaziuko Crafts Fair *(4 Mar)*, Vilnius. A feast of traditional arts and crafts marking St Casimir's Day, with stalls selling all manner of curios.
Cinema Spring *(late Mar–early Apr)*, Vilnius. One of the largest international film festivals in the Baltic region, it showcases the best foreign-language films of the year, most with English subtitles.

APRIL

Garso Galerija, Vilnius. A festival of new electronic music, often featuring radical international songwriters.
Kaunas Jazz *(late Apr)*. One of the best international jazz festivals in the country.

MAY

New Baltic Dance *(early May)*, Vilnius and Klaipėda. This eclectic event celebrates modern dance and theatre.
Poetry Spring, Vilnius. An international poetry festival and the most outstanding annual literary event in Lithuania.
Kaunas City Day *(20 May)*. A folk art fair with concerts, funfairs and fireworks.

Local folk dressed in traditional costume, Kaunas City Day festival

SUMMER

The sultry Lithuanian summer initiates great festivities. Classical music takes precedence in the warm evenings, along with jazz and blues.

JUNE

Cow-Swimming Festival, Aukštaitija National Park. A quirky custom where locals dress in folk costumes and watch as cows wearing wreaths are led into a lake to swim to the other side.
Medieval Festival, Trakai. Knights' fights with swords and battleaxes are the festival's highlight.
Joninės *(24 Jun)*. The summer solstice is celebrated all over Lithuania on St John's Day. It is also known as Rasos, meaning "of the dew", for dew's healing properties.
Pažaislis Music Festival *(Jun–Aug)*, Kaunas. Hosted at the Baroque Pažaislis Monastery, it stages music performances.

JULY

Christopher Summer Festival *(Jul–Aug)*, Vilnius. A hugely enjoyable musical fiesta with performances at different venues all over the city.
Statehood Day *(6 Jul)*. Pomp and ceremony are the hallmarks of this national holiday dedicated to the coronation of King Mindaugas.
Lake Lukštas Blues Nights features blues and jazz performers with the isolated Lake Lukštas as the backdrop.

Guards at the Presidential Palace in Vilnius, on Statehood Day

Sea Festival *(late Jul)*, Klaipėda. The freedom of the seas expressed in a carnival.

AUGUST

Christopher's Guitars, Vilnius. A festival featuring classical guitar and flamenco concerts as its highlight.

Mėnuo Juodaragis *(late Aug)*. Translated as "Black Horned Moon", this annual musical event of folk, metal and electronica is held in a different location every 3 years.

Capital Days *(late Aug–Sep)*, Vilnius. A multi-art event when Gedimino Avenue is flooded with craft and food stalls, while the squares of central Vilnius become rock and pop music venues.

AUTUMN

Autumn, which is from mid-September to December, is a visual treat. However, there are fewer annual events.

SEPTEMBER

Sirenos Theatre Festival *(Sep–Oct)*, Vilnius. Works by international and local artists are showcased.

Mushroom Festival *(late Sep)*, Varėna. The only traditional festival dedicated to mushrooms in Europe.

Fire Sculptures Festival *(21–23 Sep)*. Straw figures are set alight at night in this festival that honours Grand Duke Gediminas and also celebrates the autumn equinox.

OCTOBER

International Festival of Modern Dance *(early Oct)*, Kaunas. A festival of free-style contemporary dance, it attracts the best dancers from all over the world.

Vilnius Jazz *(mid-Oct)*. Jazz, blues and swing are performed by a host of talented contemporary Lithuanian musicians and singers at this festival.

WINTER

Lithuania looks stunning in winter. The country is often covered in a blanket of snow. However, the chill fails to curb the festive spirit.

NOVEMBER

Scanorama *(mid-Nov)*, Vilnius. Ten days of Scandinavian films take over the capital's multiplexes for this annual film festival.

DECEMBER

Christmas *(24–26 Dec)*. The festivities culminate in most homes with a 12-course meat-free meal on Christmas Eve. Christmas Day is celebrated with mass in church, and concerts.

New Year's Eve *(31 Dec)*. Celebrations and parties take place throughout the country, and at the stroke of midnight fireworks light up the sky.

JANUARY

Epiphany *(6 Jan)*, Vilnius. Shortly after New Year, a colourful procession of the Three Kings graces the streets of the Old Town.

FEBRUARY

Užgavėnės *(mid-Feb)*. People throughout Lithuania don masks of witches, devils, goats and other creatures and feast on heartwarmingly rich food in this farewell to winter.

PUBLIC HOLIDAYS

New Year's Day (1 Jan)
Independence Day (16 Feb)
Restoration of Independence (11 Mar)
Easter (Mar/April)
Labour Day (1 May)
Midsummer's Day (23 Jun)
Joninės (24 Jun)
Statehood Day (6 Jul)
Assumption Day (15 Aug)
All Saints' Day (1 Nov)
Christmas (24–26 Dec)

Musicians jamming at the Vilnius Jazz festival

THE HISTORY OF LITHUANIA

urope's last pagan stronghold, Lithuania rose as a powerful state by the late 14th century, surviving until the 16th century. It was thereafter subjugated first by the Poles and then the Russians. The long periods of occupation endured by the country stirred a reawakening of national identity in its people. An independent republic, briefly created during the inter-war era, was finally established in 1991.

At the start of the 13th century, Lithuanian tribes, such as the Samogitians in the west and Aukštaitiai in the east, began to unite in the face of regular incursions by the Germanic crusaders. The brutal attacks grew with increasing intensity before the resolutely pagan Samogitians vanquished the Knights of the Sword at the Battle of the Sun in 1236.

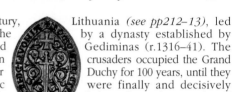

13th-century seal of the Germanic crusaders

Lithuania *(see pp212–13)*, led by a dynasty established by Gediminas (r.1316–41). The crusaders occupied the Grand Duchy for 100 years, until they were finally and decisively defeated at the Battle of Grünwald (Žalgiris) in 1410 by the powerful allied armies of Lithuania and Poland.

THE LITHUANIAN GRAND DUCHY

Duke Mindaugas (r.1235–63), who was rapidly adding territory to his base in Aukštaitija, united the tribes in 1240, crowning himself king in 1253. His acceptance of Christianity to appease the crusaders enraged the Samogitians, who murdered him, took over his land and reverted to paganism. By the beginning of the 14th century, large numbers of crusaders returned from the Middle East and joined the fight against the pagan Grand Duchy of

POLISH-LITHUANIAN COMMONWEALTH

Grand Duke Jogaila (r.1362–1434) married Jadwiga of Poland in 1386 and accepted Christianity, which led to mass baptisms throughout Lithuania in the ensuing years. The marriage

Impression of the Union of Lublin by 19th-century artist Jan Matejko

TIMELINE

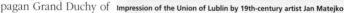

King Mindaugas (c.1203–63)

1236 Samogitian victory at the Battle of the Sun	**1253** Duke Mindaugas crowned	**1386** Lithuania and Poland unite	**1392** Grand Duchy of Lithuania reaches the Black Sea

| **1200** | | **1300** | | **1400** | | **1**|

1240 Duke Mindaugas unites Lithuania	**1316** Accession of Gediminas	**1382** Crusaders seize Samogitia	**1410** Battle of Grünwald (Žalgiris) destroys the Teutonic Knights

formed a Polish-Lithuanian alliance that endured for centuries. This proved particularly effective as a bulwark against enemies in the West and in the East. Under Grand Duke Vytautas (r.1401–30), Lithuania was able to extend its reach between the Baltic and the Black seas. Throughout the first half of the 16th century, however, a militant Russia compelled a stronger union between Lithuania and Poland, cemented at the Union of Lublin in 1569. The Commonwealth that resulted lasted for over 200 years.

Portrait of Grand Duke Vytautas on a tile

DECLINE OF THE COMMONWEALTH
When King Sigismund Augustus (r.1548–72) died without an heir, the combined position of Grand Duke of Lithuania and King of Poland became an elected one, chosen by the all-powerful nobility. Warsaw, midway between the old capitals of Vilnius and Kraków, became the base. Stefan Bathory (1533–86) was one of the most successful of these elected heads of state. Apart from founding Vilnius University, he also introduced sweeping military and judicial reforms. During the Livonian Wars (see p33), he successfully led a decisive campaign against the Russians, regaining control over Livonia in 1582.

Under the Commonwealth, Poland established its hegemony, with the Poles dominating the Lithuanian nobility. The bourgeoisie, on the other hand, were deprived of all political rights as well as the right to own land, while the peasants were forced to become serfs, subject to severe punishment if they attempted to flee.

The 17th century was a disastrous period for Lithuania, with misrule in Warsaw, plague and fires in Vilnius and a calamitous invasion by the Russians in 1655. Governed by a string of ineffective rulers and noblemen who were either deliberately divisive or simply uninterested in state affairs, the steadily weakening Commonwealth became, throughout the 18th century, little more than a puppet state to Tsarist Russia. In a series of partitions in 1772, 1793 and 1795, the vast lands of the Commonwealth were divided between Russia, Prussia and Austria, despite brave armed resistance by Lithuanian patriots. One such failed uprising was led by Jokūbas Jasinskis (1761–94). By 1795, with the final partition of the Commonwealth, Poland and Lithuania had ceased to exist.

Russians paying tribute to Stefan Bathory, a painting by Jan Matejko

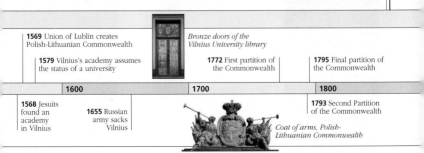

1569 Union of Lublin creates Polish-Lithuanian Commonwealth

1579 Vilnius's academy assumes the status of a university

Bronze doors of the Vilnius University library

1772 First partition of the Commonwealth

1795 Final partition of the Commonwealth

1600

1700

1800

1568 Jesuits found an academy in Vilnius

1655 Russian army sacks Vilnius

1793 Second Partition of the Commonwealth

Coat of arms, Polish-Lithuanian Commonwealth

The Grand Duchy of Lithuania

The royal seal of Vytautas

Founded in the 13th century by King Mindaugas and strengthened further by Grand Duke Gediminas in the 14th century, the Grand Duchy of Lithuania reached its greatest territorial extent under Vytautas the Great. Originally a defensive military union, the Duchy quickly started expanding eastwards and southwards, eventually stretching across much of present-day Belarus and Ukraine. The Duchy was dominated in Vilnius by a military class that later became a privileged nobility. Vilnius flourished as the capital of culture and architecture.

KEY

▨ Grand Duchy under Vytautas

THE BATTLE OF GRÜNWALD

Nothing quite symbolizes the Grand Duchy at the height of its achievements like Jan Matejko's masterpiece painted in 1878. Vytautas the Great is shown at the centre, victorious in the Battle of Grünwald (Žalgiris) against the Teutonic Knights in 1410. The Knights were decisively defeated by the combined armies of the Grand Duchy and Poland, led by Vytautas and King Jogaila, respectively.

Grand Duke Gediminas (1275–1341) *extended the Duchy's borders, moved the capital to Vilnius and built a powerful chain of defensive fortresses.*

Albert II Radvila (1595–1656), *who was descended from a long line of influential nobles, effectively ruled the Grand Duchy as Grand Chancellor of Lithuania within the Polish-Lithuanian Commonwealth.*

Grand Duke Vytautas (1350–1430), *shown here in a 17th-century portrait, is today revered as a national hero. Under his reign, the Grand Duchy grew to its greatest geographical extent covering swathes of land, between the Baltic and Black seas.*

Tile, 16th century   Coin, 16th century

SURVIVING THE CENTURIES

Artifacts found during excavations of the remains of the Royal Palace in Vilnius include decorative tiles, coins and exquisitely crafted jewellery. While the tiles and coins date from the 16th century, some of the jewellery dates back to the 14th century. The collection is likely to go on display once the newly reconstructed palace is completed.

Vilnius University, *which the Jesuits had founded as an academy in 1568, was upgraded to a university 11 years later by Stefan Bathory (1533–86), the Grand Duke of Lithuania and King of Poland.*

The icon of the Virgin Mary *at the Gates of Dawn in Vilnius is a fine example of religious painting from the period. It was originally painted on oak panels in the 1620s.*

Grand Duke Vytautas

The first book printed in the Lithuanian language *was* Catechism *(1547) by Martynas Mažvydas. Appearing in the Duchy at a time when Polish was the preferred language of the aristocracy, the book had a great appeal for the pagan rural masses.*

The Christianization of Lithuania *took place in 1387, following the union of Lithuania and Poland. However, unlike the dramatic mass conversion depicted in this 19th-century painting by Jan Matejko, many parts of Lithuania remained pagan into the 16th century.*

Napoleon's Grand Army crossing the Nemunas river in 1812

TSARIST RUSSIAN RULE

Over 120 years of occupation followed the break-up of the Commonwealth, with most of the land once governed by the Grand Duchy of Lithuania now absorbed into the Russian Empire. Resistance constantly simmered under the surface, however, and hopes of independence were revived when Napoleon marched through Kaunas and Vilnius in June 1812. These hopes were crushed six months later when the demoralized, half-frozen remnants of the French Grand Army retreated from Moscow through Vilnius.

When a rebellion led mainly by the rural nobility failed in 1831, repressive measures were launched such as the closure of Vilnius University and the enforced use of Russian in Lithuanian schools. Even harsher oppression followed another rebellion in 1863, with over 100 of the resistance leaders hunted down and hanged, while others were deported with their families to Siberia. The Russification of the whole country followed, which involved a

President Antanas Smetona (r.1926–40)

conscious eradication of all traces of traditional Lithuania. Catholic churches were converted to Orthodox ones and Lithuanian-language books in the Latin alphabet were banned. However, language and identity were kept alive by smuggling books in from East Prussia as well as the printing and circulation of the first Lithuanian-language newspapers, *Aušra* (Dawn) and *Varpas* (Bell).

NATIONHOOD REGAINED, AND LOST

As the chaos of World War I and the 1917 Revolution weakened Russia, an elected council in Vilnius declared Lithuanian independence on 16 February 1918. International recognition was slow in coming. In October 1920, Józef Piłsudski (1867–1935), the nationalist head of state of Poland, which had also regained its independence in 1918, sent an army to occupy Vilnius. The Lithuanian government was, therefore, forced to re-establish itself in Kaunas. Vilnius was indisputably Lithuania's historical capital, but by now, almost half of the city's population was Jewish, and the other half consisted of Polish-speakers. Kaunas was declared Lithuania's temporary capital and remained so until 1939. An element of pride was restored when Lithuania snatched control of Memel from a caretaker French garrison in early 1923 and renamed it Klaipėda.

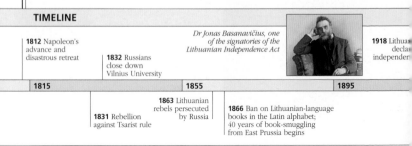

TIMELINE

1812 Napoleon's advance and disastrous retreat

1832 Russians close down Vilnius University

Dr Jonas Basanavičius, one of the signatories of the Lithuanian Independence Act

1918 Lithuan declar independen

1815	1855	1895

1831 Rebellion against Tsarist rule

1863 Lithuanian rebels persecuted by Russia

1866 Ban on Lithuanian-language books in the Latin alphabet; 40 years of book-smuggling from East Prussia begins

Adolf Hitler entering Klaipėda in 1939

Independent Lithuania was led, between 1926 and 1940, by the authoritarian Antanas Smetona. For Lithuanians, this was a time of growing prosperity as agricultural exports boomed. However, these were uneasy times, as the resurgent powers of Germany and Russia loomed on either side. Klaipėda was retaken by the Nazis in 1939 and the Red Army occupied the rest of Lithuania following an ultimatum from Moscow in 1940. The Red Army carried out mass deportations and horrific massacres. The reign of terror continued under the Nazis, who, in June 1941, launched Operation Barbarossa, the code name for Germany's invasion of the Soviet Union. An estimated 200,000 people, most of them Jews, were taken outside virtually every town and city to be executed. In 1944, as part of its Baltic Offensive, the Red Army pushed back through Lithuania. Over the next ten years, between 120,000 and 300,000 people were deported to the Siberian Gulags. A brave, but futile, partisan war was fought from the Lithuanian forests until the early 1950s.

THE REPUBLIC OF LITHUANIA

In 1988, encouraged by the greater openness of Soviet premier Mikhail Gorbachev's reforms, a group of intellectuals founded the Sąjūdis movement to rally popular support for demonstrations that had begun the previous year. The response was immediate. Peaceful protests increased and, on 11 March 1990, Lithuania declared its independence, the first of any of the Soviet republics to do so. In January 1991, Soviet tanks and troops stormed the Vilnius TV Tower, killing 14 unarmed civilians and injuring 700.

In August 1991, the failure of the hardliners' putsch in Moscow finally gave Lithuania freedom. The first presidential elections brought Algirdas Brazauskas to power. Several years of economic hardship followed, marked by rising unemployment. Lithuania's EU and NATO membership in 2004 has brought the country far greater security and prosperity.

A Lithuanian independence rally in 1989, Kaunas

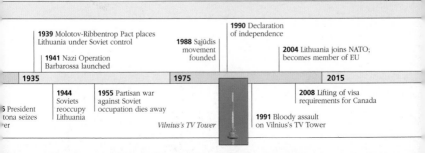

VILNIUS

Whether viewed from one of the hills that overlook the Old Town or from one of the many pavement cafés with tall spires rising all around, Vilnius is unmistakably a city of great beauty. The Old Town, on the UNESCO World Heritage list since 1994, blends Gothic and Neo-Classical styles with a breathtaking late flourish of Baroque. Vilnius is in itself an architectural monument.

The character of Vilnius, the Lithuanian capital, has been retained partly because of its isolated location. Yet, the ebb and flow of history has given it a more multicultural feel than the country's other cities.

The earliest written reference to Vilnius exists in a letter from Grand Duke Gediminas in 1323, inviting citizens from towns in Germany to settle here, pledging freedom from taxes and granting other rights. Pagan Vilnius sustained many attacks during the Northern Crusades, yet by the 14th century it had become the capital of an empire that stretched from the Baltic Sea to the Black Sea. Vilnius was reduced to being a provincial city in the Polish-Lithuanian Commonwealth, but following a period of devastating wars, invasions and fires between the early 17th and mid-18th centuries, efforts to rebuild the city resulted in the rich offshoot of the Baroque style that is typical of Vilnius today.

Vilnius regained its status as the capital of Lithuania in 1918, but only for a year. Occupied by Poland, with Lithuania's government forced to relocate to Kaunas, it declined in economic importance until the Soviets invaded it in 1939. World War II devastated Vilnius and annihilated most of its Jewish population. However, under the ensuing Soviet occupation the city expanded.

Vilnius has been transformed from a sleepy backwater to a lively, modern European capital that provides a wonderful setting for shopping, dining and nightlife. However, with Vilnius University, Town Hall Square and several carefully restored churches, the city has retained its charm.

Colourful mural by Antanas Kmieliauskas decorating the ceiling of Vilnius University's bookshop, Littera

◁ Bernardine Church rising between the Church of St Anne and the statue of Adam Mickiewicz

Exploring Vilnius

Although its Old Town is one of the largest in Europe, Vilnius is a surprisingly compact city that can easily be explored on foot. Two of the best places to begin a tour of the Old Town and its Baroque treasures are Vilnius Cathedral in the north and the Gates of Dawn in the south. Gedimino Avenue, the main shopping street where the KGB Museum is located, stretches west from Cathedral Square, while the Church of St Anne lies immediately to the east of the Old Town. Vilnius is also a good base for exploring much of Central Lithuania.

Outdoor cafés along cobblestoned Pilies Street, Old Town

SIGHTS AT A GLANCE

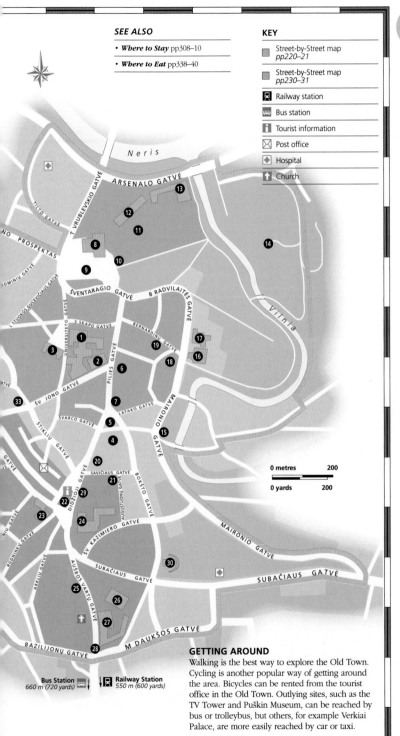

SEE ALSO

- **Where to Stay** pp308–10
- **Where to Eat** pp338–40

KEY

- Street-by-Street map *pp220–21*
- Street-by-Street map *pp230–31*
- Railway station
- Bus station
- Tourist information
- Post office
- Hospital
- Church

Neris

ARSENALO GATVĖ

T. VRUBLEVSKIO GATVĖ

TILTO GATVĖ

...NO PROSPEKTAS

Vilnia

ŠVENTARAGIO GATVĖ

B. RADVILAITĖS GATVĖ

ŠV. SKAPO GATVĖ

UNIVERSITETO GATVĖ

PILIES GATVĖ

BERNARDINŲ GATVĖ

ŠV. JONO GATVĖ

ŠVARCO GATVĖ

LATAKO GATVĖ

MAIRONIO GATVĖ

STIKLIŲ GATVĖ

SAVIČIAUS GATVĖ

DIDŽIOJI GATVĖ

AUGUSTIJONŲ GATVĖ

BOKŠTO GATVĖ

ŠV. KAZIMIERO GATVĖ

MAIRONIO GATVĖ

SUBAČIAUS GATVĖ

ARKLIŲ GATVĖ

AUŠROS VARTŲ GATVĖ

SUBAČIAUS GATVĖ

M. DAUKŠOS GATVĖ

BAZILIJONŲ GATVĖ

0 metres 200
0 yards 200

Bus Station
660 m (720 yards)

Railway Station
550 m (600 yards)

GETTING AROUND

Walking is the best way to explore the Old Town.
Cycling is another popular way of getting around
the area. Bicycles can be rented from the tourist
office in the Old Town. Outlying sites, such as the
TV Tower and Puškin Museum, can be reached by
bus or trolleybus, but others, for example Verkiai
Palace, are more easily reached by car or taxi.

Street-by-Street: Pilies Street and Vilnius University

KEY

– – – Suggested route

Narrow lanes, hidden courtyards and some of the Old Town's finest architecture make Pilies Street and nearby Vilnius University a delight to stroll around and explore. The university, which is over 400 years old, is one of the oldest in Eastern Europe. Traffic is restricted, and in summer restaurants and cafés spill out onto the streets. Souvenir stalls and shops on Pilies sell amber and interesting gifts, while the surrounding buildings are testimony to the city's long and eventful history.

Applied Arts Museum lies inside the Old Arsenal.

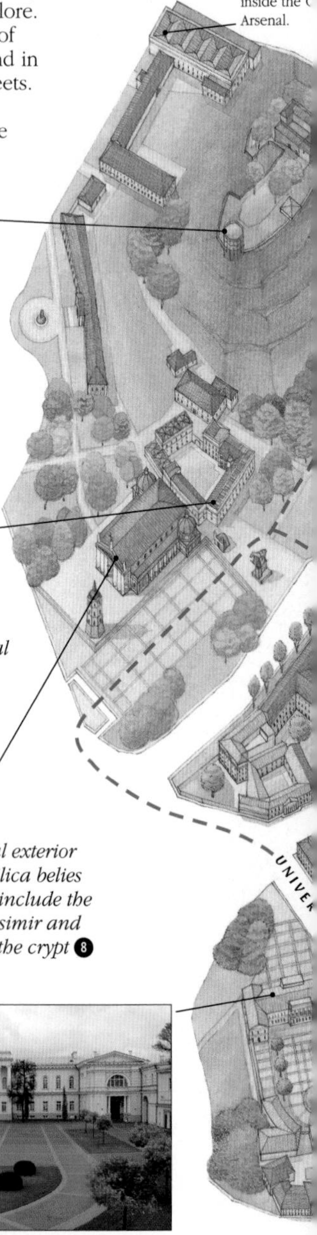

Upper Castle
The best visual introduction to Vilnius is from the viewing platform on the castle's last surviving tower. The Lithuanian flag was raised here in 1919 and in 1988 ⓫

Royal Palace
Also known as the Lower Castle, it was the main residence of the Grand Dukes and was the political and cultural heart of Lithuania ❿

UNIVER

Vilnius Cathedral
The austere Neo-Classical exterior of Lithuania's main basilica belies its hidden jewels, which include the Baroque Chapel of St Casimir and the winding passages of the crypt ❽

Presidential Palace
A 14th-century nobleman's residence, this building has hosted many historical figures. It became the Presidency in 1997 ❸

STAR SIGHTS

★ Pilies Street

★ Vilnius University

★ **Pilies Street**
With a view of the Upper Castle ever present, Pilies is one of the city's oldest streets. It was once Vilnius's commercial centre but today the street is popular with visitors hunting for amberware and other local products.

0 metres 100

0 yards 100

Church of St Anne
The flamboyant Gothic red-brick church fell victim to Napoleon's soldiers, who used it as a barracks on their way to Moscow in 1812. Fortunately, the beautiful façade has survived the turbulent centuries **17**

BERNARDINŲ GATVĖ

ILIES GATVĖ

ŠV. MYKOLO GATVĖ

St John's Church has a sweeping Baroque façade.

Littera Bookshop
This charmingly decorated bookshop at the eastern edge of the university's Sarbievijaus Courtyard also sells university souvenirs.

★ **Vilnius University**
Lithuania's largest university, it occupies a sizeable part of the Old Town. The university has over 13 courtyards and multiple buildings **1**

Vilnius University ❶
Vilniaus universitetas

Universiteto 3. **Map** 2 D3. *Tel 268 7001.* ⬚ *10am–5:30pm Mon–Sat.* ▨ *for prior booking call 268 7103.* ▥ www.vu.lt

The oldest university in Eastern Europe was founded as a Jesuit College in 1568, before becoming a school of higher education in 1579. The current campus, constructed between the 16th and 18th centuries, is a combination of different architectural styles.

The most impressive of its 13 courtyards, the Great Courtyard has open galleries dating from the 17th century, which were later lined with dedications to professors. Accessed via a passage from the western side of the Great Courtyard, the Observatory Courtyard by contrast is a serene enclosed garden from which the observatory and its zodiac symbols can be seen.

North of the Great Courtyard is the Sarbievijaus Courtyard, the oldest part of the university. At its far end, a bookshop, **Littera**, can be found. Frescoes caricaturing professors and students that decorate the interior of the bookshop were painted in 1978 by Antanas Kmieliauskas (b.1932).

Façade of St John's Church and adjoining belfry

St John's Church ❷
Šv Jono bažnyčia

Šv Jono 12. **Map** 2 D3. *Tel 611 795.* ⬚ *10am–5pm Mon–Sat.* ✝ *6pm Tue–Thu, 11am & 1pm Sun.*

At the southern edge of the university campus, the impressive façade and separate bell tower of the Church of St John the Baptist and St John the Evangelist dominate the Great Courtyard. The original Gothic church, built here in 1426, was reconstructed in 1749 in flamboyant Baroque by Jan Krzysztof Glaubitz *(see p233)*. The ten magnificent altars in faux marble with Corinthian columns illuminate the otherwise austere interior. Initially there were 22 columns, most of which were removed during further rebuilding in the 19th century. At 68 m (223 ft), the bell tower, which was given two extra tiers by Glaubitz, is the tallest structure in the Old Town.

Presidential Palace ❸
Lietuvos respublikos prezidentūra

Daukanto aikštė 3. **Map** 2 D3. *Tel 266 4154.* ⬚ *9am–5pm Sat (call in advance).* ▨ *for group tour call 266 4073.* www.president.lt

Formerly a residence for high-ranking bishops, this ornate building has existed since Lithuania's conversion to Christianity at the end of the 14th century. The palace was rebuilt in the late 1820s in the Neo-Classical style by Vasily Stasov (1769–1848), an architect from St Petersburg. It has hosted a number of important personalities, including Napoleon Bonaparte and Tsar Alexander I. The former used the palace during his doomed advance on Moscow.

The palace was later used for a variety of ceremonial purposes before becoming the Presidential Palace in 1997. When the president is in Vilnius, a flag flies showing his coat of arms.

Colourful interior of Littera, with its collection of books for leisure and study material, Vilnius University

Elegantly displayed paintings in one of the exhibition rooms, Vilnius Picture Gallery

Vilnius Picture Gallery ●

Vilniaus paveikslų galerija

Didžioji 4. **Map** 2 D4. **Tel** 212 4258. ◯ 11am–6pm Tue–Sat, noon–5pm Sun. 🖼 🖋 🚻 www.ldm.lt

The imposing, enclosed Neo-Classical courtyard of this gallery offers a reflection of 19th-century Vilnius, when these premises were used by Vilnius University and the Medical Academy. Inside, the paintings on display show how the main art movements of the 19th and early 20th centuries influenced the development of Lithuanian art. *Lithuanian Girl with Verbos* by Kanutas Ruseckas (1800–60) is an icon of the Romantic aesthetic in Lithuanian art. Similarly, the later movements of Realism and Impressionism are reflected, respectively, in intimate portraits, such as Alfredas Romeris's *Study of a Girl's Hands*, and open landscapes, such as Juozas Balzukevičius's *Across a Ryefield*.

Church of St Paraskeva ●

Šv Paraskevos cerkvė

Didžioji 2. **Map** 2 D4. **Tel** 215 3747.

Also known as Pyatnitskaya Church, this attractive little Orthodox church stands on a site that has been used for ritual and prayer for many centuries. In the mid-14th century, Grand Duke Algirdas built a church here for his Orthodox wife, before which it had been a pagan sanctuary.

Here, at the beginning of the 18th century, Peter the Great baptized a nine-year-old African slave by the name of Hannibal, later Major-General Abram Petrovich Hannibal (1696–1781), great grandfather of the Russian poet Alexander Pushkin. The current building, designed by Nikolai Chagin, dates from 1865. Closed during the Soviet period, it has been returned to the Russian Orthodox faith.

The small Russian Orthodox Church of St Paraskeva

House of Signatories ●

Signatarų namai

Pilies 26. **Map** 2 D3. **Tel** 231 4437. ◯ May–Sep: 10am–5pm Sun; Oct–Apr: 10am–5pm Tue–Sat. 🖋 🖵

The House of Signatories, with an extravagant façade, has played a crucial role in Lithuania's modern history. It

was here that, on 16 February 1918, the newly created Council of Lithuania signed the deed that restored Lithuania's independence. The Štralis Coffee House on the ground floor, created during renovation in the 1890s, was a popular meeting place for leading figures in the Lithuanian national revival.

The second-floor room, where the independence act was signed, has been re-created. Unfortunately, the displays on this historic event are a little sparse.

Šlapelis House Museum ●

Šlapelių namas-muziejus

Pilies 40. **Map** 2 D4. **Tel** 261 0771. ◯ 11am–5pm Wed–Sun (call in advance). 🖋

Presenting a journey back in time to Vilnius during the troubled first half of the 20th century, this modest, yet evocative, museum is dedicated to Marija and Jurgis Šlapelis. Although a native Polish-speaker, Marija secretly ran a Lithuanian-language bookshop on nearby Domininkonų Street while the city was under Russian, Polish, Nazi and Soviet occupations between 1906 and 1949.

On display are furnishings, newspapers, books, music sheets and postcards from this time. In addition, photographs showing a number of family reunions following the end of Soviet occupation can be found beneath 17th-century beams in what used to be the kitchen.

Vilnius Cathedral ❽
Vilniaus arkikatedra bazilika

Having taken various guises since it was first built as a Christian church on the site of a pagan temple in 1251, Vilnius Cathedral today largely dates from the late 18th century. The young architect, Laurynas Stuoka-Gucevičius, brought the fashionable French Classicist style to Baroque Vilnius, his idea for the cathedral exterior and interior being a visual re-creation of a Greek temple. Vilnius Cathedral was closed by the Soviets in 1950 and initially mooted for use as a garage for truck repairs. In 1956, however, it opened as a picture gallery. It was eventually returned to the Catholic Church in 1989 and reconsecrated a year before independence was declared.

Valavičius Chapel
Members of the Valavičius family were governors and bishops of Vilnius. Their lavish chapel was created in the early 17th century.

Stucco Sculpture
The sculpture depicting a bird sacrifice can be seen on the tympanum of the façade.

The entrance is via a huge Classical portico.

Wall Painting of the Crucifixion
The oldest surviving fresco in Lithuania, dating from the 14th century, can be found in the crypt. It was discovered in 1925.

STAR FEATURES

★ St Casimir's Chapel

★ Crypt

Statue of Luke, the Evangelist
Of the statues of the Four Evangelists on the southern façade, Luke appears with a bull, which is a symbol of service and sacrifice.

High Altar
The marvellously intricate tabernacle door on the High Altar, which was created in the 1620s, is fashioned from gold and silver. Two biblical scenes, the Last Supper and Christ Washing the Disciples' Feet, are beautifully depicted on the panel.

VISITORS' CHECKLIST

Katedros aikšė 1. **Map** 2 D3.
Tel 85261 0731. ☐ 7am–7pm daily. ☐ guided tour mandatory to visit the crypt. Enquire at the souvenir shop at the cathedral's northern entrance for timings and prices. ☐

★ St Casimir's Chapel
Italian masters created this superb chapel, one of the major Baroque jewels of Vilnius, from 1623 to 1636. Its main highlights are the marble columns, magnificent stucco figures and colourful frescoes.

★ Crypt
A sombre mausoleum holds the remains of two Grand Dukes and two wives of Sigismund Augustus (r.1548–72), the last descendant of Gediminas (r.1316–41).

ST CASIMIR (1458–84)

Casimir was the second son of a Grand Duke, whose siblings became kings and queens of European states through lineage and marriage. Pious Casimir shunned the luxuries of court life and would often go to the cathedral to pray. When he died of tuberculosis aged 25, it was rumoured that his coffin could cure disease. A fresco in St Casimir's Chapel shows how a sick orphan, who prayed beneath the coffin, was miraculously cured.

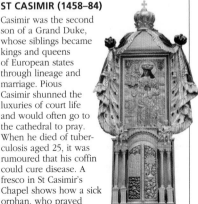

Richly decorated altar of St Casimir's Chapel

Vilnius Cathedral Belfry, Cathedral Square

Cathedral Square ❾
Katedros aikštė

Map 2 D3. 🚌 *10, 11, 33.*

The paving stones around the square show the outline of the wall around the Lower Castle, a defence that made Vilnius a 14th-century bastion against the crusades.

At the square's western end is the **Vilnius Cathedral Belfry**. It was originally part of the fortifications. There was also a western gate where Vilnius Cathedral stands today. The square's eastern end is dominated by a statue of Grand Duke Gediminas. Unveiled in 1996, it conveys the city founder's predilection for diplomacy over force. In the square's centre is a tile marked *stebuklas* (miracle), reputed to be the point where the Baltic Way *(see p39)*, the human chain linking Vilnius, Rīga and Tallinn in 1989, started from. Locals believe that turning around on it three times makes a wish come true.

Lower Castle ❿
Žemutinė pilis

Katedros 4. **Map** 2 D3. *Tel 212 7476.* 🚌 *10, 11, 33.* ⬤ *8am–5pm Mon–Fri (to 3:45pm Fri).* 📷
www.valdovurumai.lt

The buildings, including Vilnius Cathedral, the Arsenal and Royal Palace, the residence of the Grand Dukes that stood at the foot of Castle Hill and survived the sieges of the 14th century, are known as Lower Castle. In the 1520s, the Royal Palace was renovated in Renaissance style by Italian architects invited by Sigismund the Old (r.1506–48) and his wife. The palace became the hub of a vibrant cultural life. Excavations carried out here between 1987 and 2001 unearthed decorative tiles, tapestries, jewellery and armour from this period and earlier. These objects are thought to have lain buried since the palace was destroyed by Tsarist authorities in 1802 as they did not want a symbol of Lithuanian power dominating the city.

Upper Castle ⓫
Aukštutinė pilis

Arsenalo 5. **Map** 2 D3. *Tel 261 7453.* 🚌 *10, 11, 33.* ⬤ *10am–5pm Tue–Sun.* 📷

The western tower, the only remaining part of the Upper Castle complex, which once included defensive structures, is today the symbol of independent Lithuania. The viewing platform at the top provides a panorama of the spires and rooftops of the Old Town to the south, as well as a glimpse of the new skyscrapers rising to the west. A funicular offers a ride to the Upper Castle.

The original stone buildings of the Upper Castle were built in 1419, with restoration work taking place in the 1950s. According to legend, while on a hunting trip, Grand Duke Gediminas dreamed of an iron wolf howling from the hills in the park. This, his pagan priest said, was a sign that a powerful fortress should be built there. Wooden upper and lower castles and another on the adjacent hill were the result.

Lithuanian National Museum ⓬
Lietuvos nacionalinis muziejus

Arsenalo 1. **Map** 2 D3. *Tel 262 9426.* 🚌 *10, 33.* ⬤ *May–Sep: 10am–5pm Tue–Sat, 10am–3pm Sun; Oct–Apr: 10am–5pm Wed–Sun.* 📷 📷

An early 19th-century building, known as the New Arsenal, houses the Lithuanian National Museum. In front of it stands a statue of King Mindaugas, which was unveiled together with the nearby bridge in July 2003.

Western tower, the Upper Castle's lone surviving structure

Lithuanian traditional costumes on display, Lithuanian National Museum

The museum presents a glimpse of everyday life in Lithuania before World War II. Ordinary lives are evocatively documented in the exhibits that include plates and spoons, decorative boxes and perfume bottles, and even an old stone with a hollow used for pagan rituals.

The museum's main highlight is the first-floor room, which gives a pictorial history of the Lithuanian Grand Duchy from the Battle of the Sun to the 18th-century partitions (see p211).

The museum as a whole gives a concise tour of Lithuanian history from the 13th century to the present. Fascinating exhibits showcased in the museum include an executioner's sword tellingly broken into two pieces, a wonderfully ostentatious 18th-century sleigh and a handprint in iron of Peter the Great. There is also a display of folk costumes and a superb life-size re-creation of a typical Lithuanian peasant family farmstead.

Applied Arts Museum ⓭
Taikomosios dailės muziejus

Arsenalo gatvė 3a. **Map** 2 E3.
Tel *262 8080.* ☐ *11am–6pm Tue–Sat, 11am–4pm Sun.* 🖼

The 16th-century Old Arsenal houses the Applied Arts Museum, which hosts major state-sponsored exhibitions on topics mainly relating to the history of Lithuania, the Grand Duchy and sacred art.

One of the permanent exhibitions in the museum displays Lithuanian folk art from the 17th to the 19th centuries, illustrating the heavy impact that Christian themes had on traditional mediums such as sculpture. The collection includes wayside wooden crosses, shrines, saints and *rūpintojėlis* (Lithuanian folk-art representations of a weary Christ holding his head in his right hand). Particularly illuminating is the work of Vincas Svirskis

(1835–1916), a prolific craftsman who carved hundreds of shrines for rural farmsteads and villages in the Kėdainiai and Kaunas regions (see pp258–61).

Hill of Three Crosses ⓮
Trijų kryžių kalnas

Kalnų parkas. **Map** 2 E3.

A recognizable landmark and symbol of Vilnius, the three crosses on the hill adjacent to the Upper Castle are replicas of a monument destroyed by the Soviet authorities in the 1950s. Three wooden crosses were first placed here in the 16th century to commemorate, according to legend, Franciscan friars tortured and murdered by a pagan rabble. The incident took place during the rule of Grand Duke Algirdas, when Lithuania was stubbornly resisting Roman Catholic conversions. Seven of the friars were hacked to death, while the others were tied to crosses and cast into the Vilnia river.

The view of the Old Town from the crosses is unrivalled. A footbridge and a path along the Vilnia leads to steps up the hillside. An easier alternative route is via a side road leading up through the park from where T Kosciuškos Street crosses the Vilnia.

Hill of the Three Crosses, a distinguished symbol of Vilnius

Elegant façade of the Russian Orthodox Holy Mother of God Church

Holy Mother of God Church ⓯

Skaisčiausios Dievo Motinos cerkvė

Maironio 14. **Map** 2 E4. *Tel* 215 3747. 🚌 10, 11, 33. 🕆 5pm Sat, 9am Sun.

The current structure of this Russian Orthodox church, designed by Russian architect Nikolai Chagin, dates from the 19th century. One of the icons, *The Mother of God*, was brought by Tsar Alexander II, who also gave funds for the reconstruction work. For over 60 years before its renovation the church had been used as dissection rooms for the Medical Academy and as a military barracks. Just like the Church of St Paraskeva *(see p223)*, it stands where pagan Grand Duke Algirdas built a place of worship for his wife, in the 14th century.

Bernardine Church ⓰

Bernardinų bažnyčia

Maironio 8. **Map** 2 E3. *Tel* 260 9292. 🚌 10, 11, 33. 🕆 7:30am Mon–Thu; 6pm Sat; 9am (in English), 10:30am, 1pm, 5pm Sun.

In 1469, the austere Franciscan Observant friars, known as the Bernardines after their founder St Bernardino of Siena, arrived in Vilnius. The Bernardine Church, which they built in around 1525, still retains the late Gothic crystal vaulting above the aisles. In the 1770s,

a series of Baroque wooden altars and confessionals were added to the interior. However, of these only the main altar, carved by Italian craftsman Daniele Giotto, remains today. The intriguing façade combines Gothic windows and Baroque scrolls.

Both church and friary were closed after the 1863 uprising *(see p214)*, becoming barracks for Russian troops, but were eventually given back to the friars. The church's original 16th-century frescoes are being restored and include depictions of the sobriety and solemnity observed by friars, as well as St Christopher, and scenes from the Passion of Christ.

Just outside the church grounds is a statue of Adam Mickiewicz, created in 1984. In August 1987, the statue was the meeting point for the first public rally under Soviet occupation that called for Lithuania's national rights.

Church of St Anne ⓱

Šv Onos bažnyčia

Maironio 8/1. **Map** 2 E3. *Tel* 625 48011. 🚌 10, 11, 33. 🕆 8pm Mon–Sat, 9–11am Sun.

According to local folklore, this church charmed Napoleon into exclaiming how he

Church of St Anne, a Gothic gem said to have dazzled Napoleon

ADAM MICKIEWICZ (1798–1855)

"Oh Lithuania, my country, thou art like good health; I never knew till now how precious, till I lost thee." So begins *Pan Tadeusz*, the lyrical masterpiece of the great Polish Romantic poet Adam Mickiewicz. He was born into a family of Polish nobles near Nowogrodek, in present-day Belarus, three years after the partition of the Polish-Lithuanian Commonwealth. His nomadic life was dominated by a strong yearning for an idyllic lost homeland. His epic poems are full of ancient forests, groves and open landscapes.

Statue of Adam Mickiewicz, outside the Bernardine Church

Gražyna (1822), written in his youth, is about the female chief of a pagan Lithuanian tribe who outwits the cross-and-sword-wielding Teutonic Knights. The Byronesque *Konrad Wallenrod* (1828) describes these battles with even greater mastery.

wished he could take it back to Paris on the palm of his hand. St Anne's is a Gothic beauty; its ornate façade of flowing ogee arches and slender windows are a unique monument to the style in a city of Baroque. The finials and the spires are covered evenly with decorative crockets – bricks made to resemble flowers or curled leaves and so favoured by Gothic architects. One set of historians found 33 different shapes of brick used in the façade. Inside, the three Baroque altars were designed by Jan Krzysztof Glaubitz (*see p233*). The free-standing bell tower was built much later, in the 1870s.

Church of St Michael ⑱
Šv Mykolo bažnyčia

Šv Mykolo 9. **Map** 2 E3. **Tel** 261 6409. ◻ 11am–6pm Wed–Sun, 10am–1pm Mon.

The Renaissance-style Church of St Michael was built during the early 17th century, as a convent for Bernardine nuns and a mausoleum for the Sapiega family. Its interior features several of the nobles' funerary monuments. These include one to Leonas Sapiega, whose initials mark some of the crests, motifs and rosettes that decorate the ceiling. Between 1972 and 2005, the church housed the Museum of Architecture, the exhibits of which were later transferred to the Lithuanian National Museum (*see p226*).

Mickiewicz Museum ⑲
Adomo Mickevičiaus memoralinis butas-muziejus

Bernardinų 11. **Map** 2 E3. **Tel** 279 1879. ◻ 10am–5pm Tue–Fri, 10am–2pm Sat–Sun. ⬛

The legendary poet Adam Mickiewicz, who romanticized his Polish-Lithuanian homeland, stayed at this apartment, which belonged to a university professor, for a brief period in 1822. Set inside a lovely enclosed courtyard, the museum attempts to re-create the atmosphere of the era in which the poet lived.

Period furniture, which Mickiewicz himself is said to have used while writing his first folk-inspired ballads, includes a table and chair from Kaunas and a chair from Paris. Portraits of the poet are set alongside volumes of his works in various languages. The place also houses the first editions of a number of his great works. The museum often hosts literary meetings and poetry evenings.

Orthodox Church of St Nicholas ⑳
Šv Mikalojaus cerkvė

Didžioji 12. **Map** 2 D4. **Tel** 261 8559. ◻ 11am–4pm Wed–Sun. ✝ 5pm Tue–Sat, 9am Sun.

The serene, candlelit interior of the Orthodox Church of St Nicholas contrasts sharply with the bustle on Didžioji, the Old Town's main street. Originally a Gothic church dating from 1514, it passed into the hands of the Uniates, or Greek Catholics, in 1609 before getting a Baroque over-haul, including the bell tower. The church was returned to the Russian Orthodox Church in 1827. The overtly Russian Byzantine façade of the church, together with most of the interior, is an example of the change that took place in the city's religious land-scape following the doomed January 1863 uprising.

The domed chapel on the left is dedicated to Count Mikhail Muravyov (1796–1866), the governor-general who dealt harshly with the uprising's participants.

Façade, Orthodox Church of St Nicholas

Street-by-Street:Town Hall Square to the Gates of Dawn

Lithuania's distinctive Baroque architecture, known as Vilnius Baroque, can be admired in the outstanding monuments clustered around the Gates of Dawn and the Church of St Casimir. The enchanting collection of towers and sculptures was created during the 17th and 18th centuries by Italian and Polish architects and their Polish-Lithuanian noble patrons. The buildings are elegantly designed with symmetrical façades, reflecting an unmistakable Italian influence. Nonetheless, the mystical atmosphere, so unique to Vilnius, distinguishes the area from any other European city.

★ Church of St Casimir
This church was the city's museum of atheism from 1963 to 1991. The crown symbolizes St Casimir's royal lineage ㉔

Town Hall
With a bold Classical portico, the Town Hall was designed by the renowned Lithuanian architect, Laurynas Stuoka-Gucevičius ㉒

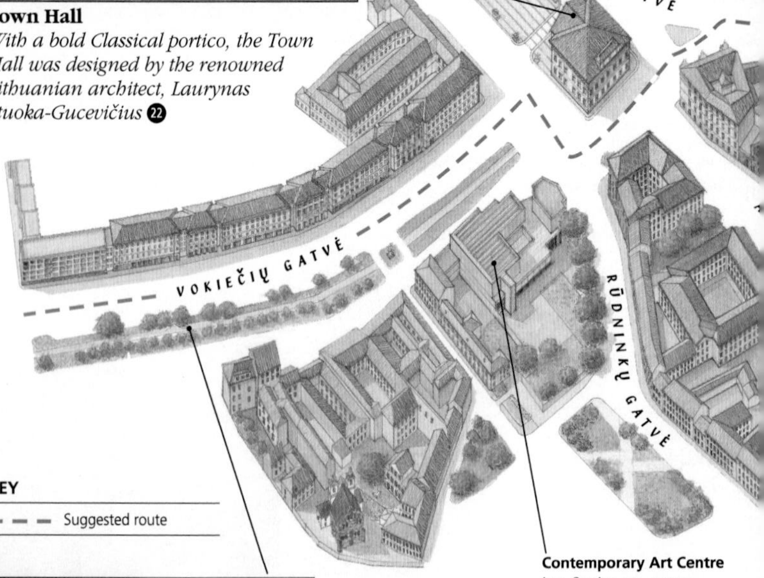

DIDŽIOJI GATVĖ

VOKIEČIŲ GATVĖ

RŪDNINKŲ GATVĖ

KEY

– – – Suggested route

Contemporary Art Centre
is a Soviet-era venue for groundbreaking modern art ㉓

Vokiečių Street
One of the city's oldest, Vokiečių Street resembles a park during the summer months, with its outdoor cafés and a pleasant central tree-lined walkway.

STAR SIGHTS

★ Church of St Casimir

★ Church of St Theresa

★ Gates of Dawn

Šv Kazimiero Street
A narrow cobblestone street named after St Casimir snakes around the back of the church towards Užupis with its jumble of roofs.

Church of the Holy Spirit

★ **Church of St Theresa**
Scenes from the life of St Theresa, revered for her mystical writings, adorn the vaulted nave of the church. The frescoes were painted in the late 18th century following a fire ㉗

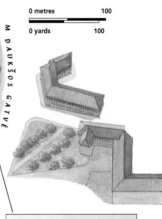

SUBAČIAUS GATVĖ

AUŠROS VARTŲ GATVĖ

M DAUKŠOS GATVĖ

BAZILIJONŲ GATVĖ

0 metres 100
0 yards 100

Basilian Gate

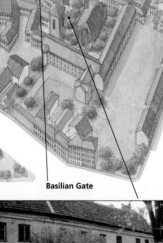

Basilian Monastery
The now dilapidated monastery complex was used as a prison to hold anti-Russian activists, including the poet Adam Mickiewicz, in the 1820s.

★ **Gates of Dawn**
A site of pilgrimage, this gateway to the Old Town protects a silver-covered painting of the Virgin Mary, said to have miraculous powers ㉘

Panoramic view of Town Hall Square, with flagpoles and church spires

Čiurlionis House ㉑
Čiurlionio namai

Savičiaus 11. **Map** 2 D4. **Tel** 262 2451. ☐ 10am–4pm Mon–Fri. Entrance from side door.

The former house of Mikalojus Konstantinas Čiurlionis (see p261) was turned into a museum in 1995, to mark the 120th anniversary of the birth of Lithuania's beloved artist and composer. Čiurlionis lived here in relative poverty with his wife Sofija, from October 1907 until June 1908, when they left Vilnius in search of success in St Petersburg.

Quite modest in scale, this museum does not attempt to rival the more extensive one dedicated to Čiurlionis in Kaunas (see p260). Instead, the museum mainly serves as an information resource and a venue to hear his chamber music concerts. Reproductions of the artist's paintings adorn the walls, as do photographs of him. Even today, Čiurlionis's grand piano stands here.

Town Hall Square ㉒
Rotušės aikštė

Didžioji 31. **Map** 2 D4. 🎭 Kaziuko Crafts Fair (Mar). **www**.vilnius rotuse.lt **Town Hall Tel** 261 8007. 🛈 Didžioji 31, 262 6470. ☐ 8am–6pm Mon–Fri.

Fully repaved in 2006, Town Hall Square was for centuries a market place and the centre of public life. It still bustles with activity, mainly during the annual Kaziuko Crafts Fair (see p208), when craft stalls line the square. The square's main building, the **Town Hall**,

was earlier the site of a court, and prisoners were marched from its cells to the square to be beheaded. The hall was constructed at the end of the 18th century and designed by the Classical architect, Laurynas Stuoka-Gucevičius (see p224). Today, the hall hosts about 200 cultural and social events around the year.

"Extreme Crafts", art exhibits at the Contemporary Art Centre

Contemporary Art Centre ㉓
Šiuolaikinio meno centras

Vokiečių 2. **Map** 2 D4. **Tel** 212 1945. ☐ noon–7:30pm Tue–Sun. 🎭 ▦ 🛈 **www**.cac.lt

The main gallery space for modern art exhibitions in Vilnius, the Contemporary Art Centre features works by both Lithuanian and international artists. The star attraction is the Fluxus Room, with a permanent exhibition dedicated to Fluxus, the radical art movement that emerged in New York in the 1960s. The room pays special tribute to the movement's creator, Kaunas-born George Maciunas (1931–78). Memorabilia evoking the populist spirit of Fluxus festivals and photographs of Maciunas fill the room.

Church of St Casimir ㉔
Šv Kazimiero bažnyčia

Didžioji 34. **Map** 2 D4. **Tel** 212 1715. 🛈 10:30am & 5:30pm Mon–Fri, noon Sun.

The city's first Baroque church, St Casimir was destroyed by fire three times after being built by the Jesuits between 1604 and 1635, prompting heavy reconstruction in the 1750s. Much of the interior was destroyed in 1812, when Napoleon's army used the church as a granary. It became a Russian Orthodox church during the 19th century and onion domes were added to it.

During World War I, it served as a Lutheran church for the German army and was then returned to the Jesuits and restored in the 1920s. The dome was rebuilt in 1942 and the crown was added. The Soviets used the church as a museum of atheism from 1963. It was reconsecrated in 1991.

Altarpiece at Church of St Casimir, depicting the saint's resurrection

Baroque Vilnius

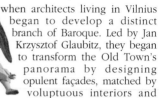

The sensual waves, rich colours and theatrical stucco figures of Baroque architecture reached Lithuania during the first half of the 17th century, replacing Gothic and Renaissance. Italian masters, invited by Lithuania's rulers, built Baroque gems such as St Casimir's Chapel *(see p225)* and the Church of St Theresa. In the mid-17th century came a second resurgence of the style, when architects living in Vilnius began to develop a distinct branch of Baroque. Led by Jan Krzysztof Glaubitz, they began to transform the Old Town's panorama by designing opulent façades, matched by voluptuous interiors and multiple altars. By the end of the 18th century Baroque had been replaced by the far more restrained values of Neo-Classicism.

Angel with golden wings, Dominican Church

St Casimir's Chapel, *in Vilnius Cathedral, is an early Baroque gem, beautified intricately with marble from Galicia and the Carpathians, lavish stucco and 17th-century frescoes.*

St John's Church (see p222), *one of Glaubitz's first works in Vilnius, boasts an overwhelming four-tier façade made up of clusters of columns. Inside there are ten interconnected altars.*

The Basilian Gate (see p234) *of the Basilian monastery was built by Glaubitz in 1761. The 18-m (59-ft) structure carries a depiction of the Holy Trinity, to which the church in the complex is dedicated.*

Church of St Theresa (see p234) *boasts radiant frescoes, glittering altars and an image of the Madonna, believed to be miraculous.*

JAN KRZYSZTOF GLAUBITZ (1700–67)

The most influential of Vilnius's late Baroque architects, Jan Krzysztof Glaubitz developed a distinct school of Lithuanian Baroque known as Vilnius Baroque. Born in Silesia, Glaubitz was a Lutheran of German origin who moved to Vilnius at the age of 37 and designed structures for all faiths in this multi-religious city. Among his most celebrated works are the magnificent façades of the Basilian Gate, St John's Church, Church of St Catherine *(see p237)*, the Church of the Holy Spirit *(see p234)* and the now destroyed Great Synagogue *(see p239)*.

Exterior of Church of St Catherine, Old Town

Ornate Baroque entranceway of the Basilian Gate

Basilian Gate ㉕
Bazilijonų vartai

Aušros vartų 7b. **Map** 2 D5.

The awe-inspiring Basilian Gate was designed in 1761 in flamboyant late Baroque style by J K Glaubitz (see p233). An all-seeing eye peers out from the central niche. The white bas-relief at the top portrays the Holy Trinity, a hint of what lies beyond the gate. The **Church of the Holy Trinity**, placed in the hands of the Uniates in 1598, stands at the centre of an enclosed court-yard. This was once a seclu-ded monastery, but in 1823 the Tsarist authorities turned it into a prison for anti-Russian revolutionaries and kept Adam Mickiewicz (see p229)

there the same year. The Uniates who live here now, are sometimes willing to show visitors round.

🔒 **Church of the Holy Trinity**
Tel 212 2578. ✝ 5:30pm Mon–Sat, 10am Sun.

Church of the Holy Spirit ㉖
Šv Dvasios cerkvė

Aušros vartų 10. **Map** 2 D5. *Tel* 212 7765. ⛔ ✝ 7am, 5pm Mon–Fri; 7am Sat; 7am, 10am Sun.

This Baroque church is the religious centre of the city's Russian Orthodox faithful. Though completed in 1634, it remains rem-arkably intact, the only alterations to the exterior being a raised façade and a new dome added in the late 19th century. The painting over the doorway depicts Sts Anthony, Ivan and Eustachius, whose remains lie within, miraculously preserved. In the 14th century, the three were Christians in the court of pagan Grand Duke Algirdas. When the pagan priests demanded that they renounce their faith, they refused and were hanged from an oak tree. They were canonized in 1547 and the nearby Church of the Holy Trinity was built in place of the oak.

Church of St Theresa ㉗
Šv Teresės bažnyčia

Aušros vartų 14. **Map** 2 D5. *Tel* 212 3513. ✝ 9am, 6:30pm daily.

Another early feature of the Baroque landscape, built from 1630 to 1655, is the Church of St Theresa, which stands in front of the Gates of Dawn. Materials like black marble in the portal and sandstone from Sweden, used to beautify its façade, were also used in the St Casimir's Chapel inside Vilnius Cathedral (see pp224–5) around the same time. This has led some researchers to believe that Italian craftsmen who designed the chapel also contributed to the Church of St Theresa. The main attraction of the church is its interior, with its frescoes and altars dating back to the second half of the 18th century. The painting on the high altar is *The Exaltation of St Theresa* by Szymon Czechowicz (1689–1775). St Theresa of Ávila in Spain inspired the formation in 1593 of the Discalced (Barefoot) Carmelites, a Roman Catholic order whose emphasis was on discipline and prayer. A convent was located next door, but today it is a hotel, the Domus Maria (see p308).

Painting, Church of St Theresa

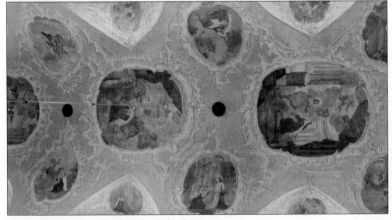

Stunning frescoes on the ceiling of the Church of St Theresa

Image of the Virgin Mary, seen through the window of the Gates of Dawn

Gates of Dawn ㉘
Aušros vartai

Aušros vartų 12. **Map** 2 D5.
Tel 212 3513. 🔲 7:30am, 9am,
10am, 5:30pm, 6:30pm Mon–Sat;
9am, 9:30am, 11am, 6:30pm Sun.
www.ausrosvartai.lt

The Classical chapel of Gates of Dawn follows the centuries-old custom of having a chapel or a religious image in every gateway to safeguard the city from outside enemies and protect departing travellers. The focus of this chapel is *The Madonna of Mercy*, an image reputed to have miracle-working powers. It was painted on oak in the 1620s and encased in silver 150 years later. The miracles attributed to it were faithfully recorded by nuns at the neighbouring Carmelite convent. Hundreds of hearts of different sizes stand out on plates of silver around the painting.

The Classical chapel that houses the image dates from 1829, when it was rebuilt from an earlier Baroque version. A flight of steps leads up to the chapel from a door in the street. A site of pilgrimage, it was one of the first stops for Pope John Paul II when he visited Lithuania in 1993.

This is the only gateway from the early 16th-century city walls to have survived. It becomes more evident when viewed from the outside where round holes that were used for cannons are still visible.

Kazys Varnelis Museum ㉙
Kazio Varnelio namai-muziejus

Didžioji 26. **Map** 2 D4. **Tel** 279
1644. 🔲 10am–4pm Tue–Sat (by
appointment only).

An extraordinary collection of modern art, maps, graphics, paintings, sculptures, vintage furniture, books and ceramics, as well as art from around the world, fill the home of the famous Lithuanian-American artist Kazys Varnelis (b.1917). Some of the rooms look truly avant-garde, mixing Italian Renaissance furniture and French Baroque with 20th-century American modern art. Other rooms have over 150 maps, including some of Lithuania dating from 1507. The book section has around 7,000 volumes of unique publications. The collection includes a number of books by famous illustrators.

Varnelis, renowned for creating optical illusions based on geometric patterns in his paintings, rarely meets visitors now.

Artillery Bastion ㉚
Bastėja

Bokšto 20/18. **Map** 2 E4. **Tel** 261
2149. 🔲 May–Sep: 10am–5pm Tue–
Sat, 10am–3pm Sun; Oct–Apr:
10am–5pm Wed–Sun.

Constructed as part of the city defences in the first half of the 17th century, the bastion had fallen into ruin by the end of the 18th century. It was used as an orphanage and the city's pre-eminent rubbish heap, and was finally cleaned up by the Germans during World War I to store ammunition. Its cool interior made it an ideal space for storing vegetables during the early Soviet period.

In 1987 it was opened as a museum. Although there is not a great deal to see, the museum holds a certain fascination for history enthusiasts. Outside, there are pleasant views of the Old Town and the hilly Užupis district.

Red-brick Artillery Bastion, dating from the 17th century

Church of St Nicholas ③①
Šv Mikalojaus bažnyčia

Šv Mikalojaus 4. **Map** 2 D4.
Tel 262 3069. 🚹 8am, 6pm Mon–
Fri; 9am Sat; 8am, 10am, 2pm Sun.

One of the oldest churches in Lithuania, the Church of St Nicholas was built when the country was still pagan. Most of its simple Gothic façade and interior dates from the 16th century. The interior is defined by the decorative brick veins of the vaulting. Some colourful paintings discovered here include a striking image of the sun.

The church has patriotic connotations for Lithuanians, as from 1901 to 1939, when Vilnius was occupied by Russia and then Poland, it was one of the few churches allowed to hold Lithuanian-language services.

In the churchyard, the statue of St Christopher carrying the Infant Christ, created in 1959, also helped to keep the spirits of the people alive. The sculptor, Antanas Kmieliauskas (b.1932), was expelled from the Association of Artists because of it. He later frescoed Littera bookshop in Vilnius University *(see p222)*.

Surviving fragment of a fresco on the ceiling of the Franciscan Church

Franciscan Church ③②
Pranciškonų bažnyčia

Trakų 9/1. **Map** 1 C4. *Tel* 261 4242.
🚹 5:30pm Mon–Sat; 10am,
11:30am Sun.

The cracked and cavernous, yet highly evocative, Franciscan Church is also known as the Church of Our Lady of the Assumption. It stands on a spot where, in the 14th century, Franciscan friars established a base on the road to Trakai *(see pp252–3)*. The Conventual Franciscans chose to settle in the poorest of urban areas, reaching out to the destitute, often outside the safety of the city walls. The Gothic main doorway dates from this earlier period, but the rest of the structure was built in the 1770s. After the 1863 uprising *(see p214)*, the church and friary were closed and used as a granary and an archive. The altars and the now unidentifiable frescoes above the nave were virtually destroyed, as was a tall Gothic bell tower that stood on Pranciškonų Street.

Dominican Church ③③
Šv Dvasios bažnyčia

Domininkonų 8. **Map** 2 D4. *Tel* 262 9595. 🚹 7am, 7:30am, 3pm, 6pm Mon–Sat; 8am, 9am, 10:30am, noon, 1:30pm, 6pm Sun.

Also known as the Church of the Holy Spirit, the current building of the Dominican Church dates from the years of repair that followed the destructive war of 1655–61 during the Russian occupation. However, a church has stood on this spot since the 14th century.

The unassuming doorway, which can be easily missed,

Lavishly decorated interior of the Dominican Church, featuring Rococo altars

belies the sumptuous interior. Figures in stucco stand out on 15 lavishly decorated Rococo altars. The altars, which are embellished with colourful paintings, also feature gilded frames and faux marble Corinthian columns – all hallmarks of the late Baroque style. The fresco-lined vestibule, which forms a passage into the nave from the street, gives the church a cavern-like quality, emphasized by the dark, candlelit interior.

During Napoleon's chaotic retreat in 1812, the friary next to the church was converted into a hospital and the crypt was used as a morgue. Today, the crypt is still full of stacks of mummified corpses from this time, preserved by the dry air. The crypt is, however, off-limits to visitors.

Movie cameras on display at the Theatre, Music and Film Museum

Façade of the Church of St Catherine, with strawberry-and-cream towers

Church of St Catherine ㉞
Šv Kotrynos bažnyčia

Vilniaus gatvė 30. **Map** 2 D3.

Originally a small wooden structure, the Church of St Catherine formed part of a Benedictine monastery in the early 17th century. The church was rebuilt in stone in 1703, almost 50 years after the Russians burned it down. The structure, as it appears today, was built and considerably expanded between 1741 and 1773. Its sophisticated design, highlighted by the delightful strawberry-and-cream twin towers, is attributed to Lithuania's

much-celebrated Baroque architect Jan Krzysztof Glaubitz (see p233).

The church suffered some damage during World War II and was reopened in 2006 after lengthy renovation. It is now regularly used as a popular venue for classical music concerts and performances. In the garden facing the church, there is a bust monument of the well-known Polish composer Stanislaw Moniuszko (1819–72), who wrote his first operas while working as an organist in Vilnius. The area to the east of the church is where a large convent for Benedictine nuns stood from 1622 until the Soviet period. The church's interior is highly decorated but not fully repaired, giving it an air of authenticity.

Theatre, Music and Film Museum ㉟
Lietuvos teatro, muzikos, kino muziejus

Vilniaus 41. **Map** 1 C4. **Tel** 231 2724. ☐ 11am–6pm Tue–Fri, 11am–4pm Sat. www.ltmkm.lt

Housed inside a 17th-century mansion once owned by the powerful Radvila family, who ruled Lithuania in the 16th century, this absorbing museum was founded

Phonograph, Theatre, Music and Film Museum

by the Ministry of Culture. The museum's expansive collection is a tribute to the Lithuanians' love of theatre and classical music. The exhibits include theatre memorabilia ranging from old costumes and puppets to stage-set pieces, mostly from the 19th and early 20th centuries. The superb collection of folk instruments features a number of kanklės (decorated Lithuanian stringed instruments related to the zither).

The space given to cinema is limited and not as informative, although there are some displays on cinematography.

Radvila Palace ㊱
Radvilų rūmai

Vilniaus 24. **Map** 1 C3. **Tel** 262 0981. ☐ 11am–6pm Tue–Sat, noon–5pm Sun. www.ldm.lt

The early 17th-century palace, once grand in size, was reduced to just one wing by the end of the Northern War (1700–21). Now an art gallery, it hosts a permanent display, including 165 portraits of members of the Radvila family. Temporary exhibitions feature little-known, but often surprisingly impressive, paintings by Lithuanian artists from the 19th and early 20th centuries.

Holocaust Museum in the Green House, annexe of the State Jewish Museum

State Jewish Museum ❸

Valstybinis Vilniaus gaono žydų Muziejus

Pylimo 4. **Map** 1 C3. **Tel** 212 7912. ☐ 9am–1pm Mon–Fri. 🖼 📷 excursions of the museum & Vilnius Old Town offered. **www**.jmuseum.lt

The hub of the city's now tiny Jewish community, this small museum displays copies of ghetto diaries and handwritten notes on the backs of cigarette packets about life in the ghetto, plus items that remained from the museum that existed before World War II. Several objects that miraculously survived from the Great Synagogue include a bas-relief of the Ten Commandments.

The museum building also hosts a Union of Former Ghetto and Concentration Camp Prisoners, a Union of Jewish War Veterans, a youth club and a newspaper in Yiddish, English, Lithuanian and Russian called *Jerusalem of Lithuania*.

Holocaust Museum ❸

Holokausto ekspozicija

Pamėnkalnio 12. **Map** 1 C3. **Tel** 262 4590. ☐ 9am–5pm Mon–Thu, 9am–4pm Fri, 10am–4pm Sun. 🖼 📷 **www**.jmuseum.lt

Located in the Green House, this annexe of the State Jewish Museum reveals some of the horror that befell the Jews of Lithuania during World War II. A display on Jewish life before the terror unfolded is followed by maps and photographs showing how and where the Holocaust was executed. Descriptions of how harsh life was in the ghettoes are followed by eyewitness accounts of the mass killings in the forests of Paneriai *(see p244)*.

Frank Zappa Statue ❸

Kalinausko 1. **Map** 1 C3.

The world's first statue of the prolific Californian rock legend Frank Zappa was created in Vilnius shortly after his death from cancer in 1993. A group of local artists wanted to test the limits of newly independent Lithuania's proclamations of democracy and freedom and were pleasantly surprised when their idea for the statue was approved. The bust was created by the then 70-year-old Konstantinas Bogdanas, known for his statues of Lenin and other notable Communists.

Bust of Frank Zappa

KGB Museum ❹

Genocido aukų muziejus

Aukų 2a. **Map** 1 C2. **Tel** 249 8156. ☐ 10am–6pm Wed–Sat, 10am–5pm Sun. 🖼 📷 📷 **www**.genocid.lt

Also known as the Museum of Genocide Victims, the KGB Museum was opened in 1992, on the ground floor of the former KGB building. In this effectively designed display area, personal stories are used to reveal the regime of terror under Stalin until 1940 and then until 1991 under the former Soviet Union.

The exhibits chronicle the Soviet occupation of Lithuania, the cattle-car deportations to Siberia and the futile efforts of the Forest Brothers *(see p118)* who fought the Soviets. Below ground, the cells were in use right up until the late 1980s and are even more overwhelming. They include tiny cells used in winter with no glass in the window and a floor filled with water, and an execution chamber displaying, under glass, the dug-up remains of victims. In 1997, the museum was taken over by the Genocide and Resistance Research Centre of Lithuania, a state institution dedicated to investigating atrocities that occurred in the country during the Nazi and Soviet occupations.

Exhibits in the corridor outside the former execution chamber, KGB Museum

Jewish Vilnius

Until it was eliminated during the Holocaust, Jewish Vilna, or Vilnius, was home to a large, influential Jewish community. About 250,000 Jews lived in Lithuania at the turn of the 19th century, compared to just 4,000 today, and 40 per cent of Vilnius's population was Jewish. By the early 19th century, Vilnius had emerged as a major centre of Jewish learning and bustled with life. The

Domed ceiling, Choral Synagogue

religious customs of the Litvaks, as Lithuanian Jews are known in Yiddish, were marked by a rigid analysis of the Talmud, the Jewish laws and traditions. As a result, other Jewish communities in Eastern Europe saw the Vilna Jews as being old-fashioned and staunch intellectuals. Decimated by World War II and ravaged further by the Soviets, Jewish Vilna is a ghostly reminder of a vanished world.

The Great Synagogue, *built in 1572, was restored with an Italian Renaissance interior by Glaubitz. The Soviets destroyed the remains of the Jewish quarter after World War II, broadening Vokiečių Street and bulldozing this awe-inspiring building.*

Jewish Vilna before World War II *had its cobbled lanes crowded with artisans' workshops and cafés. A maze of courtyards and passages that lay around Vokiečių and Žydų streets, concealed synagogues and prayer houses.*

Vilnius Choral Synagogue *is the only one in the country to survive World War II. Located on Pylimo Street 39, the synagogue started functioning in 1903. Although it was smaller in scale and simpler in design than Vilnius's other synagogues, the Choral Synagogue has an enchanting interior.*

Elijah Ben Solomon (see p36), *known as Vilna Gaon, or "genius", was a leading Talmud scholar who wrote extensive commentaries on ancient Hebrew books. He advocated an empirical study of religious scriptures over mysticism.*

A map of Vilna Ghetto *is shown on the wall at Rūdininkų 18. This is where the Jews of Vilnius were imprisoned during World War II, and the ghetto's only gate once stood.*

Further Afield

As most of Vilnius's main sites are concentrated in the Old Town, visitors often ignore the suburbs. It can be rewarding, however, to escape the bustling city centre and to discover Vilnius as a living city as well as a picturesque time capsule. A trip to the TV Tower affords excellent views on a clear day, while Vingis Park and Verkiai Palace are ideal for walking and a breath of fresh air. Paneriai and Antakalnis Cemetery, meanwhile, recount Lithuania's often tragic history.

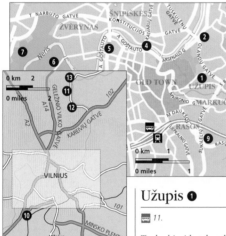

SIGHTS AT A GLANCE

Antakalnis Cemetery **3**
Calvary Church of the
    Holy Cross **11**
Church of Sts Peter and Paul **2**
Green Bridge **4**
Paneriai Holocaust Memorial **10**
Parliament **5**
Pushkin Museum **8**
Rasos Cemetery **9**
TV Tower **7**
Trinapolis Church **12**
Užupis **1**
Verkiai Palace **13**
Vingis Park and Žvėrynas **6**

KEY

■	City centre
✈	Airport
▣	Railway station
▥	Bus station
▬	Motorway
▬	Main road
═	Minor road

Užupis **1**

▥ 11.

Tucked inside a bend in the Vilnia river, Užupis translates as "Behind the River". This picturesque part of central Vilnius has narrow streets filled with cafés, art galleries and mysterious hidden courtyards. The artists who live here declared independence in 1997, with their own flag, president and independence day (1 April). Their constitution, which features articles such as "Everyone has the right to understand nothing", is nailed to a wall on Paupio Street. The statue of an angel, the symbol of Užupis, stands on nearby Užupio Street. The bizarre **Alternative Art Centre**, where the door is always open, stands by the river between Užupio and Malūnų. A stroll further east leads to the serene Bernardinų Cemetery.

The terrace of the Tores café *(see p339)* on Krivių has one of the town's best views. Another viewpoint can be found on an unmarked footpath behind the school on Krivių Street. The footpath then plunges down the Vilnia Valley into Kalnų Park.

Church of Sts Peter and Paul **2**

See pp242–3.

Antakalnis Cemetery **3**
Antakalnio kapinės

Karių kapų 11. *Tel* 234 0587.

The largest public cemetery in Vilnius brings together much of the city's modern history. Statues and memorial stones cover the verdant landscape, the crosses and tombs inscribed in Lithuanian, Russian and Polish. The main path leads past a wave of identical stone crosses dedicated to Polish soldiers who died during World War I. At the heart of the cemetery is a sweeping semicircular memorial cut into the hillside for the 14 civilians who were

Imaginatively painted façade of the Alternative Art Centre, Užupis

Graves of civilians killed by Russian tanks in 1991, Antakalnis Cemetery

killed while defending the TV Tower and the Parliament in 1991. A path to the right of the cemetery entrance leads to Soviet-era war memorials.

Green Bridge ➍
Žaliasis tiltas

The first bridge crossing the river at this point was built in the 16th century, but the current one dates from 1952, the year before Stalin's death. At its four corners stand Socialist Realist statues and reasons abound for not pulling them down. One is that they are a reminder of the ugliness of Soviet monoculture; another is that locals have come to regard them as genuine works of art. Whatever the reason, the statues of confident workers, peasants and soldiers, once built to instill optimism among the masses in a brave new Communist future, are here to stay, however odd they may seem amid Vilnius's skyscrapers.

Soviet-era statues that adorn Green Bridge

Parliament ➎
Lietuvos respublikos seimas

Gedimino 53. **Tel** 239 6060. 🚌 24.
🖳 www.lrs.lt

The far end of Gedimino Avenue is marked by the Seimas, Lithuania's

Parliament. Built in 1982, the building is typical of the late Soviet era. The similarly monumental National Library, constructed 20 years earlier, stands beside it on the other side of Independence Square.

It was in the Seimas, on 11 March 1990, that the act declaring independence from the Soviet Union was signed. During the subsequent siege, in 1991, concrete barricades and Catholic shrines were put up around the building to protect it against Soviet tanks. These were finally removed in 1993, and the remnants emblazoned with graffiti demanding freedom and democracy can still be seen on the western side of the Seimas.

Vingis Park and Žvėrynas ➏

🚌 11. 🍴 🖳 🏠

The leafy Žvėrynas district was created from the Radvila family's forest-covered hunting grounds, which were sold off from 1893 as plots of land for development. The streets are lined with old wooden villas and contemporary mansions. The silver-domed Orthodox Church of the Apparition of the Holy Mother of God (1903) looms over the Neris river. The tiny Kenesa (1922), where the Karaim

(see p253) used to congregate, stands on Liubarto Street. Vingis Park, reached via a suspension footbridge on the western side of Žvėrynas, is filled with towering pine trees and footpaths. At the centre of the park is an open-air auditorium used for concerts and, every five years, the climax to the World Lithuanian Song Festival. To the east, where the pleasant M K Čiurlionio Street meets the park, a cemetery for German soldiers killed during the two World Wars has been restored.

TV Tower ➐
Vilniaus televizijos bokštas

Sausio 13–Osios 10. **Tel** 252 5333.
🚌 49. ⏰ 10am–9pm daily. 🎫 📷
🍴 🏠 www.lrtc.net

The grand 326-m (1,070-ft) TV Tower is set against a striking backdrop of tall pines. On the ground floor, there is a small display paying tribute to those who were shot or crushed beneath Soviet tanks while trying to defend the tower on 13 January 1991. Granite markers outside show where they fell.

The tower's observation deck houses a state-run café, Paukščių Takas, at a height of 165 m (541 ft). The rotating deck makes a full circle in about 50 minutes and offers spectacular views of the area. On a clear day, visibility is 70 km (43 miles) in every direction, with views stretching into Belarus, about 40 km (25 miles) away.

Elegant TV Tower, soaring high above its surroundings

Church of Sts Peter and Paul ➋
Šv Petro ir Povilo bažnyčia

With its breathtaking interior of over 2,000 white stucco figures featuring angels and demons, biblical scenes and some gruesome historical images, the Church of Sts Peter and Paul is essentially a glorified Baroque mausoleum to its wealthy patron Michal Kazimierz Pac (1624–82). He was a Lithuanian military leader and the provincial governor of Vilnius. Pac's portrait hangs by the altar, his crest is positioned over the door and his body lies under the front steps. Built over the remains of two earlier wooden churches, the second of which was badly damaged during a brutal war with Moscow from 1655 to 1661, the church was intended to stand as a lasting monument to peace.

Twin-towered façade of the Church of Sts Peter and Paul

The interior is a fine ensemble of exquisite stucco and richly decorated chapels.

Boat-Shaped Chandelier
A late addition to the interior and a reference to St Peter's profession as a fisherman, the glass-bead chandelier was made by Latvian craftsmen in 1905.

Altar
The original high altar was replaced by The Parting of St Peter and St Paul *(1801), created by the Polish historical painter, Pranciškus Smuglevičius (1745–1807).*

STAR FEATURES

★ Chapel of the Holy Queens

★ Vaulted Nave and Cupola

★ Chapel of St Ursula

★ Chapel of the Holy Queens
The chapel to the north of the nave is rich in stucco. The female figure perched over the arch giving a coin to a beggar denotes compassion.

★ Vaulted Nave and Cupola
The exuberance of the decoration attains a dizzying scale as the nave reaches the cupola, the rectangular reliefs, flowers and cartouches, giving way to a spiral of animated angels and the face of God at the apex.

The inscription above the balcony reads "*Regina pacis funda nos in pace*" ("Queen of Peace protect us in peace"), probably a play on the patron's name.

Smiling Madonna in the Chapel of St Casimir in Vilnius Cathedral

THE ITALIAN CONNECTION
The first flowering of Lithuanian Baroque in the early 17th century took place when Lithuania's rulers invited Italian architects and sculptors to redesign the city. Matteo Castello (1560–1632) designed St Casimir's Chapel *(see p225)*. His nephew, Constante Tencalla (1590–1646), completed it, then created the façade of the Church of St Theresa *(see p234)*. Half a century later, artists Perti, Galli and Palloni arrived in Vilnius to adorn the Church of Sts Peter and Paul.

★ Chapel of St Ursula
Ursula was an English princess seized by the Huns with ten virgin companions and shot with arrows. Images of their fate are balanced by four sculptures of female saints including Mary Magdalene.

Ornate Stucco Portico
The rippling central shield above the doorway, flanked by figures of young boys, displays a fleur-de-lis, a symbol from Pac's coat of arms. The glorious stucco work adorning the entire church is attributed to the Italian masters Pietro Perti and Giovanni Maria Galli.

VISITORS' CHECKLIST

Antakalnio gatvė 1.
Tel 234 0229. 7am, 7:30am, 6pm Mon–Fri; 8:30am, 1pm Sat; 7:30am, 10am, 11:30am, 6pm Sun. Services in Lithuanian & Polish only.

Delightful wooden building of the Pushkin Museum

Pushkin Museum ⑧
Puškino memorialinis
muziejus

Subačiaus 124. **Tel** 260 0080.
🚌 10,13. ⬜ 10am–5pm Wed–Sun.
🖼 🖋

This museum is located in a
bright yellow wooden house,
which stands out on a pleasant grassy hill. It was not
the great Russian poet, but
his son Grigorij (1835–1905)
who lived here with his wife
Varvara (1855–1935). Founded
in 1940 and opened in 1948,
the museum is now home to
many volumes of Alexander
Pushkin's works and the
ground floor is furnished in
the late 19th-century style.

At the back of the house,
behind a statue of Pushkin,
are acres of tranquil grounds
and a small onion-domed
family mausoleum. Steps lead
down to a lake, and the paths
that reach out into the surrounding countryside are a
delight to explore.

Rasos Cemetery ⑨
Rasų kapinės

Rasų gatvė. **Tel** 265 6563. 🚌 31.

Revered national figures
and ordinary Vilnius folk lie
side by side in this cemetery
founded in 1769. Some of
the distinguished tombstones
include those of Jonas

Basanavičius (1851–1927),
founder of the first Lithuanian-
language newspaper *Aušra*
(Dawn), composer and
painter M K Čiurlionis *(see
p261)* and Marija and Jurgis
Šlapelis *(see p223)*. A more
controversial monument is
the tomb of the man res-
ponsible for Poland's annexa-
tion of Vilnius in 1920, Józef
Piłsudski (1867–1935). His
body lies among those of the
kings and queens of Kraków,
but by his wishes his heart
was cut out and placed
here under a granite slab.
The cemetery is spiritually
significant for the Lithuanians.
In 1956, a crowd gathered
here to protest the suppression
of the Hungarian uprising
against Soviet occupation.

Paneriai Holocaust Memorial ⑩
Panerių memorialinis
muziejus

Agrastų 17, 8 km (5 miles) SW
of Vilnius. **Tel** 868 081278. 🚉 from
Vilnius. ⬜ 9am–5pm Mon–Thu, Sun.

Centuries of Jewish culture
and tradition in Vilnius ended
at this major Holocaust site.
About 70,000 Jewish men,
women and children were
slaughtered in the forests of

Imposing tombstones of Marija and Jurgis Šlapelis at the Rasos Cemetery

For hotels and restaurants in this region see pp308–310 and pp338–40

Paneriai between July 1941 and August 1944. Around 29,000 Poles, Russians and people of other nationalities were killed, as were many of Roma and about 500 Catholic priests. The executions were carried out by Nazi units with the help of a squad of Lithuanians. The sites, including a large pit where, in 1944, the retreating Nazis attempted to destroy the last of the bodies with acid, are now an open-air memorial. The first memorial was raised here in 1948. The tiny visitor centre is closed in winter, but the rest of the site is accessible.

Fresco in a Station of the Cross, Calvary Church of the Holy Cross

Calvary Church of the Holy Cross **⓫**
Kalvarijos bažnyčia

Kalvarijų 327, 5 km (3 miles) N of Vilnius Old Town. **Tel** 269 7469.
🚌 26, 35, 36, 50. 🛐 6pm, 7pm Mon–Fri; 9am, 10:30am, noon, 1:30pm, 4pm Sun.

This twin-spire Baroque church towering over the Neris Valley was built by the Dominicans in the 1750s. The prime feature of its interior is a series of ceiling frescoes depicting the life of Christ. The main highlights are the nearby Stations of the Cross. Some 35 chapels, set along a 7-km (4-mile) hillside route, many in the Baroque style, were a popular attraction for 19th-century pilgrims. In 1962, they were destroyed by the Soviets. Several of the chapels have been re-created.

Twin-towered façade of the 18th-century Trinapolis Church

Trinapolis Church **⓬**
Šv Trejybės bažnyčia

Verkių 70. 🚌 26, 35, 36, 50.

The original wooden church lasted only 6 years before it burnt down in 1710. The solid Baroque structure that replaced it in 1722 was designed by Pietro Puttini, a Veronese architect. Following the 1831 uprising, the church was closed by the Russians and the interior destroyed. In 1849, it was converted into an Orthodox church and the Metropolitan, the city's highest-ranking Russian Orthodox personage, used the neighbouring monastery as his summer residence. In 1917, the church was returned to the Catholics and the Archbishop set up residence here. The church was closed during the Soviet era and is still not open to the public.

Verkiai Palace **⓭**
Verkių rūmai

Žaliųjų ežerių 49. **Tel** 210 2333.
🚌 35, 36, 76. 🔲 by appointment.
🎨 🎬 🍴

This once-immense Classical mansion was designed by Laurynas Stuoka-Gucevičius (1753–98) and Marcin Knackfus (1740–1821). The two distinguished architects were commissioned in 1781 to create a summer retreat for the Bishop of Vilnius. They built the palace on a site that, some 400 years previously, had been granted by Grand Duke Jogaila (see pp210–11) on his conversion to Christianity, to the new diocese of Vilnius.

The Classical gem was unfortunately short-lived. It was ravaged so much by the French army in 1812 that the subsequent owners had the central part pulled down. Only two wings of the palace survive and some decoration is still visible on the ceilings and the woodwork.

Verkiai Palace is also visited for its magnificent location. Standing on a hilltop above the Neris river, it offers a stunning view of the surrounding forests. A centuries-old legend tells how a sacred fire here was once tended by a pagan priest and beautiful virgins. The Verkiai restaurant (see p339) is located behind one of the palace wings. A winding path leads from the mansion gates down to **Vandens Malūnas**, a former watermill, which is now also a restaurant (see p338).

Vandens Malūnas, a former watermill near Verkiai Palace

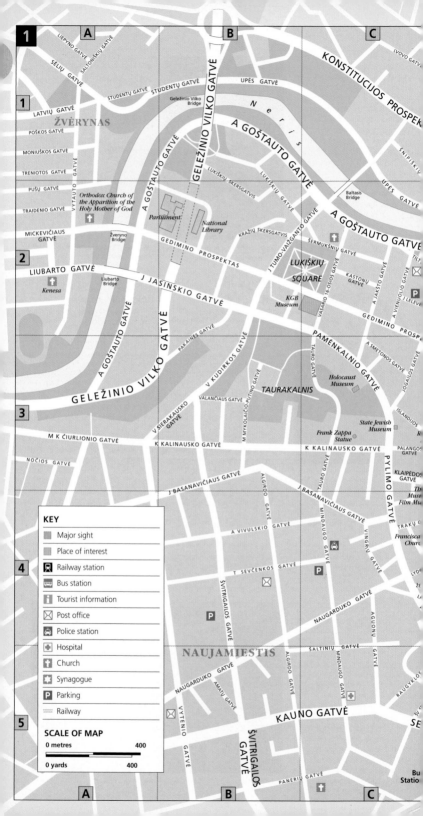

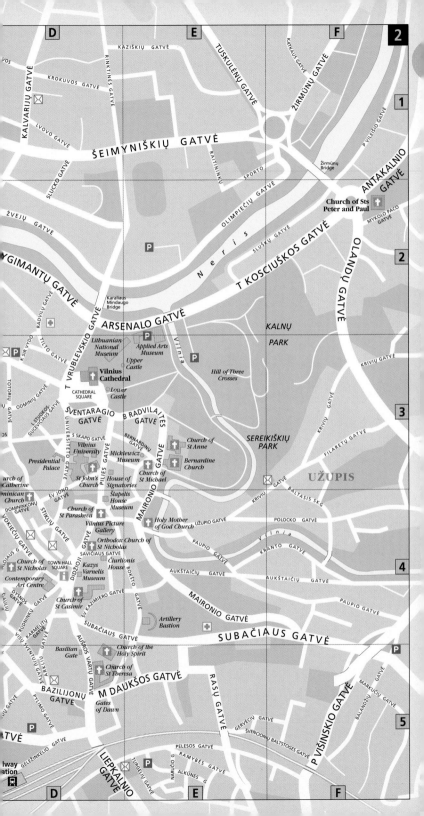

D **E** **F** **2**

KAZIŠKIŲ GATVĖ

KALVARIJŲ GATVĖ
KROKUVOS GATVĖ
RINKTINĖS GATVĖ
TUSKULĖNŲ GATVĖ
ŽIRMŪNŲ GATVĖ
KATKAUS GATVĖ

1

LVOVO GATVĖ

ŠEIMYNIŠKIŲ GATVĖ
ŠLUCKO GATVĖ
RAITININKŲ
SPORTO
OLIMPIEČIŲ GATVĖ
Žirmūnų
Bridge

ŽVEJŲ GATVĖ

ANTAKALNIO GATVĖ

P. VILEIŠIO GATVĖ

**Church of Sts
Peter and Paul**

MYKOLO PACO GATVĖ

Neris

SLUŠKŲ GATVĖ
T KOSCIUŠKOS GATVĖ

2

ŽYGIMANTŲ GATVĖ
RADVILŲ GATVĖ

OLANDŲ GATVĖ

Karaliaus
Mindaugo
Bridge
ARSENALO GATVĖ

KALNŲ
PARK

K ŠIR VYDO
TILTO GATVĖ
T VRUBLEVSKIO GATVĖ

P

Lithuanian
National
Museum
Applied Arts
Museum

P

**Vilnius
Cathedral**
Upper
Castle

Vilnia

P

KRIVIŲ GATVĖ

3

TOTORIŲ GATVĖ
ODMINIŲ GATVĖ
L STUOKOS GUCEVIČIAUS GATVĖ
SVENTARAGIO GATVĖ
UNIVERSITETO GATVĖ

CATHEDRAL
SQUARE
Lower
Castle

Hill of Three
Crosses

SEREIKIŠKIŲ
PARK

KRIVIŲ GATVĖ
FILARETŲ GATVĖ

B RADVILAITĖS GATVĖ
Bernardino
GATVĖ

Church of
St Anne

Bernardine
Church

UŽUPIS

S SKAPO GATVĖ
Vilnius
University
Mickiewicz
Museum

MAIRONIO GATVĖ

Presidential
Palace
St John's
Church
House of
Signatories
Church of
St Michael

KRIVIŲ GATVĖ
BALTASIS SKG

urch of
Catherine
ominican
Church
DOMININKONŲ GATVĖ
ŠV JONO GATVĖ
Slapelis
House
Museum

Holy Mother
of God Church

UŽUPIO GATVĖ
Vilnia
POLOCKO GATVĖ

4

VOKIEČIŲ GATVĖ
STIKLIŲ GATVĖ
Church of
St Paraskeva
Vilnius Picture
Gallery
PILIES GATVĖ
PAUPIO GATVĖ
KRANTO GATVĖ

Orthodox Church of
St Nicholas
SAVIČIAUS GATVĖ

LOJAUS G
DYMOS GATVĖ
ŠIAULIŲ
Church of
St Nicholas
Contemporary
Art Centre
TOWN HALL
SQUARE
Čiurlionis
House
Kazys
Varnelis
Museum
DIDŽIOJI

AUKŠTAIČIŲ GATVĖ
AUKŠTAIČIŲ GATVĖ

BOKŠTO GATVĖ
ŠV KAZIMIERO GATVĖ
Church of
St Casimir

MAIRONIO GATVĖ

PAUPIO GATVĖ

P

SUBAČIAUS GATVĖ
Artillery
Bastion

SUBAČIAUS GATVĖ

5

RUDNINKŲ GATVĖ
KARMELITŲ GATVĖ
VISŲ ŠVENTŲJŲ GATVĖ
AUŠROS VARTŲ GATVĖ
Basilian
Gate
Church of the
Holy Spirit

Church of
St Theresa

BAZILIJONŲ GATVĖ
PYLIMO GATVĖ

Gates
of Dawn
M DAUKŠOS GATVĖ

RASŲ GATVĖ
GERVEČIŲ GATVĖ
ŠVENČIONIŲ BALTSTOGĖS GATVĖ

P VIŠINSKIO GATVĖ
MARKUČIŲ GATVĖ
BALANDŽIŲ GATVĖ

P

GELEŽINKELIO GATVĖ
Iway
ation

LIEPKALNIO GATVĖ
TURGELIŲ GATVĖ
PELESOS GATVĖ
RAMYBĖS GATVĖ
NARUČIO G
ALKŪNES G

D **E** **F**

CENTRAL LITHUANIA

*R*olling hills, swathes of untouched ancient forest and thousands of clear lakes characterize Central Lithuania. Much of the land is protected, allowing birds, animals and plants to thrive. While Vilnius and Kaunas are the region's most vibrant cities, the less-visited towns and villages of the region, with their beautiful churches and farmsteads, also attract a number of visitors.

Lithuania's heartland is symbolized by the mysterious mounds and fort-hills of Kernavė where Mindaugas, the first king of Lithuania, is said to have united the Baltic tribes in an effort to hold back the crusading armies of the Teutonic Knights. Similarly, Trakai, with its fairytale Island Castle that once stood as the kernel of one of Europe's biggest empires, stirs romantic nationalism in Lithuanians. Kaunas, which served as the capital of independent Lithuania between the two World Wars, is often seen as the original seat of its nationhood, rather than Vilnius, the present-day capital.

Three of the country's four ethnographic regions, each with its own dialect and traditions, are located in this area. Much of Dzūkija, in the south, is thickly forested. In summer and autumn, villagers selling mushrooms or berries line the roads, particularly along the route from Vilnius to the spa town of Druskininkai. Some parts of Dzūkija, which stretches from Alytus in the west to Vilnius in the east, have large Polish-speaking communities.

Aukštaitija, which literally means "the highlands", consists of relatively high ground that is dotted with lakes. Although some forest has survived the centuries, much of Aukštaitija was used for agriculture during the 20th century. With the exception of the Russian-speaking town of Visaginas, Aukštaitija is almost exclusively Lithuanian-speaking and is the country's archaic hinterland. Centred around Marijampolė, Suvalkija, or Sūduva, is the smallest ethnographic region, with its dress and customs once influenced by Prussia as well as Poland.

Permanent display entitled "Space of Unknown Growth" at the open-air art museum, Europe Park

◁ **Picturesque view of the fairytale Island Castle at Trakai**

Exploring Central Lithuania

The well-kept roads winding through the region offer great opportunities for exploring the forests around the spa town of Druskininkai in the south as well as the lakes and villages of Aukštaitija National Park in the northeast. The best way to experience this pristine landscape is to venture off the main roads, onto the scenic minor routes connecting Trakai–Birštonas, Varėna–Marcinkonys–Merkinė and Molėtai–Ignalina. However, Central Lithuania is more than just lakes and forests. The towns are scenic and there is a good choice of old-fashioned farmsteads to visit.

Flower beds in the pedestrianized centre of Panevėžys

SIGHTS AT A GLANCE

Towns and Resorts
Alytus ⑧
Anykščiai ⑰
Birštonas ⑪
Biržai ⑮
Druskininkai ⑤
Kalvarija ⑨
Kaunas pp258–61 ⑫
Kėdainiai ⑬
Kernavė ③
Marijampolė ⑩
Molėtai Lakelands ⑱
Panevėžys ⑭
Rokiškis ⑯
Varėna ④
Visaginas ⑲

National Parks
Aukštaitija National Park pp266–7 ⑳
Dzūkija National Park ⑦
Trakai Island Castle pp252–3 ①

Sites of Interest
Europe Park ②
Grūtas Park ⑥

Rīga

Ne
Ra

⑮

Kiemėnai   A7   125

Mūša

Tetirvina

Pasvalys   G

Jonišlėlis   150

A10

Pyvesa

Pakruojis

Pušalotas

Levuo

Rozalimas

Ku

Paliūniškis

Šiauliai

A9

Šmilgiai

A17   ⑭ PANEVĖŽY

Dapšioniai

Upytė

Tros

A8

Krekenava

A2

Dotnuvėlė   144   195

Ramygala

Surviliškis

Dotnuva

Ilgižiai

Šušvė

Ukr

⑬ KĖDAINIAI

Josvainiai   Labūnava

Jurbarkas

A1   229   195

145

Daugelišiai

Didieji
Bėnai   144

Jonava

Babtai   A8

Vilkija

Nemunas   141

Nėris

A6

Liu

KAUNAS ⑫

Kaišiadorys

Ezėrėlis

Garliava   129

Ele

Maiuručiai

Jūrė   130

Slabadai

Nemunas

Pilviškiai   230

Užuogstis

A5

Kaliningrad

137

Tiesa

Prienai

⑪ BIRŠTONAS

Virbalis

A7   A16

Punia   Verknė

185

Skra

Vištytis   182

Varnupiai

⑩ MARIJAMPOLĖ

ALYTUS ⑧

200   ⑨ KALVARIJA

Šimnas   131

Liubavas

A5

Lake
Dusios   129   D

180   Merkinė

DZŪKIJA NATIONAL
PARK ⑦

Kučiūnai

Liškiava   Marcink

⑤ ⑥ GRŪTA
PARK

DRUSKININKAI ⑤

Gerdašiai

SEE ALSO

GETTING AROUND

The A1 motorway between Vilnius and Kaunas and onwards to the coast, and the A2 motorway from Vilnius to Panevėžys are the region's major arteries. Good bases for exploring are Kaunas, Druskininkai, Anykščiai and Palūšė, each of which is reachable by bus. Buses traverse Aukštaitija and Dzūkija national parks, but the best way to enjoy the surroundings is to reach the pretty villages of Zervynos and Salos II on foot. Trains go to Kaunas and Ignalina from the capital, but road transport should be taken to all other areas. There are airports at Vilnius and Kaunas.

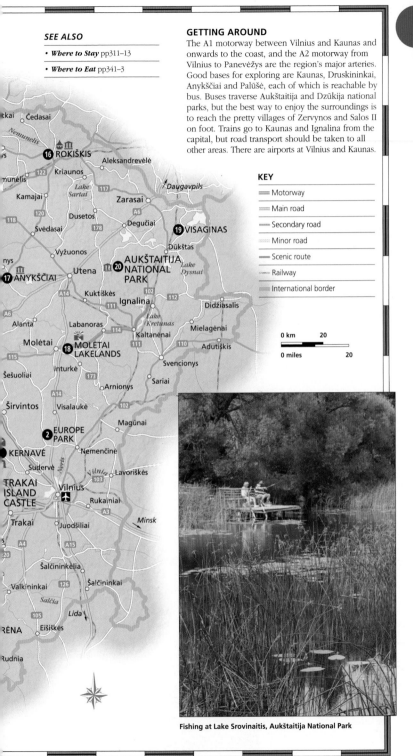

KEY

▬▬	Motorway
▭▭	Main road
▬▬	Secondary road
▭▭	Minor road
▬▬	Scenic route
▭▭	Railway
▬▬	International border

0 km   20

0 miles   20

Fishing at Lake Srovinaitis, Aukštaitija National Park

Trakai Island Castle ❶

An impressive stronghold for any invader to overcome, the Island Castle in Trakai was built as a seat of power during the reign of Vytautas the Great and completed just before the Grand Duchy's crushing victory over the Teutonic Knights at the Battle of Grünwald *(see p212)*. As Vilnius grew in importance, Trakai lost its significance and was destroyed by the Cossacks during the 1655 Russian invasion. In the late 19th century, the elegiac island ruins captured the imaginations of poets and painters during the national revival. Oddly, it was the Soviet authorities who, in the 1950s, sanctioned the reconstruction of this monument to Lithuania's glorious past. It was completed in 1987.

Dry moat, separating the main castle from the outer courtyard

The circular defence towers have 4-m (13-ft) thick bases.

★ **Lakeside Walk**
One way to appreciate Trakai's idyllic lake-filled landscape and the scale of the castle's construction, is to take the pretty walk that follows the shore of the island.

A wooden footbridge links the shore to the Island Castle.

Yachts
Between May and October yachts from the nearby Žalgiris Yacht Club are moored next to the Island Castle. They can be hired by the hour, but charges vary.

STAR SIGHTS

★ Lakeside Walk

★ History Museum

Lake Galvė
Serving as a moat around the castle, the lake has 21 tiny islands. Rowing and paddle boats can be hired along the quayside for a spectacular view of the castle.

VISITORS' CHECKLIST

Road Map D5. 🚌 from Vilnius. 🚆 from Vilnius. 🛈 Vytauto gatvė 69. **Tel** (528) 51 934. **Žalgiris Yacht Club** Žemaitės gatvė 3. **Tel** (528) 52 824. **History Museum Tel** (528) 53 946. ◻ Mar & Apr: 10am–6pm Tue–Sun; May–Oct: 10am–7pm daily; Nov–Feb: 10am–5pm Tue–Sun. 🖫 www.trakaimuziejus.lt

The Ducal Palace's keep, which is 30 m (100 ft) high, served as the residence of the Grand Duke.

★ History Museum
The museum showcases a wide array of weaponry as well as items found during excavations, including 16th-century tankards, tiles and coins.

THE KARAIM OF TRAKAI

The Karaim, a community of Turkic settlers practising a particular kind of Judaism, lend a distinctly exotic flavour to Trakai. Their ancestors were taken prisoners by Vytautas the Great on a military venture to the Crimea in 1397, and subsequently served as royal guards. The Karaim have maintained their customs and traditions. Their characteristic wooden houses, each typically with gable ends and three windows facing the street, the Karaim synagogue or Kenesa and the Karaim Museum are all on Karaimų Street. The Karaim cemetery is by Lake Totoriškiai.

Graves in the Karaim Cemetery, partially hidden by long grass

Europe Park ❷

Europos parkas

Road Map D5. *Tel (370) 237 7077.*
from Vilnius. ⬤ 10am–sunset
daily (last adm in summer: 7pm).
www.europosparkas.lt

The 55-ha (136-acre) park
contains contemporary
sculptures. The aim of its
founder, Gintaras Karosas
(b.1968), was to give an
artistic response to the French
National Geographic Institute's
statement in 1989 that a
point about 17 km (11 miles)
north is Europe's precise
geographical centre.

Around 100 works of art are
set in a landscape of forests,
hills and lakes. The American
artist Dennis Oppenheim
(b.1938) created two monumental pieces – *Chair/Pool*
and *Drinking Structure with
Exposed Kidney Pool. Double
Negative Pyramid*, by Sol
Le Wit (1928–2007), is a
reflection in concrete of
ripples on a lake. Karosas's
own work, *LNK Infotree*, is
a maze of 3,000 old TV sets.

Kernavė ❸

Road Map D5. 500. from
Vilnius. Kernius 4, (382) 47 385.
Days of Live Archaeology (Jul).
www.kernave.org

The small, sleepy village of
Kernavė overlooks the idyllic
Neris Valley, where steep-
sided fort-hills hint at the
passing of a long-lost

**Wooden steps crossing fort-hills,
Kernavė's archaeological reserve**

civilization. Archaeological
finds show that the site was
inhabited as far back as
9000 BC. In the 13th century,
Kernavė was the first capital
of the united Lithuanian tribes
and a busy trading centre.
The Northern Crusaders
ransacked the prosperous
pagan town in 1365. In 1390,
another attack was launched
by a mighty army consisting
of knights, soldiers and merce-
naries from Germany, France,
Italy and England. Henry IV
(1367–1413), the future king
of England, also participated
in the assault, from which
the town never recovered.

Today, Kernavė is Lithuania's
foremost archaeological reserve. In 2004, it was declared
a UNESCO World Heritage
Site. The protected area
comprises five large mounds,
which contained medieval
ramparts and fortifications.
Wooden steps lead to the

summits of the hills, where
there are breathtakingly
beautiful views of the
surrounding terrain.

Environs

The scenic road from Vilnius
to Kernavė passes several
villages. **Sudervė**, 20 km
(12 miles) south of Kernavė,
has an unusual white circular
church designed by
Lithuania's legendary early
19th-century Neo-Classicist,
Laurynas Stuoka-Gucevičius.

Varėna ❹

Road Map D6. 11,000.
from Vilnius. from Vilnius.
Mushroom Festival (Sep).
www.varena.lt

Surrounded on all sides
by thick forest, Varėna is
situated on the eastern
edge of Dzūkija National
Park *(see p256)*. The town is
regarded as the mushroom
capital of Lithuania. Although
a rich variety of mushrooms
grows all over the country,
here they proliferate like a
carpet on the forest floor.
One day a year, usually the
last Saturday in September,
the sleepy town springs
to life, to celebrate the
Mushroom Festival *(see p209)*.

Environs

The road from Varėna to
Marcinkonys, 22 km (14 miles)
southwest, winds pleasantly
through Dzūkija National
Park. Immediately on the

Farmstead with wooden barns, on the edge of the forest in Zervynos, near Varėna

For hotels and restaurants in this region see pp311–13 and pp341–3

Russian Orthodox Church with striking purple domes, Druskininkai

left inside the park, a road leads to **Zervynos**, a village with unpaved streets and the scenic Ūla river bubbling underneath the foliage and wooden bridges.

Druskininkai ❺

Road Map D6. 🏘 17,000. 🚆 from Vilnius. 🛈 Gardino 3, (313) 608 00. **www**.druskininkai.lt

Lithuania's foremost spa resort, Druskininkai is a haven of peace and tranquility. Main roads bypass the town, tucked inside a bend on the thickly forested Nemunas river, and noise restrictions allow peace to prevail. After thriving on 200 years of popularity, Druskininkai suffered an economic shock in the 1990s, when it found itself deprived of Polish, Belarusian and Russian tourists, who once stayed in its sanitaria.

Wellness tourism has, however, been revived since the 1990s. The sanitaria offer water and mineral mud treatments, massages, beauty programmes and fitness trails through the forest. Bike rides and long walks are possible along the Sun Path, which leads through the picturesque Ratnyčia Valley.

The boulevard-lined town centre preserves wooden villas from the 19th and early 20th centuries, mainly found on Laisvės Square. The delightful **Russian Orthodox Church** also stands in the same square. On Vilniaus Street,

some futuristic-style buildings still survive, including the now-closed Soviet-era physiotherapy treatment centre with decorative waves of solid concrete hanging in mid-air.

The serene town inspired painter and composer M K Čiurlionis (see p261), who lived here from 1890 to 1911. The **Čiurlionis Memorial Museum**, located in his family's wooden house, displays period furniture, his notebooks and copies of his artwork. Another museum in the town, the **Jacques Lipchitz Museum**, is dedicated to the Cubist sculptor who was born here in 1891.

🏛 **Čiurlionis Memorial Museum**
M K Čiurlionio 35. **Tel** (370) 313 51131. ⏰ 11am–5pm Tue–Sun. 🔒 last Tue of the month. 🖼 🎥

🏛 **Jacques Lipchitz Museum**
Šv Jokubo 17. **Tel** (313) 56 077. ⏰ call ahead for opening hours. 🖼

Grūtas Park ❻
Grūto parkas

Road Map D6. Parko 47, Grūtas village, Druskininkai. **Tel** (370) 3135 5511. ⏰ 9am–8pm daily (Jan & Feb: to 6pm; May: to 9pm; Jun–Aug: to 10pm; Oct: to 7pm; Nov & Dec: to 5pm). 🖼 🎥 🚻 🅿
www.grutoparkas.lt

Around 90 statues and busts of figures once glorified by the Soviet regime stand in alcoves on a forest trail in Grūtas village. Most of them once graced squares and gardens, before being torn down by cheering Lithuanians in 1991. The park's owner, Viliumas Malinauskas, was awarded the Ig Nobel Peace Prize in 2001, the year the park opened.

Information in English is given on each of these ideological relics. A massive metal statue of Lenin that once stood in front of the KGB building in Vilnius lost a thumb while being wrenched by a crane from its pedestal. Another statue shows Lenin with the Lithuanian Communist Party's First Secretary Vincas Mickevičius-Kapsukas. Both statues were decapitated in 1991, but their heads have been joined back. There is an image of Stalin, which once stood outside Vilnius train station until it was dismantled in 1960. Rusų Karys (Russian Soldier) is a statue made by Nazi prisoners of war from metal taken from the wrecks of German planes shot down by the Soviets. There are also statues of Red Army liberators, poets and other heroes.

Busts of Marx, Engels, Lenin and Stalin in Grūtas Park

View of the Nemunas river and surrounding area from the fort-hill at Merkinė, near Dzūkija National Park

Dzūkija National Park ❼

Dzūkijos nacionalinis parkas

Road Map D6. 🚉 *from Vilnius to Zervynos, Marcinkonys.* 🚌 *from Vilnius to Merkinė.* 🛈 *Vilniaus 3, Merkinė, (310) 57 245.* **Headquarters** *Miškininkų 61, Šilagėlių 11, Marcinkonys, (310) 44 466.* 📷 *English-speaking guides arranged in Merkinė, Marcinkonys.* www.dzukijosparkas.lt

This densely forested park covers 550 sq km (212 sq miles) of countryside. Besides an enormous area of ancient pine forest in the sandy Dainava plain, the park also covers sweeping bends in the broad Nemunas Valley. More than 200 species of flora and fauna are protected in the park, including many rare species of stork.

White stork, Dzūkija National Park

The few villages that are located in the park offer a glimpse of Eastern European life that has remained the same for a century or more. The ethnographic reserve of **Zervynos** is on the park's eastern edge.

The ancient settlement of **Merkinė** lies at the confluence of the Nemunas and Merkys rivers. A fort-hill, the site of a 14th-century castle, offers extensive vistas of the park.

Another fort-hill overlooking the Nemunas river is in the scenic hamlet of **Liškiava**, at the southwestern edge of the park. The 14th-century castle that stood here defended the Grand Duchy against the mighty Teutonic Knights. Another striking landmark is the domed 18th-century Holy Trinity Church, with a rich interior featuring seven late Baroque altars. A series of frescoes depicting images from the history of Christianity were covered in plaster in 1823 and were only restored in 1997.

In **Marcinkonys**, a village 8 km (5 miles) southwest of Zervynos, a track leads southwards to **Čepkeliai Reserve**. This area protects the country's most extensive marsh, which stretches into Belarus, and the migratory birds that stop here. Paths and raised wooden walkways reach observation platforms offering great views.

Alytus ❽

Road Map D6. 🏛 *62,000.* 🚉 *from Kaunas.* 🚌 *from Vilnius, Kaunas.* 🛈 *Rotušės aikštė 14a, (315) 52 010.* www.alytus.lt

Lithuania's sixth-largest city began as a hilltop fortress where the tiny Alytupis river trickles into the Nemunas.

The hill still offers views of both the city and the Dzūkija forests to the south.

In the centre, the **Museum of Local Lore** has a collection of 65,000 antiques. The bridge across the Nemunas has a bas-relief depicting a battle that occured here between Lithuanians and Bolsheviks in 1919. It claimed the life of Antanas Juozapavičius, the first Lithuanian officer to die in the independence struggle. His tomb lies by the **Guardian Angels' Church**.

Much of the city centre was destroyed in 1941. Soon after, all the city's 60,000 Jews were killed in Vidzgiris Forest, a site marked in 1993 by a monument of a broken Star of David. Gravestones in the city cemetery remember the Jews.

Mass of crosses in the churchyard of Guardian Angels' Church, Alytus

Environs
From Alytus, the Nemunas river sweeps towards Kaunas *(see pp258–61)* around several huge, forest-covered bends. One of these bends can be viewed from an evocative fort-hill at the far end of the quiet village of **Punia**, located 15 km (9 miles) north of Alytus.

🏛 **Museum of Local Lore**
Savanorių 6. *Tel (315) 51 990.*
◻ 9am–6pm Tue–Fri, 9am–5pm Sat. 🌐 www.alytausmuziejus.lt

Church of the Blessed Virgin Mary in Kalvarija

Kalvarija ❾

Road Map C6. 🏘 12,000.
🚆 from Kaunas. 🛈 Bažnyčios 4, (345) 60 759.

Another Lithuanian town deeply haunted by the Holocaust, Kalvarija emerged in the 17th century as a trading town on the Warsaw–St Petersburg road. Jews made up a significant part of the population, some of them wealthy merchants who exported grain to Germany, but the majority poor workers who manned several factories making brushes and medicinal alcohol. Wooden synagogues were built and, in 1803, a stone synagogue complex was constructed including a rabbi's house and *beit midrash* (a place of study and prayer).

In 1941, the Nazis and the Soviet army exterminated the entire Jewish population in town. Lithuanian and Jewish Communists were tortured, then shot on the banks of Lake Orija. The synagogue has been partially restored as a national monument.

The **Church of the Blessed Virgin Mary**, with its statues of angels and kings on the pediments above the portico and gate, was built in 1840.

Marijampolė ❿

Road Map C6. 🏘 61,000.
🚆 from Kaunas. 🚌 from Kaunas.
🛈 Kudirkos 41, (343) 51 109.
www.marijampole.lt

This town takes its name from an 18th-century monastery built for the Marian Fathers, a religious order founded in 1673. The Church of St Michael became a part of the complex in 1824, but the monastery's activities were restricted after the 1831 uprising. The church was revived by Bishop Jurgis Matulaitis (1871–1927), whose remains are marked by a tombstone and sarcophagus. During the Soviet occupation in 1944, over 6,000 residents were deported to Siberia. Anti-Soviet partisans mounted a struggle, a story told at the **Tauras District Partisans and Deportation Museum**. A cemetery on Varpio Street and a chapel on Tylioji Street remember the victims of the Soviet regime.

🏛 **Tauras District Partisans and Deportation Museum**
Vytauto 29. *Tel (370) 3435 0754.*
◻ 9am–5pm Tue–Sat. 🌐

Birštonas ⓫

Road Map D6. 🏘 4,600. 🚆 from Vilnius, Kaunas. 🛈 B Sruogos 4, (319) 65 740. 🎭 Birštonas Festival (Jun), Birštonas Jazz (Mar, alternate years). www.birstonas.lt

The secluded spa town of Birštonas is quite different from the bustling wellness centre of Druskininkai *(see p255)*. Though open to paying guests as well as patients, Birštonas's clinical sanitaria have remained trapped in a bygone era. Nonetheless, the well-ordered landscape planning and a pleasant pedestrian boulevard alongside the Nemunas river makes it a delightful town to explore. On the town's eastern edge stands Vytautas Castle Hill, the site of a hunting lodge of Grand Duke Vytautas. A large carved stone statue of Vytautas on horseback stands near the fort-hill.

Birštonas is dotted with wooden houses, which date from the mid-19th century, when the reputation of the town's mineral waters and muds began to grow. A tiny yellow building in the town centre contains a tap with free access to the rich well of water below. The town attracts a lot of visitors during Birštonas Jazz, Lithuania's oldest jazz festival. Held once every two years, the three-day marathon features a range of styles. Birštono Seklytėlė *(see p341)*, a valley-top restaurant, has a grand view of the pine-covered Nemunas.

Vytautas's statue, Birštonas

The Nemunas river seen from the promenade at Birštonas

Kaunas ⑫

Lithuania's second-largest city, Kaunas stands at the confluence of the Nemunas and Neris, the country's biggest rivers. A series of disasters hindered the city's development, including invasions by the Russians (1655), Swedes (1701) and Napoleon's Grand Army (1812). Rapid growth in the 19th century culminated in Kaunas becoming the temporary capital of newly independent Lithuania in 1919. Later, the city suffered under Nazi and Soviet occupations. Today, Kaunas is a modern city with a boulevard and a host of museums. The main historic sights are located in its well-preserved Old Town.

View of the bridge over the Nemunas river leading to the Old Town

🏛 Old Town Hall

Rotušės aikštė.
Known locally as the "White Swan" and resembling a church with its single-tiered tower, the Old Town Hall has been a marriage registry office since the 1970s. It continues to be the photogenic backdrop for newlyweds. Built in the mid-16th century, it housed merchants, magistrates and the mayor, as well as a subterranean prison. It has been used as an ammunition store, clubhouse, fire station and

Elegant Old Town Hall, locally called the "White Swan"

theatre. Town Hall Square, where it stands, was once a busy marketplace and the focal point of the Old Town.

🔒 Church of the Holy Trinity

Rotušės aikštė 22. **Tel** (37) 323 734.
🕐 10am Sun.
Built for a Bernardine convent in the late 1620s, this church has remained in good condition. Its blend of Renaissance and Gothic styles and pastel colours brighten up the northwestern corner of Town Hall Square. A redesign of the interior was completed just before the outbreak of World War II.

🔒 Church of St George

Papilès 7/9. **Tel** (37) 224 659.
🕐 6pm Mon–Fri, 10:30am Sun.
Constructed for Bernardine friars in the 15th century, this Gothic church was destroyed twice by fire before its interior was restored in the Baroque style. The church was further damaged by the Russians in the 17th century and in 1812 by Napoleon's soldiers, who used it as a warehouse. It was finally returned to the Franciscans in 1993.

🏰 Kaunas Castle

Pilies 17. **Tel** (37) 323 436.
admission with guided tour only.
The ruins of Kaunas Castle are a reminder of the strategic importance of its location, between the two rivers, Neris and Nemunas. Little is known about what stood here before the first stone structure was erected in the 13th century. Crusaders damaged the castle in 1362. Soon after reconstruction, the Teutonic Knights were dealt their decisive blow at the Battle of Grünwald (see p212) and the castle consequently fell into ruins. The structure was used as a prison in the 18th century, but was restored in the 1920s.

🏛 Pharmacy Museum

Rotušės 28. **Tel** (37) 201 569.
🕐 10am–6pm Tue–Sat.
A powder for epilepsy made from the heads of corpses, a tincture of "Venus hair" to improve one's allure and a 19th-century herbal remedy

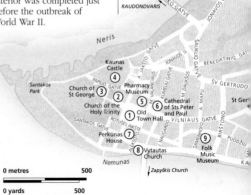

for male vitality called Erektosan are among the exhibits at this unique museum. Chilling medicinal apparatus and the occasional waxwork, such as a shaman curing a baby, add to the atmosphere. The museum also runs a homoeopathic pharmacy.

🔒 Cathedral of Sts Peter and Paul

Vilniaus 1. *Tel (37) 324 093.* 🕊 *7am, 8am, 9am, 6pm daily.*
Several reconstructions have culminated in the Gothic and Renaissance exterior of this 15th-century cathedral. The broadly late Baroque interior, however, is largely unchanged since 1800. A tombstone on the exterior of the south wall is that of Maironis (1862–1932), a priest-poet whose verse romanticized Lithuanian legends and landmarks. Inside, the sculptures surrounding the high altar are overpowering. The oldest of the cathedral's

Painting, Cathedral of Sts Peter and Paul

paintings, the 17th-century *Suffering Mother of God*, reputedly has miraculous powers.

🏛 Perkūnas House

Aleksoto 6. *Tel (37) 302 994.*
🕐 *10am–4pm Mon–Fri, 11am–1pm Sun.* 🖼
The ogee arches and pinnacles of this red-brick Gothic building, resemble Church of St Anne *(see p228),*Vilnius. It was named after Perkūnas, the pagan god of thunder, when renovation in the 19th century revealed that it may once have been the site of a pagan temple. Dating from the early 1500s, it was originally a meeting house for merchants in the Hanseatic League. Bought by the Jesuits, the house was converted into a chapel before becoming, in the 19th century, a theatre and then a school. Later, during the Soviet period, it was used as a warehouse. It is now back with the Jesuits.

VISITORS CHECKLIST

Road Map D5. 🏙 *320,000.*
✈ *10 km (6 miles) N of town.*
🚉 🚌 ℹ *Laisvės alėja 36, 323 436.* 🎷 *International Jazz Festival (Apr).* **www**.kaunas.lt

🔒 Vytautas Church

Aleksoto 3. *Tel (37) 203 854.* 🕊
6pm Tue–Thu, 10am & 6pm Sat–Sun.
Standing on the bank of the Nemunas river, this church was built on the orders of Vytautas the Great after the Holy Roman Emperor decided in 1413, much to the ire of the Teutonic Knights, that the land on the river's right bank belonged to the Grand Duchy of Lithuania. Already an army storehouse, the church was converted to serve a Russian Orthodox congregation. A full reconstruction took place after Lithuania's first independence in 1918, post World War I. In 1930, a medallion was placed in the church wall to commemorate the 500th anniversary of Vytautas's death.

Red-brick Gothic structure of Vytautas Church

🏛 Folk Music Museum

Zamenhofo 12. *Tel (837) 42 22 95.*
🕐 *Oct–Mar: 9am–5pm Tue–Sat, Apr–Sep: 10am–6pm Tue–Sat.* 🖼 🖼
This museum boasts a collection of 7,000 wind, brass and stringed instruments, including pipes and whistles. Only 500 of them are on display due to the museum's small size. The staff can give demonstrations of many of these. Stranger pieces, such as the table bass, a pine table with four strings and a pig's bladder, are also displayed.

KAUNAS

Key to Symbols *see back flap*

Exploring Modern Kaunas

Stretching eastwards from the Old Town is the city's modernized New Town. The process of its expansion began in the 19th century, and today it is as the hub of commercial and cultural life in the city. The museums and other sites are found around the heart of modern Kaunas in Laisvės (Freedom) Avenue. This broad, leafy, pedestrianized boulevard is lined with shops, pavement cafés, restaurants and bars, and is the place local people come to stroll and mingle.

View along Laisvės Avenue towards Church of St Michael

Laisvės Avenue
At the eastern end of this boulevard are the blue-silver onion domes of the Church of St Michael. Originally Russian Orthodox when it was built in the early 1890s, it was later converted to serve the Lithuanian army. A monument by the park outside the Music Theatre at Laisvės 4 marks the spot where Romas Kalanta, a Lithuanian student, set fire to himself on 14 May 1972 in protest against Soviet rule. His suicide sparked student protests, which were ruthlessly suppressed.

🏛 Mykolas Žilinskas Art Gallery
Nepriklausomybės 12. **Tel** (37) 222 853. ◯ 11am–5pm Tue–Sun. 🖼 🎥
An exile who had fled from Kaunas to West Berlin in advance of the Soviets in 1940, Mykolas Žilinskas (1904–92) later built a valuable art collection, which he donated to Kaunas in the 1970s. Besides canvases and porcelain from the 16th to the 20th centuries, including *The Crucifixion* by Rubens and some early Soviet avant-garde art, there are also pre-war paintings and sculptures by Baltic artists.

🔒 Church of the Resurrection
Žemaičių 31. **Tel** (37) 229 222. 🕯 6pm Mon–Fri; 9:30am, 11am, 12:30pm Sun.
With a 70-m (230-ft) steeple, this church was built to mark Lithuanian independence in 1918. After World War II, the Soviets turned it into a radio factory. With independence regained, the factory was evicted. After reconstruction the church was consecrated on Christmas Day 2004.

🏛 M K Čiurlionis Art Museum
V Putvinskio 55. **Tel** (37) 229 475. ◯ 11am–5pm Tue–Sun. 🖼 🎥
Housing virtually all the paintings that Čiurlionis ever produced, this museum also gives an insight into the development of art in Lithuania. With 335,000 exhibits, it is Lithuania's biggest art gallery, but there is room for only a fraction of these. Artifacts from other cultures include some oddly juxtaposed pieces from Ancient Egypt.

🏛 Vytautas the Great War Museum
Donelaičio 64. **Tel** (37) 320 939. ◯ 10am–5pm Wed–Sun. 🖼 🎥
Lithuania's national war museum exhibits weapons that the country has used to defend itself. However, the main focus of the museum is the re-creation of the story of the doomed transatlantic flight of the *Lituanica* in July 1933. The pilots Steponas Darius and Stasys Girėnas died in the crash, but the distance covered (6,411 km/3,984 miles) was the second-longest flight ever recorded. The plane's wreckage is on display.

🏛 Devil's Museum
V Putvinskio 64. **Tel** (37) 221 587. ◯ 10am–5pm Tue–Sun. 🖼 🎥 📷 📹
This museum's fine collection of representations of devils, demons and witches from Lithuania and around the world, was brought together by avid collector Antanas Žmuidzinavičius (1876–1966). A sculpture of the horned figures of Hitler and Stalin fighting over Lithuania in a pit of bones is grim, but most of the devils are shown as playful, musical and frequently drunk.

🏛 Ninth Fort
Žemaičių 73. **Tel** (37) 377 750. ◯ Apr–Oct: 10am–6pm Wed–Mon, Nov–Mar: 10am–6pm Wed–Sun. 🎥 www.9fortomuziejus.lt
The ninth in a series of fortifications constructed by Tsarist Russia to protect its western borders was built in the early 20th century, only to become a prison in 1924. During World War II, it was used for incarceration and extermination by the Nazis. The fort also housed Soviet political prisoners. Part of a farm after the war, it opened as a "museum to the victims of Fascism" in 1958. The dungeon and defence walls have displays on the Nazi and Soviet occupations.

Artillery on show at the Vytautas the Great War Museum

♙ Raudondvaris

5 km (3 miles) W of Kaunas.
🚌 from Kaunas.

Built by the crusaders in the 14th century, Raudondvaris (Red Manor) became a part of Lithuania after the Battle of Grünwald (1410). The legend says that it was presented as a gift, in 1549, by Sigismund August to Barbora Radvilaitė a year before their marriage. After her death in 1551, the castle fell into ruin and was rebuilt as a manor house in the 17th century by the Tyszkiewicz family. Its library and collection of paintings were lost during World War I. A chapel close by contains the Tyszkiewicz tombs that survived the 20th century.

A red manor with manicured lawns at Raudondvaris

♙ Pažaislis Monastery

7 km (4 miles) E of town. ⏰ 10am–5pm Tue–Fri. www.pazaislis.org

One of Eastern Europe's great Baroque monuments, Pažaislis Monastery and its central, cupola-domed Church of the Visitation of the Blessed Virgin Mary were constructed by Italian architects in the 17th century. There is finely detailed stucco work inside the church and in the corridors of the monastery, much of it framing intricate frescoes painted by the Italian artist, Michelangelo Palloni.

⛪ Rumšiškės Open-Air Museum

L Lekavičiaus 2, 15 km (9 miles) E of town. **Tel** (346) 47 392. ⏰ 10am–6pm Tue–Sat. ● 1 Nov–Easter Mon. 🎫 🛒 📷 www.llbm.lt

At Rumšiškės Open-Air Museum, traditional thatched farmsteads and other elements of village life have been carefully reassembled.

Colourful buildings and statue in the square of the Old Town, Kėdainiai

The rolling countryside overlooking Lake Kaunas creates a perfect backdrop.

♙ Zapyškis Church

15 km (9 miles) W of town.

One of Lithuania's loveliest buildings, the triangular red-brick Gothic Zapyškis Church is set in a field by the Nemunas river. Built in the 16th century, it has remained miraculously intact despite invasions and occupations.

Kėdainiai ⑬

Road Map D5. 🏠 54,000.
🚌 from Kaunas, Vilnius. 🚆 from Kaunas, Vilnius. 🛈 Didžioji 1, (347) 60 363. 📷 Cucumber Festival (Jul), Ice Cream Festival (Aug).
www.visitkedainiai.lt

With a history as a trading town on the route between Kaunas and Rīga, Kėdainiai was first mentioned in written sources in 1372. Its colourful Old Town has a series of elaborately gabled merchants' houses in the main square. Close by, the Renaissance-style Town Hall dates from 1654 and holds Kėdainiai's administrative offices. In another square, two synagogues dating from 1837 stand side by side. They were once used by the town's thriving Jewish community. Another synagogue, now the **Multicultural Centre**, holds a museum on Kėdainiai's cultural history.

Environs

Paberžė, 30 km (19 miles) north of Kėdainiai, with its delightful wooden church, was the residence of Father Stanislovas (1918–2005), a revered Tolstoyan hermit and Capuchin friar.

⛪ Multicultural Centre

Senoji rinka 12. **Tel** (347) 51 778. ⏰ 10am–5pm Tue–Sat. 🎫

M K ČIURLIONIS (1875–1911)

A tortured soul and artistic genius, Mikalojus Konstantinas Čiurlionis is Lithuania's most famous painter and composer. He started out as a prodigious composer of atmospheric symphonic and organ works, but at the age of 27 he began to study drawing. The next nine years were filled with feverish creativity. Before his early death from pneumonia, he had created around 300 works of music, painting and poetry. Many of his mystical paintings mirrored his musical compositions and some were named as pieces of music, such as *Spring Sonata* and *Funeral Symphony*. Despite their melancholy, Čiurlionis's painted and musical works can be surprisingly uplifting.

Painting by Čiurlionis, displayed at the M K Čiurlionis Art Museum

View of the wooden steps across the mounds at Kernavė's archaeological reserve ▷

Interior of the Neo-Baroque Cathedral of Christ the King, Panevėžys

Panevėžys ⑭

Road Map D5. 🏘 105,000.
🚉 from Klaipėda. 🚌 from Vilnius.
ℹ️ Laisvės aikštė 11, (45) 508 081.
www.panevezys.lt

One of Lithuania's largest cities with a modern commercial centre, Panevėžys is a crucial transport hub in the region.

South of its centre lies the **Cathedral of Christ the King**, a Neo-Baroque structure built in 1904. A sweeping painting above the altar depicts a victorious medieval Lithuanian army. A few streets north, the **Civic Art Gallery** often holds eccentric exhibitions of local modern art. East of the centre is **Glasremis**, a working gallery creating glass items.

Environs
In **Pakruojis**, 50 km (31 miles) northwest of Panevėžys, the country's largest 18th-century manor lies in a 6-ha (15-acre) park, with a five-arch stone bridge and 40 other structures.

🏛 **Civic Art Gallery**
Respublikos 3. **Tel** (45) 584 802.
⏱ 11am–6pm Wed–Sun. 🖼

🏛 **Glasremis**
J Biliūno 12. **Tel** (45) 430 403.
⏱ 10am–5pm Mon–Fri. 🛍

Biržai ⑮

Road Map D4. 🏘 28,000. 🚌 from
Panevėžys. ℹ️ J Janonio 2, (450) 33
496. **www**.birzai.lt

The small town of Biržai is best known for its traditional breweries. The local brew can be sampled in the cellar of the **Sėla Museum**, housed in the 17th-century Biržai Castle. Visitors can enjoy live folk music performed here, but should book ahead.

In 1701, Peter the Great of Russia and King Augustus II of Poland signed the pact against Sweden in this castle on the eve of the Great Northern War (see p33).

In the grounds are the ruins of an older castle, whose defences in the mid-1500s involved damming two rivers to create Lithuania's oldest man-made lake, Širvėna. A 525-m (572-yard) wooden bridge leads across the lake to Astravas Manor Park, with its sprawling 19th-century manor house, watermill and old dam.

🏛 **Sėla Museum**
J Radvilos 3. **Tel** (450) 31 883.
⏱ 10am–5:30pm Wed–Sat, 9am–
4:30pm Sun. 🖼 🛍

Rokiškis ⑯

Road Map D4. 🏘 35,000. 🚌 from
Panevėžys. 🚌 from Panevėžys, Vilnius.
ℹ️ Nepriklausomybės 8, (458) 52 261
or (458) 51 044. 🏇 Lake Sartai Horse
Race (first Sat in Feb). **www**.rokiskis.lt

Set amid glorious countryside, Rokiškis is blessed with forthills, forests and picnic sites. However, it is best known for its cheese company, Rokiškio Sūris. Having started as a small local dairy, it sells cheeses all over the Baltic region.

Rokiškis Manor House, the town's main sight, was built in 1801 by the Tyzenhaus family. The Polish architects who redesigned it in 1905 created an English-style interior, but its exterior has Baroque elements. It houses the **Rokiškis Museum**, which offers tours of the lavish Great Hall and a separate building that exhibits fine wooden folk sculptures by Lionginas Šepka (1907–85).

Environs
Kriaunos, 15 km (9 miles) southeast of Rokiškis, has a local **Historical Museum** filled with an eclectic collection of flax tools, linen fabrics, tubs and troughs. Hidden upstairs, the "loft of witches" is a coven of 400 witches, mermaids, fairies and goblins.

The island in Lake Dviragis in the village of **Salos**, 20 km (12 miles) southwest of Rokiškis, was a sanctuary for its inhabitants in the early 15th century. Now connected

Wooden bridge across the castle moat into the older castle, Biržai

Façade of Rokiškis Manor House, embellished with Baroque elements

by a bridge to the rest of the village, the island forms a calm backdrop to a Classical 19th-century manor and a Neo-Gothic wooden church.

🏛 **Rokiškis Museum**
Tyzenhauzų 5. **Tel** *(458) 52 261.*
🕐 *10am–6pm Tue–Sun.* 📷 📹

🏛 **Historical Museum**
Kriaunų village. **Tel** *(458) 41 718.*
🕐 *10am–5pm Tue–Sat.* 📷 📹

Anykščiai ⓱

Road Map D5. 🏠 *29,000.*
🚌 *from Panevėžys.* 🚌 *from Panevėžys, Kaunas.* ℹ️ *Gegužės 1, (381) 59 177.* **www**.*anyksciai.lt*
Lithuanian Narrow-Gauge Railway www.*siaurukas.eu*

Nestled in a landscape of rolling pastures, Anykščiai creates a picturesque setting for the 160-km (100-mile) **Lithuanian Narrow-Gauge Railway**. Only 68 km (42 miles) of Europe's longest functional narrow-gauge railway is in regular use today. Its locomotives pull carriages across open countryside along the Šventoji river to the scenic shores of Lake Rubikiai with its 16 islands. Tickets are sold at the tourist information centre. The old station boasts the **Anykščiai Northern Railway Museum**, providing further insights into train travel.

Environs
In **Niūronys**, 6 km (4 miles) north of Anykščiai, the **Horse Museum** hosts exhibitions on various horse-related products. Rides on real horses, around the paddock

or in a horse-drawn carriage, can be had for a small fee. There is also a mini-playground for children.

🏛 **Anykščiai Northern Railway Museum**
Vilties 2. **Tel** *(370) 38 15 4597.*
🕐 *May–Oct: 10am–5pm daily, Nov–Apr: by appointment.* 📷 📹
🖥 **www**.siaurukas.eu

🏛 **Horse Museum**
Niūronių village. **Tel** *(381) 51 722.*
🕐 *May–Aug: 9am–6pm daily, Sep–Apr: 8am–5pm daily.* 📷 📹
www.arkliomuziejus.lt

Molėtai Lakelands ⓲

Road Map D5. 🏠 *21,000.* 🚌 *from Vilnius, Daugavpils.* 🚌 *from Vilnius, Daugavpils.* ℹ️ *Inturkė 4, (383) 51 187.* 🎵 *Visagino Country Music Festival (mid-Aug).*

The lakes that extend east from the town of Molėtai are some of the Baltic region's cleanest, making it perfect for camping and swimming.

Lake Želva's Ethnocosmology Centre, Molėtai Lakelands

Forest-lined lakes with inlets, such as Baltieji and Juodieji Lakajai, and, further south, Asveja, are protected as part of the 55,000-ha (136,000-acre) Labanoras Regional Park. Molėtai is one of the oldest settlements in the country, although it has preserved very few historical monuments. The Molėtai Astronomical Observatory offers sweeping views of area. Inside, the **Ethno-cosmology Centre** displays an intriguing exhibition on the links between cosmology and the pagan rituals of the ancient Lithuanians.

Exterior of the Ignalina Nuclear Power Plant, near Visaginas

Visaginas ⓳

Road Map E5. 🏠 *22,000.*
🚌 *from Vilnius, Daugavpils.* 🚌 *from Vilnius, Daugavpils.* ℹ️ *Jenalina Ateities 23, (386) 52 597.* 🎵 *Visagino Country Music Festival (mid-Aug).*

With only 15 per cent of its population ethnically Lithuanian, Visaginas has a unique atmosphere in a country that is 85 per cent Lithuanian. It was created in 1974 to house nuclear scientists who built and then worked at the nearby **Ignalina Nuclear Power Plant**, the Baltic region's only nuclear power station.

Hidden in forests down a single road, Visaginas has no discernable centre. High-rise housing blocks cover the town from east to west. To cool the reactors at the Ignalina plant, water is pumped in from Drūkšiai, Lithuania's biggest lake.

Aukštaitija National Park ⑳

The oldest and most beloved of Lithuania's national parks, Aukštaitija National Park was established in 1974 to protect local biodiversity. About 60 per cent of the country's plant species can be found here, in addition to its ancient pine forests, fort-hills, burial mounds and old thatched cottages in villages such as Salos II. Palušė makes an ideal base for exploring the 400-sq km (154-sq mile) park. However, the park's central point, Ladakalnis Hill, is its highest, from which five lakes are visible. Rowing boats can be hired from Palušė, enabling visitors to make a circular trip or drift at a leisurely pace along the water trail.

KEY

☐ Aukštaitija National Park

0 km   2

0 miles   2

Taurapilis, one of several ancient fortifications found in the park, is situated above Lake Tauragnas, affording extensive views in all directions.

★ **Beekeeping Museum**
Sculptures of characters from Lithuanian folklore stand together on a grassy hillside with wooden hives, in the village of Stripeikiai.

★ **Ladakalnis Hill**
The best panoramic view of the park can be experienced from the hill above Lake Linkmenas. The area is noted for its mes-merizing greenery and clear lakes.

STAR SIGHTS

★ Beekeeping Museum

★ Ladakalnis Hill

★ Salos II Cultural Reserve

★ **Salos II Cultural Reserve**
The ethnographic village is arranged like a live, open-air museum, with several well-preserved timber houses.

**Unusually shaped beehives
at the Beekeeping Museum**

BEEKEEPING

Lithuanians have a long and enduring history of apiculture. Forest beekeeping, in which bees lived in tree hollows and their keepers mounted elaborate climbing apparatus to collect the honey, was widely practised in the Middle Ages. Beeswax and honey were vital to the economy in the Middle Ages. In the 15th century, a law was passed to prosecute people who harmed them, or the trees.

VISITORS' CHECKLIST

Road Map D5. 🚉 from Ignalina. 🚌 from Ignalina. 🛈 Park Headquarters and Visitors' Centre, Palušė, (386) 53 135. 🚶 on foot or by bus, offered at the Park Headquarters. Rowing boats and canoes can be hired during summer. 🖥 www.anp.lt

Trainiškis
In the village of Trainiškis stands a mighty tree believed to be more than 800 years old and said to have once been a site of pagan sacrifices.

Valčių Pervežimas Boat Way
Visitors can rent a boat for a circular trip around the park from lake to lake, going via Valčių Pervežimas, the water trail that links Lake Baluošas and Lake Dringis.

luošė

ainiškis
Valčių
rvežimas

Vaišniūnai

Lake Dringis

Gaveikėnai

e nai

IGNALINA

Lake Lūšiai

Palušė

KEY

🚉	Railway station
🚌	Bus station
🚤	Boating
🛈	Visitor information
🏛	Museum
⌗	Historic building
⚠	Campsite
☀	Viewpoint
▬	Main road
▬	Other road
—	Railway
– –	Trail
---	Water trail
▬ ▬	Park boundary
▲	Peak

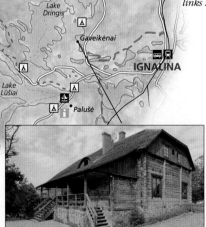

Gaveikėnai Watermill
One of several original watermills in the park, Gaveikėnai Watermill was built around 1800. Today, it houses a café.

WESTERN LITHUANIA

*I*solated for centuries, the little towns and villages of Žemaitija, the local name for the low-lying land of Western Lithuania, have a mystical atmosphere. Rustic wooden farmsteads and settlements are nestled between knolls and marshes. Klaipėda and Šiauliai are charming cities with distinct surroundings characterized by tiny, hidden lanes with a surfeit of cafés and museums.

Žemaitija is the ancient heartland of Samogitia, a medieval pagan duchy that managed to repel the innumerable incursions of its hostile, mostly Christian neighbours. With stubborn determination the Samogitians fought off the crusaders for more than 250 years, before finally being absorbed into the Grand Duchy of Lithuania in 1422. It was the last corner of Europe to be converted to Christianity and age-old rituals dedicated to pagan deities continued in more isolated parts until the 20th century.

Klaipėda, the country's only seaport city, is an ideal base for embarking on day-trips into Western Lithuania. Although the port area was secretively closed off during the Soviet era, it has since reopened to cruise ship and ferry passengers. Originally known as Memel, Klaipėda was part of Prussia and Germany for over 500 years. Some of the surviving Germanic-style half-timbered houses, once used by merchants, characterize the streets of the Old Town today.

A short ferry ride from Klaipėda lies the Curonian Spit, with its towering dunes and scenic villages like Nida. Inland, quaint little towns, such as Šilutė and Kretinga, are easily reachable and a delight to stroll around. The quiet village of Rusnė and the surrounding Nemunas Delta region attract many rare birds which breed in their lush marshes. Žemaitija National Park, close to Lake Plateliai, conceals a former Soviet missile base. Cycle paths stretch all along the Lithuanian coast from Nida up to the Latvian border and pass the coastal resorts of Palanga and Šventoji, both offering beaches, spas and all-night bars and clubs.

Pretty wooden houses along a street in Nida, a village in the Curonian Spit National Park

◁ The Nemunas river flowing amid verdant scenery, near Šilutė

Exploring Western Lithuania

The northwest corner of Lithuania offers the twin
attractions of Žemaitija National Park, with its Soviet-era
missile base, and the memorable Orvidas Garden. The
UNESCO-protected Curonian Spit, a long and narrow strip
of land between the Baltic Sea and the Curonian Lagoon,
is worth visiting for its towering dunes, charming fishing
villages, cycle paths and beaches. Western Lithuania also
gives an insight into the country's unique Catholic and
pagan mysticism, which is keenly felt in small towns
such as Tytuvėnai and Šiluva.

SIGHTS AT A GLANCE

Towns and Resorts

Jurbarkas ❾
Klaipėda pp280–81 ⓰
Kretinga ⓱
Mažeikiai ⓫
Palanga ⓲
Panemunė ❽
Plateliai ⓬
Plungė ⓮
Raseiniai ❻
Raudonė ❼
Šeduva ❸
Šiauliai pp272–3 ❶
Šilutė ㉑
Šiluva ❺
Smiltynė ⓳
Telšiai ❿
Tytuvėnai ❹

Sites of Interest

Hill of Crosses ❷
Orvydas Garden ⓭

National Parks

*Curonian Spit National Park
pp284–5* ⓴
*Žemaitija National Park
pp278–9* ⓯

Area of Natural Beauty

Nemunas Delta ㉒

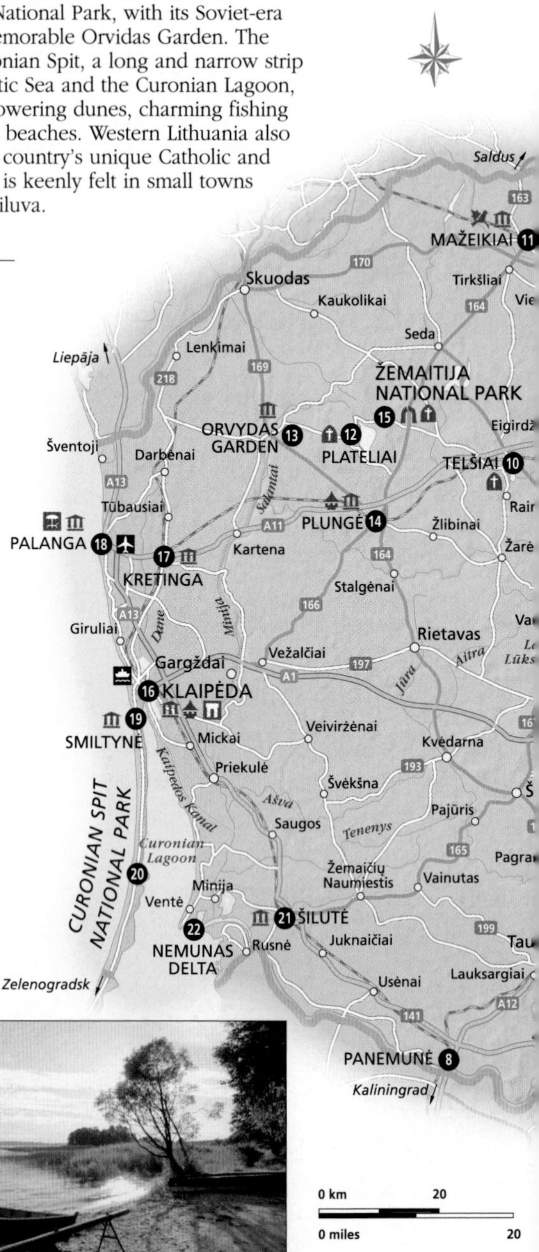

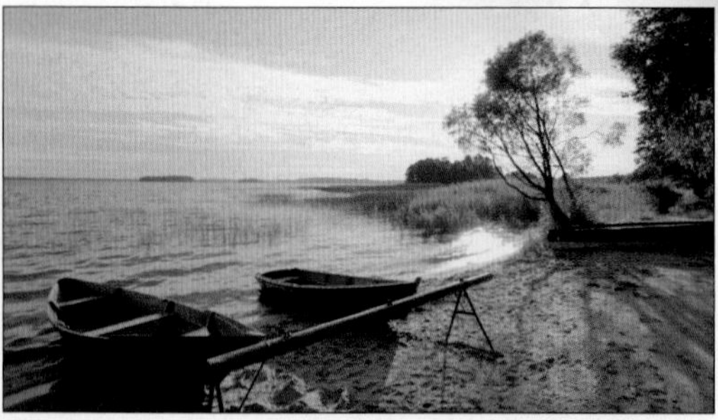

Beach on the eastern shore of Lake Plateliai, Žemaitija National Park

0 km   20

0 miles   20

GETTING AROUND

The A1 motorway between Kaunas and Klaipėda is the fastest east–west route across the region. Buses serve the region well, and good bases from which to explore it are Palanga, Kaunas, Šiauliai and Klaipėda. Trains offer a less flexible means of transport, and even the Kaunas–Klaipėda line makes a detour via Šiauliai. The regional airport, at Palanga, provides international connections, most notably with the transit hubs of Oslo and Rīga.

KEY

═══ Motorway

═══ Main road

─── Secondary road

∙∙∙∙ Minor road

⌁⌁⌁ Railway

▬▬▬ International border

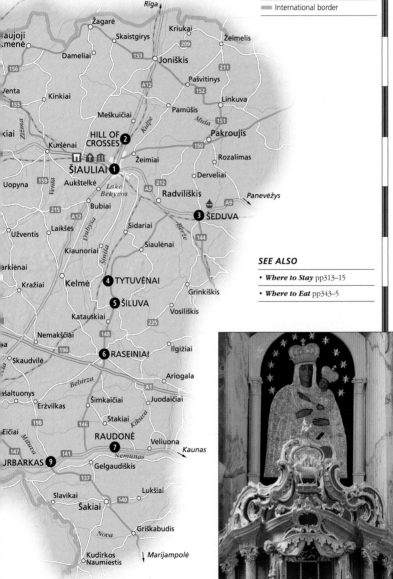

SEE ALSO

- **Where to Stay** pp313–15
- **Where to Eat** pp343–5

Painting of Madonna and Child, Tytuvėnai

Šiauliai ❶

Lithuania's fourth-biggest city, Šiauliai first appeared in historical sources in 1236, the date of the Battle of the Sun *(see p210)*. An major industrial centre since the 18th century, it saw its population rise from 6,200 in 1866 to 23,600 at the outbreak of World War I. The war destroyed more than 60 per cent of the city. Today, Šiauliai is enjoying a wave of development. New shopping centres are being built, pedestrianized streets laid and monuments renovated. The city's most attractive part, with traditional houses and museums is the Old Town.

Old bicycle outside the Bicycle Museum, a part of Aušra Museum

🏛 Aušra Museum

Vytauto 89. *Tel* (41) 526 933.
⏰ 10am–6pm Tue–Fri, 11am–5pm Sat. 🖼 🅿 *times vary; call for details.*
www.ausrosmuziejus.lt

The Aušra Museum, founded in 1923, is the oldest museum in the city. It was named in honour of the first Lithuanian newspaper. The museum is a treasure trove of art and culture with a vast collection of historical, architectural and archaeological artifacts, spread over 11 locations. The history of the daily life of the townspeople of Šiauliai is the focus of Aušra Avenue Palace,

the museum's main building. A special section is dedicated to the repressions of the Soviet post-war period.

The **Bicycle Museum** (Vilniaus 139) reveals the story of cycling in Lithuania with almost 100 bicycles on display, including a child's tricycle from 1905. Replicas of a number of historic bikes are also exhibited.

One of Lithuania's very few Art Nouveau buildings from the early 20th century, the **Chaim Frenkel Villa** (Vilniaus 74), depicts Jewish daily life in centuries past. The bulk of the city's collection of art is housed at the **Venclauskų House** (Vytauto 89), which, together with the privately run **Laiptai Gallery** (Žemaitės 83), exhibits the work of local artists such as Marcė Katiliūtė (1912–37). Her prodigious talent, creating mostly intense and haunting portraits, ended when she took her own life at the age of 25.

⛪ Cathedral of Sts Peter and Paul

Aušros Takas 3. *Tel* (41) 528 077.
⛪ 7am, 7:30am, 5pm, 6pm Mon–Sat; 8am, 9:30am, 11am, 12:30pm, 6pm Sun.

A church has stood on this spot since 1445 and the precise location of the earlier

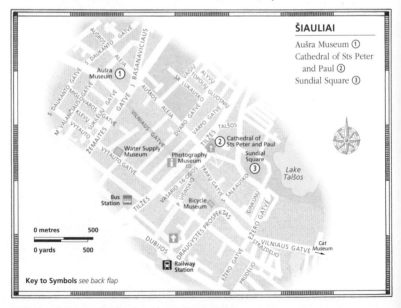

ŠIAULIAI

Aušra Museum ①
Cathedral of Sts Peter and Paul ②
Sundial Square ③

0 metres   500
0 yards   500

Key to Symbols *see back flap*

Prominent tower of the Cathedral of Sts Peter and Paul

VISITORS' CHECKLIST

Road Map C4. 🏢 *115,000.* 🚉 *Višinkio gatvė 44, S of Draugystės prospektas.* 🚌 *Tilžės gatvė 109.* ℹ️ *Vilniaus gatvė 213, (41) 523 110.* 🎪 *Saulės Žiedas Folk Festival (Jul), Šiauliai City Days (Sep).* www.siauliai.lt

🏛 Cat Museum
Žuvininkų 18. **Tel** *(41) 523 883.* ⭕ *11am–5pm Wed–Sun.* 📷

With almost 10,000 exhibits not just from Lithuania but across the world, from Austria to Zambia, this museum is a haven for cat-lovers. Established in May 1990, the museum has exhibits of cats in every conceivable pose cramming the display area. They have been crafted from porcelain, amber, marble, crystal, glass and other materials. There are cats in stained-glass windows, cats in artistic photographs, cats on postage stamps, in books and on cards. Interesting odes to cats have been collected in over 4,000 poems written in various languages. There are lamps with cats as ornamentation as well as furniture and a set of banisters with delightful feline designs.

Colourful wooden cats, Cat Museum

Hill of Crosses ➋
Kryžių kalnas

Jurgaičių village. **Road Map** C4. 🚌 *from Šiauliai.* **Tel** *(41) 370 860.* www.kryziukalnas.lt

One of Lithuania's most awe-inspiring sights, this saddle-shaped knoll in a field filled with thousands of crosses, crucifixes and rosaries is an insight into the significance of Catholicism to Lithuania.

Crosses started appearing on the hill after the ruthless suppression of the 1831 uprising against Tsarist Russian rule. By the end of the 19th century, 150 large crosses stood here, 200 by 1914, and many more by the time the Soviets came to occupy Lithuania in 1940. Seen by the atheist regime as an unnecessary religious symbol, the Hill of Crosses was hacked down in 1961, but the crosses reappeared soon after. It was bulldozed in 1973 and again in 1975, but the crosses kept appearing. Finally, the hill was left in peace. By the time Pope John Paul II visited it, in 1993, it had crosses and religious sculptures from all over the country and around the world.

wooden place of worship is marked by a metal cross. The old church was burnt down and in 1625, the existing one was built in stone to give it more permanence. Seen from afar, the cathedral's gleaming white 70-m (230-ft) tower makes the building look more modern than it actually is.

The cathedral is built in Renaissance style with some features typical of medieval architecture. Its thick walls are accompanied by details that appear to have been defensive but in fact were not. On the southern side of the cathedral is Lithuania's oldest sundial. Sts Peter and Paul Church was elevated to cathedral status in 1997.

🏛 Sundial Square
Ežero gatvė.

A sundial was erected in the square in 1986 to mark the 750th anniversary of the Battle of the Sun. The slender sundial, surmounted by a sculpture of a golden archer, towers over Lake Talšos.

Sundial Square is laid out like an amphitheatre and brings together three significant symbols for the city – the archer Šaulys, after whom, according to legend, the city was named; the sun, images of which can be found all over Šiauliai; and time, represented on the square by the numbers of the clock, 12, 3, and 6, which when brought together form the date of the battle.

Collection of crosses of all shapes and sizes at the Hill of Crosses

Šeduva ❸

Road Map C5. 🏘 *3,000.* 🚌 *from Šiauliai, Panevėžys.* 🚍 *from Šiauliai, Panevėžys.*

The little town of Šeduva is a composite of wooden houses preserved as a historic monument. One of its main sights is the twin-tower Church of the Holy Cross. Built in 1649, the church elegantly blends Renaissance and Baroque elements.

Šeduva's most delightful spot is the mid-19th-century estate of Prussian Baron Otto von Ropp, located 2 km (1 mile) east of town. Aside from the original red-brick buildings, which have given the estate the local name **Raudondvaris** (Red Manor), there is a school and a hotel, and the lakeside grounds are a pleasure to stroll through.

Environs

The grounds of **Burbiškis Manor**, 12 km (7 miles) east of Šeduva, are decorated with sculptures of lions, fauns and historical figures created in 1912 by sculptor Kazimieras Ulianskas. A dazzling display of tulips adorns the manor grounds in spring, when the Tulip Festival is celebrated.

♣ **Burbiškis Manor**
Burbiškis village. **Tel** *(422) 42 001.*
⬜ *Apr–Oct: 9am–5pm Tue–Sun.* 🏞
🎪 *Burbiškis Tulip Festival (mid-May).*

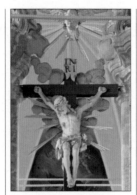

Crucifix above the altar, Friary of the Blessed Virgin Mary, Tytuvėnai

Tytuvėnai ❹

Road Map C5. 🏘 *3,000.* 🚌 *from Šiauliai.* 🚍 *from Šiauliai.* **www.**trp.lt

Once the site of a 13th-century hilltop fortress, Tytuvėnai became the secluded setting for a magnificent monastery and the church of the **Friary of the Blessed Virgin Mary** in the 1630s. The buildings were created for the Franciscans and set amid rolling hills and tranquil lakes. The courtyard of the monastery is decorated with faded frescoes, while a beautiful painting on the wooden sacristy door depicts the Resurrection.

The highlight of the church's colourful interior is an elaborate altar encircled by four Baroque figures of Franciscan saints. In the grounds, the Chapel of the Holy Stairs was modelled on the Scala Sancta (Holy Stairs) in Rome. Each of the steps, which pilgrims mounted on their knees, contains a sacred relic brought here from Jerusalem in the 1730s.

Šiluva ❺

Road Map C5. 🏘 *800.* 🚌 *from Šiauliai.* 🎪 *Šilinės Pilgrimage (Sep).*

Šiluva is one of Lithuania's great pilgrimage places. Legend has it that 400 years ago, the town was the site of a miraculous apparition of a weeping Virgin Mary holding the Infant Jesus in her arms. In the late 16th century, as Šiluva became Calvinist, its last priest buried a bundle of Catholic documents and a miracle-working painting of the Virgin Mary in an iron box in the grounds of the ruined church.

In 1610, the Virgin Mary appeared standing on a rock before children tending their herds. The box was later discovered by the rock and, as fame about the apparition grew, a wooden chapel was built close by. It was replaced in 1785 by the Church of the Nativity of the Blessed Virgin Mary. The painting of Mary, now embellished by a golden frame, was hung on the altar. The painting is concealed,

Bright evening view of the lakeside buildings at Raudondvaris, near Šeduva

Façade of the Neo-Gothic castle at the Raudonė estate, seen from across its lush grounds

except on feast days, by a 1920 painting of the Annunciation. On his visit in 1993, Pope John Paul II prayed at the church.

The obelisk-style structure of the Church of the Apparition of the Blessed Virgin Mary, which was completed in 1924, can be seen from afar.

Raseiniai's attractive main square, featuring the *Independence Statue*

Raseiniai ⑥

Road Map C5. 🏠 *37,000.* 🚌 *from Kaunas.*

An important Samogitian town, Raseiniai played a crucial role in the region's history. In 1941, the town witnessed a fierce four-day battle between hundreds of German and Soviet tanks. By the end of World War II, 90 per cent of Raseiniai had been destroyed. Miraculously, the hilltop Church of the

Ascension, built in 1729, survived the war, as did the *Independence Statue* in the town's main square. Created by Vincas Grybas (1890–1941) in 1934, the statue shows a man in a flowing cloak and bast shoes together with a bear he has tamed. The bear is a symbol of Samogitia, the independent duchy that fought the Teutonic Order in the 13th century, but it was later ceded to the Grand Duchy of Lithuania.

Raudonė ⑦

Road Map C5. **Tel** *(447) 45 445.* ⬜ *mid-Nov–mid-Apr: 10am–4pm weekly.* 📷

Originally a 16th-century family estate owned by Prussian timber merchants, the castle at Raudonė was acquired in 1810 by Platon Zubov, once a favourite consort of Catherine the Great. Catherine had played an important role in obtaining much of the Polish-Lithuanian Commonwealth during the partitions *(see p211).* After her death, the count lived in seclusion at Rundāle Palace *(see pp168–9)* in Courland.

The count's daughter gave the family castle in Raudonė its current Neo-Gothic appearance and its tall and slender fairytale tower. Destroyed by the retreating Germans at the end of World War II, the tower was rebuilt in 1968 and today offers a panoramic view of the Nemunas Valley.

Environs
Veliuona, a village 10 km (6 miles) east of Raudonė, is known for its secluded fort-hill where Gediminas *(see p212)* was reputedly slain.

Panemunė ⑧

Road Map C5. 🚌 *from Kaunas.*

Situated on the banks of the Nemunas river, Panemunė boasts a castle with two tall circular towers and red-tiled rooftops. Most of the building was erected by a family of Hungarian nobles during the reign of Stefan Bathory, the Transylvanian prince who ruled the Polish-Lithuanian Commonwealth between 1575 and 1586. Two centuries later, the castle was bought by the Polish-Lithuanian Gelgaudas family. The Tsarist authorities seized it after Antanas Gelgaudas led the 1831 uprising *(see p214).* Today, the castle belongs to the Vilnius Academy of Art.

One of the castle's tall circular towers in Panemunė

Jurbarkas  ❾

Road Map C5. 🏘 *29,000.* 🚌 *from Kaunas.* ℹ️ *Vydūno 19, (447) 51 485.* **www**.jurbarkas.lt

The ancient **Karšuva Forest**, about 3 km (2 miles) west of the tiny industrial town of Jurbarkas, is the site of one of the earliest fortresses built by the crusaders on the Nemunas river in 1259. The pagan Lithuanians erected their own castle above the Imsrė river, a tributary of the Nemunas, and both sides fought bitter battles for the next 150 years. Although nothing remains of the castles, the forest can be explored. One of Lithuania's largest and most secluded forests, the 427-sq-km (165-sq-mile) stretch has enchanting trails leading through its towering pines.

Environs
In **Gelgaudiškis**, 10 km (6 miles) east of Jurbarkas, lie the ruins of the 19th-century manor of the Gelgaudas family, the Polish-Lithuanian ancestors of actor Sir John Gielgud. The manor boasted a lavish interior with paintings, silver, crystal, bronze and porcelain works until it was ransacked during World War II. Today, the manor hosts village festivals and music evenings in its grounds.

Mount Rambynas, 60 km (37 miles) west of Jurbarkas, is a 46-m (50-yard) escarpment, and a mystical location for Lithuanians. A pagan altar that once stood here was used for rituals up until the 19th century. Today, the hill offers views over Kaliningrad.

Embellished interior of the Cathedral of St Anthony of Padua, Telšiai

Telšiai ❿

Road Map C4. 🏘 *47,000.* 🚌 *from Vilnius, Šiauliai, Klaipėda.* 🚌 *from Vilnius, Šiauliai, Klaipėda.* ℹ️ *Turgaus 21, (444) 53 010.* **www**.telsiai.lt

According to legend, Telšiai was founded by a knight named Džiugas on a hill above Lake Mastis. In 1765, the Franciscans built a church here, which became the **Cathedral of St Anthony of Padua**, after Telšiai was made a diocese in 1926. An unbroken second-floor gallery has its own altar and paintings framed by Corinthian columns. These include an altar painting of St Anthony and Infant Jesus, embellished with faux gold and held aloft by angels garbed in pink and green.

Environs
One of the worst massacres by the Soviets took place in the forests near **Rainiai**, 4 km (2 miles) southeast of Telšiai.

The terrible event took place on the nights of 24 and 25 June 1941, shortly after Nazi Germany invaded the then Soviet Union. Today, a granite cross marks the spot and the **Rainiai Chapel of Suffering**, consecrated in 1991, stands nearby. Just 30 km (19 miles) southeast of Telšiai, **Šatrija Hill** offers splendid views of the Žemaitija landscape. **Lake Lūkstas**, 40 km (25 miles) south of Telšiai, has beaches that liven up in July during the Blues Night festival.

Mažeikiai ⓫

Road Map C4. 🏘 *57,000.* 🚌 *from Šiauliai.* 🚌 *from Šiauliai.* ℹ️ *Ventos 8a, (443) 67 077.* **www**.mazeikiai.lt

A minor village in the mid-19th century, Mažeikiai rapidly grew into Lithuania's eighth-largest city by the end of the 20th century. The Vilnius–Liepāja railway, which reached Mažeikiai in 1869, was responsible for its growth.

The **Mažeikiai Museum** has displays on the town's development and regional folklore, and paintings by Alfonsas Dargis (1909–96), a Lithuanian artist who joined the New York Modernist movement.

Environs
The 4,000-ha (9,884-acre) **Kamanos State Reserve**, 20 km (12 miles) east of Mažeikiai, protects one of the region's most valuable clayfields. Richly diverse in flora and fauna, the reserve has a lower area of marshland and a higher area of lakes and tiny islands.

In **Viekšniai**, a small town 15 km (9 miles) southeast of Mažeikiai, the **Pharmacy Museum** is considered miraculous. It survived two fires that devastated the town but spared the pharmacy building.

🏛 **Mažeikiai Museum**
Burbos 9. **Tel** *(443) 26 037.*
⭕ *9am–6pm Wed–Mon.* 🖼

🌿 **Kamanos State Reserve**
Tel *(425) 59 285.* 🖼 🅿️

🏛 **Pharmacy Museum**
Tilto 3. **Tel** *(443) 37 420.* ⭕ *9am–4pm Tue–Sat.* 🖼

Rainiai Chapel of Suffering commemorating the massacre in 1941

Boats on the eastern shore of Lake Plateliai, bordering Plateliai village

Plateliai ⑫

Road Map B4. 🏚 *1,000.* 🚌 *from Plungė.* ℹ️ *Didžioji 8, (448) 49 231.* 🎭 *Shrove Tuesday Carnival (Feb/Mar).*

The administrative centre of Žemaitija National Park *(see pp278–9)*, Plateliai is a sleepy lakeside village. It has the wooden Church of Sts Peter and Paul (1744) and a park that was the grounds of a manor. The Witch's Ash, Lithuania's biggest ash tree which stands in the park, has many legends attached to it. One involves a baker who threw a loaf of bread at a witch sitting on its branches. The loaf is still visible – the knobbly bit where the branches divide.

Across the road on Didžioji Street, elaborate Shrovetide masks are displayed in the manor barn. These masks are worn during the Shrove Tuesday Carnival. The most popular destination is **Castle Island**, which takes its name from a fortress that stood on the nearest island of Pilies.

Orvydas Garden ⑬
Orvydo sodyba

Road Map B4. **Tel** *(613) 28 624.* ⏱ *June: 10am–7pm Tue–Sun, July– May: 10am–7pm Wed–Sun.* 📷

The creative work of local mystic and genius Vilius Orvidas (1952–92), this garden is one of Eastern Europe's most bizarre sights. Eclectic and enormous, it is a complex network of crosses and tombstones, boulders and tree-trunks, sculptures of odd creatures, carvings and rock paintings of pagan and religious imagery, painted missile shells and a disused Soviet tank. Hidden gardens appear out of nowhere and there is no set path, adding to the maze-like feel. The dark caverns conceal further oddities, and a pond-side hut hidden among trees is reputedly the home of pixies and gnomes.

Plungė ⑭

Road Map C5. 🏚 *39,000.* 🚂 *from Šiauliai, Klaipėda.* 🚌 *from Šiauliai, Klaipėda.* ℹ️ *Dariaus ir Girėno 27, (448) 55 108.* **www**.plunge.lt

The town of Plungė is the main gateway to Žemaitija National Park *(see pp278–9)*. One of Lithuania's most opulent manors, the well-preserved **Plungė Manor** was built by Mykolas Oginskis, a descendant of a family of Lithuanian nobles. It includes 16 sculptures of Samogitian figures and a park featuring the Thunder Oak tree, now a natural monument. The manor also houses the **Samogitian Art Museum**, which displays works by Western Lithuanian artists.

Environs
About 2,236 Jews of Plungė died in the Holocaust. Much of the killing took place in **Kaušėnai**, a village 4 km (2 miles) west of town. Here, a series of moving wooden sculptures have been carved by Jacob Bunka (b.1922), chairman of Plungė's 13-member Jewish community.

Gandinga Hill, 5 km (3 miles) southwest of Plungė, offers a panoramic view of the Žemaitija forests. A fortress, Gandinga, once stood here, built as a defence against the Teutonic Knights. Pagan burial grounds dating from the 9th century have been discovered nearby.

Another remakable outdoor museum is the **Museum of Unique Rocks** in Mosėdis, 40 km (25 miles) northwest of Plungė. Exhibits range from a display of fossils and sands inside a restored watermill to a park full of mossy boulders and crude stone sculptures. The museum was founded in 1979 by Dr Vaclovas Intas.

🏛 **Samogitian Art Museum**
Parko 1. **Tel** *(448) 52 492.*
⏱ *10am–5pm Tue–Sat.* 📷 📷

🏛 **Museum of Unique Rocks**
Salantų 2. **Tel** *(440) 76 291.* ⏱ *8am– 6pm Mon–Fri, 10am–6pm Sat–Sun.* 📷 *Nov–Apr: Sat & Sun.* 📷 📷

Plungė Manor seen across a lake, with a sculpture in the foreground

Žemaitija National Park ⓯

Shrouded in folklore and legend, the Žemaitija region was the last stretch of Europe to accept Christianity. Pagan gods were worshipped here till the 19th century, and carvings and crosses in the villages still blend Catholic and pagan imagery. Established in 1991, the Žemaitija National Park spreads across 220 sq km (85 sq miles), with its headquarters and information centre in the town of Plateliai. There are several hiking trails that meander around Lake Plateliai through isolated stretches of forest. Campsites and rural farmsteads cater to tourists.

Wild lupin with purple flowers

KEY

🛈 Visitor information

Ⓐ Campsites

☀ Viewpoint

═ Minor road

– – Hiking trail

▪ ▪ Park boundary

Barsty

Mikytai

Pūč

Visvaini

V

Plateliai

Beržoras

Lake Plateliai

Lake Beržoras

Lake Ilgis

Grigaičiai

Godeliai

Salantai

Babrungėnai

(169)

Plt

★ **Mikytai Hill and Devil's Footprint Stone**
The forest-covered "sacred hill" of Mikytai is believed by local people to be haunted. On the hill's northern slope, the Devil's Footprint Stone was once used for pagan sacrifices.

Plateliai serves as the park's main service and information centre.

Church of St Stanislav in Beržoras
This church (1746) is made of spruce logs. Its Chapels of the Cross were destroyed by the Soviets but restored in 2001.

Godeliai has a rare collection of obscure paintings and crucifixes in its Museum of Folk Art.

STAR SIGHTS

★ Mikytai Hill and Devil's Footprint Stone

★ Žemaičių Kalvarija

★ Plokštinė Former Soviet Missile Base

Mill-Gallery
A stone watermill, converted into a folk art gallery, stands in the riverside village of Babrungėnai, once famed for its beaver hunters.

★ Žemaičių Kalvarija
Churches and white Chapels of the Cross give this town a spiritual atmosphere. The Church Festival, held in July each year, is its main attraction.

0 km 2
0 miles 2

egrėnai

Žemaičių Kalvarija

Skurvydai

Platakiai

164

okštinė

VISITORS' CHECKLIST

Road Map C4. 🚌 *from Plungė to Žemaičių Kalvarija.* ℹ️ *Didžioji 8, Plateliai, (448) 49 231; to book, 86778 6576.* 🔼 **www**.zemaiti josnp.lt **Mill-Gallery** 🕘 *9am–6pm daily.* **Plokštinė Former Soviet Missile Base** 📷 *book at the park's information centre.*

Mound of Šarnelė
Excavations on this hill, in Šarnelė village, have revealed that it was a small fortified town in the third century BC.

★ Plokštinė Former Soviet Missile Base
Between 1962 and 1978, this secret Soviet rocket site, with its now rusty and overgrown silos, aimed missiles at cities in Western Europe.

FOLK LEGENDS OF LAKE PLATELIAI

Lake Plateliai had tremendous significance to the pagans of the historical regions of Samogitia and Žemaitija. Drownings occasionally occur here and according to one of the many legends associated with it, a great white horse lives in the water and takes the life of at least one swimmer every year. The water level has risen in recent times and archaeologists diving in the lake have excavated standing stones with pagan symbols under the surface. To this day, Plateliai, on the lake's western shore, celebrates many colourful traditional Samogitian festivals.

Yacht moored along the shore of Lake Plateliai

Klaipėda ⑯

First mentioned in 1252 when the Christian Livonian Order built a fortress named Memelburg at the mouth of the Danė river, Klaipėda for many centuries was an important Prussian port city called Memel. Today, as Lithuania's only sea port, Klaipėda is thriving despite serious damage during World War II and its status as a military-industrial centre during the Soviet years. For those who enjoy walking, central Klaipėda and its Old Town, with narrow, criss-crossing streets, is a delightful place to explore. Half-timbered buildings and cobbled lanes conceal gift shops, galleries and café-bars.

Visitors and local people relaxing in cafés in Klaipėda

🏛 Ännchen of Tharau

Teatro aikštė.
The heart of Klaipėda's Old Town is **Theatre Square**. A statue called *Ännchen of Tharau*, which stands in front of the theatre, is the focal point of the fountain dedicated to Simon Dach (1605–59), one of the city's distinguished personalities. Born in Klaipėda, then known as Memel, Dach became a leading Prussian poet from the late 1630s until his death. He is well known throughout Germany for his songs, hymns and dialect poems such as *Ännchen of Tharau*, written in 1637.

The original statue was created in 1912, but it mysteriously vanished on the eve of World War II. Adolf Hitler made a speech from the theatre balcony behind its original location, on 23 March 1939. In 1989, a replica

of the original *Ännchen of Tharau* statue, made by local artists, was placed in the middle of the fountain.

🏛 Castle Museum

Pilies 4. **Tel** *(46) 410 527.* ⬜ *10am–5pm Tue–Sat (to 4pm Fri).*
Not much remains of the 17th-century castle that houses the Castle Museum. The castle was built on the foundations of the 1252 fortress when Memel was part of the Duchy of Prussia. In 2002, an exhibition opened inside one of the ramparts, illustrating the development of the fortress and the city. The exhibits on display include authentic furniture and re-created models. The highlight is a Renaissance-era gold ring encrusted with diamonds. Today, this castle has become one of the most recognized symbols associated with modern Klaipėda.

Statue of *Ännchen of Tharau* in Theatre Square

🏛 Lithuania Minor History Museum

Didžioji vandens 6. **Tel** *(46) 410 524.* ⬜ *10am–5pm Tue–Sat (to 4pm Fri).*
Lithuania Minor is what the local people call East Prussia, which today is the territory of Kaliningrad as well as Klaipėda. The Lithuania Minor History Museum, inside one of the Old Town's loveliest buildings, tells the region's history. Coins, clothes, maps, postcards, old photographs and models give a glimpse of the lives and the differences between the local German- and Lithuanian-speaking communities before World War II. Situated opposite the museum is the town's old post office.

🏛 Blacksmiths' Museum

Šaltkalvių 2a. **Tel** *(46) 410 526.* ⬜ *10am–5pm Tue–Sat (to 4pm Fri).*
Black metal crosses, fences and cemetery gates in a garden beside an old working smithy are among this museum's exhibits. Some of the crosses were rescued from destruction when the Sculpture Park replaced the city's main cemetery in the 1970s. Lithuania's cross-crafting tradition, in metal and in wood, was recognized by UNESCO in 2001.

Old wooden clock inside the exceptional Clock museum

🏛 Clock Museum

Liepų 12. **Tel** *(46) 410 414; 410 413 (excursions).* ⬜ *noon–6pm Tue–Sat, noon–5pm Sun.*
A fascinating insight into the development of man's attempts to measure time, from sundials to atomic

clocks, is the focus of this unique museum. The Clock Museum was opened in 1984 inside a villa built in 1820 by John Simpson, an English merchant. Reconstructions of ancient calendars, sun, fire, water and sand clocks, and timepieces showing the changes in the faces and mechanisms of clocks from Renaissance times form the bulk of the exhibits.

The pleasant courtyard, featuring a large sundial, is a popular venue for music, dance and poetry evenings. The house next door was built by another English merchant and industrialist, Mae Lean. In 1905, it was reconstructed in the Art Nouveau style. The Neo-Gothic post office close by is another striking building in the neighbourhood.

🏛 Picture Gallery and Sculpture Park
Liepų 33. **Tel** (46) 410 412.
◯ noon–6pm Tue–Sat, noon–5pm Sun. 🖼
The city's main state-run art gallery is named after Pranas Domšaitis (1880–1965), a Lithuanian artist who was born near Königsberg and settled in South Africa in 1949. Heavily influenced by the Norwegian Symbolist painter Edvard Munch (1863–1944), Domšaitis won recognition for his art in inter-war Germany and later in South Africa. The gallery exhibits 20th-century Lithuanian art as well as a permanent exhibition of works by Domšaitis.

Dedicated to the author of the first Lithuanian book, Martynas Mažvydas (1510–63), the Sculpture Park is situated behind the gallery. Until the 1970s it was the site reserved for the city's cemetery. It covers almost 10 ha (25 acres) and is scattered mainly with

abstract and intriguing sculptures by various artists. New works are added to the park each year.

Unique creations laid out in the Sculpture Park

KLAIPĖDA

Ännchen of Tharau ①
Blacksmiths' Museum ④
Castle Museum ②
Clock Museum ⑤
Lithuania Minor History Museum ③
Picture Gallery and Sculpture Park ⑥

0 metres 200
0 yards 200

Key to Symbols *see back flap*

Kretinga ⑰

Road Map B5. 🚶 *41,000.* 🚌 *from Klaipėda.* 🚉 *from Klaipėda.*

This pretty town is based around a 17th-century Franciscan monastery, a manor house, now the **Kretinga Museum,** and gardens that stretch alongside a stream and open up into a park. The Franciscans played a major role in developing the town, particularly in independent inter-war Lithuania when they opened a college specializing in agriculture and beekeeping. They also arranged a Lourdes-style grotto in the park with an image of the Virgin Mary.

One of the highlights of the Kretinga Museum is the Winter Garden, originally built when Count Josef Tyszkiewicz reconstructed the manor in 1875. Destroyed during World War II, these gardens were re-created in 1987 and today house around 600 plants. Other museum exhibits include furniture and paintings rescued from the Tyszkiewicz mansions in Kretinga and Palanga, iron crosses that are a blend of Catholic and pagan imagery and Curonian clothing and jewellery. The Church of the Annunciation has a towering steeple and an ornate interior with 17th-century paintings.

🏛 **Kretinga Museum**
Vilniaus 20. **Tel** *(445) 77 612.*
⏲ *10am–6pm Wed–Sun.*
♿ 📷 📹 🎥
www.kretingosmuziejus.lt

View of the sandy beach with locals and visitors, Palanga

Palanga ⑱

Road Map B5. 🚶 *16,000.* ✈ *5 km (3 miles) N of town.* 🚌 *from Klaipėda.* 🚉 *from Klaipėda.* ℹ *Kretingos 1, (460) 48 811.* 🎉 *Summer Feast (Jun).* **www.**palanga.lt

The coastal town of Palanga, first mentioned in a 13th-century land partition pact between the Teutonic Order and the Livonians, became a permanent part of Lithuania in 1435. Today, it is a popular sandy resort, with its dune-and-pine-bordered beach stretching 18 km (11 miles). It also has boulevards crammed with restaurants, clubs and bars, giving it a carnival-like atmosphere. The pier, first built in 1882, is a popular spot to watch the sunset.

A Neo-Renaissance palace was built in the 1890s by the Tyszkiewicz family, with grounds created by the French landscape architect Edouard André (1840–1911). Since 1963, the palace has housed the **Amber Museum,** which exhibits 4,500 pieces, including some unusual ones such as amber with trapped prehistoric insects and plants. At the far end of the palace's grounds is **Birutės Hill,** said to be where the future wife of Grand Duke Kęstutis tended a pagan sacred fire before he wed her. Close by is one of Lithuania's best-known sculptures, *Eglė, Queen of the Grassy Snakes* (1960), inspired by a fairytale.

Environs

The quiet fishing village of **Šventoji,** 15 km (9 miles) north of Palanga, is blessed with windswept dunes. It was a thriving port in the 16th and 17th centuries. An attraction here is *Fisherman's Daughters* (1982), a statue of three girls dancing on the dunes.

🏛 **Amber Museum**
Vytauto 17. **Tel** *(460) 51 319.*
⏲ *Jun–Aug: 10am–8pm Tue–Sat, 10pm–7pm Sun; Sep–May: 11am–5pm Tue–Sat, 11am–4pm Sun.* 📷 📹 **www.**pgm.lt

Smiltynė ⑲

Road Map B5. 🚶 *100.* ⛴ *from Klaipėda.*

Officially part of Klaipėda city *(see pp280–81)*, Smiltynė is the northernmost settlement on the Curonian Spit, directly facing Klaipėda's busy port. In earlier times, the spit was the main land route used by dispatch riders, postmen and the military, between the Prussian cities of Königsberg and Memel, modern Kaliningrad and Klaipėda respectively. However, the final ferry trip was disrupted by storms or trapped ice. In 1525, an inn was established in Sandkrug (Sand Inn), as Smiltynė became known.

A string of elegant villas line the water's edge. The town's star attraction, however, is the **Sea Museum**. It is located in Kopgalis Fortress, a sea bastion built by Prussia in 1865. The

Tropical conservatory in Kretinga Museum's Winter Garden, Kretinga

Dolphins performing with trainers before an enthralled audience at the Sea Museum in Smiltynė

main highlights are the regular dolphin and sea lion shows. Permits must be purchased for photography.

🏛 **Sea Museum**
Smiltynės 3. *Tel* (46) 492 250.
⏰ Oct–Apr: 10:30am–5pm Tue–Sun; May–Sep: 10:30am–6pm Tue–Sun (Jun–Aug: to 6:30pm). 📷 🎫
📧 🌐 www.muziejus.lt

Curonian Spit National Park ⑳

See pp284–5.

Šilutė ㉑

Road Map B5. 🏠 21,500. 🚌 from Klaipėda. 🚌 from Klaipėda.
ℹ Lietuvininkų 4, Parko 2, (441) 77 785. www.silute.kryptis.lt

Originally the site of an inn for travellers riding between Klaipėda and Kaliningrad, Šilutė became a part of the German Empire in 1871. It was seized by Lithuania in 1923, but annexed by Nazi Germany 15 years later.

German influence is still visible in the low, red-tiled roofs of the public buildings. On tree-lined Lietuvininkų Street, the tiny **Šilutė Museum** displays 18th-century furniture and folk-themed exhibits. The Evangelical Lutheran Church, built in 1926, is decorated with startlingly colourful murals of biblical scenes.

Environs
Just 3 km (2 miles) northeast of Šilutė, **Macikai** was used as a German prisoner-of-war camp from 1939, then a Soviet camp for German troops after 1944, and was an official unit of the Gulag from 1948 to 1955. Today, it comprises the **Macikai Concentration Camp Museum** and a grave site.

🏛 **Šilutė Museum**
Lietuvininkų 36. *Tel* (441) 62 207.
⏰ 9am–6pm Tue–Fri, 10am–2pm Sat. 📷 🎫

🏛 **Macikai Concentration Camp Museum**
Macikai. *Tel* (441) 62 207.
⏰ 11am–3pm Tue–Sat. 🎫

Nemunas Delta ㉒

Road Map B5. 🏠 1,700. 🚌 from Šilutė. www.nemundodelta.lt

The low-lying delta of the Nemunas, Lithuania's largest river as it streams into the Curonian Lagoon, has great potential for outdoor activities. The wetlands, protected as a regional park, are a popular spot for angling and bird-watching. Every spring, when the snow and ice melt, 20 per cent of delta gets flooded, attracting 200 species of birds to breed, while hundreds of other species migrate through the area every year. A bird ringing station at **Ventė** is one of the oldest in Europe, dating from 1929.

The floods annually threaten to cut off **Rusnė**, located 11 km (7 miles) southeast of Ventė. A Lutheran church, built from 1809 to 1827, is a sign of Rusnė's East Prussian background. It was changed into a sports hall in the Soviet period, but reverted to receiving congregations in 1994. An ethnographic farmstead gives a snapshot of past life in the delta region.

Almost 8 km (5 miles) northwest from Rusnė is the village of **Minija**, situated where the Minija river meets the Nemunas Delta. The river functions as the main street in the area. Protected as architectural monuments, 19th-century wooden houses stand on both riverbanks.

Sunset view of Nemunas Delta countryside, near Šilutė

Curonian Spit National Park ⑳

A narrow 98-km (61-mile) strip of land on the Baltic Coast, the Curonian Spit (Kuršių nerija) was formed 5,000 years ago. Its landscape consists largely of pine forests, dunes and sandy beaches. The park's forests are also rich in wildlife such as roe deer, elk, foxes and wild boars. The dunes that tower over the village of Nida fall like cliffs into the Curonian Lagoon and villages have been buried beneath the shifting sands. The Curonian Spit National Park was created in 1991 to preserve the dunes, lagoons and surrounding area. The national park, which covers most of the spit, has been a UNESCO World Heritage Site since 2000.

KEY

☐ Curonian Spit National Park

★ Nida
The highly characteristic red-and-blue fishermen's cottages in Nida have remained unchanged for centuries. Some ancient weather-beaten fishing boats lie in the gardens outside the cottages.

Baltic Beach
The entire length of the spit on the side of the Baltic Sea is one long sandy beach. Areas adjacent to the villages are popular in summer, but other parts are little visited. Parking throughout the spit is allowed only at designated parking areas.

★ Parnidis Dune
Looming 52 m (171 ft) above Nida, Parnidis (Great) Dune offers stunning views and is one of the highest points on the spit. A sundial erected here in 1995 collapsed during a storm in 1999.

Vecekrug Dune, the highest wooded dune (67.2 m/220.5 ft), is bypassed by taking the cycling track.

Nida

Pre

★ Hill of Witches

Comically demonic wooden statues, such as this ghoulish figure, lurk alongside a path through the pine forest behind Juodkrantė. The statues were set up by a group of local sculptors in the 1980s.

Juodkrantė

VISITORS' CHECKLIST

Road Map B5. ⊞ Naglių 18e, Nida, (469) 52 859. ⛴ Naglių 14, Nida, (469) 51 101. *Several operators offer cruises in vessels, including a replica kurėnas. Local trips, as well as excursions across the lagoon or along the shoreline to the Dead Dunes, are available.* ℹ Taikos 4, Nida, (469) 52 345. *Bike rentals can be arranged at the centre.* 🖳 **www.**visit neringa.com or **www.**nerija.lt

Dead Dunes

These once-shifting dunes are now held in place with vegetation and offer a sanctuary to birds, animals and plants. Paths stretch from Avikalnio Dune in the north to Agilo Dune in the south.

Forest Trails

It is possible to walk or cycle the entire length of the spit. The path, marked by the dotted red line on the map, takes visitors past isolated stretches of sandy beach.

valka

KEY

⛴	Ferry port
🚏	Coach station
ℹ	Visitor information
🏛	Museum
🏖	Beach
═	Main road
- -	Trail
···	Ferry route

0 km   2

0 miles   2

STAR SIGHTS

★ Nida

★ Parnidis Dune

★ Hill of Witches

SHIFTING DUNES

In the 17th century, when the forests on the Curonian Spit were cut down to fuel industry and constant military campaigns, the mountainous dunes were released. In the Baltic winds, the sand started to shift up to 20 m (66 ft) a year in places, burying entire villages. It was only in the 19th century, when a vast number of trees were planted to reforest the area, that the moving dunes were stopped.

Parnidis Dune seen from the harbour at Nida

TRAVELLERS' NEEDS

WHERE TO STAY

Estonia, Latvia and Lithuania offer all forms of accommodation options, from luxury hotels and city-centre hostels to rural guest houses. Although there is an abundance of good-quality mid-range and budget stay options in the three capital cities of Tallinn, Riga and Vilnius, it is advisable to book well in advance during late spring, summer and early autumn. Hotels in the Baltic States share a classification code with Scandinavian countries, which has helped to improve standards throughout

Logo, Monika Centrum, Rīga

the industry. Before making a reservation, it is advisable to cross-check the establishment, since some smaller hotels, particularly those converted from Soviet-era buildings, may not live up to expectations. The elaborate network of accommodation extends to smaller towns and the countryside, where it is very easy to find a place to stay for the night. Bookings are easy as even the smallest of guest houses have their own websites, apart from being advertised through several other sources.

BOOKING

For more out-of-the-way locations, there are specialist tour operators and websites listing choices. Reservations can be made by telephone, fax and through the Internet. Local tourist information offices also help book rooms.

PRICES & PAYMENT

All major hotels accept principal credit cards for payment. Cheques and traveller's cheques, however, are rarely used in the Baltic States. It is advisable to confirm acceptable modes of payment prior to arriving, especially for rural areas. Visitors need to make sure what they are getting for their money on the hotel's website. Many hotels include breakfast and use of amenities such as a fitness centre, while other facilities, including

Three Sisters hotel *(see p294)*, a renovated house in Tallinn

saunas, can cost extra. Prices vary considerably from hotel to hotel, although there are often significant discount offers available during off-season months. It is also worth looking for special discounts or packages.

TIPPING

Generally, it is not customary to tip taxi drivers, bar staff and bellboys in the Baltic States. As a rule of thumb, tip those who provide you with good service.

LUXURY HOTELS

Tallinn, Rīga and Vilnius have a large range of luxury hotels. Often these are housed in historic buildings that have been converted to provide state-of-the-art facilities while retaining their original features. There are also several superb chain hotels that attract heads of state and other VIPs.

Swimming pools remain a rarity in the Baltic States, although fitness centres, spas and saunas are common, as is high-quality cuisine, Wi-Fi access, and in some cases, facilities for disabled guests.

Luxurious Dikļu Pils hotel *(see p307)*, a restored 19th-century manor house in the Valmiera region, Latvia

◁ **Open-air café in Cathedral Square (Doma laukums), Rīga, Latvia**

CHAIN HOTELS

Chains, such as the Radisson Blu and Reval Hotel Group, were among the first to get a foothold in the Baltic States and still occupy a leading position in the increasingly competitive market with a range of fine upmarket and mid-range hotels. The Radisson Blu Hotel Group currently boasts the largest hotel in the region with the expanded Reval Hotel Latvija *(see p302)*. The Domina Hotel Group has a couple of hotels in Tallinn and one in Rīga, while the Best Western chain has set up hotels in Estonia, Latvia and Lithuania. The more upmarket Europa chain has hotels in Rīga, Vilnius, Druskininkai and Klaipēda.

Shakespeare Boutique Hotel *(see p310)* in Vilnius

Façade of Rīga's Radisson Blu Hotel Latvija *(see p302)*

MID-RANGE HOTELS

Affordable, good quality accommodation throughout Estonia, Latvia and Lithuania is readily available. There is a wide choice of mid-range hotels available in all areas within the three Baltic States.

Most of the larger towns and cities provide a variety of mid-range hotels, although only a handful are located in the Old Town areas of Tallinn, Rīga and Vilnius. Most of the hotels can be found either in the city centre or in slightly more peripheral locations. The quality of the mid-range hotels can vary considerably so it is always sensible to make enquiries about the services, by phone or checking websites, prior to booking.

HOSTELS

Hostels were once sorely missed accommodation throughout the Baltic States, but there has been a massive growth in this type of accommodation. Budget accommodation is now widespread in all the three countries, including several centrally located hostels that are too well-appointed to be called true hostels. By far the cheapest places to stay, hostels are well suited for budget travellers.

Most hostels are of a very decent standard and have beds in communal dormitories for reasonable rates, as well as a small selection of private rooms, offered for considerably less than the average hotel rate. The majority of hostels also offer an excellent range of amenities, including Internet, kitchen facilities and assorted tours and excursions, some of which can be quite fascinating and unusual in theme.

The International Youth Hostel Association (IYHA) has comfortable hostels in the three Baltic countries. The **Estonian Youth Hostel Association** is a part of the IYHA, while in Latvia these youth hostels are known as **Hostelling Latvia**. The **Lithuanian Youth Hostelling Association** does not have an office. However, its website *(see p291)* provides contact details for hostels in different areas.

Logo of Lilija Plus Real Estate Agency

APARTMENTS & PRIVATE HOMES

Apartment rental is an excellent accommodation option that is comparatively under-used in the capital cities. Several agencies in the capital cities offer this service – **Erel Apartments & Residences** and **Goodson & Red Apartments** in Tallinn, **Lilija Plus Real Estate Agency** and **Patricia LTD** in Rīga and **Eldorado Apartments** and **Eugenijus Apartments** in Vilnius. Also available in some other major cities, apartments can range from opulent to simple and cosy, but in general all are of a very high standard. Most agency-managed apartments are in central locations. Rates are usually very competitive and the apartments often provide better facilities than those offered at a hotel in the same price range.

Rooms in private homes are limited in the capital cities but are widespread in the countryside and can usually be found through the local tourist information office. As lodging categories can occasionally be blurred in the Baltic States, this option can sometimes be more fittingly described as guest houses or family B&Bs.

Homestay B&B in Rīga, bookable through Baltic Country Holidays

GUEST HOUSES

Guest houses have become a real Baltic speciality in recent years. Often, they can be the best form of lodging in rural areas, offering cosy, clean accommodation at very reasonable rates. Most guest houses tend to be built close to a family home so a personal touch is always assured. Aesthetically, they are loosely modelled on rustic-style timber buildings and have become an integral part of the Baltic countryside. They invariably offer a range of activities for guests, such as swimming, sports and saunas, and the owners can sometimes arrange guided tours of local sights. Meals are usually optional, but a hearty, home-made breakfast or dinner costs less than similar fare in a local restaurant.

The choice of guest houses is enormous throughout the Baltic States and their availability extends to the most remote areas of each country. Bookings can be made through the rural tourism association – **Estonian Rural Tourism** in Estonia, **Baltic Country Holidays** in Latvia and **Countryside Tourism** in Lithuania.

Rural tourism has become such a popular sector in the Baltic States that many guest houses are booked out all through the summer. It is advisable to make a reservation well in advance.

CAMPSITES

Camping is an extremely popular summer pastime in Estonia, Latvia and Lithuania. As a result, there are a number of campsites scattered throughout each of the Baltic countries. These are usually very cheap and offer basic amenities such as communal showers and an on-site pub-style restaurant. However, not all camps are equipped with washing facilities and toilet blocks. Many commercial campsites also offer basic accommodation in the form of small, simple wooden huts that can house up to four people. National parks have official camping spots, which are free of charge, and many guest houses allow people to pitch tent in their grounds for a minimal fee.

In general, there is a very relaxed attitude towards camping in the Baltic States and people often camp alongside beaches and lakes and in forests in improvised campsites. For camping on private property, however, it is important to get permission from the owner beforehand.

A full list of campsites can be found on national tourism websites and rural tourism specialist websites. In Estonia, **RMK** is an efficient organization that arranges camping.

HIDDEN EXTRAS

Most decent hotels in cities throughout the three Baltic States operate in a transparent manner and will not add any hidden extras to the bill. However, it is worth checking for extra expenses such as the minibar and telephone calls, as these can be exorbitantly priced in some cases. In smaller hotels, it is a good idea to find out if breakfast is included in the room rate.

Rural guest houses tend to be peculiarly reticent about the cost of extra services. Therefore, it is advisable to check out the exact prices of

Caravans lined at Nidos Kempingas, a well-equipped campsite at Nida

Promenāde *(see p304)*, a former grain warehouse in Liepāja, Latvia

meals, drinks, saunas, guided tours, or any such additional services well in advance, to avoid any awkwardness at the time of settling the bills.

CHILDREN

Children are amply catered for in nearly all hotels and guest houses in all three countries. A number of hotels have rooms designed for families travelling with children. If not, then most hotels gladly provide extra beds for children. Many rural guest houses offer special play areas and activities for children and most decent hotels can provide cots for very young children, while babysitting services are becoming increasingly common. Some larger hotels offer special family rates that include a number of family-oriented excursions. For more information see page 381.

Disability signage

SMOKING

In keeping with the ban on smoking in public places in Estonia, Latvia and Lithuania, all hotels prohibit smoking in their public areas. Smoking is not allowed in lobbies and restaurants, although some larger hotels provide special smoking zones. These zones can be recognized by a green smoking-allowed symbol. Most hotels still offer guests a choice between smoking and non-smoking rooms, however.

DISABLED TRAVELLERS

Until recently, access and facilities for disabled travellers was limited to high-end establishments and large chain hotels. However, most major new hotels in the three capital cities have incorporated facilities for disabled guests into their design and the situation has greatly improved. In many upscale hotels, guest rooms are appointed with facilities for disabled people. It is important to remember, however, that very few rural guest houses have facilities for disabled visitors.

Modern lobby of the Radisson Blu Hotel *(see p294)* in Tallinn

DIRECTORY

HOSTELS

Estonian Youth Hostel Association
Narva mnt 16–25, Tallinn.
Tel 646 1455.
www.hostels.ee

Hostelling Latvia
Siguldas prospekts 17–2, Rīga. *Tel* 2921 8560.
www.hostellinglatvia.com

Lithuanian Youth Hostelling Association
Aušros Vartu 20, Vilnius.
Tel 6565 6571. www.lha.lt

APARTMENTS & PRIVATE HOMES

Eldorado Apartments
Vilnius. *Tel* 6991 7391.
www.apartamentai.lt

Erel Apartments & Residences
Paldiski mnt 26a, Tallinn.
Tel 663 1640. www.erel.ee

Eugenijus Apartments
Vilniaus 25–1, Vilnius.
Tel 6994 2456.
www.vilniusapartments.lt

Goodson & Red Apartments
Jõe 5, Tallinn. *Tel* 666 1650.
www.goodsonandred.com

Lilija Plus Real Estate Agency
Rīdzenes iela 25, Rīga. *Tel* 6721 6040. www.lilarealty.lv

Patricia LTD
Elizabetes iela 22, Rīga. *Tel* 6728 4868. www.patricialtd.com

GUEST HOUSES

Baltic Country Holidays
Kalnciema 40, Rīga. *Tel* 6761 7600. www.traveller.lv

Country Tourism of Lithuania
Donelaičio gatvé 2–201, Kaunas. *Tel* (37) 400 354.
www.countryside.lt

Estonian Rural Tourism
Vilmsi tänav 53b, Tallinn.
Tel 600 9999.
www.maaturism.ee

CAMPSITES

RMK
Viljandi mnt 18b, Tallinn.
Tel 676 7500. www.rmk.ee

Choosing a Hotel in Estonia

These hotels have been selected for their good value, facilities and location. They are listed by region, starting with Tallinn, followed by the rest of Estonia. Under each town or area, hotels are listed alphabetically within each price category. For Tallinn map references, see pages 82–3; for road map references see inside back cover.

PRICE CATEGORIES
The following price ranges are for a standard double room for one night during the high season. Breakfast is included, unless otherwise specified.
€ Under €40
€€ €40–€60
€€€ €60–€80
€€€€ €80–€100
€€€€€ Over €100

TALLINN

Pääsu
€

Tööstuse 47a, 13424 **Tel** *654 2013* **Fax** *625 3532* **Rooms** *24*

Located in Mustamäe, a 15-minute drive from the centre, Pääsu has a range of sparsely furnished apartments for groups with TV, refrigerator and shared showers. The owner prefers long-term bookings. There is also a café-bar as well as free parking. Buses leave regularly for the city centre. **www.paasu.ee**

Center Hotel
€€

Narva mnt 24, 10120 **Tel** *686 5202* **Fax** *686 5101* **Rooms** *55* **Map** *2 F2*

Located a short walk from Kadriorg Palace, this hotel is ideally situated for sightseeing. Although some of the cheaper rooms have shared bathrooms, most are en-suite. Facilities include free Wi-Fi, a wellness centre, a sauna and a café, where the lunch menu changes daily. **www.centerhotel.ee**

Dorell
€€

Karu 39, 10120 **Tel** *666 4333* **Fax** *666 4334* **Rooms** *30* **Map** *2 F2*

This cheap and cheerful hotel has standard rooms that are clean and comfortable, all with a pleasant café-bar and sauna. It is within walking distance of the centre or a short bus ride away. A fully equipped apartment with kitchen is also available. **www.dorell.ee**

Dzingel
€€

Männiku tee 89, 11213 **Tel** *610 5201* **Fax** *610 5245* **Rooms** *280*

Although this hotel looks a bit grim on the outside, it is another good budget option, with comfortable rooms, a restaurant, sauna and conference facilities. Located in the picturesque suburb of Nõmme, a bus ride away from the centre, it offers a good alternative view of Tallinn. **www.dzingel.ee**

Go Hotel Shnelli
€€

Toompuiestee 37, 10133 **Tel** *631 0100* **Fax** *631 0101* **Rooms** *124* **Map** *1 B2*

Next to the railway station and a short walk away from the Old Town, the seven-storey Go Hotel Shnelli is not particularly attractive on the outside but it offers decent rooms at reasonable rates. Good Old Town views from the upper floors and a charming restaurant are definite advantages. **www.gohotels.ee**

Hotel Economy
€€

Kopli 2c, 10412 **Tel** *667 8300* **Fax** *667 8301* **Rooms** *38* **Map** *1 B1*

Close to the train station and a short walk away from the Old Town, this attractive and reasonably priced hotel has light, airy and well-furnished rooms with Wi-Fi access. There is no breakfast, but for larger groups lunch and dinner can be arranged in advance. The parking is secure. **www.economyhotel.ee**

Hotel G9
€€

Gonsiori 9, 10117 **Tel** *626 7130* **Fax** *626 7100* **Rooms** *23* **Map** *2 E3*

Located on the third floor of an office building, Hotel G9 offers decent, strikingly decorated rooms at good rates. Services are limited and there is no catering on-site. However, it is only a 5-minute walk from the Old Town and is close to several restaurants, theatres, bars, casinos, cinemas and the general post office. **www.hotelg9.ee**

Lilleküla
€€

Luha 18b, 10131 **Tel** *627 1120* **Fax** *648 1333* **Rooms** *33* **Map** *1 B3*

A good option for the more budget-conscious, this modern hotel offers basically furnished but decent rooms at good rates, all of which come with Wi-Fi access. The hotel also has a pleasant little restaurant and is located about a 15-minute walk from the centre. **www.lillekulahotel.ee**

Metropol
€€

Roseni 13, 10111 **Tel** *667 4500* **Fax** *667 4600* **Rooms** *149*

Situated in the bustling port area close to the Old Town, Metropol has rather tasteful and refined rooms, all of which come with free Wi-Fi connection. There is a smart à la carte restaurant, casino, sauna and beauty salon. Free parking facilities are also available for guests. **www.metropol.ee**

Key to Symbols *see back cover flap*

OldHouse Guesthouse

Uus 22, 10111 **Tel** *641 1281* **Fax** *641 1664* **Rooms** *6*   **Map** *2 D2*

Well situated in the Old Town, this excellent-value guest house has unusually nice rooms for this price range. There is a lovely dining room with a fireplace and the kitchen is open to guests for self-catering. The owners also rent apartments. Free parking is available. **www.oldhouse.ee**

Oru Hotel

Narva mnt 120B, 10127 **Tel** *603 3300* **Fax** *601 2600* **Rooms** *51*   **Map** *2 E2*

Conveniently close to the Song Festival Grounds, Oru Hotel may look a little dull on the outside but it has pleasantly furnished and inviting rooms, all of which come with free Wi-Fi access. There is also a sauna and a decent restaurant. **www.oruhotel.ee**

Pirita Cloister Guesthouse

Merivälja 18, 11911 **Tel** *605 5000* **Fax** *605 5006* **Rooms** *20*

Just 7 km (4 miles) from the city centre, this award-winning modern guest house lies adjacent to Pirita Convent and close to the beach. The lovely rooms all come with a shower and Internet connection. Lunch and dinner have to be arranged in advance. Discounts are available from September to May. **www.piritaklooster.ee**

Romeo Family Hotel

Suur-Karja 18, 10146 **Tel** *644 4255* **Rooms** *11*   **Map** *1 C3*

This Old Town family-run hotel is excellent value, offering a range of comfortable rooms at decent rates. The owners also rent out a range of Old Town apartments, which make a great alternative to hotels. Limited parking available. **www.romeofamily.ee**

Tallink Express

Sadama 1, 10111 **Tel** *667 8700* **Fax** *667 8800* **Rooms** *163*   **Map** *2 E1*

Run by the Tallink ferry company since 2009, this smart hotel is well-positioned between the neighbouring passenger port and the city. The luxurious Tallink Spa is just next door. There's Wi-Fi throughout, a generous buffet breakfast and a children's play area. **http://hotels.tallink.com**

Tatari 53

Tatari 53, 10134 **Tel** *640 5150* **Fax** *640 5151* **Rooms** *36*   **Map** *2 D4*

A pleasant and comfortable hotel outside the city centre, Tatari 53 is within easy walking distance of the Old Town. It offers clean, nicely furnished rooms with Wi-Fi access at good rates. Allergy-free rooms are also available. Pets are allowed for a small additional charge. **www.tatari53.ee**

City Hotel Portus

Uus-Sadama 23, 10120 **Tel** *680 6600* **Fax** *680 6601* **Rooms** *107*   **Map** *2 E1*

Situated next to the D-Terminal of Tallinn's passenger port, Portus is unusually good value for money. It is within walking distance of the Old Town and shopping and entertainment centres, and offers pleasantly quirky, but comfortable, rooms with free Wi-Fi access. **www.tallinnhotels.ee**

Park Inn by Radisson Central Tallinn

Narva mnt 7c, 10120 **Tel** *669 0690* **Fax** *669 0691* **Rooms** *245*   **Map** *2 E2*

Located close to Tallinn's town centre, the Park Inn has a good choice of airy, well-appointed rooms, including large family rooms. There is a sauna, beauty salon and excellent restaurant and bar, as well as a play area for children. Children under 16 can stay for free. **www.parkinn.com**

Reval Park Hotel & Casino

Kreutzwaldi 23, 10147 **Tel** *630 5305* **Fax** *630 5315* **Rooms** *121*   **Map** *2 F3*

About a 10-minute walk away from the Old Town and overlooking a beautiful park, this hotel has an enormous casino on the ground floor. The rooms are spacious, while the suites come with Jacuzzis. Dining options include Tallinn's only all-day buffet. **www.parkhotel.ee**

Scandic Palace

Vabaduse väljak 3, 10141 **Tel** *640 7200* **Fax** *640 7299* **Rooms** *86*   **Map** *1 C3*

Scandic Palace combines Scandinavian refinement and belle époque luxury to delightful effect. The 1930s building has great views of the Old Town, while the skylight in the seventh-floor sauna is a lovely touch. There is a chic café in the lobby and an excellent Mediterranean-style restaurant. **www.scandic-hotels.com**

Sokos Hotel Viru

Viru väljak 4, 10111 **Tel** *680 9300* **Fax** *680 9236* **Rooms** *516*   **Map** *1 C2*

Located in the centre of Tallinn, Sokos is perfectly suited to everyone from families to business travellers. A wide range of excellent rooms comes with an equally impressive range of amenities. The huge complex includes a conference centre, two restaurants, a nightclub and shopping centre. **www.sokoshotels.com**

Susi

Peterburi tee 48, 11415 **Tel** *630 3300* **Fax** *630 3400* **Rooms** *99*

Although located a little way out of the city centre, Susi is well connected via a tram route. The hotel is an attractive option, thanks to its excellent amenities and large choice of rooms. It includes a restaurant, lobby bar, billiards table, beauty salon and sauna. Displays of local artwork add a touch of class. **www.susi.ee**

Kalev Spa Hotel
Aia 18, 10111 **Tel** *649 3300* **Fax** *649 3301* **Rooms** *100* €€€€ Map 2 D2

The centrally located Kalev Spa Hotel specializes in spa treatments and also boasts an enormous waterpark with three water slides and a large swimming pool. The rooms are stylishly decorated. Use of the waterpark, fitness centre and sauna facilities are included in the room rate. **www.kalevspa.ee**

My City Hotel
Vana-Posti 11/13, 10146 **Tel** *622 0900* **Fax** *622 0901* **Rooms** *68* €€€€ Map 1 C3

Set in a fine 18th-century building in a great Old Town location, this is a top-class hotel. Elegant rooms all come with free Internet connection. Services and extras include babysitting, laundry, airport transfer and complimentary newspaper. Excellent business conference facilities are available. **www.mycityhotel.ee**

Radisson Blu Hotel Tallinn
Rävala pst 3, 10143 **Tel** *682 3000* **Fax** *682 3001* **Rooms** *280* €€€€ Map 2 D4

This sleek and immaculately run hotel is located in the centre of Tallinn's business and commercial district. Great views of the city, free Internet access and free morning sauna, a healthcare centre and superb dining are just some of the additional features. **www.radissonblu.com**

Tallink City
Laikmaa 5, 10145 **Tel** *630 0800* **Fax** *630 0810* **Rooms** *332* €€€€ Map 2 E3

This sophisticated business-class hotel in the city centre has a range of spacious, well-appointed guest rooms, as well as two state-of-the-art conference rooms and superb tenth-floor meeting suites. There is an excellent restaurant buffet and the sauna is free for guests in the morning. **http://hotels.tallink.com**

Baltic Hotel Vana Wiru
Viru 11, 10140 **Tel** *669 1500* **Fax** *669 1501* **Rooms** *82* €€€€€ Map 2 D3

This trendy hotel is ideally situated in the heart of the Old Town. The beautifully furnished, pastel-coloured rooms all come with free Internet access, while the deluxe rooms have a sauna or Jacuzzi. There is also a Turkish bath and Finnish sauna, a great restaurant and a lively pub. **www.vanawiru.ee**

Kreutzwald Hotel Tallinn
Endla 23, 10122 **Tel** *666 4800* **Fax** *666 4888* **Rooms** *85* €€€€€ Map 1 A4

This hotel, with great transport links, is situated in a beautiful part of the city centre, just a short walk away from the Old Town. Sauna, gym and a free massage are included in the room rate. There is secure parking and the excellent La Bohème restaurant. **www.uniquestay.com**

Radisson Blu Hotel Olümpia
Liivalaia 33, 10118 **Tel** *669 0690* **Fax** *669 0691* **Rooms** *390* €€€€€ Map 2 D5

This 26-storey hotel has numerous extra services such as trouser presses, safes, hairdryers and slippers in its cosy rooms, along with free Internet access and spectacular views. There are fantastic restaurants, pubs and a nightclub on the premises. **www.radissonblu.com**

Schlössle
Pühavaimu 13/15, 10123 **Tel** *699 7700* **Fax** *699 7777* **Rooms** *23* €€€€€ Map 1 C2

This award-winning hotel fully deserves each of its five stars. The lavishly furnished rooms perfectly complement the splendid medieval-style interior, while the romantic restaurant is top-class. Facilities include 24-hour room service, babysitting, limousine hire and a private sauna and massage service. **www.schlossle-hotels.com**

St. Petersbourg
Rataskaevu 7, 10123 **Tel** *628 6500* **Fax** *628 6565* **Rooms** *27* €€€€€ Map 1 C2

St. Petersbourg is a small but very classy hotel in a charming Old Town location. The rooms are furnished in eclectic Art Deco style with en-suite bathrooms. The hotel restaurant specializes in Russian cuisine in keeping with the hotel's historical connection with visiting Russian aristocrats. **www.schlossle-hotels.com**

Three Sisters
Pikk 71/Tolli 2, 10133 **Tel** *630 6300* **Fax** *630 6301* **Rooms** *23* €€€€€ Map 1 C2

Tallinn's premier luxury boutique hotel is in three magnificently converted medieval houses. The beautifully fitted rooms come with flat-screen TVs and Internet connection, while the labyrinthine interior includes spiral staircases, a library with fireplace, a restaurant *(see p325)* and a supremely cosy wine cellar. **www.threesistershotel.com**

Ülemiste
Lennujaama tee 2, 11101 **Tel** *603 2600* **Fax** *603 2601* **Rooms** *130* €€€€€ Map 1 B3

An ultra-modern hotel next to the airport, Ülemiste is a great option for overnight and short-stay guests. There is a good range of rooms, as well as a fitness centre, two saunas and a decent restaurant. The summer terrace has great views of a lake. There is easy access to the city centre by car and bus. **www.ylemistehotel.ee**

The Von Stackelberg Hotel Tallinn
Toompuiestee 23, 10137 **Tel** *660 0700* **Fax** *661 6176* **Rooms** *51* €€€€€ Map 1 B3

The elegant limestone building housing this hotel was built as a residence for a German baron. Its interior is warm but stylish, and the so-called Zen rooms and apartments come with NASA-designed gravity-free chairs. All rooms have flat-screen computers and digital safes. **www.uniquestay.com**

Key to Price Guide *see p292* **Key to Symbols** *see back cover flap*

WESTERN ESTONIA

HAAPSALU Päeva Villa

🔟 €€

Lai 7, 90503 **Tel** *473 3672* **Fax** *473 3772* **Rooms** *18*
Road Map *C2*

Päeva Villa is a charming little guest house with bright and inviting rooms decorated in different themes. The restaurant serves delicious Slavic cuisine as well as Estonian dishes. Facilities include a sauna. Pets are welcome for a small extra charge. **www.paevavilla.ee**

HAAPSALU Baltic Hotel Promenaadi

P 🔟 ♿ €€€€

Sadama 22, 90507 **Tel** *473 7250* **Fax** *473 7254* **Rooms** *35*
Road Map *C2*

This delightful hotel consists of a modern extension and a converted 19th-century villa. The lovely rooms, most of which have balconies, face out on to the sea. Rowing boat and bike rental services are available. There is free Internet access in the lobby and partial Wi-Fi connection in some rooms. **www.promenaadi.ee**

HAAPSALU Fra Mare Spa Hotel

P 🔟 ♨ 🏃 ♿ €€€€€

Ranna tee 2, 90403 **Tel** *472 4600* **Fax** *472 4601* **Rooms** *115*
Road Map *C2*

Situated on the seafront, this modern hotel offers a huge range of spa and beauty treatments. The rooms are bright and airy and the whole place is suffused with a healthy atmosphere. There is an excellent pool complex, gym and even a children's playground. **www.framare.ee**

HIIUMAA ISLAND Liilia Hotel

P 🔟 €

Hiiu mnt 22, Käina, 92101 **Tel** *463 6146* **Fax** *463 6546* **Rooms** *13*
Road Map *C2*

Located in an area of stunning natural beauty, Liilia Hotel is housed in a charming building which vaguely resembles a Spanish villa. The rooms are fairly nice but simple, while the hotel restaurant and pub are delightful. Various boat trips and boat rental options are available. **www.liiliahotell.ee**

HIIUMAA ISLAND Padu Hotel

P 🔟 ♨ €€

Heltermaa mnt 22, Kärdla, 92414 **Tel** *463 3037* **Fax** *463 3023* **Rooms** *18*
Road Map *C2*

Padu Hotel is a pleasant place to stay and is a convenient base from which to explore Hiiumaa. The rooms are somewhat sparsely decorated, but the apartments are much more comfortable and cost just a little more. All rooms have balconies. The restaurant serves local wild boar. **www.paduhotell.ee**

KIHNU ISLAND Tolli Tourism Farm

🖼 P €

Sääre village, 88001 **Tel** *527 7380* **Rooms** *7*
Road Map *C2*

This authentic farmstead provides a great way to experience the rugged beauty of Kihnu, with accommodation that includes beds in a converted barn. Guests can take trips out to sea with the island's famed fishermen and there are plenty of sporting activities on offer. Village musicians can be hired on request. **www.kihnukallas.ee**

MATSULA NATIONAL PARK Algallika Center

P 🔟 €€

Mäe Farm, Rannaküla, 90115 **Tel** *5556 6088* **Fax** *5307 0921* **Rooms** *5*
Road Map *C2*

Located on a spit of land jutting out into the Matsalu Bay, this small and charming place has amazing views of the surrounding landscape. All the rooms are large and comfortable, with modern fittings and furnishings. A private sauna and spa, nature walks and horse rides are also on offer. **www.algallika.ee**

MATSULA NATIONAL PARK Altmõisa Guesthouse

P 🔟 €€

Tuulu village, 90402 **Tel** *472 4680* **Fax** *472 4681* **Rooms** *12*
Road Map *C2*

Situated on the northern shore of Matsalu Bay, this endearing guest house makes a great resting place after a long day's bird-watching or hiking trip. There are lovely views out to sea and of countless kinds of birds. The restaurant is also very good, with a health-conscious, but delicious, menu. **www.altmoisa.ee**

MUHU ISLAND Pädaste Manor

P 🔟 🗒 €€€€€

Pädaste Manor, 94702 **Tel** *454 8800* **Fax** *454 8811* **Rooms** *24*
Road Map *C2*

The hotel in Pädaste Manor has a heliport and has become famous after much high-profile media coverage. Its combination of refined luxury and rustic charm is certainly irresistible. Beautiful rooms, sumptuous food and a range of spa treatments make a perfect package. Ferry pick-up service is also available. **www.padaste.ee**

PALDISKI Laulasmaa Resort

P 🔟 ♨ 🏃 🗒 ♿ €€€€

Puhkekodu 4, 76702 **Tel** *687 0800* **Fax** *687 0801* **Rooms** *150*
Road Map *C1*

Situated on a beautiful sandy bay just 30 minutes from Tallinn, this is an excellent resort with a superb wellness institute and spa facilities. More than half the rooms have balconies, and there are special allergy-free rooms as well. The resort's surroundings are fantastic for walking and cycling. **www.laulasmaa.ee**

PÄRNU Lepanina

P 🔟 ♨ 🏃 ♿ €€€

Kabli village, 86002 **Tel** *446 5024* **Rooms** *34*
Road Map *D2*

Lepanina is a pleasant seafront hotel some 52 km (32 miles) from Pärnu and 12 km (7 miles) from the Latvian border. Family rooms can sleep two children and all rooms have a balcony and view of the sea. Facilities include a sauna complex, swimming pool, restaurant, lobby bar, tennis courts and a mini golf course. **www.lepanina.ee**

PÄRNU Scandic Rannahotell
P ∥ &   €€€
Ranna pst 5, 80010 **Tel** *443 2950* **Fax** *443 2918* **Rooms** *62*   **Road Map** *D2*

Scandic Rannahotell is an elegant seafront hotel, equipped with modern facilities. It has an excellent à la carte restaurant and a rooftop terrace for warmer weather. Some rooms have sea views and balconies. Sauna, massage and beauty therapies are available. Free parking for guests. **www.scandic-hotels.com**

PÄRNU Ammende Villa
P ∥   €€€€€
Mere pst 7, 80010 **Tel** *447 3888* **Fax** *447 3887* **Rooms** *24*   **Road Map** *D2*

A glorious Art Nouveau house, Ammende Villa has been converted into a luxury hotel. The rooms are beautifully furnished in authentic period style, while the service is second to none. The hotel is close to the beach and a short walk from the Old Town. Car rental is available. **www.ammende.ee**

PÄRNU Strand Spa & Conference Hotel
P ∥ ≋ &   €€€€€
Tammsaare pst 35, 80010 **Tel** *447 5370* **Fax** *447 5371* **Rooms** *187*   **Road Map** *D2*

The largest hotel in Pärnu, Strand Spa & Conference Hotel is close to the sea and city centre. Its spa and large swimming pool are free for guests, as is the popular Spa nightclub. Massage and beauty treatments are also available. The hotel specializes in organizing large conferences. **www.strand.ee**

PÄRNU Tervise Paradiis
P ∥ ≋ ⅍ 目 &   €€€€€
Side 14, 80010 **Tel** *447 9219* **Fax** *445 1601* **Rooms** *122*   **Road Map** *D2*

Warm and stylish rooms and a recreational atmosphere make Tervise Paradiis a good family option. The hotel boasts the largest waterpark in Estonia, as well as a huge swimming pool, bowling alley and a well-equipped fitness centre. It also has a good restaurant. **www.terviseparadiis.ee**

SAAREMAA ISLAND Kaali Visitors' Centre
P   €
Kaali village, Kaali Meteorite Crater, 94102 **Tel** *459 1184* **Rooms** *10*   **Road Map** *C2*

The Kaali Visitors' Centre offers comfortable guest house-style accommodation in a great location. The hotel can arrange excursions to Kuressaare and other major sights in Saaremaa, as well as boat trips to nearby islands, horse-riding and cycling. Transport available on request. **www.kaali.kylastuskeskus.ee**

SAAREMAA ISLAND Grand Rose Spa Hotel
P ∥ ≋ ⅍ &   €€
Tallinna 15, Kuressaare, 93811 **Tel** *666 7000* **Rooms** *65*   **Road Map** *C2*

This hotel offers comfortable accommodation. Allergy-free rooms, as well as those with facilities for disabled guests are included. The spa and sauna centre is beautifully designed and offers guests free access between 8am and 10pm. **www.grandrose.ee**

SAAREMAA ISLAND Loona Manor
⎙ P ∥   €€
Loona, Kihelkonna, 93401 **Tel** *454 6510* **Rooms** *10*   **Road Map** *B2*

Situated at the gateway to Vilsandi National Park, Loona Manor is a perfectly adequate hotel with cosy and well-furnished attic rooms as well as grounds for camping. Guided tours around the park are available, including a memorable trip to Vilsandi Island on a huge truck, especially popular with bird-watchers. **www.loonamanor.ee**

SAAREMAA ISLAND Nasva Yacht Club Hotel
P ∥ &   €€
Nasva village, 93822 **Tel** *454 4044* **Fax** *454 4028* **Rooms** *21*   **Road Map** *C2*

Located in a fishing village 10 km (6 miles) from Kuressaare, this hotel resembles a ship on the outside and has a maritime theme on the inside. The rooms are bright and cheerful and all have balconies. The restaurant is reasonable but there are better places to eat in Kuressaare. **www.saaremaa.ee/nasvahotel**

SAAREMAA ISLAND Välja Tourism Farm
⎙ P   €€
Hiievälja village, Angla Windmills, 94202 **Tel** *563 28956* **Rooms** *7*   **Road Map** *C2*

Situated on the less explored side of Saaremaa, Välja Tourism Farm is an excellent base for exploring this beautiful region. Comfortable rooms are on offer in quaint, farmstead-style surroundings. Camping is also available. Leisi, the nearest town, is almost 7 km (4 miles) away. **www.valja.maaturism.ee**

SAAREMAA ISLAND Georg Ots Spa Hotel
P ∥ ≋ ⅍ 目 &   €€€
Tori 2, Kuressaare, 93815 **Tel** *455 0000* **Fax** *455 0001* **Rooms** *91*   **Road Map** *C2*

The interior of this award-winning hotel is minimalist, though warm and intimate. The swimming pool is a master-piece of design. An excellent range of spa and beauty treatments and top-notch dining are also on offer. The hotel is also close to all the main sights in Kuressaare. **www.gospa.ee**

SAAREMAA ISLAND Lepametsa Tourist Farm
⎙ P   €€€
Nasva Küla, 93822 **Tel** *454 4159* **Rooms** *4 cabins*   **Road Map** *B2*

Located near Kuressaare, this charming property is within walking distance of beaches and forests, and surrounded by greenery and nature. There are several wooden cabins to rent, each with cooking facilities. For a small extra cost, you can also use the sauna, or hire bicycles or canoes. **www.lepametsa.ee**

SAAREMAA ISLAND Vanalinna Võõrastemaja
P ∥   €€€
Kauba 8, Kuressaare, 93812 **Tel** *455 5309* **Rooms** *14*   **Road Map** *C2*

A home-like hotel that is good value for money. The rooms are unexceptional but comfortable, while the two attic rooms have a more romantic and rustic feel. The hotel restaurant offers excellent food at reasonable prices. **www.vanalinna.ee**

Key to Price Guide *see p292* **Key to Symbols** *see back cover flap*

SAAREMAA ISLAND Pilguse Manor €€€€

Jõgela village, 93301 **Tel** *524 0033* **Fax** *454 5441* **Rooms** *15* **Road Map** *C2*

This relaxing family-run hotel is surrounded by stunning scenery. The comfortable rooms tastefully incorporate rustic elements. The hotel has free Wi-Fi access for guests. If weather permits, a prepacked country picnic on Katri Cliff is a great option. The area is perfect for hiking and cycling. **www.pilguse.ee**

SAAREMAA ISLAND Saaremaa Spa Hotel Rüütli €€€€

Pargi 12, Kuressaare, 93813 **Tel** *454 8100* **Fax** *454 8199* **Rooms** *93* **Road Map** *C2*

Located next to the town park and the marina, this large spa hotel is a good option for families. Children's facilities include a play area and a designated pool in the water centre. There is also a squash court, sauna complex and plenty of health and beauty therapies, including water aerobics. **www.sanatoorium.ee**

SAAREMAA ISLAND Oti Manor **P** €€€€€

Oti, 94501 **Tel** *511 7773* **Rooms** *5* **Road Map** *C2*

Oti Manor has been beautifully transformed into a charming hotel consisting of five suites, each of which is furnished on a different theme. The hotel is 8 km (5 miles) from the town of Orissaare and 50 km (31 miles) from Kuressaare. A stunning beach is within easy reach. **www.otimanor.ee**

SOOMAA NATIONAL PARK Riisa Rantso **P** €

Riisa village, 86802 **Tel** *556 94270* **Rooms** *5* **Road Map** *D2*

This rustic ranch is located in the middle of Soomaa National Park, next to the Hallista River. Three wooden cabins offer comfortable and charming accommodation. There are numerous extras available, such as Finnish and Russian-style saunas, boat trips, bicycle hire, tent hire and even a home-cooked dinner. **www.riisarantso.ee**

VORMSI ISLAND Elle-Malle Guesthouse **P** €

Hullo village, 91301 **Tel** *473 2072* **Rooms** *12* **Road Map** *C1*

This is a charming and restful guest house that feels far from the bustle of the modern world. The main guest house has several rustic-looking but cosy rooms, while a narrow windmill on stilts has been converted into a romantic double room. Excellent local food is offered at great prices. **www.ellemalle.com**

VORMSI ISLAND Rumpo Mäe Farm **P** €

Rumpo village, 91309 **Tel** *472 9932* **Rooms** *14* **Road Map** *C1*

This charmingly converted farmstead makes an excellent place to stay. It is close to the sea and is well situated for hiking and cycling. The rooms are simple but pleasant. Self-catering facilities are available. Guests can also pitch a tent in the grounds. **www.rumpomae.ee**

EASTERN ESTONIA

KUREMÄE Wironia **P** €€

Rakvere 7, 41531 **Tel** *336 4200* **Fax** *336 1210* **Rooms** *21* **Road Map** *E1*

This simple, but pleasant, hotel is 20 km (12 miles) away from the spectacular Pühtitsa convent and close to several other areas of interest. The average-priced rooms are bright and cheery and there is a nice pub and restaurant with outdoor seating in summer. A good base for exploring the region. **www.wironia.ee**

LAHEMAA NATIONAL PARK Merekalda Guesthouse **P** €€

Neeme tee 2, Käsmu, 45601 **Tel** *323 8451* **Rooms** *7* **Road Map** *D1*

This relaxing guest house has five snug apartments and two double rooms. Rates do not include breakfast, although light breakfasts can be ordered, and the closest restaurant is in nearby Võsu. The stunning surroundings are a dream for hikers and cyclists. No pets are allowed. **www.merekalda.ee**

LAHEMAA NATIONAL PARK Rannaliiv Guesthouse €€

Aia 4, Võsu, 45501 **Tel** *323 8456* **Fax** *323 8456* **Rooms** *13* **Road Map** *D1*

Situated near a beautiful beach, Rannaliiv Guesthouse is a comfortable place to pass a few days. It has homely rooms with balconies and a pleasant garden for guests to sit in during summer. There is also a sauna and swimming pool, and hall with a fireplace for groups. **www.rannaliiv.ee**

LAHEMAA NATIONAL PARK Park Hotel Palmse €€€

Vihula district, Palmse, 45202 **Tel** *322 3626* **Fax** *323 4167* **Rooms** *27* **Road Map** *D1*

Park Hotel has sparsely furnished, but bright and cheerful rooms housed in the converted distillery of Palmse Manor. The beautiful surroundings and central location in Lahemaa National Park make it an attractive option. There is a great beer cellar and rustic-style sauna for guests. **www.phpalmse.ee**

LAHEMAA NATIONAL PARK Sagadi Manor **P** €€€€

Sagadi village, Sagadi, 45403 **Tel** *676 7888* **Fax** *676 7880* **Rooms** *28* **Road Map** *D2*

The hotel is located on the grounds of the beautiful Sagadi Manor estate. The charming en-suite rooms are housed in the loft of converted stables. A hostel across the courtyard offers sparse but comfortable accommodation at more modest rates. Bicycle rental options are available. **www.sagadi.ee**

NARVA King
`P` `11`   €€

Lavretsovi 9, 20307 **Tel** *357 2404* **Fax** *357 2404* **Rooms** *23*   **Road Map** *E1*

King is a charming, rustic-style hotel in the centre of town. The tastefully furnished rooms are comfortable and lavish and each comes with free Wi-Fi access. The restaurant, set over two floors, is excellent. Excursions are also available. **www.hotelking.ee**

NARVA Narva Hotel
`P` `11` `&`   €€€

Puškini 6, 20308 **Tel** *359 9600* **Fax** *359 9603* **Rooms** *51*   **Road Map** *E1*

Excellently located close to the bus and railway stations, this establishment is close to all of Narva's most famous historic monuments. While the hotel's exterior is rather modest, the rooms are very clean and comfortable and some come with Internet connection. **www.narvahotell.ee**

NARVA-JÕESUU Narva-Jõesuu Spa Hotel
`P` `11` `≋` `&`   €€€

Aia 3, 29002 **Tel** *359 9521* **Fax** *359 9525* **Rooms** *144*   **Road Map** *E1*

Offering a wide range of therapy treatments, this delightful spa hotel is a relaxing getaway. There is an excellent swimming pool and sauna, while the beautiful beach is only a short walk away. The hotel's reception staff can arrange excursions to nearby Narva and the Ontika Coast, among other leisure activities. **www.narvajoesuu.ee**

ONTIKA COAST Toila Spa Hotel
`P` `11` `≋` `大` `&`   €€€€

Ranna 12, 41702 **Tel** *334 2900* **Fax** *334 2901* **Rooms** *280*   **Road Map** *E1*

A modern nine-storey spa hotel surrounded by sea and forest, this highly professional establishment specializes in health and wellness treatments. There is a huge range of quality accommodation, including apartments and a nearby camping site. The bathing pools are nicely designed in mock-Roman style. **www.toilaspa.ee**

OTEPÄÄ Pühajärve Spa Hotel
`P` `11` `≋` `大` `&`   €€€

Pühajärve, 67414 **Tel** *766 5500* **Fax** *766 5501* **Rooms** *98*   **Road Map** *E2*

This spa hotel is beautifully located and offers an excellent range of wellness and beauty treatments. There is also a sizeable swimming pool, bowling alley, gym and billiards room. Best of all, though, are the stunning natural surroundings. Pets are welcome. **www.pyhajarve.com**

PÕLTSAMAA Heleni Maja Guesthouse
`11` `P`   €

Pajusi 12, 48106 **Tel** *776 2720* **Fax** *776 2721* **Rooms** *15*   **Road Map** *D2*

Situated in the tranquil environs of Põltsamaa, this is a pleasant, if rather functional, guest house. The rooms are clean and comfortable and the restaurant is similarly low-key. A pool table and sauna are available for evening relaxation. **www.helenimaja.ee**

PÕLVA Hotel Pesa
`P` `11` `≋`   €€

Uus 5, 63308 **Tel** *799 8530* **Fax** *797 0833* **Rooms** *24*   **Road Map** *E2*

Hotel Pesa is a congenial place with unexceptional, but comfortable, rooms and a good restaurant. Wi-Fi access is limited to the lobby and selected rooms. The hotel boasts a swimming pool, fitness centre and sauna. Among the many activities on offer is an excellent culture and nature tour. **www.kagureis.ee**

RAKVERE Wesenbergh
`P` `11`   €€

Tallinn 25, 44311 **Tel** *322 3480* **Fax** *322 3387* **Rooms** *47*   **Road Map** *D1*

Named after an old local castle, this elegant little hotel also has a separate villa. Some rooms are provided with a private sauna. There is a gym and aerobics hall. In addition to a restaurant, café and a grill-house, Wesenbergh also has a 24-hour lobby bar. **www.wesenbergh.ee**

RÕUGE Rõuge Suurjärv Guesthouse
`P` `&`   €€

Metsa 5, 66201 **Tel** *785 9273* **Rooms** *16*   **Road Map** *E2*

This home-like guest house is a great base from which to explore the beautiful region. The rooms are simple but comfortable and a rustic-style breakfast is served. Lunch and dinner can be arranged on request. A real country sauna is also available. The area is fantastic for hiking. **www.maremajutus.ee**

SANGASTE MANOR Sangaste Castle Hostel
`▤` `P` `11`   €€

Lossiküla village, 67001 **Tel** *767 9300* **Fax** *767 9303* **Rooms** *10*   **Road Map** *D2*

One of the most striking manor houses in Estonia, Sangaste Castle has charming high-ceilinged rooms which resonate with history. The restaurant is similarly authentic-looking, although its menu is fairly basic. The castle boasts a museum and tower, plus beautiful gardens to explore. **www.sangasteloss.ee**

SETUMAA Piusa Ürgoru Holiday Home
`▤` `P`   €€

Väiko-Härma village, 65334 **Tel** *528 9134* **Rooms** *6*   **Road Map** *E2*

This pleasant village-like ensemble consists of a main house, a converted granary and several simple log cabins at a lower price. The beautiful surrounding countryside and local places of interest make it a good choice. There is also a campsite and trout fishing is possible throughout the summer. **www.puhkemaja.ee**

SILLAMÄE Hotel Krunk
`P` `11`   €€

Kesk 23, 40231 **Tel** *392 9030* **Fax** *392 9035* **Rooms** *21*   **Road Map** *E1*

Situated right in the middle of town, Hotel Krunk is a good example of Stalinist Neo-Baroque architecture and is an intriguing place to stay. The hotel was constructed during the Soviet era and was then a guest house. The spacious rooms all have Internet connection. The hotel also has a good restaurant and a sauna. **www.krunk.ee**

SUUR MUNAMÄGI Haanjamehe Farm
Vakari, 65101 **Tel** *786 6000* **Fax** *786 6001* **Rooms** *14*   **Road Map** *E2*

This delightfully converted farmstead gives a real taste of rural life. The rooms are lovely and there is a staggering range of activities on offer, from excursions to local sights, to canoeing and amusing obstacle courses. The wonderful wooden restaurant is a great place to unwind. **www.haanjamehetalu.ee**

TAEVASKOJA Taevaskoja Holiday Centre Hostel
Taevaskoja, 63202 **Tel** *5373 6406* **Rooms** *30*   **Road Map** *E2*

This hostel is not exactly luxurious, but it is cheap and cheerful. Guests can make use of the self-catering facilities. There is also a volleyball court, sauna and rock-climbing wall. It is a good base from which to go for trekking and canoeing. **www.taevaskoja.ee**

TARTU Tartu Hotel
Soola 3, 51013 **Tel** *731 4300* **Fax** *731 4301* **Rooms** *58*   **Road Map** *E2*

A reasonable budget option for a night or two, Tartu Hotel is located on the periphery of the city centre and offers rooms at a good price. The whole hotel has Wi-Fi access. The sauna can take groups of up to 15 people at one time. **www.tartuhotell.ee**

TARTU Terviseks B&B
Raekoja Plats 10, 51003 **Tel** *565 5382* **Rooms** *5*   **Road Map** *E2*

A friendly B&B located right on the Town Hall Square, Terviseks is a great budget option. It offers private rooms for those who enjoy the sociable elements of hostels, like the big kitchen and living room, but also want some privacy. There's a total of 24 beds available. **www.terviseksbbb.com**

TARTU Hansa Hotel
Aleksandri 46, 51004 **Tel** *737 1800* **Fax** *737 1801* **Rooms** *22*   **Road Map** *D1*

Strategically located close to the Tartu river, Hansa Hotel resembles an old merchant's house or a row of stores. This comfortable and modern hotel retains its period charm. The rooms are lovely, with a neat decor and facilities, such as TV and telephone. Special rooms for disabled guests are available. **www.hansahotel.ee**

TARTU Pallas
Riia mnt 4, 51004 **Tel** *730 1200* **Fax** *730 1201* **Rooms** *61*   **Road Map** *E2*

This slightly unusual but charming hotel sits atop a sleek commercial building in the centre of town and offers great views. The wonderfully decorated rooms are all inspired by famous Estonian artists. The restaurant is decent and serves a range of set menus. **www.pallas.ee**

TARTU Barclay
Ülikooli 8, 51003 **Tel** *744 7100* **Fax** *744 7110* **Rooms** *49*   **Road Map** *E2*

An elegant 1912 Art Nouveau building, the Barclay hotel served as the headquarters of the Red Army during Soviet times. The rooms are extremely comfortable, if unimaginatively furnished. The hotel has an excellent location in the centre of town. **www.barclay.ee**

TARTU Draakon
Raekoja plats 2, 51003 **Tel** *744 2045* **Fax** *742 3000* **Rooms** *40*   **Road Map** *E2*

Located right on Town Hall Square, Draakon is a plush hotel mainly catering to businessmen and high-end tourists. The suites come with their own saunas. All rooms have Internet connection. There is an elegant Baroque-style restaurant and an atmospheric medieval-style beer cellar restaurant. **www.draakon.ee/eng**

VILJANDI Hotel Centrum
Tallinna 24, 71008 **Tel** *435 1100* **Fax** *435 1130* **Rooms** *27*   **Road Map** *D2*

Hotel Centrum is located on the third floor of the Centrum shopping centre. The rooms are comfortable, though sparsely decorated. A sauna, massage parlour and beauty salon are open to guests. The excellent restaurant *(see p329)* is a bonus. **www.centrum.ee**

VILJANDI Grand Hotel Viljandi
Tartu 11/Lossi 29, 71004 **Tel** *435 5800* **Fax** *435 5805* **Rooms** *49*   **Road Map** *D2*

Housed in a 1938 Art Deco building, the Grand Hotel is decidedly opulent for its small-town setting. It has an impressive gym, a sauna divided into a Turkish bath and Finnish sauna and a very good restaurant. Check with the helpful staff about local excursions and cultural events. **www.ghv.ee**

VÕRU Kubija Hotel
Männiku 43a, 65603 **Tel** *786 6000* **Fax** *786 6001* **Rooms** *56*   **Road Map** *E2*

Kubija is a bright, welcoming and uniquely furnished hotel that takes special care of its guests. It even includes a sleep centre offering expert advice and diagnoses on sleeping problems. A good range of wellness treatments as well as plenty of fascinating local excursions can be found here. **www.kubija.ee**

VÕRU Tamula Hotel
Vee 4, 65609 **Tel** *783 0430* **Fax** *783 0431* **Rooms** *25*   **Road Map** *E2*

Located on the sandy shores of Lake Tamula, Tamula Hotel is a bright and pleasant establishment. The suites have a private sauna. The hotel also has tennis courts, while bike rental is available for exploring the nearby town of Võru. There is a pub and nightclub beside the hotel. **www.tamula.ee**

Choosing a Hotel in Latvia

These hotels have been selected for their good value, facilities and location. They are listed by region, starting with Rīga, followed by the rest of Latvia. Under each town or area, hotels are listed alphabetically within each price category. For Rīga map references, see pages 160–61; for road map references see inside back cover.

PRICE CATEGORIES
The following price ranges are for a standard double room for one night during the high season. Breakfast is included, unless otherwise specified.

Ⓛ Under 30 Ls
ⓁⓁ 30–50 Ls
ⓁⓁⓁ 50–80 Ls
ⓁⓁⓁⓁ 80–110 Ls
ⓁⓁⓁⓁⓁ Over 110 Ls

RĪGA

KB   Ⓛ

Krišjānis Barona iela 37, LV-1011 **Tel** *6731 2323* **Fax** *6731 6953* **Rooms** *11*   **Map** *2 E3*

Named after Krišjānis Barons, a collector of Latvian folk songs, this B&B is owned by his great-grandson. The renovated Art Nouveau building is bright and spacious, while the bedrooms are basic but good value. The studio in the attic has a kitchenette. **www.kbhotel.lv**

Baltvilla   🅿 🍴 ▤ ♿   ⓁⓁ

Senču prospekts 45, LV-2164 **Tel** *6784 0640* **Fax** *6799 0888* **Rooms** *37*

Just 30 minutes from the centre of Rīga, this hotel on the edge of Lake Baltezers opened in 2007. It specializes in providing both medical and spa treatments for its guests, with good facilities for those with disabilities or allergies. The rooms are comfortable and stylish. **www.baltvilla.lv**

B&B Rīga   🅿   ⓁⓁ

Ģertrūdes iela 43, LV-1011 **Tel** *6727 8505* **Fax** *6729 7594* **Rooms** *18*   **Map** *2 E2*

This family-run B&B is located in a quiet courtyard a short walk from the Old Town. The apartment-style rooms come in a range of sizes, although the smallest do not include cooking facilities. The largest are very good value for big groups. Breakfast is served at a café across the road. **www.bb-riga.lv**

Days Hotel   🅿 🍴 ▤   ⓁⓁ

Brīvības iela 199c, LV-1039 **Tel** *6716 6000* **Fax** *6716 6001* **Rooms** *135*   **Map** *2 F1*

This oddly curvy building is a short tram ride from the Old Town, but its location means that its rooms are reasonably priced. The decor is groovy 1960s retro, with a range of different colour schemes in the bedrooms. The terrace is a pleasant place for cocktails in summer. **www.dayshotelriga.com**

Homestay   ▤ 🅿   ⓁⓁ

Stokholmas iela 1, LV-1014 **Tel** *6755 3016* **Rooms** *4*

Located in the upmarket Mežaparks district, a 20-minute tram ride from the Old Town, Homestay is well worth the journey. The owners, a Latvian and a New Zealander, are very attentive towards their guests. The rooms are cosy and the breakfast is excellent. **www.homestay.lv**

Laine   🅿 🍴   ⓁⓁ

Skolas iela 11, LV-1010 **Tel** *6728 8816* **Fax** *6728 7658* **Rooms** *38*   **Map** *2 E2*

Housed in an Art Nouveau building, tucked away in a quiet street, this hotel is a great budget find. The bright and welcoming rooms show a Scandinavian influence and have paintings on the walls. Safes, Wi-Fi access, hairdryers and minibars are provided. The cheapest rooms have shared facilities. **www.laine.lv**

Rīga   🅿 🍴 ♿   ⓁⓁ

Aspazijas bulvāris 22, LV-1050 **Tel** *6704 4222* **Fax** *6704 4223* **Rooms** *236*   **Map** *2 D4*

With a prime spot on the edge of the Old Town, this local landmark has been open since 1956. A little of the Soviet era lingers despite renovation. However, it has all the facilities of a large hotel such as Wi-Fi access, a business centre and sauna. The lobby includes a currency exchange, bar and jewellery store. **www.hotelriga.lv**

Albert   🅿 🍴 ▤ ♿   ⓁⓁⓁ

Dzirnavu iela 33, LV-1010 **Tel** *6733 1717* **Fax** *6733 1718* **Rooms** *246*   **Map** *2 E4*

The Albert in question is Einstein, and this theme is subtly present throughout this popular hotel in the main Art Nouveau district. The stylish rooms each contain a quote from the famous scientist, and there are atom motifs in the carpets. Bedrooms are simple but comfortable, decorated in calming colours. **www.alberthotel.lv**

Clarion Collection Hotel Valdemars   🅿 🍴 ▤ ♿   ⓁⓁⓁ

Valdemara iela 23, LV-1010 **Tel** *6733 4462* **Fax** *6733 3001* **Rooms** *83*   **Map** *2 D2*

Located in a splendid Art Nouveau building on the edge of the Quiet Centre, this Scandinavian-style hotel offers free use of the sauna and hot tub, as well as a complimentary evening meal. Rooms are simple but comfortable, and service is friendly. Free Wi-Fi. **www.valdemars.lv**

Key to Symbols *see back cover flap*

Domina Inn
Pulkveža brieža 11–13, LV-1010 **Tel** *6763 1800* **Fax** *6763 1801* **Rooms** *88* **Map** *1 C1*

Situated in the city's main Art Nouveau district, this elegant hotel is itself architecturally impressive. Rooms vary somewhat in size, but are all modern and come with a safe, minibar and broadband Internet access. Allergy-free bedrooms are also available. Use of the sauna and Jacuzzi costs extra. **www.dominahome.com**

Ekes Konventa
Skārņu 22, LV-1050 **Tel** *6735 8393* **Fax** *6735 8395* **Rooms** *11* **Map** *2 D4*

Right in the centre of the Old Town, this building has an interesting history. It was a guest house for travellers in the 15th century and later housed the widows of guild members. The downside is that rooms are small and noise tends to carry, which may cause problems for light sleepers. **www.ekeskonvents.lv**

Elizabete Hotel
Elizabetes iela 27, LV-1010 **Tel** *6750 9292* **Fax** *6750 9291* **Rooms** *20* **Map** *2 D2*

Housed in a restored 18th-century wooden building, this quiet and stylish hotel offers a range of accommodation options. The decor in the rooms ranges from warm to muted tones. One of the rooms has a washing machine and tumble dryer, while some have bathtubs. **www.elizabetehotel.lv**

Europa Royale

Krišjānis Barona 12, LV-1050 **Tel** *6707 9444* **Fax** *6707 9449* **Rooms** *60* **Map** *2 E3*

This 19th-century residence became a hotel in 2006, and has retained its original features. Everything about it is plush – parquet floors, high ceilings, huge doors, stained-glass windows and wooden staircases. The Presidential Suite has a private door to the restaurant. There is also a casino, sauna and Jacuzzi. **www.europaroyale.com**

Garden Palace

Grēcinieku iela 28, LV-1050 **Tel** *6722 4650* **Fax** *6735 9749* **Rooms** *66* **Map** *1 C4*

With an abundance of old-fashioned elegance, this is a well-priced option for visitors looking for a little luxury. The decor is a tasteful combination of cream and gold, set off by crystal chandeliers and vases of flowers. The suites are well appointed, while rooms at the top have terraces. **www.hotelgardenpalace.lv**

Gutenbergs
Doma laukums 1, LV-1050 **Tel** *6781 4090* **Fax** *6750 3326* **Rooms** *38* **Map** *1 C3*

This cosy hotel is just around the corner from the Dome Cathedral. Rooms in the new wing have the most character, with wooden beams and interesting trinkets. In summer, there is dining on the rooftop terrace, with live Latvian music on weekend evenings and during Sunday brunch. **www.gutenbergs.lv**

Hanza
Elijas iela 7, LV-1050 **Tel** *6779 6040* **Fax** *6779 6044* **Rooms** *80* **Map** *2 E5*

A renovated residential building in the Moscow District, a short walk beyond the Central Market, Hanza is a good choice if being absolutely central is not essential. Rooms are comfortable, with formal beige decor, heated bathroom floors and Wi-Fi. Streetside rooms have a view of Jesus Church. **www.hanzahotel.lv**

Hotel Justus
Jauniela iela 24, LV-1050 **Tel** *6721 2404* **Fax** *6721 2406* **Rooms** *45* **Map** *1 C4*

This stylish Old Town hotel is partially housed in the 14th-century former monastic dormitories of the nearby cathedral. Many rooms have the original brick walls exposed, some of which feature murals painted by the monks. Rooms are furnished with antique fittings that are all available for purchase. **www.hoteljustus.lv**

Kolonna
Tirgoņu iela 9, LV-1050 **Tel** *6735 8254* **Fax** *6735 8255* **Rooms** *41* **Map** *1 C4*

A central and affordable option. The rooms of Kolonna are clean and spacious, but often oddly shaped because they have been fitted into a historic building, evidence of which can be seen in exposed sections of wall. The hotel also provides Wi-Fi access. **www.hotelkolonna.com**

Konventa Sēta
Kalēju iela 9/11, LV-1050 **Tel** *6708 7501* **Fax** *6708 7515* **Rooms** *141* **Map** *2 D4*

Named after the convent court in which it is set, this hotel benefits from a very convenient location in the Old Town. Although many of the rooms in the complex of medieval buildings are quite plain, some have features such as old wooden joists. Apartments with kitchenettes are also available. **www.konventa.lv**

Maritim Park
Slokas iela 1, LV-1048 **Tel** *6706 9000* **Fax** *6706 9001* **Rooms** *227* **Map** *1 A5*

Located on the opposite side of the Daugava river, this large but quiet hotel is popular with business travellers and has a good link by tram to the Old Town. Rooms are modern and clean, coming in a range of sizes. The Bellevue restaurant *(see p332)* on the tenth floor, one of Rīga's most expensive, has superb views. **www.maritim.lv**

Metropole
Aspazijas bulvāris 36, LV-1050 **Tel** *6722 5411* **Fax** *6721 6140* **Rooms** *41* **Map** *2 D4*

Open since 1871, this is the elder statesman of Rīga's hotel scene. It is conveniently located on the edge of the Old Town, although street-facing rooms can be noisy. The spacious, Scandinavian-style rooms come equipped with Wi-Fi, minibar and trouser press. **www.metropole.lv**

Monika Centrum

Elizabetes iela 21, LV-1010 **Tel** *6703 1900* **Fax** *6703 1901* **Rooms** *80*   **Map** *2 D2*

An attractive Neo-Gothic building, reminiscent of a castle and located in the main Art Nouveau district, this hotel offers spacious and cosy rooms within easy reach of the Old Town. Suites come with four-poster beds, and facilities include free Wi-Fi, sauna and fitness centre. Breakfast is a hearty buffet. **www.centrumhotels.com**

Old City Boutique Hotel

Teatris 10, LV-1050 **Tel** *6735 6060* **Fax** *6735 6061* **Rooms** *65*

This modern hotel spans two connected buildings, with rooms of uniformly high quality, although the bathrooms are on the small side. Exposed stone walls enhance the appeal of the medieval buildings, while the hotel's only suite has its own sauna, Jacuzzi and rooftop terrace. **www.oldcityhotel.lv**

Radi un Draugi

Mārstaļu iela 3, LV-1050 **Tel** *6782 0200* **Fax** *6782 0202* **Rooms** *76*   **Map** *2 D4*

An excellent budget choice in the centre of the Old Town, this popular hotel should be booked well in advance. Owned by British-Latvians, it is a no-frills place with basic but comfortable and clean rooms. The name means "friends and family", something which the helpful staff take to heart. **www.draugi.lv**

Radisson Blu Daugava

Kuģu iela 24, LV-1048 **Tel** *6706 1111* **Fax** *6706 1100* **Rooms** *361*   **Map** *1 B4*

This classy hotel, on the left bank of the Daugava river, has spacious rooms and excellent facilities, including a swimming pool – something very unusual in Rīga. A shuttle bus runs to the House of Blackheads every hour during the day. **www.radissonblu.com/hotel-riga**

Radisson Blu Hotel Latvija

Elizabetes iela 55, LV-1010 **Tel** *6777 2222* **Fax** *6777 2332* **Rooms** *571*   **Map** *2 D2*

Once an Intourist hotel where foreign guests were accommodated and spied upon, the building has been extensively renovated and is now counted among Rīga's leading hotels. The funky Skyline Bar *(see p365)* on the 26th floor is a big tourist draw, with fantastic views and a good cocktail list. **www.radissonblu.com**

Vecrīga

Gleznotāju iela 12/14, LV-1050 **Tel** *6721 6037* **Fax** *6721 4561* **Rooms** *16*

A friendly hotel located in a quiet part of the Old Town, this 18th-century town house retains plenty of old-world charm alongside facilities such as minibars and satellite TV. There is also outdoor dining in summer. The reception area proudly displays photographs of a visit by the Dalai Lama in 2000. **www.vecriga.lv**

Islande

Ķīpsalas iela 20, LV-1048 **Tel** *6760 8000* **Fax** *6760 8001* **Rooms** *205*   **Map** *1 A3*

A 20-minute walk from the Old Town, this large and modern hotel is located on the left bank of the Daugava river. The rooms are simple and reflect Scandinavian influence, and many have excellent views. The ninth-floor Arctic Lights restaurant looks out over the city. Spa treatments are also on offer. **www.islandehotel.lv**

Neiburgs

Jauniela 25–27, LV-1050 **Tel** *6711 5522* **Fax** *6755 9562* **Rooms** *55*   **Map** *2 D4*

The wealthy descendants of the family who lived here in the early 1900s have returned to restore its Art Nouveau exterior and much of the interior too. There are several apartments, with a separate kitchen and living area, as well as spacious rooms. The beds are superbly comfortable. **www.neiburgs.com**

Bergs

Elizabetes iela 83/85, LV-1050 **Tel** *6777 0900* **Fax** *6777 0940* **Rooms** *38*   **Map** *2 D2*

A very stylish addition to the fashionable Berga Bazārs shopping precinct, this boutique hotel has won numerous awards in publications such as the *Tatler* and *Condé Nast Traveller*. Rooms are large and comfortable, and the service is professional; the only downside is that the place can be noisy at weekends. **www.hotelbergs.lv**

Dome Hotel and Spa

Miesnieku iela 4, LV-1050 **Tel** *6750 9010* **Fax** *6750 9009* **Rooms** *15*   **Map** *1 C3*

A small slice of luxury in Old Rīga, this five-star boutique hotel housed in a 17th-century building is the place to treat yourself. Spa and massage treatments and a Turkish steam bath are available, while the rooftop terrace offers views of the Old Town and Rīga Cathedral. **www.domehotel.lv**

Grand Palace

Pils 12, LV-1050 **Tel** *6704 4000* **Fax** *6704 40014* **Rooms** *56*   **Map** *1 C3*

A classy option popular with celebrities, this hotel has two acclaimed restaurants, a sauna, gym and a cosy lobby bar with antler chandeliers. Bedrooms are elegantly decorated in blue, white and gold and equipped with Wi-Fi, a minibar, safe and pay TV. Bathrooms have tubs and heated floors. **www.grandpalaceriga.com**

Radisson Rīdzene

Reimersa iela 1, LV-1050 **Tel** *6732 4433* **Fax** *6732 2600* **Rooms** *95*   **Map** *2 D3*

Formerly the exclusive domain of the Communist elite, this 1980s hotel is considered one of the best in town. The sauna and fitness centre on the top floor have glass walls with excellent views of the nearby park, while the glass pyramid covering the restaurant is a local landmark. **www.radissonblu.com**

Key to Price Guide *see p300* **Key to Symbols** *see back cover flap*

WESTERN LATVIA

BAUSKA Kungu Ligzda

Rīgas iela 41, LV-3901 **Tel** *2952 2333* **Rooms** *11* **Road Map** *D4*

This is a modern hotel, although it was originally an 18th-century manor house. There is an extensive garden stretching down to the river, and meals are served on the terrace in summer. There are several luxury rooms as well as standard rooms. Breakfast and parking are included. **www.kunguligzda.viss.lv**

DUNDAGA Pūpoli

Gipka iela, LV-3270 **Tel** *2655 4001* **Rooms** *4* **Road Map** *C3*

This wooden guest house is ecologically run. Meals can be provided by arrangement, while there is also a kitchen for guests to use. Other facilities include a sauna and plunge pool. Berry- and mushroom-picking trips can be arranged in season. **www.dundaga.lv/pupoli/en**

ENGURE Villa Elizabete

Jūras iela 88, LV-3113 **Tel** *2911 7510* **Fax** *6316 1421* **Rooms** *7* **Road Map** *C3*

Small, clean double bedrooms as well as a larger deluxe room in the attic are offered at this wooden guest house. There is plenty to keep visitors busy, including basketball and bicycle hire. For children, there is a playground at the back, including a sandbox, swing and slide. **www.villaelizabete.lv**

JAUNMOKU PILS Jaunmoku Pils

Tume, LV-3139 **Tel** *2618 7442* **Rooms** *5*

The former hunting residence of George Armistead, Rīga's mayor from 1901 to 1912, this red-brick manor house has appealing rooms with slightly old-fashioned furnishings. The public areas are decorated with hunting trophies, while antique stoves add to the charm. It's a popular place for weddings in the summer. **www.jaunmokupils.lv**

JAUNPILS Jaunpils Pils

Tukuma rajons, LV-3145 **Tel** *6310 7082* **Rooms** *7* **Road Map** *C4*

In addition to several basic rooms, this castle offers four atmospheric and individualistic places to stay. The Baron's Room is the most impressive, with a four-poster bed, Jacuzzi, under-floor heating and fireplace. The other three have a selection of these features. Tiled floors and exposed walls add further character. **www.jaunpilspils.lv**

JELGAVA Zemgale

Rīgas iela 11, LV-3002 **Tel** *6300 7707* **Fax** *6300 7710* **Rooms** *34* **Road Map** *C4*

Just across the Lielupe river from the city's main tourist sights, this hotel is part of a recreation complex offering tennis, ten-pin bowling and ice-skating. Rooms are on the small side, but clean and modern, and staff are friendly and helpful. There are two cafés in the complex. **www.zemgale.info**

JŪRMALA Eiropa

Juras iela 56, LV-2015 **Tel** *6776 2211* **Fax** *6776 2299* **Rooms** *47* **Road Map** *D4*

This family hotel has been tastefully converted from a former luxury villa. It is situated conveniently close to the beach and the town centre. The location is quiet, and some rooms are self-catering. The staff is very pleasant and helpful, and the buffet breakfast, included in the rates, is good. **www.eiropahotel.lv**

JŪRMALA Jūrmala Spa

Jomas iela 47/49, LV-2015 **Tel** *6778 4415* **Fax** *6778 4411* **Rooms** *190* **Road Map** *C3*

This renovated Soviet-era block is a welcome addition to the hotel scene in Jūrmala. The style is retro-chic, with extensive use of natural materials, including stone in the bathrooms. The spa facilities are excellent and medical consultations are available. The bar on the 11th floor offers panoramic views. **www.hoteljurmala.com**

JŪRMALA Amber Sea

Dzintaru prospekts 68, Dzintari, LV-2015 **Tel** *6775 1297* **Fax** *6714 6601* **Rooms** *40* **Road Map** *C3*

Tastefully decorated, predominantly in chocolate, red and cream, this is a very stylish option away from the busy resort of Majori. Rooms are spacious and the suites very large, some with access to a terrace. The restaurant is also classy. Prices rise considerably during the peak summer period. **www.amberhotel.lv**

JŪRMALA Baltic Beach

Jūras iela 23/25, Majori, LV-2015 **Tel** *6777 1400* **Fax** *6776 4044* **Rooms** *165* **Road Map** *C3*

Although its wedge-shaped exterior is quite uninspiring, the Baltic Beach is one of Jūrmala's top hotels. Rooms come in a range of different sizes and degrees of luxury. The spa centre offers a long list of massages and treatments, as well as medical consultations. Staff have a reputation for being rather dour. **www.balticbeach.lv**

KANDAVA Kandava

Sabiles iela 3, 14 km (9 miles) E of Sabile, LV-3120 **Tel** *2640 6733* **Fax** *6318 1643* **Rooms** *10* **Road Map** *C3*

This centrally located hotel offers clean, comfortable and very basic rooms with red sheets and curtains. Most rooms have TVs, although, without satellite or cable, the viewing options are limited. The restaurant downstairs is fashionable, with retro furnishings and glowing oval lights in the floor and the bar. **www.hotelkandava.lv**

KOLKA Vītoli
Kolkas pagasts, Dundagas novads **Tel** *2913 5764* **Fax** *6791 4763* **Rooms** *7*   **Road Map** *C3*

This modest but cosy guest house includes a kitchen for patrons' use and a fireplace. Located in the picturesque Slītere National Park, it is just 200 m (220 yds) from the sea and 3 km (2 miles) from Cape Kolka. Motorboat excursions to the cape can be organized in advance. Shared bathrooms. **www.lai-ripo.lv/atputa**

KULDĪGA Virkas Muiža
Virkas iela 27, LV-3301 **Tel** *2206 0780* **Fax** *6332 2787* **Rooms** *18*   **Road Map** *B3*

This 17th-century wooden manor house 1 km (half a mile) from the centre of Kuldīga is a good budget option. Rooms are simple but comfortable, and the surrounding yard has picnic areas and a playground. The buffet breakfast is not included in the price. **www.hotelvirka.lv**

KULDĪGA Metropole
Baznīcas iela 11, LV-3301 **Tel** *6335 0588* **Fax** *6335 0599* **Rooms** *14*   **Road Map** *B3*

Built as a hotel in 1919 and subsequently used for other purposes, the Metropole was gutted by fire in 1997. The interior has been fully renovated, with stylishly minimal decor and sloping ceilings lending the rooms character. The classy restaurant has an extensive wine list and a terrace for summer dining. **www.hotel-metropole.lv**

LIEPĀJA Libava
Vecā ostmala 29, LV-3401 **Tel** *6342 9714* **Fax** *6342 5319* **Rooms** *7*   **Road Map** *B4*

From the spacious lobby to the immaculate bedrooms, this canal-side hotel provides an affordable slice of luxury. Guests can take advantage of a discount in the basement spa, relax on cream leather sofas in the conservatory, or try the restaurant's adventurous menu. There is a working pier alongside the hotel. **www.libava.lv**

LIEPĀJA Poriņš
Palmu iela 5, LV-3401 **Tel** *2915 0596* **Fax** *6342 8602* **Rooms** *20*   **Road Map** *B4*

This boutique hotel is stylish without being intimidating. Rooms have Scandinavian furnishings, wicker-finished wardrobes and stencilled walls. A glass lift provides wheelchair access, and parking is off the street. The dining room is unique, with one wall made from stacked birch logs. **www.porins.lv**

LIEPĀJA Promenāde
Vecā ostmala 40, LV-3401 **Tel** *6348 8288* **Fax** *6348 8588* **Rooms** *42*   **Road Map** *B4*

Retaining elements of the late 19th-century grain warehouse in which it is housed, this canal-side hotel is both cosy and modern. The lobby doubles as an art gallery, and the restaurant has a view of the canal. There is also a business centre and mooring space for yachts. **www.promenadehotel.lv**

MEŽOTNE Mežotnes Pils
Mežotnes pagasts, LV-3918 **Tel** *6396 0711* **Fax** *6396 0725* **Rooms** *21*   **Road Map** *D4*

Built from 1797 to 1802, but partly destroyed in World War II, this exquisitely restored manor house has a Neo-Classical interior. Rooms range from singles to family apartments, with tasteful wooden furniture and wallpaper reminiscent of the 19th century. The grounds are also impressive. **www.mezotnespils.lv**

NĪCA Nīcava
Nīcas pagasts, LV-3473 **Tel** *6348 6379* **Rooms** *6*   **Road Map** *B4*

Convenient for exploring Lake Pape Nature Reserve, this hotel offers rooms in an old post house. The decor is a little dated but rooms are clean and large; some are huge. The restaurant and less formal café share a menu which includes some hearty traditional Latvian dishes. **www.nicava.lv**

PĀVILOSTA Vēju Paradīze
Smilšu 14, LV-3466 **Tel** *2644 6644* **Rooms** *17*   **Road Map** *B4*

Rooms in this comfortable motel have wooden floors and exposed beams. Most bedrooms are doubles with en-suite facilities, but some can accommodate up to four people and have shared bathrooms. Facilities include a sauna and café, with a terrace for dining in summer. **www.vejuparadize.lv**

PEDVĀLE Firkspedvāle
Sabiles novads, LV-3295 **Tel** *6325 2249* **Rooms** *5*   **Road Map** *C4*

This manor house was part of the estate that forms the Pedvāle Open-Air Museum. The rooms have plenty of character, with wooden beams and photographs on the walls, although they would not suit visitors seeking luxury. Food is served in the pub nearby. There is also a sauna. **www.pedvale.lv**

ROJA Dzintarkrasts
Žocene, LV-3279 **Tel** *2860 0600* **Fax** *2937 0274* **Rooms** *19*   **Road Map** *C3*

Guests at this family-friendly complex can choose to stay in either a hotel room or cottage, and there is space for tents and caravans. Accommodation in the modern wooden buildings is comfortable and clean. Facilities include a good restaurant, sauna and swimming pool, and numerous activities are available. **www.dzintarkrasts.lv**

ROJA Rēderi
"Vejkalni", Kaltene, LV-3264 **Tel** *6322 0558* **Fax** *6781 1113* **Rooms** *11*   **Road Map** *C3*

This wooden-construction hotel has bright, spacious rooms offering views of the sea, which is just 300 m (330 yds) away. The adjoining stone house has a simple café, and sauna facilities are also available. The surrounding area has a number of nature trails that are worth exploring. **www.hotelrederi.lv**

Key to Price Guide *see p300* **Key to Symbols** *see back cover flap*

RUNDĀLE Baltā Māja

Pilsrundāle, LV-3921 **Tel** *6396 2140* **Rooms** *10*   **Road Map** *D4*

When restoring the run-down servants' quarters of Rundāle Palace, the owners left plenty of the original features such as paved floors and tiled stoves. Most rooms have shared bathrooms, although two have en-suite facilities. High-quality home-cooked Latvian dishes are served in the cosy restaurant. **www.kalpumaja.lv**

TALSI Saule

Saules iela 19, LV-3201 **Tel** *2917 7071* **Rooms** *6*   **Road Map** *C3*

This pleasant guest house is run along environment-friendly lines. Rooms have wooden floors and pine furniture, while the Black Room features antique furniture made from dark wood, including an ornate 120-year-old bed. There are views of Lake Talsi from the terrace. Organic breakfast is served. **www.saulehotel.lv**

TĒRVETE Laima

Tērvete Nature Park, LV-3728 **Tel** *2949 5041* **Rooms** *6*   **Road Map** *C4*

With an excellent location within the nature park, this guest house offers basic bedrooms with en-suite facilities. All rooms have a TV and DVD player. Facilities include a sauna and pool table; bicycles are also available to hire. The ground-floor café boasts a bizarre mix of carpeted walls, mirrors, tiles and rocks. **www.laima.viss.lv**

TUKUMS TLH

Stadiona iela 3, LV-3101 **Tel** *6312 2299* **Fax** *6310 7464* **Rooms** *47*   **Road Map** *C3*

Part of an outwardly uninspiring, but modern, recreation centre, this hotel offers simple, affordable and clean rooms. The centre also includes an ice-skating arena, sauna, café, gym and even a hairdressing salon. The bedrooms are located away from the other facilities and, thus, tend to remain quiet at night. **www.tlh.lv**

VENTSPILS Olimpiskā Centra

Lielais prospekts 33, LV-3601 **Tel** *6362 8032* **Fax** *6362 8032* **Rooms** *68*   **Road Map** *B3*

Part of the city's Olympic Centre, incorporating tennis courts, swimming pool, skate park and many other facilities, this hotel offers very good value for money. The rooms are devoid of character, with vertical blinds contributing to an office-like feel, but they are clean and comfortable. **www.hotelocventspils.lv**

VENTSPILS Raibie Logi

Lielais prospekts 61, LV-3601 **Tel** *2914 2327* **Rooms** *8*   **Road Map** *B3*

Aptly named Raibie Logi, translated as "vivid windows", this early 20th-century wooden building is decorated in jolly colours both inside and out. It offers clean rooms with pine furniture and laminated floors, with little touches such as sweets left on pillows. Light meals may be served in addition to breakfast. **www.raibielogi.lv**

VENTSPILS Vilnis

Talsu iela 5, LV-3602 **Tel** *6366 8880* **Fax** *6366 5054* **Rooms** *52*   **Road Map** *B3*

A decent three-star option for those wishing to stay outside the city centre, Vilnis is on the right bank of the Venta river. The hotel is geared towards business travellers. There is a classy restaurant with a grand piano, small aquarium and long wine list. **www.dzintarjura.lv**

EASTERN LATVIA

AGLONA Aglonas Cakuli

Ezera iela 4, LV-5304 **Tel** *2933 3422* **Fax** *6532 1465* **Rooms** *7*   **Road Map** *E4*

This friendly, family-run guest house with a rustic feel is located on a quiet residential road beside Lake Cirišs. Rooms are small, with somewhat cramped bathrooms. Breakfasts are hearty and the owners are keen to help their guests. Fishing equipment is available for hire, and there is ice fishing in winter. **www.aglonascakuli.lv**

DAUGAVPILS Leo

Krāslavas iela 58, LV-5403 **Tel** *6542 6565* **Fax** *6542 5325* **Rooms** *5*   **Road Map** *E4*

A regular winner of local tourist board awards, Leo is a small and centrally located hotel housed in a well-restored building. Organized in a motel style, the five rooms are arranged around the small car park. The clean, comfortable and reasonably sized rooms have en-suite bathrooms. The staff are friendly and helpful.

DAUGAVPILS Sventes Muiža

Alejas 7, Svente, LV-5473 **Tel** *6542 7822* **Fax** *6549 7322* **Rooms** *12*   **Road Map** *E4*

Sventes Muiža is an impressively restored manor house, complete with wooden floors and old tiled stoves. Each room is named after a month of the year and decorated accordingly. Facilities include two saunas, an outdoor pool and a separate smoking room. There is also a museum of military vehicles. **www.sventehotel.lv**

DAUGAVPILS Villa Ksenija

Varšavas iela 17, LV-5404 **Tel** *6543 4317* **Rooms** *6*   **Road Map** *E4*

Standard bedrooms in this restored mansion, which dates from 1876, are tastefully decorated, although not as elegant as the common areas. The white bedding is, however, notably crisp. The executive suite has its own sauna and Jacuzzi. Hotel services include laundry, ticket booking and a concierge. **www.villaks.lv**

GAUJA NATIONAL PARK Lāču Miga

Gaujas iela 22, Līgatne, LV-4110 **Tel** *2913 3713* **Rooms** *20*   **Road Map** D3

This hotel takes its name, "Bear's Den", rather seriously, with teddy bears of all sizes placed throughout the wooden building. It is well above par for rural Latvia, with superior rooms equipped with sofas and large bathtubs. The restaurant Lāču Miga (*see p336*) is worth visiting in its own right. **www.lacumiga.lv**

GAUJA NATIONAL PARK Province

Niniera iela 6, Cēsis, LV-4101 **Tel** *6412 0849* **Rooms** *5*   **Road Map** D3

This small guest house is close to Maija Park, a short walk from the centre of town. The rooms are simple but cosy and clean. The restaurant, located in a conservatory and with a terrace for summer, is popular with locals. There is also a playground for children. Breakfast is not included. **www.province.lv**

GAUJA NATIONAL PARK Kārļa Muiža

Drabešu pagasts, Cēsis, LV-4138 **Tel** *2616 5298* **Rooms** *8*   **Road Map** D3

Housed in a converted 19th-century estate building, this place offers accommodation in apartments of different sizes, each with a kitchen. Breakfast is available on request. The hotel has 30 ha (74 acres) of land, and bicycles, quad bikes and boating equipment can be hired. Transfers and babysitters can be provided. **www.karlamuiza.lv**

GAUJA NATIONAL PARK Kolonna Hotel Cēsis

Vienības laukums 1, Cēsis, LV-4101 **Tel** *6412 0122* **Fax** *6412 0121* **Rooms** *40*   **Road Map** D3

Excellently located in the centre of town, the rooms are neutrally decorated, and some have pleasant views of the park in front. Studio rooms are worth the additional cost. The formal restaurant is only open in summer, while the café in the basement operates year-round. **www.hotelkolonna.com**

GAUJA NATIONAL PARK Sigulda

Pils 6, Sigulda, LV-2150 **Tel** *6797 2263* **Fax** *6797 3157* **Rooms** *44*   **Road Map** D3

One of the few establishments in town to enjoy a central location, this hotel offers unexceptional rooms at a reasonable price. The common areas are more interesting, particularly the small indoor bridges which link the 100-year-old hotel to its more modern annexe. There is paid Wi-Fi access. **www.hotelsigulda.lv**

GAUJA NATIONAL PARK Spa Hotel Ezeri

Sigulda pagasts, Sigulda, LV-2150 **Tel** *6797 3009* **Fax** *6797 3880* **Rooms** *29*   **Road Map** D3

A modern hotel influenced by Scandinavian design, featuring a lot of wood. The spa centre includes indoor and outdoor pools, saunas and aroma baths and offers a range of massages. The restaurant, with a pleasant terrace for summer dining, serves Modern European cuisine. The gardens are attractive when in bloom. **www.hotelezeri.lv**

IKŠĶILE Meidrops

Rīgas iela 18, LV-5052 **Tel** *6503 6547* **Fax** *6503 0612* **Rooms** *16*   **Road Map** D3

A well-appointed riverside hotel and recreation centre on the route between Rīga and Daugavpils, with facilities including a swimming pool, sauna, Jacuzzi and children's playground. The restaurant is housed in a log cabin. There are views from the hotel of the ruins of Ikšķile Church, the oldest in Latvia. **www.meidrops.lv**

JĒKABPILS Hercogs Jēkabs

Brīvības iela 190, LV-5201 **Tel** *6523 3433* **Fax** *6523 3433* **Rooms** *6*   **Road Map** D4

This 19th-century red-brick building beside the Daugava river has an excellent location in the centre of town. Rooms are spacious and decorated in soothing pastel shades; some have sloping ceilings and wooden pillars. Many of the rooms offer stunning views of the river. The restaurant downstairs is cosy. **www.jnami.lv**

KOKNESE Orinoko

Kokneses pagasts, LV-5113 **Tel** *2663 7918* **Fax** *6512 0417* **Rooms** *14*   **Road Map** D4

Bedrooms here are clean, bright and airy. The views of the surrounding area are excellent, and the hotel has a motorboat that guests can use. There are also volleyball and badminton nets. The restaurant serves fresh fish. **www.orinoko.lv**

KRĀSLAVA Priedaine

Klusā iela 2, LV-5601 **Tel** *2643 0798* **Rooms** *5*   **Road Map** E4

This small and popular guest house is located on the bank of the Daugava river, just across from the centre of town. Fishing can be arranged here, as can raft trips along the Daugavas Loki, a series of bends in the Daugava river. The area around it is a nature reserve.

LIELVĀRDE Lielvārdes Osta

Krasta iela 2, LV-5070 **Tel** *2915 0107* **Rooms** *4*   **Road Map** D4

With mooring for boats on the Daugava river, this friendly hotel boasts Lielvārdes Osta (*see p337*), one of the best restaurants in town. There are only four apartments (all with kitchen facilities), so you might need to book well in advance. **www.lielvardesosta.lv**

LIMBAŽI Bīriņu Pils

Bīriņi, LV-4014 **Tel** *6402 4033* **Rooms** *127*   **Road Map** D3

Built in 1860 in Neo-Gothic style, this manor house has been immaculately restored. The bedrooms in the main building are usually available only for events such as weddings; other guests stay in the gardener's house, which is also luxurious. Boats, bicycles and horses are available for hire. **www.birinupils.lv**

Key to Price Guide *see p300* **Key to Symbols** *see back cover flap*

LUDZA Cirmas Ezerkrasts

Zvirgzdenes pagasts, LV-4600 **Tel** *2833 2523* **Fax** *6462 2756* **Rooms** *18*   **Road Map** *E3*

The centrepiece of this recreation complex is a row of attractive log cabins overlooking Lake Cirmas, each with a living room, including fireplace, TV and sofa-bed, kitchen and three bedrooms. There is also a guest house with three double rooms, a kitchen and shared bathroom. **www.cirmasezerkrasts.lv**

LUDZA Ludza

1 Maija iela 1, LV-5701 **Tel** *2910 4055* **Rooms** *10*   **Road Map** *E3*

This bright-blue three-storey building in the centre of Ludza is one of the only places to stay in town. It manages to squeeze in a sauna, Jacuzzi, gym and café, as well as banquet and conference facilities. The ten rooms are simple but comfortable, and events are often held on weekends. **www.hotelludza.lv**

PREIĻI Pie Pliča

Raiņa bulvāris 9, LV-5301 **Tel** *2912 1689* **Fax** *6530 7075* **Rooms** *10*   **Road Map** *E4*

Housed in the town's first hospital, an attractive wooden building with a veranda, Pie Pliča is the most highly regarded hotel in Preiļi. Many bedrooms are located under the eaves, and are simple but pleasant. Antique jugs and agricultural implements are displayed in the communal areas. There is also a sauna.

RĀZNA Rāzna

28 km (17 miles) S of Rēzekne, LV-4622 **Tel** *2999 4444* **Fax** *6466 7288* **Rooms** *30*   **Road Map** *E4*

Located on the banks of Lake Rāzna, this hotel complex is one of Latvia's largest recreation centres and includes spacious hotel rooms as well as two well-appointed villas. Activities available include boat and bicycle rental, fishing and horse-riding. The sauna has a glass wall for viewing the lake. **www.razna.lv**

RĒZEKNE Latgale

Atbrīvošanas alēja 98, LV-4601 **Tel** *6462 2180* **Fax** *6462 2180* **Rooms** *80*   **Road Map** *E4*

This Soviet-era block has been extensively renovated, offering a range of decent rooms at good prices. The local tourist information office is located within the building, as is one of the best restaurants in town, also called Latgale *(see p337)*. There is also a bar with pool tables in the basement. **www.latgalehotel.lv**

RĒZEKNE Kolonna Hotel Rēzekne

Brīvības iela 2, LV-4600 **Tel** *6460 7820* **Fax** *6460 7825* **Rooms** *41*   **Road Map** *E4*

This hotel has retained its original impressive 1940s façade but has been significantly modified inside. Rooms are clean and businesslike in appearance, with international TV and Wi-Fi access. There is also a beauty salon. The city's main attractions are a 15-minute walk away. **www.hotelkolonna.com**

SALACGRĪVA Rakari

Svētciems, LV-4033 **Tel** *6407 1122* **Fax** *2721 7254* **Rooms** *40*   **Road Map** *D3*

Signposted by a giant yellow chair in a roadside field, this fully-featured recreation complex includes a hotel and restaurant in a huge barn-like building, 16 cottages (each for four people) and space for camping. Equipment can be hired for windsurfing and kitesurfing boards. Cross-country skiing in winter. **www.rakaricamp.lv**

SAULKRASTI Medzābaki

Medzābaki-2, Carnikavas pagasts, LV-2163 **Tel** *6714 7070* **Fax** *6714 6066* **Rooms** *40*   **Road Map** *D3*

With a wonderful location on the edge of Lake Lilaste, this complex includes a large thatch-roofed hotel, 13 self-contained holiday cottages and leisure facilities perfect for children. Unspoilt beaches on the Baltic Coast are just a 10-minute walk across the sand dunes. **www.medzabaki.lv**

SAULKRASTI Minhauzena Unda

Ainažu iela 74, LV-2160 **Tel** *6795 5198* **Fax** *6795 4599* **Rooms** *40*   **Road Map** *D3*

A former Soviet-era children's rehabilitation centre in the middle of a pine forest and named after Baron Münchhausen, this hotel offers basic accommodation just 5 minutes' walk from the shore of the Baltic Sea. Conference facilities are available, and concerts take place here during Saulkrasti Jazz. **www.minhauzenunda.lv**

STĀMERIENA Vonadziņi

Skolas iela 1, LV-4406 **Tel** *6447 1151* **Fax** *6447 1151* **Rooms** *17*   **Road Map** *E3*

This recreation centre alongside Lake Ludza incorporates two thatch-roofed wooden guest houses and a bath-house with a sauna, pool and two bedrooms. The pleasant bedrooms come in a range of sizes, some with fantastic lake views. A wide range of activities are on offer, including boating and horse-riding. **www.vonadzini.lv**

VALMIERA Wolmar

Tērbatas iela 16a, LV-4200 **Tel** *6420 7301* **Fax** *6420 7305* **Rooms** *30*   **Road Map** *D3*

Taking the former name of the city, this large hotel with spacious rooms is a short walk from the main tourist sights. Unusually for a provincial Latvian hotel, the reception desk sells essentials such as toothpaste. The stylishly retro café is decorated with illuminated maps of Latvia. **www.hotelwolmar.lv**

VALMIERA Dikļu Pils

Dikļi, LV-4223 **Tel** *6420 7480* **Fax** *6420 7485* **Rooms** *30*   **Road Map** *D3*

Every room in this beautifully restored late 19th-century manor house is luxurious. There are many options for relaxation, with a sauna, steam room, whirlpool bath, swimming pool and billiards room with pool and snooker tables. There are plans to develop the 20 ha (50 acres) of parkland for sports and recreation. **www.diklupils.lv**

Choosing a Hotel in Lithuania

These hotels have been selected for their good value, facilities and location. They are listed by region, starting with Vilnius, followed by the rest of Lithuania. Under each town or area, hotels are listed alphabetically within each price category. For Vilnius map references, see pages 246–7; for road map references see inside back cover.

PRICE DETAILS
The following price ranges are for a standard double room for one night during the high season. Breakfast is included, unless otherwise specified.

ⓛ Under 150 Lt
ⓛⓛ 150–300 Lt
ⓛⓛⓛ 300–450 Lt
ⓛⓛⓛⓛ 450–600 Lt
ⓛⓛⓛⓛⓛ Over 600 Lt

VILNIUS

Litinterp

Bernardinų 7, 01124 **Tel** *212 3850* **Fax** *212 3559* **Rooms** *16*   **Map** *2 E3*

Boasting a prime spot close to the Church of St Anne, this two-star hotel offers perhaps the cheapest and smallest rooms in the Old Town. However, it is a peaceful spot to spend a night. The rooms are well equipped, with refrigerator, tea- and coffee-making facilities and phone. Some rooms have en-suite bathrooms. **www.litinterp.com**

Paupio Namai

Paupio 31a, 01134 **Tel** *264 3113* **Fax** *264 3112* **Rooms** *25*   **Map** *2 F4*

A range of budget accommodation, from shared dormitories to basic, clean apartments with en-suite bathrooms, characterizes Paupio Namai. One of Vilnius's few genuine hostels, this huge house on the edge of the Užupis district, a few steps from the Old Town, has a communal kitchen and laundry room. **www.paupio-hostel-vilnius.com**

Amicus

Kaminkelio 15, 02182 **Tel** *237 5880* **Fax** *283 3980* **Rooms** *20*

A modern-looking mansion located midway between the airport and city centre, this is a pleasant economy-class hotel, with helpful English-speaking staff. Facilities include a bar-restaurant and a sauna that can be hired by the hour. Guests should opt for a taxi rather than a bus to get to town. **www.amicushotel.lt**

Domus Maria

Aušros vartų 12, 01129 **Tel** *264 4880* **Fax** *264 4878* **Rooms** *39*   **Map** *2 D5*

One of the loveliest budget options in Vilnius, this former nunnery, tucked unobtrusively in a quiet courtyard, is close to the Gates of Dawn, with some rooms overlooking this landmark. Every room has a TV, Internet connection and en-suite bathroom. Some rooms have bathrooms adapted for disabled guests. **www.domusmaria.lt**

Ecotel Vilnius

Slucko 8, 09312 **Tel** *210 2700* **Fax** *210 2707* **Rooms** *166*   **Map** *2 D2*

Situated on a quiet street across the river from the Old Town, Ecotel is a pleasant and unfussy two-star hotel. All rooms come with en-suite bathroom and TV. There are special rooms for guests with disabilities or allergies. With magnificent views of Vilnius, it is popular with both leisure and business travellers. **www.ecotel.lt**

Europa City Vilnius

Jasinskio 14, 01112 **Tel** *251 4477* **Fax** *251 4476* **Rooms** *128*   **Map** *1 B2*

A tranquil place amid some of the capital's noisiest roads, modern-looking Europa City Vilnius is a perfect business-class hotel. It features comfortable rooms and spacious, well-appointed meeting rooms. The Old Town is about a 15-minute walk away, best accessed down Gedimino Avenue. **www.groupeuropa.com**

Grata Hotel

Vytenio 9/25, 03113 **Tel** *268 3300* **Fax** *213 2760* **Rooms** *101*   **Map** *1 B5*

Tucked away in a fairly quiet street, this well-located hotel is just a 20-minute walk away from the Old Town. The elegant rooms are all equipped with flat-screen computers with free Internet access, as well as satellite TV, telephone, minibar, and complimentary tea- and coffee-making facilities. **www.gratahotel.com**

Saulès Namai

Saulès 15/23, 10310 **Tel** *210 6112* **Rooms** *9*   **Map** *1 A1*

Those who prefer cosy B&Bs to large hotels should choose this family-run, quiet option. Rooms are comfortable and attractively furnished. There's a large kitchen and living room with fireplace for guests to use, and a pretty, leafy garden. **www.saules-namai.com**

Senatoriai

Tilto 2a, 01101 **Tel** *212 6491* **Fax** *212 6372* **Rooms** *11*   **Map** *2 D3*

An unassuming guest house, Senatoriai retains its simplicity, despite its location close to Vilnius Cathedral. Heavy wooden furnishing and flooring give it an ornate, old-fashioned feel. Standard services, including Wi-Fi access, laundry services and airport transfer, are available. **www.senatoriai.lt**

Key to Symbols *see back cover flap*

Apia

P   ⑩⑩⑩

Šv Ignoto 12, 01120 **Tel** *212 3426* **Fax** *212 3618* **Rooms** *12*   **Map** *2 D3*

This tiny hotel is essentially an intimate guest house with an unbeatable location amid the spires of the Old Town. The rooms lack safes and minibars, but free access to the Internet and free parking facilities are available. Rooms at the front face an often-crowded street, but those at the back face a quiet courtyard. **www.apia.lt**

Barbacan Palace

P ⑪ 🗉 🖑   ⑩⑩⑩

Bokšto 19, 01126 **Tel** *266 0840* **Fax** *266 0841* **Rooms** *49*   **Map** *2 E4*

This hotel is tucked away in one of the Old Town's darker, less visited lanes. Its best rooms boast a fine view across Užupis. Facilities include air-conditioned rooms and free Internet connection. It also has the odd distinction of having a bowling alley in the basement. **www.barbacan.lt**

Dvaras

P ⑪ 🗉   ⑩⑩⑩

Tilto 3-1, 01101 **Tel** *210 7370* **Fax** *261 8783* **Rooms** *8*   **Map** *2 D3*

A classy guest house close to Vilnius Cathedral, Dvaras means, "manor house". However, the interiors resemble a richly designed country cottage, with creaky floors, thick carpets and elegant furnishings. Excellent meals are served in a cosy but little-visited cellar restaurant. **www.dvaras.lt**

Grybas House

P   ⑩⑩⑩

Aušros vartų 3a, 01129 **Tel** *261 9695* **Fax** *212 2416* **Rooms** *10*   **Map** *2 D5*

This family-run guest house offers unpretentious, spacious rooms spruced up with personal touches. Heated bathroom floors and Wi-Fi Internet access are among its perks. Importantly for the Old Town, there is also secure parking in the courtyard. Prices are very reasonable for the location. **www.grybashouse.com**

Novotel Vilnius

⑪ 🗺 🋤 🗉 🖑   ⑩⑩⑩

Gedimino 16, 01103 **Tel** *266 6200* **Fax** *266 6201* **Rooms** *159*   **Map** *1 B2*

Despite its massive size, this relatively new addition to Gedimino Avenue maintains an intimate feel in its rooms, with tea- and coffee-making facilities and spacious bathrooms. The gorgeous views from the upper floors are an added attraction. The French-style restaurant, Garden Brasserie, serves well-prepared meals. **www.novotel.com**

Reval Hotel Lietuva

P ⑪ 🗺 🋤 🗉 🖑   ⑩⑩⑩

Konstitucijos, 09308 **Tel** *272 0200* **Fax** *272 6210* **Rooms** *291*   **Map** *1 C1*

One of Vilnius's lofty landmarks, the concrete-block Lietuva has been transformed by the pan-Baltic Reval Hotels chain into a radiant Scandinavian masterpiece. Friendly staff, Wi-Fi access, a lively lobby, a stunning view from the top-floor bar and the superb Riverside restaurant *(see p340)* add to the experience. **www.revalhotels.com**

Rinno

P   ⑩⑩

Vingrių 25, 01141 **Tel** *262 2828* **Fax** *262 5929* **Rooms** *17*   **Map** *1 C4*

A luxurious three-star hotel on the edge of the Old Town, Rinno is enthusiastically rated by many guests and has a high number of return visits. The rooms are cosy and spotless, the bathrooms huge and the service professional. Free Wi-Fi, secure parking and an optional bodyguard service are also available. **www.rinno.lt**

Scandic Hotel Neringa

P ⑪ 🗺 🗉 🖑   ⑩⑩⑩

Gedimino 23, 01103 **Tel** *268 1910* **Fax** *261 4160* **Rooms** *60*   **Map** *1 B2*

A fantastic combination of space, light and practicality is evident at the Scandic Hotel Neringa. The Nordic region's leading hotel chain renovated the age-old Hotel Neringa in 2001, preserving much of its original design. There is a mini-pool and sauna, besides a 1960s-themed retro disco called Neringa Café-Bar. **www.scandic-hotels.com**

Amberton Hotel

P ⑪ 🗺 🗉   ⑩⑩⑩⑩

Stuokos-Gucevičiaus 1, 01120 **Tel** *210 7461* **Fax** *210 7460* **Rooms** *77*   **Map** *2 D3*

A gleaming structure overlooking Cathedral Square, the Amberton has rooms with tea- and coffee-making facilities, Wi-Fi Internet access and TVs, as well as heated bathroom floors. Sofi L, the hotel's restaurant, prides itself on its fresh seafood flown in from Italy. **www.citypark.lt**

Artis Centrum Hotels

P ⑪ 🗺 🗉   ⑩⑩⑩⑩

Liejyklos 11/23, 01120 **Tel** *266 0366* **Fax** *266 0377* **Rooms** *120*   **Map** *2 D3*

Located in the very centre of the Old Town, Centrum Hotels Artis places a heavy accent on fine furnishings and oil paintings. It is a lovely place, with impressively sized rooms, Wi-Fi and conference facilities. All the main attractions as well as the shopping and business streets are within walking distance. **www.centrumhotels.com**

Atrium

⑪ 🗺 🗉   ⑩⑩⑩⑩

Pilies 10, 01123 **Tel** *210 7777* **Fax** *210 7770* **Rooms** *28*   **Map** *2 D3*

Sumptuously spacious suites and apartments, together with a location close to Vilnius Cathedral, are the main selling points of Atrium. The standard rooms are small but reasonably priced for the place. The ground floor has an excellent Argentinian-themed restaurant, El Gaucho Sano *(see p340)*. **www.atrium.lt**

Conti

P ⑪ 🗺 🗉   ⑩⑩⑩⑩

Raugyklos 7/2, 01140 **Tel** *251 4111* **Fax** *251 4100* **Rooms** *88*   **Map** *2 C5*

Located on the edge of the Old Town, Conti offers spa breaks and special packages for newly-weds. For regular guests, there is little missing in the comfortable rooms, particularly the luxury room. The garret rooms are an excellent low-cost option for those travelling alone. **www.contihotel.lt**

Crowne Plaza Vilnius

Čiurlionio 84, 03100 **Tel** *274 3400* **Fax** *274 3411* **Rooms** *108*   **Map** *1 A3*

A towering five-star hotel where the upper floors offer sweeping views of the cityscape. The in-house amenities are extensive, but Wi-Fi is only available on some floors. There is also a restaurant on the 16th floor. The pine-covered Vingis Park is close by and the Old Town is a 20-minute walk away. **www.cpvilnius.com**

Europa Royale Vilnius

Aušros vartų 6, 01129 **Tel** *266 0770* **Fax** *261 2000* **Rooms** *51*   **Map** *2 D5*

With a fantastic location close to the Gates of Dawn, Europa Royale Vilnius is a tastefully designed four-star hotel with innovatory facilities such as in-room spas, beauty treatments and babysitting services. The Druskininkai restaurant *(see p341)* serves delightful cuisine. **www.europaroyale.com**

Grotthuss

Ligoninės 7, 01134 **Tel** *266 0322* **Fax** *266 0323* **Rooms** *20*   **Map** *1 C4*

Luxury furniture, goose-feather beds and en-suite bathrooms with Spanish tiles and heated floors add a touch of glamour to the usual facilities such as Wi-Fi access, minibar, TV and safe. A location on one of Old Town's tranquil cobblestoned streets and a superb restaurant are further attractions. **www.grotthusshotel.com**

Holiday Inn Vilnius

Šeimyniškių 1, 09312 **Tel** *210 3000* **Fax** *210 3001* **Rooms** *134*   **Map** *2 E1*

Efficient and professionally run, Holiday Inn Vilnius stands on a busy city intersection, although the rooms have blackout curtains and soundproof windows. Guests can select from a variety of pillows from the pillow menu. Prices are high, in relation to the hotel's location. **www.holidayinnvilnius.lt**

Mabre Residence

Maironio 13, 01124 **Tel** *212 2087* **Fax** *212 2240* **Rooms** *40*   **Map** *2 E4*

One of the Old Town's most enchanting hotels, Mabre Residence is set in a former monastery. Fully enclosed in a peaceful courtyard, it is surrounded by church spires. The hotel's beauty centre offers facials, manicures and massages. Its restaurant, Steakhouse Hazienda, serves good steak, wine and beer. **www.mabre.lt**

Narutis

Pilies 24, 01123 **Tel** *212 2894* **Fax** *262 2882* **Rooms** *50*   **Map** *2 D3*

Each plush room here is individually decorated in luscious colours. Unique frescoes, wall paintings, original 16th-century beamed ceilings and Gothic vaults add to its charm. French designer Anne Toulous selected soft, noise-absorbing carpets for the rooms and corridors. Two suites even have a *hammam* and Jacuzzi. **www.narutis.com**

Ramada Vilnius

Subačiaus 2, 01127 **Tel** *255 3355* **Fax** *255 3311* **Rooms** *55*   **Map** *2 E4*

One of the Old Town's newest hotels, Ramada Vilnius is part of the Wyndham Hotel Group. The well-appointed rooms have DVD players and satellite TV, as well as free high-speed Internet access and a minibar. Some of the rooms facing the street may be noisy. **www.ramadavilnius.lt**

Shakespeare Boutique Hotel

Bernardinų 8/8, 01124 **Tel** *266 5885* **Fax** *266 5886* **Rooms** *31*   **Map** *2 E3*

The Shakespeare Boutique Hotel, with its Sonnets restaurant *(see p340)*, is a favourite among regular visitors to Vilnius. A tasteful emphasis on art and literature and polite service sets it apart. Each room is stocked with a selection of books. There are rooms named after James Joyce, Oscar Wilde and Leo Tolstoy. **www.shakespeare.lt**

Best Western Naujasis Vilnius

Konstitucijos 14, 09308 **Tel** *273 9595* **Fax** *273 9500* **Rooms** *114*   **Map** *1 C1*

Set amid the skyscrapers of the capital's new business district, Best Western Naujasis Vilnius is clean and efficient. It has a decent restaurant, a small fitness centre, sauna and pool and all the in-room facilities expected of a four-star hotel. Visitors should note that rooms facing the front tend to be noisy well into the night. **www.hotelnv.lt**

Le Meridien Villon Resort

19 km (12 miles) N of Vilnius, Highway A2, 03005 **Tel** *273 9700* **Fax** *273 9730* **Rooms** *192*

Set amid rolling countryside, Le Meridien Villion Resort is a sprawling resort hotel. All rooms as well as the hotel's Le Paysage restaurant *(see p343)* overlook lakes and forests. A golf course and Lithuania's biggest conference centre contribute to the feeling of space. **www.lemeridien.lt**

Radisson SAS Astorija

Didžioji 35/2, 01128 **Tel** *212 0110* **Fax** *212 1762* **Rooms** *120*   **Map** *2 D4*

One of Vilnius's best hotels, the Radisson SAS Astorija provides a broad range of professionally delivered services and amenities. The Brasserie Astorija *(see p340)* serves modern international cuisine, while Astorija Bar offers panoramic views of the Old Town. **www.vilnius.radissonsas.com**

Relais & Châteaux Stikliai

Gaono 7, 01131 **Tel** *264 9595* **Fax** *212 3870* **Rooms** *43*   **Map** *2 D4*

An opulent five-star hotel on one of the Old Town's most charming narrow streets, this place exudes elegance. The rooms boast beautiful upholstery in rich fabrics and luxurious en-suite bathrooms. This is where royalty and stars come to stay, particularly in the breathtaking King Mindaugas Suite. **www.stikliaihotel.lt**

CENTRAL LITHUANIA

ALYTUS Dzūkija

`P` `ii` ⓛ

Pulko 14/1, 62001 **Tel** *(315) 51 345* **Rooms** *32* **Road Map** D6

All rooms in Dzūkija reflect the ambience of a typical cottage in rural Lithuania, with creaky furniture and canvases of rural scenes. However, this is the biggest hotel in Alytus, situated in the town centre. All rooms have satellite TV and separate bathrooms. **www.hoteldzukija.lt**

ALYTUS Senas Namas

`P` `ii` ⓛⓛ

Užuolankos 24, 62111 **Tel** *(315) 53 489* **Fax** *(315) 51 643* **Rooms** *25* **Road Map** D6

Opened in 1997, the three-star Senas Namas is one of the more comfortable and professionally run hotels in town. Located in a quiet neighbourhood close to the town centre, it is also among the region's best. All rooms have an en-suite bathroom, Internet access and a refrigerator that doubles as a minibar. **www.senasnamas.lt**

ANYKŠČIAI Mindaugo Karūna

`P` `ii` 🛏 🚲 ♿ ⓛⓛ

Liudiškių 18, 29130 **Tel** *(381) 58 520* **Fax** *(381) 58 640* **Rooms** *27* **Road Map** D5

This three-star hotel at the Mindaugo Karūna leisure and sports centre is clean and contemporary. Nestled on the eastern edge of Anykščiai at the base of a hill named "Light of Good Fortune", and close to a thick oak forest, the hotel reflects tranquillity. Only the suites and deluxe rooms have Internet access. **www.mindaugokaruna.lt**

AUKŠTAITIJA NATIONAL PARK Šakarva

🛏 `P` ⓛ

Šakarva, 30204 **Tel** *(370) 6871 6136* **Rooms** *10* **Road Map** E5

A set of comfortable wooden cottages amid the beautiful scenery of Lake Ilgis, Šakarva, within the national park, is best visited in summer. The highlight, however, is the bath house on wheels, which is a mobile hot tub that can be delivered to the national park's campsite. Guide services are available on request. **www.sakarva.lt**

AUKŠTAITIJA NATIONAL PARK Žuvedra

`P` `ii` 🛏 ⓛⓛ

Mokyklos 11, Ignalina, 30119 **Tel** *(386) 52 314* **Rooms** *10* **Road Map** E5

Situated just outside Aukštaitija National Park, Žuvedra is a pretty lakeside hotel in the town of Ignalina. All rooms come with self-regulated heating, and guests can also visit the saunas and baths at the relaxation centre. The deluxe rooms, which face the outdoor terrace and the lake, are the best. **www.zuvedra.com**

AUKŠTAITIJA NATIONAL PARK Miškiniškės

`P` `ii` ⓛⓛⓛ

Kazitiškio sen, 30252 **Tel** *(370) 6160 0692* **Rooms** *15* **Road Map** E5

A gorgeous and expansive farmstead deep in the Lithuanian countryside, Miškiniškės provides a combination of comfort and isolation. Its delightful cabins and family cottages built of logs are well-equipped. The on-site restaurant prepares all kinds of meals, including delicious game dishes. **www.miskiniskes.lt**

BIRŠTONAS Audenis Guest House

`P` `ii` ⓛⓛ

Lelijų 3, 59207 **Tel** *(319) 61 300* **Fax** *(319) 61 301* **Rooms** *9* **Road Map** D6

This placid hotel resembles a modern residence. Well located close to the spa resort of Birštonas, Audenis Guest House has a selection of sparsely decorated, but comfortable rooms, with TV, telephone, minibar and Internet access. Fans and ironing facilities are available on request. **www.audenis.lt**

BIRŠTONAS Sofijos Rezidencija

`P` ⓛⓛ

Jaunimo 6, 59206 **Tel** *(319) 45 200* **Fax** *(319) 45 201* **Rooms** *14* **Road Map** D6

While the exceptional decoration in every room may seem extravagant to some, the four-poster beds, silk and satin quilts, and Renaissance-style paintings may make others feel like royalty. Its multicuisine restaurant serves good food in a unique ambience. **www.sofijosrezidencija.lt**

BIRŠTONAS Sonata

`P` `ii` ⓛⓛ

Algirdo 34, 59204 **Tel** *(319) 65 825* **Rooms** *20* **Road Map** D6

This hotel is tucked away in the quietest corner of town, on the banks of the Nemunas river. The rooms, decorated in subtle pastel shades, reflect the surrounding calm. A wide variety of optional facilities such as horse-riding, tennis and canoeing are available, but most guests prefer to just relax in this peaceful environment. **www.sonata.lt**

DRUSKININKAI Dalija

`P` ⓛ

Vasario 16-osios 1, 66118 **Tel** *(313) 51 814* **Rooms** *11* **Road Map** D6

The best budget option in the spa resort town of Druskininkai, Dalija is a 19th-century wooden building. Its basic rooms and wood-panelled walls have an old-fashioned, rustic charm. All rooms come with a shower room and toilet, as well as facilities such as kettle, fridge and a TV showing the local channels. **www.dalijahotel.lt**

DRUSKININKAI Regina

`P` `ii` 🛏 ⓛⓛ

T Kosčiuškos 3, 66116 **Tel** *(313) 59 060* **Fax** *(313) 59 061* **Rooms** *40* **Road Map** D6

Located in the town centre, Regina has a spa centre, aqua park and pleasure grounds, and is among Druskininkai's more comfortable hotels. The rooms are modestly sized but immaculately furnished. The Regina restaurant *(see p341)* offers a choice of excellent European dishes and has floor-to-ceiling windows. **www.regina.lt**

DRUSKININKAI Spa Vilnius

K Dineikos 1, 66165 **Tel** *(313) 53 811* **Fax** *(313) 59 019* **Rooms** *177*   **Road Map** *D6*

Popularly regarded as Druskininkai's premier wellness centre, Spa Vilnius offers a wide range of massages, water and mud baths as well as exercise facilities. The eight-storey, four-star hotel is a refreshing and sparklingly clean retreat. It is a favourite with families because of its in-house nanny and kids' games room. **www.spa-vilnius.lt**

DRUSKININKAI Europa Royale Druskininkai

Vilniaus 7, 66119 **Tel** *(313) 42 221* **Fax** *(313) 42 223* **Rooms** *101*   **Road Map** *D6*

Housed in a renovated 19th-century building, this hotel is part of the four-star Europa chain. It is directly connected to one of the resort's best spas, so that curative muds, mineral waters and beauty treatments are just a few steps away. There is a good restaurant, a café and a summer courtyard. **www.europaroyale.com**

KAUNAS Kaunas Archdiocese Guesthouse

Rotušės 21, 44279 **Tel** *(37) 322 597* **Fax** *(37) 320 090* **Rooms** *21*   **Road Map** *D5*

Although the rooms at this guest house are simple and sparsely furnished, they are clean and boast spectacular views of the surrounding Old Town. Internet access is available and there are many good restaurants nearby. It is, therefore, a good choice for the budget-conscious. **www.kaunas.lcn.lt**

KAUNAS Apple Economy Hotel

M Valančiaus 19, 44275 **Tel** *(37) 321 404* **Rooms** *14*   **Road Map** *D5*

A convenient Old Town location, cosy atmosphere and reasonable rates make the Apple Economy Hotel a very pleasant budget option for a short stay in Kaunas. Breakfast is not included in the room rate but can be ordered for a small charge. The hotel also has a small souvenir museum. **www.applehotel.lt**

KAUNAS Nemunas Tour

Gėlių 50, Ringaudai, 44324 **Tel** *(37) 563 766* **Fax** *(37) 563 863* **Rooms** *6*   **Road Map** *D5*

A short drive from Kaunas and the Via Baltica motorway, Nemunas Tour is a comfortable and well-run guest house. It offers a huge range of activities from organized sightseeing to sports and is a good way to experience the best of the countryside and city. Hearty home-made meals can be ordered. **www.nemunastour.com**

KAUNAS Daugirdas

T Daugirdo 4, 44279 **Tel** *(37) 301 561* **Fax** *(37) 301 562* **Rooms** *48*   **Road Map** *D5*

Located a stone's throw from most of Kaunas's sights, Daugirdas is a four-star hotel housed in a tastefully restored building. The comfortable, well-furnished rooms are well equipped, with Internet access, minibar and even air conditioning. Its Gothic-style basement, decorated with frescoes, has three restaurants. **www.daugirdas.lt**

KAUNAS Sfinksas

Aukštaičių 55/19a, 03000 **Tel** *(37) 301 982* **Fax** *(37) 301 983* **Rooms** *12*   **Road Map** *D5*

Although Sfinksas is a short drive away from the city centre, it is a pleasant, though slightly quirky, place to stay. Each room is uniquely decorated, while the overall eccentric design is a good example of Baltic idiosyncracy. The restaurant is excellent and the staff are exceptionally helpful. **www.sfinksas.lt**

KAUNAS Best Western Santakos

J Gruodžio 21, 44293 **Tel** *(37) 302 702* **Fax** *(37) 330 2700* **Rooms** *92*   **Road Map** *D5*

Set in an elegant historic red-brick building in the heart of the Old Town, this four-star hotel offers quality. The wonderful interiors and cosy rooms are matched by excellent service and a range of facilities. The restaurant is among the best in Kaunas and serves artfully garnished dishes in a Persian-themed ambience. **www.santaka.lt**

KAUNAS Park Inn Kaunas

K Donelaičio 27, 44240 **Tel** *(37) 306 100* **Fax** *(37) 306 200* **Rooms** *206*   **Road Map** *D5*

Opened in 2008, this is sprawling, contemporarily designed hotel has the city's biggest conference centre, with eight halls that can together seat up to 1,000 people. The hotel's Diverso restaurant serves fresh Mediterranean cuisine while the Ginger bar offers fine service. **www.parkinn.com**

KĖDAINIAI Grėjaus Namas

Didžioji 36, 57257 **Tel** *(34) 751 500* **Fax** *(34) 767 154* **Rooms** *18*   **Road Map** *D5*

Perhaps the best place to stay in the sleepy town of Kėdainiai, this boutique hotel is well appointed and elegantly furnished. It is housed in an 18th-century building constructed by Scots. The business and deluxe rooms are air conditioned and there is also a special room for disabled guests. **www.grejausnamas.lt**

MARIJAMPOLĖ Sudavija

Sodo 1a, 68295 **Tel** *(343) 52 995* **Fax** *(343) 52 926* **Rooms** *10*   **Road Map** *C6*

Excellently located in an attractive part of the town centre, Sudavija is popular among businesspeople and tourists. The well-appointed rooms, with satellite TV channels and telephones, reflect a cosy, homey ambience. The on-site restaurant serves good food and the service is efficient. **www.sudavija.com**

MOLĖTAI LAKELAND Apple Island

Lake Grabuostas, Žalvariai village, 33284 **Tel** *(383) 50 073* **Rooms** *10*   **Road Map** *D5*

Ideal for families or groups, this well-equipped and well-run campsite offers a range of two- and four-bed wooden huts. Pitches for camper vans and tents are also available. There is a huge choice of sports and leisure activities on offer. A great place for wholesome, rugged countryside fun. **www.appleisland.lt**

Key to Price Guide *see p308* **Key to Symbols** *see back cover flap*

MOLÉTAI LAKELAND Belvilis

Molétų raj Kirneilė village, 33166 **Tel** *(383) 51 098* **Fax** *(383) 51 099* **Rooms** *20* **Road Map** *D5*

A luxurious lakeside complex of beautifully designed rooms and cottages, Belvilis is an ideal place for a relaxing or a romantic getaway. It has a fine restaurant, spa and beauty treatments as well as a complex of swimming pools and baths. Given its quality and idyllic surroundings, it is excellent value for money. **www.belvilis.lt**

PANEVÉŽYS Romantic

Kranto 24, 35173 **Tel** *(45) 584 860* **Fax** *(45) 581 162* **Rooms** *73* **Road Map** *D5*

An hour's drive from Vilnius and only a short one from the Via Baltica motorway, Romantic is undoubtedly among the few decent hotels in Panevėžys. Housed in a thoroughly refurbished historic building in the town centre, the hotel has a lovely swimming pool, gym and spa centre, along with a quality restaurant. **www.romantic.lt**

TRAKAI Akmeninė Rezidencija

Bražuolės village, 21100 **Tel** *(370) 6114 3111* **Fax** *(528) 25 186* **Rooms** *10* **Road Map** *D5*

This rustic-style hotel, a complex of five hotel rooms and five villas, is a divine getaway with great views of Trakai Castle. It offers cosy accommodation with lakeside Russian baths and top-quality dining. Water sports are available in summer, while in winter the lake turns into a giant ice-skating rink. **www.akmenineuzeiga.lt**

TRAKAI Trasalis

Gedimino 26, 21118 **Tel** *(528) 51 588* **Fax** *(528) 51 589* **Rooms** *103* **Road Map** *D5*

A comfortable hotel and entertainment centre, Trasalis has well-furnished rooms with Internet connection and all the usual modern facilities. It boasts a mini aquapark, spa centre, bowling and two pleasant restaurants. The hotel also offers an array of sightseeing excursions and sports activities. **www.trasalis.lt**

VARĖNA Vila Ula

Burokaraistėlės village, 65383 **Tel** *(370) 6799 3318* **Fax** *(370) 3745 7579* **Rooms** *15* **Road Map** *D6*

Conveniently situated for exploring Dzūkija National Park, Vila Ula nestles by a lake, surrounded by forests. It is one of the many countryside retreats that are springing up across Lithuania. Both two-bed and four-bed rooms are available, as well as a fabulous sauna. **www.vilaula.lt**

VISAGINAS Gabriella

Jaunystės 21, 31230 **Tel** *(386) 70 171* **Fax** *(386) 70 151* **Rooms** *17* **Road Map** *E5*

Although not the most charming of hotels, Gabriella is clean and comfortable and has enough facilities to make a stay in Visaginas pleasant. All rooms come with Internet connection and satellite TV. The restaurant is surprisingly cosy, while the spa centre is small but relaxing. **www.gabriella.lt**

WESTERN LITHUANIA

CURONIAN SPIT NATIONAL PARK Santauta

Kalno 36, Juodkrantė, 93102 **Tel** *(469) 53 348* **Fax** *(469) 53 349* **Rooms** *45* **Road Map** *B5*

One of the best and cheapest budget options on the Curonian Spit, Santauta has fairly rudimentary rooms, but that does not affect the jovial family-holiday atmosphere. The building itself has the aura of a wooden, Eastern European mountain chalet. **www.santauta.lt**

CURONIAN SPIT NATIONAL PARK Ąžuolynas

L Rėzos 54, Juodkrantė, 93101 **Tel** *(469) 53 310* **Fax** *(469) 53 316* **Rooms** *79* **Road Map** *B5*

Perhaps the closest to a resort hotel on the Curonian Spit, Ąžuolynas, directly facing the lagoon, has a swimming pool and waterslide for families to enjoy. It also has a Turkish bath, besides a tennis court and fitness centre. A heath path over the dunes leads to the Baltic Sea. **www.hotelazuolynas.lt**

CURONIAN SPIT NATIONAL PARK Inkaro Kaimas

Naglių 26–1, Nida, 93123 **Tel** *(469) 52 123* **Rooms** *3* **Road Map** *B5*

Reflecting the gaudy reds and blues of a traditional Nida fisherman's home, the wooden apartments of Inkaro Kaimas are delightfully positioned on the edge of the Curonian Spit. The rooms are tastefully decorated and come with satellite TV and a kitchenette. Only a few rooms have air conditioning. **www.inkarokaimas.lt**

CURONIAN SPIT NATIONAL PARK Kuršių Kiemas

Miško 11, Juodkrantė, 93102 **Tel** *(469) 53 004* **Fax** *(469) 53 114* **Rooms** *20* **Road Map** *B5*

This charming and elegant building, tucked away from the rest of Juodkrantė down a pine-shrouded road, has been a hotel since 1895. Originally called the Hotel Bachmann, it was a retreat for well-off Prussians. Today, the well-equipped rooms are comfortable, some with balconies and kitchenettes. **www.neringatravel.lt**

CURONIAN SPIT NATIONAL PARK Linėja

Taikos 18, Nida, 93121 **Tel** *8657 44 968* **Rooms** *37* **Road Map** *B5*

Named after the twin flower, a plant typical of the Curonian Spit region, the three-star Linėja sits on a slope above the town of Nida. Guests can choose between catering or non-catering accommodation. The rooms are cosy and suitable for families. Bowling, billiards and cycling are among the resort's activities. **www.linejanida.lt**

CURONIAN SPIT NATIONAL PARK Litorina

Nidas–Smiltynė 19, Nida, 05872 **Tel** *(469) 52 528* **Fax** *(469) 51 102* **Rooms** *19*   **Road Map** *B5*

Unusual for the Curonian Spit, Litorina is located on the Baltic Coast rather than with the other settlements by the lagoon. It is a classy resort hotel with tennis, sauna and gym facilities and evening entertainment. The serene and secretive location makes it popular with the Lithuanian elite. **www.litorina-dubingiai.lt**

CURONIAN SPIT NATIONAL PARK Nerija

Pamario 13, Nida, 93124 **Tel** *(469) 52 777* **Fax** *(469) 52 777* **Rooms** *57*   **Road Map** *B5*

A three-star hotel, Scandinavian-style Nerija exudes space and openness, with high-ceilinged rooms, large beds, generous windows and balconies overlooking the pine forest. Tennis, volleyball and basketball courts are nearby, while the ground-floor restaurant provides a romantic setting for dinner. **www.neringahotels.lt**

CURONIAN SPIT NATIONAL PARK Nidos Kempingas

Taikos 45a, Nida, 93121 **Tel** *(469) 52 045* **Rooms** *10*   **Road Map** *B5*

Lithuania's best-organized and most popular campsite, Nidos Kempingas also has a selection of rooms and a spacious split-level apartment – the latter with kitchenette, modern bathroom with heated floor and a security system. The range of daytime activities for families and children is hard to beat. **www.kempingas.lt**

CURONIAN SPIT NATIONAL PARK Villa Banga

Pamario 2, Nida, 93124 **Tel** *(469) 51 139* **Fax** *(469) 52 762* **Rooms** *7*   **Road Map** *B5*

Exuding peace and tranquillity, Villa Banga is a gorgeous thatch-roofed building right in the centre of Nida, close to the Curonian Lagoon. Its rooms are replete with wooden furniture and come with kitchenettes. Breakfast is optional and may cost extra. Bikes and skis can be hired, depending on the time of year. **www.nidosbanga.lt**

CURONIAN SPIT NATIONAL PARK Nidus

G D Kuverto 15, Nida, 93123 **Tel** *(469) 52 001* **Fax** *(469) 50 016* **Rooms** *26*   **Road Map** *B5*

Situated midway between the beach destinations and the town of Nida, Nidus is a 15-minute walk from the beaches and the town centre. Guests rooms, which are clean and painted in warm colours, all have a balcony. Bike rental, a pleasant restaurant and a smart conference room are among the facilities on offer. **www.nidus.lt**

KLAIPĖDA Park Inn by Radisson Klaipėda

Minijos 119, 93231 **Tel** *(46) 380 803* **Fax** *(46) 482 030* **Rooms** *84*   **Road Map** *B5*

For drivers using the nearby port or business travellers on a budget, the modern high-rise Park Inn Klaipėda offers comfort, safety and efficiency in equal measure. All rooms have colour-coded lighting to create an ambience to match the mood of the guests. Some rooms are also equipped for disabled visitors. **www.parkinn.com**

KLAIPĖDA Klaipėda

Naujoji Sodo 1, 92118 **Tel** *(46) 404 372* **Fax** *(46) 404 373* **Rooms** *307*   **Road Map** *B5*

Commonly referred to as the K-Centre, this hotel consists of two skyscrapers, both of which are city landmarks. One of them, constructed in the Soviet-era style, is archaic yet comfortable. The second is very modern, with stunning views, sunken baths and split-level suites. **www.ambertonhotels.com**

KLAIPĖDA Preliudija Guest House

Kepėjų 7, 91247 **Tel** *(46) 310 077* **Fax** *(46) 492 785* **Rooms** *6*   **Road Map** *B5*

Located in the middle of the criss-cross lanes of the Old Town, this lovely guest house is a bargain. The building dates back to the 1850s and is a protected architectural monument. The rooms, however, appear stylishly modern, and come with free Internet access. Dry-cleaning and laundry services are available. **www.preliudija.com**

KLAIPĖDA National Hotel

Žvejų 21, 91247 **Tel** *(46) 211 111* **Fax** *(46) 416 172* **Rooms** *50*   **Road Map** *B5*

Overlooking the Old Town, with its romantic sights and a multitude of noisy nightlife options, the National could not have a better location. However, even for guests who need solitude, this four-star hotel, with its unrivalled services and soundproof windows, is an ideal choice. **www.nationalhotel.lt**

KLAIPĖDA Navalis

Manto 23, 92234 **Tel** *(46) 404 200* **Fax** *(46) 404 202* **Rooms** *28*   **Road Map** *B5*

Housed in a refurbished 1863 building, this four-star hotel has retained most of its architectural features. The symbolic bow of a boat in the reception area and the general ambience reflects the hotel's naval theme. The decor is formal, but restful, in soft, warm colours with mahogany and beech furniture. **www.navalis.lt**

KLAIPĖDA Vecekrug

Jūros 23, 92125 **Tel** *(46) 301 002* **Fax** *(46) 312 262* **Rooms** *23*   **Road Map** *B5*

Named after the highest point on the Curonian Spit, Vecekrug is distinguished by its combination of friendly staff and modern structure. The rooms have soundproof windows, Internet connection, minibar and bathrooms with heated floors. A wall of windows overlooks the coast while other rooms face a quiet street. **www.vecekrug.lt**

KLAIPĖDA Radisson Blu Hotel Klaipėda

Šaulių 28, 92231 **Tel** *(46) 490 800* **Fax** *(46) 490 815* **Rooms** *74*   **Road Map** *B5*

With rooms decorated in 19th-century New England maritime style, Radisson Blu Hotel Klaipėda sets high standards. Free Wi-Fi access, a top-notch restaurant and cocktail bar, as well as steam bath and fitness studio with superb equipment, complete the picture. **www.radissonblu.com/hotel-klaipeda**

Key to Price Guide *see p308* **Key to Symbols** *see back cover flap*

NEMUNAS DELTA Ventainė

Marių 7, Ventės village, Kintųdoyen, 99361 **Tel** *(441) 68 525* **Fax** *(441) 47 422* **Rooms** *27* **Road Map** *B5*

A snug hotel, campsite and leisure centre on the shores of the Curonian Spit, Ventainė is close to the bird-ringing station at Ventė and a short drive from the Nemunas Delta. Boats, jet-skis, tennis courts and multiple saunas can all be rented. The small on-site restaurant sometimes closes early. **www.ventaine.lt**

PALANGA Kungis Inn

Užkanavės 32, 00169 **Tel** *(460) 56 310* **Rooms** *7* **Road Map** *B5*

Tucked away in the heart of a pine forest near Palanga International Airport and a short walk from the beach, Kungis Inn is an excellent budget option. The accommodation, though fairly basic, boasts thick carpets, bathrooms with heated floors and charcoal barbeque grills on the balcony.

PALANGA Alanga

S Nėries 14, 00134 **Tel** *(460) 49 215* **Fax** *(460) 49 316* **Rooms** *47* **Road Map** *B5*

The imaginative colours of the rooms and apartments, together with comfortable furniture, make Alanga a joy to stay in. A swimming pool, along with Finnish and Turkish saunas, makes it even more inviting. The staff are polite and professional. **www.alanga.lt**

PALANGA Chateau Amber

Naglio 17, 00136 **Tel** *(614) 39 919* **Fax** *(8656) 02 596* **Rooms** *8* **Road Map** *B5*

With gently swaying pines in the background and windows overlooking the sea and golden dunes, Chateau Amber appears more like a fairytale house. It is virtually on the beach, making the seaview from some of the rooms unbeatable, especially at sunset. There is also an on-site mini-spa. **www.chateauamber.lt**

PALANGA Mama Rosa Villa

Jūratės 28a, 00133 **Tel** *(460) 48 581* **Fax** *(460) 48 580* **Rooms** *8* **Road Map** *B5*

Sumptuously decorated in classic English style, the rooms at Mama Rosa Villa have lovely wrought-iron beds and sleek, shiny bathrooms. With its tastefully designed interiors, this place could indeed be an English country cottage. The service is courteous and the exclusive restaurant and sauna complex a delight.

PALANGA Vanagupė

Vanagupės 31, 00169 **Tel** *(460) 41 199* **Fax** *(460) 31 199* **Rooms** *98* **Road Map** *B5*

This plush five-star beach hotel has an unbeatable range of luxury services, a classy restaurant and a sprawling spa centre. It is perfect for couples on a romantic weekend. Its L'Ambra Rossa restaurant serves classic European cuisine. **www.vanagupe.lt**

PLUNGĖ Beržas

Minijos 2/Telšių 2 **Tel** *(448) 56 840* **Fax** *(448) 56 840* **Rooms** *10* **Road Map** *C5*

Although the rooms of Beržas have a faded, rustic charm, the hotel offers some of the most comfortable beds to be found between Klaipėda and Šiauliai. Breakfast is available for an extra charge. The hotel tries hard to make guests feel welcome in this sleepy town. **www.berzas.goo.lt**

ŠEDUVA Prie Ežero

Raudondvaris village, Radviliškio raj, 82213 **Tel** *(422) 44 430* **Fax** *(422) 44 436* **Rooms** *15* **Road Map** *C5*

On the Panevėžys road, a few kilometres away from Šeduva, this three-star lakeside hotel is also one of the more pleasant accommodation options in these parts. Most rooms have satellite TV. For those on a budget, a boarding school across the lake rents out rooms in summer. **www.hotelprieezero.lt**

ŠIAULIAI Saulininkas

St Lukauskio 5a, 76236 **Tel** *(41) 436 555* **Fax** *(41) 421 848* **Rooms** *13* **Road Map** *C4*

An affable hotel with reasonably priced rooms, Saulininkas is set in a quiet neighbourhood a few blocks from the Church of Sts Peter and Paul. The sauna and pool can be booked ahead for evening parties and the gym is used by locals. The restaurant also delivers food to rooms. **www.saulininkas.com**

ŠIAULIAI Grafaitės Svetainė

Aušros 1, Ginkūnai, 81493 **Tel** *(41) 589 120* **Fax** *(41) 502 152* **Rooms** *23* **Road Map** *C4*

There are two streets in Šiauliai named Aušros. This one is out of the city centre in the direction of the Hill of Crosses, making it convenient for pilgrims or for those who wish to visit this Catholic landmark. Harmoniously furnished, the little guest house has well-equipped rooms. **www.hotelgrafaite.com**

ŠIAULIAI Šaulys

Vasario 16–Osios 40, 76351 **Tel** *(41) 520 812* **Fax** *(41) 520 911* **Rooms** *41* **Road Map** *C4*

Safe and secure, with bright and comfortable rooms, Šaulys is not exactly upmarket, yet it offers the classiest rooms in Šiauliai. The on-site restaurant has a reasonable wine list, the pool and sauna are refreshing and the staff can help arrange ticket reservations and do laundry, all for a small extra charge. **www.saulys.lt**

ŽEMAITIJA NATIONAL PARK Linelis

Paplatelės, 90483 **Tel** *(655) 77 666* **Fax** *4484 9422* **Rooms** *33* **Road Map** *C4*

By far the most pleasant accommodation in Žemaitija National Park, Linelis is situated on the northeastern shore of Lake Plateliai and has its own beach. Activities on offer include pedalos, sailing and even diving excursions. A small on-site spa is another highlight. **www.linelis.lt**

WHERE TO EAT

Restaurant culture in Estonia, Latvia and Lithuania has changed dramatically in recent years. Although traditional food is still very popular, there has been a huge increase in all kinds of new restaurants specializing in everything from an eclectic international cuisine to quality pizza. The considerable rise in the diversity and standards of restaurants is comparable across the three Baltic States, although the variety of eating places is much higher in the capital cities. A few other large cities

Sign for a café in the Old Town, Vilnius

and popular resort towns also have a fairly impressive choice of dining options. Good food is an integral part of Baltic culture and the abundance of traditional-style restaurants in each country attests to the pride many people take in their national cuisine. Traditional Baltic food may not be particularly subtle, but it is tasty and makes for a hearty meal. It is often best enjoyed in the countryside where portions are generous and ingredients tend to be deliciously fresh.

TYPES OF RESTAURANTS

Restaurants and cafés in the Baltic States are locally referred to as *restoran* and *kohvik* in Estonia, *restorāns* and *kafejnīca* in Latvia, and *restoranas* and *kavinė* in Lithuania. Both types of establishments vary widely in the type of food they offer.

Restaurants can either be very luxurious and modern establishments or basic food-and-beer places that do not differ significantly from pubs. Similarly, cafés can be pleasant and stylish. Most of them offer a decent but cheap meal of hearty proportions. Sometimes they act as a meeting place for local drinkers. All cafés have a good selection of alcohol on sale. Most modern bars often have a small but good-quality menu which is available until late.

Modern interior of Vincent's restaurant *(see p332)* in Rīga

A café in Town Hall Square in the Old Town, Tallinn, Estonia

Locally-run pubs are known as *kõrts* in Estonia, *krogs* in Latvia and *baras* in Lithuania. Although rare in Tallinn, Rīga and Vilnius, pubs are common in small towns and in the countryside. Sometimes, they are rustically furnished places that offer an excellent standard of traditional food and local beer. Fast food has not really taken off in the Baltic States and can only be found in central locations in the capitals.

DINING HOURS

The rise in restaurant culture has seen a proliferation of restaurants which keep similar opening hours throughout the Baltic States. They open between 10 and 11am and close between 11pm and midnight. In small towns, restaurants are more likely to open later

Bakery sign in Trakai, Lithuania

and close earlier, and in tourist resorts some restaurants are open only during summer months. Big breakfasts are rare in the Baltic States. Until quite recently, the only breakfast food available were pastries or pancakes. These days, however, restaurants offer a range of breakfasts, including variations on the English fry-up. Lunch is still the main meal of the day for many people. Nonetheless, eating out has become such a recreational habit that restaurants often fill up in the evenings, although people tend to eat early, normally between 6 and 9pm.

Café culture is big in the Baltic States. Most cafés open any time from 8 to 10am and close around 9 or 10pm, although in small towns they often close earlier. In more remote places, many cafés

Atmospheric street restaurant in the Old Town, Vilnius, Lithuania

remain closed on Sundays. Pubs and cafés always have an array of snacks available.

MENUS

English-language menus are commonplace in the capital cities and tourist resorts. In small towns and the countryside, however, such menus are much scarcer. Most people in the Baltic States speak some English, so it may be possible to ask for help in deciphering the menu. After Russian, German is the most common language in Latvia and Estonia. Consequently, menus often come with German or Russian translations.

Menu, Tallinn's Admiral restaurant *(see p322)*

VEGETARIANS

Meat is integral to Baltic cuisine, although there is an increasing choice of vegetarian (*vegetaarlane* in Estonian, *veģetārie* in Latvian and *vegetaras* in Lithuanian) dishes on offer in most decent restaurants. However, these vegetarian menu options are limited to the capital cities.

RESERVATIONS

Reservations are usually made by phone, although in some cases they can be made via the Internet. It is unnecessary to make lunchtime bookings, but it is sensible to reserve a table for dinner, particularly on a Friday or Saturday evening, in a good restaurant in one of the capital cities.

PAYING

Restaurant prices have gone up considerably in the Baltic States, but are still comparatively lower than in other European countries. The cost of alcohol is also notably lower than in other European countries. Prices are highest in the capitals, particularly in tourist spots. Tax is always included in the price. Cover charges are quite rare, and usually only apply to restaurants or bars which include special live music sets. Cafés are the most affordable eating option, but many only accept cash. However, credit and debit card payment is becoming common throughout the Baltic States.

TIPPING

Tipping is a relatively new concept to the Baltic States. Service charges are usually included in the bill. However, some leading restaurants add a service charge to the total, which should be clearly indicated. Tipping is only expected in larger establishments with table service. The general rule is to leave 10 per cent or less of the total bill. Tipping in cafés and bars is rare.

CHILDREN

Although children are welcome in restaurants, only a few popular chains offer provisions such as half-portions. In centrally located establishments in bigger towns and cities, however, menus for children are becoming more common. It is usually possible to arrange for something off the menu to meet the children's needs.

DISABLED VISITORS

Few restaurants, besides the new ones, offer easy access for disabled people in the Baltic States. The situation, however, is improving. Tallinn is slightly ahead of Vilnius and Riga in this regard. Hotel restaurants remain a good option for disabled visitors as they have more facilities.

SMOKING

Smoking in enclosed public spaces, such as restaurants, bars, clubs, hotel lobbies, buses and trains, is banned in the Baltic States. The only option for smokers is to sit at an outdoor table in the summer, although some restaurants even prohibit outdoor smoking. However, a few cigar bars have been licensed to allow smoking.

Log-cabin restaurant at the LIDO Atpūtas Centrs *(see p330)* in Rīga

The Flavours of Estonia, Latvia and Lithuania

Traditional Baltic cooking is hearty and filling, designed to satisfy after hard physical labour and during long, gloomy winters. In the past, staple dishes were mostly soups and porridges made with grains such as barley, although coastal communities also ate fresh and preserved fish. Meat was usually reserved for festivals. Today it is central to most dishes, typically accompanied by boiled potatoes and rye bread. Popular seasonings include garlic, onions, caraway seeds and dill. Baltic cuisines have been influenced by those of neighbouring countries, particularly Russia and Germany in Estonia and Latvia, and Poland in Lithuania.

Bunch of fresh dill

Basket of wild mushrooms gathered in the woods of Latvia

MEAT, POULTRY & GAME

Pork is on almost every Baltic menu, whether breaded and fried like a schnitzel or in the form of bacon and sausages. Roast pork has long been a festive treat. Pork fat is also eaten, often accompanied by rye bread, and several dishes, such as Lithuanian *liežuvis* (cow's tongue), stem from

a time when no part of the animal could be wasted. Chicken and beef are also widely available, while game, such as wild boar, hare and venison, may be found both in rural and in upmarket urban restaurants.

FISH & SEAFOOD

Fishing has a venerable history in the Baltic States, with the long coastlines of Estonia and Latvia and an extensive network of rivers and lakes throughout the region. Many traditional recipes fell out of use during the Soviet era when most fish was exported. The Baltic sprat, in particular, was canned and eaten throughout the Soviet Union. Today, fish is usually prepared by frying or baking, but is also smoked and salted. The prevalence of this in Estonia is said to show a link with Scandinavian traditions.

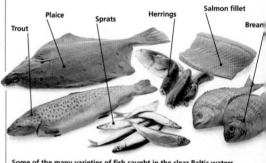

Trout   Plaice   Sprats   Herrings   Salmon fillet   Bream

Some of the many varieties of fish caught in the clear Baltic waters

BALTIC DISHES AND SPECIALITIES

The long list of Baltic soups and porridges includes Latvian *putra* (porridge with pork fat, often with meat or smoked fish added). Popular sausages include Lithuanian *vėdarai*, made from pig's intestines stuffed with potato. Estonia is noted for *verevoorst* (blood sausage) and *verleib* (blood bread). Latvia's signature dish is *pelēkie zirņi* (grey peas with bacon). Lithuania's *kugelis* (grated potato pudding often incorporating bacon, onion and eggs) is served with sour cream. A favourite Lithuanian snack is *kepta duona*, also known as *grauzdini* (fried rye bread with garlic) in Latvia and served with cheese. Throughout the region, you can sample Russian-style *pelmeni* (dumplings).

Red caviar on rye bread

Pīrāgi *(Latvia)* and pirukas *(Estonia)* are small leavened pasties, usually filled with bacon or cabbage.

Stalls in the bustling market square in Vilnius, Lithuania

Popular freshwater fish include pike, eel and elvers. Caviar is also available, including the relatively affordable red variety.

FRUIT & VEGETABLES

The Baltic climate limits the cultivation of fruit and vegetables, and they are not strongly represented in traditional recipes. By far the most common vegetable is the potato, introduced in the 18th century and now served at almost every meal. Other accompaniments include simple salads, often just cucumber and tomato. Mushrooms are popular and, every autumn, people roam the forests to gather mushrooms either to eat or to sell (see p373). Cepe is preferred, although varieties such as chanterelle and

rozites caperata, meaning "gypsy mushrooms", are also picked.

Local apples, plums and pears appear in fruit pies and tarts, but the true fruit bounty of the region is its berries and currants. Picking

Freshly picked redcurrants at an Estonian farm

berries is a popular summer pastime (see p373). They are eaten raw, made into tarts, puddings or compotes, or preserved for the winter.

DAIRY PRODUCE

Dairy products feature strongly in Baltic cuisine. Local butter is held in high regard, while Estonian *kefir* (fermented cow's milk) and Latvian *rūgušpiens* (curdled milk) are also very popular. Caraway cheese is eaten by Latvians, especially in midsummer. The most ubiquitous dairy product is sour cream. A base for many Baltic sauces, it is also poured directly on to a wide range of dishes.

ON THE MENU

Kartupeļu pankūkas (Latvia) Potato pancakes.

Kibinai (Lithuania) Mutton and onion pies, a speciality of the Karaim community.

Šližikai (Lithuania) Biscuits served with poppy seed milk, on Christmas Eve.

Rosolje (Estonia) Herring, meat, beetroot and apple salad, in a whipped cream and mustard dressing.

Seljanka (Estonia) and *Soļanka* (Latvia) A soup made with meat, pickled vegetables or fish, which has Russian origins.

Zrazai (Lithuania) Thin beef rolled with onion, bread and often mushrooms, then baked.

Šaltibarščiai *(Lithuania) is a chilled soup made of beetroot, cucumber, chopped egg,* kefir *and dill.*

Cepelinai, *or "zeppelins", are meat-stuffed potato dumplings in a sour cream, onion and bacon sauce.*

Pannkoogid, *huge, fluffy pancakes served with a berry compote, show the influence of Russian cuisine.*

What to Drink

Beer is popular in the Baltic States and several of the region's breweries date back to the 19th century. Vodka is not as popular as it was during the Soviet era, although it is still widely drunk and both local and Russian brands are available. The region also has some unusual spirits and liqueurs made with herbs. Although wine-drinking does not have a distinguished history, imported wine is available in restaurants and many affordable local sparkling wines are available. The most prominent traditional soft drink, *kali* in Estonia, *kvass* in Latvia or *gira* in Lithuania, has been claimed as a historical forerunner of strong beer. Customarily made from rye bread and very mildly alcoholic, it is a refreshing alternative to aerated drinks such as cola.

Viru Valge vodka

Rīga Black Balsam, Latvia

Bobelinė, Lithuania

WINES

Although the Baltic States are not a major wine producing region, both Latvia and Lithuania produce sparkling wines, such as Rīga Šampanietis and Alita Šampanas respectively. In Estonia, mulled red wine, known as *hõõgvein* or *glögg*, is popular in winter. Served warm, it has a spicy taste due to the cinnamon and cloves used to flavour it. Fruit wines, such as Põltsamaa Kuldne, which is made from apples, are also common.

Latvia has the distinction of being in the *Guinness Book of World Records* for the northernmost open-air vineyard in the world. Sabile vineyard, Vīna kalns (*see p178*), has a long history of viniculture, but production stopped during the Soviet occupation. It has been restarted but is very limited and often the only chance to try the wine is by attending the annual wine festival in summer.

SPIRITS & LIQUEURS

The best-known Estonian liqueur is the sweet-tasting Vana Tallinn, which has ingredients such as citrus oils, cinnamon, vanilla and rum. It can be drunk neat but is worth trying in coffee or over ice cream. It is also used to make cocktails or mixed with white wine or champagne. Vodka is also popular in Estonia, and Viru Valge is the most common local brand. In addition to the original version, it is available in flavoured varieties such as vanilla, lemon and watermelon.

For visitors to Latvia, Rīga Black Balsam is an unmissable drink and makes a popular souvenir, although perhaps as much for its ceramic bottle as for the liquid inside. Developed in 1752 as a medicinal tonic, it is composed of a top-secret list of ingredients and is an acquired taste. Occasionally drunk neat, it is often mixed with cola, hot blackcurrant juice or vodka. Specialist shops, and some bars, also sell Latvian liqueurs such as the caraway-flavoured Allažu Ķimelis.

Lithuania has a range of herbal liqueurs, including Trejos Devynerios. Concocted by a pharmacist in the late 19th century, Trejos Devynerios was listed as a legal patent medicine between the two World Wars. Vodka-drinkers may want to try Starka, which is distilled from rye grain, while other traditional drinks are honey-based mead and *bobelinė*, a liqueur made with cranberry juice. In rural areas throughout the region, local people brew their own, very potent vodka. Visitors should be wary of this, as it is usually of low quality and there have been cases where batches have been contaminated with methanol. In Lithuania, a legitimate drink takes the name of this illegal vodka, Samanė, but is not as strong.

Vana Tallinn liqueur

BEER

After independence in 1991, the region's state breweries were privatized and many of them were subsequently bought by large international corporations. Baltic Beverages Holdings, jointly owned by Carlsberg and Scottish & Newcastle, owns several of the region's biggest brands, such as Saku in Estonia, Aldaris in Latvia and Utenos and Švyturys in Lithuania. The Finnish company

Rīgas sparkling wine, Latvia

Põltsamaa Kuldne fruit wine, Estonia

Glögg mulled wine, Estonia

Olvi has bought Cēsis, which is Latvia's oldest brewery, A Le Coq in Estonia and Ragutis in Lithuania. Also in Lithuania, Kalnapilis is owned by the Danish Brewery Group. These major brands predominate in both bars and shops, although some of the more popular international beers are also available in the three countries. The two main categories are light (*belein* in Estonian, *gaišais* in Latvian and *šviesus* in Lithuanian) and dark (*tume* in Estonian, *tumšais* in Latvian and *tamsus* in Lithuanian). However, the major breweries have diversified their ranges and produce everything from very light US-style ice beers to rich and dark porters such as Ragutis, a chocolate porter. Lager-drinkers will certainly find a light beer to suit their palate, although visitors often find the dark beers appealing.

The arguably more interesting products of small and medium-sized breweries do make it into some bars, particularly in the area where they are produced and in the capital cities, and larger supermarkets also often have a decent range. Estonia's islands produce stronger drinks than most of the mainland breweries, and Saaremaa *õlu* is particularly well received. Interesting breweries in Latvia include Užavas, which produces unpasteurized beers that cannot be stored for long and are not exported. Other brands worth looking out for are Valmiermuižas, Tērvetes and Bauskas. The LIDO chain of restaurants brew

Saku Brewery, producer of some of the most popular beer in Estonia

their own brand of beer, with a microbrewery on the premises of the huge LIDO Recreation Centre, just outside Rīga. In Lithuania, the Biržai region is known for its long-standing brewing traditions and is home to several breweries, including the popular Rinkuškiai, which has both light and dark beer.

SOFT DRINKS

The most popular soft drink in the Baltic States is a drink traditionally made from fermented rye bread and sometimes flavoured with fruit or herbs, alternatively called *kali*, *kvass* and *gira*. Strictly speaking, it is not a soft drink and is beer-like, although it has a very low alcohol content, usually about 1 per cent. It vanished from the market at the time of the collapse of the Soviet Union because of concerns about the conditions of its production and storage, since it used to be dispensed from large outdoor tanks. Once reintroduced, it proved a threat to the market dominance of Coca-Cola, which responded by buying the drink manufacturers in the three countries, who now produce Linnuse Kali, Pilskalna Kvass and Bajorų Gira.

Today, this mass-produced drink is usually made from malt extract and flavourings. Another common lunchtime drink across the region is *kefir*, a very mildly alcoholic fermented milk, which is one of the key ingredients of *šaltibarščiai* (*see p319*).

Kefir, fermented milk, Lithuania   **Kvass, malted drink, Latvia**

A very popular soft drink in Estonia is Tartu Limonaad, while Latvia has the very rustic *bērzu sula*, made from birch sap. It is fermented in a barrel with barley seeds sprinkled on top and sometimes rye bread crusts are added. Traditional flavourings for the juice include peppermint and sprigs of blackcurrant, while more modern additions include lemon or orange zest, raisins and cinnamon. Something else to look out for in Latvia is *veselība*, which is a soft drink sold in vessels akin to beer bottles and advertised as being fortified with an abundance of vitamins.

Saku Originaal, Estonia   **Aldaris Zelta, Latvia**   **Kalnapilis Grand, Lithuania**   **Švyturys Gintarinis, Lithuania**

Choosing a Restaurant in Estonia

Chosen for their impressive food, location and value
for money, these restaurants cover a wide price range.
They are listed by area, starting with Tallinn. Restaurants
within the same price category appear in alphabetical
order. For Tallinn map references, see pages 82–3; for
road map references see the inside back cover.

PRICE DETAILS
Based on the price per person of a
three-course meal with half a bottle
of wine, including cover charge,
service and tax.
€ Under €10
€€ €10–€20
€€€ €20–€30
€€€€ €30–€40
€€€€€ Over €40

TALLINN

African Kitchen   €€
Uus 32–34, 10111 **Tel** 644 2555   **Map** 2 D2

The restaurant's vibrant and lively interior is matched by the excellent food, which is the most authentic African
cuisine in the Baltic States. African Kitchen is a hip, fun place to eat, with an impressively diverse menu of fresh-
tasting, spicy and exotic fare.

Clayhills Gastropub   €€
Pikk 13, 10123 **Tel** 641 9312   **Map** 1 C2

The latest addition to the Tallinn pub scene is this friendly, handsome two-floor gastropub which, true to its name,
has a focus on good-quality food as well as beer and wine. There's a selection of pastas, grilled meats, burgers and
salads, as well as cheap and tasty snacks. Popular with local students and artists.

Kompressor   €€
Rataskaeru 1, 101223 **Tel** 646 4210   **Map** 1 C2

This restaurant is always packed with young people, and the menu reveals why: it serves huge and tasty pancakes,
with a variety of sweet and savoury fillings, for a very low price. Its a great place to recharge your batteries if you
are exploring Old Town. Seating is at large communal tables.

Pizza Americana   €€
Müürivahe 2, 10146 **Tel** 644 8837   **Map** 2 D3

A small restaurant, Americana specializes in thick-crust, American-style pizzas, which come with a huge variety of
toppings. The restaurant itself is small but popular, probably due to the sheer dimensions of the pizzas. Pizza and
wine can also be delivered anywhere in Tallinn.

Von Krahli Aed   €€
Rataskaevu 8, 10123 **Tel** 626 9088   **Map** 1 C2

This chic establishment is an ideal choice for a fresh meal or light snack. The emphasis here is on healthier eating,
so there is a reasonable list of vegetarian options, while items that contain gluten, eggs or dairy are indicated on the
menu. Good food at reasonable prices.

Admiral   €€€
Lootsi 15, 10151 **Tel** 662 3777   **Map** 2 F1

This restaurant offers a unique dining experience aboard an old steamer docked in the Tallinn passenger port. The
elegant but cosy interior boasts great views of the harbour and city through portholes, while the Balkan cuisine is
of high quality. The ship can also be chartered for cruises.

Alter Ego   €€€
Roseni 8, 10111 **Tel** 5456 0339   **Map** 2 D2

Situated in the fashionable Rotermanni Quarter (see p73), Alter Ego offers Mediterranean-style food, with a heavy
Spanish influence. The menu is full of top-notch offerings, such as the Estonian fillet mignon with a 17-year-old
Oloroso sherry glaze. The wine list is immense, and all breads, ice creams and sorbets are made in-house.

Amarillo   €€€
Viru väljak 4, 10111 **Tel** 680 9280   **Map** 1 C2

Amarillo serves good Tex-Mex food in a relaxed environment. The menu covers everything from burritos and fajitas
to burgers and pizzas, and food can be made especially spicy on request. Lactose and gluten-free dishes are highlighted on the menu. A popular place that mostly attracts families and large groups.

Artemis   €€€
Pikk 35, 10133 **Tel** 644 1114   **Map** 1 C2

Artemis is an authentic, Greek-owned and run restaurant with all the frills. The plastic grapevines only add charm
to the homeliness of the place. The menu includes staple favourites such as moussaka and dolmades, among others.
It is one of the few places that serve ouzo, a Greek aniseed-flavoured liqueur.

Key to Symbols see back cover flap

Balalaika
Paldiski mnt 4, 10149 **Tel** *667 7120*   €€€

Map *1 A3*

Located in the Meriton hotel, this Russian restaurant serves all that you would expect – caviar, blinis and stroganoff – and more. The unique selling point here, though, is the cold *zakuska* buffet, which is set up inside an 18th-century carriage made in St Petersburg. A large selection of vodka is also on offer.

Beer House
Dunkri 5, 10123 **Tel** *644 2222*   €€€

Map *1 C2*

A restaurant-cum-microbrewery, Beer House really does resemble an old German-style beer house. The menu includes six kinds of sausage, along with some good meaty main courses. This place also serves the only unpasteurized beer in the country. There is live music and a sauna for up to 20 people.

Controvento
Vene 12/Katariina käik, 10123 **Tel** *644 0470*   €€€

Map *2 D2*

Hidden away in the beautiful Katariina Passage, Controvento is a hugely popular Italian restaurant because of its outstanding food and thoroughly charming atmosphere. The restaurant has excellent pizza and pasta along with a good choice of meat and fish dishes. Book ahead at weekends.

Golden Dragon
Pikk 37, 10133 **Tel** *631 3506*   €€€

Map *1 C2*

Unarguably the best Chinese restaurant in Tallinn, Golden Dragon is housed in a cosy cellar with an extensive whitewashed vaulted ceiling. The vast menu is a dream for vegetarians, and the portions are gratifyingly large. Some Thai dishes are on offer as well. Usually fills up at weekends.

Grillhouse Daube
Rüütli 11, 10130 **Tel** *645 5531*   €€€

Map *1 C3*

Spread over two floors, Grillhouse Daube is an extremely pleasant place with welcoming staff. The quality menu offers a good selection of tender steaks as well as satisfying pasta and fish dishes. There are also some good-value and delicious set meals for groups of four or more.

Kuldse Notsu Kõrts
Dunkri 8, 10123 **Tel** *628 6567*   €€€

Map *1 C2*

Specializing in Estonian cuisine, Kuldse Notsu Kõrts is a charming cellar restaurant with an interior humorously described as "nouveau-rustic" by the owners. The menu abounds with meat, particularly pork, but there are some vegetarian options such as the Farm Girl's Stew.

Must Lammas
Sauna 2, 10140 **Tel** *644 2031*   €€€

Map *1 C3*

Must Lammas, meaning "black sheep", is a refreshingly modern Georgian restaurant, rather than the usual folksy one. The ultra-stylish interior does not, however, detract from the superb Caucasian cuisine. Try the spicy lamb soup for starters, with a classic Georgian wine such as Saperavi.

Park Avenue
Kreutzwaldi 23, 10147 **Tel** *630 5305*   €€€

Map *2 F3*

Part of the Reval Park Hotel & Casino (*see p293*), Park Avenue is as sleek as its New York namesake. It offers a buffet of set hot, cold and sweet selections or a combination of all three from lunchtime until 5am. There is also an à la carte menu. The summer terrace has great views.

Sakura
Sakala 20, 10152 **Tel** *648 4477*   €€€

Map *2 E2*

Popular with locals, Sakura boasts an impressive range of quality Japanese food served up by kimono-clad Estonian waitresses. The interior has a pleasant ambience and the service is excellent. Private rooms are available for larger groups or special parties. Sushi can be ordered to take away.

Turg
Mündi 3, 10146 **Tel** *641 2456*   €€€

Map *1 C2*

Turg means "market" in Estonian, which provides the theme for this popular cellar restaurant. The stalls, carts and crowds give it a bustling market feel by day, but by night it is a more subdued, candlelit place. The menu offers a number of meat dishes.

Vanaema Juures
Rataskaevu 10/12, 10123 **Tel** *626 9080*   €€€

Map *1 C2*

Meaning "grandma's place", Vanaema Juures definitely lives up to its name. It is an exceptionally cosy and homely cellar restaurant decorated with 1920s and 30s period furniture. The excellent Estonian-style cuisine is stylishly served and reasonably priced. Try the roast elk, a local speciality.

Elevant
Vene 5, 10123 **Tel** *631 3132*   €€€€

Map *2 D2*

Elevant offers outstanding and imaginative fusion-style Indian fare that includes Ayurveda dishes and cross-over European elements such as moose soup and wild boar kebab. The extensive menu has plenty for vegetarians as well as more traditional Indian food. The interior is wonderfully relaxing.

Horisont Restaurant & Bar €€€€

Tornimäe 3, 10145 **Tel** *624 3000* **Map** *2 E3*

Situated on the 30th floor of Swissôtel Tallinn, this top-class restaurant offers amazing views across the city, but the food is better still, and the service is beyond compare. Try the monkfish with chorizo, shrimps and pesto risotto, but be sure to save room for the coconut soufflé. Closed Sun & Mon.

Maikrahv €€€€

Raekoja plats 8, 10146 **Tel** *631 4227* **Map** *1 C2*

One of the more reasonably priced and refined medieval-style restaurants in Tallinn, Maikrahv is set in an atmospheric arched hall under Town Hall Square. The menu offers a good selection of tasty international dishes. There is a great summer terrace and a hall to accommodate large groups.

Olde Hansa €€€€

Vana turg 1, 10140 **Tel** *627 9020* **Map** *1 C3*

A tourist attraction in its own right, Olde Hansa is an immensely enjoyable experience. Huge traditional dishes are served by waiting staff in medieval costumes in a candlelit atmosphere, while an ensemble plays live traditional music. The menu is reputed to be based on carefully researched recipes.

Oliver €€€€

Viru väljak 3, 10140 **Tel** *630 7898* **Map** *2 D3*

Oliver does a roaring trade simply by being on one of the most popular tourist routes in Tallinn. It is a pleasant-looking, if unremarkable, cellar restaurant which offers a good selection of grilled dishes, from Cajun ribs to steak tartare, along with a couple of vegetarian dishes.

Troika €€€€

Raekoja plats 15, 10146 **Tel** *627 6245* **Map** *1 C2*

One of Tallinn's best Russian restaurants, Troika occupies a great spot on Town Hall Square. The beautiful vaulted interior creates an atmospheric fusion of medieval Tallinn and Slavic exuberance. The somewhat pricey menu offers the usual Russian classics with some exotic additons, such as bear stroganoff.

Balthasar €€€€€

Raekoja plats 11, 10146 **Tel** *627 6400* **Map** *1 C2*

With superb views and a supremely elegant interior, Balthasar's speciality is an outstanding garlic-themed menu. The restaurant is named after Balthasar Russow, who wrote *Chronicle of Livonia* on the premises. Even some desserts contain garlic, but garlic-free dishes are also available.

Bocca €€€€

Olevimägi 9, 10123 **Tel** *641 2610* **Map** *1 C2*

Sleek and minimalist, Bocca is a favourite with Tallinn's in-crowd. The suitably stylish menu includes some excellent pastas and fillets, along with delicacies such as vineyard snails with Fontina and Gorgonzola sauce and rabbit ravioli in mushroom sauce. The lighting is wonderfully atmospheric.

Dominic €€€€€

Vene 10, 10123 **Tel** *641 0400* **Map** *2 D2*

Combining a café with an Italian-inspired menu, a restaurant with a French menu and a cosy little wine cellar, Dominic is a stylish establishment with exceptionally good food. The historic and tastefully converted building dates back to the 14th century.

Egoist €€€€€

Vene 33, 10123 **Tel** *646 4052* **Map** *2 D2*

Unashamedly opulent, Egoist specializes in old-fashioned haute cuisine in an aristocratic salon-style interior. Choose from favourites such as lobster carpaccio or pan-fried foie gras, or try something from the new menu of Estonian dishes. The *kama* (yoghurt made from four grains and sour cherries) is exquisite.

Fish & Wine €€€€€

Harju 1, 10146 **Tel** *662 3013* **Map** *1 C3*

Fish & Wine is an ultra-hip restaurant for good reason. Its suberb menu is one of the most innovative in the area and changes regularly. Set in a three-storey building facing Niguliste Church, it also enjoys a prime location. The extensive menu features imaginative fusion cuisine. The ground-floor bar is a great weekend hangout.

Gloria €€€€€

Müürivahe 2 **Tel** *640 6800* **Map** *3 C3*

Opened in 1937, Gloria has very stylish 1930s European interiors decked out with Art Nouveau originals and artifacts from the owner Dimitri Demjanov's private collection. The food is served by very attentive waiters and waitresses. Gloria also serves fantastic wine from its own cellar and Cuban cigars.

La Bonaparte €€€€€

Pikk 45, 10133 **Tel** *646 4444* **Map** *1 C2*

This highly esteemed French restaurant is set in a beautifully restored medieval merchant's house and has catered for French presidents. With dishes such as duck fillet with raspberry syrup and shark fillet with caramel-lime sauce, it is truly first-rate. The cellar offers more secluded dining.

Karl Friedrich
  €€€€€

Raekoja plats 5, 10146 **Tel** *627 2416* **Map** *1 C2*

Overlooking Town Hall Square, Karl Friedrich offers fantastic European cuisine in luxurious but refined surroundings. Its claim to fame is the culinary use of capsicums. The à la carte menu is served in four tastefully furnished rooms on the second floor, while there is a more casual lounge on the first floor and a cosy cellar pub as well.

Three Sisters Restaurant Bordoo
€€€€€

Pikk 71/Tolli 2, 10133 **Tel** *630 6300* **Map** *1 C2*

One of the most luxurious restaurants in Tallinn, Three Sisters simply oozes luxury. The food is excellent and can be enjoyed on the terrace or in the charming courtyard in summer. The private Angels Room has an 18th-century ceiling fresco, while the wine cellar stores over 300 wines.

WESTERN ESTONIA

HAAPSALU Blu Holm
€€

Sadama 9/11, 90502 **Tel** *472 4406* **Road Map** *C2*

Among the highlights of the elegant and spacious Blu Holm are its outstanding service and sleek interior. The excellent fish dishes are subtly enhanced by the wonderful view of the sea. Folk music and dance performances are a regular feature of the restaurant.

HAAPSALU Central
€€

Karja 21, 90502 **Tel** *473 5595* **Road Map** *C2*

Housed in a big 19th-century wooden building, this restaurant has a great view of the local castle and serves traditional Estonian food. Colourful murals enrich the overall historic ambience. The cosy beer cellar is charmingly furnished and makes a good place for a family dinner, so a quiet evening cannot be guaranteed.

HAAPSALU Restaurant Bergfeldt
  €€

Ranna tee 2, 90403 **Tel** *472 4606* **Road Map** *C2*

With its excellent facilities and seaviews, Restaurant Bergfeldt is an attractive dining option. The menu is a collection of international dishes including some Estonian fare. The Panoramic Hall offers exceptional views of the town, and the outdoor Terrace Café is a pleasant option in summer.

HAAPSALU Haapsalu Kuursaal
€€€

Promenaadi 1, 90502 **Tel** *475 7500* **Road Map** *C2*

Housed in a beautiful late-19th-century wooden building, Haapsalu Kuursaal is one of the best and most popular restaurants in Haapsalu. The excellent food is largely thanks to the efforts of the young and eager-to-please chefs from a local vocational college. The place offers great views and atmosphere.

HIIUMAA ISLAND Liilia Hotel Restaurant
€€

Hiiu mnt 22, Käia, 92101 **Tel** *463 6146* **Road Map** *C2*

This restaurant, a part of the Liilia Hotel *(see p295)* and situated adjacent to Pullu Pub, has a friendly atmosphere. The fare includes plenty of local meat and fish dishes that have been specially created to suit a variety of tastes. Pork steak with banana and apple, locally caught fish, and a few vegetarian options are included.

HIIUMAA ISLAND Vetsi Tall
€€

Kassari, 92111 **Tel** *462 2550* **Road Map** *C2*

Vetsi Tall is located in the tastefully renovated stable of Kassari manor and resembles an old-style inn. There is an enticing range of traditional Estonian meals, including smoked fish, as well as many more European-style dishes. The atmospheric Gentry Room has a lovely fireplace.

KIHNU ISLAND Kurase Keskus Café
€

Sääre village, 88005 **Tel** *525 5172* **Road Map** *C2*

The only eatery in Kihnu Island, this humble café serves a surprisingly decent fare. It offers a number of local specialities, including the island's famed fish dishes. It's open only in summer. Ask about the open-air dining room where local fish is served.

MATSALU NATIONAL PARK Amanda Puhvet
€€

Üdruma village, 90701 **Tel** *5563 2853* **Road Map** *C2*

Amanda Puhvet is a lovely little out-of-the-way place located en route to Saaremaa and Matsalu National Park. A large wooden bird-watching tower right outside makes it hard to miss. The filling fare includes hearty soups, decent main courses and special dishes for children.

MATSALU NATIONAL PARK Roosta Holiday Village Restaurant
€€

Tuksi, 91202 **Tel** *472 5190* **Road Map** *C2*

Part of a lovely ensemble of vacation cottages in the northwest of the country, this restaurant has a good mixture of Estonian and international dishes. There is a sizeable breakfast buffet each morning for guests and a restful summer terrace with delightful views.

MUHU ISLAND Muhu Restaurant

Liiva village, 94701 **Tel** *459 8160*   **Road Map** *C2*

Situated in the heart of the island, Muhu Restaurant is a charming, friendly place. The walls are lined with traditional blankets along with other local paraphernalia. The eclectic menu is prepared with local produce and includes ostrich meat which comes from a nearby farm. Open only in summer.

MUHU ISLAND Alexander – Pädaste Manor Restaurant

Pädaste manor, 94702 **Tel** *454 8800*   **Road Map** *C2*

This restaurant is part of the top-quality Pädaste Manor hotel *(see p295)*, a converted manor house by the sea. The menu is surprisingly innovative, with some outstanding fish dishes. The chef prefers to use local produce and many herbs and vegetables are grown in the manor's grounds.

PALDISKI Valge Laev

Rae 38 **Tel** *604 5039*   **Road Map** *C1*

Valge Laev has been Paldiski's only restaurant for some time. The maritime-themed interior is rather charming, although the food is standard Estonian pub fare. However, it is very filling and suits the somewhat surreal surroundings of the town.

PALDISKI Laulasmaa Resort Restaurant

Puhkekodu 4, 76702 **Tel** *687 0870*   **Road Map** *C1*

This restaurant has a pleasant ambience, with herbs used to adorn the tables. The menu is not extensive but the food is good quality and includes some wonderful dishes, such as the pork fillet with grilled garden vegetables, or cottage cheesecake with berries.

PÄRNU Must Pärl

Supluse 22, 80042 **Tel** *442 6902*   **Road Map** *D2*

This marine-themed restaurant has wave-like walls and a shell-shaped stage for weekend dance performances. The food is fairly standard although the reasonable prices and pleasant atmosphere make Must Pärl a worthwhile place to visit. It has a good outdoor terrace.

PÄRNU Pärnu Kuursaal

Mere pst 22, 80010 **Tel** *442 0368*   **Road Map** *D2*

This lively and popular place is set in an attractive late 19th-century seafront building. The tavern's menu has something for most tastes. The main courses are stodgy but satisfying and include meat dishes and local favourites such as herring and sour cream, grilled sausage and perch in beer pastry.

PÄRNU Postipoiss

Vee 12, 80011 **Tel** *446 4864*   **Road Map** *D2*

A Russian restaurant that offers an authentic taste of Russia, with everything from *blini* (pancakes) and *pelmeni* (dumplings) to *solianka* (Russian beef soup) on the menu. There is also a pretty decent home-made beer to wash it all down. Despite the quaint rustic interior, weekend nights are usually very lively.

PÄRNU Cafe Grand

Kuninga 25, 80014 **Tel** *444 3412*   **Road Map** *D2*

This classy restaurant gives a glimpse of what Pärnu high society looked like in the 1920s, at the peak of the Estonian national awakening. Bow-tied waiting staff serve German-influenced specialities. Etiquette classes are available for those who want to match their behaviour to the decor.

PÄRNU Restaurant Strand

Tammsaare pst 35, 80010 **Tel** *447 5370*   **Road Map** *D2*

This sleek, modern restaurant has some extremely good dishes on offer, although the menu is not exactly huge. Try rounding off one of the excellent main courses with the intriguing roasted Camembert and cloudberry jam for dessert. The hotel complex also includes a popular nightclub.

PÄRNU Seegi Maja

Hospidali 1, 80011 **Tel** *443 0550*   **Road Map** *D2*

In spite of its unreliable doorways and rafters, this beautifully restored Old Town house is one of the most charming and atmospheric restaurants in Pärnu. Good, medieval-themed food is served in generous portions on earthenware dishes. The place also offers fantastic home-made beer.

PÄRNU Ammende Villa

Mere pst 7, 80010 **Tel** *447 3888*   **Road Map** *D2*

Ammnede Villa offers luxury dining that perfectly suits the opulent Art Nouveau surroundings. Exquisite French and Mediterranean food is served up in three halls with immaculate attention to detail. The sea breeze-swept summer terrace looks out over pleasant residential surroundings.

SAAREMAA ISLAND Kaali Tavern

Kaali Meteorite Crater, 94102 **Tel** *459 1182*   **Road Map** *C2*

Located very close to the Kaali meteor impact site, Kaali Tavern is a perfect resting place after a long day's sight-seeing. The tavern is housed in a creamery, and embellished with locally-made limestone and metalwork decorative elements. The place offers decent food in very pleasant surroundings. Open only in summer.

Key to Price Guide *see p322* **Key to Symbols** *see back cover flap*

SAAREMAA ISLAND Restoran Vaekoda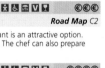

Tallinna mnt 3, 93811 **Tel** *453 3020*   **Road Map** *C2*

Housed in a 17th-century building known as the Weigh House, in the centre of the Old Town, Vaekoda Pub is a popular place with locals and tourists. The food is much above average for a pub while the amiable atmosphere makes for a lively and fun evening.

SAAREMAA ISLAND Suur Töll Tavern

Lilbi, 93826 **Tel** *454 5404*   **Road Map** *C2*

The tavern's decor is inspired by the folklore about the friendly giant of Saaremaa, Suur Töll, and his wife Piret. Suur Töll Tavern is part of a charming holiday village just 3 km (2 miles) from Kuressaare. The place serves a variety of hearty Estonian fare and has a special menu for children.

SAAREMAA ISLAND Grand Rose Spa Hotel

Tallinna 15, 93811 **Tel** *666 7000*   **Road Map** *C2*

This cosy cellar restaurant is one of the best places in town. Its arched brick ceiling and partitioned rooms provide an intimate setting, while the medieval-style feel to the place creates an interesting atmosphere. The excellent menu includes a few local Saaremaa specialities.

SAAREMAA ISLAND Hotel Saaremaa Restaurant

Mändjala, 93822 **Tel** *454 4100*   **Road Map** *C2*

With its idyllic location overlooking Mändjala beach and excellent cuisine, this restaurant is an attractive option. The food ranges from gourmet-style Estonian cuisine to health food-style minimalism. The chef can also prepare a special evening picnic package for the beach.

SAAREMAA ISLAND Georg Ots Spa Restaurant

Tori 2, 93815 **Tel** *455 0000*   **Road Map** *C2*

This restaurant offers wonderfully inventive cuisine that strikes a perfect balance between health and sumptuousness. There is also a range of rich pasta dishes for those unconcerned with counting calories. The open-air terrace has a great view of the bay during the summer season.

VORMSI ISLAND Krog No 14

Hullo, 91301 **Tel** *4724 330*   **Road Map** *C2*

Located in a Swedish-style wooden house that is so characteristic of Vormsi Island, Krog No 14 is a friendly family-run place that serves authentic Estonian home-cooked food. Large groups should book in advance. There is also a very cosy bar which stays open until midnight at weekends.

EASTERN ESTONIA

KUREMÄE Wironia Pub

Rakvere 7, 41531 **Tel** *336 4202*   **Road Map** *E1*

This cheery place is ideal for a meal after a long day of sightseeing. The food is fairly typical of Estonian pub fare and includes meat, fish and salad. There are some good main courses such as schnitzel, meat-and-spuds, pancakes and other hearty local favourites. There is a nice little pub with cosy wooden benches and pool tables next door.

LAHEMAA NATIONAL PARK Kaminasaal

Rakvere tee 13, Võsu, 45501 **Tel** *5648 2286*   **Road Map** *D1*

Situated in one of the most beautiful parts of Lahemaa, this is a lovely little restaurant. The rustic interior is the main attraction, although the food strikes a perfectly decent balance between local and European tastes. There are outdoor tables in summer and an open fire in winter. Bookings in advance only.

LAHEMAA NATIONAL PARK Lahemaa Kohvikann

Palmse village, 45405 **Tel** *323 4148*   **Road Map** *D1*

Run by a friendly German-Russian couple, this simple, cheery restaurant near the Lahemaa National Park has an outdoor deck and serves hearty German-influenced dishes with tasty sauces and sides. The large variety of options, such as fish, grilled meats, pastas and burgers, should please just about anyone.

LAHEMAA NATIONAL PARK Sagadi Manor Restaurant

Sagadi village, Sagadi, 45402 **Tel** *676 7888*   **Road Map** *D2*

With its splendid interior and beautiful surroundings, the Sagadi Manor Restaurant is an immensely enjoyable experience. The menu includes specialities made with local game and fowl, as well as the famous Sagadi carrot cake. The first-floor terrace has magnificent views in summer.

LAHEMAA NATIONAL PARK Viitna Kõrts

Viitna, 45202 **Tel** *520 9156*   **Road Map** *D1*

Located along the Tallinn-Narva motorway, and by a main entry road to the centre of Lahemaa, this old-style tavern is a popular resting place for travellers. The food consists mainly of variations on potato, meat and fish dishes, but it is well made, filling and tastes great in the atmospheric surroundings.

NARVA 100% China

Tallinn mnt 6b, 20304 **Tel** *357 5099*

Road Map *E1*

One of the best restaurants in Narva, this pleasant little place boasts the only Chinese chef in the region, ensuring that the food is more or less authentic. The extensive menu includes many vegetarian options, something of a rarity in strictly non-vegetarian Estonia.

NARVA German Pub

Puškini 10, 20308 **Tel** *359 1548*

Road Map *E1*

A popular place with locals, German Pub offers hearty Estonian-style food in a relaxed environment. The rustic-looking cellar has a somewhat incongruous gallery of boxing photographs on proud display. It becomes a boisterous pub late at night.

NARVA Petchki Lavochki

Tallinna mnt 19, Narva, 21006 **Tel** *357 9333*

Road Map *E1*

This is a restaurant attached to Café Geneva, a popular nightspot in the Geneva entertainment complex. The food is mostly Russian fare, such as cabbage soup, pelmeni, pickled foods and blini pancakes. From 3pm to 4pm during the week, there is a 20 per cent happy hour discount.

NARVA Salvadore

Puškini 28, 20306 **Tel** *688 1105*

Road Map *E1*

The centrally located Salvadore is a safe bet for a good meal that is a decent blend of Estonian and European dishes. The home-made pasta and risotto are worth trying. There is also a children's menu featuring the Matroskin Cat Sandwich, named after a famous Russian cartoon. The sandwich consists of rye bread, ham and butter.

ONTIKA COAST Mio Mare

Ranna 12, Toila, 41702 **Tel** *334 2915*

Road Map *E1*

Part of the Toila Spa Hotel *(see p298)*, Mio Mare is a low-key restaurant that has a fantastic menu. The main courses mostly feature exquisitely prepared meat and fish dishes. At weekends, the restaurant remains open till late, with accordion music and local bands.

OTEPÄÄ Karupesa Hotel Restaurant

Tehvandi 1a, 67406 **Tel** *766 1500*

Road Map *E2*

A pleasant little place with romantic lighting and cosy tables. The food is mostly meat-based, though there is also a set vegetarian menu. The restaurant has a bar with billiard tables, as well as a tennis court outside which is turned into an ice-skating rink during winter.

PAIDE Paide Restoran

Keskväljak 15, 72711 **Tel** *5698 8777*

Road Map *D2*

Given the paucity of dining options in a parochial town like Paide, this restaurant is a decent place for a good meal. Situated in the town centre, it is a cheery little eatery that serves up a menu of typical small-town fare, largely including generous portions of meat, fish and salad.

PÕLTSAMAA Rivaal

Veski 1, 48106 **Tel** *776 2620*

Road Map *D2*

A lovely little riverside restaurant in the middle of town, Rivaal has a good range of Estonian-style dishes on offer. Large groups can be catered for. The nearby castle has a famous wine-tasting cellar and there is also a charming rose island a short walk away.

PÕLVA Pesa Hotel Restaurant

Uus 5, 63308 **Tel** *799 8530*

Road Map *E2*

About as good a place to eat as you will find in a provincial Estonian town. Unusually, the menu includes some decent vegetarian choices as well as generic Estonian and European dishes. The Sun Terrace is a pleasant place to eat, while the cosy pub stays open until late.

PÕLVA Põlva Restaurant

Kesk 10, 63308 **Tel** *799 9037*

Road Map *E2*

This establishment in the centre of town consists of a bistro, restaurant and bar. The interior is curiously charmless and the food is typical of a small town, though the menu is extensive enough for even the most fastidious visitor to find something to suit his or her liking.

RAKVERE Katariina Kelder

Pikk 3, 44307 **Tel** *322 3943*

Road Map *D1*

This restro-bar is located on the oldest street in Rakvere and is one of the best places in town for a satisfying meal. The food is more imaginative than local pub fare, and usually consists of a piece of meat with a small serving of salad. The nearby castle ruins provide a good way of walking off dinner.

SETUMAA Hirve Café

Silla 4, Värska, 64001 **Tel** *797 6105*

Road Map *E2*

Located in a holiday centre, Hirve Café mostly attracts visitors to the Setu Farm Museum. The menu is typical rural Estonian food with plenty of soup, potatoes and roasts. A range of sandwiches and other snacks makes it a good place for a quick bite.

Key to Price Guide *see p322* **Key to Symbols** *see back cover flap*

SILLAMÄE Krunk €€

Kesk 23, 40231 **Tel** *392 9030* **Road Map** *E1*

This Soviet-era hotel restaurant *(see p299)* has a strangely elegant and refined air about it. The food is the best in town, dressing up the usual meat and fish dishes with at least a veneer of style. Popular international dishes are served with fries. Live music at weekends adds to the ambience.

SUUR MUNAMÄGI Suur Munamägi Tower Café €

Haanja Village, 65101 **Tel** *525 1364* **Road Map** *E2*

It is definitely worth visiting this renovated glass-fronted café for a refreshing cold drink or cup of coffee simply because it is the highest point in the Baltic States and offers a truly breathtaking view. The place mainly serves basic refreshments. Remains open till 8pm during the summer.

SUUR MUNAMÄGI Café Suur Muna €€

Haanja village, 65101 **Tel** *786 6000* **Road Map** *E2*

Café Suur Muna is a pleasant rural café with a small but decent menu. Its idyllic surroundings can be admired from the lovely wooden terrace. Taking inspiration from the name of the area, Suur Munamägi (Big Egg Hill), the menu of this café features several egg dishes.

TARTU Eduard Vilde Lokaal €€

Vallikraavi 4, 30103 **Tel** *734 3400* **Road Map** *E2*

A typical Irish-style pub, although much brighter than usual, Eduard Vilde Lokaal has big windows and light coloured walls. The huge menu at this cheerful eatery includes Irish-themed dishes such as beef and Guinness pie as well as burgers and curries.

TARTU Kalinka €€

Ülikooli 10, 51003 **Tel** *730 5997* **Road Map** *E2*

With dishes such as pork neck baked with apples and a signature dessert of whipped cream and jam mousse, Kalinka offers a taste of authentic Russian cuisine in an intimate, tavern-style environment. All the staple Russian classics are there as well. The enclosed courtyard is a great spot to eat in during the summer.

TARTU Tsink Plekk Pang €€

Küütri 6, 51007 **Tel** *730 3415* **Road Map** *E2*

This excellent Old Town restaurant-cum-bar is spread out over four floors and has a relaxed and enjoyable atmosphere. The Asian-themed menu includes a choice of Chinese food, sushi and a few Indian dishes. A great place to come for a drink too.

TARTU Atlantis €€€

Narva mnt 2, 51009 **Tel** *738 5495* **Road Map** *E2*

Atlantis occupies a glass-fronted building overlooking the Emajõgi river and forms part of a complex that includes a popular nightclub. The restaurant itself is bright, comfortable and elegantly furnished. The eclectic menu features some excellent fish dishes. The panoramic view of Tartu is another bonus.

TARTU La Dolce Vita €€€

Kompanii 10, 51007 **Tel** *740 7545* **Road Map** *E2*

This likeable little restaurant has an enormous selection of salads, pizzas and main courses. The pizzas are baked in the only wooden oven in Tartu, while the delightful interior is reminiscent of a genuine trattoria. The outdoor terrace looks out over a lovely park.

VILJANDI Hotel Centrum Restaurant €€

Tallinna 24, 71008 **Tel** *435 1140* **Road Map** *D2*

The restaurant at Hotel Centrum *(see p299)* offers great views of Viljandi's main street from its fourth-floor vantage point. It is a modern and comfortable place to eat in, with a menu that is arguably the best in town. It also has a better-than-average wine list for the provinces.

VILJANDI Suur Vend Pub €€

Turu 4, 71003 **Tel** *433 3644* **Road Map** *D2*

A friendly and welcoming pub with an eclectic and suprisingly good menu that offers everything from breaded broccoli to wok-fried pork and chicken. There is regular live music and even a cosy sauna which can be booked by the hour, on the premises.

VÕRU Õlle 17 €€

Jüri 17, 65609 **Tel** *785 8588* **Road Map** *E2*

Õlle 17 is the only Irish-style pub in Võru. The friendly, relaxing environment includes a lounge area and a comfortable separate room for smokers. There is a range of fresh-tasting, well-made pub food, including meat and salads, along with an unusually large selection of beers, including Guinness.

VÕRU Ränduri Pub €€

Jüri 36, 65603 **Tel** *786 8050* **Road Map** *E2*

Ränduri Pub is situated on a main road running through the centre of town. With its traditional-looking wood and brick interior, it is a comfortable spot and has a decent range of Estonian pub-style food, including meat and fish dishes and salads at good prices. Plenty of parking space is available.

Choosing a Restaurant in Latvia

These restaurants have been selected for their food, good value and location. They are listed by region, starting with Rīga, followed by the rest of Latvia. Under each town or area, hotels are listed alphabetically within each price category. For Rīga map references, see pages 160–61; for road map references see the back cover.

PRICE DETAILS
The following price ranges are based on the cost of a meal for two, including service tax but excluding alcoholic drinks.
Ⓛ Under 10 Ls
ⓁⓁ 10–15 Ls
ⓁⓁⓁ 15–20 Ls
ⓁⓁⓁⓁ 20–25 Ls
ⓁⓁⓁⓁⓁ Over 25 Ls

RĪGA

Alus Sēta   ⓁⓁ
Tirgoņu iela 6, LV-1050 **Tel** *6722 2431*   **Map** 1 C4

The most central branch of the popular LIDO chain of self-service Latvian restaurants, Alus Sēta serves authentic local cuisine in a farmhouse setting. Popular dishes include shashlik and grey peas, teamed with the restaurant's own brand of beer or tasty Užavas ale.

Citi Laiki   ⓁⓁ
Brīvības iela 41, LV-1010 **Tel** *6724 0592*   **Map** 2 F1

Housed in a wooden building dating from 1824, Citi Laiki offers Latvian dishes in a rustic environment complete with local antiques. Unlike many of the capital's Latvian restaurants, it is not owned by the LIDO group and has table service instead of a buffet. Traditional folk music performances are among the weekend highlights.

Dzirnavas   ⓁⓁ
Dzirnavu iela 74/76, LV-1050 **Tel** *6728 4228*   **Map** 2 E4

Popular for offering Latvian cuisine at reasonable rates, Dzirnavas is one of several LIDO restaurants in the capital. The buffet spread is lavish, with plenty of salad options as well as favourites such as shashlik. The decor has a medieval feel, with exposed brickwork and torches hanging from the walls.

Fazenda   ⓁⓁ
Baznīcas iela 14, LV-1010 **Tel** *6724 0809*   **Map** 2 E2

An old wooden building in the Central District is home to this cute restaurant and bakery. The interior looks like Grandmother's country house, complete with floral wallpaper, antique furniture and brick stoves. The menu features simple but fresh international dishes with a Latvian flavour. Breakfast is served until 2pm on weekends.

LIDO Atpūtas Centrs   ⓁⓁ
Krasta iela 76, LV-1019 **Tel** *6750 4420*   **Map** 2 D5

Part of the LIDO chain of recreation centres, this massive log cabin with an amusement park, ice-skating rink and live folk music performances is a tourist attraction in its own right. The buffet boasts over 500 items, including many traditional Latvian dishes. There is also a sit-down restaurant and a large beer hall.

Osīriss   ⓁⓁ
Krišjānis Barona iela 31, LV-1011 **Tel** *6724 3002*   **Map** 2 E3

A sophisticated and atmospheric café with an excellent international spread, Osīris has a predominantly artistic clientele and hosts regular art exhibitions. The fireplace and foreign newspapers help to make it a cosy hangout, and the classical music playing in the background adds to the ambience. Reservations are recommended for dinner.

Vērmanītis   ⓁⓁ
Elizabetes iela 65, LV-1050 **Tel** *6728 6289*   **Map** 2 D2

Located on the edge of Vērmanes Garden, this branch of the ubiquitous LIDO chain of restaurants is decorated like a farmhouse with staff dressed in traditional Latvian costumes. Self-service Latvian staples, such as meat, potatoes, rice and salads, are available at reasonable prices. Pizzas and other fast food are available in the cellar.

Aragats   ⓁⓁⓁ
Miera iela 15, LV-1001 **Tel** *6737 3445*   **Map** 2 F1

Specializing in authentic Armenian dishes, this Caucasian restaurant has a homely ambience with very friendly staff. Favourites include shashlik and *hashlama* (mutton and vegetable soup), as well as a range of wines from the region. Sweet coffee completes this traditional meal.

Dada   ⓁⓁⓁ
Kalēju iela 30, LV-1050 **Tel** *6710 4433*   **Map** 2 D4

Taking its name from an avant-garde artistic movement, Dada displays a playful irreverence in its decor, mismatched cutlery and staff uniform. Most people come here for its Mongolian Barbecue section, where visitors can pick from a selection of meat, seafood, vegetables, noodles and sauces which the chef will stir-fry.

Key to Symbols *see back cover flap*

Kitchen

Maskavas iela 12–1, LV-1063 **Tel** *2027 2827* **Map** *2 D5*

With its location in the red-brick warehouses next to the Central Market, you can be sure the food in this vibrant restaurant is fresh. The menu changes regularly, as the chefs take their inspiration from the seasonal produce sold nearby. For a dose of modern Latvian art, pop into the adjoining KIM? Contemporary Art Centre. Closed Sundays.

Raw Garden

Skolas iela 12, LV-1010 **Tel** *2778 0489* **Map** *2 E2*

This is Rīga's first and only raw-food restaurant, although it actually serves a mix of raw and cooked dishes. The focus is on vegan, seasonal, foraged and local produce. The brightly coloured interior will put you in a good mood, while the smoothies will keep your body happy.

3 Pavāri

Torņa iela 4, LV-1050 **Tel** *2037 0537* **Map** *1 C3*

The brainchild of the eponymous "three chefs", who are among the country's most promising, 3 Pavāri is one of the more exciting dining experiences in the city. The friendly chefs offer up a modern take on seasonal Latvian dishes using modern cooking technology, *sous vide* cooking and a bit of liquid nitrogen.

Biscuit

A Pumpura iela 3, LV-1010 **Tel** *6779 9222* **Map** *2 D2*

Elegance abounds at this upmarket restaurant in the Quiet Centre. While Italian cuisine is the order of the day, there is a Russian flavour to the place, since the head chef and interior designer were recruited from Moscow. Fresh Mediterranean seafood and Angus steaks are the highlights on an eclectic menu.

Democratic Wine Bar Garage

Elizabetes iela 83/85 (Berga Bazaars), LV-1050 **Tel** *2662 8833* **Map** *2 E3*

The former garage of the Berga Bazaars is now a trendy wine bar, serving a Latvian interpretation of tapas, along with a great selection of Italian and Argentinian wines to accompany an international menu that changes daily. The friendly staff have a democratic, "never say no" policy, meaning the menu is flexible.

Honkonga

Valdemāra iela 61, LV-1050 **Tel** *6781 2292* **Map** *1 A3*

Among the better Chinese restaurants, Honkonga serves authentic spicy food instead of the bland options commonly available in Rīga. It is very atmospheric, with delightful decor and Chinese music creating a soothing background. A very popular place, it is especially busy during weekends.

Ķiploku Krogs

Jekaba 3/5, LV-1050 **Tel** *6721 1451* **Map** *1 C3*

Taking its name seriously, Ķiploku Krogs, which means "garlic bar", has garlic in almost every dish, including the ice cream. In fact, the menu labels the few dishes that do not contain the pungent ingredient. The results are less gimmicky than might be expected, with some very exciting choices.

Palete

Gleznotāju iela 12/14, LV-1050 **Tel** *6721 6037*

A favourite with both foreign visitors and local people, this cosy restaurant in the Vecrīga hotel *(see p301)* serves an eclectic international menu ranging from Cajun to Italian. There is something to suit most tastes, but seafood is a speciality. Paintings and an open fireplace in winter add to its old-world charm.

Alus Ordenis

Raiņa bulvāris 15, LV-1050 **Tel** *6781 4190* **Map** *2 D3*

This beer cellar serves rural Latvian dishes, with some unique treats such as *cuku pupas* (broad beans in butter sauce), bulls' testicles and boiled pigs' trotters. A wide range of locally brewed beer is also available. The food is authentic but more expensive than at similar Latvian restaurants.

Bellevue

Skolas iela 1, LV-1048 **Tel** *6706 9040* **Map** *2 E2*

An upmarket option on the left bank of the Daugava river, Bellevue sits on the 11th floor of the Maritim Park hotel *(see p302)* and offers a plush ambience and impressive views of the riverfront and Old Town. Specializing in European cuisine, the chef serves gourmet dishes to a well-heeled clientele.

Benjamiņs

Barona iela 12, V-1000 **Tel** *6707 9444* **Map** *2 E3*

Housed in an opulent 19th-century building, this elegant restaurant, in the Europa Royale hotel *(see p301)*, retains many of its original features, such as stained-glass windows and parquet floors. The menu offers international dishes, complemented by an extensive wine list which includes some sought-after vintages.

Bergs

Elizabetes iela 83/85, LV-1050 **Tel** *6777 0957* **Map** *2 D2*

Located in the Bergs boutique hotel *(see p302)*, this restaurant is among Rīga's classiest dining venues. Overseen by one of the city's most esteemed chefs, Kaspars Jansons, the food here is good and the service attentive. Its eclectic menu highlights modern European and fusion cuisine, served in an intimate setting.

Bon Vivant

Mārstaļu iela 8, LV-1050 **Tel** *6722 6585*

Map *2 D4*

The decor of this Belgian restaurant resembles a 1930s brasserie. Bon Vivant is a cosy place to tuck into steamed mussels and fries or sausages sold by the half-metre. The food here is accompanied by a decent selection of beers, each served in its own special glass.

Da Sergio

Tērbatas iela 65, LV-1001 **Tel** *6731 2777*

Map *2 E3*

The chefs at Da Sergio, considered one of the best Italian restaurants in the city, make their pizzas in a wood-fired oven. There is also an extensive menu of authentic pasta and seafood dishes. The Mediterranean atmosphere here is maintained by a strictly Italian music policy, with a wine list to match.

Fish Restaurant Le Dome

Miesnieku iela 4, LV-1050 **Tel** *6755 9884*

Map *1 C3*

Voted the best fish restaurant in the Baltics (*Baltic Times*, 2011), this is an intimate space on a quiet street in the Old Town. Part of the Dome Hotel and Spa (*see p302*), the restaurant specializes in freshly caught Baltic fish and locally grown produce. The fish soup is a must.

Gastronome

Brīvības iela 31, LV-1000 **Tel** *6777 2391*

Map *2 F1*

Despite the rapid development of restaurants in Rīga over the past years, seafood options are scarce, making this combined shop and restaurant a welcome addition. Situated in the Radisson Blu Hotel Latvija (*see p302*), Gastronome's open kitchen serves delectable grilled fish and oyster dishes, as well as freshly baked pastries and pies.

Indian Raja

Skarņu 7, LV-1050 **Tel** *6722 3240*

Map *2 D2*

While many of Latvia's Asian restaurants cater to local tastes by toning down their dishes, Sue's Indian Raja serves authentic cuisine from around the subcontinent. As a result, it is arguably more popular with expatriates than locals, and consistently wins plaudits from critics and visitors. Chicken tikka masala is the chef's speciality.

La Boheme

Alunana iela 2a, LV-1010 **Tel** *6732 1938*

Map *1 C4*

As it is situated opposite the British Embassy, it is appropriate that Angus beef is one of the star dishes here, although the menu is fully international. Unusual vegetables which feature include Jerusalem artichokes. In addition, there is a generous use of alcohol in many dishes.

Lidojošā Varde

Elizabetes 31a, LV-1010 **Tel** *6732 1184*

Map *2 D2*

One of Rīga's oldest expatriate hangouts, Lidojošā Varde, which means "flying frog", is so named because of the frog decorations in all its three cellar rooms. It is especially popular with staff from the nearby embassies. The straightforward menu comprises burgers, ribs, salads and pasta.

Melnie Mūki

Jāņa sēta 1, LV-1050 **Tel** *6721 5006*

Map *2 D2*

Housed in a former cloister, with a chef who worked for a former Latvian president, Melnie Mūki (Black Monks) is renowned for its eclectic menu, available at surprisingly reasonable prices. The service is attentive and the atmosphere is relatively formal. It is wise to reserve in advance, as it is popular among local diners.

Nieburgs

Jauniela iela 25–27, LV-1050 **Tel** *6711 5522*

Map *1 C4*

The spacious white interior, with ample glass and modern lighting, contrasts with the elaborate Art Nouveau exterior and gives a Scandinavian feel to the decor. The menu is largely Latvian. Although the style and environment is definitely Old Town, prices are pleasantly suburban.

Ostas Skati

Matrou iela 15, LV-1048 **Tel** *2669 3693*

Map *1 C4*

As Kipsalu Island becomes more gentrified, suitably expensive restaurants have started opening. Arrive at this restaurant by boat in summer, or walk across the ice in the winter, for grills of a wide variety of fish or meat. Heat lamps mean that the terrace is open in spring and autumn as well as summer.

Rozengrāls

Rozena 1, LV-1050 **Tel** *6722 0356*

Map *1 C4*

Among the few restaurants in the city that still prepare food from old recipes, Rozengrāls attracts attention for the late 13th-century cellar it inhabits. Today, traditionally dressed staff serve strictly medieval fare. Venison soup, perch stuffed with prunes and oven-baked veal in sea-buckthorn sauce are some of the house specialities.

Vincent's

Elizabetes iela 19, LV-1000 **Tel** *6733 2634*

Map *2 D2*

With celebrity chef Mārtiņš Rītiņš at the helm, Vincent's has been a staple of Rīga's restaurant scene since it opened in 1994 and continues to attract most of the foreign dignitaries and celebrities who pass through the city. Adventurous international dishes are offered alongside a menu of classy versions of traditional Latvian fare.

Key to Price Guide *see p330* **Key to Symbols** *see back cover flap*

WESTERN LATVIA

DUNDAGA Jūras Sapņi
🚶 🎵 🚗 Ⓥ ⒼⒼ

*Vīdāles iela 2, LV-3270 **Tel** 2946 2622* **Road Map** *C3*

There are few dining options in Dundaga, and Jūras Sapņi is one of the best. The decor has a seaside theme, with palm trees, a large mural and a grotto in one corner. The food covers the standard Latvian fare of pork, chicken and potatoes. There is also a separate children's menu.

ENGURE Cope
♿ 🎵 🚗 ⒼⒼ

*Ricteļu dzirnavas, LV-3113 **Tel** 2244 0094* **Road Map** *C3*

This wooden guest house next to Ridelļi Watermill includes a pleasant café, making it a convenient stop for visitors en route to Lake Engure. The flour which is still produced at the mill is used in several dishes on the menu, including the delicious pancakes. Boats can be hired here for a cruise along the lake.

JAUNMOKU PILS Liepaleja
🚶 🎵 🚗 Ⓥ ⒼⒼⒼ

*Tume, LV-3139 **Tel** 6310 7125*

Housed in Jaunmoku Pils *(see p303)*, Huberts is decorated with hunting trophies. The kitchen specializes in game and wildfowl and the menu has signature dishes such as "Potato Pancakes to the Taste of the Major-domo's Wife". Children's dishes are served in animal shapes.

JELGAVA La Tour de Marie
♿ Ⓥ 🍷 ⒼⒼⒼⒼ

*Akademijas iela 1, LV-3001 **Tel** 6308 1392* **Road Map** *C4*

On the seventh floor of the Holy Trinity Church tower, the only part that remains, is the city's finest restaurant. Bare brick walls and windows in the clock faces add to the atmosphere, and the view is one of the best you'll find while dining in Latvia. The menu mixes French and Latvian cuisine; the beef fillet in mango sauce is a highlight.

JŪRMALA Aquarius
♿ 🚗 🍷 ⒼⒼⒼⒼⒼ

*33 Bulduru prospekts, Bulduri, LV-2010 **Tel** 6775 1071* **Road Map** *C3*

A surprisingly stylish dining option, slightly off the tourist trail in Bulduri, Aquarius derives its name from the fish tank behind the bar. The menu is an assortment of adventurous Asian and European dishes. The excellent food is complemented by music and chic decor. The extended wine list also has half-bottle options.

JŪRMALA MaMa
♿ 🚗 Ⓥ 🍷 ⒼⒼⒼⒼⒼ

*Tirgoņu iela 22, LV-2015 **Tel** 6776 1271* **Road Map** *C3*

Just off the main pedestrain street of Majori, this restaurant in the Boutique Hotel MaMa has twice been voted the best hotel restaurant in Jūrmala. The eclectic interior and Mediterreanean menu combine to create one of the best dining experiences in the city. There is also a special menu for your pets. Closed Mon & Tue Oct–Apr.

JŪRMALA Pegasa Pils
🎵 🚗 Ⓥ ⒼⒼⒼⒼⒼ

*Jūras iela 60, Majori, LV-2015 **Tel** 2923 6425* **Road Map** *C3*

Housed in a restored wooden Art Nouveau building with a distinctive corner tower, this restaurant close to the Dzintari concert hall is one of the best choices in Majori. Food is international fare with many fish dishes, as well as pasta options. There is live music on weekend evenings.

JŪRMALA Villa Joma
🚶 ♿ 🚗 ⒼⒼⒼⒼⒼ

*Jomas iela 90, LV-2015 **Tel** 6777 1999* **Road Map** *C3*

This pastel-coloured restaurant is bright and airy and considered among the best eateries in Jūrmala. The menu is helpfully displayed outside the restaurant and includes international favourites that change according to the season. In addition to the wine list, cocktails are also served at the bar.

KOLKA Mazkrūziņi
📋 🚗 Ⓖ

*Kolkas rags, LV-3275 **Tel** 2917 4944* **Road Map** *C3*

This little eatery is the only option for food in Kolka. Situated at the cape, not in the village itself, the "Little Cup" café serves typical Latvian and fish dishes in plastic containers, to be enjoyed on the open terrace or at the nearby beach. The local fish stew is the speciality, cooked over an open fire. Only open in the summer season (May–Sep).

KULDĪGA Stenders Pica
🚶 ♿ 🎵 🚗 Ⓥ ⒼⒼⒼⒼ

*Sūvu 2, LV-3301 **Tel** 6332 3763* **Road Map** *B3*

Housed on the first floor of a former granary, Stenders offers an array of standard Latvian dishes and is very popular locally for its signature pancakes. The cosy open-air terrace makes an excellent spot for scenic views of the city, particularly appealing on a summer's day.

KULDĪGA Metropole
♿ 🚗 Ⓥ 🍷 ⒼⒼⒼⒼⒼ

*Baznīcas iela 11, LV-3301 **Tel** 6335 0588* **Road Map** *B3*

Housed in the Metropole hotel *(see p304)*, this restaurant is the most upmarket dining option in town. The menu comprises regular Latvian and international dishes, with fish and game sourced from farms in the region. The hotel's wine list is extensive, and the basement has a bar.

LIEPĀJA ČiLi Pica Jaunā

Jauna Ostmala 3–5, LV-3401 **Tel** *6340 7500*   **Road Map** *B4*

Although part of a Lithuanian chain, rapidly spreading throughout Latvia, this restaurant does Italy proud by producing fresh pizzas that have never seen a deep freeze or microwave. Fruit salads made out of fresh fruits, rather than tinned ingredients, are a further bonus.

LIEPĀJA Olīve

Klaipēdas iela 104c, LV-3401 **Tel** *2666 0935*   **Road Map** *B4*

Hidden away on the second floor of the Baata shopping centre, this modern restaurant centres around an open kitchen that serves up a wide range of fusion dishes. The design is as eclectic as the menu, featuring a jungle growing down from the ceiling and a large sculpture of a slumbering panther.

LIEPĀJA Libava

Vecā ostmala 29, LV-3401 **Tel** *6342 9714*   **Road Map** *B4*

Emphasizing local cuisine, the restaurant specializes in fish and seafood. The menu includes signature dishes such as fine fish broth and the local speciality *Liepājas menciņi* (cod). With white walls and red leather chairs, it is a pleasant place to dine.

LIEPĀJA Pastnieka Māja

Fr Brīvzemnieka 53, LV-3401 **Tel** *6340 7521*   **Road Map** *B4*

This brick and timber building is located in a quiet street close to the centre of town. The structure may be old, but the restaurant's decor is resolutely modern. The menu largely sticks to the Latvian standards and the drinks list includes several local beers. There is also a large terrace.

MEŽOTNE Mežotnes Pils

Mežotnes pagasts, LV-3918 **Tel** *6396 0711*   **Road Map** *D4*

This pleasant dining room in the Mežotnes Pils hotel *(see p304)* offers spectacular views of the palace grounds. The food is less grand than the surroundings might suggest. The modest menu comprises simple Latvian cuisine, including *escalope* (thin slivers of meat or fish), available at reasonable rates. It is best to book in advance.

NĪCA Nīcava

Nīcas pagasts, LV-3473 **Tel** *6348 6379*   **Road Map** *B4*

The restaurant is divided into a main dining room, with the entry from the Nīcava hotel *(see p304)* and a conservatory, with its entrance around the side of the building. The Latvian menu is the same in each and includes a selection of traditional dishes such as pork knuckle roasted and served with horseradish.

PĀVILOSTA Pub Āķagals

Dzintaru iela 3, LV-3466 **Tel** *2916 1533*   **Road Map** *B4*

The ornate wooden decor of this pub extends even to its quirky bar made from logs. Taking advantage of its proximity to the sea, the restaurant specializes in smoked and fresh fish dishes and also serves Latvian cuisine. There is an in-house sauna and a cosy fireplace for cold winter days.

PEDVĀLE Dāre

Pedvāles Brīvdabas Mākslas Muzejas, LV-3294 **Tel** *6325 2273*   **Road Map** *C4*

Only a short drive from Sabile and located close to the entrance to the Pedvāle Open-Air Museum, this café serves up a decent selection of Latvian favourites in a relaxed atmosphere. Art is sometimes exhibited inside the café. The pleasant outdoor terrace is a favourite dining venue in summer.

ROJA Dzintarkrasts

Žocene, LV-3264 **Tel** *2860 0600*   **Road Map** *C3*

Tastefully furnished with dark-wood tables and wicker chairs, this sophisticated restaurant is part of the Dzintarkrasts holiday complex *(see p304)*. The menu includes traditional Kurzeme dishes, such as sorrel soup with fried bacon and slices of boiled egg, and dark bread soup with dried fruit and whipped cream.

ROJA Otra Puse

Jūras iela 6, LV-3264 **Tel** *2947 7602*   **Road Map** *C3*

Local cuisine is on offer at this restaurant in the Otra Puse recreation complex. A wide selection of fish dishes, including some that are smoked in the on-site smokehouse, and other regional delicacies are served in a pretty stone and wood building, just 200 m (220 yds) from the beach. Live music on Saturdays. Closed Mon–Thu Oct–May.

RUNDĀLE Baltā Māja

Rundāle, LV-3921 **Tel** *6396 2140*   **Road Map** *D4*

The Baltā Maja *(see p305)* is about 200 years old. In addition to bed and breakfast offered to guests, there is an excellent café serving authentic home-cooked Latvian food in an endearing farmhouse-style dining room. The black bread and berry dessert served here is unmissable. Book ahead.

RUNDĀLE Rundāles Pils

Rundāle, LV-3921 **Tel** *6396 2195*   **Road Map** *D4*

Conveniently located for visiting Rundāle Palace, this restaurant occupies the Duke of Courland's former kitchens. The Latvian food here is fantastic but the vegetarian menu is comparatively sparse. The restaurant is open all year, but off-season (November–April) visitors must give prior notice if they wish to dine.

SABILE Zviedru Cepure

Piltiņa, Matkules pagasts, LV-3132 **Tel** 2640 5405
Road Map *C3*

Just 3.5 km (2 miles) from Sabile is the Zviedru Cepure ("Swedish Hat") recreation centre, named after a mound where a Swedish commander, his wife, 200 soldiers and their horses were buried. As well as offering skiing, horse riding and a toboggan run, the centre has a log-cabin café serving hearty Latvian dishes and hot wine in the winter.

TALSI Martinelli

Lielā iela 7, LV-3201 **Tel** 6329 1340
Road Map *C3*

A fireplace and wooden beams impart a cosy farmhouse-feel to this popular restaurant. Traditional Latvian pork, chicken and fish dishes are served, along with age-old family recipes such as peeled barley penny buns with soup. The owners have a wine shop next door with an interesting stock.

TUKUMS Ledus Halle

Stadiona iela 3, LV-3101 **Tel** 6310 7470
Road Map *C3*

The dining options in Tukums are limited, but one of the best is in the ice-skating hall in the historic centre, not far from the train and bus stations. Ledus Halle houses a hotel and a restaurant that serves typical Latvian cuisine – from soups and salads, to meat, fish and even vegetarian dishes.

VENTSPILS Buginš

Lielā iela 1/3, LV-3601 **Tel** 2926 4215
Road Map *B3*

With wooden beams and old photographs adorning the wall, this lively place attempts to emulate the setting of a cosy rural log cabin. However, the TV in the main room somewhat disturbs the effect. The food, mostly standard Latvian, is decent. The service, however, is not particularly quick.

VENTSPILS Melnais Sivēns

Jāņa iela 17, LV-3602 **Tel** 6362 2396
Road Map *B3*

The most atmospheric dining option in Ventspils, Melnais Sivēns is housed in the basement of the city's Livonian Order castle. It serves interesting medieval cuisine, such as black pudding with apple and cranberry marmalade, and spice-marinated pork with sorrel sauce, in a candlelit ambience.

VENTSPILS Skroderkrogs

Skroderu iela 6, LV-3601 **Tel** 6362 7634
Road Map *B3*

This cosy cafe takes its inspiration from its location in Skroderu iela, or "Tailors' Street". The tables have been made from old sewing machines and irons, and other tools of the rag trade adorn the walls. The menu is a mix of local and international, with one of the highlights being the pork fillet pickled in the local Užavas beer.

EASTERN LATVIA

AGLONA Upenīte

Tartakas iela 7, LV-5304 **Tel** 2631 2465
Road Map *E4*

A member of the European Network of Regional Culinary Heritage, the Upenīte guest house offers one of the more interesting dining venues in Aglona. The dining room is styled after a medieval tavern and specializes in curd pancakes made according to a traditional Latgallian recipe. Dining is by appointment only.

DAUGAVPILS Gubernators

Lāčplēša 10, LV-5403 **Tel** 6542 2455
Road Map *E4*

This lively cellar pub has plenty of choice on the menu, which is available both in French and English. The Russian influence on the city is clear, as *pelmeni* (dumplings) are served as well as the usual Latvian dishes of pork, potato and black peas. Russian Baltika beer is on offer alongside other options.

DAUGAVPILS Plaza

Gimnazijas iela 46, LV-5403 **Tel** 6540 4900
Road Map *E4*

Situated on the tenth floor of the Latgola hotel in central Daugavpils, the Plaza restaurant offers a fantastic panorama of the city. The white tablecloths and Mediterranean dishes bring a touch of class in a city with limited dining options. Breakfast is served from 7am, and there is live music every Friday evening.

DAUGAVPILS Villa Ksenija

Varšavas 17, LV-5404 **Tel** 6543 4317
Road Map *E4*

Styled as a mansion house, this restaurant has an elegant dining room with a sideboard bearing a wide choice of brandy and single-malt scotch. The food is international in its scope, with particular emphasis on fish dishes. There is a prominent fireplace with framed collections of mounted butterflies on the walls.

GAUJA NATIONAL PARK Sarunas

Rīgas iela 4, Cēsis, LV-4101 **Tel** 6410 7173
Road Map *D3*

This centrally located restaurant specializes in pizzas. However, there is also a separate menu of Russian-style meals that taste more Latvian than Russian. The red seating, lights embedded in the floor and visible air conditioning, make the place resemble a trendy bar. Friday and Saturday nights are enlivened by DJs.

GAUJA NATIONAL PARK Lāču Miga

Gaujas iela 22, Līgatne, LV-4110 **Tel** *2913 3713*   **Road Map** *D3*

Located in the hotel of the same name *(see p306)*, this restaurant is bear-themed and is signposted by orange paw prints. Wooden furniture and white leather chairs give the place a modern look, while the menu offers high-quality international dishes. Open only on weekends.

GAUJA NATIONAL PARK Zaļumnieka Piestātne

Pils iela 9, Sigulda, LV-2150 **Tel** *2915 0104*   **Road Map** *D3*

This budget bistro and pizzeria in the centre of Sigulda serves a wide range of Latvian and international offerings, including pasta dishes and hamburgers. While the exterior is unimpressive, the interior is bright and filled with wooden furniture and decorative sculptures. There is outdoor seating in summer and a playground for the kids.

GAUJA NATIONAL PARK Kolonna Hotel Cēsis

Vienības laukums 1, Cēsis, LV-4101 **Tel** *6412 0122*   **Road Map** *D3*

A varied menu of Latvian cuisine is served in the rather formal dining room of Kolonna Hotel Cēsis *(see p306)*. Lamb, beef and pork grills, as well as fresh fish and seafood, are among its staples. However, it is only open during summer. The more casual and cheaper Café Popular in the basement is open year-round.

GAUJA NATIONAL PARK Aparjods

Ventas iela 1a, Sigulda, LV-2150 **Tel** *6797 4414*   **Road Map** *D3*

Themed on a farmhouse, Aparjods has a warm interior decorated with sepia photographs and cane and wood furnishings. Alongside traditional Latvian cuisine, more adventurous European dishes, such as snails, are also available. It is a popular dining venue despite being outside the town centre.

GAUJA NATIONAL PARK Kunga Rija

Krimuldas pagasts, Turaida, LV-2147 **Tel** *2923 5741*   **Road Map** *D3*

Food is served in a relaxed atmosphere on the mezzanine and ground floors of this restaurant which resembles a large log cabin. The menu is quite adventurous for provincial Latvia, featuring dishes such as fried salmon trout in a herb crust with plums and a rosé wine sauce.

GAUJA NATIONAL PARK Spa Hotel Ezeri

Siguldas pagasts, Sigulda, LV-2150 **Tel** *6797 3009*   **Road Map** *D3*

The modern dining room in the Spa Hotel Ezeri *(see p306)* has a Scandinavian-influenced decor. The short yet interesting menu comprises modern European cuisine. It is an excellent place to dine, even for those not staying at the hotel or using the spa facilities. Closed on Mondays during the winter season.

GULBENE Lacītēs

Rankas pagasts, LV-4416 **Tel** *2659 9997*   **Road Map** *E3*

A cut above most Latvian roadside eateries, this modern log cabin with a thatched roof is a pleasant restaurant. The Latvian menu offers local dishes with children's options and non-alcoholic cocktails. The staff are friendly and helpful. There is a watermill, Lacītēs Ūdensdzirnavas, close by.

IKŠĶILE Meidrops

Rīgas iela 18, LV-50522 **Tel** *6503 0466*   **Road Map** *D3*

Located in a prime spot on the banks of the Daugava river, the restaurant in the Meidrops hotel *(see p306)* is a modern log cabin with thatched roof. Great attention has been paid to detail with decorative metalwork by a local artisan. Meals such as smoked duck salad with mushrooms and spinach are served on handmade dishes.

JĒKABPILS Uguntiņa

Pasta 23b, LV-5201 **Tel** *6523 1907*   **Road Map** *D4*

A favourite among locals, this bustling restaurant offers a wide selection of Latvian dishes such as pork, potatoes and black beans, as well as a few more unexpected items such as sushi. The menu is only in Latvian, but the staff are usually very helpful with deciphering it.

JĒKABPILS Hercogs Jēkabs

Brīvības iela 182, LV-5201 **Tel** *6523 3433*   **Road Map** *D4*

This restaurant, set by the Daugava river, is a cosy spot for both lunch and dinner, with a menu that includes Latvian staples such as pork chops. It is more of a pub than a restaurant, with simple wooden chairs and tables as well as a few comfortable leather sofas.

KOKNESE Vino Rosso

Koknesies pagasts, LV-5113 **Tel** *2921 2909*   **Road Map** *D4*

Located on the bank of the Daugava river, this restored warehouse is part of the Bilstiņi manor complex in Koknese. The restaurant serves Mediterranean cuisine, including antipasti, with a menu that changes weekly. The wine list has choices complementing specific dishes.

KRĀSLAVA Mārīte

Tirgus 2, LV-5601 **Tel** *6562 2634*   **Road Map** *E4*

In the absence of any genuine restaurants in town, this centrally located café is popular with locals. The name Mārīte means "ladybird", and this is reflected in the predominantly scarlet decor. The menu is straightforward, covering the usual Latvian basics of chicken, pork and fish. There is live music on Friday evenings.

Key to Price Guide *see p330* **Key to Symbols** *see back cover flap*

LIELVĀRDE Lielvārdes Osta

Krasta iela 2, LV-5070 **Tel** *2915 0107*   **Road Map** *D4*

Part of the Lielvārdes Osta boutique hotel *(see p306)* on the Daugava river, this restaurant is undoubtedly one of the best in the region. The well-presented international fare is served in a cosy dining room with a roaring fire in winter. The bar has been made from the bow of a boat.

LIMBAŽI Bīriņu Pils

Bīriņi iela, LV-4014 **Tel** *6402 4033*   **Road Map** *D3*

Housed in the brick-lined cellar of Bīriņi manor house, Bīriņu Pils *(see p306)* is a pleasant hotel restaurant. However, it is slightly out of the way for those not staying at the hotel. The menu is limited and mostly covers simple Latvian meat dishes. Children's options are also available.

PREIĻI Levaž

Kooperativa iela 1c, LV-5301 **Tel** *2632 6577*   **Road Map** *E4*

One of the few places to eat in Preiļi, this small cafeteria serving typical regional and national fare is among the best options. Known locally as "the glasshouse", it is famous for its bright orange interior and glass walls, as well as the small winter garden inside, giving the impression of sitting inside a tropical greenhouse.

RĒZEKNE Latgale

Atbrīvošanas aleja 98, LV-4600 **Tel** *2616 4444*   **Road Map** *E4*

This restaurant, on the ground floor of the Latgale hotel *(see p307)*, is an appealing dining venue. The relatively formal setting with plush furnishing is brightened up with large windows. The restaurant's menu has a wide range of Latvian dishes, though vegetarian options are limited.

RĒZEKNE Rozalija

Brīvības iela 2, LV-4601 **Tel** *6460 7820*   **Road Map** *E4*

This restaurant in the Kolonna Hotel *(see p307)* is one of the more stylish and upmarket options in the city. The menu contains regional dishes such as cold beetroot soup, herring with *biezpiens* (cottage cheese) and stewed cow's tongue with mashed potato, as well as an international selection. Breakfast is served daily.

RĒZEKNE Little Italy

Atbrīvošanas aleja 100, LV-4600 **Tel** *6462 5771*   **Road Map** *E4*

Centrally located Little Italy is a favourite with locals. This first-floor restaurant has pleasant views and a menu that features a wide selection of Italian favourites. There are 30 types of pizza, in addition to pasta and other dishes. Desserts include an unusual folded pizza filled with fruit.

SALACGRĪVA Zvejnieku Sēta

Rīgas iela 1, LV-4033 **Tel** *6404 1440*   **Road Map** *D3*

The fishing boat and nets displayed outside are a clue to the specialities of this restaurant. However, in addition to fish and other seafood, it serves salads and soups. Conveniently located in the centre of town, Zvejnieku Sēta is a pleasant place to sample hearty local fare.

SALACGRĪVA Rakari

Svētciems, just off Via Baltica (Rīga–Tallinn), LV-4033 **Tel** *6407 1122*   **Road Map** *D3*

Part of a well-equipped recreation complex *(see p307)* that includes a hotel, guest houses and camping grounds, Rakari serves Latvian favourites in a large brick and timber building. Visible from the main road just south of Svētciems, its landmark is a giant yellow chair in a field.

STĀMERIENA Vonadziņi

Skolas iela 1, LV-4406 **Tel** *6447 1151*   **Road Map** *E3*

Attractively situated by Lake Ludza, the restaurant in the Vonadziņi hotel *(see p307)* makes an excellent refreshment stop for those touring the area. The restaurant is part of a complex of log buildings with thatched roofs, and there are plenty of recreation possibilities as well as a menu of international dishes.

VALMIERA Rātes Vārti

Lāčplēša iela 1, LV-4201 **Tel** *6428 1942*   **Road Map** *D3*

Located conveniently close to the Simona church and the local museum, this restaurant has a far wider menu than would normally be expected in a small town. The warm couscous salad is excellent, and the prices very reasonable. Many visitors lunch here en route between Rīga and southern Estonia.

VALMIERA Dikļu Pils

Dikļu pagasts, LV-4223 **Tel** *6420 7480*   **Road Map** *D3*

The impeccably restored Dikļu Pils *(see p307)* houses this restaurant, with a formal, though not stifling, ambience. The food here consists of an interesting array of Latvian and international dishes emphasizing seasonal and local ingredients, such as fish from nearby Lake Burtnieku. The menu is more suited to vegetarians.

VECPIEBALGA Jumurdas Muiža

Jumurda, 19 km (12 miles) S of Vecpiebalga, LV-4844 **Tel** *6487 1791*   **Road Map** *D3*

This restaurant is part of a lakeside hotel complex developed from manor buildings. The modern European cuisine blends rural culinary traditions with urban sophistication. The summer terrace offers brilliant lakeside views and has a retractable roof that is useful in case of bad weather. By appointment only.

Choosing a Restaurant in Lithuania

These restaurants have been selected for their food, good value and location. They are listed by region, starting with Vilnius, followed by the rest of Lithuania. Restaurants are listed alphabetically within each price category. For Vilnius map references, see pages 246–7; for road map references see the back cover.

PRICE DETAILS
The following price ranges are the based on the cost of a meal for two, including service tax but excluding alcoholic drinks.
Ⓛ Under 55 Lt
ⓁⓁ 55–65 Lt
ⓁⓁⓁ 65–75 Lt
ⓁⓁⓁⓁ 75–85 Lt
ⓁⓁⓁⓁⓁ Over 85 Lt

VILNIUS

Art Cafe Crêperie   Ⓥ   Ⓛ
Aušros Vartų 4 **Tel** *6830 8771*   **Map 1 C3**

This café serves delicious *crêpes* and coffee rather unusually through the window of an old bus. The café interior is old-fashioned and simple. There are a variety of *crêpe* fillings on offer, including the Alchemikas, or Alchemist, which consists of strawberries, bananas and Nutella.

Briusly   Ⓥ   Ⓛ
Islandijos 4 **Tel** *6914 1205*   **Map 1 C3**

Named after Kung Fu culture's most famous fighter, Briusly serves simple and tasty Pan-Asian meals at surprisingly affordable prices. This informal restaurant's modestly sized premises can get crowded with trendy young locals in the evening. It is one of the few places in Vilnius that serves hot curry.

Čili Kaimas   🚻 🎵 🖥 Ⓥ   Ⓛ
Vokiečių 8 **Tel** *231 2536*   **Map 2 D4**

Offering Lithuanian food in a vast barn-style venue complete with farming implements and a tree growing through the middle, Čili Kaimas is loud, kitsch and hugely popular. Two menu options are provided, one offering better food at higher prices. The vodka snacks followed by pigs' trotters and stuffed intestines must be sampled.

Forto Dvaras   🚻 Ⓥ   Ⓛ
Pilies 16 **Tel** *6561 3688*   **Map 2 D3**

This restaurant employs a team of local culinary experts to regularly check the ingredients and kitchen implements for authenticity. Diners can choose between the village atmosphere upstairs and the cavernous cellar theme restaurant with a menu demonstrating that there is more to Lithuanian food than *cepelinai* (stuffed dumplings).

Gras'as   🎵 🖥   Ⓛ
Vokiečių 2 **Tel** *212 2031*   **Map 2 D4**

As its name suggests, Gras'as uses grass as the main feature of its interior design, especially on the walls. Despite their simplicity, dishes commonly take a while to prepare, but the merry evening atmosphere and the bizarre decor keep visitors occupied during the wait. Meals here are good value for money.

Grill Brazil   🚻 Ⓥ   Ⓛ
Saltoniškių 9 **Tel** *219 5977*   **Map 1 B2**

Grill Brazil is the first Brazilian restaurant in the Baltic States, and is located in the Panorama shopping centre. There's a buffet, with sausages, poultry, pork and salads, where you can eat as much as you want, and waiters walk around with large *churrasco* (meat on skewers). It's a great place for a fun, relaxing meal.

Mambo Pizza   🖥 Ⓥ   Ⓛ
Upės 6 **Tel** *656 82408*   **Map 1 C2**

Situated near the Reval Hotel Lietuva *(see p309)*, Mambo Pizza serves possibly the tastiest pizzas in Vilnius. In summer, tables are laid around the exterior windows amid the lush green expanse along the Neris river. Evenings attract a youthful crowd and the place sometimes turns into a lively nightclub.

Transylvania   Ⓥ   Ⓛ
Totorių 22/3 **Tel** *262 2301*   **Map 2 D3**

The casual pub-style Transylvania serves an unusual spread of inexpensive but authentic Carpathian dishes, with decor to match and rock music playing in the background. The menu is surprisingly long, with a fair smattering of vegetarian as well as meat dishes, such as Dacian roast and pepper steak served with flaming absinthe.

Užupio Klasika   Ⓥ   Ⓛ
Užupio 28 **Tel** *215 3677*   **Map 2 E4**

A tiny, romantic café fashioned out of a living room, Užupio Klasika is a pleasant spot for a long, intimate rendezvous, partly because dishes often take a painfully long time to arrive. Meals are carefully created by a single chef, so more than a handful of guests can slow things down. The food is, however, well worth the wait.

Key to Symbols *see back cover flap*

Vandens Malūnas

Verkių 100 **Tel** *271 1666*

The delightful setting of this restored 19th-century watermill is a lush valley just below Verkiai Palace. The indoor seating by the fireplace in winter is as lovely as sitting by the rushing water in spring and summer. The food is simple Lithuanian cuisine, but it undoubtedly complements the location.

Barcelona

Linkmenų 5/66 **Tel** *203 0030*

Not far from the capital's new business district, Barcelona is the only Spanish restaurant in Vilnius. Highlights include paella, which takes precisely 20 minutes to prepare and is served steaming in a pan, as well as tapas and sangria. The decor is slightly stark, but the lively weekend evenings warm things up.

Belmontas

Belmonto 17 **Tel** *6861 6656*

Nestled in the Vilnius Valley, just a 10-minute taxi ride from the Old Town, Belmontas is an enjoyable year-round choice consisting of three restaurants. Vila Gloria offers fireside dining with good wines, Joanos Carinovos Smuklė is a far less ceremonious barn-style eatery and Belmono Kriokliai has a summertime barbecue.

Cozy

Dominikonų 10 **Tel** *261 1137*

Map *2 D4*

Located in the heart of the Old Town, Cozy is one of the city's hippest café-restaurants with a DJ-bar. The contemporary jazz music complements the subtly lit interiors decorated with Buddhas and framed black-and-white photographs. It serves decent European cuisine and set lunches. The lounge-style DJ-bar is an ideal spot to unwind.

Didžioji Kinija

Konstitucijos 12 **Tel** *263 6363*

Map *1 C1*

Of the many Chinese restaurants scattered around the city, Didžioji Kinija is probably the best. It serves generous helpings of delicious food in almost overflowing plates. The main dishes are placed in the centre of the table. For the sake of variety, order two or three different dishes. The restaurant's candle-lit ambience is romantic.

Dubliner

Dominikonų 6 **Tel** *243 0807*

Map *2 D4*

Most Irish-style pubs in the Baltic States make do with serving Guinness and hanging a few pictures of Oscar Wilde on their walls. Fortunately Dubliner is not limited to this cliché. Fabulous Irish boxty is served here alongside chicken tikka and scrumptious pies. Attentive service and a relaxed, casual atmosphere complete the picture.

IdaBasar

Subačiaus 3 **Tel** *262 8582*

Map *2 E4*

This restaurant presents a choice between a reasonably priced atrium café and a more classy, less-frequented gourmet restaurant in the cellar. The food served in the café, such as the *tarte flambée* or onion tart, is cheap, filling and tasty, especially when teamed with Lithuanian beer. The European fare served downstairs is more refined.

Prie Katedros

Gedimino 5 **Tel** *6057 7555*

Map *1 B2*

Prie Katedros is a microbrewery and the interior decor of vats, metal ducts and tubes adds to the feeling of it being like a factory. The atmosphere is warm and jovial, the fare tasty. The honey beer that is brewed in-house is delicious, and honey-flavoured dishes such as the honey steak are a perfect accompaniment.

Saint Germain

Literatų 9 **Tel** *262 1210*

Map *2 D3*

Modestly sized but hugely popular with expatriates, Saint Germain blends an excellent choice of wines, impressive food and a Provence-style atmosphere. Salmon and *dorado* (mahi mahi) are cooked to perfection and cheeses are given ample prominence. The outdoor seating beneath the spires of the Old Town is especially popular.

Tores

Užupio 40 **Tel** *6564 9032*

Map *2 E4*

The outdoor terrace at Tores, with its sweeping view of the Old Town spires, the Upper Castle and surrounding parks, makes it worth the price. It is a lovely spot for a pre-dinner drink-with-a-view. The fish dishes and desserts are reasonable, but the menu and service never quite live up to the scenic wonders.

Verkiai

Žaliųjų ežerų 49 **Tel** *210 2333*

Tucked away behind one of the two surviving wings of Verkiai Palace, just north of the Vilnius city limits, is the wonderful Verkiai restaurant. It looks especially enchanting in summer, when the flowers surrounding the outdoor pavilion are in full bloom. The decor is subtle and the food enjoyable without being ostentatious.

Miyako

Konstitucijos 7a **Tel** *248 7060*

Map *1 C1*

Housed on the top floor of the elegant and thoroughly post-modern Europa shopping centre, Miyako has a restaurant with a sushi bar with subtle Japanese ambience. The restaurant's sashimi is delectable and cuts of fish are superb. Another highlight is the soup with crispy asparagus.

Riverside

Konstitucijos 20 **Tel** *272 6272*

Map 1 C1

Black lacquered furniture with drapes and a decor in warm earthy hues makes this restaurant housed in the Reval Hotel Lietuva *(see p309)* cosy. The big open kitchen is still an attraction and the food is always a delight. Seafood is the focus of the extensive menu. For wine, guests can peruse vintages at the restaurant's central wine station.

Sonnets

Bernardinų 8/8 **Tel** *266 5885*

Map 2 E3

Exuding elegance, Sonnets is housed in the Shakespeare Boutique Hotel *(see p310)*. Seating ranges from snug sofas by the bar and fine-dining tables in the library to the less formal balcony. The menu reads like Dante's *Inferno*. "Aleksandr", a mix of chestnuts, Gorgonzola and baked fig, is the restaurant's signature dessert.

Sue's Indian Raja

Odminių 3 **Tel** *266 1887*

Map 2 D3

An old Vilnius favourite, Sue's Indian Raja is among the most reliable restaurants in town that serve authentic Indian cuisine. Ably managed by a retired Indian Air Force officer, the delicious korma and wonderfully spicy *jalfrezi* blend with less familiar enchantments for the palate. Occasional live Indian music recitals add to the atmosphere.

Da Antonio

Vilniaus 23 **Tel** *262 0109*

Map 1 C2

Opened as Vilnius's first quality Italian restaurant in 1997, Da Antonio combines an intimate elegance with traditional cooking. Pizzas are prepared in a wood-fired oven, pasta is created on the premises and the wines are an imaginative selection from Italy. Reproductions of Italian art add the final touch to the ambience.

El Gaucho Sano

Pilies 10 **Tel** *210 7773*

Map 2 D3

Although not quite as authentically Argentinian as it advertises itself to be, El Gaucho Sano, in the Atrium hotel *(see p309)*, prepares some of the best steaks in Vilnius. Thick cuts of meat, served on wooden carving boards with a choice of sauce dips, makes it a carnivore's favourite. South American red wine served here suits the cuisine.

Garden Brasserie

Raugyklos 4a **Tel** *233 5648*

Map 2 C5

Novotel Vilnius's *(see p309)* restaurant knows how to serve a crème brûlée. The French-trained chefs never add too much spice in their creations, preferring instead to allow the ingredients to retain their natural flavour. Another highlight is the Sunday buffet, a family-friendly tradition. Closed from June to August.

La Mama

Didžioji 28 **Tel** *260 9009*

Map 2 D4

Housed inside an upmarket mini-entertainment centre in the Old Town, La Mama lays special emphasis on steaks and roasts. The menu ranges from a choice of beef, duck and ostrich to delicious grilled salmon and tuna steak. Seating by the windows offers a pleasant view of Town Hall Square.

Medininkai

Aušros vartų 8 **Tel** *86008 6491*

Map 2 D5

The restaurant at the Europa Royale Vilnius *(see p310)* has an atmospheric courtyard for dining in summer and an evocative cellar for chillier weather. The chef likes to call her dishes Lithuanian fusion, but in reality Medininkai serves international cuisine with a certain panache. Service may sometimes seem tardy.

Brasserie Astorija

Didžioji 35/2 **Tel** *212 0110*

Map 2 D4

One of the classiest restaurants in Vilnius and with the most cordial service, Brasserie Astorija is at the Radisson SAS Astorija *(see p310)*. The chef emphasizes the use of fresh, healthy ingredients in his cooking. Every course is a delight, especially the seafood, and the wine list is exceptional. The glass vestibule is great for people-watching.

La Provence

Vokiečių 22 **Tel** *262 0257*

Map 2 D4

This classy restaurant, with quality of service and prices to match, reputedly offers the most exquisite gourmet fare in town. Visited mostly by diplomats and entrepreneurs, La Provence stand out on account of its reliability at blending superb Mediterranean and French cuisine with unmatched presentation makes.

Stikliai

Gaono 7 **Tel** *264 9580*

Map 2 D4

Housed in Relais & Châteaux Stikliai *(see p310)*, this restaurant offers a choice of two different venues. The exquisite restaurant, with a French accent, serves jacket potatoes and great goulash besides desserts such as chocolate ice cream in gold leaf. The less pretentious beer hall in the cellar serves European and Lithuanian cuisine.

Tokyo

Vienuolio 4 **Tel** *261 5195*

Map 1 C2

Located within the Grand Casino World complex, Tokyo ranks among the best Japanese restaurants in the Baltic States. Optionally served with excellent sake, the sushi, sashimi and tempura are first-rate, and the *hamachi* and tuna cuts superb. The bustling casino seems miles away from Tokyo's relaxed interior.

Key to Price Guide see p338 **Key to Symbols** see back cover flap

CENTRAL LITHUANIA

ALYTUS Dzūkų Svetainė

Rotušės 16 **Tel** *(315) 73 780* **Road Map** D6

Fairly nondescript from the outside, this is one of the more reliable spots in this part of Dzūkija for a basic home-cooked meal. Local specialities include pork roast with mushrooms and *koldūnai* (meat dumplings roasted with cheese and sauce). Locally made cheeses are used in snacks that go well with wine or beer.

ANYKŠČIAI Mindaugo Karūna

Liudiškių 18 **Tel** *(381) 58 520* **Road Map** D5

This fine-dining restaurant is located in a hotel and sports centre off the Molėtai road, on the town's eastern edge. Well-prepared European dishes are served with a fair selection of European wines as well as locally made wines and brandies. An amiable oak-furnished pub sits in the same complex.

ANYKŠČIAI Romuvos Parkas

20 km (12 miles) E of Anykščia, Žaliosios village, Svedasų region **Tel** *(381) 57 747* **Road Map** D5

Part of the Romuva Park Hotel and leisure complex, this small, intimate restaurant rustles up pleasant European and Lithuanian fare that suitably complements the panoramic view of the pine forest. A sunroom can be reserved for small groups and diners can use the equally sunny patio in good weather.

AUKŠTAITIJA NATIONAL PARK Baras Palūšė

Vasario 16-osios g 16 **Tel** *(386) 47 473* **Road Map** D5

Standard, though hearty, Lithuanian fare is served at this modest wooden house in the Aukštaitija National Park. However, in addition to the staple beer and fried pork, filling portions of *cepelinai* (stuffed dumplings) and good rye bread are also available.

BIRŠTONAS Birštono Seklytėlė

Prienų 10 **Tel** *(319) 65 800* **Road Map** D6

Stunning views are the main attraction at Birštono Seklytėlė, perched on a platform above the densely forested Nemunas Delta region. It may be hard to find a table at the edge, but the seating inside this airy Scandinavian-style lodge is just as pleasant. The food is hearty, with the usual emphasis on chicken, pork and beef.

BIRŠTONAS Sonata

Algirdo 34 **Tel** *(319) 65 825* **Road Map** D6

Hidden away by the banks of the Nemunas river in the quiet spa town of Birštonas, the windows of this hotel restaurant peer out onto a lush pine forest. The spectrum of meals on offer is gratifyingly broad, the presentation conscientious and without any of the reliance on mayonnaise common in Lithuania outside the cities.

BIRŽAI 19-tas Kilometras

Raubonių village, Pasvalys, 19 km (11 miles) from the Latvian border **Tel** *(451) 39 676* **Road Map** D4

Located on the Via Baltica motorway to Riga, 19-tas Kilometras rustles up canteen-style cutlets, pancakes and salads. This is less a place to dine than a convenient stop to break the journey between capital cities, but the home-made apple pie and *tinginys* chocolate cake available here are very popular.

DRUSKININKAI Kolonada

Kudirkos 22 **Tel** *(313) 51 222* **Road Map** D6

Sophisticated jazz, blues and classical music are played at this lovingly restored, 80-year-old colonnade building tucked inside a landscaped park. Lavishly renovated and re-opened in 2004, this modern restaurant and music club now provides delicious meals. Very popular with artists and intellectuals.

DRUSKININKAI Regina

Kosciuškos 3 **Tel** *(313) 59 060* **Road Map** D6

The Regina hotel *(see p311)* boasts one of the biggest restaurants in this spa resort. The huge floor-to-ceiling windows add to the sense of space. In summer, the dining area sprawls onto a large patio, providing a sense of Druskininkai's restorative and peaceful environment. The menu contains a broad range of European cuisine.

DRUSKININKAI Europa Royale Druskininkai

Vilniaus 7 **Tel** *(313) 42 221* **Road Map** D6

Venison and duck are the staples at this steeply priced restaurant at Europa Royale Druskininkai *(see p312)*. The dishes are carefully prepared and exquisitely presented and the service is as attentive as can be found anywhere outside Vilnius. The glaring white decor makes even a speck of dirt unthinkable.

KAUNAS Bernelių Užeiga

Valančiaus 9 **Tel** *(37) 20 0913* **Road Map** D5

Generous helpings of authentic Lithuanian food are served in this restaurant, located within the confines of the Old Town. The interior evokes the feel of a country tavern and the exterior, in gaudy purple peppered with bright red flowers, makes it hard to miss. This 18th-century building is a protected architectural monument.

KAUNAS Keturi Metų Laikai

Mickevičiaus 40b **Tel** *(37) 223 253*   **Road Map** *D5*

Literally translated as "four seasons", Keturi Metų Laikai used to serve traditonal Lithuanian food, but now serves a variety of meals. It is a quaint little café, best for lunch, beer, snacks or coffee and cake. The prices here are very reasonable, making it a favourite among budget travellers.

KAUNAS Tado Blindos Smuklė

Kęstučio 93 **Tel** *(37) 202 993*   **Road Map** *D5*

Named after Lithuania's very own Robin Hood, who roamed the woods and forests of Northern Lithuania in the mid-19th century, the Tado Blindos Smuklė is a lively and unsophisticated eatery that is popular with both the young and old. Meat dishes dominate the menu, along with tasty stews and broths.

KAUNAS Didžioji Siena

Kumelių 7 **Tel** *(37) 220 585*   **Road Map** *D5*

Didžioji Siena, with its refined ambience, is the most reasonably priced option for Chinese food in Kaunas. The menu provides some vegetarian choices, but excels in exotic seafood dishes. The set lunch menus make this a convenient option midway through a tour of the Old Town.

KAUNAS Ramzis II

Daukšos 29 **Tel** *(37) 324 301*   **Road Map** *D5*

A slice of Egypt tucked down a side street in the Old Town, Ramzis II serves both authentic and Western versions of Egyptian cuisine and provides hookahs and hosts belly-dancing shows during weekends. A restaurant to be enjoyed rather than taken too seriously, as exemplified in the menu, which features "Viagra soup".

KAUNAS Pompėja

Putvinskio 38 **Tel** *(37) 422 055*   **Road Map** *D5*

With clay floor tiles and mock-classical Roman frescoes, Pompėja conjures up the spirit of ancient Rome. An unlikely combination of haute cuisine and sizeable portions means that the broadly Mediterranean dishes on offer should satisfy demanding appetites. Weekend evenings see lively entertainment programmes.

KĖDAINIAI Grėjaus Namas

Didžioji 36 **Tel** *(347) 51 500*   **Road Map** *D5*

One of the loveliest restaurants in Central Lithuania, Grėjaus Namas is housed in the Old Town hotel of the same name *(see p312)*. Set within the building's subtly decorated cellars, the restaurant offers fish dishes bathed in home-made sauces and the choicest cuts of beef and pork in an optional whiskey sauce.

KERNAVĖ Pušynėlis

Verkšionys, near Dūkštai **Tel** *204 0115*   **Road Map** *D5*

Situated above a stunning, thickly forested bend in the Neris river, Pušynėlis commands a stunning view, which is its primary attraction. The food cannot quite match the panorama, but a children's playground makes this an attractive destination for families.

MARIJAMPOLĖ Sudavija

Sodo 1a **Tel** *(343) 52 995*   **Road Map** *C6*

In the quiet retreat that is the Sudavija hotel *(see p312)* is a snug dining room with white tablecloths, a warm fireplace, a piano and delicious home-cooked food. A restaurant of the same name once stood on Kęstučio Street in pre-war Marijampolė and this newer incarnation continues its legacy of good food and a homely ambience.

PANEVĖŽYS Forto Dvaras

Savaitiškio 61, Babilonas Shopping Centre **Tel** *(45) 442 887*   **Road Map** *D5*

The Panevėžys branch of the reliable Forto Dvaras chain is decorated in Lithuanian-homestead style with wooden clocks and framed old photographs adorning the walls. Calorific traditional local food such as *cepelinai* (stuffed dumplings) and potato pancakes is available here. The service is friendly.

PANEVĖŽYS VIP Martini Club

Respublikos 70 **Tel** *(45) 469 090*   **Road Map** *D5*

A great place to combine an evening meal with a night on the town, the VIP Martini Club puts special emphasis on dancing. Dishes available here are generally light, such as hot chicken salad, although the beefsteak with mush-rooms is filling and rather good. Open on Friday and Saturday, from 9pm to late.

PANEVĖŽYS Deja vu

Kranto 24 **Tel** *(45) 584 859*   **Road Map** *D5*

The only classy restaurant in Panevėžys is located inside the Romantic hotel *(see p313)*. Its interior of ferns and flowers, rich oil paintings and murals, soft furniture and tableware help maintain the hotel's name. The dishes are refined and stylishly presented. The outdoor terrace looks out onto the Nevėžis river and its former riverbed.

TRAKAI Kybynlar

Karaimų 29 **Tel** *(528) 55 179*   **Road Map** *D5*

Traditional Karaim dishes served here include beef, lamb, chicken, vegetables and fresh fish baked in crisp pastry. Karaim decorative patterns and colours pervade the interior, but tastefully and never kitsch. *Kibinai* (savoury pastry) is a favourite, preferably accompanied by strong drink, but the *šišlik* (steak) is fabulous too.

Key to Price Guide *see p338* **Key to Symbols** *see back cover flap*

TRAKAI Senoji Kibininė

Karaimų 65 **Tel** *(528) 55 865* **Road Map** *D5*

The first Karaim eating house in Trakai, this old barn has been in existence for several years. It is informal and hugely popular considering the fact that there are only two items on the menu: *kibinai* pastries and *čenakai* (stewed cabbage hotpot). Guests should try both accompanied with beer in summer and vodka at other times.

TRAKAI Trakų Dvarkiemis

Užukampis village **Tel** *(618) 88 880* **Road Map** *D5*

Nestled amid the forests and fields on the road from Vilnius to Trakai, this wooden mansion, though quirky from the outside, offers a unique dining experience. It offers a healthier approach to Lithuanian cuisine with plenty of leafy salads and vegetarian and meat options. A popular stop for families.

TRAKAI Akmeninė Rezidencija

Bražuolės village, 30 km (19 miles) N of Vilnius Airport **Tel** *(614) 8698 30544* **Road Map** *D5*

Hard to find due to the absence of any signposts, this is a delightfully elusive hideaway hotel and restaurant, captivatingly situated on the shores of Lake Akmena. Two of the tables stand on a pier, the others above the grassy banks. Caucasian spices give the dishes an exotic aroma and the wines suit them.

TRAKAI Apvalaus Stalo Klubas

Karaimų 53a **Tel** *(528) 55 595* **Road Map** *D5*

Perched at the water's edge directly facing Trakai's Island Castle, this restaurant benefits from having one of Lithuania's prettiest views. The menu ranges from gourmet French to Lithuanian national flavours with delights ranging from duck to tiger prawns along with some excellent wines that complement the food superbly.

VILNIUS–KLAIPĖDA MOTORWAY Bajorkiemis

Karčiupio village, 15 km (9 miles) from Kaunas **Tel** *(37) 440 770* **Road Map** *D5*

A voluminous roadside inn, Bajorkiemis features a substantial menu of filling Lithuanian dishes. A playground for children lies at the back and numerous pathways stretch into the forest towards Lake Kauno Marios. This is a convenient break for those returning from the coast.

VILNIUS–KLAIPĖDA MOTORWAY Tvirtovė Prie Didžiulio

Dėdeliškių village, 20 km (12 miles) W of Vilnius **Tel** *243 2389* **Road Map** *D5*

Located near the motorway to Kaunas is a modern-day brick-built castle, with three floors of restaurant space. Though massive in size and tastelessly decorated, it serves good, unpretentious food and Lithuanian beer with a fine view of the surrounding lakes and countryside.

VILNIUS–MOLĖTAI ROAD Žaldokynė

Raudondvaris village, 17 km (11 miles) N of Vilnius **Tel** *250 2289* **Road Map** *D5*

An adventure in traditional Lithuanian food can be found on the road to Molėtai. A thatched barn-like mansion conceals a maze of dining rooms with a very complicated floor plan. Much care goes into the varieties of *cepelinai* (stewed dumpling) dishes on offer. Fifty varieties of potato were tested before the right types were found.

VILNIUS–PANEVĖŽYS MOTORWAY Le Paysage

Motorway A2, 17 km (11 miles) N of Vilnius **Tel** *273 9628* **Road Map** *D5*

Set within the upmarket Le Meridien Villon Resort *(see p310)*, Le Paysage is a destination in its own right. Its tall, curved windows overlook the rolling countryside. The French cuisine is exquisite, particularly the seafood and the fabulous array of French cheeses. Combine the trip with a visit to the hotel's Oasis Spa.

VISAGINAS Grilis

Sedulinos 5b **Tel** *(386) 32 692* **Road Map** *E5*

In the extraordinary town of Visaginas, perhaps the best location for a meal or an evening drink is Grilis. The dishes served here are broadly Lithuanian even though, as everywhere else in town, little else except Russian is spoken. In good weather, the rooftop terrace offers fine views.

WESTERN LITHUANIA

CURONIAN SPIT NATIONAL PARK Baras po Vyšniom

Naglių 10, Nida **Tel** *(469) 52 906* **Road Map** *B5*

Edged by a garden of cherry trees and evenly cut grass, Baras po Vyšniom is a pretty wooden chalet on Nida's most enticing street. Home-cooked meals available here go well with local beer or a glass of wine. Especially popular in the summer months, it is advisable to book ahead.

CURONIAN SPIT NATIONAL PARK Lyra

Preilos 15/1, Preila **Tel** *(469) 55 105* **Road Map** *B5*

A modest seasonal restaurant, Lyra is located in Preila, one of the Curonian Spit's smaller fishing villages. The back-garden dining area that faces onto the lagoon is a good spot to view the seascape. The dishes here are filling and there is a special menu for children.

CURONIAN SPIT NATIONAL PARK Vella Bianca

Rėzos 1a, Juodkrantė **Tel** *(469) 50 013*   **Road Map** B5

One of the finest restaurants on the Curonian Spit, with panoramic views of the lagoon and Juodkrantė harbour, Vella Bianca boasts excellent Italian cuisine and a range of fine wines. Exploiting the location, it presents fabulous seafood creations, although its meat, pasta and home-made pizza dishes are also superb.

KLAIPĖDA Senoji Hansa

Kurpių 1 **Tel** *(46) 400 056*   **Road Map** B5

The dominant attraction of Senoji Hansa is its prime location and outdoor seating. This is more a sunny spot for a midday snack, a coffee or a beer than for a romantic evening meal, but the dishes on offer are Lithuanian in style, much of them fried, and the service is as relaxed as most of the holidaymakers.

KLAIPĖDA Anikės Kuršiai

Sukilėlių 8/10 **Tel** *(46) 314 471*   **Road Map** B5

This little restaurant makes use of its attractive Old Town location and summertime outdoor seating to serve authentic Curonian cuisine to passing tourists. Curonian coffee and home-made cranberry juice complement set meals, enough for two, based largely on smoked ham, herring, sauerkraut and sour milk.

KLAIPĖDA Ferdinandas

Naujoji Uosto 10 **Tel** *(46) 313 681*   **Road Map** B5

One of Klaipėda's two Russian restaurants, Ferdinandas is a short walk along a busy road from the Old Town but is worth the effort, as it presents a quaint and authentic Russian feel. The menu includes soups with pies, stuffed pork and *dičj*, a dish of roasted fowl that was once the mainstay of Tsar-style cuisine.

KLAIPĖDA Petit Marseille

Žvejų 4a **Tel** *(46) 430 472*   **Road Map** B5

Reflecting the same winning characteristics as Saint Germain *(see p339)*, its partner restaurant in Vilnius, the Petit Marseille features a wonderful selection of French food and wine, delicious cheeses and satisfying desserts. The Old Town location and outdoor seating by the Danė river add to the charm, making it a relaxing dining spot.

KLAIPĖDA Stora Antis

Tiltų 6 **Tel** *(46) 493 910*   **Road Map** B5

A lovely old-fashioned brick cellar in the Old Town, Stora Antis specializes in Russian cuisine and has, in recent years, welcomed many popular Russian cultural figures to its candlelit lair. *Pelmeni* (stewed dumplings) and *borsch* (beetroot soup) feature on the menu, along with seafood and steak and some surprisingly good wines.

KLAIPĖDA Navalis

H Manto 23 **Tel** *(46) 404 200*   **Road Map** B5

With wide windows facing onto Klaipėda's bustling shopping street, freshly made coffee and Wi-Fi, this café, housed at the Navalis hotel *(see p314)*, is very popular with visitors. There is also a fine-dining restaurant that prepares divine fish and seafood dishes served with exotic sauces, as well as delicious desserts.

KLAIPĖDA San Marino

Žvejų 21/1 **Tel** *(46) 404 445*   **Road Map** B5

One of Klaipėda's most tasteful dining options, San Marino is located in the Europa Royale Klaipėda *(see p314)*. The occasional sculpture and Corinthian column hint at ancient Rome. The fancy Italian dishes served here are perfectly suited for amorous candlelit dinners for two and the choice of wine is among the best in Klaipėda.

KLAIPĖDA Sinbado Oazė

Didžioji Vandens 20 **Tel** *(46) 470 444*   **Road Map** B5

Delightful on every level, Sinbado Oazė is one of Old Town Klaipėda's dining surprises. The Middle Eastern food is fabulous yet reasonably priced and the ambience very relaxed. The belly-dancing performances in the dimly lit interior in the evenings are charming. The option of outdoor dining is also available, but the inside is far cosier.

KRETINGA Pas Grafą

Vilniaus 20 **Tel** *(445) 51 366*   **Road Map** B5

The elegant café-restaurant Pas Grafą, inside the winter gardens of Count Tiškevičius's 19th-century palace in Kretinga, is perfect for coffee and a light snack. Exotic plants and vines hang from the ceiling, making it a delightful stop, especially in winter. Closed on Mondays.

NEMUNAS DELTA Ventainė

Ventė village, Šilutės region **Tel** *(441) 68 525*   **Road Map** B5

A restful, isolated hotel, campsite and aqua park, Ventainė offers everything from Roman baths to tennis. Its restaurant is one of the few places in these parts to serve a cooked meal. The view of the Curonian Lagoon adds to the list of attractions and a well-stocked bar keeps the place humming during summer evenings.

NIDA Sena Sodyba

Naglių 6/2 **Tel** *(469) 52 782*   **Road Map** B5

Sena Sodyba is set back slightly from bustling Naglių street, giving the impression of a private dining spot set in a private back garden. The service is pleasantly alert, but it is the freshness of the food, particularly the fish dishes and the fish soup, that is the real highlight of this popular dining venue. Open only from June to August.

Key to Price Guide *see p338* **Key to Symbols** *see back cover flap*

NIDA In Vino

Taikos 32 **Tel** *(655) 77 997* **Road Map** *B5*

Fabulously positioned, In Vino is a laid-back wine bar that serves a wide choice of alcoholic and soft drinks made from grapes. The views from In Vino are gorgeous, but the menu comes second to the extensive wine list. It is possible to ask the management to keep an unfinished bottle for a return visit a day or two later.

NIDA Prūsų Rūmai

Naglių 29 **Tel** *(469) 52 578* **Road Map** *B5*

One of Nida's more popular eating venues, the Prūsų Rūmai is popular with both families and tourist groups for serving satisfying portions of broadly European dishes. The ingredients are fresh and the fish is bought straight from local fishermen. The nautical-themed decor inside is predictable but not too cheesy.

NIDA Ešerinė

Naglių 2 **Tel** *(469) 52 757* **Road Map** *B5*

Strategically placed in the loveliest corner of Nida, this restaurant serves delicious food in a friendly atmosphere. The Hawaiian-style straw parasols juxtaposed with elegant furniture outside is eye-catching. However, the interior is far more brash, giving Ešerinė the feel of a beer-swilling British pub.

PALANGA Elnio Ragas

J Basanavičiaus 25 **Tel** *(460) 53 505* **Road Map** *B5*

Brazenly decked out with hunters' trophies and a lurid mural dedicated to the joy of the hunt, the Elnio Ragas tempts diners with roe deer and boar meat, served with the predictable potatoes and vegetables. Beer is the beverage of choice here, with fewer wine options.

PALANGA Alanga

S Nėries 14 **Tel** *(460) 49 215* **Road Map** *B5*

Housed in the Alanga hotel *(see p315)*, this restaurant is a haven of sophisticated calm. The decor of fish tanks, painted seashells and sand-coloured walls are ample reminders of its close proximity to the beach. It offers excellent European cuisine and a range of decent international wines.

PALANGA 1925 Senolių Užeiga

J Basanavičiaus 4 **Tel** *(460) 52 526* **Road Map** *B5*

A snug wooden chalet located in a bustling corner of town, 1925 Senolių Užeiga rustles up delicious breakfasts of omlettes and porridge, tasty bar snacks and more substantial meals. The sausages and chips served here will surely please kids. A friendly atmosphere, reliable food and sheltered setting beneath trees makes this a favourite.

PALANGA Žuvinė

J Basanavičiaus 37a **Tel** *(460) 48 070* **Road Map** *B5*

Far more than just another restaurant on Palanga Beach, this wonderful fish restaurant has a menu that features an impressive variety of fish and seafood, from simple herring to a glorified salmon *carpaccio* and the finest black caviar. There is even a scrumptious surf-and-turf tiger-prawn steak.

ŠIAULIAI Juonė Pastogė

Aušros al 31a **Tel** *(41) 524 926* **Road Map** *C4*

Perhaps Šiauliai's most enjoyable Lithuanian restaurant, Juonė Pastogė serves a wide array of traditional food. Situated in a fairly quiet part of town, it is also a music club featuring a lively programme, and is very popular with families. In summer a spacious, green yard opens up as an extension of the dining area.

ŠIAULIAI Medžiotojų Užeiga

Dubijos 20 **Tel** *(41) 524 526* **Road Map** *C4*

With a bar made out of cowhide and old photographs of hunters with their trophies, game is undoubtedly the focus of Medžiotojų Užeiga. It is possible to order in advance for an entire roasted boar served on a tray of salad. Much smaller dishes are available too, including fish.

ŠIAULIAI Arkos

Vilniaus 213 **Tel** *(41) 520 205* **Road Map** *C4*

A high-ceilinged cellar-based café-bar that takes its cuisine seriously, Arkos concentrates on fish in summer and meats ranging from beef to ostrich in winter. The menu also comes with wine recommendations and desserts are worth leaving room for. It also hosts live music on Friday and Saturday.

ŠILUTĖ Rambynas

Lietuvininkų 68a **Tel** *(441) 77 055* **Road Map** *B5*

One of the biggest restaurants serving Šilutė's needs, Rambynas is centrally located on the town's main street. It is also a morning café, bar and nightclub. Weekend nights even include a programme of adult entertainment. The food, which is also available as home delivery, is standard filling fare.

ŽEMAITIJA NATIONAL PARK Linelis

Paplatelės village, Plungė region **Tel** *(655) 77 666* **Road Map** *C4*

Part of the lovely Linelis hotel *(see p315)* and aqua park on the shores of Lake Plateliai, this restaurant manages to be delightfully cosy both in summer and in the depths of winter. Candles and romantic music light up the evenings spent amid the ancient forest. The menu includes both national and European dishes, and some good wines.

SHOPPING IN ESTONIA

Traditional handicrafts and souvenirs can be found all over Estonia. The country's retail sector is, in general, quite uniform outside the major towns of Tallinn, Tartu and Pärnu. Shopping malls have had a considerable impact on smaller towns and the same stores and brand names fill out the bulk of these identikit malls. Despite this, towns and villages are good places to find local

Viking, sold in souvenir stalls

specialities, including handicrafts, locally woven textiles such as blankets and rugs, and high-quality organic honey from local farms. Most towns hold small markets where visitors can find food and household items. Antique stores also stock some interesting objects. Prices are usually lower outside Tallinn. Estonian chocolate, alcohol and cigars are readily available in most supermarkets.

Stockmann, one of the best department stores in Estonia

OPENING HOURS

Most shops are generally open from 10am to 6 or 7pm on weekdays, and from 10am to 5pm on Saturdays and Sundays. Shopping centres usually open from 10am to 8 or 9pm daily. In small towns and villages, opening hours are more erratic at weekends, with many shops only opening for half a day or staying closed. Grocery stores normally keep longer hours, and in Tallinn there are several 24-hour convenience stores.

HOW TO PAY

All large stores and the majority of small shops throughout Estonia accept most major credit and debit cards. Retail outlets prominently display logos for accepted credit and debit cards. Visitors may be asked for proof of identity when paying with a credit card. However, most market stalls and out-of-the-way places accept only krooni *(see p385)*.

RIGHTS & REFUNDS

In Estonia, all goods come with a two-year warranty under EU law. However, after a period of six months from the date of purchase, the customer might be asked to prove that the defect existed at the time of buying and was not introduced later. Warranties are only effective on production of a valid receipt.

Refunds remain discretionary on the part of the seller, although most major stores will provide a refund as long as there is no damage to the goods and the receipt is produced. Legal guidance can be sought from the Consumer Centre of Estonia *(see p349)*, which protects consumer rights in the case of cross-border purchases.

VAT EXEMPTION

Nearly all goods and services are subject to 20 per cent VAT, which is always included in the display prices. Non-EU citizens can claim a VAT refund on some goods over €127. Ask the shop for a VAT refund cheque, which then needs to be stamped by customs. You can get a refund at Tallinn Airport, or check www.globalrefund.com for locations.

SALES

Throughout Estonia, sales are usually held in the middle and at the end of a season, although the most significant reductions are reserved for the New Year sales. Watch out for a sign in shop windows, which may read as *allahindlus* (discount), *soodusmüük* (sale), *lõpumüük* (final sale), or *tühjendusmüük* (everything must go).

MARKETS

Just about every Estonian town has a market, known as *turg*, although they often only sell fruit, vegetables, household goods and other everyday items. There is little in the way of souvenirs or curios to be found in these markets. Kuressaare market in Saaremaa is a rare exception. It also sells trinkets, such as dolomite-carved objects, in addition to the local produce. For Estonian mementos the best bet is to attend one of the annual folk or town festivals held across the

Trendy clothes displayed in the window of a Kaubamaja store in Tartu

country. Impromptu markets are set up with stalls selling an array of local delicacies, quirky gifts and a fascinating range of handicrafts, including colourful ceramics, stained glass and woodcarvings.

DEPARTMENT STORES & SHOPPING MALLS

The country's best department stores, such as Stockmann and Kaubamaja *(see p349)*, are in Tallinn, although Kaubamaja has opened a huge department store in Tartu. Shopping malls are far more prevalent and are springing up in town centres and suburbs all around the country at a phenomenal rate.

Malls are good for essentials, but they offer little for the discerning shopper.

Supermarkets, such as Selver and Rimi, are extremely common throughout Estonia. These enormous hypermarkets sell just about everything one can think of, from everyday household items to an extensive collection of alcohol, chocolates, cigarettes and music.

REGIONAL SPECIALITIES

Visitors can buy a number of popular local products from all over Estonia. The country has a stunning selection of regional specialities that make ideal souvenirs. In Tallinn,

traditional items, such as hand-knitted mittens and socks, lace, ceramics, amber, leather-bound books, silverware and objects carved out of limestone, are widely available. Kihnu Island *(see p101)* is famed for its colourful and elaborately patterned handmade rugs, as well as thick woollen fishermen's jumpers made by the island's inhabitants.

In southeastern Estonia, home to the Setu people *(see p120)*, one can purchase authentic examples of the embroidered shawls and ornate jewellery that are unique to their culture. The Setu were also the only people in Estonia to commonly use pottery which is sold in several ceramics shops. Today, pottery fairs peddle their wares in the main Setu towns. The use of dolomite is unique to Saaremaa Island *(see pp92–5)*. Dolomite is used to make a wide range of souvenirs, such as carved ashtrays, pestles and mortars. Muhu Island is famous for its embroidered handmade slippers and bright orange knitwear. Pärnu *(see pp98–9)* is known for its linen and the most popular souvenirs in the coastal resort of Haapsalu *(see pp88–9)* are hand-woven and beautifully patterned white shawls.

Visitors purchasing beautifully crafted cane baskets from a local market

Shopping in Tallinn

Tallinn has witnessed a proliferation of sleek new shopping malls in recent years. Most international brand names can be found alongside a considerable range of popular Scandinavian brands. Tallinn's Old Town, which has some exclusive fashion boutiques and speciality art shops, is also one of the best places in the capital for gift shopping and souvenir hunting. Almost every street has something in the way of traditional handicrafts, such as ceramics, glassware, linen, wooden utensils and toys. There are plenty of stores and market stalls which specialize in art, antiques, jewellery, amber, knitted woollens, patchwork quilts and interesting knick-knacks. The Christmas Market in Town Hall Square is especially popular and brings together virtually every imaginable Estonian product.

Colourful ceramic collection at the stylish Bogapott studio

Russian dolls and amber jewellery for sale on one of Tallinn's souvenir stalls

MARKETS

Tallinn's main market, the open-air Central Market, offers a glimpse into the everyday life of the city's inhabitants. Stalls full of fresh produce may not offer much variety for the average souvenir-hunter, but the Central Market's bustling atmosphere is worth the experience. Those interested in shopping can try and haggle. The market selling knitwear at the corner of Viru and Müürivahe covers a sizeable stretch of the Old Town wall and is a great place to find a gift. Uus Käsitööturg, a popular stall in the market, has a good selection of traditional handicrafts and souvenirs. The Christmas Market in Town Hall Square (see pp58–9), which runs through December, features everything from knitwear and decorative items to marzipan.

HANDICRAFTS

Much more than just souvenirs aimed at tourists, Estonian handicrafts are synonymous with a traditional way of life that persists even today. Tallinn abounds with a bewildering variety of handicrafts. Wooden toys and utensils are particularly common as are a wide range of ceramics, including candle-holders modelled after the Old Town buildings. Traditionally woven rugs are still made today, some of which are more like works of art with their beautiful and elaborate patterns.

Bogapott, an exclusive ceramics studio, and **Galerii Kaks**, with its wide range of textiles, are worthy of a visit. **Nukupood** stocks handmade toys as well as dolls dressed in traditional folk costumes of Estonia. In **Katariina Gild**, craftsmen can be seen creating handicrafts, jewellery and ceramics. **A-Galerii** has a dazzling selection of local handmade jewellery.

ART & ANTIQUES

Tallinn's contemporary art scene offers plenty of galleries and small shops that stock all manner of attractive oil paintings, graphic art, textiles, sculpture and off-beat ceramics.

The city has several antique stores selling everything from Soviet-era paraphernalia to exorbitantly priced Russian icons. Emerging only in the 1990s, antique shops have quickly become a fascinating and flourishing retail niche.

Woven baskets, knitting wool and textiles at the Town Hall Square market

Special permission is needed to take some objects out of the country, so check with the shop manager before buying. With a stunning range of bronze items, silverware and crystals, **Reval Antiik** and **Shifara Art & Antiques** are among Tallinn's best antiques stores.

BOOKS & MUSIC

The best bookstore in Tallinn for English-language books is **Apollo**. This outlet has a range of gift-books relating to Estonian culture and history, as well as a small selection of Estonian novels translated into English. Look out for the English translation of *The Czar's Madman* and *Treading Air* by Jaan Kross (1920–2007), the esteemed Estonian writer.

Estonia's wealth of choral and classical music also makes for a great gift. CDs of the works of renowned composers, such as Heino Eller (1887–1970), Eduard Tubin (1905–82) and Arvo Pärt *(see p23)*, are widely available, as are folk music and choral music compilations. **Lasering**, one of the leading music stores in Tallinn, has an impressive selection of various kinds of music and a separate section on classical music.

Apollo, Tallinn's primary bookstore, stocks a range of gift-books

FOOD & DRINK

Estonian food products are ubiquitous and can usually be found in any supermarket. Rye bread is a local staple, as are sprats, smoked fish and

Kaubamaja store, one of Tallinn's leading shopping venues

cheese, *halvah* and blood sausage, during the Christmas season. Try the gourmet section at **Kaubamaja** for variety. For chocolate-lovers, Kalev, Estonia's largest and oldest chocolate and confectionary producer, offers a wide range of luxury chocolates with picturesque prints of Tallinn on the box. These chocolates can be bought from local food stores. Real chocolate connoisseurs should try the handmade delicacies at **Anneli Viik**. There are also numerous bakeries selling delicious pastries and cakes. **Stockmann**, one of the largest department stores, also stocks cakes, bagels and savouries.

Logo of Kalev chocolate

Vana Tallinn *(see p320)*, a very sweet, brown liqueur, is considered to be the national drink of Estonia. Those without a sweet tooth may prefer it mixed with coffee, while some people even drink it with milk. In terms of sheer consumption, beer is by far the most popular drink in Estonia. Saku Originaal is the dominant brand, but Tartu Alexander and A Le Coq beers are popular brews as well. There is an abundance of locally made, as well as quality imported, vodka which is considerably cheaper than in other European countries. Saare Džinn, a gin flavoured with berries from the Estonian islands, is good too. **Liviko**, one of Estonia's leading alcohol producers, has stores all over Tallinn.

DIRECTORY

DIRECTORY

HANDICRAFTS

A-Galerii
Hobusepea 2. **Tel** 646 4101.

Bogapott
Pikk jalg 9. **Tel** 631 3181.
www.bogapott.ee

Galerii Kaks
Lühike jalg 1. **Tel** 641 8308.

Katariina Gild
Vene 12. **Tel** 644 5365.

Nukupood
Raekoja plats 18. **Tel** 644 3058.

ART & ANTIQUES

Reval Antiik
Sulevimägi 1. **Tel** 644 0747.
www.reval-antique.ee

Shifara Art & Antiques
Vana-posti 7. **Tel** 644 3536.
www.shifara-antique.ee

BOOKS & MUSIC

Apollo
Estonia pst 9. **Tel** 633 6000.
www.apollo.ee
One of several branches.

Lasering
Pärnu mnt 38. **Tel** 627 9279.
www.lasering.ee
One of several branches.

FOOD & DRINK

Anneli Viik
Pikk 30. **Tel** 644 4530.
www.anneliviik.ee

Kaubamaja
Gonsiori 2. **Tel** 667 3100.
www.kaubamaja.ee

Liviko
Mere pst 6. **Tel** 683 7745.
www.liviko.ee
One of several branches.

Stockmann
Liivalaia 53. **Tel** 633 9539.
www.stockmann.ee

RIGHTS & REFUNDS

Consumer Centre of Estonia
Kiriku 4. **Tel** 646 0123.
www.consumer.ee

SHOPPING IN LATVIA

Numerous supermarkets and shopping centres have opened in major towns and cities throughout the country since 1991. However, Rīga undoubtedly has the country's largest range of shopping options. This is particularly true when it comes to items likely to be of interest to visitors, although outside the capital it is usually possible to find typical handicraft items such as amber jewellery and embroidered knitwear. Museum gift

Handmade crochet hat

shops are normally good places to pick up interesting mementos when a town or village lacks a dedicated souvenir retailer. Several workshops across the country allow visitors to watch artisans at work and even make their own pottery, woodwork and other items to take home. Latvian markets cater mostly to local people, but can still be fascinating places to visit. Local honey, chocolate, beer or a bottle of Black Balsam can make excellent gifts.

OPENING HOURS

Most shops in Latvia open around 10am. Small shops close around 6 or 7pm, while bigger malls and shopping centres usually stay open until 10pm. Many small shops remain closed on Sundays.

HOW TO PAY

In cities and large towns, it is possible to pay with debit cards and major credit cards such as MasterCard or VISA. Some places will also accept American Express and Diners Club. In smaller towns and villages cash payment in the local currency, the lat (see p386), may be the only option.

It is rare for traveller's cheques to be accepted as payment outside Rīga, the capital city, although those issued by major companies can usually be exchanged at most banks.

VAT EXEMPTION

Visitors from non-EU countries are entitled to a VAT refund of up to 12 per cent, provided that the items were purchased in a shop displaying the "Tax Free" logo and the total price of purchases made from the shop was at least 30.50 lats. Identification must be shown at the point of purchase, and a Global Refund receipt completed. Purchased items cannot be used until the receipt is stamped by a customs official when leaving the country. The VAT can be reclaimed at

the customs zone in the airport or the land borders with Russia, at Terehova and Grebņeva. For departures from other locations, the receipt should be stamped and sent to Global Blue Latvia (see p353) along with the visitor's bank details within six months.

SALES

Although locally made items are fairly cheap compared to those in EU countries, prices for imported goods tend to be high in Latvia, a situation which has not been helped by high inflation. One way of picking up a bargain is to visit the end-of-season sales, when shops reduce their prices.

MARKETS

Most Latvian towns have regular or even daily markets, although they are rarely

aimed at tourists and are most useful for everyday food purchases. However, some markets, such as the covered market hall in Liepāja (see pp180–81), which is a throwback to the Soviet era, are extremely atmospheric. In the summer months, some markets, like the ones in Jūrmala, sell souvenirs as well as fresh produce.

DEPARTMENT STORES & SHOPPING MALLS

Most sizeable towns have at least one department store or supermarket. Several malls and shopping centres have been built in important cities such as Rīga, Ventspils, Liepāja and Daugavpils. Some of these malls are located in the outskirts of the cities, while others are more central and easy to access. The larger retailers include Rimi, Maxima and Mego.

Collection of fresh produce for sale at the Central Market, Rīga

Handcrafted items displayed at the Ludza Handicrafts Centre, Eastern Latvia

HANDICRAFTS

Traditional Latvian handicrafts include handmade linen, amber jewellery, woodwork and knitwear embroidered with popular Latvian folk symbols. Motifs from the natural world, such as the sun, stars or trees, are commonly used as part of the repertoire of geometric designs found on many handcrafted goods. A particularly attractive example is the *Lielvārdes josta*, a long red-and-white woven belt which features symbolic patterns, and is a part of Latvian wedding costumes. These belts are available in souvenir shops in Rīga, and can be seen on display at the Pumpurs Museum in Lielvārde, or even made to order.

Visitors can watch artisans at work in several places, such as the House of Craftsmen in Liepāja. The Handicrafts Centre in Ludza has workshops where visitors can try their hand at crafting items themselves. Musical instruments can be purchased from the Musical Instruments Workshop in Gaigalava.

The Smithy of Ancient Jewellery in the New Castle in Cēsis calls itself a workshop of experimental archaeology,

A bar of Laima, Latvia's favourite chocolate

with master craftsman Daumants Kalniņš making replicas of ancient designs. Another place to find handicraft items is the branch of Tornis in the tower of Turaida Castle near Sigulda.

FOOD & DRINK

Available in many varieties, Laima *(see p353)* chocolate has been made in Latvia for decades and is among the country's most popular buys. Another common gift is Rīga's Black Balsam, a herbal liqueur which is supposed to have medicinal properties, which comes in attractive ceramic bottles. Visitors usually prefer it in cocktails or with blackcurrant juice rather than neat.

Beer also makes a good gift. Latvians are enthusiastic beer-drinkers so there are several brands to choose from. The most popular ones are internationally owned, but more unusual brews include the yeasty Užavas, which is made near Ventspils.

ART & ANTIQUES

Genuinely valuable Latvian antiques are not easy to find, partly because the 20th century saw many of them destroyed or lost during war

and occupation. In spite of this, antique shops are well worth exploring, especially because they often stock interesting items. The best place to buy art is in commercial art galleries. A licence, which is available at most shops, is usually required before genuine antiques can be exported. The shops are helpful with the paperwork.

AMBER

Amber jewellery is a popular Latvian souvenir, despite the fact that resin is less commonly discovered in Latvia than Lithuania. It is readily available in tourist areas, such as Jūrmala, and in some museum shops.

Buyers should be aware that not all amber is genuine, as various plastics are used to emulate it. Visitors spending a large sum of money on amber objects should ask for a certificate of authenticity, and it is generally safer to buy from an established shop rather than a street-seller.

ROADSIDE STALLS

In the countryside, especially in rural Latgale, it is common to see stalls at the side of the road selling fresh produce. Latvian honey is particularly delicious and also makes a good gift.

Shopping in Rīga

Once a member of the powerful Hanseatic League *(see p32)*, the Latvian capital has had a distinguished mercantile history. Although its harbour is no longer one of the most important in the region, commerce has flourished since the restoration of independence, with boutiques and department stores springing up throughout the city. Specialist shops can be found all over the Old Town and in shopping malls, while major high-street brands are available in Centrs. Souvenir shops, mostly found in the Old Town, sell handicrafts of variable quality including linen, amber jewellery and knitwear. Handmade chocolates and Rīga Black Balsam, the city's signature drink, are popular gifts.

DEPARTMENT STORES & SHOPPING MALLS

The years since independence have witnessed the development of many shopping centres and department stores as well as the renovation of stalwarts such as the 1920s **Galerija Centrs**.

Upmarket boutiques and galleries can be found at **Berga Bazārs**, a 19th-century enclave of shops, offices, restaurants and apartments. The **Galleria Rīga** shopping mall is the hub of designer fashion, while **mc²** has stores specializing in gourmet food and home accessories. For more basic shopping there is **Stockmann**, on the edge of the Old Town.

MARKETS

Housed in five huge zeppelin hangars, Rīga's Central Market has most of its indoor space dedicated to food, while the stalls and kiosks selling CDs, clothes and electrical goods are outside. Also of interest is the covered outdoor antique and organic food market on the second and fourth Sunday of each month at Berga Bazārs. Latvians love to give flowers and the city's main Flower Market is open 24 hours a day, through the year.

MUSIC

Folk music was a key part of the National Awakening Movement (1856), although in the years since independence it has become harder to find a sizeable clientele for folk recordings. Rīga's best music outlet is **Upe**, a chain owned by the former frontman of folk-rock band Jauns Mēness. Upe specializes in folk music from Latvia and beyond, and also has a wine bar. **Randoms** is perhaps the biggest music shop in the Baltic States. Cheap CDs can be bought at the Central Market, although bootleg versions are rife.

Decorative wall lamp

CLOTHING & JEWELLERY

Handwoven garments, lace items and knitwear are popular souvenirs. Designer clothes are available at upmarket stores, while smaller shops sell traditional woollen garments. **Tines** sells handmade wool and linen items in traditional designs, while modern styles from up-and-coming designers can be found at **Latvijas Modes Klase** in Berga Bazaars.

In addition to countless places selling amber necklaces and bracelets, there are several shops offering more unusual jewellery. The stylish **Tornis** stocks pieces inspired by ancient Latvian designs, as well as more modern styles.

HANDICRAFTS

There are numerous souvenir shops in the Old Town stocking items such as linen and wooden toys. In some cases, however, these are mass-produced rather than handmade. More unique and practical gifts can be found in **Riija**, which offers ecologically produced crafts and household items. **Tine** boasts a wide range of souvenirs, while more can be found in the open-air **Egle** craft market. Some shops also sell Russian objects such as *matryoshka*, wooden dolls of various sizes that are placed one inside the other.

ART & ANTIQUES

There are many commercial art galleries in Rīga and the tourist information office can provide an up-to-date list. **Māksla XO** is one of the city's most highly regarded

A shopper browsing for souvenirs at Art Nouveau Rīga

Amber jewellery displayed in a shop window

galleries. **Art Nouveau Rīga**, a leading souvenir shop, offers attractive reproductions, along with scarves, mugs and other objects inspired by early 20th-century designs. The shop is conveniently located at the end of Alberta iela, a street with the city's most impressive Art Nouveau buildings.

Rīga also has a fine selection of antique shops, mostly clustered around Brīvības iela. Upmarket emporiums include **Doma Antikvariāts**, while the chaotic **Retro A** is packed with a bewildering range of Soviet memorabilia. Religious icons and musical instruments are available at **Volmar**.

AMBER

Rīga has dozens of shops selling amber jewellery. Hard to miss is **Amber Line**, which has numerous branches all over the city. **IG Romuls**, under the town hall, sells amber jewellery in traditional and more modern styles, designed by two generations of the Romuls family. Amber can also be bought from street stalls and even in the Central Market, but be aware that such items might not be the genuine article.

FOOD & DRINK

Laima has been one of Latvia's leading chocolate brands since 1870. It is also a popular store for chocolate. In recent years, however, its position has been challenged by the more upmarket **Emils Gustavs Chocolate**, which has stores all over Rīga, including one in the Valters un Rapa bookshop.

For something more traditional, many varieties of honey are available for tasting at the **Jāṇa Bišu** Honey Room, along with other bee-related products. **Desa & Co** (Sausage & Company) is one of the few places in the city to taste deer, wild pig and bison, all raised on their farm in the Latvian countryside, along with other locally produced ecological items. The famous Rīga Black Balsam also makes a popular gift, which probably has as much to do with the ceramic bottles it comes in as with the drink itself. It is widely available throughout the city.

Rīga Black Balsam

DIRECTORY

DEPARTMENT STORES & SHOPPING MALLS

Berga Bazārs
Dzirnavu iela 84.
www.bergabazars.lv

Galerija Centrs
Audēju iela16.
Tel 6701 8018.
www.galerijacentrs.lv

Galleria Rīga
Dzirnavu iela 67.
Tel 6750 8000.
www.galleriariga.lv

mc²
Krasta iela 68a. *Tel* 6700 6868. www.mc2.lv

Stockmann
13 Janvāra iela 8.
www.stockmann.lv

MUSIC

Randoms
Kaļķu iela 4. *Tel* 6722 5212. www.randoms.lv

Upe
Vaļņu iela 26. *Tel* 6720 5509. www.upeveikals.lv

CLOTHING & JEWELLERY

Latvijas Modes Klase
Elizabetes iela 85a.
Tel 2779 1635.
www.modesklase.eu

Tines
Vāgnera iela 5. *Tel* 2542 4477. www.tines.lv

Tornis
Grēcinieku iela 11–2.
Tel 6722 0270.
www.balturotas.lv

HANDICRAFTS

Egle
Kaļķu iela 1a. *Tel* 2550 5268. www.spogulegle.lv

Riija
Tērbatas iela 6/8. *Tel* 6728 4828. www.riija.lv

Tine
A Mierovica iela 6–2.
Tel 6721 6728.

ART & ANTIQUES

Art Nouveau Rīga
Strēlnieku 9.
Tel 2836 7112.

Doma Antikvariāts
Doma laukums 1a.
Tel 6781 4401.

Māksla XO
Elizabetes iela 14.
Tel 2948 2098.

Retro A
Tallinas 54. *Tel* 6731 5306.

Volmar
Krāmu iela 4.
Tel 6721 4278.

AMBER

Amber Line
Torņa iela 4. *Tel* 6732 5058. www.amberline.lv

IG Romuls
Ratslaukums 1. *Tel* 2655 5363. www.romuls.lv

FOOD & DRINK

Desa & Co
Maskavas iela 4. *Tel* 6721 6186. www.zemitani.lv

Emils Gustavs Chocolate
Aspazijas bulvāris 24.
Tel 6722 8333.
www.emilsgustavs.com

Jāṇa Bišu
Pēterbaznīcas iela 17.
Tel 6722 4355.
www.daugmalesmedus.lv

Laima
Audēja iela 16. *Tel* 6710 4431. www.laima.lv

VAT EXEMPTION

Global Blue Latvia
www.global-blue.com

SHOPPING IN LITHUANIA

Souvenirs and gifts available in Lithuania usually consist of traditional arts and handicrafts made from local materials such as amber, ceramics and wood. Beautiful handmade flax or linen table-cloths and throw blankets, garments and soft toys are often available at reasonable prices. The shops and stalls of the Old Towns in the larger cities as well as the various resorts are flooded with most of these objects.

Mushrooms and berries for sale

Handicrafts of a superior quality and in greater variety can be found at specialist shops, which are commonly located close to the major tourist sights. Food and drink in Lithuania are distinctive in taste. The local cheeses and smoked meats on offer are varied and delicious. The wide choice of Lithuanian alcohol, such as *trauktinės*, often described as a bitter brandy, as well as vodka and beer, are great souvenirs to carry back home.

OPENING HOURS

Shops in Lithuania are usually open from 9 or 10am until 6pm on weekdays. Some gift and souvenir shops open at 10am. Food shops and supermarkets belonging to larger chains often open at 8am and close late in the evening.

The Soviet-era practice of closing for an hour for lunch is slowly fading and a handful of supermarkets are open 24 hours a day. Many shops open on Saturdays until 4pm, and some in tourist areas and in large city and town centres are open on Sundays as well. In smaller towns and villages, local stores close early so visitors should avoid leaving shopping until the evening.

HOW TO PAY

As in the other countries of the Baltic region, almost all shops in Lithuania accept major international credit and debit cards. Some smaller retail outlets may accept only the local currency. Bargaining is rarely practised except at some market and souvenir stalls, but visitors are welcome to try.

VAT & TAX-FREE SHOPPING

In Lithuania sales tax, known locally as *pridėtinės vertės mokestis* (PVM), is levied on most goods at a flat rate of 21 per cent. By law, visitors from non-EU nations can claim a refund of sales tax from

customs when they leave the country, provided they have completed a tax-free shopping cheque, available at stores where the "Tax-Free Shopping" sign is displayed. Shoppers should have their passport with them at the time of purchase. VAT can be paid back only if the outward journey is made by air, road or sea; rail is exempt. Visitors need to spend a minimum of 200 litas, including VAT, in a shop in one day to claim the refund of sales tax.

DEPARTMENT STORES & SHOPPING MALLS

To meet the growing demands of local consumers, sprawling modern shopping complexes are being constructed in Vilnius as well as in most of Lithuania's large towns and cities. The malls are replacing the old department stores

dating from the Soviet era, whose interiors were usually adapted in the 1990s to fit the needs of small traders.

Shopping malls have a main anchor tenant, which tends to be one of the leading nationwide supermarket chains. As a result, the range of goods available is practically the same as that found in the rest of Europe. For more authentic shops, visit the Old Towns in the major cities.

AMBER

Lithuanian artisans have applied great imagination to the crafting of amber, an indisputable part of the country's cultural heritage. They fashion it into jewellery, lampshades, writing materials and a great range of other objects.

Amber comes in browns, greens and other colours, besides the more familiar

Europa *(see p356)*, a stylish shopping mall in Vilnius

Souvenir stall on Theatre Square, Old Town, Klaipėda

yellow. It is also available as original polished stones, of which the most valuable and exquisite are those that have insects, plants, leaves and feathers preserved in the fossilized resin.

HANDICRAFTS & REGIONAL SPECIALITIES

Lithuanian craftsmen make all manner of objects out of wood, such as handcarved spatulas and spoons, and grotesque masks of devils and witches, whose distorted, freakish faces are traditionally displayed every Shrovetide. A far more acceptable wooden memento is the *rūpintojėlis*, a constantly worrying Christ-like figure who sits with his chin on one hand. Another religiously themed souvenir commonly made out of wood is the crucifix.

For the musically inclined, handcarved musical instruments, such as the alluring Lithuanian *kanklės*, or zither, make an ideal gift. Russian *matryoshka* dolls can be easily bought from local markets.

Some of the most original items of clothing that can be bought in Lithuania are made of flax. Shirts and blouses, dresses and hand-crocheted hats are all widely available, particularly in the capital's gift and souvenir shops. A hand-woven *juosta*, which is a sash or waistband often used in a wedding attire besides being used as a traditional form of

fortune-telling, is also widely available and makes a good souvenir to take home.

The agricultural nature of Lithuania has helped in preserving many local customs and traditions. Black ceramics, in the form of pots, jugs, cups and figures, are among the specialities of the southern region of Dzūkija. Further north, Aukštaitija is known for its rich tradition of music and instruments, especially its horns and pipes. In the west, the people of Žemaitija value their religious images, miniatures and shrines, which often incorporate traditional pagan symbols.

Cognac bottles on display

FOOD & DRINK

Traditional foods of all kinds are sold in Lithuanian shops, including *blynai* (a thin potato

pancake similar to a crêpe with both sweet and savoury fillings), *spurgos* (doughnuts), smoked and steamed cheeses and a range of products made from curd and sour milk.

Smoked meats are usually sold as long, thick sausages or, even more authentically, bound in balls. The best local fish to buy is herring, normally marinated and sold in sealed packets. Some supermarkets also have cafés where a traditional Lithuanian meal of *cepelinai* (potato dumplings), as well as *kugelis* (baked potato pudding) and *vėdarai* (potato sausage) can be sampled. Lithuanian rye bread, such as the widely used black bread or the greyer *palangos*, can be bought from local stores. Traditional *šakotis* (tree cake) and *tinginys* (handmade cakes) are commonly available. Mushrooms and forest berries can also make unusual gifts, but visitors need a customs clearance to carry them back. Local favourites, such as *starka* (aged, caramel-coloured vodka), or *trejos devynerios* (herbal panacea), should not be missed. The best of the many varieties of *degtinė* include the excellent gold-topped Lithuanian vodkas, while the company Alita makes a popular eponymous brand of brandy. Švyturys Premium Pils and the Švyturys Ekstra Draught are both very fine bottled beers. For more information on food and drinks see pages 318–21.

***Matryoshka* dolls for sale at one of the many souvenir stalls in Lithuania**

Shopping in Vilnius

The main streets of the Old Town are lined with countless souvenir shops, stalls and galleries that specialize in the national favourites of amber, linen, wood and ceramics. Many of the better-quality craft shops and art galleries are also hidden in the Old Town's labyrinth of narrow lanes and courtyards, so it is worth exploring off the beaten track. Away from the Old Town, Gedimino prospektas (avenue) has a number of clothing stores, bookshops and several shopping centres, while bigger malls with huge spaces for fashionable shopping can be found further afield. With so many choices, Vilnius has evolved into a shopper's paradise.

MARKETS

The most extraordinary market in Lithuania is **Gariūnai**, located next to Vilnius's towering water-heating facility, about 5 km (3 miles) southwest of the city centre. The market sells everything from cheap clothes, shoes, toys, toiletries and cosmetics to food, gadgets and even cars. Traders come from far and wide to sell their wares and, unlike at other markets in the country, bargaining is widely practised in Gariūnai. It is open from sunrise to lunchtime every day of the week except Mondays. The best time to visit the market is during the weekend.

At the southern edge of the Old Town, near the bus and train stations, is **Halės Market**,

One of the paintings for sale on Pilies gatvė

which mostly stocks a variety of fresh fruit and vegetables, cheese, meat and cakes.

FASHION & CLOTHING

The spruced-up Gedimino prospektas is the best place to shop for clothes and footwear. **Gedimino 9**, one of the new mini-malls dotting the avenue, boasts the Baltic region's first Marks & Spencer and Lindex stores. However, most of the outlets for more expensive brands tend to be found in the Old Town along Vokiečių and Didžioji gatvė (street). Vilnius also has its own treasured and highly sought-after designers with their individual boutiques, such as **Ramunė Piekautaitė**. Perhaps Lithuania's most visually impressive shopping mall is **Europa**, which brands itself as a fashion and style centre.

TRADITIONAL ARTS & CRAFTS

Shops and stalls selling traditional Lithuanian arts and crafts are most easily found along Pilies, Didžioji and Aušros vartų streets. Prices vary, so it is best to scan the market stalls before buying anything. Quaint outlets selling handmade artifacts at cheaper rates are tucked away in the narrow lanes leading off the Old Town artery.

Linen & Amber Studio, an efficiently designed chain of gift shops, is among the best places to find handicrafts made of amber and flax. These shops stretch up the entire length of Pilies gatvė and beyond; the one on Stiklių gatvė is among the largest.

Market stall displaying traditional amber jewellery in Vilnius's Old Town

For those interested in gifts and accessories made by local textile artists, a good destination is **Aukso Avis**. Funky felt hats, bags and jewellery, screen-printed shirts, garments and silk-printed wall pieces can be purchased here. Visitors can also craft their own souvenirs on the spot. **Sauluva** is one of the best and most reliable options as it stocks an assortment of Lithuanian handicraft items made of wood, ceramics, glass, dried flowers and amber.

Inside the elaborately frescoed Littera bookshop, Vilnius University

ART GALLERIES

Vilnius has an astonishing range of imaginative gift ideas displayed in a number of small art galleries, such as **Rūtos Galerija**. Quirky paintings, colourful plates designed with old photographs, vases and curios for shelves and mantelpieces cover the gallery space. At the **Artists' Union Exhibition Hall**, next to the Contemporary Art Centre *(see p232)*, original artwork, hand-decorated cards and a fine range of Lithuanian and non-Lithuanian art books are the main attractions. Many upscale galleries in Vilnius mount shows of the work of Lithuania's foremost painters and sculptors. These works are regularly offered for sale.

Colourful painting at an art gallery

The bohemian district of Užupis is lined with a surfeit of galleries and gift shops. Among them, **Užupio Galerija**, a working gallery selling metal and enamel pieces, is most interesting.

BOOKS & MUSIC

Vilnius has a large number of small, yet very intriguing, bookstores. Most of them sell locally published English-language reference books, coffee-table books, original as well as translated local and international fiction besides maps and postcards. **Vaga** has a whole upper floor which has a good collection of books in English.

Littera *(see p222)*, the bookshop within the Vilnius University complex, is attractive and has a lively atmosphere. It is worth visiting as much for the stunning frescoed walls and ceiling as it is for its books.

There is a lack of a single, all-encompassing record store in Vilnius. However, Muzikos Bomba in the Europa mall has a fair collection of Lithuanian and international music. It also sells music under its own record label. Fans of jazz, blues and rock should not forget to visit **Thelonious**, a quirky basement store in the Old Town stacked with records, CDs and old-fashioned hi-fi equipment. The **Humanitas** bookstore has a fine selection of art books in English as well as a small collection of local music CDs.

DIRECTORY

MARKETS

Gariūnai Market
Vilnius–Kaunas highway.

Halės Market
Pylimo & Bazilijonų street corner.

FASHION & CLOTHING

Europa
Konstitucijos 7a.
Tel 204 7109.
www.pceuropa.lt

Gedimino 9
Gedimino 9. **Tel** 262 9812. **www**.gedimino9.lt

Ramunė Piekautaitė
Didžioji 20. **Tel** 231 2270.

TRADITIONAL ARTS & CRAFTS

Aukso Avis
Savičiaus 10.
Tel 261 0421.

Linen & Amber Studio
Didžioji 5. **Tel** 262 4986.
www.lgstudija.lt
One of several branches.

Sauluva
Literatų 3 & Šv Mykolo 4.
Tel 212 1227.
www.sauluva.lt

ART GALLERIES

Artists' Union Exhibition Hall
Vokiečių 2. **Tel** 261 9516.
www.galerija-lds.lt

Rūtos Galerija
Vokiečių 28. **Tel** 231 4537.

Užupio Galerija
Užupio 3–I. **Tel** 231 2318.
www.uzupiogalerija.lt

BOOKS & MUSIC

Humanitas
Dominikonų 5.
Tel 249 8392.
www.humanitas.lt

Littera
Vilnius University, Universiteto 5.
Tel 212 7786.

Thelonious
Stiklių 12.
Tel 212 1076.

Vaga
Gedimino 50. **Tel** 249 8121. **www**.vaga.lt

ENTERTAINMENT IN ESTONIA

Logo of Vanemuine concert hall, Tartu

Estonia has a strikingly dynamic and eclectic entertainment scene. The larger towns and cities, especially Tartu and Pärnu, have a crowded cultural calendar as well as a good nightlife scene. Classical music lovers are spoiled for choice all through the year as a range of nationwide and local concerts takes place, given by a fine selection of national and international performers. Saaremaa Island hosts many classical music festivals throughout the summer. Estonians are fond of wining and dining, which plays an integral part in their social lives. A vast array of rustic-style pubs can be found in major towns and cities, offering a hearty meal, a friendly environment and sometimes vibrant, toe-tapping folk music. Smaller towns, such as Haapsalu, Narva and Kuressaare, have numerous bustling nightclubs and bars. A major part of Estonia's cultural life revolves around folk festivals, with almost every town hosting some kind of celebration throughout the year. For entertainment in Tallinn refer to pages 360–61.

A jam session in progress at the Viljandi Early Music Festival

INFORMATION

A good starting point for news about local concerts and events is the nearest tourist information office. *The Baltic Times* also offers information on arts and entertainment. All Estonian towns have their own websites, which usually carry listings of what is happening when. The publication *In Your Pocket* covers Tallinn, Tartu, Pärnu and other major Estonian cities.

BOOKING & PRICES

Bookings for cultural events can be made at the venue or through ticket agencies. **Piletilevi**, the biggest ticketing agency, offers both online booking and ticket purchase. A number of retail outlets throughout Estonia also offer the same service, particularly at the Selver supermarket chain and Statoil petrol stations.

CLASSICAL MUSIC & BALLET

Estonia has an outstanding tradition of classical music and recitals are regularly hosted all over the country. Tartu's main concert venue, the **Vanemuine**, stages theatre, classical music performances, ballet, comedy, musicals and special shows for children. Pärnu Concert Hall *(see p98)* hosts a wide range of concerts and music events.

Logo of Illusioon nightclub, Tartu

MUSIC FESTIVALS

A number of festivals are organized to promote modern and traditional music. Vilandi's annual Suure-Jaani Music Festival is held to commemorate popular composers Mart Saar and Villem Kapp, while Muhu Island's Juu Jääb Music Festival, held in June, was established to explore the connections between traditional and world music. Other events that draw large numbers of local and international musicians are the Viljandi Early Music Festival and the Saaremaa Opera Days. For indie music fans, the highlight is the annual Plink Plonk festival in Tartu. **Eesti Muusika-festivalid** has the details of all nationwide festivals available online.

NIGHTLIFE

Tartu has an impressive range of pubs, clubs and bars to choose from. One of the best-known nightclubs is **Atlantis**,

Brightly lit up exterior of Tartu's favourite nightclub, Atlantis

Performers at one of the many folk festivals held in Estonia

while the most exclusive is **Illusioon**. Another favourite is the **Eduard Vilde Lokaal**, which has consistently attracted a huge clientele. The occasional live performances that take place at **Kink Konk** give it a casual, bohemian feel.

Pärnu also has a lively nightlife. **Lime Lounge** is a stylish place for a drink, while **Postipoiss** is a restaurant-cum-pub with frequent live music. The slickest nightclub in town is **Bravo**, while **Mirage**, another club, is often packed.

In Narva, head for the **German Pub** for a drink in enjoyable surroundings. **Africa** is the biggest and most popular pub in Haapsalu and doubles up as a disco during weekends. Kuressaare has a good choice of quality restaurants, pubs and bars. With an attractive outdoor deck, the **John Bull Pub** is cheerful.

FOLK FESTIVALS

Some of the most important festivals take place in July. Of these, the Viljandi Folk Festival is the biggest, attracting vast numbers of dancers, musicians and singers each year. Another is the Hiiu Folk Festival in Hiiumaa *(see pp90–91)*, which has a particularly authentic ambience created by its rustic setting.

August is also a busy month. The splendid Narva Historic Festival stages an enactment of the Great Northern War *(see p33)* in Narva. Obinitsa hosts several festivals celebrating Setu culture *(see p120)*. The White Lady Days,

held on the August full moon, is a festival filled with merry-making in the grounds of the castle in Haapsalu *(see p88)*.

CINEMA

Films are shown in their original language with Russian subtitles, though the choice of films outside Tallinn is decidedly poor. Most reasonably large towns have a small cinema which shows the latest blockbusters a few weeks after being shown in the capital. Hollywood films are regularly shown at Pärnu's single-screen **Mai Cinema**. Tartu's trendy **Kino Ekraan**, located in a shopping mall, is part of the same chain as **Forum Cinemas Astri**.

The Black Nights Film Festival *(see p49)*, celebrated in November and December, travels to Tartu, Viljandi, Narva, Jõhvi and Kärdla, while Pärnu has a small film festival of its own in July.

Poster for an Estonian-language film, *Sigade Revolutsioon*

DIRECTORY

BOOKING & PRICES

Piletilevi
www.piletilevi.ee

CLASSICAL MUSIC & BALLET

Vanemuine
Vanemuise 6, Tartu. **Tel** 744 0100.
www.vanemuine.ee

MUSIC FESTIVALS

Eesti Muusikafestivalid
www.festivals.ee

NIGHTLIFE

Africa
Tallinna mnt 1, Haapsalu.
Tel 473 3969. www.africa.ee

Atlantis
Narva mnt 2, Tartu.
Tel 738 5485. www.atlantis.ee

Bravo
Hommiku 3, Pärnu. **Tel** 5344 3887. www.bravoclub.ee

Eduard Vilde Lokaal
Vallikraavi 4, Tartu. **Tel** 734 3400.
www.vilde.ee

German Pub
Puškina 10, Narva. **Tel** 359 1548.
www.germanpub.ee

Illusioon
Raatuse 97, Tartu. **Tel** 742 4341.
www.illusion.ee

John Bull Pub
Pärgi tänav, Kuressaare.
Tel 505 6216.

Kink Konk
Vallikraavi 4, Tartu.
www.kinkkonk.ee

Lime Lounge
Hommiku 17, Pärnu. **Tel** 449 2190. www.limelounge.ee

Mirage
Rüütli 40, Pärnu. **Tel** 447 2404.
www.mirage.ee

Postipoiss
Vee 12, Pärnu. **Tel** 446 4864.
www.trahterpostipoiss.ee

CINEMA

Forum Cinemas Astri
Tallinna 41, Narva. **Tel** 1182.
www.superkinod.ee

Kino Ekraan
Riia 14, Tartu. **Tel** 740 4020.
www.superkinod.ee

Mai Cinema
Papiniidu 50, Pärnu. **Tel** 443 9451. www.maikino.ee

Entertainment in Tallinn

Entertainment in Tallinn is astonishingly vibrant. Its classical music and opera performances are world renowned and a major tourist draw. In recent years, the city has also started to attract some big international pop artists, although its local live-music scene is far more enjoyable. A plethora of venues in Tallinn regularly host rock, jazz, blues and alternative music performances by local bands. The city's pulsating nightclub scene covers diverse genres, from mainstream pop to underground club music. There is a large choice of places to enjoy a drink. These usually stay open late into the night and range from ultra-chic lounge bars to good old-fashioned, pint-in-hand pubs. Theatre in Tallinn is generally of a very high quality, but is mostly performed in Estonian, except during international festivals.

A scene from *Carlo Gozzi Il Corvo* at the Tallinn Linnateater

INFORMATION

Visitors can check *Tallinn In Your Pocket*, *The Baltic Times* and *Piletilevi (see p359)* for upcoming events in the city.

THEATRE

Tallinn has a proud tradition of theatre and the flagship Estonian Drama Theatre *(see p72)* does a fine job of preserving the national repertoire. The **Tallinn Linnateater** specializes in contemporary work. The best place for serious theatre-lovers is the **Von Krahl Theatre**, the leading avant-garde theatre, though English translations are rare. It often stages various intensely visual multimedia productions. Russian-speakers can visit the **Russian Drama Theatre**, which puts on a range of classic and contemporary Russian theatre.

CLASSICAL MUSIC, OPERA & DANCE

Concerts by the Estonian National Symphony Orchestra, which are often held in the Estonian Concert Hall *(see pp72–3)* and the Estonian National Opera, regularly sell out thanks to their consistently high-quality performances and productions. However, there are also wonderful chamber and choral concerts held in churches and other more intimate Old Town locations every week, such as Niguliste Church *(see pp64–5)*, the House of Blackheads *(see p66)* and the **Estonian Music Academy**. The best of both contemporary Estonian as well as international dance performances are usually hosted at **Kanuti Gildi Saal**.

ROCK, POP, JAZZ & BLUES

Live-music lovers are spoiled for choice in Tallinn. **Café Amigo** attracts the biggest local rock, pop and blues bands and holds nightly performances. **Von Krahl Baar** is one of the best places in the city to experience the local alternative music scene, while the industrial setting of the **Rock Café** has a diverse range of live music ranging from blues to funk. Most of the popular international acts that come to Tallinn play at the outdoor Song Festival Grounds *(see p78)*. **No99** hosts cosy jazz concerts on Fridays and Saturdays, as well as some jazz acts during the Jazzkaar festival *(see p48)*.

PUBS & BARS

Tallinn's Old Town is packed with bars and pubs of every imaginable size and description. There are several well-acclaimed Irish and English-style pubs, such as **Molly Malone's** and **Scotland Yard**, which are as much favoured by expats as by foreign visitors. Stylish and classy lounge bars are also extremely popular among the city's well-heeled. Some of the best venues include the chic **Déjà Vu** and the extravagant **Lounge 24**, which affords spectacular views from the 24th floor of the Radisson SAS *(see p294)*. There are

Logo of Molly Malone's pub

Atmospheric interior of the stylish Déjà Vu lounge bar

Parlament, one of Tallinn's most popular nightspots

CINEMA

In Tallinn, films are screened in their original language with subtitles. The diversity of choice has dwindled due to the arrival of the multi-screen **Coca-Cola Plaza** and **Solaris**, which show the latest Hollywood blockbusters and Estonian films. Art-house and independent house films are screened at the impressive **Sõprus** and **Kino Artis**. The Black Nights Film Festival (see p49) is a cinema-lover's treat, when the best in world cinema gets a rare screening in smaller cinemas.

also several smaller, cosier pubs scattered around the Old Town, which are far less frequented by boisterous visitors. Intimate places, such as **Hell Hunt**, Tallinn's first real tavern, and the **Drink Bar**, which occasionally features live bands, offer an amiable atmosphere for a chat over a relaxing drink.

NIGHTCLUBS

The amazing choice and variety of nightclubs draws people from far and wide to Tallinn. Most of the city's best clubs are situated in the Old Town, or within walking distance of it. Many, such as Café Amigo, Déjà Vu and **Parlament**, are just good, simple, fun places and are equally popular with locals and foreign visitors. For the most exclusive hangouts head to **Club Privé** or **BonBon** and marvel at the preening clientele. Serious clubbers can try the portside **Arena 3**.

Visitors should find out more about a place rather than walking into the first nightclub they come across. It is advisable that visitors choose a nightclub carefully. There are some dubious nightclubs in Tallinn, which should be avoided by travellers.

Movie posters displayed at the Coca-Cola Plaza

DIRECTORY

THEATRE

Russian Drama Theatre
Vabaduse väljak 5.
Tel 641 8246.
www.veneteater.ee

Tallinn Linnateater
Lai 23.
Tel 665 0800.
www.linnateater.ee

Von Krahl Theatre
Rataskaevu 10.
Tel 626 9090.
www.vonkrahl.ee

CLASSICAL MUSIC, DANCE & OPERA

Estonian Music Academy
Rävala 16. *Tel* 667 5700.
www.ema.edu.ee

Kanuti Gildi Saal
Pikk 20. *Tel* 646 4704.
www.saal.ee

ROCK, POP, JAZZ & BLUES

Café Amigo
Hotel Viru, Viru väljak 4. *Tel* 680 9380.
www.amigo.ee

No99
Sakala 3. *Tel* 668 8798.

Rock Café
Tartu mnt 80d.
Tel 681 0878.
www.rockcafe.ee

Von Krahl Baar
Rataskaevu 10/12.
Tel 626 9090.
www.vonkrahl.ee

PUBS & BARS

Déjà Vu
Vana Viru 8. *Tel* 5688 4455. www.dejavu.ee

Drink Bar
Väike-Karja 8.
Tel 644 9433.

Hell Hunt
Pikk 39. *Tel* 681 8333.
www.hellhunt.ee

Lounge 24
Radisson Hotel, Rävala pst 3. *Tel* 682 3424.
www.madissoni.ee

Molly Malone's
Mündi 2.
Tel 631 3016.
www.baarid.ee

Scotland Yard
Mere pst 6e.
Tel 653 5190.
www.scotlandyard.ee

NIGHTCLUBS

Arena 3
Sadama 6.
www.arena3.ee

BonBon
Mere pst 6e.
Tel 5400 5411.
www.bonbon.ee

Club Privé
Harju 6.
Tel 631 0580.
www.clubprive.ee

Parlament
Ahtri 10.
Tel 611 6145.
www.clubparlament.com

CINEMA

Coca-Cola Plaza
Hobujaama 5.
Tel 680 0684.
www.superkinod.ee

Solaris, Kino Artis
Estonia Pst 9.
Tel 630 4111.

Sõprus
Vana-Posti 8.
Tel 644 1919.
www.kinosoprus.ee

ENTERTAINMENT IN LATVIA

Latvia's major cultural events are concentrated in Rīga, although the dynamic festival calendar includes plenty of reasons to explore the country beyond the capital. A few concerts and events are scheduled through the year, but visitors need to consult a website or the tourist board as they are not regular. The major exception is Liepāja, which has a vibrant cultural life and its own symphony orchestra. The city is also considered the home of Latvian rock

Traditional chamber music, Rīga

bands and DJs perform in clubs every evening. There are also some good rock clubs in addition to numerous bars that host live music. The seaside resort of Jūrmala is another hotspot during summer. Here, many bars and clubs open only for the tourist season and the Dzintari Concert Hall hosts concerts ranging from classical to pop. Valmiera, considered to be the cultural capital of the Vidzeme region, is another lively city. For entertainment options in Rīga see pages 364–5.

One of Rīga's tourist offices, which has details of events in the capital

INFORMATION

Tourist information offices in Rīga provide details of entertainment in the capital and the rest of the country, while regional tourist offices focus on local areas. Online resources include the **Latvian Culture Portal**, which has a searchable nationwide calendar, and **Latvijas Koncerti** for classical-music events.

BOOKING & PRICES

Tickets for cultural events are generally very affordable in Latvia, and bookings can be made at the venue or through a ticket agency. **Biļešu Paradīze** has offices in several of Rīga's shopping centres and major venues as well as concert halls and

cultural centres around Latvia. Tickets can be delivered internationally for an extra fee. **Ticket Service** has an even larger network of outlets, including at many post offices, Narvesen stores and Statoil petrol stations. Tickets can be booked online and collected from a sales office, or delivered to an address within Latvia. Both agencies' websites have instructions in English, although most event descriptions are only in Latvian.

THEATRE

Most theatrical performances are in Latvian or Russian. **Liepāja Theatre** produces a mix of intimate drama and expansive theatrical works. The building's restored Art Nouveau and Neo-Classical interior is well worth a look. There are also occasional travelling performances at

Saulkrasti Open-Air Stage and at the open-air stage in Reņķa Gardens, Ventspils.

CLASSICAL MUSIC & OPERA

The **Latvian Music Information Centre** is a good resource for details of musical performances across the country. Some of the best classical music concerts take place at annual events, such as the International Early Music Festival, which includes outdoor concerts in Rundāle Palace (see pp168–9) and Bauska Castle (see pp166–7).

In Jūrmala, the Dzintari Concert Hall (see p171) stages very high-quality events from June to August, on Saturdays. Liepāja's Holy Trinity Church (see p180) hosts organ recitals. The **Liepāja Symphony Orchestra** specializes in romantic music and hosts

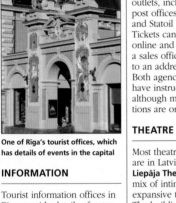

Scene from *Uncle Vanya*, by Anton Chekhov, performed at Liepāja Theatre

View of the open-air theatre near Rundāle Palace

concerts throughout Latvia in major cities such as Rīga, Valmiera and Cēsis.

With the exception of special events, such as the annual Sigulda Opera Festival, there are few chances to see opera outside Rīga. The Latvian National Opera does leave the capital to perform elsewhere in Latvia, but only occasionally. Venues for these shows include cultural centres in several towns and **Krustpils Open-Air Stage** near Jēkabpils.

ROCK, POP & ALTERNATIVE

The liveliest music scene outside the capital is in Liepāja, which boasts **Latvia's 1st Rock Café**, a four-floor building with pool tables, dining indoors and outdoors and live music every night. Another option is **Fontaine Palace**, which features a mixture of bands and DJs. It has a more relaxed bar downstairs, and a fast food outlet next door. The summer sees performances on Liepāja's open-air stage **Pūt Vējiņi**, as well as the Summer Sound festival *(see p132)* in July.

Jūrmala hosts plenty of live music in summer. The programme at the Dzintari Concert Hall features popular Latvian and Russian musicians. The major Russian-language pop competition, New Wave, held every July, attracts huge crowds, while the biggest music festival, **Positivus**, takes place near Salacgrīva and features bands from all over the globe *(see p133)*. The schedule at the open-air stage in Ogre, on the way to Daugavpils, includes rock and pop acts, while the nightlife

in Jelgava is enlivened by **Jelgavas Baltie Krekli**. Like its sister club, Četri Balti Krekli in Rīga, it has a strictly-Latvian music policy.

JAZZ

Regular jazz nights are scarce outside Rīga, but local tourist offices may provide information. **Saulkrasti Jazz Festival** is an important event in the calendar, as is the **Sigulda Jazz Festival** in Liepāja.

Latvia's 1st Rock Café in Liepāja, fronted by its signature guitar

BARS & CLUBS

Most places in Latvia have at least a couple of bars, of which some turn into discos on weekend nights. Some of the better ones include Latvia's 1st Rock Café and Fontaine Palace, both in Liepāja.

CINEMA

State funding for Latvian films has almost dried up and many cinemas have closed since independence. Most cinemas tend to screen Hollywood movies with Latvian and Russian subtitles. Cēsis Castle hosts the annual **Cēsis Historical Film Festival** in August.

Entertainment in Rīga

Since independence Rīga has been working hard to recapture its reputation as the cultural capital of the Baltic region. Apart from world-class performances of opera, ballet and classical music, the city also has a thriving live-music scene. Local bands play diverse genres from jazz to rock, often alongside international performers. The summer months see a few festivals offering music and more, but in winter there is usually some form of cultural event or other taking place regularly. The city is also renowned for its energetic nightlife. On Friday and Saturday nights, many Old Town bars buzz with foreign visitors, though it is not difficult to find a peaceful place for a drink among local people. Clubs, which range from small and hip to huge and mainstream, stay open throughout the night.

INFORMATION

Most hotels in Rīga stock an assortment of free pocket-sized magazines containing listings and other information, of which the best is *Rīga This Week*. The affordably priced and comprehensive bi-monthly *Rīga In Your Pocket* is available to browse or download as a PDF from the company's website. The Latvian Culture Portal *(see p363)* website is also helpful.

THEATRE

Theatre performances are mainly in Latvian or Russian, making them of limited interest to most visitors. The **Latvian National Theatre**, housed in a Neo-Classical building, has a significant place in Latvian history, as independence was declared here on 18 November 1918. The **Dailes Theatre**, directed by Eduards Smiļģis (1886–1966) for 40 years, puts on a range of productions, from traditional to experimental. Other options include the **New Rīga Theatre** and the **Russian Drama Theatre**. Rīga's most important theatre festival is Homo Novus, held in September, usually every alternate year. It concentrates on experimental theatre and dance.

OPERA & BALLET

Since the 18th century, Rīga has maintained a strong tradition of opera and ballet. The **Latvian National Opera** has an imposing Neo-Classical building with a Baroque interior. It is the venue for world-class performances that are usually in their original language with subtitles in Latvian and English. The building that houses the Latvian National Opera is also home to the Rīga Ballet. The strong ballet tradition established during the Soviet period continues today.

Although the National Opera closes in the summer, there are special performances in August. Tours of the building are also available for a minimum of ten people.

CLASSICAL MUSIC

There are a number of concert venues in Rīga, including the Dome Cathedral *(see p142)*, which hosts regular recitals. **Ave Sol** hosts chamber and choral music performances. The Latvian Philharmonic Orchestra performs at the Great Guild *(see p145)*, while chamber music is played at the Small Guild. **Spīķeri Concert Hall**, located in the warehouses next to Rīga's Central Market, is a contemporary venue for classical music and is the home of the Sinfonietta Rīga chamber orchestra.

ROCK, POP & ALTERNATIVE

Major international artists perform at the **Arēna Rīga**, while local bands play at a host of smaller venues. **Kaļķu Vārti** is noted for booking some of the country's top artistes. **Depo** features alternative music from ska to metal and **Sapņu Fabrika** offers a range of diverse genres from world music to rock. **Četri Balti Krekli** offers strictly Latvian music.

JAZZ & BLUES

The best blues venue in the city is **Bites Blūza Klubs**, which has live music on weekend evenings. It also serves surprisingly good food, while the photographs on the walls are testament to the number of international performers who have visited over the years. The small **Hamlets** club hosts jazz performances, as does the upmarket **Carpe Diem** restaurant. **Rīgas Ritmi** (Rīga's Rhythms) organizes concerts featuring local and international jazz, blues and world musicians at various venues throughout the year.

A lavishly decorated hall of the Latvian National Theatre

BARS & CLUBS

With a wide range of bars and clubs, Rīga has a swinging nightlife. **Balzambārs** is a popular place to try the eponymous drink in various cocktails. **Skyline Bar** in the Radisson Blu Hotel Latvija *(see p302)* is one of the favourite bars in town. **I Love You** attracts a youthful local crowd, while **Paddy Whelan's** Irish pub is a favourite among expats.

The best-known nightclubs, **Pulkvedim Neviens Neraksta** and **Club Essential** feature DJs on the weekend, while **Folkklubs Ala** offers a mix of folk bands and more traditional music.

Rīga's gay scene remains low-profile. **XXL**, the only well-advertised gay club, has live shows on Friday and Saturday nights. **Golden**, a gay-friendly bar, plays house music in a warm ambience.

CASINOS

Although there are numerous establishments that describe themselves as casinos, most provide only slot machines. Establishments with gaming tables include the **Olympic Voodoo Casino** in the Radisson Blu Hotel Latvija *(see p302)* and the **Royal Casino**. It is compulsory to register at casinos, so you must be sure to carry valid photo ID.

CINEMA

There are several multi-screen cinemas in Rīga, mostly offering Hollywood films. The largest is the **Coca-Cola Forum**, which has 14 halls and several cafés. **Splendid Palace**, the city's first cinema house, has been renovated and also shows non-Hollywood films. **K Suns** is the best place for art-house cinema.

Sweeping view of Rīga from Skyline Bar, Reval Hotel Latvija

DIRECTORY

THEATRE

Dailes Theatre
Brīvības iela 75.
Tel 6727 0463.
www.dailesteatris.lv

Latvian National Theatre
Kronvalda bulvāris 2.
Tel 6700 6337.
www.teatris.lv

New Rīga Theatre
Lāčplēša iela 25.
Tel 6728 0765.
www.jrt.lv

Russian Drama Theatre
Kaļķu iela 16.
Tel 6722 4660.
www.trd.lv

OPERA & BALLET

Latvian National Opera
Aspāzijas bulvāris 3.
Tel 6707 3777.
www.opera.lv

CLASSICAL MUSIC

Ave Sol
Citadeles iela 7. *Tel 6718 1637.* www.avesol.riga.lv

Spīķeri Concert Hall
Maskavas iela 4/1.
Tel 6721 5018.
www.sinfoniettariga.lv

ROCK, POP & ALTERNATIVE

Arēna Rīga
Skanstes iela 21.
Tel 6738 8200.
www.arenariga.com

Četri Balti Krekli
Vecpilsētas iela 12.
Tel 6721 3885.
www.krekli.lv

Depo
Vaļņu iela 32. *Tel 6721 1374.* www.klubsdepo.lv

Kaļķu Vārti
Kaļķu iela 11a.
Tel 6722 4576.
www.kalkuvarti.lv

Sapņu Fabrika
Lāčplēša 101.
Tel 2201 1811.
www.sapnufabrika.lv

JAZZ & BLUES

Bites Blūza Klubs
Dzirnavu iela 34a.
Tel 6733 3123.
www.bluesclub.lv

Carpe Diem
Meistaru iela 10–12.
Tel 6722 8488.
www.carpediem.lv

Hamlets
Jāņa sēta 5. *Tel 6722 9938.* www.hamlets.lv

Rīgas Ritmi
www.rigasritmi.lv

BARS & CLUBS

Balzambārs
Torņa iela 4.
Tel 6721 4494.

Club Essential
Skolas iela 2.
Tel 6724 2289.
www.essential.lv

Folkklubs Ala
Smilšu iela 16. *Tel 2779 6914.* www.folkklubs.lv

Golden
Ģertrūdes iela 33–35.
Tel 2550 5050.
www.mygoldenclub.com

I Love You
Aldaru iela 9. *Tel 6722 5304.* www.iloveyou.lv

Paddy Whelan's
Grēcinieku iela 4.
Tel 6721 0150.

Pulkvedim Neviens Neraksta
Peldu iela 26–28. *Tel 6721 3886.* www.pulkvedis.lv

Skyline Bar
Radisson Blu Hotel Latvija,
Elizabetes iela 55.
Tel 6777 2222.

XXL
Kalniņa iela 4. *Tel 6728 2276.* www.xxl.lv

CASINOS

Olympic Voodoo Casino
Radisson Blu Hotel Latvija,
Elizabetes iela 55.
Tel 6782 8777.

Royal Casino
Tērbatas iela 7.
Tel 6709 2299.

CINEMA

Coca-Cola Forum
Janvara iela 8.
www.forumcinemas.lv

K Suns
Elizabetes iela 83–85.
www.kinogalerija.lv

Splendid Palace
Elizabetes iela 61.
www.splendidpalace.lv

ENTERTAINMENT IN LITHUANIA

Lithuania offers its visitors a wide variety of entertainment, with something for everybody. Most cities have a strong cultural tradition. Panevėžys has a popular drama theatre, while the residents of Klaipėda are more inspired by music, embracing both improvised and traditional jazz, blues and operetta. Trakai and Kernavė provide scenic backdrops to summer events, including medieval festivals of archery and swordfighting

Sign for a nightclub in Palanga

and mystical celebrations of the summer solstice. Lively pop festivals sometimes brighten up summer resorts such as Palanga and Juodkrantė. Outside Vilnius the entertainment options tend to be limited, although Klaipėda provides some atmospheric venues for live music. Baroque and chamber music concerts are regularly performed throughout the year in many of Lithuania's churches. For entertainment options in Vilnius see pages 368–9.

INFORMATION

The English-language *In Your Pocket* guides, found in hotels, at newsstands and online, cover most of Lithuania's livelier towns. Despite its name, *VilniusNOW!*, found in four- and five-star hotels of the capital, occasionally lists events outside Vilnius.

Lithuania has a large number of visitor's information centres with English-speaking staff and English-language leaflets, booklets and up-to-date local information. All of Lithuania's towns and cities have their own dedicated websites, which usually contain schedules and information on culture and events.

BOOKING & PRICES

The booking service **Bilietai** has kiosks in most concert venues and shopping centres in major cities, where tickets can be bought with credit cards or cash. Tickets can also be booked by telephone or through a website and can be collected from a sales office, or delivered to any address in Lithuania. Prices usually vary anywhere between 30 and 100 litas per person.

THEATRE

Lithuanian theatre developed during the period of independence between the World Wars, producing young and talented playwrights such as Balys Sruoga and Kazys Binkis. Vilnius has a

Imposing exterior of the Klaipėda State Drama Theatre in Klaipėda

particularly strong theatre culture, although an equal passion for theatre exists outside the city.

The **Klaipėda State Drama Theatre**, which dates from 1819, is Lithuania's oldest theatre building and the most famous outside Vilnius. In Panevėžys, the **Juozo Miltinio Drama Theatre** is named after legendary stage actor and director Juozas Miltinis (1907–94), who taught actors to reject conservatism and to draw on their own life experiences while acting.

CLASSICAL MUSIC

Kaunas has several concert halls that feature music regularly. The **Kaunas State Musical Theatre** and the **Great Hall** of Vytauto Didžiojo University are among the preferred venues, but the Kaunas City Symphony Orchestra and Kaunas State Choir also perform at less formal venues including the Mykolas Žilinskas Art Gallery (*see p260*). Some churches host classical music recitals that often have no entry charges.

Zapyškis Church (*see p261*), outside Kaunas, and the famous Church of the Holy Trinity (*see p234*), near Anykščiai, are some of the more atmospheric venues in the countryside.

On the coast, the **Klaipėda State Music Theatre** holds a wide array of classical music concerts, opera and other performances. The Panevėžys Civic Art Gallery (*see p264*) and the Kėdainiai Multicultural Centre (*see p261*) also hold regular concerts.

Beautiful exterior view of the Kaunas State Musical Theatre

MUSIC FESTIVALS

Several music festivals have grown in popularity over the years. The magnificent Baroque Pažaislis Monastery complex *(see p261)*, near Kaunas, forms the backdrop to the annual **Pažaislis Music Festival**. The **Edvard Grieg and M K Čiurlionis Festival**, hosted in Kaunas each spring, features classical music concerts. The **Muzikinis Pajūris** (Musical Seaside) festival of opera and symphony takes place every summer in Klaipėda.

NIGHTLIFE

Club life is not limited to the capital city. Klaipėda has an increasingly lively and varied nightlife. A popular place is **Pabo Latino**, a branch of the successful club of the same name in Vilnius. Newer venues are gradually taking the place of the duller bars and discos in and around the Old Town. They offer casinos, concerts and restaurants, besides dance floors. Kanto Street also has some spirited bars full of fun and revelry.

Kaunas has a mix of low-key bars such as **BO** in the Old Town and the swinging **Nautilus Centre**, a club frequented by the young. The other party-town in Lithuania is the coastal resort of Palanga, where in summer the entire area around Basanavičiaus gatvė (street) turns into a pulsating open-air disco from dusk virtually until dawn.

Colourfully lit interior of a nightclub on Basanavičiaus Street in Palanga

JAZZ, BLUES & FOLK MUSIC

Jazz features prominently in the country's cultural scene. Among the best jazz festivals is Kaunas Jazz *(see p208)*. **Kurpiai** in Klaipėda also hosts jazz and blues performances. Folk music features at the Days of Live Archaeology in Kernavė *(see p254)*, in July.

CINEMA

Movies screened in Lithuania are shown in their original language, which means that they can be enjoyed by locals and visitors. Only one modern multiplex, the **Forum Cinemas**, exists in both Vilnius and Kaunas. However, other cities have decent cinemas, such as **Cinamon** in Klaipėda.

DIRECTORY

BOOKING & PRICES	CLASSICAL MUSIC	MUSIC FESTIVALS	Pabo Latino

BOOKING & PRICES

Bilietai
www.bilietai.lt

THEATRE

Juozo Miltinio Drama Theatre
Laisvės 5, Panevėžys.
Tel (45) 584 614.
www.miltinio-teatras.lt

Klaipėda State Drama Theatre
H Manto 45.
Tel (46) 314 453.
www.kldteatras.lt

CLASSICAL MUSIC

Great Hall
S Daukanto 28,
Kaunas.
Tel (37) 327 869.

Kaunas State Musical Theatre
Laisvės alėja 91,
Kaunas.
Tel (37) 227 113.

Klaipėda State Music Theatre
Danės 19.
Tel (46) 397 404.

MUSIC FESTIVALS

Edvard Grieg and M K Čiurlionis Festival
www.kaunofilharmonija.lt

Muzikinis Pajūris
www.muzikinis-teatras.lt

Pažaislis Music Festival
www.pazaislis.lt

NIGHTLIFE

BO
Muitinės 9-1, Kaunas.

Nautilus Centre
Savanorių 124, Kaunas.
Tel (37) 338 228.

Pabo Latino
Žvejų 4, Klaipėda.
Tel (46) 403 040.

JAZZ, BLUES & FOLK MUSIC

Kurpiai
Kurpių 1a, Klaipėda.
Tel (46) 410 555.

CINEMA

Cinamon
www.cinema.lt

Forum Cinemas
www.forumcinemas.lt

Entertainment in Vilnius

The range of entertainment on offer in Vilnius has changed rapidly in recent years. Trendy clubs and lounge bars have sprung up, but, at the same time, there has been a resurgence of traditional folk singing and dancing. *Sutartinės*, music with rural roots, helped sustain national identity through the periods of occupation and, today, it has made a comeback in folk-themed restaurants. Classical music was promoted during the Soviet period, but it was also significant in the 20th-century national revivals. Classical music, opera and ballet performances in Vilnius are excellent. Live music is played in several key venues frequented by a small but enthusiastic and faithful crowd. Tourist information points provide news on most cultural events.

A scene from the play *Three Sisters* at the State Small Theatre of Vilnius

INFORMATION

VilniusNOW! is available free of charge in four- and five-star hotels, while *Vilnius In Your Pocket*, which also covers upcoming events, is available in most of the city's hotels. It is also sold in shops and kiosks. Brochures and leaflets of cultural events can be found at the capital's tourist information centres. Posters are another source of information.

Tickets for concerts, opera, ballet and plays can be purchased at the appropriate venue or booking kiosks. Tickets for all major events in Lithuania can be bought online from **Bilietai LT**.

THEATRE

The residents of Vilnius have a passion for theatre. Productions by two of the country's most outstanding directors, Oskaras Koršunovas and Eimuntas Nekrošius, are highly recommended. The **Lithuanian National Drama Theatre** and the more avant-garde **State Small Theatre of Vilnius** provide pre-recorded English translation for some performances, which can be heard using headphones.

CLASSICAL MUSIC, OPERA & BALLET

Vilnius has a good classical music scene. Both the opulent **National Philharmonic** and the contemporary **Congress Palace** hold superb concerts. Chamber music concerts are often held at the atmospheric St Catherine's Church *(see p237)* and, occasionally, at St Casimir's Church *(see p232)*.

On weekdays during term time, students and professors at the Lithuanian Academy of Music often give free-of-charge recitals at different venues in the city.

The standard of opera and ballet is generally high in Vilnius, although the repertoire is fairly conservative. In addition to classical performances, the innovative choreography of the **Anželika Cholina Dance Theatre** attracts big audiences and is very popular among locals and visitors. The famous **National Opera & Ballet Theatre** is funded by Lithuania's Ministry of Culture. Tickets for its performances often sell out quickly and it is advisable to visit the ticket office to check on availability.

FOLK MUSIC

Lithuania's folk music can be heard in folk-themed restaurants, which are as popular with locals as they are with visitors. For an authentic experience, enjoy the music with a traditional meal of meat-and-potatoes and Lithuanian beer at venues such as the cavernous Čili Kaimas *(see p338)* or the atmospheric **Marceliukės Klėtis**. Folk festivals are often played out in the courtyards and halls of Vilnius University *(see pp220–21)*, or in more low-key spots such as the **Teachers' House**.

ROCK, BLUES & POP

Several outstanding Lithuanian rock and pop performers play regularly at atmospheric venues such as **Tamsta Club**,

A classical music concert in progress at the Congress Palace

Live band playing at the Tamsta Club in the Old Town

Brodvėjus and the **Forum Palace**. Names to look out for include the punky Biplan, the singer and songwriter Andrius Mamontovas and the more soulful Jurga. International artistes on tour tend to play at the modern **Siemens Arena** or the less pretentious **Utenos Entertainment Centre**, which doubles as an ice rink.

JAZZ

With a small but fanatical following, jazz forms an inextricable part of the Lithuanian lifestyle. During the Soviet era, jazz was associated with freedom. The birth of Lithuania's modern jazz scene was at a recital in 1961, by 17-year-old pianist Vyacheslav Ganelin at the Academy of Music, which mesmerized the audience. Ganelin still makes rare appearances in Vilnius, often with saxophonist Petras Vyšniauskas. Another big name to look out for is singer-flautist Neda Malūnavičiūtė.

The best jazz in town is showcased at the **Vilnius Jazz** festival, which is held in October *(see p209)*.

NIGHTLIFE

Though a little quieter than many other European capitals, Vilnius has an abundance of bars and clubs featuring a variety of music genres and both local and international DJs. Uproarious **Bix** is for heavy metal fans, while **Gravity**, located inside a Soviet-era bomb shelter, attracts the best DJs. A little more central are **Paparazzi**, popular for its friendly atmosphere and wide range of cocktails, and **Pabo Latino**, a nightclub specializing in Latin rhythms. Bands often play live at **Žaltvykslė**.

CINEMA

Vilnius has two modern multiplex cinemas, both operated by Forum Cinemas *(see p367)*. One of them is housed in the Coca-Cola Plaza, while the other is in the Akropolis shopping centre. Films from other countries are usually screened in their original language with Lithuanian subtitles. Lithuanian films do not usually have English subtitles. Art-house cinemas have all but disappeared. A rare survivor, however, is **Skalvija**.

DIRECTORY

INFORMATION

Bilietai LT
www.bilietai.lt

THEATRE

Lithuanian National Drama Theatre
Gedimino 4.
Tel 262 1593.
www.teatras.lt

State Small Theatre of Vilnius
Gedimino 22.
Tel 249 9869.
www.vmt.lt

CLASSICAL MUSIC, OPERA & BALLET

Anželika Cholina Dance Theatre
Šimulionio 4–103.
Tel 6883 4181.
www.ach.lt

Congress Palace
Vilniaus 6–14. *Tel 261 8828.* www.lvso.lt

National Opera & Ballet Theatre
Vienuolio 1.
Tel 262 0727.
www.opera.lt

National Philharmonic
Aušros vartų 5.
Tel 266 5216.
www.filharmonija.lt

FOLK MUSIC

Marceliukės Klėtis
Tuskulėnų gatvė 35.
Tel 5272 5087.

Teachers' House
Vilniaus 39.
Tel 262 3514.
www.kultura.lt

ROCK, BLUES & POP

Brodvėjus
Vokiečių 4.
Tel 210 7208.
www.brodvejus.lt

Forum Palace
Konstitucijos 26.
Tel 263 6666.
www.forumpalace.lt

Siemens Arena
Ozo 14.
Tel 247 7576.
www.siemens-arena.lt

Tamsta Club
Subačiaus 11.
Tel 212 1185.
www.tamstaclub.lt

Utenos Entertainment Centre
Ąžuolyno 9.
Tel 242 4444.

JAZZ

Vilnius Jazz
www.vilniusjazz.lt

NIGHTLIFE

Bix
Etmonų 6. *Tel 262 7791.*

Gravity
J Jasinskio 16.
Tel 249 7966.

Pabo Latino
Trakų 3. *Tel 262 1045.*

Paparazzi
Totorių 3. *Tel 212 0135.*

Žaltvykslė
Pilies 11. *Tel 268 7173.*

CINEMA

Skalvija
A Goštauto 2–15.
www.skalvija.lt

OUTDOOR ACTIVITIES AND SPECIALIST HOLIDAYS

Bereft of dramatic peaks and raging rivers, the Baltic States nevertheless abound with subtle charms and this has helped develop rural tourism in the three countries. Exploring the lakes and rivers allows the scenery to unfold at a leisurely pace, while back on land, the forests are perfect for rambling. Fishing, berry- and mushroom-picking and bird-watching are among the most popular activities and can easily be arranged by reputed tour operators. The opportunities for those who wish to discover the region on horseback are endless, with excursions for both novices and experienced riders. Winter changes the landscape, and skiing, ice-skating, snowboarding and snowmobiling take over. For visitors who simply want to relax, the region has a series of stylish spa resorts which draw on decades of tradition. Brewery tours tempt those impressed by local beer. However, the infrastructure varies from region to region and it is best to contact a reputed tour operator.

INFORMATION

In the Baltic States, most tourist information centres have lists of both state-run and private tour operators, who organize a variety of outdoor activities depending on the time of the year. Most companies have their own dedicated websites *(see p375)*.

RURAL TOURISM

Development of rural tourism as an organized activity began in the mid-1990s with support from the Ministry of Agriculture along with other organizations. It has now become one of the biggest tourist attractions in the Baltic region, and it is often advisable to arrange for accommodation well in advance. Bookings can be made through the various rural tourism associations *(see p291)*, such as Estonian Rural Tourism, Country Holidays and Countryside Tourism of Lithuania.

BIRD-WATCHING

Located on major migration routes, with a high proportion of fish-rich wetlands and little intensive farming, the Baltic States are an ideal destination for bird-watchers. Ducks, geese, swans, corncrakes, bitterns, common coots and white storks are easily spotted.

It has been estimated that around 50 million waterfowl, including most of the world's tundra swans and barnacle geese, visit Estonia's coastal wetlands every spring. The peak time for bird-watching is the beginning of May at sites such as Matsalu National Park *(see p89)*. The autumn migration is at its best in October

Bird-watching tower near Lake Lubans, Latvia

at Põõsaspea Cape, close to Haapsalu. Several tour operators, including **Estonian Nature Tours**, arrange bird-watching trips. For further information contact **Estonian Ornithological Society**.

Good bird-watching spots in Latvia include Gauja National Park *(see pp186–9)* and Lake Lubans *(see p198)*. The **Engure Ornithological Centre**, situated in Lake Engure *(see p172)*, has been monitoring and protecting duck populations since 1958. The **Latvian Birding** website keeps up-to-date lists of sightings in the country.

Over 330 species of birds can be spotted in Lithuania, including great snipes, white-tailed eagles, ferruginous ducks, corncrakes and aquatic warblers, among which are endangered species that breed in the country. The main

Latvia's Ķemeri National Park, home to a large number of birds

Cyclists on a winding path in Gauja National Park, Latvia

migration route follows the coast and crosses the Curonian Spit, and a particularly good spot is the Vente Horn on the tip of the Nemunas Delta National Park (see p283). The biggest draws are the migrations in spring and autumn, mainly between September and early October. Early spring is a good time to observe seabirds, owls, woodpeckers and grouse, while the largest number of species can be spotted during the breeding season between late May and early June. The **Lithuanian Society of Ornithologists** also arranges bird-watching tours.

HIKING & TREKKING

Despite their lack of hilly terrain, the Baltic States attract walkers with their extensive forests, attractive rivers, lakes and rural calm. The relatively high chance of spotting wildlife such as roe deer, wild boar, moose and wolves also draws a number of walkers here. Each country has a good selection of well-marked trails with campsites and guest houses along the way, and local tourist offices can suggest routes or arrange guides for visitors.

In Estonia, Lahemaa National Park (see pp106–107) has trails of varying lengths covering a diverse terrain. There are also pleasant routes surrounding Tartu (see pp114–15) and on the islands of Saaremaa (see pp92–3) and Hiiumaa (see pp90–91). A more unusual activity is bog-walking in Soomaa National Park (see pp100–101).

Latvia's Gauja National Park is good for walking, particularly along the well-marked Līgatne Nature Trail (see p189). There are also numerous short trails in the Tērvete Nature Park (see p167) and visitors looking for hills might head for the Latgale Uplands (see p198). Tour companies, such as **Eži**, organize walking trips in Valmiera (see p190).

Lithuania has almost 300 hiking trails, of which around 170 are in regional or national parks. Dzūkija National Park (see p256) is a favourite and some of its paths and facilities have been especially adapted for disabled visitors. Short, well-signposted walks include the 5-km (3-mile) long Šeirė Nature Trail and the route through the Čepkelių bog from the park's headquarters.

Walking trail in the picturesque Tērvete Nature Park, Latvia

Among the Lithuanian companies offering walking trips, the **Nemunas Tour** is one of the most popular.

CYCLING

The relatively flat terrain and breathtaking scenery of the Baltic States makes cycling a pleasant way to get around. However, mountain bikers will find little to challenge their skills. It is not all smooth riding, though, as some roads are in poor condition. A popular international route is the EuroVelo route 10, which runs along the north of Estonia through Tallinn, across to the islands of Hiiumaa and Saaremaa via ferry, on to Rīga and then

A cycle sign at Vaide, Latvia

further south to Klaipėda. Bicycle rental is easy in Estonia and Latvia, while in Lithuania there are hire outlets in the larger towns and cities. A good point of contact for all three countries is **BaltiCCycle**, a non-profit organization which provides details of organized tours, bicycle rental and self-guided cycling. It is also possible to hire a bike in one Baltic country and return it in another.

In Estonia, popular areas for cycling include Lahemaa National Park and the islands of Muhu (see p91), Saaremaa and Hiiumaa. **City Bike** is a notable organization that provides cycling tours and rental services in Estonia.

Easy rides in Latvia include the route from Rīga to Jūrmala (see pp170–71), while the best opportunity for mountain biking is in the Gauja Valley near Sigulda (see p188). There are marked biking routes around Kuldīga (see p179) and from Cēsis (see p188–9) to Valmiera; Eži arranges trips in the latter area.

The Lithuanian section of the international Baltic Coast route includes an attractive stretch between Palanga (see p282) and Klaipėda (see pp280–81). There is also a marked route along the coast of the Curonian Lagoon to the Nemunas Delta National Park.

Riders practising their equestrian skills, Pärnu, Estonia

HORSE-RIDING

Horses are a common sight in the rural areas of the Baltic States, especially in Latvia's Latgale region, where traditional ploughing methods still persist alongside mechanized farming. Horses can be hired at most horse-breeding farms; some farms also offer instruction. It may be possible to hire carriages, traps and even horse-drawn sleighs during winter.

The sandy tracks of Lahemaa National Park are popular for horse-riding in Estonia. One unusual option is the **Tihuse Riding Farm** on the island of Muhu, where guests can also participate in ploughing fields with the help of horses. Visitors to the Tori Stud Farm *(see p101)*, in Estonia, can enjoy a tour of the farm in a

horse-drawn carriage. In Latvia, tourist attractions offering horse-riding include the Līgatne Nature Trail. Disabled visitors may be interested in riding therapy at **Kavalkāde** in Jūrmala. One of Lithuania's most renowned horse-breeding farms, **Žagarė Stud Farm**, about 34 km (21 miles) north of Šiauliai, has stalls built and decorated with materials from England at the end of the 19th century.

FISHING

Fishing is a very popular year-round activity in the Baltic States. In winter, hardy local people trek out onto frozen lakes and cut holes in the ice. Common fish include perch, brown trout, pike, carp, bream, tench and grayling. Fishing permits are

required throughout the region, and additional licences are required for some areas. Major tour operators can provide or assist visitors in obtaining the required permits.

Estonia's long coastline offers numerous angling opportunities. Inland, several companies organize fishing trips to Lake Peipsi *(see p123)* and Lahemaa National Park. A good starting point is the **Tallinn Fishing Club**, which issues permits that can otherwise be difficult to arrange. The club's staff provide assistance, although most of them speak only Estonian.

In Latvia, Lake Engure and Lake Kaņieris in Ķemeri National Park *(see p170)* are particularly good for pike. There are also many other suitable lakes in the Latgale and Vidzeme regions, and fish farms around the country. The **Latvian Fishing Association** can provide information on fishing sites, and permits are usually easy to obtain.

The key spots in Lithuania are in the east of the country, particularly near Ignalina in the Aukštaitija National Park *(see pp266–7)* and Molėtai Lakelands *(see p265)*, and in the south. The Nemunas river is also popular, particularly around the town of Rusnė, as is the Curonian Spit *(see pp284–5)*. Most fishing tackle shops and park offices sell licences; otherwise they are available from the **Department of Water Resources**.

Fishermen angling from the banks of the Lielupe river in Jelgava, Latvia

MUSHROOM- & BERRY-PICKING

Picking berries in spring and mushrooms during autumn are popular activities in the Baltic States. In fact, mushrooms are often a source of income in rural areas.

Often, the best way to arrange mushroom- and berry-picking is to ask your hotel or guest house to organize it. It is advisable to take a local along for guidance on both where to look and which varieties of mushroom are edible and tasty. The Estonian Rural Tourism website has details of farms which can offer mushroom- and berry-picking. The Džukija and Aukštaitija national parks offer some of the best opportunities. Visitors must bear in mind that it is usually illegal to pick the cranberries which grow on peat bogs. Berry-picking with **Vaskna Turismitalu** near Võru also teaches visitors how to make traditional alcoholic Christmas drinks. The website of Countryside Tourism of Lithuania has useful information on mushroom- and berry-picking. The **Žervynos Hostel** can also help with arrangements for the same.

WINTER SPORTS

With long winters usually providing several months of snow coverage, it is not surprising that cross-country skiing is popular. What may be more unexpected is the number of downhill ski runs in a region where the highest point is just about 318 m (1,043 ft) above sea level. Although the Baltic States do not attract hardcore skiers and snowboarders, there are adequate opportunities for those who enjoy the sport.

In Estonia, some of the best skiing, snowboarding, snowmobiling, snowtubing and ski-jumping are found around Otepää *(see p118)*, such as at **Kuutsemäe Resort**. Cross-country skiing is also possible at the Soomaa National Park. Details for winter activities are listed on the Estonian Rural Tourism website *(see p291)*.

Canoeing in Soomaa National Park, Estonia

A premier spot for downhill skiing in Latvia is **Žagarkalns**, located close to Cēsis, but there are numerous other options listed in the Baltic Country Holidays website *(see p291)*. Visitors seeking adventure should try the bobsleigh run in Sigulda operated by **Taxi Bob**. In Lithuania, Ignalina is a favoured destination for skiers. The **Lithuanian Winter Sports Centre** is one of several options in the area, with four downhill pistes, cross-country skiing and a skating rink. For ice-skating on frozen lakes, including Trakai, visitors may contact **Kempingas Slėnyje**. **Camping Villa Ventainė** regularly organizes snowmobiling and ice-fishing on the Curonian Lagoon.

Enthusiasts enjoying skiing in Kuutsemäe, Otepää, Estonia

WATER ACTIVITIES

With hundreds of rivers and lakes, and an extensive coastline, the Baltic States offer ample opportunities for canoeing, kayaking, windsurfing and rafting. The lack of any serious rapids may deter keen white-water enthusiasts, but it is perfect for leisurely river excursions.

Canoeing is one of the best ways to explore the wilderness of Soomaa National Park in Estonia, where visitors can also try to build *haabjas* (longboats). A number of water activities are provided by **Vesipapp**, **Surf Paradise** and **Reimann Retked**. Of the Baltic countries, Latvia has the most developed water tourism and the Gauja river is a popular spot. Specialist operator **Campo** offers a range of river trips and **Pāvilosta Marina** arranges catamaran sailing lessons. In Lithuania, the Aukštaitija region, with almost 300 lakes linked by waterways, allows tour companies to create multi-day sailing trips. Elsewhere, the **Trakai National Sports and Health Centre** offers kayaking, canoeing, yachting and diving. Similarly, the **Zarasai Water Sports Centre** offers waterskiing and windsurfing. Klaipėda's **Oktopusas** diving centre arranges dives in lakes and the Baltic Sea.

Latvian ice-hockey player in action in an IIHF World Championship match

SPECTATOR SPORTS

The Baltic States are among the few parts of Europe where football is not the dominant spectator sport. The region's most enthusiastic football fans are the Estonians, and their national team has improved in recent years. However, the biggest sport in Estonia is basketball, for which major fixtures can be seen at the **Kalev Stadium**.

In Latvia, the most popular sport is ice hockey, particularly since the national team beat Russia in the 2000 Ice Hockey Championships. Many of the best players are members of overseas teams, making domestic games a little lacklustre, but support is enthusiastic at international games at the **Arena Rīga**. Visitors to Daugavpils will find the city in the thrall of speedway racing. Enthusiasts should not miss a visit to the **Lokomotive Stadium**.

The most popular spectator sport in Lithuania is basketball. The national team has won a bronze medal at the Olympic Games three times and was the European champion in 2003. Žalgiris Kaunas and Lietuvos Rytas Vilnius are the leading domestic teams. To watch players practising, visit the **Siemens Arena**.

GOLF

Soviet Russians were not keen on golf, so the sport is relatively new to the region and there are few good courses.

In Estonia, a number of golf clubs are members of the **Estonian Golf Association**. The **Estonian Golf & Country Club** is seeking to be a part of the PGA Tour. There are 18-hole courses in Otepää, Saaremaa and Tallinn, the last of which is well maintained.

The premier course in Latvia is at the **Ozo Golf Club** on Rīga's outskirts, while the country's other 18-hole course is **Saliena**, located between Rīga and Jūrmala. Golf clubs in Lithuania with 18-hole courses include **Sostinių** and **Europos Centro**. There are also plans to open a golf complex near Klaipėda, featuring an additional spa hotel.

SPA BREAKS

There have been health resorts in the Baltic States since the 19th century, although there is evidence of mud and spring water being used in folk medicine much earlier. The resorts were hugely popular during the Soviet era, drawing visitors from across the former Soviet Union for relaxation or medical treatment. There was a decline in the spa industry after independence. However, since then new spa hotels have opened and older ones have been renovated. Treatments are cheaper than in Western Europe, and there are special deals in winter.

There are several spa hotels on the Estonian islands and also establishments within, and close to, the capital, such as the **Kalev Spa**, a huge facility on the edge of the Old Town, and **Meriton Spa**. The **Estonian Spa Association** represents several of the country's spas.

The main spot for a spa break in Latvia is Jūrmala, a string of seaside towns providing everything from lively bars to secluded beaches. Another good choice is the Spa Hotel Ezeri *(see p307)*.

In Lithuania, the best spas can be found in Druskininkai *(see p255)*, one of which is **Spa Vilnius**. Palanga is also a popular spa destination.

BREWERY TOURS

Beer brewing has a celebrated history in the Baltic States, and there are several brewery tours available in the region. Try **A Le Coq Brewery** in Estonia or the **Užavas** or **Valmiermuižas** facilities in Latvia. Lithuania has the best choice of breweries open to the public, including **Utenos**, **Švyturys**, **Volfas Engelman**, **Kalnapilis** and **Rinkuškiai**.

Entrance to the Spa Vilnius, one of the best spas in Druskininkai, Lithuania

DIRECTORY

BIRD-WATCHING

Engure Ornithological Centre
Tel 742 2195.
www.eedp.lv

Estonian Nature Tours
Linnuse tee 1, Läänemaa.
Tel 477 8214.
www.naturetours.ee

Estonian Ornithological Society
Veski 4, Tartu.
Tel 742 2195.
www.eoy.ee

Latvian Birding
www.putni.lv

Lithuanian Society of Ornithologists
Naugarduko 47–33, Vilnius. *Tel 8521 30498.*
www.birdlife.lt

HIKING & TREKKING

Eži
Beātes iela 30a, Valmiera, Latvia. *Tel 6420 7263.*
www.ezi.lv

Nemunas Tour
Gėlių 50, Ringaudai, Lithuania. *Tel 3756 3766.*
www.nemunastour.com

CYCLING

BaltiCCycle
Tel 6995 6009.
www.bicycle.lt

City Bike
Uus 33, Estonia.
Tel 683 6383.
www.citybike.ee

HORSE-RIDING

Kavalkāde
Skautu iela 2, Jūrmala, Latvia. *Tel 2940 6955.*

Tihuse Riding Farm
Hellamaa, Muhu, Estonia.
Tel 514 8667.
www.tihuse.ee

Žagarė Stud Farm
Žagariškų k, Žagarė, Lithuania. *Tel 4266 0860.*

FISHING

Department of Water Resources
Juozapavičiaus 9, Vilnius.
Tel 5272 3786.

Latvian Fishing Association
Stabu iela, Rīga.
Tel 6731 6943.

Tallinn Fishing Club
Pärnu mnt 42.
Tel 525 4488.

MUSHROOM- & BERRY-PICKING

Vaskna Turismitalu
Haanja vald, Võrumaa, Estonia. *Tel 782 9173.*

Žervynos Hostel
Tel 3103 9583.

WINTER SPORTS

Camping Villa Ventainė
Ventės k, Lithuania.
Tel 4416 8525.
www.ventaine.lt

Kempingas Slėnyje
Slėnio 1, Trakai, Lithuania.
Tel 5285 3880.
www.camptrakai.lt

Kuutsemäe Resort
Tel 766 9007.
www.kuutsemae.ee

Lithuanian Winter Sports Centre
Sporto 3. *Tel 3865 4193.*
www.lzsc.lt.

Taxi Bob
Peldu iela 2, Sigulda, Latvia. *Tel 2924 4948.*
www.taxibob.lv

Žagarkalns
Tel 2626 6266.
www.zagarkalns.lv

WATER ACTIVITIES

Campo
Kronu 23d, Rīga.
Tel 2922 2339.
www.campo.laivas.lv

Oktopusas
Šilutės 79, Klaipėda, Lithuania. *Tel 4638 1850.*
www.godive.lt

Pāvilosta Marina
Ostmalas 4, Pāvilosta,

Latvia. *Tel 6349 8581.*
www.pavilostamarina.lv

Reimann Retked
Tel 511 4099.
www.retked.ee

Surf Paradise
Ristna, Hiiumaa, Estonia.
www.paap.ee

Trakai National Sports and Health Centre
Karaimų 73, Lithuania.
Tel 5285 5501.

Vesipapp
Tel 511 9117.
www.vesipapp.ee

Zarasai Water Sports Centre
Laukesos village, Zarasai, Lithuania. *Tel 3855 3426.*
www.poilsiobaze.lt

SPECTATOR SPORTS

Arena Rīga
Skanstes iela 21.
Tel 6738 8200.
www.arenariga.lv

Kalev Stadium
Juhkentali tänav 12, Tallinn. *Tel 644 5171.*

Lokomotive Stadium
Jelgavas iela 54, Daugavpils, Lithuania.
www.lokomotive.lv

Siemens Arena
Ozo 14a, Lithuania.
Tel 5247 7576.
www.siemensarena.lt

GOLF

Estonian Golf Association
Tel 504 1792.
www.golf.ee

Estonian Golf & Country Club
Manniva küla, Jõelähtme, Harjumaa. *Tel 602 5290.*
www.egcc.ee

Europos Centro
Girijos village, Lithuania.
Tel 6162 6366.
www.golflub.lt

Ozo Golf Club
Milgravja 16, Rīga.
Tel 739 4399.
www.ozogolf.lv

Saliena
Egļuciems, Babītes Pagasts, Latvia. *Tel 716 0300.*
www.salienagolf.lv

Sostinių
Pipiriškių k, Pastrėvio sen, Lithuania. *Tel 6199 9999.*

SPA BREAKS

Estonian Spa Association
Sadama 9–11, Haapsalu.
www.estonianspas.eu

Kalev Spa
Aia 18, Tallinn. *Tel 649 3300.* www.kalevspa.ee

Meriton Spa
Toompuiestee 27, Estonia.
Tel 667 7111.
www.meritonhotels.com

Spa Vilnius
Dineikos k 1, Druskininkai.
Tel 3135 3811.
www.spa-vilnius.lt

BREWERY TOURS

A Le Coq Brewery
Tähtvere 56–62, Tartu, Estonia. *Tel 744 9711.*
www.alecoq.ee

Kalnapilis
Taikos avenue 1, Panevėžys, Lithuania.
Tel 4550 5219.
www.kalnapilis.lt

Rinkuškiai
Alyvų 8, Birži, Lithuania.
Tel 4503 5293.
www.rinkuskiai.lt

Švyturys
Kūlių vartų 7, Klaipėda, Lithuania. *Tel 4648 4000.*
www.svyturys.lt

Utenos
Pramonės 12, Utena, Lithuania.
www.utenosalus.lt

Užavas
Užavas pagasts, Ventspils, Latvia. *Tel 2921 9145.*
www.uzavas-alus.lv

Valmiermuižas
Dzirnavu iela 2, Valmiera, Latvia. *Tel 2026 4269.*
www.valmiermuiza.lv

Volfas Engelman
Kaunakiemio 2, Kaunas, Lithuania. *Tel 8007 2427.*
www.volfasengelman.lt

SURVIVAL GUIDE

PRACTICAL INFORMATION

After so many years of being excluded from the map of Europe, the Baltic States of Estonia, Latvia and Lithuania are now drawing a great number of eager visitors to discover the region's hidden treasures. These countries are extremely visitor-friendly destinations that offer a wealth of historic sights and cultural activities as well as great natural beauty, good food and fascinating insights into the region's complex past. Each country has a well-developed network of tourist

Logo, Estonian Ministry of Foreign Affairs

information centres that often extends into small towns and offers an abundance of useful literature to help visitors get the best out of their trip. Moreover, with the region's capitals only a relatively short drive away from each other, it is easy to explore the Baltic States either individually or as a whole. Tour operators are growing in number and offer a good variety of packages. The practical information below and on pages 380–81 covers each of the three Baltic States.

WHEN TO VISIT

The best time to visit the Baltic States is from May to October, when the weather is generally pleasantly warm and, quite often, surprisingly hot or cool, but rarely cold. It is an ideal time to explore the region's natural wonders by visiting one of the many national parks or taking long treks in the countryside, camping or going swimming in the sea or one of the numerous lakes. Nearly all the best festivals take place in summer, while some small museums and historic sights are only open between May and September.

The Old Towns of Tallinn and Rīga are especially crowded at the peak of summer due to their compact size. Vilnius's larger Old Town, however, is less cramped. Autumn is often splendid in

Impressive building of the French Embassy in Rīga, Latvia

Street café close to Vilnius Cathedral, Vilnius, Lithuania

the Baltic States, but the weather can abruptly turn chilly as early as October.

The capitals are also very atmospheric in winter, when they are blanketed in snow, although winter temperatures can plunge significantly at any time. The worst time to visit is January, the coldest month, and the rainy month of April, when the snow melts into a mass of sludge.

VISAS & PASSPORTS

Citizens of EU-member states, the USA, Canada, Australia and New Zealand only need a valid passport for entry into Estonia, Latvia and Lithuania for a period of up to 90 days in a half-year period. Those wishing to stay beyond the permitted 90 days will need to apply for a national

long-term visa or a residence permit. Visitors from other countries should enquire at the relevant embassy or consulate for visa requirements before travelling. The official websites of the Ministry of Foreign Affairs for each of the three countries offers information on visa regulations.

CUSTOMS REGULATIONS

EU citizens are not subject to customs regulations, provided they adhere to EU guidelines. All visitors should check for any customs duty or special permission required to export a cultural object, before buying it. For detailed information on all these guidelines, entrance regulations and visa cost, it is advisable to visit the official website of the European Commission.

◁ Shops and cafés lining a cobblestoned street in Tallinn's Old Town, Estonia

Visitors at the tourist information office in Tallinn, Estonia

TOURIST INFORMATION

Estonia, Latvia and Lithuania have a remarkably well-developed network of tourist information centres supported by an equally advanced structure of tourism websites. All cities and most major towns have a tourist information office, which is usually located in or close to the town square. In the case of very small towns, the office is often situated in a museum or within some other historic building. Tourist offices in cities and larger towns are open from 9am to 6pm on weekdays. The offices are open for shorter hours on Saturdays and are usually open on Sundays. In remote places, opening hours are more erratic and it is advisable to check in advance.

Tourist offices are staffed by friendly English-speaking local people, who are always eager to promote their area

Logo, Lithuanian Tourism

and can offer information on accommodation, museums, historic sights, nature trails, entertainment and restaurants. Free brochures covering local and national sights and events are available at these offices, which also sell more detailed maps, postcards and guide-books at nominal rates. For a full list of all tourist information offices across each country, visit their websites. Latvia and Lithuania also have tourist information centres in London, Finland, Germany, Sweden and Russia.

BUSINESS HOURS

Throughout Estonia, Latvia and Lithuania, banks and state institutions are generally open from 9am to 5 or 6pm. Private businesses are increasingly working longer hours and are open from 9am to any-where between 6 and 8pm. For opening hours of shops see pages 346, 350 and 354.

For opening hours of shops see pages 346, 350 and 354.

Imposing exterior of the Hipoteku Bank in Limbaži, Latvia

DIRECTORY

VISAS & PASSPORTS

Estonia
www.vm.ee

Latvia
www.am.gov.lv

Lithuania
www.urm.lt

CUSTOMS REGULATIONS

www.ec.europa.eu

TOURIST INFORMATION

www.visitestonia.com
www.latvia.travel
www.tourism.lt

EMBASSIES & CONSULATES IN TALLINN

Canada
Toomkooli 13. *Tel* 627 3311.
www.canada.ee

United Kingdom
Wismari 6. *Tel* 667 4700.
www.ukinestonia.fco.gov.uk

United States
Kentmanni 20. *Tel* 668 8100.
http://estonia.usembassy.gov

EMBASSIES & CONSULATES IN RĪGA

Australia
Vilandes iela 7. *Tel* 6732 0509.

Canada
Baznīcas iela 20/22.
Tel 6781 3945.

France
Raina bulvāris 9. *Tel* 6703 6600.

United Kingdom
J Alunana iela 5. *Tel* 6777 4700.
www.ukinlatvia.fco.gov.uk

United States
S Velsa 1. *Tel* 6710 7000.

EMBASSIES & CONSULATES IN VILNIUS

Australia
Vilniaus 23. *Tel* 212 3369.

Canada
Jogailos 4. *Tel* 249 0950.
www.canada.lt

United Kingdom
Antakalnio 2. *Tel* 246 2900.
www.ukinlithuania.fco.gov.uk

United States
Akmenų 6. *Tel* 266 5500.
www.usembassy.lt

Exhibition on the Lithuanian partisans, in the KGB Museum *(see p238)* in Vilnius, Lithuania

MUSEUMS, CHURCHES & HISTORIC SIGHTS

Museums in the Baltic States keep rather erratic hours, so it is advisable to check opening times before visiting. Usually, they open from 10am to 5 or 6pm during summer, although in some cases they open at 11am or even mid-day. Monday is the official closing day for most museums, though some are also closed on Tuesdays. Nearly all museums open on Saturdays and many on Sundays. However, tour operators often arrange for museums to open.

Other sights, such as castles and churches, tend to have fairly regular opening hours in summer, between 9 or 10am and 4 or 5pm, Tuesday to Saturday. In winter, however,

St Nicholas's Orthodox Cathedral *(see p181)* in Liepāja, Latvia

many museums open for shorter hours or just remain closed. Some historic sights can only be visited as part of a guided tour. Organizers often try to accommodate single visitors into a group.

DISCOUNT CARD SCHEMES

A cost-effective way of exploring Tallinn, Vilnius and Rīga is to purchase a city card. The Tallinn Card costs €6 for 6 hours, €24 for 24 hours, €28 for 48 hours and €32 for 72 hours. It entitles holders to free entrance to 40 major museums and tourist sights, free sightseeing tours, usage of public transport and admission to a range of entertainment venues, including a bowling centre, water park and a major nightclub. It can also get visitors a discount in many restaurants and shops. The card is on sale at tourist information centres, hotels, travel agents, Tallinn Airport, Tallinn Port and online. The Rīga Card costs 12 lats for 24 hours, 14 lats for 48 hours and 18 lats for 72 hours. It entitles holders to free admission to many museums, a walking tour of the Old Town and a discount at a range of hotels. There are two types of Vilnius City Card, 24 hours and 72 hours. The card entitles

KONTROLES TALONS

Ticket to St Peter's, Rīga

holders to free public transport (both buses and trolleybuses), free entry to museums and discounts on tours, accommodation and restaurants.

ADMISSION CHARGES

In all three Baltic States, admission charges vary considerably depending on the type of museum and where it is located. Most museums away from the capitals are quite reasonably priced. Ticket prices in Tallinn, Rīga and Vilnius are more expensive, but still reasonable. Students and senior citizens can obtain discounts. State museums in Estonia offer free entrance on the last Saturday of each month. In Latvia, state museums give free admission on the last Wednesday of each month, and in Lithuania many museums do not charge any entrance fee on Wednesdays.

WHAT TO WEAR

The chilly winters in the Baltic countries make thick layers of clothing, as well as gloves, hats and thick-soled waterproof shoes necessary. In summer, lightweight garments are usually adequate, but it is best to carry a jacket for the evenings. In spring, carry an umbrella. Comfortable footwear is recommended for walking on the cobbled streets of Rīga and Tallinn.

TRAVELLING WITH CHILDREN

The Baltic States are extremely child-friendly. Most parks have play areas and some even have a range of distractions, such as bouncy toy castles and trampolines. Many traditional-style taverns and ethnographic museums also provide some wonderfully old-fashioned play apparatus for children. Some hotels offer childcare facilities. For information on eating out with children *see page 317.*

DISABLED TRAVELLERS

Although there has been a significant improvement in recent years, Estonia, Latvia and Lithuania are not very well equipped in providing facilities for disabled people. Most of the new upmarket hotels and restaurants have taken disabled travellers' needs into consideration, but such places are a distinct minority. Owing to their historic structure, the Old Towns of the three capital cities are extremely difficult for disabled people to negotiate. In Tallinn, there are several steep, winding cobble-stoned streets, and Rīga's Old Town is also predominantly cobbled. Although very little of Vilnius's Old Town is cobbled, it is still difficult

Children playing at the Seaside Open-Air Museum *(see p177),* Ventspils, Latvia

to get around in many places due to the extremely narrow streets and pavements.

Public transport is another major obstacle as trams, trolleybuses and trains do not provide wheelchair access in Tallinn and Rīga, and only a very limited number of buses do. The situation is better in Vilnius, where a large number of buses and trolleybuses have access for disabled people. For information on access for disabled travellers in hotels, *see page 291.*

Signpost at
Limbaži, Latvia

LANGUAGE

Both Latvian and Lithuanian belong to the Baltic family of languages. Estonians speak a Finno-Ugric dialect, which is

closer to Finnish. German is quite commonly spoken as a second language in all three Baltic States, while virtually everybody is fluent in Russian. However, communicating in English in the capital cities is seldom a problem – most people speak it to some extent. Knowledge of English is less widespread in rural areas. For common words and phrases used in the three languages, refer to the Phrase Book on pages 427–9.

MEASURES & ELECTRICAL APPLIANCES

The Baltic States all use the metric system. The mains voltage is 230 volts in Estonia and Lithuania and 220 volts in Latvia. Standard Continental European two-pin plugs are used. Although UK plug adapters are available, they are not easy to find, so it is advisable to bring any necessary adapters with you.

LOCAL TIME

The clocks of the Baltic States are set to Eastern European Standard Time and are two hours ahead of Greenwich Mean Time (GMT+2) and seven hours ahead of Eastern Standard Time (EST+7). Clocks go forward one hour on the last Sunday in March and go back one hour on the last Sunday in October.

View of the cobbled Viru Street in Tallinn's Old Town

Personal Security and Health

Estonia, Latvia and Lithuania are generally safe countries, with relatively rare instances of theft and mugging. However, visitors should remain vigilant in the capitals, particularly in and around the Old Towns. Generally, Tallinn, Rīga and Vilnius are far safer than many other Western capitals, although the same precautions should be exercised as in any other major city in the world. The quality of medical care is improving, though at present it may fall short by European standards. Pharmacies in bigger cities are open all day and all three countries provide free emergency care.

Busy western end of Basanavičiaus Street in Palanga, Lithuania

POLICE

The Estonian *politsei* (police) usually wear a dark blue jacket and trousers, black boots and a baseball-like cap. They drive white cars with a blue stripe and the word *politsei* written on the side doors and bonnet. In Tallinn, the police have a significant street presence, especially in the Old Town, during summer. The municipal police force wear dark green uniforms and have limited powers. Therefore, the state police should be contacted to report a crime.

In Latvia, the *policija* (police) wear dark blue uniforms consisting of a suit-like jacket with epaulets and a maroon tie, although when on patrol they mostly wear dark blue overalls with a luminous yellow vest and broad cap. The Latvian police drive white cars with a grey stripe along the side. The Rīga municipal police usually wear all-black uniforms and patrol the Old Town, although they have limited powers of arrest. In an emergency, it is best to call the state police.

In Lithuania, the *policija* (police) uniform consists of a dark green jacket and trousers, black boots and a cap. They drive white cars with a green stripe along the side and "police" written in large letters across the car's bonnet.

GENERAL PRECAUTIONS

Although the vast majority of visitors to the Baltic States do not have any problems with theft, it always helps to take some basic precautions to safeguard valuables. Car theft remains a persistent problem in all three Baltic States, so park in central and well-lit areas, and keep expensive objects hidden from view. Using a guarded parking lot is safer still.

Pickpocketing is a minor problem, but still take care of your wallets and handbags.

In Rīga, avoid using the tunnels around Central Station at night; use the traffic light crossings instead. It is also a good idea to avoid using ATMs in quiet spots at night. Also, never carry large amounts of cash around with you while visiting popular tourist destinations.

PERSONAL SAFETY

As anywhere, using common sense is the best way to ensure your personal safety. Never accept drinks from strangers, no matter how affable they might seem, and never accept invitations from people to go with them to another bar or nightclub. Be vigilant and avoid disreputable-looking clubs, as a number of scams can happen in such places. It is advisable to carry a mobile phone, with a record of all emergency numbers.

Avoid drinking excessively. There are a handful of thugs in each of the Baltic capitals, who make a point of preying on inebriated foreigners as they stumble out of bars in the early hours and head back to their hotels, although they normally target solitary people. Also, refrain from ostentatious behaviour, such as carrying luxury items.

Estonian police car

Latvian police car

HEALTH CARE

Standards of health care in the Baltics are now at least equal to those in other European countries, if not better. EU citizens will be treated free of charge provided they bring their Health Insurance card (EHIC) with them, together with another form of photographic identification. Visitors from outside the EU will find the charges very reasonable. Most pharmacies stock international drugs.

Private clinics exist in all major cities and are an option if you require non-emergency treatment. Tallinn, Vilnius and Rīga all have a choice of

Interior of the Town Hall Pharmacy *(see p60)*, in Tallinn's Old Town

standard Western European clinics that are significantly cheaper than private clinics in the West. Check to see if your existing insurance policy covers all emergencies. If not, it is advisable to take out travel insurance. EU citizens with an EHIC card are entitled to free treatment in Estonia, Latvia and Lithuania.

As there are virtually no significant health risks in the Baltic States, precautionary immunization is not mandatory. However, there is the risk of acquiring tick-borne encephalitis, so if you are planning to spend any length of time in a forest in summer, you should get vaccinated against it. In Tallinn, Rīga

Exterior of the Medical Diagnostic Centre, Vilnius

and Vilnius, tap water is safe to drink, but is best avoided as it does not taste very good. Bottled mineral water is better.

PHARMACIES

Minor ailments and accidents can often be treated by staff at a local pharmacy (*apteek* in Estonian, *aptieka* in Latvian and *vaistinė* in Lithuanian), which will usually stock a large selection of international drugs as well as many herbal medicines that are produced locally. Pharmacies generally open from 8am to 7 or 8pm on weekdays and until 3 or 4pm on Saturdays. There are a few 24-hour pharmacies in Tallinn, Rīga and Vilnius.

DIRECTORY

EMERGENCY IN ESTONIA

Ambulance
Tel 112.

Fire
Tel 112.

Police
Tel 112.

Roadside Assistance
Tel 1888.

MEDICAL HELP IN TALLINN

24-Hour Pharmacy
Tõnismägi 5.
Tel 644 2282.

Qvalitas Swedish-Estonian Medical Centre
Parnu mnt 102c.
Tel 605 1500.
www.qvalitas.ee

Tallinn Central Hospital
Ravi 18.
Tel 622 7070.
www.itk.ee

Tallinn Mustamäe Hospital
J Sütiste 19.
Tel 617 1300.
www.regionaalhaigla.ee

EMERGENCY IN LATVIA

Ambulance
Tel 03, 112.

Fire
Tel 01, 112.

Police
Tel 02, 112.

Roadside Assistance
Tel 1888.

MEDICAL HELP IN RĪGA

24-Hour Pharmacy
Audēju 20.
Tel 6721 3340.

ARS
Skolas 5. *Tel 6720 1007.*
www.ars-med.lv

Paul Stradiņš Clinical University Hospital
Pilsoņu 13.
Tel 6706 9600.
www.stradini.lv

Rīga Hospital Number One
Bruņinieku 5. *Tel 6727 0491.* www.1slimnica.lv

EMERGENCY IN LITHUANIA

Ambulance
Tel 03, 112.

Fire
Tel 01, 112.

Police
Tel 02, 112.

Roadside Assistance
Tel 1888.

MEDICAL HELP IN VILNIUS

24-Hour Pharmacy
Gedimino pr 27.
Tel 261 0135.

Baltic-American Medical and Surgical Clinic
Antakalnio 124. *Tel 234 2020.* www.bak.lt

Vilnius University Emergency Hospital
Šiltnamių 29.
Tel 216 9140.

Banking and Currency in Estonia, Latvia and Lithuania

The Baltic States have a thriving banking sector and stable currencies which have been pegged firmly to the euro. Estonia joined the Eurozone on 1 January 2011, with Latvia and Lithuania expected to join in 2014. The best and most convenient way to obtain local currency is by withdrawing it from debit accounts using the ATMs of major banks. Banks and *bureaux de change* offer money-changing services. The rate may vary considerably, so it is wise to check in advance before you travel to the Baltic States.

BANKING HOURS

In Estonia and Latvia, banks are usually open from Monday to Friday between 9am and 6pm. Major banks in big cities stay open on Saturdays, from 9am to 2pm in Estonia and from 10am to 3pm in Latvia. In Lithuania, opening hours vary, with bank branches operating from 8am to 5pm on weekdays. Banks in big cities open on Saturdays from 8am to 3pm or 10am to 5pm, and, in rare cases, for a few hours on Sundays.

ATMS

There is an extremely wide network of ATMs in the Baltic States, spread across most major town centres and the capital cities. Some petrol stations have ATMs and most small towns have at least two or three. Most ATMs have English-language options and accept all major international credit and debit cards, such as **MasterCard**, **Visa Electron**, VisaPlus and Cirrus/Maestro, and you can withdraw cash with no additional charges. However, most of the ATM cash machines issue notes of high denominations.

Distinctively signposted *bureau de change* **in Latvia**

BANKS & BUREAUX DE CHANGE

Estonia, Latvia and Lithuania have a staggering number of banks. The biggest is the Swedish-owned, pan-Baltic **Swedbank**. It has branches in just about every town as well as many branches and ATMs in the cities. Sampo Bank and **SEB** are major banks in Estonia. In Latvia, **Latvijas Banka**, SEB, Citadele and Nordea are well established. In Lithuania, Vilniaus Bankas (SEB) and **Lietuvos Bankas** have the largest

One of the many 24-hour ATMs of Snoras, a bank in Lithuania

network. Banks usually charge between 2 and 3 per cent commission for changing money.

Bureaux de change are extremely widespread in the three capitals and are open long hours 7 days a week. They offer rates competitive to the banks, except in Estonia, where commission can be as high as 25 per cent. Changing money in hotels in all three countries should also be avoided, as they often offer unfavourable exchange rates.

CREDIT CARDS AND TRAVELLER'S CHEQUES

Traveller's cheques are best avoided as very few banks now change them and they are unheard of in shops. As there is a wide network of ATMs across all three countries, either cash or a credit card is a preferable option.

All the major credit cards are widely accepted, except in the smallest shops and cafés. Some museums outside the capitals also require cash payment. Bus and train fares must usually be paid in cash, both at the stations and on board.

ESTONIAN CURRENCY

The Euro (€) is the common currency of the European Union. It went into general circulation on 1 January 2002, initially for twelve partici-pating countries. Estonia joined in 2011, with the kroon phased out later that year. EU members using the Euro as sole official currency are known as the Eurozone. Several EU members have opted out of joining this common currency. Euro notes are identical throughout the Eurozone countries, each one including designs of fictional architectural structures. The coins, however, have one side identical (the value side), and one side with an image unique to each country. Both notes and coins are exchangeable in each of the participating Euro countries.

Bank Notes

Euro bank notes have seven denominations. The €5 note (grey in colour) is the smallest, followed by the €10 note (pink), €20 note (blue), €50 note (orange), €100 note (green), €200 note (yellow) and €500 note (purple). All notes show the stars of the European Union.

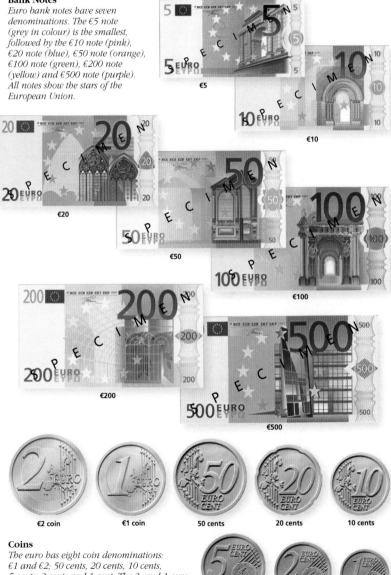

€5

€10

€20

€50

€100

€200

€500

€2 coin

€1 coin

50 cents

20 cents

10 cents

Coins

The euro has eight coin denominations: €1 and €2; 50 cents, 20 cents, 10 cents, 5 cents, 2 cents and 1 cent. The 2- and 1-euro coins are both silver and gold in colour. The 50-, 20- and 10-cent coins are gold. The 5-, 2- and 1-cent coins are bronze.

5 cents

2 cents

1 cent

LATVIAN CURRENCY

Latvia's monetary unit is the lat, commonly abbreviated as Ls. One lat is divided into 100 santims. Lats were introduced in the country in 1993, replacing the Latvian rouble, which was used for a short period after Latvia regained its independence. In 2005, the currency entered the Exchange Rate Mechanism II and lat was then fixed to the euro. In small towns and villages, it is sometimes difficult to get change for high-denomination notes. Be aware that visitors have reported a scam in which Lithuanian currency is given as change, as they resemble their Latvian counterpart but are lower in value. There are plans to adopt the euro soon.

Banknotes
Latvian banknotes are available in denominations of 5, 10, 20, 50, 100 and 500 lats. All these notes usually have signature prints of an oak leaf.

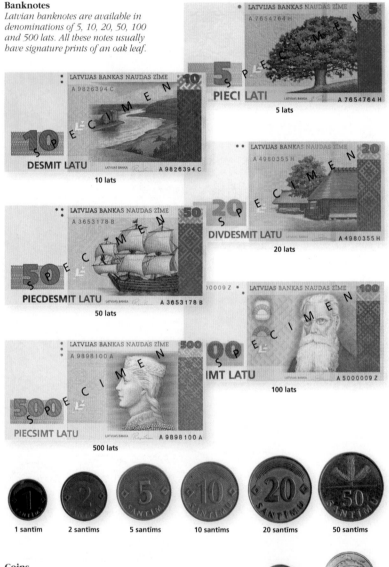

5 lats

10 lats

20 lats

50 lats

100 lats

500 lats

1 santīm   2 santīms   5 santīms   10 santīms   20 santīms   50 santīms

Coins
Latvian coins come in denominations of 1, 2, 5, 10, 20 and 50 santims, and 1 and 2 lats. Some gold and silver commemorative coins are also in circulation.

1 lat   2 lats

LITHUANIAN CURRENCY

The national currency of Lithuania is the litas, which is usually abbreviated as Lt. First issued by the Bank of Lithuania in 1922 after World War I, the litas was recalled from circulation after Lithuania was annexed by the Soviets in 1940. The litas was reintroduced in 1993, following a period of transition from the rouble to the litas. One litas consists of 100 centų. The obverse of all coins bears their value and the reverse bears the national coat of arms.

The litas has become a stable currency since it was pegged to the euro in 2002. The euro is to be adopted by Lithuania, but this is unlikely to happen before 2015. Foreign currency can easily be exchanged in banks or in *bureaux de change*.

Banknotes

Lithuanian banknotes currently in circulation are issued in denominations of 10, 20, 50, 100, 200 and 500 litų (or litai).

10 litų

20 litų

50 litų

100 litų

200 litų

500 litų

1 centas   2 centų   5 centų   10 centų   20 centų   50 centų

Coins

Lithuanian coins come in the following denominations: 1 centas and 2, 5, 10, 20 and 50 centų (or centai) and 1 litas and 2 and 5 litų. On the reverse side is the national emblem of the vytis, *a sword-wielding knight on horseback.*

1 litas   2 litų   5 litų

Communications in Estonia, Latvia and Lithuania

The three Baltic States have a highly developed communications network, which is almost on par with that of Western Europe. Mobile phone usage is extremely high, broadband Internet access is widespread and the national postal services are generally dependable. International courier services also operate in all three countries. The absence of high mountains and the flat terrain in the Baltic countries ensure good mobile phone coverage, although there are blind spots in remote areas. International calling cards are easily available. While travelling, one of the best ways of keeping in touch is by email, although in parts of the Latvian and Lithuanian countryside, public Internet access is rare and Wi-Fi access far more limited than in Estonia.

PUBLIC TELEPHONES

The public telephone system in the Baltic States is of a good standard. Most payphone booths accept pre-paid phonecards, which are readily available from kiosks, post offices and supermarkets. English-language instructions on how to operate the payphone are often posted inside. Discounts on international calling cards are also available from many kiosks. In an effort to win back customers lost to mobile phones, local rates have been kept low but call prices to mobile as well as international numbers are high. In Latvia, some centrally located phone booths offer Wi-Fi access at a range of up to 100 m (109 yards). Hotels charge more than the going rate.

MOBILE PHONES

GSM mobile phone networks have complete coverage in the Baltic States. If you want to use your mobile, however, you should check with your service provider. It is best to inquire about incoming call costs, which can often be exorbitant. The main mobile networks have partnerships with Western European service providers such as Orange and Vodafone. Another option is to buy a pre-paid SIM card from a local provider and insert it into the handset for relatively cheap call and SMS rates.

Estonian postbox outside the Central Post Office, Tallinn

POSTAL SERVICES

Mail services in the Baltic States are efficient and very dependable. Post offices provide a range of services at competitive postal rates. Mail can be sent *poste restante* to any post office in the Baltic region, but a passport is usually essential to collect it.

Postcards should be bought in post offices, as they are cheaper than in most shops.

INTERNET

Internet cafés are abundant and cheap in most major cities and towns in the Baltic States. Nearly all hotels have Internet connections and many cafés and restaurants have Wi-Fi access. In smaller towns they are signposted with an "@" sign. Almost all hotels have fax facilities, and faxes can also be sent through the central post offices.

ENGLISH-LANGUAGE MEDIA

There is one pan-Baltic, English-language newspaper: *The Baltic Times* comes out every Thursday and covers news, business, arts and entertainment across the Baltic States. It includes weekly entertainment listings and information on concerts, exhibitions and films. *In Your Pocket* (around €2) provides comprehensive and well-researched write-ups on everything from restaurants and bars to nightclubs and shopping, as well as up-to-date information on musem opening times. Both publications are widely available at kiosks and some retail outlets. Free listings magazines come and go in all three capitals and are available at hotel reception desks.

European editions of British and American newspapers, such as *The Financial Times,* the *International Herald Tribune* and *The Guardian* are readily available in Tallinn, Rīga and Vilnius.

Customers at a newspaper kiosk in Ventspils, Latvia

Communications in Estonia

Estonia's communications infrastructure is very efficient. All phone lines are digital, ensuring high-quality connections and easy-to-make international calls. Internet and mobile phone usage is particularly high. A staggering range of services can be paid for through mobile phones, including parking charges. The post offices offer a range of express delivery options, including a special pan-Baltic option. There are over 1,000 Wi-Fi areas covering a vast stretch of the country, including the main islands and even some beaches. However, Internet access is limited in the provinces.

One of the many payphone booths in the Old Town, Tallinn

MAKING A PHONE CALL

Estonia has an extremely simple and efficient digital telephone network. In 2004, the country did away with all city codes, as a result of which all landline numbers are now seven digits. The code for Estonia is 372. To call abroad from an Estonian line, dial the international code 00, followed by country code.

To call a number within Estonia, dial the number as it is, as there are no city codes in effect. Landline numbers have seven digits and charges for landline calls are cheaper than those to mobile phones.

Public payphones only accept *telefoniputka* (pre-paid cards), which come in denominations of €2, €3 and €6 units, and are available at kiosks and post offices. International calls can also be made using pre-paid cards, but the rates are high.

MOBILE PHONES

Estonian mobile numbers all begin with 5 and usually have seven or eight digits. The main mobile phone operators are **EMT**, Elisa and the pan-Baltic **Tele2**. EMT Simpel and Tele2 both offer pre-paid SIM cards, which are useful for visitors planning to stay in Estonia for any significant length of time.

POSTAL SERVICES

The state-owned Estonian *postkontor* (post office) is an efficiently run enterprise. It has 500 outlets around the country opening from 9am to 6 or 7pm on weekdays, and between 9am and 3pm on Saturdays. The **Tallinn Central Post Office** is open till 8pm on weekdays, and 6pm on Saturdays. It is also open till 3pm on Sundays.

Eesti Post (Estonian Post) is the only provider of universal postal services in Estonia. It offers traditional services such as delivering letters, parcels and periodicals, besides express, warehousing and transportation facilities. Postboxes are orange and marked "Eesti Post".

INTERNET & EMAIL

Internet cafés, locally known as *internetikohvik*, are widespread in Tallinn and Tartu. In smaller towns, there may only be one or two and they are often crowded with children playing computer games.

Wi-Fi Internet logo, Estonia

Prices generally range from €1–€2 for 30 minutes. All public libraries offer free Internet access, although only for 15 minutes at a time, and in smaller towns, this is the only option available. There are over 350 Wi-Fi hotspots in Tallinn, many of which are free, usually in hotel lobbies, cafés, pubs, parks and petrol stations. There are distinctive black-and-orange signs to help spot places offering Wi-Fi access.

DIRECTORY

USEFUL NUMBERS

Collect Calls
Tel 16116.

Directory Enquiries
Tel 1182.

Operator
Tel 165.

MOBILE PHONES

EMT
www.emt.ee

Tele2
www.tele2.com

POSTAL SERVICES

Eesti Post
www.post.ee

Tallinn Central Post Office
Narva mnt 1. *Tel 661 6616.*
www.post.ee

INTERNET ACCESS

www.wifi.ee

DIALLING CODES

- All Estonian mobile phone numbers begin with 5. All others are landline numbers.
- To make an international call from Estonia, dial 00 and then the country code and number.
- To call Estonia from overseas, use the international access code 00 followed by Estonia's country code, which is 372.

Communications in Latvia

The telephone and mail networks in Latvia are both efficient and reliable, although some post office branches need modernization. Nevertheless, post offices are present in most towns and villages of significant size. Public telephones are also common, despite the popularity of mobile handsets. Internet access is excellent in Rīga and other major cities, with Wi-Fi hotspots in many cafés and hotels, and it is improving rapidly throughout the country.

A Plus Punkts kiosk selling SIM-card packages and top-up credit, Rīga

DIRECTORY

USEFUL NUMBERS

Directory Enquiries
Tel 1188.

PUBLIC TELEPHONES

Lattelekom
www.lattelecom.lv

POSTAL SERVICES

Latvijas Pasts
Brīvības bulvāris 32.
Tel 6750 2815.
www.pasts.lv

MAKING A PHONE CALL

The partly state-owned **Lattelekom** no longer has a monopoly on landlines, but remains the only operator of public telephones. Most public telephones need either a *telekarte* (phonecard), which can be purchased in denominations of 2, 5 and 10 lats at post offices and newsstands, or with a major credit card. For international calls, it is better to purchase a pre-paid calling card, which allows connection through a toll-free number and gives automated instructions in many languages.

Since August 2008, all valid landline numbers have eight digits; the additional digit is a zero after the third digit. To make a local call to an old seven-digit landline number, prefix the number with 6. If it is a mobile phone number prefix it with 2. Latvia has no area dialling codes.

MOBILE PHONES

Latvia's relatively flat terrain helps ensure excellent signal coverage in all the major cities. Today, more Latvians have mobile phones than landlines and Lattelekom is the main service provider.

Visitors who intend using their mobile phones should contact network operators to enable roaming. If there are partnership agreements between the visitor's service provider and the local network, roaming charges are cheaper. If not, both incoming and outgoing international calls are charged at a premium rate.

To avoid roaming charges altogether, purchase a local SIM card issued by a local network operator. This is possible only if the handset is unlocked, as some operators lock phones to specific networks. SIM card packages and top-up credit are available at newspaper kiosks and supermarkets.

Signpost for an Internet café in Rīga

POSTAL SERVICES

Letters and packages weighing up to 10 kg (22 lbs) are handled by the state-owned **Latvijas Pasts** (Latvia Post). Main post offices are usually open between 8am and 7pm on weekdays, and from 8am to 4pm on Saturdays. The largest branch in Rīga, at Brīvības bulvāris (avenue) 32, tends to stay open for longer hours, while smaller post offices in villages and cities, such as Jēkabpils and Ludza, often open for shorter hours. Letters and postcards can also be mailed using the bright yellow postboxes.

INTERNET & EMAIL

Most towns have at least one Internet café, variously called a *datorsalon, interneta kafenica* or *interneta clubs*. Prices vary between 0.50 santīm and 1 lat per hour. In villages or very small towns, the library may be the only place with public Internet access. Many hotels offer Wi-Fi access. Internet facility may be available for free or may require a pre-paid Lattelekom card.

DIALLING CODES

- All toll-free numbers in Latvia begin with 8 and all fee-based numbers start with 9.
- To make a call to Latvia from an overseas number, first dial the international access code 00 followed by Latvia's country code (371), and then the landline or mobile phone number.

Communications in Lithuania

The widespread network of telephone and mail services in Lithuania is very efficient. The huge popularity of mobile phones has ensured that public phones are, in fact, rarely used, although they still stand in good working order in many cities, towns and villages. Post offices can be found in all towns and larger villages. Internet usage is fast becoming popular and finding an access point is seldom a problem in most big cities.

Phone card, available with the service provider, Teo LT

MAKING A PHONE CALL

The landline telephone network in Lithuania is run by the private company **Teo LT**. Its payphones are card-operated and easy to use. Cards can be bought at post offices and newsstands, in denominations of 9, 13 and 30 litai. Call tariffs vary according to the time of day, but it is usually about 2 litai per minute for calls made to other countries in Europe or the USA. Telephone rates in hotels vary widely, so it is best to check before making a call.

Lithuania has a complicated system of telephone codes with specific city codes, which can be confusing for most visitors. To make a call from a landline to another landline in the same city or area, dial only the number. If the number is in another city or area add 8 plus the area code before the number. To call a local mobile or landline number from a mobile or landline number overseas, use the international access code followed by the number. To call a local mobile from a local mobile number, prefix the number with 8. For making calls to a landline number from a local mobile number, dial 8, the city code and then the number.

MOBILE PHONES

There are currently three mobile phone operators in Lithuania – **Omnitel**, **Bité** and **Tele2**. Mobile phone users who wish to avoid roaming costs can buy a SIM card from one of these service providers. Available at newspaper kiosks, these SIM cards help cut local call rates and also reduce international call costs.

POSTAL SERVICES

Lithuania's postal service is very punctual. *Paštas* (post offices) can be found almost everywhere in the country. They open from 8am to 6pm on weekdays and 9am to 2pm on Saturdays. **Vilnius Central Post Office** opens from 7:30am to 7pm on weekdays and 9am to 4pm on Saturdays. A postage stamp for a postcard to any EU country costs 2.45 litai.

It is best to register letters and parcels for a small extra fee. The main post office in every city offers a *poste restante* service for receiving mail. To collect it, you will need to show your passport.

INTERNET & EMAIL

Internet cafés tend to be used mostly by youngsters enjoying computer games. They can be found in many cities and are often located in cellars, rather than standing as recognizable cafés. Hotels offer Internet access to guests, but some provide only a plug-in point for a laptop. Prices for access are reasonable and connections are generally speedy.

DIRECTORY

USEFUL NUMBERS

Directory Enquiries
Tel 118.

PUBLIC TELEPHONES

Teo LT
www.teo.lt

MOBILE PHONES

Bité
www.bite.lt

Omnitel
www.omnitel.lt

Tele2
www.tele2.lt

POSTAL SERVICES

Vilnius Central Post Office
Gedimino 7. *Tel 261 6759.*
www.post.lt

DIALLING CODES

- Lithuania's city codes include 5 for Vilnius, 37 for Kaunas, 46 for Klaipėda, 313 for Druskininkai, 460 for Palanga and 469 for Nida.
- To call Lithuania from overseas, dial the international access code 00, followed by Lithuania's country code (370) and the local number.

An everyday scene inside the Vilnius Central Post Office

TRAVELLING TO ESTONIA

It is easy to reach Estonia by air, as several major international carriers from many European cities provide links to Tallinn, the capital of Estonia. The country is also well served by ferries, with regular services to Tallinn and the island of Saaremaa. In Tallinn, the ferry port and main railway station are conveniently located close to the Old Town and city centre, while the airport

Logo of Estonian Air, the national carrier

and coach station are only a short taxi or bus ride away. The city has good coach connections with the rest of Europe, although travelling by coach can be slow. Reaching Estonia from Western Europe by train is almost impossible, as the only international service is from Russia. However, a pan-Baltic train, Rail Baltica, is being planned and may be operational by 2016.

Gleaming interior of Lennart Meri Tallinn Airport

ARRIVING BY AIR

The sleek-looking **Lennart Meri Tallinn Airport** is the only Estonian airport with regular scheduled flights. In recent years, the airport has become a regional hub with approximately 12 airlines using the airport, including major carriers such as **Finnair**, **airBaltic** and **Lufthansa**.

Founded in 1991, **Estonian Air** is the country's national carrier. Based in Tallinn, it offers a good standard of services in both business and tourist class. The airline has direct links with several major European destinations as well as some Estonian cities and islands. Visitors from outside Europe need to catch a connecting flight from cities such as London, Helsinki, Copenhagen or Stockholm.

As a consequence of the EU "open-skies" policy implemented in 2004, several

low-cost carriers, such as **easyJet**, now provide daily flights to Tallinn from London.

FROM TALLINN AIRPORT TO THE CITY CENTRE

Lennart Meri Tallinn Airport is about 3 km (2 miles) from the city centre. Taxis wait outside and the ride to the city centre costs around €10. Bus number 2 takes up to 15 minutes to reach the centre and costs around €1.50. It leaves every 20 minutes Monday to Saturday, and every 30 minutes on Sunday.

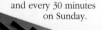
Taxi stand near Lennart Meri Tallinn Airport

OTHER ESTONIAN AIRPORTS

Estonia's other airports are situated in Pärnu, Kuressaare and Kärdla. These are serviced by small regional airlines with connections to Tallinn. There are special summer flight services from Sweden to Saaremaa Island and from Finland to Tartu.

In 2009, Tartu Airport was upgraded and now receives regular flights from Riga and Stockholm.

ARRIVING BY SEA

Estonia is very well served by ferry, with Tallinn's **Passenger Port** (*reisisadam*) handling about 7 million passengers a year. The main line **Tallink** has routes to Helsinki (Finland), Rostock (Germany) and Stockholm (Sweden), while other carriers, such as **Viking Line** and Eckerö Line are accessible from Helsinki and Stockholm. Linda Line runs a hydrofoil service to Helsinki.

Travellers from Helsinki are spoiled for choice, with a range of catamarans and ferries making the crossing. The Passenger Port is within walking distance of Tallin's Old Town and a taxi ride should cost between €3 and €5, although it is close enough to walk. The local bus no. 2 connects the port with the city centre, bus station and airport. Tallinn is also included in a choice of Baltic Sea cruises.

Tallink shuttle on its way to Rīga from Helsinki

Pärnu and Saaremaa Island are also included in some cruise ship itineraries.

ARRIVING BY COACH

International coach routes to Estonia are provided by **Lux Express** and **Ecolines**, which operate connections between Tallinn and Berlin, Munich, Kaliningrad, Warsaw and St Petersburg, among others. International coaches arrive at **Tallinn Bus Station** (*bussijaam*), which is a short taxi ride from the city centre. Alternatively, catch the numbers 2 or 4 trams, or numbers 17, 17a or 23 buses from the main bus station into the city centre. Passengers travelling to Tallinn by bus from Rīga or Vilnius can get off at the more central Viru väljak bus stop. There are also limited international coach connections with Pärnu, Narva and Tartu. The coach network is efficiently run and cheap. Services are clearly posted in coach and bus stations.

Luxury coach of Eurolines, Europe's largest coach network

ARRIVING BY TRAIN

Tallinn's main railway station, Balti Jaam, is a short walk away from the Old Town. There is a nightly train to Moscow. Tickets should be pre-booked, since Russian visa specifications insist on dates of entry and exit. In 2010, the Tartu–Volga line reopened, making it possible to travel from Tallinn to Riga. There are plans to build the Rail Baltica route to Warsaw.

ARRIVING BY CAR

Since 2007, when the Baltic States agreed to the Schengen Agreement (under which systematic border controls were abolished), there are no border restrictions for Schengen visa-holders. Crossing the border from Latvia is easy, especially for EU passport-holders. The border crossing with Russia is slower and border guards are likely to scrutinize your documents. To bring along your own car into Estonia, the Vehicle Registration document, an international driving permit and a valid Green Card insurance policy are mandatory.

ARRIVING BY HELICOPTER

Copterline's 12-seater helicopter service between Helsinki and Tallinn takes 18 minutes. There are about 13 hourly services between 7am and 8pm, from Monday to Saturday. Tallinn's heliport is a 5-minute drive from the city centre. A minibus service is available.

DIRECTORY

AIRLINES

airBaltic
www.airbaltic.com

Czech Airlines
www.czechairlines.com

easyJet
www.easyjet.com

Estonian Air
www.estonian-air.ee

Finnair
www.finnair.com

Lufthansa
www.lufthansa.com

AIRPORTS

Kärdla Airport
www.kardla-airport.ee

Kuressaare Airport
www.kuressaare-airport.ee

Lennart Meri Tallinn Airport
Lennujaama 1.
Tel 605 8888.
www.tallinn-airport.ee

Pärnu Airport
www.parnu-airport.ee

Tartu Airport
www.tartu-airport.ee

FERRY COMPANIES

Tallink
www.tallink.ee

Viking Line
www.vikingline.fi

FERRY PORT

Passenger Port
Sadama 25. *Tel* 631 8550.
www.portoftallinn.com

COACH COMPANIES

Ecolines
www.ecolines.ee

Lux Express
www.luxexpress.eu

COACH STATION

Tallinn Bus Station
Lastekodu 46. *Tel* 680 0900.
www.bussireisid.ee

HELICOPTER

Copterline
www.copterline.com

Getting Around Estonia

The best way of getting around Estonia is by car, as all the main sights are, at most, a few hours' drive away from each other. The country's rail network is cheap but with a limited reach and often frustratingly slow. A far better public transport option is the country's well-developed bus system, which links all the major towns and cities as well as the remote parts of the country. However, rural bus services are sparse, and the buses tend to crawl along at no more than about 30 kmph (19 mph). Alternatively, there is a good range of ferries serving the islands but many of these do not run in winter, when the sea freezes over. Some regular domestic flights connect Estonia's mainland cities, and there are regular air connections to several islands.

Local train waiting at Tallinn railway station

TRAVELLING BY TRAIN

Estonia's rail network is the least efficient way to see the country. Services have been so reduced that the choice of destinations is limited. There are rail routes between Tallinn and Narva, Tartu, Pärnu and Viljandi, and an electric train runs between Tallinn and Paldiski ten times a day. It is usually advisable to catch a *kiirrong* (fast train), although these are still relatively slow compared to those in Western Europe. However, there are now express trains, with first-class carriages, between Tallinn and Tartu. **Edelaraudtee** runs inter-city passenger services and **Elektriraudtee**, belonging to the same company, runs local electric trains.

It is best to buy *pilet* (tickets) on board, although some can be bought online or at the ticket offices in Tallinn. There are no passes for rail travel. Timetables are rarely printed or updated and services are usually posted on large display boards at the stations.

TRAVELLING BY BUS

The bus network in Estonia is efficiently run and is good value for money. Inter-city buses run regularly and are generally comfortable. Some companies run express routes, which avoid endless stops in small towns and villages. Route operators include **SEBE** and **Taisto**. The Tartu–Tallinn route is the busiest and most convenient, with coaches departing every hour until late at night. Tickets can be bought from the bus station or the driver on boarding. On busier routes, it is best to buy tickets in advance. Although ticket prices vary, they are generally very reasonable, but slightly higher than that for rail travel. The fares of buses bound for the islands are usually higher as they always include the price of the ferry crossing. To check bus schedules visit **Bussireisid**'s website.

Luggage is usually carried onto the bus and passengers may have to pay a small additional fee to stow any large items in the compartment underneath the bus.

TRAVELLING BY FERRY

The Estonian islands are well served by a number of car and passenger ferry connections. There are also regular services between Rohuküla harbour (near Haapsalu), Heltermaa (on Hiiumaa Island) and Vormsi. Virtsu harbour (north of Pärnu) has hourly connections with Muhu Island, which is linked with nearby Saaremaa Island by road. Saaremaa itself is connected with Hiiumaa from Triigi harbour in the northeast. Saaremaa has a special summertime ferry service to Ventspils in Latvia. Check **Saaremaa Shipping Company**

Bussireisid's air-conditioned inter-city express bus en route from Tartu

Ferry from Virtsu on its way to Saaremaa Island

Limited's official website for route details. **Veeteed** runs a ferry service between Pärnu and the islands of Kihnu and Vormsi, although the service is less regular. In summer, ferries tend to quickly fill up and passengers can be left waiting in long queues if they don't reserve their tickets well in advance. Passengers travelling by car should reach the harbour about 20 minutes before the scheduled departure time.

Isn winter, ferry services are often cancelled in the event of the sea freezing over, although officially designated ice roads are established if the ice is thick enough.

TRAVELLING BY AIR

Estonian Air, the country's national carrier (*see p392*), operates domestic flights that connect the major cities. **Avies** also runs a few daily flights between Tallinn, Kuressaare and Kärdla. It is best to book well in advance because their planes are very small and can only seat up to seven passengers. There are also some flights from Pärnu Airport to Kuressaare and Kihnu which are reasonably priced, and a good option in winter when the sea is frozen. Tartu Airport has connections to Riga and Stockholm. Kärdla acts mainly as a stopover point for chartered flights in Europe. The daily domestic service to Tallinn is the only regular service coming from the airport at Kärdla.

TRAVELLING BY CAR

Driving is by far the best way to get around Estonia. Conditions are generally good on main roads and distances are relatively short. However, country roads are severely potholed and dirt roads are also common in many rural parts of the country.

There are no motorways and overtaking is the norm. It is mandatory by law to drive with the headlights on at all times of the day. Wearing a seatbelt is compulsory for drivers as well as passengers. The speed limit is 50 kmph (31 mph) in built-up areas and 90 kmph (56 mph) on the main roads. In Estonia, drinking alcohol and driving is illegal. By law, winter tyres must be fitted between December and March.

Petrol stations are quite rare in remote places so it is advisable to fill up on petrol when leaving a city or town.

CAR HIRE

There are numerous car rental firms, including **Avis**, **Budget**, **Europcar**, **Hertz** and **National**. A local company, **Easy Car Rent**, also offers good deals. All require a major credit card and a valid international driver's licence. Rental rates are comparable to those in Western Europe. Outside Tallinn, there are few rental options except in major towns. However, some of the Tallinn-based chains can organize car hire in other parts of the country.

Autorent Terminal of Avis, a global car rental chain

Getting Around Tallinn

Most of the main sights in Tallinn are within comfortable walking distance of each other. The Old Town is so compact that it can easily be covered on foot. Public transport in Tallinn is cheap and efficient. It is made up of an integrated network of trolleybuses, buses and trams serving sites away from the city centre. Cycling is another good way of getting around the city. In general, Tallinn's transport options are very good, and there is no need for a car unless you plan to take a day trip or explore the outer parts of the city.

BUSES, TROLLEYBUSES & TRAMS

Tallinn's public transport system operates daily between 6am and midnight. Buses are the best way to reach the airport and other outlying areas. The terminal for many routes is in Viru Keskus, the central shopping mall. The nine trolleybus lines mainly connect to residential areas near the centre. The main stops are on Vabaduse väljak and Balti Jaam. Trams follow the main arteries in and out of the city centre. The four tram lines running across the city converge at the Hobujaama stop on Narva maanti (road).

Bus sign, Tallinn

The same tickets can be used on all three systems and schedules in English can be found at the **Tallinn Bus Company**'s website. As drivers only sell single tickets at a premium, it is best to buy tickets, either individual or as booklets, at kiosks. Tallinn Card *(see p380)* holders are entitled to unlimited travel on all public transport.

MINIBUSES

Minibuses, or route-taxis as they are often called, are a faster option for travellers. They connect the city centre to outlying residential areas. These white vans, operated by many small private companies, follow set routes, picking up and dropping off passengers at any spot they request along the route. Most minibuses leave from a stop at Estonia puiestee (boulevard) just opposite the Estonian Drama Theatre. Destinations are usually displayed in the window. Tickets cost between €1 and €2 depending on how far the destination is. Tickets can only be purchased from the drivers on boarding.

DRIVING

Driving around Tallinn may be a little disorienting for visitors. There are several confusing one-way systems and traffic jams are common during rush hour. Also, tram tracks are often in the middle of the road. Drivers have to stop and wait for a tram when it pulls in at a station so that passengers can safely alight. Driving conditions are especially difficult at night because of the dangerous habit of overtaking on narrow roads and speeding. The speed limit in Tallinn is 50 kmph (31 mph), except for some larger roads where the limit is 70 kmph (43 mph).

PARKING

There are plenty of parking options in Tallinn, though it can be hard to find a good spot in the heart of the city during weekdays. In the city centre, paid parking is in force between 7am and 7pm on weekdays and 8am and 3pm on Saturdays, although the first 15 minutes are free. Tickets can be bought from street-side machines or kiosks or, in some areas, by using a

Tram, a convenient mode of transport for short hops around Tallinn

A taxi waiting in a cobblestoned street in the Old Town, Tallinn

mobile phone, following instructions posted on signs. Rates range from around €1 per 15 minutes to €4.60 per hour. The Old Town has a seven-day, 24-hour paid-parking in effect, which starts at €0.75 per 15 minutes. A relatively convenient option might be to leave your car at one of several centrally located guarded parking lots. These range in price from about €0.75 to €1.90 per hour. In the summer months, paid parking is also in effect in the Pirita istrict.

TAXIS

There is an abundance of taxis in Tallinn, although it is best to take one from a taxi stand or to book one in advance from reputed companies such as **Tulika Takso**, **Tallink Takso** or **Reval Takso**. Taxi stands can be found near large hotels, major intersections and also next to the Estonian Drama Theatre. Hailing a taxi on the street is risky, as there are many dishonest taxi drivers who overcharge foreign visitors. However, legislation has been introduced to help improve the situation. All taxi drivers are obliged to display their prices in English, on the vehicle's rear right-hand window, and to provide a receipt on request. If the driver fails to give a receipt, the passenger is legally entitled not to pay the fare.

Starting fares normally range from €2.25 to €4.50, with a rate of about €0.50 per kilometre, although prices can vary considerably from operator to operator. It is advisable to ask the driver for an approximate price before

starting your journey and ensure that the meter is running. All fares must be paid in euros.

CYCLING

Getting around Tallinn by bicycle is a good option, although it is not so practical in the cobbled streets of the Old Town. There are plenty of bicycle rental firms in the city, such as **CityBike**, that offer a wide range of organized tours accompanied by a guide. It is also possible to rent a bicycle and take off by yourself. As there are hardly any bicycle lanes in Tallinn, special care should be taken when cycling along congested streets.

WALKING

Walking is the ideal way to experience the busy streets of Tallinn's Old Town and the city centre. In general, Tallinn is a pedestrian-friendly environment, although a good road map is useful to avoid getting lost in its labyrinthine streets. A huge number of

walking tours are available from most hotels and tourist information centres.

VELOTAXI

Velotaxis, or bicycle-taxis, are a novel way of seeing the city. They operate from March to October and cost around €2.25 for an adult and €0.95 for a child, and can be ordered on the **Velotaxi** website.

DIRECTORY

BUSES, TROLLEYBUSES & TRAMS

Tallinn Bus Company
www.tak.ee

TAXIS

Reval Takso
Tel 601 4600.
www.reval-takso.ee

Tallink Takso
Tel 640 8921.
www.tallinktakso.ee

Tulika Takso
Tel 612 0001.
www.tulika.ee

CYCLING

CityBike
Tel 5111 819.
www.citybike.ee

VELOTAXI

Velotaxi
Tel 5811 6051.
www.velotakso.ee

Fascinatingly novel velotaxi, available for hire in Tallinn

TRAVELLING TO LATVIA

Most visitors arrive in Latvia by air, at Rīga International Airport. Since independence there has been a rapid growth in the number of European cities directly linked to Rīga, mainly because of the arrival of low-cost carriers that raised the capital's profile as a destination for weekend breaks. In contrast, the country's regional airports are little used for

Arrivals sign at Rīga Airport

international passenger flights. For those who wish to avoid air travel and who have more time, there are sea routes from Germany and Scandinavia, besides comfortable trains and coaches from other parts of the Continent. Arriving by car is also perfectly feasible, provided the driver has the correct documents and is willing to tackle a variable road network.

ARRIVING BY AIR

The majority of passengers arrive at **Rīga International Airport**, which is connected to most Western European cities as well as to Prague, Moscow, Kiev, Tallinn, Vilnius and Warsaw. Services at the airport include a currency exchange and ATMs, which remain open until the last flight arrives.

The country's national carrier, **airBaltic**, was established in 1995 and offers some very affordable flights. Rīga is also served by other major airlines including **LOT**, **SAS**, **Lufthansa** and **Finnair**. Several low-cost carriers, such as **Wizz Air** and **Ryanair**, also fly to Rīga from various European cities.

There are very few direct flights to Latvia from the USA, New Zealand, Canada or Australia. Visitors often transfer at another European airport such as Copenhagen or Helsinki. It may be more economical to arrange a long-haul flight to a transport hub such as London, along with a separate onward flight.

Exterior view of Rīga International Airport

FROM RĪGA AIRPORT TO THE CITY CENTRE

Rīga Airport is located about 8 km (5 miles) from the city centre. The cheapest way to reach the city is by taking a bus from outside the airport terminal. Bus 22 runs approximately every 10 to 20 minutes, from 5:45am to midnight, and takes 30 minutes to reach Abrenes iela (street); stops along the way include 11 Novembra krastmala and the Central Railway Station. airBaltic operates the Airport Express every 30 minutes, from

5:30am to 12:30pm; it costs 3 lats. Taxis reach the city centre in 15 minutes.

OTHER LATVIAN AIRPORTS

The other international airports are in Ventspils and Liepāja. Neither is much used by scheduled passenger services.

ARRIVING BY SEA

Passenger ferries take longer than air travel, though crossing the Baltic Sea has its own appeal. Ferries operated by Tallink *(see p393)* connect Rīga to Stockholm (Sweden). **Scandlines** connects Liepāja to Lübeck (Germany), and Ventspils to Nynashamn (Sweden) and Lübeck. Rīga's main **Ferry Terminal** can be reached by trams 5, 7 or 9 from the bus station or outside the National Opera. There are marinas at Rīga, Jūrmala, Liepāja, Pāvilosta, Salacgrīva and Ventspils for those with their own boats. The Latvian Coast website offers information.

Express bus waiting outside Rīga International Airport

Passengers queuing up outside the ticket office at a bus station

ARRIVING BY COACH

This is the best way to travel between the three Baltic capitals. International carriers, such as **Ecolines**, **Lux Express** and **Nordeka** run services between Riga and several other European cities. Hansabuss operates three times a day. Rīga's main bus terminal, Autoosta, is five minutes south of the Old Town.

Travelling by coach costs less than travelling by air. However, the difference in fare is negligible except during the peak season. International coaches are equipped with air conditioning and reclining seats, but can be uncomfortable for long journeys.

ARRIVING BY TRAIN

The main railway station in Rīga, Central Railway Station, is located south of the Old Town. Although there are no trains from Vilnius to Rīga, there are international rail routes that head east towards Moscow, Vitebsk, Odessa and St Petersburg. The most comfortable way to travel on most routes is a *kupeja* (four-bunk

compartment). However, there are more luxurious two-bunk compartments on the trains from Moscow.

ARRIVING BY CAR

Since the Schengen Agreement *(see p393)*, there are no border controls between Estonia, Latvia and Lithuania. Entering from Russia or Belarus may take several hours.

It is essential to bring along the vehicle's registration document, a valid third-party insurance policy and either a European driving licence or an International Driving Permit. Vehicles must be in roadworthy condition and it is compulsory that you have a first-aid kit, fire extinguisher and hazard-warning triangle in your vehicle at all times. From December to March, winter tyres must be used, and between September and April, drivers should fit spiked tyres.

ARRIVING BY BICYCLE

Since Latvia acceded to the Schengen Agreement, cycling into Latvia has been simple from Estonia or Lithuania. The flat landscape makes it an attractive option during summer. Carry appropriate spares and a waterproof jacket.

There are two EuroVelo cycle routes passing through Latvia, though they are not always well marked, and much of the riding is on country roads. EV10 follows the Baltic coastline, while EV11 crosses the Estonian border at Valka and traverses Eastern Latvia to Daugavpils.

Passenger train passing through lush pine forests of the Latvian countryside

Getting Around Latvia

The public transport network in Latvia is extensive and affordable. Travelling by coach tends to be quicker than by train, although the buses are often old and can be uncomfortable. Major urban areas and places of interest to visitors usually benefit from frequent coach services. However, in the countryside, there may be only one bus or train per day in each direction. This means that visitors who wish to get off the beaten path will find it difficult to rely on public transport. Car hire is a popular choice, despite the variable state of the roads in the country. The combination of a flat landscape and relatively short distances makes cycling pleasant, especially in good weather.

Commuters entering the Central Railway Station, Rīga

TRAVELLING BY TRAIN

Trains tend to take a little longer than buses to reach their destinations, but the journey is slightly more comfortable, especially if travellers bring along cushions for the hard benches. However, the windows rarely open, making the carriages stuffy in summer. The heating can be erratic.

The most useful routes are from Rīga to Jūrmala Beach, Jelgava and destinations in Gauja National Park. There are also train services to places further afield such as Valmiera, Daugavpils and Rēzekne. Rail enthusiasts should take the narrow-gauge line between Alūksne and Gulbene.

TRAVELLING BY COACH

Regular coach services run between most large towns and cities. Other places are less frequently served, therefore careful planning is important to visit several towns in a single day. Although more expensive than travelling by train, travelling by bus is still good value. For overnight journeys, it is advisable to carry a blanket or sleeping bag.

Autoosta (Rīga's Central Bus Station) runs services to Bauska, Cēsis, Sigulda, Daugavpils, Liepāja, Valmiera and Ventspils. If the journey starts at a major station, it is best to buy a ticket before boarding. Otherwise tickets can be purchased from the driver. If your luggage is very large, you may have to pay to stow it in the luggage compartment, but otherwise it is normal to take it on board.

UNDERSTANDING TIMETABLES

Outside of Rīga, it can be difficult to find station staff who speak English. Timetables are written on boards at the railway station and are also available by telephone and on the Internet. Details of several common routes are also available in the publication *Rīga in Your Pocket (see p403)*. For further enquiries visit the **Latvian Railways** website.

Timetables at train or bus stations rarely include timings of return journeys from various destinations. Express buses are generally indicated by the letter "E", while the equivalent for trains is indicated by three-digit route numbers. *Pietur* indicates that a train or bus stops at a particular destination, while *nepietur* means that it does not. Buses and trains listed as *darbdienās* run on weekdays, and the days of the week are often listed by their initial. Latvian stations number their *perons* (platform) and *ceļš* (track) separately.

TRAVELLING BY CAR & MOTORCYCLE

Bringing or renting a vehicle is an excellent way to see Latvia for those who come

One of the many extra-long public buses typical of Daugavpils

Typical car rental sign at the Domestic Airport, Rīga

for short trips, or wish to visit out-of-the-way corners of the country. However, neither car rental nor petrol is cheap, and road conditions vary dramatically. Most major routes are in an acceptable state, but minor roads can be in poor condition. Many are surfaced with gravel or dirt. In winter, gritting is not widespread, and some minor roads become impassable without a sturdy four-wheel-drive vehicle.

Latvians tend to drive aggressively and overtaking on blind corners is common. Congestion is rare outside the capital. The legal blood alcohol limit is 0.05 per cent, with a ten-day prison sentence for exceeding it. Seat belt use is mandatory in the front seats, as well as in the rear if fitted, and crash helmets must be used on motorcycles. It is compulsory to drive with the headlights switched on at all times. The speed limit is 50 kmph (31 mph) in built-up areas and 90 kmph (56 mph) elsewhere. Traffic police cannot always be spotted outside towns and cities, but they are strict about speeding and collect fines on the spot. Remember to ask for a receipt if you are fined.

In the countryside, changes in speed limit are not always signposted and it is up to the driver to notice signs indicating built-up areas. These are white rectangles usually bearing the name of the town or village.

Signposting is poor across the country, making it essential to buy a good roadmap. For vehicle breakdown and towing, it is advisable to contact **SOS Motor Club**. On major roads, *degvielas*

stacija (service stations), are often open 24 hours, but in rural areas it can be hard to find a place to refuel.

Parking is usually easy outside Rīga, although some cities, notably Daugavpils and Liepāja, have parking meters in certain areas. There is also a fee of 1 lat to enter Jūrmala, collected at a roadside booth.

CAR HIRE

Vehicle hire is most easily arranged in Rīga, although other towns and cities have hire offices. Most international car rental companies are represented in the capital, and many of them have offices at the airport. They are many smaller companies as well. Check the condition of the vehicle and the insurance cover provided. Car hire services are operated by companies such as **Budget Rent A Car**. Most companies stipulate a minimum age for the person hiring the car. Requirements state that the driver should have held a licence for at least a year. The driver may also need to leave his credit card details or a large deposit.

Bumpy road sign at Krāslava

TRAVELLING BY BICYCLE

Cycling is a good way to get around the relatively flat terrain of Latvia. Bicycles can be hired in many towns and cities. The tourist information board can provide details of cycle routes, such as the popular and easy trail from Rīga to Jūrmala and routes in Gauja National Park and its surrounding valley. There are also two European Cycle Routes in Latvia, one of which, part of the EuroVelo 10, runs along the entire coast.

Bicycles are permitted on trains, although you need to buy a ticket for them. There are designated areas at the end of each carriage, marked with a bicycle symbol.

Cyclists riding through a field of dandelions in Gauja National Park

Getting Around Rīga

Rīga's compact Old Town is a pleasure to wander around and is best explored on foot. The cobbled streets, however, can prove difficult for those with mobility problems. Several hotels are located within the Old Town, while many others are within easy walking distance. It is also a short walk to the unmissable Art Nouveau district from the city centre. Attractions further afield, such as the Latvian Ethnographic Open-Air Museum, can be reached via the city's extensive network of buses, minibuses, trolleybuses and trams. Tickets are available on board, while passes valid for various lengths of time can be purchased from newspaper kiosks. Taxis are readily available outside the Old Town.

Passengers boarding a bus at Rīga Bus Station

BUSES, TROLLEYBUSES & TRAMS

With several bus, trolleybus and tram routes, Rīga's public transport system is a cheap and efficient way of getting around the Old Town. It brings many museums, hostels and hotels within easy reach of the town centre and also offers access to the zoo, the Song Festival grounds and to several large parks.

There are timetables at the various bus stops, but usually no route maps are shown, therefore it is advisable to carry one when travelling. Public transport on most routes runs between 5:30am and 11:30pm, with some services operating hourly throughout the night. Autoosta *(see p401)* is close to both the Central Railway Station and Central Market. Other transport hubs include the stretch in front of the Orthodox Cathedral.

Various organizations merged in 2005 to form a single body responsible for public transport, **SIA Rīgas Satiksme**. Until 2009 different payment systems operated for buses, trams and trolleybuses but now they have finally been integrated. There is a single fare of 0.70 lats paid to the driver on boarding. There is no extra charge for luggage. However, it is better to purchase your ticket first from a kiosk. The *etalon* smart card covers five, ten or twenty journeys at a discount. Public transport is free to holders of a **Rīga Card** *(see p380)*.

MINIBUSES

Rīga's *mikroautobuss* (minibus) network runs along the major boulevards and out into the suburbs, and usually offers great comfort and speed. The main stops are outside the Central Railway Station and the Orthodox Cathedral. Tickets cost marginally more than those for other public transport.

DRIVING

Driving in Rīga is seldom a pleasant experience, marred by heavy traffic during peak hours and aggressive drivers. Petrol stations are readily found, and roads tend to be in good condition, with just a few potholes.

It is worth noting that you must not pass a tram that has its doors open, since this might endanger passengers, and you must be aware not to block the tram lines.

PARKING

Parking can be difficult to find in the city centre. It is also expensive. Rates are 1.40 lats for the first hour and 2 lats per hour on the streets of the Old Town. For those who really need a car, it is best to choose a hotel with parking space.

TAXIS

Taxis are abundant in Rīga and are a comfortable, though relatively expensive, way of getting around. They do not come in a standard colour, although all official cabs have yellow licence plates. From 6am until

Taxis for hire outside Rīga International Airport

midnight, the meter starts at 0.4 lats and rises by 0.35 lats per kilometre. After midnight, the meter starts at 0.6 lats, increasing by 0.4 lats per kilometre. A better price can be obtained by calling a reputed company such as **Rīga Taxi** or **Rīgas Taxometru Parks**. It is also better to book a taxi in advance, rather than hire one in the street. Taxis waiting outside the upmarket hotels tend to be more expensive.

Passengers must note that drivers often refuse to accept a fare of less than 3 lats, and try to charge at least that much to take passengers from the bus or railway station to a nearby hotel. Visitors must ensure that the meter is used, or at least negotiate a fare in advance, before entering the taxi. It is rarely difficult to find a taxi during the day, while at night taxis congregate at each end of Kaļķu iela.

Pedestrians at a zebra crossing, Aspazijas bulvāris

Cycling in Rīga, a quick and easy way of getting around the city

CYCLING

Getting around Rīga by bicycle is a good option, despite the Old Town's cobbled streets and the heavy traffic in other parts of the city. One of the more pleasant places for a ride is the pristine suburb of Mežaparks *(see p156)*. **Eat Rīga** can offer help with bicycle rental in the city.

WALKING

The Old Town is relatively small, with plenty of recognizable landmarks, making the walk manageable as well as enjoyable in spite of the cobblestoned streets. It is particularly pleasant to wander around in summer, when many streets and squares are lined with terrace seating outside bars and cafés, and the weather is more suitable for walking. The area immediately north of the Old Town is home to some impressive Art Nouveau buildings and several smart shops and restaurants. The main street in Rīga's Art Nouveau district is Elizabetes iela, which intersects with Brīvības bulvāris (avenue). In addition, Alberta and Strēlnieku iela also feature examples of this style.

The Rīga Card *(see p380)* offers free entry to many museums, a free walking tour of the Old Town, and free public transport within Rīga and Jūrmala. Since public transport is already so cheap in the country, investing in the card is worthwhile only if visitors are interested in the walking tour or in visiting several museums in a single day. The card is available in hotels, Rīga Airport and the tourist information offices.

MAPS

The most widely available map of the city is published by Jāņa Sēta, at a scale of 1:20,000 with the centre shown at a detailed 1:7000. A much smaller version of the map is included in the popular *Rīga In Your Pocket* guide, but it is only detailed enough if you do not plan to stray far from the centre. However, the guide also indicates public transport routes.

DIRECTORY

BUSES, TROLLEYBUSES & TRAMS

SIA Rīgas Satiksme
Tel 8000 1919.
www.rigassatiksme.lv

TAXIS

Rīga Taxi
Tel 8000 1010. www.taxi.lv

Rīgas Taksometru Parks
Tel 8383. www.rtp.lv

CYCLING

Eat Rīga
Tel 2246 9888.
www.eatriga.lv

CITY CARD

Rīga Card
Tel 6721 7217. www.rigacard.lv

MAPS

Rīga In Your Pocket
Laipu iela 8–9a. *Tel* 6722 0580.
www.inyourpocket.com

TRAVELLING TO LITHUANIA

The quickest and easiest way to reach Lithuania is by air. Most airlines fly to Vilnius, which has direct connections with many European cities. Some international flights arrive at Kaunas and Palanga airports. Lithuania has only one sea port, at Klaipėda, which offers a limited number of passenger ferry services across the Baltic Sea to Germany and Scandinavia. By land, it is best to travel to Lithuania

Klaipėda port logo

by coach. There are regular departures from London, Paris and other European capitals. However, getting to Lithuania by car is long and hazardous given the bad roads in Poland. A daily train service links Warsaw with Kaunas and Vilnius, with a change at Sestokai, on the Polish-Lithuanian frontier. Lithuania is not covered by Eurail or InterRail, making travelling by train from Western Europe expensive.

ARRIVING BY AIR

Lithuania is well connected with Europe and, via major European transport hubs such as London, Copenhagen and Amsterdam, to the rest of the world. Connectivity has improved, with flights to and from Vilnius timing in well with intercontinental flights. Since March 2008, the control of internal borders among the Schengen states, which also include Estonia, Latvia and Lithuania, was abolished.

Opened in 1944, **Vilnius Airport** is the arrival point for most flights. It is the only airport among the Baltic capitals to have maintained its original appearance of a formulaic erstwhile Soviet-era terminal. Services at the airport include car rental offices, currency exchange, cafés and newspaper kiosks that also sell bus tickets.

airBaltic offers increased services between Riga and Vilnius, and direct services from Vilnius to several European cities including Amsterdam, Copenhagen, Dublin and London. British Airways pulled out of serving Vilnius due to low-cost airline competition. As a result, major international flights and low-cost carriers from around 40 cities arrive in Lithuanian airports. These include almost all the capitals of Western Europe, as well as Prague, Moscow, Minsk, Gomel, Kiev, St Petersburg, Tbilisi, Kaliningrad, Baku, Tel Aviv and other cities further east. Other European carriers that serve Vilnius, include

International check-in hall at Vilnius Airport

Austrian Airlines, Czech Airlines, Estonian Air, Finnair, Lufthansa, Ryanair and **SAS**.

From the United States, the most common routes to Lithuania are via Warsaw, then on to Vilnius with **LOT**; Stockholm or Copenhagen, then on to Vilnius with SAS; or Helsinki, then on to Vilnius with Finnair. Czech airlines fly via Prague.

Canadian visitors tend to fly via Frankfurt and Brussels with Lufthansa.

Travelling from Australia or New Zealand also requires multiple carriers, and it is worth shopping around for the best prices.

airBaltic has implemented a one-way ticket system, which ensures the prices of tickets depend directly on demand. The traditional "Sunday rule", with prices being higher on weekdays than on the weekends, does not hold true, as the

majority of tickets are purchased on the Internet. In accordance with inter-national agreements, most airline services operate a system of reduced rates for children, students and pensioners as well as pre-arranged groups.

FROM VILNIUS AIRPORT TO THE CITY CENTRE

Vilnius Airport is located 5 km (3 miles) south of the city centre. There is a train from the airport to Vilnius Main Station, which takes about 7 minutes, although buses also operate. Tickets are cheaper if bought at airport kiosks.

The bus stop and taxi rank are both outside the arrivals area. The official rate for taxis into town is about 25 litai, but tourists will find it difficult to pay less than 50 litai. Taxis take 20 minutes to reach the city centre.

OTHER LITHUANIAN AIRPORTS

The airports at Kaunas and Palanga have scheduled international flights, although they are fairly limited compared to those at Vilnius Airport. New terminals are being built at both the airports in an effort to make them better equipped. From Kaunas Airport, shuttle bus number 120 goes to Savanorių prospektas (avenue) and the Old Town, while bus number 29 goes to the bus station. A minibus shuttle travels twice daily between Kaunas Airport and Vilnius connecting all Ryanair flights, as that is the only carrier operating in Kaunas at the moment. For information on airport bus services, log on to **Ollex**. There are hourly buses from **Palanga Airport** to Palanga and many buses operate between Palanga and Klaipėda. airBaltic offers its passengers free minibus services from Palanga Airport to Klaipėda. Buses head north from the airport to Liepāja in Latvia.

ARRIVING BY CAR

As Lithuania is part of the Schengen zone, there are no restrictions to entering it from Schengen countries. Drivers entering the country by car do not need an international driver's licence, but it is essential to carry the vehicle's registration documents, insurance papers, a passport and a licence from their country. All cars must carry a first-aid kit and fire extinguisher.

International cargo and passenger carrier sailing out of Klaipėda

ARRIVING BY SEA

Lithuania's only commercial maritime harbour, **Klaipėda State Sea Port**, is linked by ferry to ports in Germany, Sweden and Denmark. There are connections between Klaipėda and Kiel and Mukran in Germany, Copenhagen-Fredericia, Aabenraa-Aarhus in Denmark and Karlshamn in Sweden.

ARRIVING BY COACH

Lithuania has an extensive network of roads connecting the country to neighbouring states. It is fairly simple to reach Lithuania by bus or coach from Estonia or Latvia as there are numerous crossing points. There are express passenger coaches from Vilnius to Rīga and Tallinn, as well as other cities including Warsaw, Berlin, Prague, Vienna, Kaliningrad and Moscow. On the other hand, the journey from countries such as Germany or the UK is very long and the inconvenience is best avoided.

Airport terminal building, Palanga Airport in Western Lithuania

DIRECTORY

AIRLINES

airBaltic
See p393.

Austrian Airlines
www.austrian.lt

Czech Airlines
www.czechairlines.com

Finnair
See p393.

LOT
See p399.

Lufthansa
See p393.

Ryanair
See p399.

SAS
See p399.

AIRPORTS

Kaunas Airport
Karmėlava. *Tel (37) 399 396.*
www.kaunas-airport.lt

Palanga Airport
Liepojos pl 1. *Tel (460) 52 020.*
www.palanga-airport.lt

Vilnius Airport
Rodūnios kelias 10a. *Tel 273 9305.* www.vilnius-airport.lt

AIRPORT BUS SERVICES

Ollex
www.ollex.lt

FERRY INFORMATION

Klaipėda State Sea Port
www.portofklaipeda.lt

Getting Around Lithuania

Lithuania's excellent road network makes it very easy to get around. Buses are the fastest and most convenient mode of public transport in the country. Express buses link virtually every town in Lithuania and are also a great way to see the countryside. Trains are cheaper, but also less frequent and with far fewer routes. The roads in Lithuania are some of the best-maintained in Central and Eastern Europe, which often makes hiring a car the most comfortable way to travel. The country's relatively flat landscape, punctuated by low hills, makes it ideal for cycling as well.

International luxury coach at the bus station in Panevėžys

TRAVELLING BY BUS

Buses form the main mode of Lithuania's public transport network. The privately owned bus company **Toks** operates comfortable buses on more than 50 routes countrywide as well as 11 international routes for **Eurolines**. Although travelling by bus is usually a little more expensive than by train, buses are quicker and connect more places.

Schedules are written on signs at the head of each stand, as well as inside the bus station building. Express buses, marked by an "E" in the schedules, sometimes operate on intercity routes, bypassing smaller towns and villages along the way. Many of the bus services to the coast, for instance to Palanga or Nida, are seasonal and operate in summer only. For more information on frequency of services check the official website for Toks.

Vilnius Bus Station is the country's biggest bus transport hub, although **Kaunas Bus Station** also has links with various European cities.

Tickets can be bought at ticket desks in bus stations in larger towns, although you can also buy them from the driver on boarding, especially on minor routes. In summer, or during weekends when services are more regularly used, it is worth buying tickets in advance. Tickets have to be paid for in cash and there are no facilities for reserving them by telephone or on the Internet. Disabled passengers, senior citizens over the age of 70 and children below the age of ten, are entitled to a 50 per cent discount. Pre-school children travel free. Groups of ten passengers or more get price reductions if travel is arranged in advance.

TRAVELLING BY TRAIN

The national rail network is run by **Lietuvos Geležinkeliai** (Lithuanian Railways). The main routes are from Vilnius to Šiauliai and Klaipėda, Vilnius to Visaginas, which passes by Ignalina and Aukštaitija National Park, Šiauliai to Panevėžys and Rokiškis, and the comparatively speedy and regular Vilnius to Kaunas route. The Vilnius to Varėna line continues to Dzūkija National Park before heading into Belarus. One of the most enjoyable and scenic train journeys in Lithuania is on the Narrow-Gauge Railway, which runs from Panevėžys to Lake Rubikiai.

All train tickets must be purchased at the ticket desks at railway stations. Reductions are available for young children, pensioners and also disabled passengers.

Lithuania's *autobusų stotis* (bus stations) and *traukinių stotis* (railway stations) are generally located close to one another and are within easy walking distance of the town centre. Theft is rare, although it is best to keep an eye on your belongings. Risk to personal safety is seldom an issue when travelling in Lithuania, but security guards are often deployed at Vilnius Bus Station.

However, bus and train stations place little emphasis on cleanliness and hygiene, although the stations at Vilnius and Kaunas have now been modernized. At

Narrow-Gauge Railway, one of the most scenic and enjoyable train journeys

Well-maintained ticket office in the railway station, Vilnius

the larger railway stations it is also possible to leave your baggage at the left luggage room for a small fee, or deposit the luggage in a self-service locker.

TRAVELLING BY CAR

Roads in Lithuania are excellent by post-Soviet standards, and present no special problems to drivers. There are different categories of roads, with different speed restrictions. The highest category of roads in Lithuania is the motorway, but there are only two of these, Kaunas to Klaipėda (A1), and Vilnius to Panevėžys (A2). Although the Vilnius–Kaunas and Kaunas–Klaipėda roads look the same, the former stretch is not the "motorway" class because of its hilly terrain. There are no toll roads in Lithuania except through the Curonian Spit National Park.

Lithuanian regulations state that every car must carry a small fire extinguisher, a first-aid kit, a reflective warning triangle and reflective safety vest. It is mandatory for passengers to wear seat belts. Motorists must use headlights at all times, both during the day and night. The traffic police may not be able to speak fluent English but are stringent about rules and can collect fines on the spot.

The maximum permissible speed limit on motorways is 130 kmph (81 mph) from May to October and 110 kmph (68 mph) for the rest of the year, the exception being the Vilnius–Kaunas motorway where the speed limit remains 110 kmph (68 mph). The speed limit in built-up areas is 50 kmph (31 mph), but drivers are rarely stopped for speeding unless they exceed a speed of 60 kmph (37 mph).

Drunken driving is a punishable offence and local authorities sometimes use roadblocks and breathalyzer tests as enforcement tools.

CAR HIRE

A large number of local and well-known international car hire companies offer a wide range of vehicles for rental in Lithuania. Some have desks at Vilnius Airport and upmarket hotels. Many others can be found in Vilnius city centre. Local firms, such as **Aunela**, have a range of newer and older Western makes of cars. The minimum rental period is usually 24 hours. Payments for car hire can be made both with cash or through any major credit card.

DIRECTORY

TRAVELLING BY BUS

Eurolines
See p393.

Kaunas Bus Station
Vytauto 24. *Tel* (37) 409 060.

Toks
www.toks.lt

Vilnius Bus Station
Sodų 22. *Tel* 8900 01661.
www.toks.lt/en/schedule

TRAVELLING BY TRAIN

Lietuvos Geležinkeliai
www.litrail.lt

CAR HIRE

Aunela
www.aunela.lt

ROAD SIGNS

Signposting on motorways, country roads and minor roads is comprehensible. When entering a town or village, the settlement's name appears on a sign with black lettering on a white background. This indicates that drivers must slow down to the speed limit for built-up areas. Small blue signs near road junctions in Vilnius city centre point the way to streets, sights and landmarks. Key road signs to look out for are those regulating speed, controlling roadside parking and preventing right or left turns. These are often monitored by traffic police.

Part of Klaipėda's recently modernized road network

Getting Around Vilnius

The best way to explore Vilnius is on foot as most sights such as churches, museums, restaurants and cafés are within easy walking distance of each other. It is only a short walk to the main sights from the city's main thoroughfare, Gedimino Avenue. Vilnius's Old Town is among the biggest in Europe and much of the city's inner traffic is kept to roads that circle its boundary. To reach the sights and restaurants that lie outside the city centre, a reliable network of trolleybuses and buses exists. Taxi services are usually trustworthy. However, getting around by road is best avoided at rush hour.

blockades, adding to drivers' woes in the short term. With the rise in the number of vehicles, tailgating and overtaking have become standard practice. Central Vilnius has an extensive one-way system, which can be quite tricky to negotiate without a road map.

PARKING

Multi-storey car parks in Vilnius are few. Most often drivers use roadside parking. In the city centre, drivers can use controlled parking between 8am and 6pm, using a pay-and-display machine. Parking is more expensive in the Old Town. Failing to pay results in a wheel-clamp, a lengthy wait and then a very heavy fine.

In parked cars, all objects including bags and clothing should be locked out of sight.

Modern trolleybus, part of Vilnius's public transport network

BUSES & TROLLEYBUSES

Vilnius has a very dependable network of trolleybuses and buses with frequent services that span the city. Some of the older vehicles are now being replaced with modern ones. However, public transport is best avoided during rush hour, when trolleybuses and buses are crowded.

A detailed map of the city's bus routes is available on the **Vilnius Transport** website. The timetables for every *stotelė* (stop) can be viewed by clicking "*autobusų*" for buses and "*troleibusų*" for trolley-buses. Few services run between 11pm and 5am.

A standard *bilietas* (ticket) is valid on both buses and trolley-buses. This must be bought in advance at a kiosk or from the driver on boarding, and then validated by punching it in one of the machines on board. Passes for one, three and ten days are available. Penalties for travelling without a valid ticket are high.

DRIVING IN VILNIUS

Traffic density has increased rapidly in Vilnius in recent years, resulting in traffic

congestion during peak hours, especially early mornings and late evenings. The problem is further compounded by the erstwhile Soviet city planning. The lack of roads is a serious issue that Vilnius's city council is struggling to solve with the help of EU funds. However, road construction causes further

TAXIS

Taxis are easily available in Vilnius, although during rush hour and late on weekend evenings it may be necessary to call several companies before finding a free cab. Ordering a taxi by telephone is cheaper than hailing one on the street. The average charge is 2 litas per kilometre,

View of a busy road in Vilnius during peak traffic hour

Martono Taksi, an expensive but reliable option

though prices are higher at night. Companies such as **Romerta** and **Ekipažas** are generally reliable. All taxis must have a working meter, so check the initial reading as you get in.

CYCLING

Conditions for cyclists vary considerably around the city. Bicycle routes are clearly marked on many of the pavements in the Old Town, along roads such as Gedimino and Konstitucijos avenues and into districts such as Žvėrynas and Vingis Park. EuroVelo route 11 is an Eastern European cycle route that runs through the eastern Baltic region, taking in Vilnius and Tartu. It has now been extended to Vilnius from the southwest to the northeast, towards Verkiai. However, cycling along roads that do not have bicycle lanes is not recommended. Bicycles can be rented at **Baltic Cycle**.

WALKING

Each sight is just a few steps from the next one, allowing visitors to experience the Old Town's magnificent architecture from close quarters. There are many pedestrianized streets and, despite the occasional reckless driver, traffic is rarely a hindrance.

Crossing roads in Vilnius can sometimes be hazardous. At many crossings a "red man" and "green man" guide pedestrians on when to cross. However, at road junctions, there are traffic lights just for cars. When at a pedestrian crossing without lights, cars must give way to pedestrians, but they do not always do so.

Gedimino Avenue is the city's main street for shopping, festivals and parades, besides being an attraction in itself. Stretching from Cathedral Square in the east to Žvėrynas in the west, it becomes pedestrianized in the evenings and night. The lush districts of Žvėrynas and Užupis are on either sides of the Old Town. The former leads to the splendid views of the Neris river and Vingis Park, reachable by a pedestrian bridge. A walk to Užupis may culminate in a breathtaking panorama at the Tores restaurant *(see p339)*, the peaceful Bernadinų Cemetery or as far as even Belmontas and the Church of Sts Peter and Paul.

Visitors walking down Pilies Street towards Upper Castle, Old Town

SIGHTSEEING TOURS

Tour guides in Vilnius are professional and speak fluent English. A typical sightseeing tour arranged by **Senamiesčio Gidas** or **Mano Gidas** includes a trip to the Old Town, Užupis and the Church of Sts Peter and Paul. Customized tours can also be arranged.

Travel agencies such as **Visit Lithuania** also arrange guided tours as well as accommodation and transport. **West Express** organizes specialized tours, such as Jewish Vilnius.

CAR HIRE

A convenient alternative for getting around the city and taking day trips to nearby attractions such as Trakai is to hire a car. International car rental companies, such as **Europcar**, **Avis** and **Hertz**, and local companies, such as Aunela, offer insured vehicles.

DIRECTORY

BUSES & TROLLEYBUSES

Vilnius Transport
Sodų 22. **Tel** 216 0054.
www.vilniustransport.lt

TAXIS

Ekipažas
Šv Stepono 33a. **Tel** 233 7958.
www.ekipazastaksi.lt

Romerta
Garsioji 9. **Tel** 275 6969.
www.romerta.lt

CYCLING

Baltic Cycle
Vytenio 6–110. **Tel** 6995 6009.
www.bicycle.lt

SIGHTSEEING TOURS

Mano Gidas
Krokuvos 59-1a. **Tel** 6123 4000.
www.manogidas.eu

Senamiesčio Gidas
Aušros vartų 7. **Tel** 6995 4064.
www.vilniuscitytour.com

Visit Lithuania
L Stuokos-Gucevičiaus 1.
Tel 262 5241.
www.visitlithuania.net

West Express
A Stulginskio 5. **Tel** 255 3255.
www.westexpress.lt

CAR HIRE

Avis
See p395.

Europcar
See p395.

Hertz
See p395.

General Index

Acknowledgments

Dorling Kindersley would like to thank the many people whose help and assistance contributed to the preparation of this book.

Contributors
Howard Jarvis has been editor-in-chief for several publications including *The Baltic Times*, *VilniusNOW!* and *Baltic Stand By*. He has been a regular contributor for the Jane's Information Group since 2000.

John Oates, winner of the Guardian newspaper's Young Travel Writer of the Year award, has contributed to numerous newspapers, magazines and guidebooks.

Tim Ochser has been living in Rīga since 2001 where he works as a freelance journalist. He also contributes to Latvian media and has written several Latvian plays.

Neil Taylor is a writer, a tour operator and a consultant. He writes for British newspapers on the Baltics and has published several guidebooks on the region.

Fact Checkers
Eat Latvia, Nicholas Archdeacon, Joel Dullroy, Irja Luks, Brigita Pantelejeva, Nat Singer

Proofreader
Deepthi Talwar

Indexer
Ajay Lal Das

Design and Editorial
Managing Editor Douglas Amrine
Managing Art Editor Jane Ewart
Senior Editor Michelle Crane
Production Controller Lousie Daly
Picture Research Ellen Root
DTP Designer Natasha Lu

Additional Photography
Peter Dennis, Rose Horridge, Rajnish Kashyap, Ian O'Leary.

Additional Illustrations
Chapel Design & Marketing Ltd

Cartography
Casper Morris, Stuart James

Cartographic Research
Netmaps

Special Assistance
Dorling Kindersley would like to thank the following for their assistance: Sonata Šiaučiulytė at Vilnius Tourist Information Centre

Revisions Team
Emma Anacootee, Claire Baranowski, Marta Bescos, Imogen Corke, Joel Dullroy, Anna Freiberger, Maite Lantaron, Carly Madden, Alison McGill, Vikki Nousiainen, Lucy Richards, Ellen Root, Sands Publishing Solutions, Susana Smith, Neil Taylor

Photography Permissions
Dorling Kindersley would like to thank the following for their assistance and kind permission to photograph at their establishments:
Ainaži Naval College Museum, Andrejs Pumpurs Museum, Anton Hansen Tammsaare Museum, Aqua Park, Arsenal Museum of Art, Art Nouveau in Rīga, Aviation Museum, Beekeeping Museum, Bicycle Museum, Calvary Church of the Holy Cross, Cathedral of Christ the King, Cathedral of St Anthony of Padua, Cathedral of St Mary the Virgin (Toomkirik), Cathedral of Sts Boris and Glebe, Cat's House, Church of St Casimir's, Church of St Theresa, Church of Sts Peter and Paul, Coca Cola Plaza, Tallinn, Contemporary Art Centre, Dauderi, Déjà Vu Lounge Bar, Tallinn, Dome Cathedral, Dominican Church, Dominican Monastery, Old town, Dundaga, Europa Mall, Vilnius, Folk House of the Livs, Franciscan Church, Friary of the Virgin Mary, Tytuvenai, House of Blackheads, KGB Cells Museum, KGB Museum, Vilnius, Kohtla Underground Mining Museum, Kiek in de Kök, Tallinn, Kumu Art Museum, Latgale Culture and History Museum, The Latvian Ethnographic Open-Air Museum, Latvian Museum of Photography, Rēzekne, Liepāja Museum, Lithuanian National Museum, Littera Bookshop, Vilnius University, Mentzendorff House, The Mihkli Farm Museum, Mikalojus Konstantinas Čiurlionis National Museum of Art, Motor Museum, Museum of the Barricades of 1991, Museum of Decorative Arts and Design, Museum of History and Applied Arts, Preiļi, Museum of Horns, Museum of Rīga's History and Navigation, Niguliste Church, Tallinn, Palmse Manor House, Pedvāle Open-Air Museum, Peter The Great House Museum, The Palanga Amber Museum, Photo Museum, Tallinn, Porcelain Museum, Powder Tower/Latvian War Museum, Railway Station, Vilnius, Rundāle Palace, Latvia, Sea Museum-Aquarium and Dolphinarium in Smiltynė, Setu Village Museum (Lake Peipsi), Shakespeare Boutique Hotel, Skaistkalne Roman Catholic Church, Skyline Bar (Reval Hotel, Latvia), St Anne's Basilica, St John's Church, Tallinn International Airport, Tamsta Club, Tērvete Nature Park, Theatre, Music and Film Museum, Town Hall Pharmacy in Tallinn, Trakai Island Castle, Tukums, Vilnius Cathedral, Vilnius Picture Gallery, Vilnius University, Vincents Restaurant, Rīga, Vytautas The Great War Museum, Žemaitija National Park

Picture Credits

Key: a-above; b-below/bottom; c-centre; f-far; l-left; r-right; t-top.

The publisher would like to thank the following individuals, companies, and picture libraries for their kind permission to reproduce their photographs:

Works of art have been reproduced with the kind permission of the following copyright holders:

The Offering 1909 by M. K. Ciurlionis, Tempera on canvas, 71 x 78.5. Inv. No Ct- 172 © Mikalojus Konstantinas Čiurlionis National Museum of Art; Funeral Symphony II from the cycle of 7 paintings by M. K. Ciurlionis, 1903 Pastel on paper, 62.3 x 73. Inv. No Ct-107 © Mikalojus Konstantinas Čiurlionis National Museum of Art Tarvas 2002 by Tauno Kangro, 9 x 4 x 2m, bronze, Rakvere on the Castle Hill, Estonia 112bc

4CORNERS IMAGES: Cozzi Guido 249b

AKG-IMAGES: 32cl, 34br, 36tr, 36-37c, 50crb, 51tl, 135bc, 136tc, 215tl; Erich Lessing 30, 212-213c; RIA Nowosti 39t, 39c, 212cl; ALAMY IMAGES: A.P. 84, 163b, 181br; Urmas Ääro 45b, 102; Stuart Abraham 42br; Ace Stock Limited 17br, 93crb, 291bc; AllOver photography 206b; Arco Images 233cb; Andrew Barnes 26bc; Caro 202bl, 206tr; China Span/Keren Su 183b; Content Mine International 129b, 131tr; Gary Cook 187tl; Kitt Cooper-Smith 27ca; Dennis Cox 2-3; Danita Delimont 12bc, 24br, 131br, 174-175, 371tl, 401br; Ilja Dubovskis 284cl; Cody Duncan 19cr; Sindre Ellingsen 253tl; Maciej Figiel 27tl, 27cla; Peter Erik Forsberg 45c; FotoIJ 54; Johan Furusjö 133bl; Christopher Griffin 69cr; Andrew Harrington 85b; Simon Hathaway 318cl; Pete Hill 390cla; Ula Holigrad 18cr; Peter Horree 3c; !hotimagery! 248; Imagebroker 19cl, 93tl, 80tr, 138; Imagebroker/ Michael Zegers 398cr; Images&Stories 129c; INSADCO Photography 388c; InterFoto Pressebildagentur 201c; Jevgenija 187br; Michael Juno 288c; Stanislovas Kairys 239bl; Christian Klein 363tl; Stan Kujawa 319c; Yadid Levy 37cr, 243tl; Robin Mckelvie 110crb, 172bl; The Natural History Museum 27tc; Natural Visions 26br; Kari Niemeläinen 397br; Indrek Parli 48bl; PCL 133tl; Pictorial Press Ltd 22cl; Les Polders 58br; The Print Collector 125c; Robert Harding Picture Library Ltd 130t,/Yadid Levy 376-7; Joeri De Rocker 362cl; Jonathan Smith 24cla; David Soulsby 394cl; Sylvia Cordaiy Photo Library Ltd 362tc; Vario images GmbH & Co.KG/Stefan Kiefer 395br; Tiit Veermae 17tr, 18tr, 47t, 57cr, 96-7, 106clb, 110cra, 117br; Martyn Vickery 20br, 68clb, 243tr, 356b; Visual&Written SL 70tl; World Pictures 47br; Sven Zacek 92cla, 103b APOLLO RAAMATUD: 349bl; AUKSTAITIJOS SIAURASIS GELEZINKELIS: 406br.

BANK OF ESTONIA: 385tl, 385tr, 385cla, 385cra, 385cl, 385cr, 385clb, 385cb, 385cb(1), 385crb, 385bl, 385bc, 385br, 385fbr; BANK OF LATVIA: 386cla, 386cra, 386cl, 386cr, 386clb, 386crb, 386br, 386fbr; BANK OF LITHUANIA: 31c, 39bl; BOGAPOTT: 348tr THE BRIDGEMAN ART LIBRARY: King Charles XII (1682-1718) of Sweden, on horseback, 1702 (engraving) (b/w photo), Picart, Bernard (1673-1733)/Bibliotheque Nationale, Paris, France, Archives Charmet/The Bridgeman Art Library 33br, Catherine the Great, 1793, Lampi, Johann Baptist I (1751-1830)/ Hermitage, St. Petersburg, Russia,/The Bridgeman Art Library 34bl, Arms of the Hanseatic League (stone), German School/© Museum of London, UK,/The Bridgeman Art Library 134bc, Shipping off a Baltic Port (oil on canvas), Larsen, Carl E. (1823-59) & Neumann, Carl Johan (1833-91)/ Private Collection, Bourne Gallery, Reigate, Surrey/The Bridgeman Art Library 135crb Bussi Reisid: 394br.

CLUB ILLUSION: 358c; CORBIS: Niall Benvie 370bl; Christophe Boisvieux 57br; Epa/Toms Kalnins 207br,/Kay Nietfeld 119bc,/Ljubo Vukelic 39bc; Franz-Marc Frei 202cl; Jon Hicks 40-1, 232t; Robert Harding World Imagery/Yadid Levy 21tr; Hans Georg Roth 364bl; Sygma/ Gérard Rancinan 22bl; Peter Turnley 215crb; Zefa/Goebel 16cl, 203br.

DANITA DELIMONT STOCK PHOTOGRAPHY: Janis Miglavs 11br, 182; Keren Su 216, 217b; VYDAS DOLINSKAS: 213tl, 213tc.

ESTONIAN AIR: 392tc.

FOCUS: Kaido Haagen 24clb; Tiit Hunt 90tl; Jarek Jõepera 10cl, 19cra, 46tl, 119cra, 119clb, 119crb, 123tr; Didzis Kadaks 26crb, 171br, 186bc; Mati Kose 49cr; Arnold Kristjuhan 19ca; Heinrich Lukk 29br; Kalju Suur 23tc, 23cra, 25tl, 53tl; Tiina Tammet 75tl; Andres Teiss 44, 359tl, 361tl, 373tr; Toomas Tuul 10br, 11t, 15tr, 46br, 48tc, 48cr, 74cl, 89b, 92bl, 93bl, 94cl, 101br, 105cr, 106cla, 107cra, 113br, 321tr, 358br, 372tl, 373bc, 395tl; Tips International/ Didier Givois/ Vandystadt 119tc.

GETTY IMAGES: AFP/Tim Sloan 137bc,/Ilmars Znotins 130br,/Stringer 37br; AFP/Petras Malukas/ Stringer 207tl; De Agostini 204; Hulton Archive/ Austrian Archives/Imagno 212br; Hulton Archive/ Stringer 36br, 136clb, 214c; Jeff Gross 374tl; Robert Harding World Imagery/Gary Cook 12tl; Stu Forster 23bl; Time & Life Pictures/Ben Martin 196bl,/David Rubinger 137tl; THE GRANGER COLLECTION, NEW YORK: Ullstein Bild 137crb.

HOWARD JARVIS: 220cl.

ILGI BAND: 25tr.

JONATHAN SMITH PHOTOGRAPHY: 24-5c, 208bc, 209tl, 268, 269b, 319tl, 366cr.

KALEV CHOCOLATES: 349c; LINAS KARDASEVICIUS: 262-263; KAUBAMAJA STORE: 349tc; KGB CELLS MUSEUM: 115cb; KLAIPEDA CLOCK MUSEUM: 280crb.

THE LATVIAN ETHNOGRAPHIC OPEN AIR MUSEUM: Uldis Veisbuks 159cla, 159clb, 159cra; ARCHIVE OF THE LATVIAN TOURISM DEVELOPMENT AGENCY: 140cl, 198cl, 198bc; LIEPAJA THEATRE: 362br; LILIJA PLUS LTD.: 289cb; LITHUANIAN NATIONAL TOURISM OFFICE: 379c; LITHUANIA STATE DEPARTMENT OF TOURISM: 212tl; DAOYONG LIU: 16ca; LONELY PLANET IMAGES: Jonathan Smith 208cl.

MARY EVANS PICTURE LIBRARY: 9c, 34tl, 52c, 134bl, 287c; Mary Evans Iln Pictures 41c; Rue Des Archives 377c; MIKALOJUS KONSTANTINAS ČIURLIONIS NATIONAL MUSEUM OF ART: 22cra; MOLLY MALONE'S: 360c; MONIKA CENTRUM: 288tc.

NATIONAL AERONAUTICS AND SPACE ADMINISTRATION: 14cl; NATIONAL GEOGRAPHIC IMAGE COLLECTION: Klaus Nigge 18bl; NATUREPL.COM: Niall Benvie 19crb; William Osborn 19clb; Igor Shpilenok 19bc; Artur Tabor 18br; NORTH WIND PICTURE ARCHIVES: 26cl

PALANGOS TOURISM INFORMATION CENTRE: Tomas Smilingis 27br JOAN PARENTI: 275br; PATRICIA TOURIST OFFICE RIGA– WWW.RIGALATVIA.NET: 402br; PHOTOGRAPHERS DIRECT: Andrew Bain Photography 200-201, Peter Erik Forsberg 346cl, Didzis Kadaks 153; James A. Krug 8-9, Stefan Sollfors Photography 132tc, Wandering Spirit Travel Images/Louise Batalla Duran 55b; PHOTOLIBRARY: Niall Benvie 124-125; Jon Arnold Travel/Peter Adams 13tl; JTB Photo 128, 347b; Roland Marske/Voller Ernst 205b; PHOTOSHOT: NHPA/Lee Dalton 18cb; PRIVATE COLLECTION: 22tr, 24tr, 33tl, 33crb, 34cb, 35c, 35cb, 35bc, 36cl, 36bl, 38tl, 50ca, 51cr, 52tl, 77tr, 79cl, 79cr, 79bl, 99cr, 135tc, 198cra, 210c, 210crb, 210bc, 211tc, 211crb, 212bl, 213tr, 213bl, 213br, 214br, 239cl, 239cr; PROMENADE HOTEL: 291tl.

ERIKS REMESS: 13br; REUTERS: Alexander Demianchuk 119br; RĪGA OPERA FESTIVAL: 132bl; AIVAR RUUKEL: 100cl, 100cla, 100br, 101cl.

SALACGRVAS NOVADA TIC: 190cr; SCANPIX BALTICS: 133cr; F64 23crb, 132cr; LT 25cr; Postimees/Lauri Kulpsoo 19tc,/Henn Soodla 19cla; SIGADE REVOLUTSIOON LLC: 359bc; STAROVER.EE: Piirissaare 122bc; STATE SMALL THEATRE OF VILNIUS: Dmitrij Matvejev 368cl; SUPERSTOCK: Age Fotostock 148tl,/Wojtek Buss 257cl; Yoshio Tomii 49bl.

COURTESY OF THE TALLIN CITY MUSEUM: 73c; TALLIN CITY THEATRE: Siim Vahur 360cl; TEATER VANEMUINE: 358tc; TOPFOTO.CO.UK: The British Library/HIP 214tl; TRAVEL-IMAGES. COM: A. Dnieprowsky 43br, 165tr, 184bl; G. Frysinger 243br.

VILNIUS CONGRESS CONCERT HALL: 368br; VILNIUS JAZZ FESTIVAL: Vytautas Suslavicius 209bl.

JONATHAN WASSERSTEIN: 72crb.

WIKIMEDIA COMMONS: 23cl, 118br; WIKIPEDIA, THE FREE ENCYCLOPEDIA: 20cl, 22crb, 38cb, 38bc, 51bc, 378tc; GNU Free Documentation License 26bl, 37tl, 51crb, 52br, 53bl, 211bc [http:// en.wikipedia.org/wiki/Wikipedia:Text_of_the_ GNU_Free_Documentation_License]; U.S. Department of Defense 53bc.

Front Endpaper: ALAMY: A.P. ftl, Urmas Ääro tl, FotoIJ fcl, !hotimagery! bl, Imagebroker ftr; DANITA DELIMONT STOCK PHOTOGRAPHY: Janis Miglavs fbr, Keren Su br; JONATHAN SMITH PHOTOGRAPHY fbl.

Cover Picture Credits

Front–Alamy Images: Simon Reddy. Back–Alamy Images: Thomas Cockrem bl; Jaak Nilson cla; Dorling Kindersley: Nigel Hicks clb; Linda Whitwam tl; Spine–Alamy Images: Simon Reddy t.

All other images © Dorling Kindersley
For further information see: www.dkimages.com

SPECIAL EDITIONS OF DK TRAVEL GUIDES

DK Travel Guides can be purchased in bulk quantities at discounted prices for use in promotions or as premiums. We are also able to offer special editions and personalized jackets, corporate imprints, and excerpts from all of our books, tailored specifically to meet your own needs.

To find out more, please contact:
(in the US) **SpecialSales@dk.com**
(in the UK) **travelspecialsales@uk.dk.com**
(in Canada) DK Special Sales at **general@ tourmaline.ca**
(in Australia) **business.development@ pearson.com.au**

Phrase Book: Estonian

In Emergency

Help!	**Appi!**	*Aupy!*
Stop!	**Peatuge!**	*Beb-atu-gay!*
Call a doctor!	**Kutsuge arst!**	*Coot-soo-gay arst!*
Call an ambulance!	**Kutsuge kiirabi!**	*Coot-soo-gay keer-awbi!*
Call the police!	**Kutsuge politsei!**	*Coot-soo-gay po-leet-say!*
Call the fire department!	**Kutsuge tuletõrje!**	*Coot-soo-gay too-lei-tur-ye!*
Where is the nearest telephone?	**Kus on lähim telefon?**	*Coos onn la-bim telefon?*
Where is the nearest hospital?	**Kus on lähim haigla?**	*Coos onn la-bim bigh-glaa?*

Communication Essentials

Yes	**Jah**	*Yah*
No	**Ei**	*Ey*
Please	**Palun**	*Pa-loon*
Thank you	**Aitäh**	*Ai-tab*
Excuse me	**Vabandage**	*Va-ban-da-gay*
Hello	**Tere**	*Te-re*
Goodbye	**Head aega**	*Heyad ayga*
Good night	**Head õhtut**	*Heyad ewb-toot*
morning	**hommik**	*bom-mik*
afternoon	**pärastlõuna**	*pa-rawst-lew-na*
evening	**õhtu**	*ewb-tu*
yesterday	**eile**	*eilay*
today	**täna**	*ta-naw*
tomorrow	**homme**	*bom-may*
What?	**Mida?**	*Meeda?*
When?	**Millal?**	*Meelal?*
Why?	**Miks?**	*Meeks?*
Where?	**Kus?**	*Coos?*

Guidelines for Prounciation

The Estonian alphabet consists of the following letters: a, b, d, e, f, g, h, i , j, k, l, m, n, o, p, r, s, š, z, ž, t, u, v, õ, ä, ö, ü. The letters c, q, x, y, z are used only in proper names (of places and people) and in words borrowed from foreign languages. Unlike English, all letters in Estonian are pronounced (for example: the silent k in "knee").

Some letter sounds:

a	as in the "u" in cut
b	similar to "p" in English
g	similar to "k" in English
j	as in the "y" in yes
r	like in English, but rolled
š	"sh"
ž	as in the "s" in pleasure
õ	like the "o" in own
ä	as in the "a" in bat
ö	similar to the "u" in fur
ü	as in the "u" in cube

Some letter combination sounds:

ai	as in the "ai" in aisle
ei	as in the "ei" in vein
oo	as in the "a" in water
uu	as in the "oo" in boot
öö	as in the "u" in fur

Some points to remember:
• Usually the first syllable of a word is stressed. However, quite a few words with foreign origins and some native Estonian words, such as *aitäh*, don't follow this pattern.
• Vowels and consonants can be short (written with one letter), long or extra long (written with two letters).

Useful Phrases

How are you?	**Kuidas läheb?**	*Cooi-das la-beb?*
Very well, thank you.	**Aitäh, väga hästi.**	*Ai-tab, va-ga bas-ti.*
Pleased to meet you.	**Meeldiv tuttavaks saada.**	*Mayl-div too-taw-vawks saa-daw.*
See you soon!	**Varsti näeme!**	*Vaarsti nay-me!*
Is there … here?	**Kas siin on …?**	*Cos scene onn …?*
Where can I get …?	**Kust ma saaksin …?**	*Coost ma sawk-sin …?*
How do you get to?	**Kuidas minna …?**	*Cooi-dass min-na …?*
How far is …?	**Kui kaugel on …?**	*Cooi cow-kel onn …?*
Do you speak English?	**Kas te räägite inglise keelt?**	*Cos tay ra-gi-tay ing-li-say keylt?*
I can't speak Estonian.	**Ma ei oska eesti keelt.**	*Maw ey oska eysti kaylt.*
I don't understand.	**Ma ei saa aru.**	*Maw ey saa aru.*
Can you help me?	**Kas saate mind aidata?**	*Cos saw-tay meend eye-data?*
Please speak slowly.	**Palun rääkige aeglaselt.**	*Pa-loon ra-ki-gay ayg-la-selt.*
Sorry!	**Vabandust!**	*Va-ban-doost!*

Useful Words

big	**suur**	*suur*
small	**väike**	*vayke*
hot	**kuum**	*coom*
cold	**külm**	*kewlm*
good	**hea**	*be-ya*
bad	**halb**	*balb*
enough	**küllalt**	*cool-alt*
well	**hästi**	*basti*
open	**avatud**	*aw-va-tud*
closed	**suletud**	*soo-laytud*
left	**vasak**	*vaw-sawk*
right	**parem**	*paw-rem*
straight	**otse**	*ot-say*
near	**lähedal**	*la-bay-dawl*
far	**kaugel**	*kaw-gbell*
up	**ülal**	*oolal*
down	**all**	*all*
early	**vara**	*va-raw*
late	**hilja**	*bill-yaw*
entrance	**sissepääs**	*see-say-pa-es*
exit	**väljapääs**	*val-yaw-pa-es*
toilet	**tualett**	*too-a-lett*
free/unoccupied	**vaba**	*vaw-baw*
free/no charge	**tasuta**	*taw-soo-taw*

Making a Telephone Call

Can I call abroad from here?	**Kas ma saan siit välismaale helistada?**	*Cos maw sawn seet va-lees-maw-lay bay-lees-taw-da?*
I would like to call collect.	**Tahaksin helistada vastaja kulul.**	*Taw-baw-ksin bay-lees-taw-da vaus-taya koo-lool.*
local call	**kohalik kõne**	*kobaw-lik kew-ne*
I'll ring back later.	**Helistan hiljem tagasi.**	*Hay-lees-tawn beel-yem taw-gaw-si.*
Could I leave a message?	**Kas ma saaksin teate jätta?**	*Cos maw sawk-seen tyate ya-taw?*
Could you speak up a little, please?	**Kas saate natuke valjemini rääkida?**	*Cos saw-tay naw-too-kay vawl-ye-meenee ra-ki-daw?*

Shopping

How much is this?	**Kui palju see maksab?**	*Cooi pawl-yu say mawk-sab?*
I would like …	**Tahaksin …**	*Taw-bawk-sin …*
Do you have …?	**Kas teil on …?**	*Cos tayl onn …?*
I'm just looking.	**Vaatan lihtsalt.**	*Vaw-tan libt-sawlt.*
Do you take credit cards?	**Kas krediitkaardiga saab maksta?**	*Cos kre-diit-kawrd-eega sawb mawk-sta?*
What time do you open?	**Mis kell teil avatakse?**	*Mees kell tayl a-vaw-tawk-say?*
What time do you close?	**Mis kell teil suletakse?**	*Mees kell tayl su-lay-tawk-say?*
this one	**see**	*cee*
that one	**too**	*toe*
expensive	**kallis**	*kaw-lees*

cheap	odav	oh-dav
size	suurus	soo-rus
antique dealer	antiigipood	an-tiiki-pode
souvenir shop	suveniiripood	sou-ve-niiri-pode
bookshop	raamatupood	raw-maw-too-pode
café	kohvik	koh-fik
chemist	apteek	ap-tayk
newspaper kiosk	ajalehekiosk	a-ya-le-he-kii-osk
department store	kaubamaja	cow-ba-mawya
market	turg	toorg

Staying in a Hotel

Have you any vacancies?	Kas teil on vaba tuba?	Cos tayl onn vawba too ba?
double room	kahene tuba	ka-bay-ne tooba
with double bed	laia voodiga	la-ya vo-diga
twin room	kahe voodiga tuba	ka-bay vo-diga too
single room	ühene tuba	ew-bene too-ba
non-smoking	mittesuitsetajatele	meetay-sooitse-ta-ya-lay
room with a bath/shower	tuba vanniga/dušiga	too-ba vaw-niga/doosh-iga
porter	portjee	port-ye
key	võti	vew-ti
I have a reservation.	Mul on reserveeritud.	Mool onn re-se-veri-tood.

Sightseeing

bus	buss	boos
tram	tramm	trawm
trolley bus	troll	trol
train	rong	row-ng
bus stop	bussipeatus	boo-si-peya-toos
tram stop	trammipeatus	tra-mi-peya-toos
art gallery	kunstigalerii	koonsti-gale-ree
palace	palee	pa-lay
castle	loss	lowss
cathedral	katedraal	caw-tay-dral
church	kirik	kee-reek
garden	aed	eye-ed
library	raamatukogu	raw-maw-too-kogu
museum	muuseum	mu-seum
tourist information	turismiinfo	too-ris-me-info
closed for public holiday	külastajatele suletud	koo-las-taya-tayle soo-le-tood
holiday	puhkepäev	pooh-ke-payev
travel agent	reisibüroo	ray-see-bu-rob

Eating Out

A table for ... please	Palun üks laud ... inimesele	Pa-loon ooks la-ood ...eenee-me-selay
I want to reserve a table.	Tahaksin reserveerida lauda.	Taw-bawk-sin re-ser-veri-da la-ooda.
The bill, please	Palun arve	Pa-loon arvay
I am a vegetarian.	Olen taimetoitlane.	Olayn tai-may-toyt-lanay.
I'd like ...	Tahaksin ...	Ta-bawk-sin...
waiter/waitress	kelner/ettekandja	kel-ner/etay-kandya
menu	menüü	men-oo
wine list	veinimenüü	veini-men-oo
chef's special	firmaroog	feer-ma-rogue
tip	jootraha	yot-rawba
glass	klaas	klas
bottle	pudel	poo-del
knife	nuga	noo-ga
fork	kahvel	kawf-fel
spoon	lusikas	loo-si-kaws
breakfast	hommikusöök	bom-miku-sook
lunch	lõuna	lewna
dinner	õhtusöök	eub-tu-sook
main courses	praed	prayed
starters	eelroad	el-rowad
vegetables	köögiviljad	koo-gi-vilyad
desserts	magustoidud	maw-gus-toy-dud
rare	pooltoores	pole-toe-res
well done	küps	cewps

Menu Decoder

äädikas	a-di-kaws	vinegar
aurutatud	ow-ru-tawtud	steamed
friikartul	free-kartool	chips
grillitud	grilly-tud	grilled
jäätis	ya-tis	ice cream
juust	youst	cheese
kala	kaw-la	fish
kana	kawna	chicken
kartul	kar-tool	potatoes

kaste	kaws-tey	sauce
keedetud	kay-day-tud	boiled
klimbid	klim-bid	dumplings
kohv	k-oh-v	coffee
kook, saiad	coke, sigh-ad	cake, pastry
koor	core	cream
küüslauk	koos-lauk	garlic
lambaliha	lawm-ba-leeba	lamb
leib/sai	layb/sei	bread
liha	lee-ba	meat
loomaliha	lo-ma-leeba	beef
mereannid	mayrey-awnid	seafood
mineraalvesi	min-e-rawl-vaysi	mineral water
muna	moona	egg
õli	ewli	oil
õlu	ewlu	beer
pannkook	pawn-coke	pancake
peekon	paykon	bacon
piim	peem	milk
pipar	peepar	pepper
pirukas	piru-kaws	pie
praeliha	praey-leeba	steak
praetud	praeytud	fried
punane vein	poo-naw-nay vein	red wine
puuvili	puu-veelee	fruit
puuviljamahl	puu-vil-ya-mawbl	fruit juice
riis	rees	rice
rull	rule	roll
salat	sawlat	salad
sealiha	seya-leeba	pork
seened	say-ned	mushrooms
sink	sink	ham
šokolaad	sbok-o-lawd	chocolate
sool	sole	salt
suhkur	subkoor	sugar
suitsukala	suit-soo-kawla	smoked fish
supp	soup	soup
tee	te	tea
täidetud	tayde-tood	stuffed
valge vein	val-gay vein	white wine
vorst	vorst	sausage
võileib	voi-layb	sandwich

Numbers

0	null	nul
1	üks	ewks
2	kaks	kawks
3	kolm	colm
4	neli	ne-li
5	viis	viis
6	kuus	kuus
7	seitse	say-tsey
8	kaheksa	kaw-bex-a
9	üheksa	ew-bex-a
10	kümme	kewmme
11	üksteist	eux-taste
12	kaksteist	kawks-taste
13	kolmteist	colm-taste
14	neliteist	nayli-taste
15	viisteist	viis-taste
16	kuusteist	kuus-taste
17	seitseteist	saytse-taste
18	kaheksateist	kawbeksaw-taste
19	üheksateist	ewbeksaw-taste
20	kakskümmend	kawks-kew-mend
30	kolmkümmend	colm-kew-mend
40	nelikümmend	nayli-kew-mend
50	viiskümmend	viis-kew-mend
60	kuuskümmend	kuus-kew-mend
70	seitsekümmend	say-tse-kew-mend
80	kaheksakümmend	kaw-beksa-kew-mend
90	üheksakümmend	ew-beksa-kew-mend
100	sada	sa-da
1000	tuhat	too-bawt

Time

one minute	üks minut	ewks minut
hour	tund	toond
half an hour	pool tundi	pole toondi
Sunday	pühapäev	pew-ba-payev
Monday	esmaspäev	esmas-payev
Tuesday	teisipäev	taysi-payev
Wednesday	kolmapäev	kolma-payev
Thursday	neljapäev	nelya-payev
Friday	reede	re-de
Saturday	laupäev	lauw-payev

Phrase Book: Latvian

In Emergency

Help!	Palīgā!	Pu-lee-gaa!
Stop!	Apstāties!	Up-staat-eas!
Call a doctor!	Izsauciet ārstu	Iz-souts-eat abr-stoo!
Call an ambulance!	Izsauciet ātro palīdzību!	Iz-souts-eat aa-troa pu-leedz-ee-boo!
Call the police!	Izsauciet policiju!	Iz-souts-eat po-lits-ee-yoo!
Call the fire department!	Izsauciet ugunsdzēsējus!	Iz-souts-eat oo-goons-dseb-say-oos!
Where is the nearest telephone?	Kur ir tuvākais telefons?	Koor ir too-vaak-ais tel-e-fons?
Where is the nearest hospital?	Kur ir tuvākā slimnīca?	Koor ir too-vaak-aa slim-neets-u?

Communication Essentials

Yes	Jā	Yaa
No	Nē	Neh
Please	Lūdzu	Loodz-oo
Thank you	Paldies	Pul-deas
Excuse me	Atvainojiet	Ut-vy-noa-yeat
Hello	Sveiki / Labdien	Svay-key / lub-dean
Goodbye	Uz redzēšanos	Ooz redz-ee-shun-oas
Good night	Ar labu nakti	Ur lub-oo nukt-i
morning	rīts	reets
afternoon	pēcpusdiena	pebts-poos-dea-nu
evening	vakars	vu-kars
yesterday	vakar	vu-kar
today	šodien	sboa-dean
tomorrow	rīt	reet
What?	Ko?	Kuah?

> ### Guidelines for Prounciation
>
> Latvian is, for the most part, a phonetic language and the stress is almost always on the first syllable. Each letter and vowel combination (dipthong) has a particular sound, as indicated below:
>
> #### Vowels
> Either short or long (with a macron):
> | | |
> |---|---|
> | a | like "u" in "under" |
> | ā | like "a" in "star" |
> | e | like "e" in "bed", or "a" in "cat" |
> | ē | like "ai" in "hair", or "a" in "glad" |
> | i | like "i" in "sit" |
> | ī | like "ee" in "feet" |
> | o | like "o" in "corn", or "oa" in "oar" |
> | u | like "oo" in "book" |
> | ū | like "oo" in "school" |
>
> #### Dipthongs
> | | |
> |---|---|
> | ai | like "i" in "line" |
> | au | like "ow" in "cow" |
> | ei | like "ay" in "clay" |
> | ie | like "ea" in "clear" |
> | oi | like "oy" in "boy" |
> | ui | like "ui" in "ruin" |
>
> #### Consonants
> Same as English, except for:
> | | |
> |---|---|
> | c | like "ts" in "hats" |
> | č | like "ch" in "church" |
> | dz | like "ds" in "hands" |
> | dž | like "j" in "joke" |
> | ģ | like "d" in "duty" |
> | j | like "y" in "yellow" |
> | ķ | like "c" in "cute" |
> | ļ | like "li" in "million" |
> | ņ | like "n" in "new" |
> | r | like "r" in "run" |
> | š | like "sh" in "shut" |
> | ž | like "s" in "treasure" |

When?	Kad?	Kud?
Why?	Kāpēc?	Kaa-pebts?
Where?	Kur?	Koor?

Useful Phrases

How are you?	Kā jums klājas?	Kaa yooms klaa-yus?
Very well	Ļoti labi	Lyot-ee lu-bi
Pleased to meet you.	Prieks iepazīties.	Preaks ea-pu-zeet-eas.
See you soon!	Uz drīz redzēšanos!	Ooz dreez redz-e-shun-oas!
Is there ... here?	Vai šeit ir ....?	Vi shayt eer ...?
Where can I get ...?	Kur es varu dabūt ...?	Koor es vu-roo du-boot ...?
How do you get to?	Kā es varu tikt līdz?	Kaa es vu-roo tikt leedz?
How far is ...?	Cik tālu atrodas ...?	Tsik taa-loo ut-roa-dus ...?
Do you speak English?	Vai jūs runājat angliski?	Vy yoos roon-aa-yut ung-lees-kee?
I can't speak Latvian.	Es nerunāju latviski.	Es ne-roon-aa-yoo lut-vees-kee.
I don't understand.	Es nesaprotu.	es ne-sup-roat-oo.
Can you help me?	Vai varat man palīdzēt?	Vy vu-rut mun pu-leedz-ebt?
Please speak slowly.	Lūdzu, runājiet lēnām.	Loodz-oo roon-aa-yeat lebn-aam.
Sorry!	Atvainojiet!	ut-vy-noa-yeat!

Useful Words

big	liels	leals
small	mazs	muzs
hot	karsts	kabrsts
cold	auksts	owksts
good	labs	lubs
bad	slikts	slikts
enough	pietiekami	pea-teak-um-ee
well	vesels	vas-als
open	atvērts	ut-vebrts
closed	slēgts	slebgts
left	kreisi	pu krays-i
right	labi	pu lu-bi
straight	taisni	tai-sni
near	tuvu	toov-oo
far	tālu	taal-oo
up	augšā	owg-shaa
down	lejā	lay-aa
here	šeit	sbayt
there	tur	toor
early	agri	ug-ri
late	vēlu	vebl-oo
entrance	ieeja	ea-ey-u
exit	izeja	iz-ey-u
toilet	tualete	toou-le-te
free/unoccupied	brīvs	breevs
free/no charge	bezmaksas	bez-muk-sus

Making a Telephone Call

Can I call abroad from here?	Vai no šejienes var zvanīt uz ārzemēm?	Vy noa sbay-ean-ess vur zvun-eet ooz aar-zem-ebm?
I would like to call collect.	Es gribu, lai maksā zvana saņēmējs.	Es grib-oo, lai muks-aa zvu-nu suny-eb-mebs.
local call	vietējā saruna	veat-ay-aa su-roo-nu
I'll ring back later.	Es atzvanīšu vēlāk.	Es ut-zvun-ee-shoo vebl-aak.
Could I leave a message?	Vai es varu atstāt ziņu?	Vy es vuroo ut-staat ziny-oo?
Could you speak up a little, please?	Lūdzu, runājiet mazliet skaļāk?	Loodz-oo, roon-aa yeat muz-leat skuly-aak?

Shopping

How much is this?	Cik tas maksā?	Tsik tus muk-saa?
I would like ...	Es vēlētos ...	Es veb-leb-toas ...
Do you have ...?	Vai Jums ir ...?	Vy yooms ir ..?
I'm just looking.	Es tikai skatos.	Es tik-ai skut-oas.
Do you take credit cards?	Vai es varu maksāt ar kredītkarti?	Vy es vu-roo muk-saat ur kred-eet-kurti?
What time do you open?	Cikos tiek atvērts veikals?	Tsik-oas teak ut-vebrts vay-kuls?

What time do you close?	Cikos tiek slēgts veikals?	*Tsik-oas teak slebgts vay-kuls?*
this one	šo	*shoa*
that one	to	*toa*
expensive	dārgs	*daargs*
cheap	lēts	*lebts*
size	izmērs	*iz-mebrs*
antique dealer	antikvariāts	*un-teek-vur-i-aats*
souvenir shop	suvenīru veikals	*soo-ve-near-oo vay-kuls*
bookshop	grāmatu veikals	*graa-mut-oo vay-kuls*
café	kafējnīca	*ku-fay-neets-u*
chemist	aptieka	*up-teak-u*
newspaper kiosk	avīžu kiosks	*u-veezb-oo kee-osks*
department store	universālveikals	*oo-ni-ver-saal-vay-kuls*
market	tirgus	*tir-gus*

Staying in a Hotel

Have you any vacancies?	Vai jums ir brīvas istabas?	*Vy yooms ir breev-us is-tu?*
double room with double bed	istaba ar divvietīgu gultu	*is-tu-bu ur div-veat-ee-goo gool-too*
twin room	divvietīga istaba	*div-veat-ee-gu is-tu-bu*
single room	vienvietīga istaba	*vean-veat-ee gu is-tu-bu*
non-smoking	nesmēķētāju	*ne-smee-kyeb-taay-oo*
room with a ...	istaba ar vannu/dušu ...	*is-tu-bu ur vun-oo/doosb-oo ...*
porter	portjē	*port-yay*
key	atslēga	*ut-sleb-gu*
I have a reservation	Man ir pasūtīts	*mun ir pus-oo-teets*

Sightseeing

bus	autobuss	*ow-to-boos*
tram	tramvajs	*trum-vuys*
trolley bus	trolejbuss	*trol-ay-boos*
train	vilciens	*vilts-eans*
bus stop	autobusa pietura	*ow-to-boos-u pea-too-ru*
tram stop	tramvaja pietura	*trum-vuy-u pea-too-ru*
art gallery	mākslas galerija	*maak-slus gul-e-ree-yu*
palace/castle	pils	*pils*
cathedral	katedrāle	*kut-e-draa-le*
church	baznīca	*buz-neets-u*
garden	dārzs	*daarzs*
library	bibliotēka	*bib-li-oa-te-ku*
museum	muzejs	*mooz-ays*
tourist information	tūristu informācija	*toor-is-too in-for-maats-i-ya*
closed	slēgts	*slehgts*
holiday	brīvdiena	*breev-dea-nu*
travel agent	ceļojumu aģentūra	*tsely-oy-oo-moo udy-en-toor-u*

Eating Out

A table for ... please.	Galdiņu .... personām, lūdzu.	*Guld iny oo...pebr soa naam, loodz oo.*
The bill ...	Rēķinu ...	*Rebky-i-noo ...*
I am a vegetarian.	Es esmu veģetārietis.	*Es as-moo vedy-e-taar-ea-tis.*
I'd like ...	Es vēlos ...	*Es veb-loas ...*
waiter/waitress	oficiants / oficiante	*of-its-i-unts/of-its-i-unte*
menu	ēdienkarte	*eb-dean-kurt-e*
wine list	vīnu karte	*veen-oo kurt-e*
chef's special	īpašais šefpavāra ieteikums	*ee-push-ais sbef-pu-vaa-ru eat-ay-kums*
tip	dzeramnauda	*dzer-um-now-du*
bottle	pudele	*poo-de-le*
knife	nazis	*nu-zis*
fork	dakša	*duk-shu*
spoon	karote	*kur-oa-te*
breakfast	brokastis	*broa-kus-tis*
lunch	pusdienas	*poos-dea-nus*
dinner	vakariņas	*vuk-ur-iny-us*
main courses	galvenie ēdieni	*gul-ven-ea eb-dea-ni*
starters	uzkodas	*ooz-koa-dus*
vegetables	dārzeņi	*daarz-eny-i*
desserts	saldie ēdieni/deserti	*sul-dea ee-dea-ni/dess-er-ti*
rare	asiņains	*us-iny-ains*
well done	labi sacepts	*lu-bi suts-apts*

Menu Decoder

alus	*ul-oos*	beer
augļu sula	*ow-gly-oo soo-la*	fruit juice
baltvīns	*bult-veens*	white wine
bekons	*bek-ons*	bacon
cepts	*tsepts*	fried
cūkgaļa	*tsook-guly-u*	pork
cukurs	*tsoo-koors*	sugar
desa	*des-u*	sausage
etiķis	*et-iky-is*	vinegar
frī kartupeļi	*free kur-too-pely-i*	chips
grilēts	*gril-ebts*	grilled
jēra gaļa	*yebr-u guly-u*	lamb
jūras veltes	*yoor-us vel-tes*	seafood
kafija	*kuf-i-yu*	coffee
kartupeļi	*kur-too-pely-i*	potatoes
kūpinātas zivis	*koop-in-aat-us ziv-is*	smoked fish
krējums	*kray-ooms*	cream
liellopa gaļa	*leal-loap-u guly-u*	beef
maize	*maiz-e*	bread
mērce	*mebr-tse*	sauce
minerālūdens	*min-er-aal-oo-dens*	mineral water
ola	*oal-u*	egg
pankūka	*pun-koo-ku*	pancake
piens	*peans*	milk
pildīts	*pild-eets*	stuffed
pipars	*pi-purs*	pepper
rīsi	*rees-i*	rice
saldējums	*sul-day-ums*	ice cream
sāls	*saals*	salt
salāti	*sul-aa-ti*	salad
sarkanvīns	*sur-kun-veens*	red wine
siers	*sears*	cheese
šķiņķis	*sbkyinky-is*	ham
smalkmaizīte	*smulk-maiz-ee-te*	pastry
šokolāde	*sbok-o-laa-de*	chocolate
steiks	*stayks*	steak
tēja	*tbey-u*	tea
tvaicēts	*tvai-tsebts*	steamed
vārīts	*vaar-eets*	boiled
vista	*vis-tu*	chicken
zivis	*ziv-is*	fish
zupa	*zoop-u*	soup

Numbers

0	nulle	*nooll-e*
1	viens	*veans*
2	divi	*di-vi*
3	trīs	*trees*
4	četri	*cbet-ri*
5	pieci	*peat-si*
6	seši	*se-sbi*
7	septiņi	*sept-iny-i*
8	astoņi	*us-toany-i*
9	deviņi	*dev-iny-i*
10	desmit	*des-mit*
11	vienpadsmit	*vean-puds-mit*
12	divpadsmit	*div-puds-mit*
13	trīspadsmit	*trees-puds-mit*
14	četrpadsmit	*cbet-r-puds-mit*
15	piecpadsmit	*peats-puds-mit*
16	sešpadsmit	*sesb-puds-mit*
17	septiņpadsmit	*sept-iny-puds-mit*
18	astoņpadsmit	*us-toany-puds-mit*
19	deviņpadsmit	*dev-iny-puds-mit*
20	divdesmit	*div-des-mit*
30	trīsdesmit	*trees-des-mit*
40	četrdesmit	*cbet-r-des-mit*
50	piecdesmit	*peats-des-mit*
60	sešdesmit	*sesb-des-mit*
70	septiņdesmit	*sept-iny-des-mit*
80	astoņdesmit	*us-toany-des-mit*
90	deviņdesmit	*de-viny-des-mit*
100	simts	*simts*
1000	tūkstotis	*took-stoa-tis*

Time

one minute	viena minūte	*vean-u min-oo-te*
hour	stunda	*stoon-du*
half an hour	pus stunda	*poos stoon-du*
Sunday	svētdiena	*sveet-dea-nu*
Monday	pirmdiena	*pirm-dea-nu*
Tuesday	otrdiena	*oa-tr-dea-nu*
Wednesday	trešdiena	*tresb-dea-nu*
Thursday	ceturtdiena	*tset-oort-dea-nu*
Friday	piektdiena	*peakt-dea-nu*
Saturday	sestdiena	*sest-dea-nu*

Phrase Book: Lithuanian

In Emergency

Help!	Gelbėkit!	*Galbekit!*
Stop!	Sustokit!	*Soostokit!*
Look out!	Atsargiai!	*Aatsaargyai!*
Call a doctor!	Kvieskit gydytoją!	*Kvieskit geedeetoyaa!*
Call an ambulance!	Kvieskit greitąją!	*Kvieskit greitaayaa!*
Call the police!	Kvieskit policiją!	*Kvieskit politsiyaa!*
Call the fire department!	Kvieskit gaisrinę!	*Kvieskit gīsrine!*
Where is the nearest telephone?	Kur yra artimiausias telefonas?	*Koor eeraa artimyowsyaas telefonaas?*
Where is the nearest hospital?	Kur yra artimiausia ligoninė?	*Koor eeraa artimyaausyaa ligonine?*

Communication Essentials

Yes	Taip	*Taip*
No	Ne	*Ne*
Please	Prašom	*Praashom*
Thank you	Ačiū	*Aachyoo*
Excuse me	Atsiprašau	*Aatsipraashoa*
Hello	Sveiki	*Sveiki*
Goodbye	Viso gero	*Viso gero*
Good night	Labanakt	*Laabaanaakt*
morning	rytas	*reetaas*
afternoon	popietė	*popiete*
evening	vakaras	*vaakaraas*
yesterday	vakar	*vaakar*
today	šiandien	*shyaandien*
tomorrow	rytoj	*reetoy*
What?	Kas?	*Kaas?*
When?	Kada?	*Kaadaa?*
Why?	Kodėl?	*Kodel?*
Where?	Kur?	*Koor?*

Useful Phrases

How are you?	Kaip sekasi?	*Kaip sakaasi?*
Very well, thank you.	Ačiū, labai gerai.	*Aachyoo, laabai gerai.*
Pleased to meet you.	Malonu susipažinti.	*Maalonoo soosipaazhinti.*
See you soon!	Iki greito pasimatymo!	*Iki greito paasimaateemo!*
Is there ... here?	Ar čia yra ...?	*Ar che eeraa ...?*
Where can I get ...?	Kur galiu gauti ...?	*Koor galyoo gowti ...?*
How do you get to ...?	Kaip nuvykti iki ...?	*Kaip nooveekti iki ...?*
How far is ...?	Koks atstumas iki ...?	*Koks aatstoomaas iki ...?*
Do you speak English?	Ar kalbate angliškai?	*Ar kaalbaate aangliskai?*
I can't speak Lithuanian.	Aš nekalbu lietuviškai.	*Aash nekaalboo lietoovishkai.*
I don't understand.	Aš nesuprantu.	*Aash nesoopraantoo.*
Can you help me?	Ar galite man padėti?	*Ar gaalite maan paadeti?*
Please speak slowly.	Prašau kalbėti lėčiau.	*Praashoa kaalbeti lechyoa.*
Sorry!	Apgailestauju!	*Aapgilestowyoo!*

Useful Words

big	didelis	*didelis*
small	mažas	*maazhaas*
hot	karštas	*karshtaas*
cold	šaltas	*shaaltaas*
good	geras	*geraas*
bad	blogas	*blogaas*
enough	gana	*gaanaa*
well	gerai	*gerai*
open	atidarytas	*aatidareetaas*
closed	uždarytas	*oozbdareetaas*
left	kairė	*kīre*
right	dešinė	*dashine*
straight	tiesiai	*tiesyai*
near	šalia	*shaalyaa*
far	toli	*toli*
up	aukštyn	*owkshteen*
down	žemyn	*zhemeen*
early	anksti	*aanksti*
late	vėlai	*velai*
entrance	įėjimas	*eeyeyimaas*
exit	išėjimas	*isheyimaas*
toilet	tualetas	*tuaaletaas*
free/unoccupied	laisva/neužimta	*līsvaa/neoozbimtaa*
free/no charge	nemokamai	*nemokamai*

Making a Telephone Call

Can I call abroad from here?	Ar galiu iš čia paskambinti į užsienj?	*Ar gaalyoo ish che paaskaambinti ee oozbsienee?*
I would like to call collect.	Aš norėčiau paskambinti abonentui jo sąskaita.	*Aash norechyoa paaskaambinti aabonentui yo saaskitaa.*
local call	vietinis pokalbis	*vietinis pokaalbis*
I'll ring back later.	Aš pats vėliau paskambinsiu.	*Aash paats velyoa paaskaambinsyoo.*
Could I leave a message?	Ar galiu palikti žinutę?	*Ar gaalyoo paalikti zhinoote?*
Could you speak up a little, please?	Ar galite kalbėti šiek tiek garsiau?	*Ar gaalite kaalbeti shiek tiek garsyoa?*

Shopping

How much is this?	Kiek tai kainuoja?	*Kiek tai kīnuoyaa?*
I would like ...	Aš norėčiau ...	*Aash norechyoa ...*
Do you have ...?	Ar turite ...?	*Ar toorite ...?*
I'm just looking	Aš tik žiūriu	*Aash tik zhyooryoo*
Do you take credit cards?	Ar priimate kreditines korteles?	*Ar priimaate kreditines korteles?*
What time do you open?	Kada pradedate darbą?	*Kaadaa praadedaate darbaa?*

Guidelines for Prounciation

Lithuanian has a complicated wandering accent that can change whenever a word changes its ending, as is seen with "*mato matoe*" (he/she/it/they see) and "*matau matoe*" (I see).

Diphthongs hold the sound longer than that of a simple vowel:
ai like "a" in "made" or "i" in "child"
au like "ow" in "cow" or "o" in "note"
ei like "a" in "made"
ie like "ie" in "sienna"
ui like "ooey" in "gooey"
uo like the word "woe"

Vowels have only one sound:
a like "a" in "father"
e like "e" in "bet"
ę like "a" in "man"
ė like "a" in "made"
i like "i" in "bit" but before an "a", "o", or "u", it is sounds like the "y" in "canyon"
y like į
o like "o" in "boat"
u like "oo" in "wood"
ą, į, ų, and ū just hold the sound of a, i, and u longer

Any consonant before an "e", "i", or "y" is palatalized or softened like "n" in "bunion". Consonants that do not sound like their English counterparts include:
c like "ts" in "Betsy"
č like "ch" in "chunk"
j like "y" in "yellow"
š like "sh" in "shot"
ž like "s" in "measure"
g is always hard like in "go"
r is trilled on the tip of the tongue.

What time do you close?	Kada baigiate darbą?	*Kaadaa baigyaate darbaa?*
this one	šitas	*shitaas*
that one	anas	*aanaas*
antique dealer	antikvariatas	*aantikvaryaataas*
bookshop	knygynas	*kneegeenaas*
department store	universalinė parduotuvė	*ooniversaaline parduotoove*
market	turgus	*toorgoos*
newspaper kiosk	spaudos kioskas	*spoados kyoskaas*
souvenir shop	suvenyrų parduotuvė	*sooveneeroo parduotoove*

Staying in a Hotel

Have you any vacancies?	Ar turite laisvų kambarių?	*Ar toorite lisvoo kaambaryoo?*
double room	dvivietis	*dvivietis*
with double bed	kambarys	*kaambarees*
twin room	kambarys su dviem lovom	*kaambarees soo dviem lovom*
single room	vienvietis kambarys	*vienvietis kaambarees*
non-smoking room with a bath/shower	nerūkantiems kambarys su vonia/dušu	*nerookaantiems kaambarees soo vonyaa/dooshoo*
porter	nešikas	*neshikaas*
key	raktas	*raaktaas*
I have a reservation.	Mano vardu rezervuotas.	*Maano vardoo rezervuotaas.*

Sightseeing

bus	autobusas	*owtoboosaas*
tram	tramvajus	*traamvaayoos*
trolley bus	troleibusas	*troleiboosaas*
train	traukinys	*troakinees*
bus stop	autobusų stotelė	*owtoboosoo stotale*
tram stop	tramvajaus stotelė	*traamvaayoas stotale*
art gallery	meno galerija	*mano gaaleriyaa*
palace	rūmai	*roomai*
castle	pilis	*pilis*
cathedral	katedra	*kaatedraa*
church	bažnyčia	*baazhneechyaa*
garden	sodas	*sodaas*
library	biblioteka	*biblyotekaa*
museum	muziejus	*moozieyoos*
tourist information	turizmo informacija	*toorizmo informaatsiyaa*
closed for public holiday	nedirbama – valstybinės šventės	*nedirbama – vaalsteebines shventes*

Eating Out

A table for ... please	Ar yra staliukas ...	*Ar eeraa staalyookaas ...*
I want to reserve a table.	Norėčiau rezervuoti staliuką.	*Norechyaa rezervuoti staalyookaa.*
The bill, please!	Prašom sąskaitą!	*Praashom saaskitaa!*
I am a vegetarian.	Aš vegetaras.	*Aash vegetaraas.*
I'd like ...	Norėčiau ...	*Norechyaa ...*
waiter/waitress	padavėjas/padavėja	*paadaaveyaas/paadaaveyaa*
menu	meniu	*menyoo*
wine list	vynų sąrašas	*veenoo saaraashaas*
chef's special	rekomenduojama paragauti	*rekomenduojaamaa paraagowti*
tip	arbatpinigiai	*arbaatpinigyai*
glass	stiklinė	*stikline*
bottle	butelis	*bootelis*
knife	peilis	*peilis*
fork	šakutė	*shaakoote*
spoon	šaukštas	*showkshtaas*
breakfast	pusryčiai	*poosreechyai*
lunch	pietūs	*pietoos*
dinner	vakarienė	*vaakariene*
main courses	pagrindiniai patiekalai	*paagrindinyai paatiekaalai*
starters	pirmieji patiekalai	*pirmieyi paatiekaalai*
desserts	desertai	*desertai*
rare	pušalis	*pooszhaalis*
well done	gerai išvirtas	*gerai ishvirtaas*

Menu Decoder

actas	*aatstaas*	vinegar
alus	*aaloos*	beer
arbata	*arbaataa*	tea
baltas vynas	*baaltaas veenaas*	white wine
bekonas	*bekonaas*	bacon

bifšteksas	*bifshteksaas*	steak
blynas	*bleenaas*	pancake
cukrus	*tsookroos*	sugar
dešra	*dashraa*	sausage
duona	*duonaa*	bread
druska	*drooskaa*	salt
ėriena	*erienaa*	lamb
grietinėlė	*grietinele*	cream
įdarytas	*eedareetaas*	stuffed
jautiena	*yowtienaa*	beef
jūros gėrybės	*jyooros gereebes*	seafood
kava	*kaavaa*	coffee
kepenėlės	*kepeneles*	liver
keptas ant grotelių	*kaptaas aant grotalyoo*	grilled
keptas	*kaptaas*	fried/roasted
keptuvėje/orkaitėje	*keptooveye/orkaiteye*	
kiauliena	*kyoalienaa*	pork
kiaušinis	*kyoashinis*	egg
košė	*koshe*	porridge
kumpis	*koompis*	ham
ledai	*ledai*	ice cream
mėsa	*mesaa*	meat
mineralinis vanduo	*mineraalinis vaanduo*	mineral water
padažas	*paadaazhaas*	sauce
pienas	*pienaas*	milk
pipirai	*pipirai*	pepper
pyragas	*peeraagaas*	pie/cake
raudonas vynas	*roadonaas veenaas*	red wine
rūkyta žuvis	*rookeetaa zhoovis*	smoked fish
ryžiai	*reezhyai*	rice
salotos	*saalotos*	salad
šokoladas	*shokolaadaas*	chocolate
sumuštinis	*soomooshtinis*	sandwich
sūris	*sooris*	cheese
sriuba	*sryoobaa*	soup
vaisių sultys	*visyoo sooltees*	fruit juice
virtas	*virtaas*	boiled
virtas garuose	*virtaas garuose*	steamed
virtiniai	*virtinyai*	dumplings
vištiena	*vishtienaa*	chicken
žuvis	*zhoovis*	fish

Numbers

0	nulis	*noolis*
1	vienas	*vienaas*
2	du	*doo*
3	trys	*trees*
4	keturi	*ketoori*
5	penki	*penki*
6	šeši	*sheshi*
7	septyni	*septeeni*
8	aštuoni	*aashtuoni*
9	devyni	*deveeni*
10	dešimt	*dashimt*
11	vienuolika	*vienuolikaa*
12	dvylika	*dveelikaa*
13	trylika	*treelikaa*
14	keturiolika	*ketooryolikaa*
15	penkiolika	*penkyolikaa*
16	šešiolika	*sheshyolikaa*
17	septyniolika	*septeenyolikaa*
18	aštuoniolika	*aashtuonyolikaa*
19	devyniolika	*deveenyolikaa*
20	dvidešimt	*dvideshimt*
30	trisdešimt	*trisdeshimt*
40	keturiasdešimt	*ketooryaasdashimt*
50	penkiasdešimt	*penkyaasdashimt*
60	šešiasdešimt	*shashyaasdashimt*
70	septyniasdešimt	*septeenyaasdashimt*
80	aštuoniasdešimt	*aashtuonyaasdashimt*
90	devyniasdešimt	*deveenyaasdashimt*
100	šimtas	*shimtaas*
1000	tūkstantis	*tookstaantis*

Time

one minute	minutė	*minoote*
hour	valanda	*vaalaandaa*
half an hour	pusvalandis	*poosvaalaandis*
Sunday	sekmadienis	*sekmaadienis*
Monday	pirmadienis	*pirmaadienis*
Tuesday	antradienis	*aantraadienis*
Wednesday	trečiadienis	*trechyaadienis*
Thursday	ketvirtadienis	*ketvirtaadienis*
Friday	penktadienis	*penktaadienis*
Saturday	šeštadienis	*sheshtaadienis*

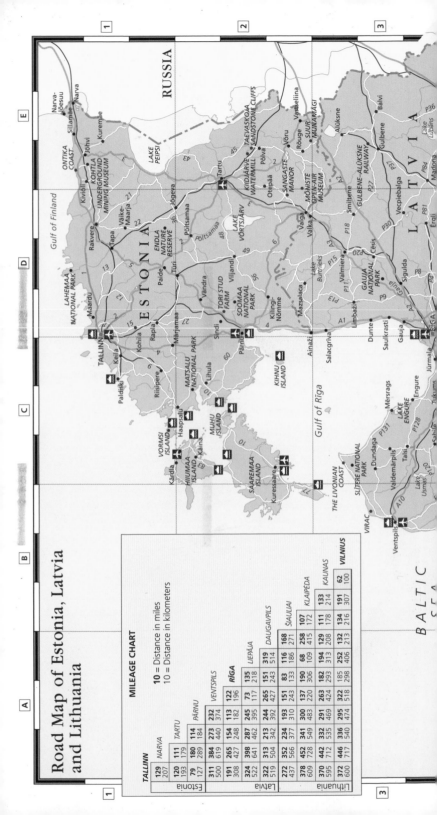

Road Map of Estonia, Latvia and Lithuania

MILEAGE CHART

10 = Distance in miles
10 = Distance in kilometers

	TALLINN	NARVA	TARTU	PÄRNU	VENTSPILS	RĪGA	LIEPĀJA	DAUGAVPILS	ŠIAULIAI	KLAIPĖDA	KAUNAS
NARVA	129 / 207										
TARTU	120 / 193	111 / 179									
PÄRNU	79 / 127	180 / 289	114 / 184								
VENTSPILS	311 / 500	265 / 427	384 / 619	232 / 374							
RĪGA	191 / 308	154 / 248	273 / 440	113 / 182	122 / 196						
LIEPĀJA	324 / 522	287 / 462	398 / 641	245 / 395	73 / 117	135 / 218					
DAUGAVPILS	313 / 504	213 / 342	265 / 427	193 / 310	319 / 514	151 / 243	168 / 271				
ŠIAULIAI	322 / 519	234 / 377	341 / 549	193 / 310	151 / 243	83 / 133	116 / 186	68 / 109			
KLAIPĖDA	378 / 609	352 / 566	452 / 728	300 / 483	137 / 220	190 / 306	258 / 415	190 / 306	107 / 172		
KAUNAS	370 / 595	442 / 712	332 / 535	291 / 469	194 / 313	129 / 208	182 / 293	129 / 208	111 / 178	134 / 216	
VILNIUS	372 / 600	446 / 717	336 / 540	295 / 474	252 / 406	185 / 298	322 / 518	133 / 214	132 / 213	191 / 307	62 / 100

Estonia · Latvia · Lithuania